WORK-RELATED ATTITUDES

Kathryn M. Bartol

J. Richard Hackman

Richard T. Mowday

Greg R. Oldham

Dennis W. Organ

Patricia C. Smith

ORGANIZATIONAL DESIGN, STRUCTURE, DEVELOPMENT

Chris Argyris

Richard L. Daft

Paul R. Lawrence

William Ouchi

(Continued inside back cover)

BEHAVIOR IN ORGANIZATIONS

Understanding and Managing the Human Side of Work

Second Edition

ROBERT A. BARON
PURDUE UNIVERSITY

WITH THE SPECIAL ASSISTANCE OF

Jerald Greenberg
OHIO STATE UNIVERSITY

Allyn and Bacon, Inc. BOSTON LONDON SYDNEY TORONTO

Managing Editor: Bill Barke
Composition Buyer: Linda Cox
Cover Coordinator: Linda Knowles Dickinson
Cover Designer: Christy Rosso
Text Designer: Nancy Murphy, East of the Sun
Photo Research: East of the Sun
Senior Editorial Assistant: Alicia Reilly

LIBRARY OF CONGRESS CATALOGING-IN-PUBLICATION DATA
Baron, Robert A.
   Behavior in organizations.

   Includes bibliographical references and index.
   1. Organization behavior.   I. Greenberg,
Jerald.   II. Title.
HD58.7.B37   1986   658.3   85–13533
ISBN 0–205–08660–8

PHOTO CREDITS   Page 11 (clockwise from upper left) © Harry Wilks / Stock, Boston; David S. Strickler / The Picture Cube; © Sylvia Johnson 1982 / Woodfin Camp & Associates; © Mike L. Wannemacher / Taurus Photos. Page 41 (left) Alan Carey / The Image Works; (right) © Burk Uzzle 1984 / Woodfin Camp & Associates; (below) Wide World Photos. Page 47 (below) photo by Talbot D. Lovering. Page 64 (left) © Ulrike Welsch; (right) © Frank Siteman 1984 / The Picture Cube. Page 83 (left) © Elizabeth Hamlin 1980 / Stock, Boston; (right) © Alan Carey / The Image Works. Page 146 photo courtesy of Procter and Gamble. Page 156 © John J. Krieger, Jr. / The Picture Cube. Page 211 (top) David Powers / Stock, Boston; (below) Alan Carey / The Image Works. Page 224 Wide World Photos. Page 243 (left) © Raimon / The Picture Cube; (center) Alon Reininger / Woodfin Camp & Associates; (right) Wide World Photos. Page 269 Frank J. Staub / The Picture Cube. Page 311 (left) © Russell Abraham 1975 / Stock, Boston; (right) George Bellerose / Stock, Boston. Page 323 Alan Carey / The Image Works. Page 327 (top) Ellis Herwig / The Picture Cube; (below) © Frank Siteman 1985 / The Picture Cube. Page 351 (left) Wide World Photos; (right) Wide World Photos. Page 367 Terry McCoy / The Picture Cube. Page 446 Mark Antman / The Image Works. Page 483 (left) Alan Carey / The Image Works; (right) David S. Strickler / The Picture Cube.

Printed in the United States of America
10 9 8 7 6 5 4 3   89 88 87

To Sandra, who brought light into my dark

SPECIAL INSERTS

CONTENTS

v

vi

A NOTE FROM THE AUTHOR

A Personal Search for Excellence, or Why Different *Should* Be Better

How should an author approach the task of revising his or her work? After eighteen years of university teaching, plus exposure to hundreds of texts and revisions, I'm convinced that two contrasting strategies exist. One approach—clearly the more popular strategy—rests on the following assumption: materials already present in a book are quite acceptable, by and large, and should remain unchanged. This view implies a revision process in which new materials are added at appropriate points, while much of the structure and content remain unaltered. A second, and less common, approach follows the belief that nothing already in a book is sacred; in fact, almost everything can be (and perhaps should be) improved. This view suggests a revision process in which large sections or even entire chapters are rethought, reorganized, and rewritten.

In my own writing, I've always opted for the latter approach. Some of my friends attribute this behavior to the fact that I'm a confirmed workaholic, but I feel that it actually stems from two personal convictions: (1) all human endeavors are imperfect and can, with a little hard work, be improved; (2) if I ever reach the point at which I stop learning from my colleagues or from my own experience, and at which I feel no desire to transmit new insights to students, it will be time to retire!

Largely as a result of these beliefs, in revising this text extensive changes and reorganizations have been made. Since all of these may not be readily apparent from a brief glance through the book, it may be helpful to summarize them here.

Changes in Content

First and foremost, I have made a large number of changes in content. These alterations are based on suggestions and feedback from many colleagues. Most comments I received about the first edition were gratifyingly positive. However, others indicated that the text could be improved (1) by devoting more attention to organizational behavior itself, and somewhat less to the basic psychological processes underlying it; and (2) by expanding coverage of the "macro" side of O.B.—such topics as organization theory and contingencies in organization design. In order to take account of these recommendations, I have instituted the following changes.

Addition of a new chapter on group dynamics. Group processes play a key role in many forms of organizational behavior. For this reason, it seems important to represent them more adequately in this edition. Accordingly, a new chapter dealing with group dynamics has been included. It deals with such topics as the structure of work groups (their cohesiveness and norms, various roles within them), individual productivity in groups, and group performance itself.

Addition of a new chapter on the contextual dimensions of organization design. In recent years, growing attention has been directed to the complex interplay between the external environment and technology, on the one hand, and organizational structure and function, on the other. A new chapter summarizes both classic and recent research on these important topics, and so expands coverage of various aspects of organization theory and related topics.

Inclusion of many new topics. In order to represent the breadth of modern O.B., as well as its rapid progress in recent years, literally dozens of topics not covered in the first edition are included now. Among these are the following:

organizational socialization
mentorship
organizational commitment
citizenship behaviors
assessment centers
burnout
stress and unemployment
organizational communication and organizational performance
policy model of organizational innovation
workflow integration
routine and nonroutine technologies
comparable worth
resource-dependence view of intraorganizational power
interorganizational coordination
structure of multinationals
interface conflict-solving model

Thorough Up-Dating of All Materials

While some might disagree, I firmly believe that O.B. has become increasingly sophisticated in recent years. For this reason, it seems important to make a text such as this one as current in content as possible. Therefore, I have engaged in thoroughly up-dating every chapter. As a result of these efforts, more than 50 percent of the citations included are from 1980 or later, and approximately 33 percent are from 1983, 1984, and 1985. Of course, at the same time, I have retained coverage of classic materials—theories and findings whose value has been confirmed by the test of time.

Changes in Special Features

The first edition of this text contained several special features designed to enhance its appeal and usefulness to students. In this edition, I have refined several of these features and have added others as well.

Changes in Special Inserts. I have retained the three types of inserts (boxes) used in the first edition: Focus on Behavior, From the Manager's Perspective, and Case in Point. However, several changes involving these have been made.

First, virtually all such inserts are new to this edition. Second, fewer are presented in each chapter. This reflects comments from students and colleagues to the effect that too many boxes interrupt the flow of reading, and interfere with overall comprehension of the chapter material. Third, all inserts are carefully cited in the text by statements such as "Please refer to the Focus insert on page 303." Such comments tell students just when to read each insert, and they tie each box more closely to the text topic they illustrate.

Improvements in in-text aids: Special attention has been devoted to improving a wide range of in-text aids. For example, efforts have been made to improve the special labeling on all graphs and charts—labeling that calls attention to the key findings being presented. Second, the "mix" of illustrations has been altered, again in response to feedback from colleagues and students. Slightly fewer cartoons and photos—but more flow charts and diagrams—are included. Finally, chapter opening stories are tied more closely to chapter content, and more entries are included in the glossary than in the first edition. Together, all these changes are designed to make the book easier to read and to understand.

Better Balance between Basic Knowledge and Application

O.B. is clearly scientific in its basic orientation, and this fact was strongly reflected in the first edition. In addition, though, it is intimately concerned with application—with using the knowledge it acquires to further both individual and organizational goals. This fact receives somewhat greater emphasis in the current edition. Specifically, more attention is now directed (when appropriate) to the question of how the principles, theories, and findings described can be put to actual use. Similarly, more examples of such application are included throughout. The result, I believe, is a better balance between these two basic themes of our field than was true in the first edition.

Changes in Ancillary Materials

Teaching O.B. can be a difficult and time-consuming task. For this reason, I have attempted to provide *substantially* improved assistance to colleagues faced with this assignment. Thus, this new edition is accompanied by two ancillary items that will, I believe, prove quite helpful:

- *A Comprehensive Test Bank*, by Jerald Greenberg, Ohio State University.
- *An Extensive Instructor's Manual*, by Angelo S. DeNisi, University of South Carolina, and Robert D. Goddard, Appalachian State University.

A Concluding Comment and Another
Request for Help

As I have tried to suggest, the above changes did *not* emerge from a vacuum—
nor even simply from my own ponderings. Rather, they were suggested by feedback
from many students and colleagues. Therefore, I wish to request your aid in this
regard again. Only *your* feedback, after all, can inform me whether, and to what
extent, I have indeed improved this text. So, please don't hesitate: share your views
and ideas with me as often and in whatever form you wish. I'll be sincerely grateful
for such input, and promise to take it carefully to heart.

ACKNOWLEDGEMENTS:
SOME WORDS OF THANKS

In preparing this text, I have been assisted by many talented, gracious people.
While I can't possibly hope to thank all of them, I would like to express my sincere
appreciation to a few whose aid has been most valuable.

First, my sincere thanks to the colleagues listed below, who read and commented upon the book as it took shape. Their suggestions were thoughtful, informative, and constructive, and I have tried to follow them as closely as possible:

- Angelo S. DeNisi, University of South Carolina
- Ralph Katerberg, University of Cincinnati
- Jack Kondrasuk, University of Portland
- Marilyn Hazzard Lineberger, Emory University
- Robert W. Moore, Management Consultant, Boulder City, Nevada
- Paula M. Popovich, Ohio University
- James M. Tolliver, University of New Brunswick

Second, I'd like to express my appreciation to my good friend Jerry Greenberg
for preparing three chapters, and for contributing to the project in many other ways.
As in the past, it has been a pleasure working with him.

Third, my thanks to Alicia Reilly for her tremendous aid in developing the
Instructor's Manual, to Angelo DeNisi for overseeing its preparation and pulling it
together, and to the many colleages who contributed cases, exercises, and other
elements to it. (These contributions are, of course, acknowledged in the manual
itself.)

Fourth, my thanks to Paula Carroll, at Allyn and Bacon, for her excellent
efforts as production manager, and to Linda Dickinson for a very attractive cover.

Fifth, yet another tip of my hat to Ziggy (Bill) Barke. Once again, his enthusiasm, energy, and good fellowship has been invaluable from start to finish. In
fact, I don't know what I'd do without him!

Sixth, I am sincerely grateful to Terry Mitchell, Karl Vesper, and my other
colleagues in the Department of Management and Organization at the University of
Washington for the hospitality they extended to me during my visit. My task of

revising the book was greatly facilitated by their assistance, and I want to acknowledge it, with thanks, here.

And finally, my sincere thanks to Nancy Murphy, for an internal design even more attractive than the ones she has provided in the past (hard to believe, but true!), for a great job of photo research, and for other contributions too numerous to remember, let alone list here! We're a team of long standing, and I hope we can continue to work together for many years to come.

To all of these outstanding people, and to many others as well, my warmest, personal *"Thanks!"*

Robert a. Baron

PART I

UNDERSTANDING ORGANIZATIONAL BEHAVIOR

CHAPTER 1

THE FIELD OF ORGANIZATIONAL BEHAVIOR: What It Is and What It Does

Individuals, Groups, and Organizations: The Three Foundations of Organizational Behavior   Organizational Behavior and the Scientific Method   O.B. in Action: Putting Knowledge to Work   Organizational Behavior: A Working Definition

ORGANIZATIONS: Their Nature and Impact

Organizations: A Working Definition   Organizations: Their Structure and Impact

ORGANIZATIONAL BEHAVIOR: A Capsule Memoir

Scientific Management: The Beginnings   Human Relations: Work Settings as Social Systems   Organizational Behavior in the 1980s: Optimistic, Sophisticated, Integrative

IN QUEST OF UNDERSTANDING: Research Methods in Organizational Behavior

Natural Observation: Basis for Insight   The Survey Method: Knowledge Through Self-Report   Experimentation: Knowledge Through Intervention   The Correlational Method: Knowledge Through Systematic Observation   Theory: Essential Guide to Organizational Research

USING THIS BOOK: A Displaced Preface

SPECIAL INSERTS

CASE IN POINT   "We Just Don't Do Things That Way Around Here"
FROM THE MANAGER'S PERSPECTIVE   Understanding Research: Some
   Practical Benefits

Organizational Behavior: An Introduction

Sigma Industries has a problem, and it can be summarized in a single word: *turnover.* In recent years, an alarming proportion of the bright young people hired have quit. In fact, many have stayed only a few months before packing their belongings and moving to what they view as greener pastures. The situation has gotten so bad that John Rinaldi, Head of Personnel, has just been raked over the coals by Margaret Bemming, C.E.O. at Sigma. Now, he's meeting with his own staff to try to find a solution to this persistent problem.

"I just don't understand it," John begins. "Our salaries are higher than the industry average, and our working conditions are among the best around. Yet we keep losing these good people. What's wrong?"

"Beats me!" exclaims Carol Sanders, John's second-in-command. "With that new bonus plan in place, there's not much else we can give 'em."

"Yes, but we've got to do *something*—and fast. Meg was boiling when I left her. I've never seen her so angry." At this point, there is much head shaking and sighing in the group. Then, the silence is broken by a small voice from the back of the room.

"I hope I'm not interrupting or anything," it says with hesitation, "but I've got an idea." All eyes focus on the speaker, Bret Harding, a junior member of the staff. "I've done a lot of the exit interviews with these people, and I think I know what's bothering them. It isn't so much the conditions here—those are O.K. It's the gap between what they expect and what they find."

"Just what do you mean by that?" asks John, scowling.

Undeterred, Bret continues. "Well, I get the feeling that our recruiters paint *too* glowing a picture of Sigma—one we can't hope to match. The way they describe it, everyone here gets to do the kind of work they like best, promotions are fast and practically guaranteed, and everyone is deliriously happy—stuff like that. When new people arrive and find that things don't match this description, they're disappointed. Even worse, some feel they've been misled. That makes them mad, and the next thing you know, they're looking for another position . . ."

"Hmm . . ." John remarks, stroking his chin. "You may just have something there. I've always felt that some of our recruiters go too far. They want to get the best people for us, but they make Sigma sound like some kind of paradise on earth! Maybe they're really setting us up for trouble by promising more than we can deliver. . . ."

"Can you believe it?" Chris Feinberg exclaims as she bursts into Tom Radinsky's office. "Those crumbs, those rotten crumbs!" They're really out to get us this time!"

"Hey, take it easy," Tom murmurs in his most soothing voice. "What's up? Why are you so angry?"

"It's those people in Finance again. They've adopted a new policy—without asking *us*, of course. This is it: any customer who's been late in paying an invoice during the past twelve months no longer qualifies for our ninety-days-same-as-cash arrangement. What do you think of that?"

Now it's Tom's turn to boil over. "What! I can't believe it!" How could they do that to us! Don't they know how this'll affect sales? Every one of our competitors will have an edge. We'll probably lose the Crawford account right off. Then we can kiss that big Allied deal good-bye. Why would our own people do this to us? Don't they want us to move our products?"

"Some days, Tom, I really wonder," Chris replies. "They just keep their heads buried in those accounts all the time—I don't think they ever give a thought to our real business, or to sales. I know that they're rated on maximizing cash flow and cutting losses. But heck, *we're* evaluated on total volume. Anyway, you can forget about a bonus this year—we'll be lucky to make quota, let alone exceed it—"

At this point, a strange gleam comes into Chris's eyes. "O.K., if that's their game, so be it. We can't change things now. But I'm not going to take this lying down. I know a few tricks that can send those guys up the wall, yes indeed. And I'm going to use every one. They can't hurt us like this and get away with it . . . I'll show *them!*"

Things have recently gone from bad to worse for R. B. Hastings, Inc., a large retail chain. And the reason for its problems is clear for all to see: a reluctance (or inability) to change. In the past, Hastings had been a giant in its industry. Sales rose steadily, profits climbed, and the company seemed headed for permanent prosperity. The formula responsible for this success was simple. Hastings opened small stores near the center of moderate-sized towns and cities. And, it sold inexpensive merchandise for people of modest means. For decades, this approach worked, and worked very well. Twenty years ago, however, clouds began to gather on the corporate horizon. Growing numbers of people moved to the suburbs, where they were followed by several of Hastings' competitors.

Hastings itself, however, decided to stay put: it refused to open stores in the new shopping centers and enclosed malls. Similarly, growing prosperity had produced an "up-market" shift in consumer tastes. Again, Hastings failed to adjust; it continued to sell the same old mix of modestly-priced merchandise. Most recently, Hastings had decided not to honor national credit cards. This decision had driven even die-hard Hastings customers into the arms of its competitors, who *did* accept these cards.

All of these policies stemmed from Hastings' "culture of conservatism." The company viewed itself as an outpost of stability in a changing world, and took great pride in doing things "the old way." While this adherence to tradition won the loyalty of some customers, it alienated many others. For example, buyers for the company, ever cautious, often ignored new trends or styles. The result: Hastings became known—especially among young shoppers—as a store where last year's fashions and products were offered at this year's prices! No wonder the company was in trouble. It had shut its eyes to major change, and was now paying the price. Could it survive? Was there a place for it in the modern retailing environment? Or should it give up and either liquidate or seek a merger? These were the questions currently facing management, employees, and stockholders. . . .

As you can readily see, something is seriously wrong in each of these organizations. In the first, unrealistic expectations among new employees are contributing to a high level of turnover. In the second, conflict between two departments seems likely to reduce sales and generate lasting feelings of ill will. In the third, a reluctance to adjust to changing environmental conditions threatens the very existence of a large and previously successful company. In short, each of these organizations suffers from problems that reduce its efficiency, performance, and overall effectiveness. Unfortunately, such difficulties are far from rare. On the contrary, they are a basic fact of life in modern organizations (see Figure 1.1, page 6). Thus, you are almost certain to encounter them in your own career, as well as within the covers of this book.

Of course, calling attention to such difficulties is one thing; resolving them is quite another. How can this complex task be accomplished? How, in short, can organizations maximize their productivity while maintaining the satisfaction and wellbeing of the persons who compose them? In the past, managers and others possessing authority within (or over) organizations found it necessary to deal with such questions largely through informal means. That is, they had to rely upon common sense, trial and error, or the proverbial "wisdom of the ages" in handling organization-based problems. Such an approach, we hasten to add, was far from worthless. In the hands of talented, energetic persons, it often yielded impressive results. Thus, even in ancient times, some organizations were highly successful in accomplishing their major goals, and some produced high morale among their members (e.g., consider the Roman army or the construction "industry" of ancient

FIGURE 1.1   *Danger: Problems Ahead.*
As suggested by this cartoon, modern organizations—and the people in them—face many problems. (Source: Drawing by Richter; © 1981 The New Yorker Magazine, Inc.)

Egypt). All too often, though, this informal approach proved ineffective. Trial and error, after all, is costly, and it offers no guarantee of success. Similarly, while common sense sometimes provides valuable insights into human behavior, it is far from infallible in this regard, and sometimes it leads us seriously astray.

While the limitations of an informal, common-sense approach to organizational problems were always apparent, they became even more painfully obvious during the late nineteenth and early twentieth centuries. At that time, rapid industrialization, major technological advances, and sheer growth in size both intensified long-standing difficulties and created many new ones. Faced with these chaotic conditions, thoughtful managers and scholars began a search for other, perhaps more effective, means of dealing with them. Fortunately, one new approach was soon suggested by the emergence of several fields, known collectively as the **behavioral sciences.** These new disciplines (e.g., psychology, sociology, political science) attempted to add to knowledge of human behavior through the use of rigorous scientific methods; and, as they quickly discovered, this tactic really *worked*. Within a few short decades, the behavioral sciences had contributed important new insights into human behavior and human society. This rapid progress, in turn, soon raised another intriguing possibility: Why not apply the knowledge and methods of these fields to the task of understanding organizations and solving their complex problems? As this idea took shape, the field of **organizational behavior** itself was born.[1] Needless to add, it didn't spring fully formed onto the intellectual stage. Rather, it went through many shifts in direction and content before adopting its modern perspective.[2] We will consider some of these later in this chapter. At present, though, organizational behavior (O.B.) is an active, vigorous field, with two major goals: (1) increased understanding of organizations and behavior within them, and (2) application of this knowledge to the solution of many practical problems, and the enhancement of organizational effectiveness. You can gain some idea of the breadth and diversity of modern organizational behavior by examining the questions in Table 1.1. Please note: these are only a small sample of the many topics currently addressed by our field.

In the chapters that follow, we will address every issue raised in Table 1.1, as well as many others. Before turning to these varied topics, however, it is important to provide you with certain background information—a foundation that will prove useful in the remainder of the book. Thus, we will use the rest of this initial chapter for completing several basic tasks.

First, we will define the field of organizational behavior, indicating what it is and just what it seeks to accomplish. Second, we will comment on the nature of organizations and the ways in which they shape the attitudes, actions, and values of persons within them. Third, we will briefly trace the origins and development of organizational behavior. Fourth, we will consider the manner in which our field

TABLE 1.1   *O.B.: A Sample of the Questions It Addresses.*
Modern O.B. seeks information useful in answering all of these questions.

(1) Are there actually conditions under which leaders are unnecessary?
(2) Do female managers differ from male managers in important ways? Or is the existence of such differences basically a myth?
(3) How do individuals learn about the "right" way to behave in an organization? (That is, how do they become *socialized* into it?)
(4) What sources of bias operate in the appraisal of employees' performance?
(5) Is information carried by the grapevine and other informal channels of communication accurate?
(6) What are the best techniques for training employees in their jobs?
(7) What tactics can be used to convert destructive organizational conflict into more constructive encounters?
(8) How do individuals (or groups) acquire power and influence within an organization?
(9) What conditions cause people to suffer from "burnout?" What can be done to prevent such reactions?
(10) How can resistance to change within an organization be overcome?
(11) How do new technologies affect the structure and effectiveness of organizations?
(12) What steps can be taken by American businesses to compete more effectively against their Japanese counterparts?
(13) What factors lead persons to feel satisfied or dissatisfied with their jobs?
(14) Are individuals or committees better at making complex decisions?

attempts to "do its thing"—the specific techniques it uses to add to existing knowledge about organizations and organizational processes. Finally, we will describe the structure of this book, and call your attention to several of its special features.

THE FIELD OF ORGANIZATIONAL BEHAVIOR: WHAT IT IS AND WHAT IT DOES

In a sense, we have already offered a definition of organizational behavior: as a field, it seeks increased understanding of human behavior in organizational settings. As far as it goes, this statement is both accurate and useful. Unfortunately, though, it does not go quite far enough. In fact, it omits mention of several key aspects of modern O.B. deserving of our careful attention. These relate to (1) the specific kinds of knowledge O.B. seeks, (2) its basic approach to gaining such knowledge, and (3) the use to which this information is put once it is obtained.

Individuals, Groups, and Organizations: The Three Foundations of Organizational Behavior

What kinds of knowledge does O.B. seek? The answer to this question is suggested by the three incidents on pages 4 and 5. As you may recall, the first focused on the impact of false expectations among new employees on their high rate of turnover. The second was concerned with conflict between two departments within a single company; and the third examined the dire effects resulting from a company's failure to adapt to changing environmental conditions. In short, the first story focused on individuals, the second on groups, and the third on an entire organization. Which of these levels of analysis is essential for thorough knowledge of organizational behavior? The answer should be obvious: all three. To fully understand why people act and think as they do in organizational settings, we must know something about them as individuals (e.g., their attitudes, perceptions, motives), something about the groups to which they belong (e.g., their leaders, politics, norms), and something about their total organization (e.g., its culture, values, structure). Careful attention to each of these factors is a central theme in modern O.B. and this should be fully reflected in any definition of the field.

Organizational Behavior and the Scientific Method

Earlier, we noted that organizational behavior took its "entrance cue" from the developing behavioral sciences. It built on the basic principle, first established in these fields, of applying scientific methods to the study of complex human phenomena. Given this fact, it is not surprising that modern O.B. is largely scientific in orientation. It, too, seeks increased knowledge through an empirical, science-based approach. We will have more to say about this strategy in a later section of this chapter, where we describe several of the specific methods used in organizational research. At this point, however, we wish to call your attention to another fact. While O.B. is basically scientific in orientation, it is far from rigid in this regard. Most practitioners in the field fully agree that carefully conducted research, carried out in accordance with basic scientific principles, is the best single way of adding to our store of knowledge about organizational behavior. At the same time, though, they also recognize the complexities of applying such methods in actual organizations, and the limitations this implies. Further, many believe that important ideas and valuable insights can sometimes be gained through less formal means (e.g., from the comments and observations of experienced, practicing managers). Please don't misunderstand: such sources of information are *not* viewed as a substitute for the findings of systematic research. But there is some feeling, in our field, that they *can* be useful, and should not be totally ignored. In sum, while O.B. is certainly scientific in orientation it is, perhaps, a bit less defensive about this perspective than other disciplines. In our view, this can often be a "plus."

O.B. in Action: Putting Knowledge to Work

Knowledge, it is often said, is a wonderful thing. To this we would simply add: but knowledge that can be *used* is even better! While this sentiment is not an official motto for O.B., it is certainly one of its guiding principle. There is general agreement in our field that knowledge about organizations and organizational behavior, once acquired, should be put to practical use. Further, there is also agreement that it should be used in two major ways. First, it should contribute to enhanced organizational effectiveness. Productivity, efficiency, and product quality should all benefit from such applications. Second, it should contribute to enhanced wellbeing among organization members. Knowledge about organizational behavior, in short, should be used to improve the quality of work life, increase job satisfaction, and further the career development of individuals. It is important to note that there is no contradiction between these two goals. On the contrary, there has recently been growing realization that they actually go hand in hand.[3] In any case, "application" cannot readily be separated from "basic knowledge" where O.B. is concerned; the two are intimately—and consistently—intertwined.

Organizational Behavior: A Working Definition

Putting our comments up to this point together, we can now offer the following formal definition of O.B.: *Organizational behavior is the field that seeks enhanced knowledge of behavior in organizational settings through the scientific study of individual, group, and organizational processes, the goal of such knowledge being the enhancement of both organizational effectiveness and individual wellbeing.*

Since definitions are somewhat abstract, we have represented this one graphically in Figure 1.2. Please examine this flow chart carefully; in one sense, it provides a general road map for the remainder of this text.

ORGANIZATIONS: THEIR NATURE AND IMPACT

The phrase "organizational behavior" has two distinct parts. Yet, in our comments so far, we have focused mainly on the "behavior" aspect, while largely ignoring the "organization" component. At this point, we will restore needed balance by focusing directly on organizations themselves. First, we will offer a definition of this term, and in this way indicate just what organizations are. Second, we will examine some of the ways in which organizations shape the actions of persons within them.

Organizations: A Working Definition

Which of the photos in Figure 1.3 shows an organization? If you answered "The ones in A and B," think again. Actually, all the groups shown can be labeled organizations. To see why this is so, consider the following definition: *An organization is any social structure or system consisting of two or more persons who are interdependent and who work together in a coordinated manner to attain common goals.* In sum, organizations consist of persons who interact with one another (directly or indirectly), whose fates are somewhat linked (what happens to one

FIGURE 1.2   *O.B.: A Working Definition.*
O.B. seeks to add to our knowledge about behavior in organizational settings through the scientific study of individual, group, and organizational processes. Further, it seeks to apply such knowledge to the enhancement of both organizational effectiveness and individual wellbeing.

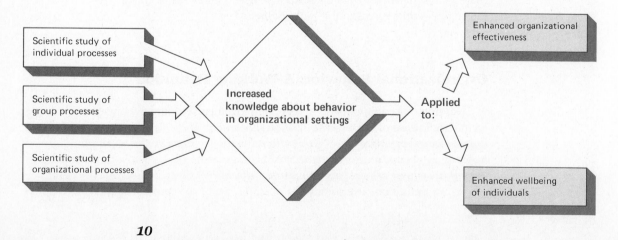

FIGURE 1.3 *Organizations Take Many Forms.*
Which of these qualify as being an organization? While you might find this fact mildly surprising, the answer is: all of them. All represent social systems in which individuals work together to attain shared goals.

affects what happens to the others), and who work together in order to achieve shared goals.

As you can see, this definition is quite broad in scope. Thus, it applies equally well to giant corporations (top left), government agencies (top right), informal clubs (bottom left), and symphony orchestras (bottom right). The key factor to keep in mind is *not* sheer size. Rather, it is whether the persons involved work together in a coordinated manner to attain shared goals. If they do, the term "organization" may well apply; if they do not, it is probably inappropriate.

One additional point: because of its deep commitment to the practical application of knowledge, O.B. usually focuses most of its attention on work-related organizations (e.g., ones in business, government, or industry). For this reason, this text, too, will concentrate on such organizations. But, as we hope will soon become apparent, many of the principles and findings discussed apply to organizations generally, and can be extended beyond the world of work. Thus, while much of our attention throughout this text will be work-organization *focused,* it will by no means be work-organization *bound.*

Organizations: Their Structures and Impact

One executive known to the author frequently remarks: "A business is only as good as its people."[4] What he means by this comment is that it is the actions, motivation, and commitment of the persons within an organization that largely determine its fate. Certainly, this is true; organizations *are,* after all, composed of individuals. Yet, this is only part of the total picture. While individuals shape organizations and determine their outcomes, they, in turn, are often profoundly affected by these complex social systems. In short, organizational behavior is very much a two-way street in which individuals affect the organization and the organization affects individuals. There are several reasons why this is so.

First, organizations generally have a formal **structure,** an internal arrangement of divisions, departments, work teams, and so on.[5] This internal structure (often represented by an *organizational chart* such as the one in Figure 1.4) specifies how tasks and responsibilities are to be divided, how communication should take place, and where power or authority rests. Thus, it often exerts a profound effect upon the persons working within a given organization, determining the kinds of work they do, with whom they communicate, and to whom they report. While every organization has some form of internal structure, however, specific ones may differ greatly in this regard. For example, some adopt a system in which few intermediate levels separate the lowest rung on the corporate ladder from the highest—their *chain of command* is short. In contrast, others develop a structure in which many levels separate such positions—their chain of command is long. Similarly, in some organizations, many subordinates report to a single supervisor—the *span of control* is wide. In others, only a few subordinates report to a single supervisor—the span of control is narrow. We could go on to describe many other aspects of organizational structure; however, we will return to this topic in more detail in Chapter 14. By now, the main point should be clear: the way in which a given organization is structured or "put together" can greatly affect the persons within it.

It's important at this point to consider two additional facts about organizational structure. First, its development is in no way a random process. Rather, organizational structure is often shaped by the specific *technologies* used by an organization (e.g., the knowledge, processes, and facilities it requires to attain its goals or produce desired outputs), and the *environment* in which it operates (e.g., the competitors it must face, general political and economic conditions). Again, we will return to such factors later (in Chapter 15). Second, the formal structure of an organization does not always closely match its informal structure. For example,

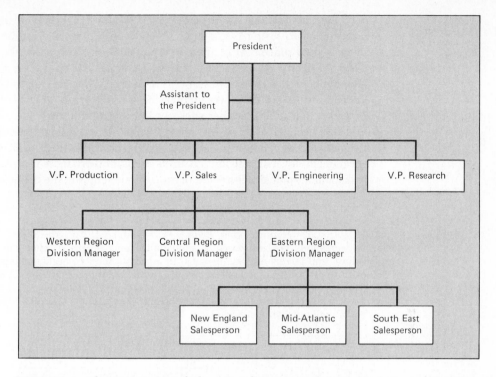

FIGURE 1.4 *The Organizational Chart: Road Map to an Organization's Formal Structure.* The formal structure of an organization is often represented by a diagram such as this one—generally known as the *organizational chart.* Whatever its precise form, an organization's structure often exerts powerful effects upon the persons within it.

information often flows more freely through the informal "grapevine" than through formal channels. Similarly, persons who seem to have authority over others may, in fact, be mere figureheads who receive rather than give orders. As we will see at several later points, the informal structure of an organization is often more important than the formal one shown on the organizational chart, and this can have major implications for the persons at work within it.

A second major way in which organizations influence the behavior and attitudes of their members is through what has come to be termed their **culture.** As complex social systems, organizations usually develop beliefs, perspectives, and intricate sets of *norms*—rules indicating how organizational members *should* behave in various situations or *should* perform various functions. Together, the influence of such factors on individuals can be profound. Indeed, organizational culture, especially when coupled with formal *organization policy* and the specific *role requirements* of various jobs, can often outweigh personal preferences or style. For example, consider an individual who moves from a job at one government agency to a position at another. In the first, members of the general public were perceived largely as petty nuisances, to be gotten rid of as quickly as possible. Also, a degree of rudeness in dealing with such people was implicitly accepted as necessary. Because of this set of beliefs and norms, the individual in our example is accustomed to losing her temper when dealing with the public, and to "putting them in their place." At her new job, however, she learns that the organization has a very different set of values: "Be polite at all costs," is one guiding principle; "Remember—we're here to serve" is another. As she becomes aware of these new, informal rules, our employee changes her behavior; after all, she doesn't want to act in a way that will make her stick out like a sore thumb.

It is because of these and related factors that organizations often have a life of their own, independent of the persons who compose them. Indeed, over the years, specific employees come and go, until an entire work force is replaced. Yet, because of organizational structure and organizational culture, the behavior and attitudes of

FIGURE 1.5 *Organizational Behavior: Very Much a Two-way Street.*
Organizations are composed of individuals, and generally reflect the motives, attitudes, values, and talents of these persons. In addition, though, organizations have a life of their own, apart from individuals. Thus, they exert strong effects upon their members through their policies, culture, and formal structure. (Note: Individuals are represented as separate from the Organization solely for purposes of clarity in this diagram. Obviously, they belong *inside*, not outside, the circle.)

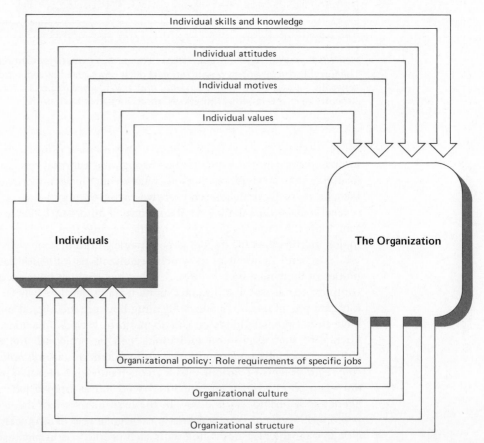

the new members quickly come to resemble those of the persons they replaced. In a word, they are soon *socialized* into the organization, and adopt its prevailing norms and values.[6] It is largely for this reason that we must view organizational behavior as a two-way street. To understand it fully, we must grasp not only how individuals affect an organization, but also how organizations themselves mold and shape the persons within them. (Please see Figure 1.5 for a summary of these suggestions. And for a concrete example of organizational culture in operation, see the **Case in Point** on page 16.)

ORGANIZATIONAL BEHAVIOR: A CAPSULE MEMOIR

In the late 1980s, the notion that the "human side" of work (and organizations) is important is far from surprising. Most people in the business world realize that communication, motivation, cooperation, influence, and many other person-based processes play a key role in organizational functioning. It is somewhat surprising to learn, therefore, that this idea is relatively new. It took form only during the present century, and did not gain widespread recognition among practicing managers until recent decades. Why did this perspective take so long to develop? And where did it originate? We will now focus on these and related questions.

Scientific Management: The Beginnings

How can productivity be improved? This issue has puzzled managers since ancient times. In a key sense, the modern field of organizational behavior can be traced to this question. To understand why this is so, we must return to the closing decades of the nineteenth century—a period of rapid industrialization and technological change. At that time, the prevailing view of work was much as it had remained throughout recorded history. The jobs being performed were what really mattered; the people who performed them were much less important. In accordance with this perspective, many engineers set about the task of applying the new technological knowledge now at their disposal to the development of ever-more efficient machines. The rationale behind such activities was straightforward: if the means of production could be improved, wouldn't efficiency, too, automatically increase? Much to their surprise, the answer was "no." Sometimes shiny new equipment enhanced productivity, but sometimes it did not. Faced with such outcomes, a growing number of managers came to a new conclusion: while machines *are* important, they are only part of the total picture. The people who run them too must also be considered. Efforts to apply this basic idea soon led to *time and motion studies*—attempts to design jobs so that they could be performed in the most efficient manner possible.

The process did not stop there, however. Growing concern with the human side of work soon paved the way for emergence of a major new approach—one

"We Just Don't Do Things That Way Around Here . . ."

Bud Johnson is waiting to see Paul Selman, director of his sales region, and he's really excited. Bud has just returned from his third trip as a field representative for Bartlett Systems, Inc., a young but rapidly growing producer of computer software, and he's almost overflowing with good news. Against all odds, he has just landed two—count 'em!—two major orders for the company. He can hardly wait to share the good news, and literally jumps to his feet when Paul opens the door and beckons him inside.

Motioning him to a seat, Paul begins: "Well, how'd it go? Did you make out all right with all your travel arrangements?"

"Oh yeah, sure, fine. But let me tell you my news: I got a big order from Dunwood Co."

Paul looks pleased. "No kidding! Good work. They're a tough nut to crack. Which system did they take?"

"The 600 series. It turned out to be just what they need. All I had to do was point out the pluses of our package, and they were sold."

"Nice going, nice going," Paul comments with a smile. "You're really off to a good start. Anything else?"

Bud smiles; here's his big moment. "Oh nothing much . . . just an order from an outfit called IPC."

"IPC!" Paul exclaims, almost falling off his chair. "You got an order from IPC! Why, they're practically married to Unicomp. What a breakthrough! How'd you do it?"

"Well, I have to admit it wasn't easy," Bud says, hoping to make this moment of triumph last. "That Unicomp rep, Jennifer O'Reilly, is pretty sharp. She's had them all sewed up for a long time. But when I mentioned that I'd heard some rumors about Unicomp being acquired, they started to listen."

Paul looks surprised. "Unicomp's being bought out? Where did you hear that? I don't know anything about it."

"Oh, I didn't really hear it, I just kind of made it up. See, the way I figure it, they're really concerned about getting stuck with systems they can't use. So I played that card for all it was worth—and it worked."

Now Paul is looking angry rather than surprised. "You mean you just made it up? You told them a deliberate lie just to get the order?"

Bud is taken aback; this isn't the reaction he expected. But he forges bravely ahead. "Yeah, that's what I did. You know what they say, all's fair in love, war, and sales . . ."

Paul leans forward in his chair, and the look in his eyes, plus the way he is gripping the edges of his desk, warn Bud that the storm is about to break: "Look, we just don't do things that way around here. We've got a reputation for integrity and honesty, and we're not going to have idiots like you blowing it for us. You'd better learn the ropes, my boy, or you're not long for this job!"

Questions

(1) Do you think Bud knew about his company's position concerning honesty when dealing with customers? If so, why did he choose to ignore it?

(2) Assume that Bud did not know of this position or rule. What might account for this lack of knowledge on his part?

(3) Do you think the company's position makes sense? Or, given the highly competitive nature of its business, should it be changed?

(4) If you were Bud, what would you have done? Would you try to close the order at all costs and in any manner? Or would you stick to the company's norms (rules) even if this prevented a sale?

known as **scientific management.** Although it was practiced by many persons, its most famous advocate was Frederick W. Taylor. In a book entitled *The Principles of Scientific Management,* Taylor outlined the key features of his new approach.[7] It, too, was concerned with maximizing efficiency and getting the most work possible out of employees. Thus, scientific management emphasized the importance of effective *job design,* efforts to plan work tasks in a systematic manner. In addition, it contained two new features that, taken together, focused attention on employees as well as on their work.

First, Taylor suggested that workers be carefully selected and trained for their jobs. In this regard, he broke with the traditional view holding that employees are basically interchangeable cogs who can easily be shuffled from job to job. Second, he recognized the importance of motivation in work settings. Indeed, he firmly believed that efforts to raise worker motivation might result in major gains in productivity. His view concerning the basis of such motivation was, by modern standards, quite naive. Briefly, he assumed that work motivation stems mainly from the desire for gain (i.e., money). Today, in contrast, it is realized that people actually seek many goals through their work—everything from enhanced status through personal fulfillment. While he was mistaken about the nature of motivation in work settings, Taylor *did* grasp the importance of this key factor. This, as we're sure you can see, was a major step forward.

To repeat: scientific management was primarily concerned with raising efficiency and output—*not* with enhancing worker satisfaction or morale. But it did begin to recognize the importance of considering people in work settings, especially their abilities, training, and motives. In this way, it opened the door to further attention to the human side of work, and contributed to the emergence of an independent field of organizational behavior.

Human Relations: Work Settings as Social Systems

While scientific management directed some attention to the importance of human behavior at work, it should be obvious that it did not go far enough in this respect. Good job design and high motivation are indeed important factors where productivity is concerned; yet they are only part of the total picture. Performance is also strongly affected by many other factors, such as relations among employees, communication between these persons and management, attitudes toward specific jobs and the organization generally, and the quality of leadership provided by supervisors. Today, these facts seem so obvious they hardly bear repeating. In the past, however, this was not the case. In fact, it actually took some dramatic and unexpected research findings to call the complex, social nature of work and work settings to the attention of practicing managers. The research that accomplished this key task is usually known as the *Hawthorne studies,* and given its importance in the history of our field, it is worth describing here.

The Hawthorne studies: An overview.   In the mid-1920s a series of fairly typical scientific management studies were begun at the Hawthorne plant of the Western Electric Company outside Chicago. The purpose of the research was simple: to determine the impact of level of illumination on worker productivity. Several groups of female employees took part. One group worked in a *control room* where the level of lighting was held constant; another worked in a *test room* where brightness of the lighting was systematically varied. Results were quite baffling: productivity increased in both locations. Further, there seemed to be no orderly link between level of lighting and performance. For example, output remained high in the test room even when illumination was reduced to that of moonlight—a level so dim that workers could barely see what they were doing!

Puzzled by these findings, officials of Western Electric called in a team of experts headed by Elton Mayo. The results they uncovered proved to have a major impact on the developing field of organizational behavior.[8] In an initial series of studies (known as the *Relay Room experiments*), Mayo and his colleagues examined the impact of thirteen different factors on productivity. These included length of rest pauses, length of work day and work week, method of payment, place of work, and even a free mid-morning lunch. Subjects were again female employees who worked in a special test room. Once more, results were quite mysterious: productivity increased with almost every change in work conditions. Indeed, even when subjects were returned to initial, standard conditions, productivity continued to rise (refer to Figure 1.6).

As if these findings were not puzzling enough, additional studies soon added to the confusion. For example, in one investigation (known as the *Bank Wiring Room study*), male members of an existing work group were carefully observed by members of the research team. No attempts were made to alter the conditions under which they labored, but they were interviewed by another investigator during non-work periods. Here, results were quite different from those in the earlier studies. Productivity did *not* rise continuously. On the contrary, it soon became apparent that workers were deliberately restricting their output. This was revealed both by observations of their work behavior (e.g., all men stopped work well before quitting time) and by interviews (almost all admitted that they could easily do more if they wished). Why was this the case? Why did these workers restrict their own output, while those in the Relay Room experiments did not? Gradually, Mayo and his colleagues arrived at the answer: in reality, work places are complex *social systems.* In order to fully comprehend behavior in them, it is necessary to understand worker attitudes, communication among employees (as well as with management), and a host of other factors.

Armed with his insight, Mayo and his associates were soon able to interpret the puzzling findings obtained in their research. First, with respect to the Relay Room experiments, it was clear that productivity rose because subjects reacted favorably to the special attention they received. In short, they knew they were being observed, and because they enjoyed such attention, their motivation—and so their productivity—rose. In contrast, output was held low in the Bank Wiring Room study because of other factors. The men in that group feared "working themselves out of a job" and raising the amount they were expected to complete each day if their productivity was too high. To avoid such outcomes, they established informal but powerful rules about behavior on the job—rules that held production to low levels.

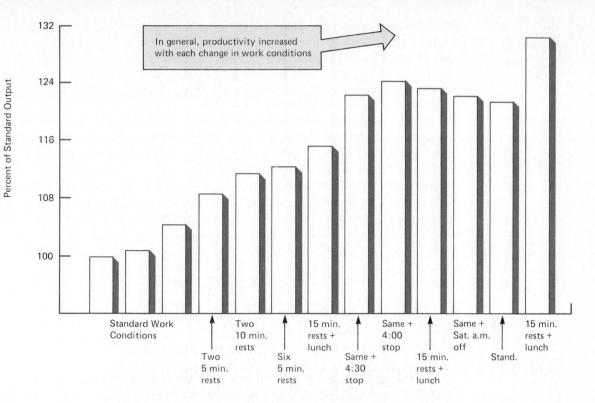

In general, productivity increased with each change in work conditions

Percent of Standard Output

132
124
116
108
100

Standard Work Conditions

Two 5 min. rests

Two 10 min. rests

Six 5 min. rests

15 min. rests + lunch

Same + 4:30 stop

Same + 4:00 stop

15 min. rests + lunch

Same + Sat. a.m. off

15 min. rests + lunch

Stand.

FIGURE 1.6   The Hawthorne Project: Some Puzzling Results.
In one portion of the famous Hawthorne project, female employees were exposed to a number of changes in work conditions. Surprisingly, virtually every one of these alterations brought about an increase in productivity. This finding and other results of the project indicate that job performance is strongly affected by many social factors (e.g., relations between employees, their work-related attitudes, norms concerning on-the-job behavior). (Source: Based on data from Roethlisberger and Dickson, 1939; see Note 8.)

The Hawthorne studies: Their implications and impact.   By modern research standards, the Hawthorne studies were seriously flawed. For example, no attempt was made to assure that participants were representative of all workers in their plant, or of all manufacturing personnel generally. As a result, findings could not readily be generalized. Similarly, contrasting procedures were applied to different groups of workers (e.g., males and females; persons performing different jobs). Because of this fact, it is impossible to determine whether the results observed stemmed from changes instituted by the researchers, from differences between various groups of subjects, or both. (See our discussion of experimentation below.)

Despite these flaws, however, the Hawthorne studies exerted impressive, lasting effects. Together, they underscored the fact that full understanding of behavior in work settings requires knowledge of many factors ignored by scientific management and earlier views—factors relating to complex aspects of human behavior. As recognition of this basic principle grew, a new perspective known as the **human**

relations approach took shape.[9] This perspective devoted far more attention to human needs, attitudes, motives, and relationships than had previously been the case. In addition, it recognized the fact that lasting gains in productivity and satisfaction can be achieved only through appropriate changes in these and related factors. In this way, it established a close link between the emerging field of organizational behavior and several behavioral sciences (e.g., psychology, sociology)—a link that has persisted, and even strengthened, in the intervening years. While the human relations perspective itself was gradually replaced by even more sophisticated views (see below), several of its ideas and concepts contributed to the development of the modern field of organizational behavior. Since O.B., in turn, has exerted important effects upon the practices adopted by many organizations, an intriguing fact is now clear: the workers in that long vanished plant outside Chicago probably had greater and more lasting effects upon the entire world of work than most of them would ever have dreamed possible.

Organizational Behavior in the 1980s: Optimistic, Sophisticated, Integrative

To recapitulate: once it was widely realized that work settings are really complex social systems, and that behavior in them is shaped by a wide range of individual, group, and organizational forces, the stage was set for the emergence of an independent, science-oriented field of organizational behavior. Such a field was not long in taking shape. While no ribbon-cutting ceremonies were held to mark its entry upon the scene, it was very much a going concern by the early 1950s, in fact if not always in name. Indeed, by that time, active research programs concerned with topics still central to O.B. (e.g., leadership, motivation) were well under way. Since its emergence, O.B. has continued to develop in many ways so that currently, it is as diverse and varied as the processes it seeks to unravel. At this point, a quick glance at some of its major characteristics may prove useful.

O.B. and the human resources model.   Suppose that you approached a large group of managers and asked each one to describe his or her basic view of human nature. What type of answers do you think you would receive? Unfortunately, even today, many of the replies would be negative in tone. Some of the persons questioned might suggest that human beings are basically lazy and either unwilling or unable to accept much responsibility. Further, they might note that the key role of managers is that of giving such persons direction—keeping them on track, so to speak. This traditional view, often known as **Theory X,** has prevailed for centuries, and is still very much with us today.

In contrast, other persons you question might report a more positive view of human beings and human behavior. These managers would reject the notion that most people are basically lazy. Instead, they would contend that under appropriate conditions people are just as capable of working hard and accepting responsibility as they are of "goofing off." Indeed, they might add that for many individuals, work serves as a primary source of satisfaction. In accordance with this more optimistic perspective—often known as the **human resources model** or **Theory Y**—such managers might further describe their primary task as that of identifying the conditions that tend to encourage such favorable outcomes, and assuring that they exist within their units or organization.[10]

Which of these contrasting perspectives, Theory X or Theory Y, is adopted by modern O.B.? As you can probably guess, the second. Most individuals working in our field currently believe that employees *can* demonstrate many desirable behaviors at work, provided appropriate conditions exist. But please note: acceptance of this human resource model does *not* imply acceptance of the naive belief that employees will always or even usually be responsible and productive. Rather, it simply recognizes the fact that they react to conditions around them. If these are favorable (e.g., they are treated with respect and enjoy good relations with management and coworkers), they may work hard, accept responsibility, and show many other desirable actions. However, if conditions are negative (e.g., they feel exploited and do not have confidence in their supervisors), they may adopt far less positive patterns. In short, modern O.B. does not view the world of work through rose-tinted glasses. At the same time, though, it does assume that there are no built-in reasons why work cannot be pleasant and satisfying, or why employees cannot be encouraged to show constructive actions on the job. In this respect, it is more optimistic than older perspectives that preceded its appearance.

O.B. and the contingency approach: Realizing that there are, in fact, no simple answers.   No discussion of the nature of modern O.B. could be complete without mention of one more of its defining characteristics: acceptance of the **contingency approach** or perspective.[11] While this approach itself is both complex and sophisticated, its central conclusion can be simply stated: where organizational behavior is concerned, there are—alas!—no simple answers. The processes studied by O.B. are too complicated and are affected by too many different factors to permit us any such luxury. Thus, according to the contingency approach, there is no single best style of leadership, method of communication, technique for motivating employees, or internal organizational structure. Instead, the most successful style, method, technique, or structure varies from situation to situation, and from one set of circumstances to another.

Because of its awareness of such complexity, answers offered by the contingency approach tend to include such phrases as "under some conditions . . .", "it depends . . .", or "assuming all other factors are equal . . . ." Needless to note, persons seeking simplicity or a hard-and-fast "cookbook" formula for managing organizational behavior find such replies disappointing. Indeed, they sometimes grumble about the inability of O.B. to offer "straight answers." There is a key reason why such complaints, understandable as they are, should be taken with a grain of salt: growing evidence suggests that the conclusions reached by the contingency approach are much closer to the truth than those inspired by simpler "single answer" approaches. For this reason, the contingency perspective, although the subject of some criticism, has gained widespread acceptance in O.B.[12] Thus, we will encounter it, and specific theories it has generated, at several later points in this book.

O.B. as a uniquely integrative field. A final feature of modern O.B. worthy of mention is its uniquely *integrative* nature. As we have already noted, O.B. draws upon the principles and findings of several related fields (e.g., psychology, sociology, communication). But it does much more than just this: it also *integrates* this information (as well as findings from its own research) into a unified framework for comprehending behavior in organizational settings. In this respect, it is unique. The fields closely related to O.B., and on which it often draws, tend to focus almost exclusively on a single level of analysis. For example, psychology directs its attention primarily to processes involving individuals. Social psychology often focuses on events occurring within groups. And sociology (from which much of *organizational theory* derives), concentrates on social structures and institutions. To a large extent, each of these fields focuses on its chosen level of analysis while either ignoring or at least deemphasizing the others. This is definitely *not* the case in O.B. In contrast, it actively seeks to *integrate* information from all three levels. We should note that within O.B., some division exists between scholars interested primarily in individual and group processes (those with a *micro* orientation) and ones interested mainly in processes involving organizations themselves (those with a *macro* orientation). Members of both "camps" fully agree, however, that adequate comprehension of organizational behavior requires attention to, and integration of, information relating to all three levels. That is, they agree that individuals and groups play a central role in the functioning of organizations, and that organizations, in turn, shape the attitudes, values, and actions of individuals and groups. Thus, O.B. is indeed integrative in its outlook. Because of this fact, it offers a unique contribution not provided by any other field of study.

...RSTANDING:
...DS IN
...BEHAVIOR

...ve already noted, is essentially scientific in orientation. ...to our knowledge of organizations and behavior within ...scientific methods widely employed by the behavioral ...in this section, we will acquaint you with several of these ...will explain just how scientists wishing to add to our ...nal behavior actually proceed.[13] Please note: our main ...ning you into an expert in research methodology. Rather, ...ng you with a basic grasp of the logic underlying these ...uch knowledge will prove useful to you in several ways, ...t any organizational research yourself. Our reasons for ...marized in the **Manager's Perspective** insert on page ... After you do, your own ideas about the practical value of ...of research may change considerably!

A Methods:

1) Natural Observation:
   Basis for insight.

2) Survey Method: knowledge
   through Self-Report.

3) Experimentation:
   knowledge thro' Intervention

4) The Correlation Method:
   Knowledge through
   systematic Observation

Understanding Research: Some Practical Payoffs

"O.K.," you may now be thinking, "so I'll read this section and maybe—just maybe—I'll understand it. Then I'll know something about research. So what? What'll that buy me?" While we understand why you may feel this way, we don't agree with these sentiments. On the contrary, we feel that there are important reasons for having a working knowledge of research methods, even if you never intend to use them yourself. Basically, these reasons fall under two major headings.

First, knowing something about such methods will make you a more effective evaluator (and user) of research findings. At many points in the future, you will read or hear statements about organizational behavior. Some of these will be based solely on common sense, and you already know how to interpret these: with a great degree of caution. Others, though, will be based on the results of research studies. For example, you may read in a magazine that, according to recent research, companies whose C.E.O.'s are under the age of forty are much more successful than ones whose C.E.O.'s are over the age of sixty. Similarly, you may hear at a staff meeting that, according to "the latest findings," employees really don't prefer flexitime arrangements; most would rather stick to the standard 9-to-5 pattern. How should you react to such statements? Our suggestion is: with a healthy degree of skepticism! First, as we pointed out earlier in this chapter, where behavior in organization is concerned, there are no simple answers. Thus, you should question hard-and-fast conclusions on this basis alone. Second, you should ask, "Just how was this knowledge obtained?" Research, like all human endeavors, can vary greatly

in quality. Before accepting its conclusions, therefore, you should seek to learn something about the way it was conducted. And this, of course, is where a working knowledge of research methods will come in handy: it will help you evaluate the basis for such statements and decide whether to accept or discount them. In short, a basic grasp of research methods will help you separate valid findings from ones that should be doubted. This can often be of considerable practical value.

Second, having such knowledge at your disposal may well yield another benefit: it will make you a more sophisticated and versatile manager. Obviously, no one can be an expert in everything. But there *is* something to be said for having a basic idea of what people in other fields do, and being able to "speak their language," at least to a degree. A basic knowledge of research methods may prove useful to you in this respect. For example, in the years ahead, you may well find yourself having to interact with professionals in the field of organizational behavior. Such persons are often called in as consultants, to help organizations deal with various problems. Knowing something about research methods may be useful to you in such cases. At the least, it will help you to communicate with these experts and to understand the basic strategies they use in trying to solve practical problems.

In sum, basic knowledge about research methods is far from an exercise in empty academics. On the contrary, we suggest that having such information will prove useful to you in several important respects. And given the highly competitive nature of the business world today, we can all use every edge we can get!

Natural Observation: Basis for Insight

Perhaps we should begin by noting that there is some disagreement about whether this first method—**natural observation**—should actually be considered scientific in nature. The reason for this is simple: scientific research usually strives for *objectivity* and a *systematic approach.* Unfortunately, both of these goals are difficult to obtain in natural observation. When using this method, an investigator visits one or more organizations and through careful observation of events, actions, and outcomes within them, attempts to reach conclusions about complex organizational processes or problems. In some cases the researcher may actually join the organization and observe it from the inside (a procedure known as **participant observation**). More often, the investigator observes the organization without actually participating in its activities.[14] In either case, it may be difficult for the observer to proceed in a fully systematic manner: the unpredictable nature of events in a busy organization may interfere with such plans. Similarly, because the observer is very close, both psychologically and physically, to the events he or she records, total objectivity, too, may be difficult to maintain. While these problems are certainly serious, they do not, by themselves, render natural observation useless. On the contrary, when carried out by skilled investigators, this method can serve a unique function in organizational research. Specifically, it can call attention to factors and relationships that have previously been ignored, and so serve as a major source of new insights. In this respect, natural observation may be of considerable value.

The Survey Method: Knowledge Through Self-Report

A second major technique for conducting organizational research is the **survey method**. In this approach, individuals respond to questions about some aspect of their own behavior, or some aspect of their organization. The questions are often presented on a printed form or questionnaire. Sometimes, however, they are posed during face-to-face interviews. In either case, the data collected involve subjects' self-reports of their current views, beliefs, feelings, or attitudes.

Surveys can be used to study many different issues—almost any topic an investigator can imagine. To mention just a few examples, they can gather information about employees' level of job satisfaction or motivation, their reactions to pay plans or supervisors, and even their personal experience with prejudice or sexual harrassment. This flexibility in content, plus great ease of use, represent major advantages of the survey method. Along with such benefits, however, come certain drawbacks. Perhaps the most important of these centers around the fact that survey data consist entirely of self-reports—individuals' own answers to the questions asked. For this reason, the accuracy of survey results depends very heavily upon the honesty and frankness of the persons who respond. If they wish to conceal their true views and feelings, or to present themselves in a favorable light, the findings obtained can be quite misleading. Thus, it is crucial to win the good will and cooperation of participants when using the survey method.

If such cooperation is obtained, surveys can be quite revealing. Thus, they have been, and will almost certainly continue to be, a major technique for acquiring new information about behavior in organizational contexts. (See Table 1.2 for an example of a survey questionnaire.)

TABLE 1.2   *The Survey Method: One Example.*
A survey that might be used to study one aspect of organizational behavior. This particular questionnaire is designed to assess individuals' beliefs concerning the stressfulness of their jobs.

Place a check mark next to each statement that describes your current job.

_____ I don't have enough responsibility.	_____ I have too much responsibility.
_____ I have too much training for my job.	_____ I wish I had more training so that I could do my job better.
_____ My job lacks variety.	
_____ I often have too much time on my hands.	_____ I don't have enough time to complete my work.
_____ My job is not challenging.	
_____ I don't have enough work to do much of the time.	_____ I find my job too challenging.
_____ I am bored by the routine nature of my job.	_____ I don't have time to visit with friends because of my work load.
_____ I have to force myself to stay alert.	_____ I often find the pace of my job over-whelming.
_____ Sometimes, I have to search for things to do.	_____ My work continues at such a fast pace that I don't have time to recover.
	_____ I find that I often have to take work home with me.

Experimentation: Knowledge Through Intervention

Suppose that after reading the best-selling book *Dress for Success,* an O.B. researcher became interested in the following question: When individuals go on job interviews, how should they dress?[15] Further, imagine that no firm or clear evidence on this question currently exists. How could she go about answering this question? One possibility is as follows: she could conduct an appropriate *experiment.*

Unfortunately, many persons seem to feel that experimentation is a complex and mysterious process—one well beyond their grasp. In fact, its basic logic is surprisingly simple and involves only two major steps: (1) some factor believed to affect behavior is systematically varied, either in its presence or strength, and (2) the effects of such variation upon some aspect of behavior are studied. The basic logic behind these procedures can be simply stated. If the factor varied actually affects organizational behavior, then persons exposed to different levels or amounts of it should also show differences in the way they act. For example, exposure to a small amount of the factor in question should result in one level of behavior; exposure to a larger amount should result in a different level, and so on. But please take note: this reasoning is correct only if all other factors that might also affect the behavior under study are held constant. If additional ones are allowed to vary, it is impossible to tell just why any differences in behavior occur. They might then stem from the factor we have chosen to vary, from other factors we have overlooked, or some combination of the two. (Incidentally, the factor systematically varied by a researcher is usually termed the **independent variable**; the aspect of behavior studied, and which it is assumed to affect, is known as the **dependent variable**.)

Admittedly, these comments have been somewhat abstract. To clarify matters, therefore, let's return to the example mentioned above, and see just how an organizational researcher might conduct an experiment concerned with the impact of style of dress on the outcome of job interviews. Actually, there are several ways in which to proceed in this instance. One interesting approach would be as follows. The researcher might arrange for a number of personnel managers to interview a job applicant. In reality, the applicant would be an accomplice of the investigator. (To keep matters simple, let's assume that only one person—a female—plays this role.) The applicant would then be instructed to dress in one of three distinct styles before reporting to each interview: (1) a very *informal* manner (she would wear old jeans and a rumpled shirt), (2) a neat but *traditionally feminine* manner (she would wear a frilly blouse, dangling jewelry, and a skirt), or (3) a neat and *professional* manner (she would wear a tailored suit, simple jewelry). After each interview, the personnel manager involved would be asked to rate the applicant on a special form provided by the researcher. Separate questions on this form would involve ratings of the applicant on several job-related dimensions (e.g., her motivation, talent, intelligence, potential for future success), as well as specific recommendations about hiring this person. The ratings assigned to the applicant when dressed in each of the three different styles would then be compared. (Note, by the way, that the accomplice's style of dress at each interview would be determined in advance in some random manner, such as by a table of random numbers). If style of dress does indeed affect ratings of job applicants, it would be expected that ratings received by the accomplice would differ across the three style-of-dress conditions. For example, as shown in Figure 1.7, she might receive higher ratings when dressed in a neat but traditionally feminine manner than when dressed informally. Further, she might receive the highest ratings of all when "dressed for success" in a professional style. If such results were obtained, it could be concluded (at least tentatively) that the way people dress when going on a job interview *does* matter—a finding of practical importance to both interviewers, who could try to avoid being unduly influenced by this factor, and to applicants, who may want to take this into account when selecting their wardrobe. (Incidentally, actual research on this topic indicates that style of dress does indeed exert such effects.[16])

Of course, the study could have turned out in some other way. For example, the applicant might have received equal ratings in the traditionally feminine and professional conditions. (Perhaps frilly blouses and dangling jewelery are back in style.) Or, style of dress might turn out to have little or no impact on the applicant's ratings: only her qualifications and personality really matter. Regardless of the precise results, though, the basic logic—and purpose—of the research project would remain the same. In order to determine whether a particular factor (independent variable) affects some aspect of work-related behavior, two basic steps are employed: (1) this factor is varied systematically, and (2) the impact of such variations on participants' behavior is carefully noted.

At this point, we should hasten to add that the experiment described above is the simplest type that can be performed. Only one factor was varied in order to examine its effects upon behavior. In many cases, O.B. researchers seek to study the impact of several independent variables at once. They do so because in most real-life situations, behavior is affected by many factors rather than only one. Moreover, the *interactions* between such factors may be of crucial importance. That is, the way in which one factor influences behavior may depend, quite strongly, on some other factor. Continuing with the example above, a job applicant's style of dress may be only one of the factors affecting the ratings she receives. Another could be her

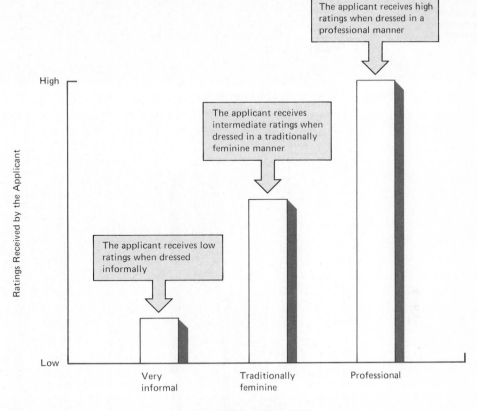

High ─

Ratings Received by the Applicant

Low ─

The applicant receives high
ratings when dressed in a
professional manner

The applicant receives
intermediate ratings when
dressed in a traditionally
feminine manner

The applicant receives low
ratings when dressed
informally

Very
informal

Traditionally
feminine

Professional

Applicant's Style of Dress

FIGURE 1.7   *Experimentation: A Simple Case.*
In a hypothetical experiment, a job applicant (actually an accomplice of the researcher)
dressed in one of three different styles when reporting for an interview. Results indicate that
she received highest ratings from interviewers when dressed in a professional manner, and
lowest ratings when dressed in a very informal style.

actual qualifications. Moreover, these two factors might interact, so that, for example, style of dress exerts larger effects upon interviewer ratings when the applicant has minimal qualifications than when she has excellent ones (refer to Figure
1.8, page 28). Similarly, various aspects of her personality (e.g., her apparent level
of friendliness or confidence) may also affect interviewers' reactions to her, and may
also interact with style of dress. By varying several factors at once in an experiment,
it is often possible to obtain more accurate and complete information about some
aspect of organizational behavior than could be obtained if such factors were
studied one at a time, in isolation. For this reason, many studies described in later
portions of this book will be ones in which several factors—not just one—were
systematically varied at once. Regardless of the number of independent variables
studied, however, the basic underlying strategy remains the same: each is systematically varied in order to determine whether, and to what degree, such changes
affect some important aspect of organizational behavior.

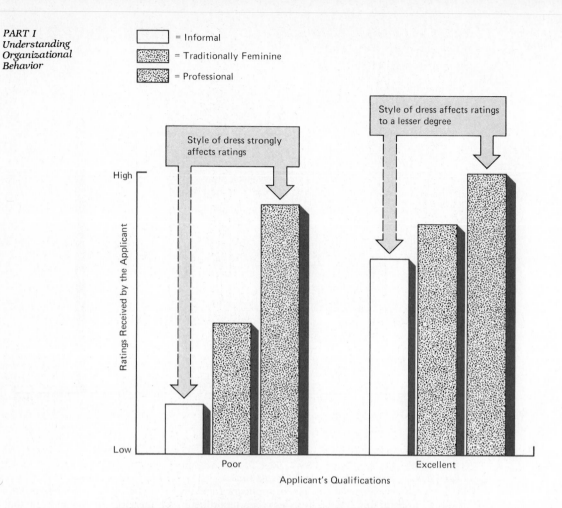

☐ = Informal

▨ = Traditionally Feminine

▨ = Professional

Style of dress strongly affects ratings

Style of dress affects ratings to a lesser degree

High

Ratings Received by the Applicant

Low

Poor   Excellent

Applicant's Qualifications

FIGURE 1.8 *Interaction Between Variables: An Example.*
When a job applicant's qualifications are poor, the style in which she dresses exerts a strong effect upon the ratings she receives from interviewers. When her qualifications are excellent, in contrast, style of dress has much less impact upon these ratings. In sum, these two factors—style of dress and job qualifications—*interact* in determining ratings of the applicant.

A final note of caution: this discussion has not considered several basic issues that arise when actual experiments are performed (e.g., are the persons who take part in the study representative of a larger group to whom the results are to be generalized?) Because of such matters, conducting experiments on organizational behavior is often more difficult than you might at first suspect. Despite these complications, though, experimentation remains a basic tool of the field of O.B., and for good reason: the results it yields often add substantially to our understanding of behavior in organizational settings.

The Correlation Method: Knowledge Through Systematic Observation

As we have just pointed out, experimentation is a valuable technique for conducting organizational research. In fact, many experts believe it is the single most effective method available. Despite this fact, however, there are many situations in which it simply cannot be used. Practical or ethical constraints may rule out the possibility of performing an appropriate experiment, even if such a project can be readily imagined. For example, suppose that an O.B. researcher has reason to suspect that certain styles of management are more effective than others in inducing high levels of commitment and performance among employees. Can he put this prediction to experimental test? Only if the managers in one or more companies are willing to let him alter their behavior at will—an unlikely outcome, to say the least. Similarly, imagine that a researcher believes that certain types of stress produce burnout among employees. Can he now arrange to expose different individuals to varying levels of such conditions (e.g., low, moderate, high), in order to determine whether burnout rises in the manner that he predicts? Obviously not; such procedures might harm the participants and so would be unethical. In these and many other cases, experimentation is not feasible because of either practical or ethical constraints.

Fortunately, when such conditions are encountered, it is not necessary for researchers to throw up their hands in despair and surrender. Instead, they can turn to an alternative approach known as the **correlational method.** Briefly, this technique involves careful observation of two or more variables in order to determine if they are related in some manner. If changes in one are found to be consistently associated with changes in the other (e.g., as one rises, so does the other), evidence for a link between them is obtained. Please note: in contrast to experimentation, *no attempt is made to vary one of these factors in order to observe its effects upon the other.* Instead, naturally occurring variations in both are observed in order to learn whether they tend to occur together in some way. To see how the correlational method can be applied to the study of organizational behavior, let's return to the topic examined above—the impact of applicants' style of dress on the ratings they receive in job interviews.

Here, the basic procedures would be quite simple. A researcher interested in this topic would arrange to visit the employment offices of many different companies. In each, she would observe applicants as they appear for interviews, rating their style of dress along one or more dimensions (e.g., unprofessional–professional; neat–sloppy). Needless to state, the researcher would try to make these observations without calling applicants' attention to her activities. Next, she would obtain the ratings assigned to each person by the interviewers. In a final step, she would compare these two variables—her ratings of applicants' style of dress and the reactions they received from interviewers—to see if they are related. Note once again that she would *not* attempt to vary any applicant's style of dress; nor would she intervene in the interview situation in any manner. Rather, she would simply gather data on both factors (style of dress, interview ratings) and then observe whether they are in fact related. Again, many different patterns of results are possible. For example, it might be found that the more professional the applicants' style of dress, the higher the ratings they receive. Or, it might be noted that ratings increase with "professionalism," but only up to a point; beyond this, they level off and show no further rise. Whatever the nature of the relationship uncovered, it might be summarized as a *correlation*—a number (derived from statistical procedures) indicating the strength and direction of the link. (Correlations range from −1.00 to +1.00. Negative numbers indicate inverse relationships; as one factor rises, the other falls, or vice versa. Positive numbers indicate direct relationships: as one factor rises [or falls], the other does likewise.)

The correlation method offers several key advantages. First, it can readily be employed in a wide range of settings—including actual, functioning organizations. Second, it can be applied to topics and issues that cannot be studied by direct experimentation for ethical or practical reasons. Third, if carefully and skillfully conducted, it may permit researchers to uncover important relationships without affecting or interfering with ongoing activities in any way. In contrast, of course, experimentation requires some type of intervention or change. Given these advantages, you may now be wondering why O.B. researchers ever prefer experimentation. Doesn't it involve a lot of extra work for very little gain? The answer is that despite its many "pluses," the correlational method suffers from one major drawback which should not be overlooked: it is usually not very effective in establishing cause-and-effect relationships. Specifically, the fact that changes in one variable are accompanied by changes in another does *not* guarantee that changes in the first *caused* changes in the second. The opposite may be true or, even worse, changes in both may actually be produced by changes in some other factor not taken into account.[17] For example, imagine that systematic observation reveals that the less hair on the heads of male managers, the higher their position in their companies. One interpretation of this finding might be that hair loss causes promotions—not a very reasonable suggestion to say the least. Another is that promotions, with all the extra worry and pressures they involve, cause hair loss. This is a bit more convincing, but not much. Finally, there is another possibility: both hair loss and promotions stem from another factor: increasing experience on the job—and age! In short, there is no causal link between these two variables; rather, both are affected by another factor.

In this case, it is easy to see that the third alternative is the most reasonable one. In many other instances, though, such a choice is more difficult. For example, suppose that in the example above, our researcher finds that the more professional the style of dress of job applicants, the higher the ratings they receive from interviewers. Does this mean that a professional style of dress causes high ratings? Not necessarily. It is also possible that people who adopt this style possess greater confidence, more maturity, and better judgment than persons who dress in an unprofessional manner. It might well be *these* factors, not style of dress itself, that is producing the observed results. In sum, the moral for researchers—and for consumers of research findings—is clear. Always be on guard against interpreting even a strong correlation between two variables as evidence for a direct causal link between them. As suggested by the cartoon in Figure 1.9, jumping to such conclusions can be quite misleading.

FIGURE 1.9   *Why Correlation Does Not Necessarily Imply Causation.*
As shown in this cartoon, the fact that changes in one variable are accompanied by changes in another does not necessarily imply that there is a causal link between them. Although winters may indeed have gotten colder in the years after Nixon left office, it seems very unlikely that his departure from the White House caused this change in climate. (Source: © **1978 by Newspaper Enterprise Association, Inc.**)

Theory: Essential Guide to Organizational Research

By this point, you should have a good grasp of the basic methods used by O.B. researchers to answer questions about behavior in organizational settings. You may still be wondering, however, about a related issue: where do these questions come from? How do researchers select specific topics for detailed study? Actually, there are several answers to this question. For example, on some occasions, the idea for a research project is suggested by informal observation of organizations and the activities occurring within them. On others, it is suggested by the findings of previous research, which raised intriguing questions or left others unanswered. Perhaps the most important source of research ideas, though, can be stated in a single word: **theory**. Briefly, theory represents attempts by scientists to answer the question "why?" It involves efforts to understand precisely *why* certain events occur as they do, or *why* various processes unfold in a specific manner. Thus, theory goes beyond mere observation or description; it seeks explanation. The attainment of comprehensive, accurate theories is a major goal of all fields of science, and O.B. is no exception. Thus, a great deal of research in our field is concerned with efforts to construct, refine, and test such frameworks. But what, exactly, are theories? And what is their value to O.B.? Perhaps the best means of answering such questions is through a concrete example.

Imagine that we observe the following: when people work together in a group, each member exerts less effort on the joint task than when they work alone. (This is known as *social loafing*, and will be discussed in detail in Chapter 8.) The observation just described is certainly useful by itself. After all, it allows us to predict what will happen when individuals work together, and it also suggests the possibility of intervening in some manner to prevent such outcomes. These two accomplishments—*prediction* and *intervention* (*control*)—are major goals of science. Yet, the fact that social loafing occurs does not explain *why* it takes place. It is at this point that theory enters the picture.

In older and more advanced fields such as physics or chemistry, theories often consist of mathematical equations. In O.B. and related fields, however, they usually involve verbal statements or assertions. For example, a theory designed to account for social loafing might read as follows. When persons work together, they realize that their outputs will not be individually identifiable, and that all participants will share in the responsibility for the final outcome. As a result, they conclude that they can get away with taking it easy, and so exert less effort on the task. Note that this theory, like all others, consists of two parts: several basic concepts (e.g., individual effort, shared responsibility) and statements concerning the relationships between these concepts.

Once a theory has been formulated, a crucial process begins. First, predictions are derived from the theory. These are developed in accordance with basic principles of logic, and are known as **hypotheses**. Next, these predictions are tested in actual research. If they are confirmed, confidence in the accuracy of the theory is increased. If, instead, they are disconfirmed, confidence in the theory may be weakened. Then, the theory may be altered so as to generate new predictions and these, in turn, are made the subject of research. In short, the process is a continuous one, involving the free flow of information between a theory, predictions derived from it, and the findings of ongoing research. (Please see Figure 1.10 for a summary of this process.)

We will have reason to touch on many different theories in later portions of this book. As each is presented, try to keep these two points in mind: (1) such theories

FIGURE 1.10. *The Continuing Interplay Between Theory and Research.*
Once a theory is formulated, it is tested through direct research. If predictions derived from it are confirmed, confidence in the theory's accuracy is increased. If predictions derived from it are disconfirmed, however, confidence in the theory's accuracy is reduced. Then it may either be modified so as to generate other predictions, or it may be rejected.

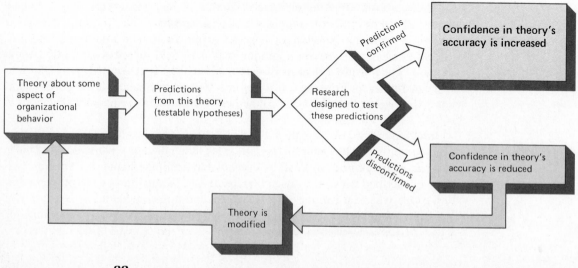

are designed to explain key aspects of organizational behavior, and (2) they should be accepted as valid only to the extent that predictions from them are confirmed in careful research.

USING THIS BOOK: A DISPLACED PREFACE

Before concluding, we would like to comment briefly on several features of this text. Usually, such information is included in the Preface. Since many people skip reading such messages these days, though, we feel that presenting it here makes good sense.

First, we'd like to mention the book's overall organization. It begins by focusing on processes that underlie individual behavior in organizational settings (e.g., motivation, learning, perception). Next, it shifts to processes centered largely in groups (e.g., leadership, communication, conflict). Finally, it turns to processes involving entire organizations (e.g., organizational structure and the ways it is shaped by technology and the environment; organizational change and development).

Second, we wish to call your attention to several aspects of this text designed to make it easier and more convenient for you to use. Each chapter is preceded by an outline showing the major topics covered. All chapters end with a summary of important points, and a glossary that defines key terms and concepts. Such terms are printed in **dark type like this** the first time they are used. The book also contains three distinct types of inserts or "boxes." One of these is labeled *From the Manager's Perspective* (see the one on page 23). Inserts of this type point out applications and implications of materials covered for actual management policy or decisions. Another type of insert is called *Focus on Behavior*. These boxes present descriptions of recent studies or lines of investigation we feel are of special interest. They are included to give you a feel for the kind of progress being made in O.B. at the present time. The third type of insert is labeled *Case in Point* (see page 16). Boxes of this type present brief cases designed to illustrate various aspects of organizational behavior. They are included to help emphasize important links between text materials and situations you may well encounter in the years ahead.

To conclude: we hope that these and other features of this text will help us to communicate knowledge about organizational behavior to you in a manner you will find interesting—or at least bearable! Further, we hope that they will permit some of our own excitement with the field to come through in an undistorted way. To the extent these goals are reached, we'll be satisfied that as authors and teachers, we have done our part. The rest, of course, is up to you!

SUMMARY

The field of **organizational behavior** (O.B.) seeks enhanced knowledge of behavior in organizational settings through the scientific study of individual, group, and organizational processes. Its major goals involve the application of such knowledge to the enhancement of organizational effectiveness and individual wellbeing.

Organizations are social structures or systems in which two or more persons work together in a coordinated manner to reach common goals. While organizations are strongly affected by the persons who compose them, they also exert strong effects, in turn, upon these individuals. Specifically, organizations often shape the behavior and attitudes of their members through their formal *structure* and through *organizational culture*.

In a sense, O.B. is very old, for every civilization has shown interest in understanding behavior in organizations. However, it is only during the past hundred years that a systematic, science-oriented approach to this topic has emerged. *Scientific managment*—one early predecessor of modern O.B.—stressed the importance of designing jobs so that they could be performed as efficiently as possible. In contrast, the *human relations approach* emphasized the key role of social factors in work settings. This perspective was stimulated, in part, by the famous *Hawthorne studies*. Modern O.B. itself is highly diverse, but it is characterized by acceptance of the *human resources model*, the *contingency approach*, and by its *integrative* nature.

In their efforts to comprehend the organizational behavior, O.B. researchers make use of several methods. **Natural observation** involves careful study of events, actions, and processes occurring within a specific organization. The **survey method** makes use of interviews or questionnaires, which ask individuals to provide information about some aspect of their own behavior or some feature of their organization. **Experimentation** involves procedures in which one or more factors *(independent variables)* are systematically varied in order to determine if such changes affect various aspects of organizational behavior *(dependent variables)*. In contrast, the **correlational method** involves careful observation of two or more variables in order to determine if changes in one are accompanied by changes in the other. While the correlational method is highly efficient and can be employed in situations where practical or ethical constraints make experimentation impossible, it suffers from one major drawback: ambiguity with respect to cause-and-effect relationships.

Theories, in science, consist of two major parts: basic concepts and assertions regarding relationships between these concepts. They represent attempts to explain the occurrence of various phenomena. Once a theory is formulated, predictions derived from it are subjected to test in research. If these predictions are confirmed, confidence in the theory is increased. If they are disconfirmed, the theory may be rejected, or altered so as to generate new predictions.

KEY TERMS

behavioral sciences: Several fields (e.g., psychology, sociology, political science) that seek increased knowledge of human behavior and human society through the use of scientific methods.

contingency approach: A perspective suggesting that organizational behavior is affected by a large number of interacting individual, situational, and organizational factors. According to this approach, there are no simple answers to complex questions about organizations and behavior within them.

correlational method: A basic method of research involving systematic observation of two or more variables in order to determine whether changes in one are accompanied by changes in the other(s).

dependent variable: The variable in an experiment (usually some aspect of behavior) that is studied in order to determine whether it is affected in any manner by variations in one or more other variables (ones that are systematically variaed by a researcher).

experimentation: A basic method of research in which one or more factors are systematically varied to determine if such changes exert any impact upon one or more other variables.

human relations approach: A perspective on management and organizational behavior that recognizes the importance of social factors and processes (e.g., communication, influence, leadership) in work settings.

human resources model: A view suggesting that under appropriate circumstances employees are fully capable of working productively and accepting responsibility.

hypotheses: Propositions open to direct scientific test. Often, hypotheses are derived, through logic, from theories. On other occasions, they are suggested by informal observation or the findings of previous research.

independent variable: The factor that is systematically varied in an experiment in order to determine whether such changes affect one or more other variables (usually, aspects of behavior).

natural observation: A research method involving observation of naturally occurring events, activities, and outcomes within an organization.

organization: A social structure consisting of two or more persons who are interdependent and who work together in a coordinated manner to attain common goals.

organizational behavior (O.B.): The field that seeks enhanced knowledge of behavior in organizational settings through the scientific study of individual, group, and organizational processes.

organizational culture: Refers to the shared beliefs, values, and norms of a given organization.

organizational structure: The internal arrangement of an organization, including its division into separate departments and the allocation of tasks and responsibilities among them.

scientific management: An early approach to management and organizational behavior emphasizing the importance of effective job design and employee motivation.

survey method: A research method in which individuals respond to questions about some aspect of their own behavior or some aspect of their organization.

theory: Efforts, by scientists, to explain natural phenomena. Theories generally consist of two major parts: basic concepts and assertions regarding the relationships between these concepts.

Theory X: A traditional view of behavior in work settings, holding that most persons are lazy and irresponsible. The major task for managers is that of providing them with direction and enforcing discipline.

Theory Y: *See* **human resources model.**

NOTES

1. L. G. Bolman and T. E. Deal (1984). Modern approaches to understanding and managing organizations. San Francisco: Jossey-Bass.

2. D. McGregor (1960). *The human side of enterprise.* New York: McGraw-Hill.

3. M. A. Von Glinow, M. J. Driver, K. Brousseau, and J. B. Prince (1983). The design of a career oriented human resource system. *Academy of Managment Review, 8*, 23–32.

4. R. A. Baron (1985). *Understanding human relations: A practical guide to people at work:* Newton, MA: Allyn and Bacon.

5. W. A. Randolph and G. G. Dess (1984). The congruence perspective on organization design: A conceptual model and multivariate research approach. *Academy of Management Review, 9*, 114–127.

6. G. R. Jones (1983). Psychological orientation and the process of organizational socialization: An interactionist perspective. *Academy of Management Review, 8*, 464–474.

7. F. W. Taylor (1911). *The principles of scientific management.* New York: Harper & Brothers.

8. F. J. Roethlisberger and W. J. Dickson (1939). *Management and the worker.* Cambridge: Harvard University Press.

9. See Note 2.

10. See Note 2.

11. P. R. Lawrence and J.W. Lorsch (1967). *Organization and environment.* Cambridge: Harvard University Press.

12. C. B. Schoonhoven (1981). Problem with contingency theory: Testing assumptions hidden within the language of contingency "theory." *Administrative Science Quarterly, 26*, 349–377.

13. R. L. Daft (1983). Learning the craft of organizational research. *Academy of Management Review, 8*, 539–546.

14. H. Mintzberg (1973). *The nature of managerial work.* New York: Harper & Row.

15. S. Forsythe, M. F. Drake, and C. E. Cox (1985). Influence of applicant dress on interviewer's selection decisions. *Journal of Applied Psychology, 70*, 374–378.

16. See Note 15.

17. T. R. Mitchell (1985). An evaluation of the validity of correlational research conducted in organizations. *Academy of Management Review, 10*, 192–205.

PART II

INDIVIDUAL PROCESSES

CHAPTER 2

Learning: Adapting to the World Around Us

Chris Folay and Beth Laurenti are driving home from work. It's Friday afternoon, and Beth is in good spirits, happily looking forward to an exciting weekend. For Chris, though, it's another story. Her face is glum, and she stares out the window without uttering a word. Noticing her friend's unhappy mood, Beth asks:

"Hey, Chris, what's wrong? You look like doom-and-gloom itself!"

"Oh, it's my assistant, Tom. I just can't figure him out, and it's getting me down."

"What do you mean?" Beth asks.

"Well, he's just a puzzle, that's all. For months he'll do good work—so good that I'm really proud of him. Then, just when I'm certain he's ready for promotion, he falls apart. I just can't understand it."

"Yeah, that's strange," Beth agrees. "Why do you suppose he acts that way?"

"Darned if I know. As soon as I start praising his work or mentioning the word promotion, he seems to choke up and do something real dumb. Like this week—he really made a mess of the Martin deal. It's going to take some real maneuvering on my part to get it straightened out."

"Hm . . . you know," Beth comments, "I think I've got an idea. I don't know Tom well, but it's my impression that he's not the kind of guy who likes responsibility. So maybe when you begin mentioning promotion, he gets worried that he'll have to take on more than he can handle."

At this remark, Chris turns and stares at her friend, a puzzled look on her face. Beth notices her expression, but forges on.

"Also, I know that Tom's real happy here. If he gets a promotion, won't he have to move out West? Maybe that's bothering him too."

Chris is silent for a moment but then, stroking her chin, she replies. "You know, I never thought of it that way before. I always assumed that *everyone* wants a promotion when they can get it. Now that you mention it, though, I'm not sure about Tom . . ."

"Well, that could be it," Beth answers. "I've heard of stranger things. Anyway, you know the old saying 'One person's meat, another's poison.' What seems like a plum to you might be a real disaster to him. That could be the key to understanding his behavior. He's just learned to avoid things he really doesn't want."

At first glance, Tom's behavior probably struck you, too, as somewhat puzzling. After all, why would anyone want to stay an assistant instead of gaining a promotion and advancing his career? Tom's actions lost much of their mystery, however, once we took note of the basic process mentioned by Beth: **learning.** What this refers to, of course, is our ability to profit from experience—our capacity to gain the skills, behaviors, and information we need to function in a complex world and reach our major goals. For Tom, the key goal was somewhat surprising: avoiding a promotion and the changes it would bring (e.g., a cross-country move, increased responsibility). In other cases, and with other persons, both the behaviors and goals might be very different; yet, the basic process would remain much the same.

But what, precisely, is learning? Generally, it is defined as follows: *learning is any relatively permanent change in behavior produced by experience.*[1] Thus, it involves changes in the way we behave, think, or feel resulting from our continued contact with the world around us. Note that learning should not be confused with temporary changes such as those produced by drugs, illness, or fatigue. Similarly, it is *not* synonymous with "improvements" in behavior or performance. As we have already seen, learning can often yield undesirable as well as desirable outcomes. (While Tom may have been happy to stay where he was, his errors probably proved costly to Chris, his supervisor, and to his company.)

You are probably already familiar with learning as a basic process. Most of us have faced the task of acquiring new skills or studying for exams. But there is a good chance that you do not yet appreciate the breadth of its impact or its key relevance to organizational behavior. In a sense, the impact of learning cannot be overstated. It seems to play a role in virtually everything we do, from reading these words and falling in love to learning to drive and forming our major values (see Figure 2.1). Similarly, it exerts powerful effects on a wide range of organizational processes—acquiring job-related skills, "plugging into the grapevine," and understanding the complexities of organizational politics, to name just a few. It is because of these effects that we have chosen to consider learning very early in this text. In order to acquaint you with its basic nature, and to provide a firm foundation for many discussions in later chapters, we will proceed as follows.

First, we will describe two basic forms of learning—**operant conditioning** and **modeling.** While others exist (e.g., *Pavlovian* or *classical conditioning*), these are the forms most central to organizational behavior. Second, we will indicate how

40

FIGURE 2.1 *Learning: Key Process in Human Behavior.*
Learning plays an important role in virtually all human activities, including the ones shown here.

knowledge about these types of learning has been put to practical use in efforts to change or modify various aspects of organizational behavior. Third, we will comment briefly on the role of learning in other important processes: *employee training* and *organizational socialization*. (Information on an additional learning-related topic—*mentorship*—will be included in a special **Focus** insert.)

OPERANT CONDITIONING: LEARNING BASED ON CONSEQUENCES

Operant conditioning, a form of learning with important implications for organizational behavior, is based upon a simple principle: behavior usually produces some kind of consequences. For example, meeting an important deadline set by your supervisor may result in praise, a bonus, or promotion. Failing to meet it may lead to criticism—or worse! Similarly, threatening your opponent during negotiations will probably make this person angry, and may reduce the chances of an agreement. Treating him or her in a conciliatory way may produce opposite effects (i.e., increase the likelihood of an agreement). Because of the *contingency* that often exists between what we do and the outcomes we experience, we often learn to act in specific ways.

First, we learn to engage in behaviors that produce positive outcomes—ones we find pleasant or desirable. Thus, we often acquire actions that permit us to acquire money, status, approval, and satisfaction of our physical needs. Such stimuli are termed **positive reinforcers,** and their effect upon behavior is straightforward: generally, they strengthen responses that precede them or lead to their occurrence. The impact of positive reinforcement can be readily observed in many organizational settings. For example, the young manager who is rewarded for a job well done by praise and recognition from his supervisor is likely to work even harder on future occasions. Similarly, a salesperson who succeeds in closing a major deal through the use of some specific tactic is likely to use it again in the future: after all, it seems to work! In these and countless other cases, the basic principle remains the same: people show increased tendencies to perform behaviors that help them attain (or at least move closer to) positive, desired outcomes.

Second, we learn to perform actions that permit us to avoid *unpleasant* outcomes or to escape from them once they occur. Thus, we acquire responses that help us in avoiding harsh physical conditions (e.g., intense heat or cold), criticism from superiors, "loss of face" in front of others, cuts in pay, and similar results. Outcomes of this type are termed **negative reinforcers,** and again, their impact upon behavior is clear: in general, they strengthen responses that lead to their removal or termination. The impact of negative reinforcement can be readily observed in many organizations. For example, production workers often acquire complex techniques for "looking busy" while goofing off, and so avoid criticism from their supervisors. Similarly, it is the rare secretary or administrative assistant who does not know how to soothe his or her boss, and so escape from prolonged temper outbursts.

Finally, we also learn to avoid engaging in behaviors that lead to or produce negative outcomes. In short, we learn to refrain from performing actions that are *punished*. Please note: **punishment** is *not* identical to negative reinforcement. In the case of punishment, we learn to avoid negative outcomes by withholding behaviors we would like to perform (e.g., we don't tell our boss just what we think of her, even when she makes us angry). In the case of negative reinforcement, in contrast, we learn to perform responses that prevent or terminate the occurrence of unpleasant outcomes (e.g., we learn how to avoid getting into situations in which we'd like to tell her just what we think of her). The basic principles involved in positive reinforcement, negative reinforcement, and punishment are summarized in Figure 2.2; please examine them carefully.

As we noted at the start of this discussion, operant conditioning has important implications for the field of O.B. In fact, procedures derived from its basic principles have often been used to produce desirable changes in a wide range of organizational behavior and organizational processes.[2,3] We will return to these applied (and often successful) efforts below. Before doing so, however, it is essential to acquaint you with a few additional facts about the nature of operant conditioning itself— so please read on.

FIGURE 2.2 *Positive Reinforcement, Negative Reinforcement, and Punishment: An Overview.*
As shown here, positive reinforcers strengthen behaviors that lead to their occurrence, while negative reinforcers strengthen responses that lead to their removal or termination. Punishment suppresses responses that lead to unpleasant outcomes.

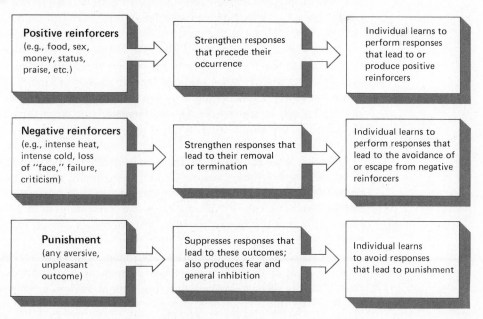

Operant Conditioning:
Some Key Aspects

Several aspects of operant conditioning are far from surprising. For example, the greater the number of occasions on which a given behavior is followed by positive reinforcement, the stronger the tendency to perform that behavior. Thus, the more often a young woman working for the Internal Revenue Service is praised by her supervisor for wringing additional taxes out of citizens, the more diligently will she work at this task on future occasions. Similarly, the shorter the delay between performance of a given response and reinforcement for it, the stronger the tendency to perform this activity. Thus, continuing the example, if the young auditor is praised by her supervisor as soon as she returns to the office with each taxpayer's check in hand, the impact will probably be greater than if he waits several days before delivering such verbal rewards.

While the impact of the factors we have just mentioned is fairly straightforward, there is another, far less obvious aspect of operant conditioning deserving of our attention. This involves the pattern and regularity with which positive or negative reinforcers are presented and is generally referred to as **schedules of reinforcement.** Such schedules often exert profound effects upon behavior and represent one of the most important components of operant conditioning.

Schedules of reinforcement: The when and why of rewards. As you already know from your own experience, reinforcement does not always follow a particular response. For example, studying hard for an exam sometimes yields a high grade— but sometimes it does not. Flattering a potential client sometimes helps in winning a large order, but occasionally it may backfire and produce opposite results. And apologizing sincerely for errors often "turns off" criticism from your boss quite quickly, but again, not always (e.g., he may be in an especially rotten mood). In many cases, the occurrence or absence of reinforcement following a given form of behavior seems to be quite random; indeed, there may be no way of knowing, in advance, whether some action will or will not yield the desired outcomes. In others, though, the delivery of reinforcers is governed by definite rules. These are known as *schedules of reinforcement,* and can take an almost infinite number of forms.[4] The simplest of these is a schedule in which every response is followed by a reward—a pattern known as *continuous reinforcement.* Aside from this relatively rare situation, though, the most basic schedules are ones in which the occurrence of reward is governed by a single rule. Four distinct schedules of this type exist.

In the first, the **fixed interval schedule,** the occurrence of reinforcement depends largely on the passage of time. Specifically, some predetermined interval must elapse after a response has been reinforced before such a reward is available once again. Schedules of this type are quite common in organizational settings. For example, many businesses pay their employees on a fixed interval schedule (e.g., once a week, once a month). Similarly, performance reviews usually occur once or twice a year, on a fixed schedule. Fixed interval schedules of reinforcement often result in a highly distinctive pattern of behavior. Individuals exposed to such conditions typically show a low rate of responding immediately after receiving a reward. Then, as the time when reinforcement can be obtained again approaches, they gradually respond at a faster and faster rate (refer to Figure 2.3). Thus, right after

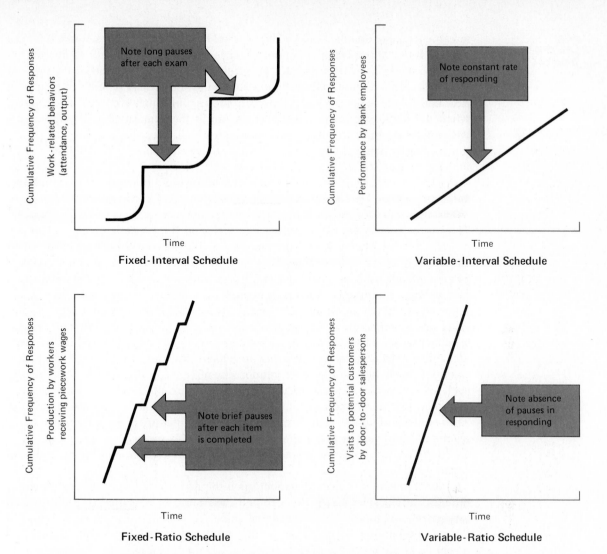

FIGURE 2.3 *Basic Schedules of Reinforcement: A Summary of Their Effects.*
Patterns of behavior (rates of responding) that might be observed under fixed interval, variable interval, fixed ratio, and variable ratio schedules of reinforcement. Note that the steeper the lines, the higher the rate of responding by the persons involved.

payday, work-related activities such as attendance, effort, and output may all drop to low levels. As the time of the next paycheck rolls around, however, all of these activities may increase in frequency. Similarly, it is common to observe increased effort and productivity as the time for the annual performance review approaches; after it is over, many people relax, and reduce their output.

The availability of reinforcement is also controlled mainly by the passage of time in a **variable interval schedule.** Here, though, the period that must elapse between reinforcements varies around some average value. In some cases, reinforcement can be obtained after a short period has passed. In others, a much longer interval must elapse before it again becomes available. As a result of this uncertainty, variable interval schedules generally yield steady and moderate rates of responding (see Figure 2.3). A good example of the impact of such schedules is provided by the actions of most bank employees. Since they can't tell, in advance, when the bank examiners will appear to audit their books (they usually arrive without prior notice), such persons must keep their records in good order at all times. Only by doing so can they avoid the negative outcomes that will follow should major errors exist.

3) The occurrence of reinforcement is determined in a different manner in **fixed ratio schedules.** Here, after one response has been reinforced, a specific number of additional responses must be performed before another reinforcement is presented. Thus, it may be necessary for persons exposed to such a schedule to respond 10, 80, or even 300 times before receiving the next reward. Fixed ratio schedules are quite common in organizational settings. For example, many companies employ piecework pay systems in which employees earn a fixed amount of money for completing a set number of items or operations. Similarly, many managers employ informal schedules in which they permit their subordinates to take a break and relax after completing a specified number of work units (e.g., after painting a specific number of walls; after packing a set number of boxes). Fixed ratio schedules often yield a pattern of behavior in which individuals respond at a constant rate, but pause briefly after each reinforcement (refer to Figure 2.3). Apparently, such pauses occur because they quickly learn that the first few responses immediately after reinforcement rarely bring additional rewards. Because of the high rates of responding they generate, fixed ratio schedules are often attractive to management. They may be less popular with workers, however, especially when they feel that the ratio between responses (effort) and reinforcements (pay) is set too high.

4) Reinforcement is also dependent upon the number of responses performed in **variable ratio schedules.** Here, though, the number of responses that must be performed varies around some average value. Thus, reinforcement sometimes follows a small number of responses, while on other occasions it may result only after a very large number have been emitted. As you might guess, such uncertainty as to just when reinforcement will occur often results in high and constant rates of responding (refer to Figure 2.3). A dramatic illustration of this pattern is provided by gamblers who choose to play slot machines. Since these devices pay off after swallowing a variable number of coins, gamblers can never know when they will be lucky. Thus, they often respond at a very high rate—as high as their funds permit! But variable ratio schedules operate in many other contexts, too. For example, door-to-door salespersons have no way of knowing how many potential customers they must visit before making a sale. As a result, they often rush from house to house and block to block at a very high rate (see Figure 2.4). In sum, where variable ratio schedules are involved, the old phrase "hope springs eternal" seems to apply—and to apply very well.

As we have tried to suggest, these simple schedules of reinforcement seem applicable to many real-life situations. But do they actually produce the effects described above? Research findings suggest that, often, they do.[5] For example, several studies designed to compare the impact of various schedules on the behavior

FIGURE 2.4   *Variable Ratio Schedules in Action: The Case of Door-to-Door Salespersons.*
Because they can never be certain when they will make a sale, door-to-door salespersons
often show a high and steady rate of calling on prospective customers.

of employees indicate that when organizational rewards are made contingent upon
the performance of specific responses (i.e., when ratio schedules are employed),
high levels of the desired behaviors often result. However, when such rewards are
made contingent on the passage of time (i.e., when interval schedules are used),
employees emit desired behaviors at a lower rate. In short, consistent with the
patterns shown in Figure 2.3, ratio and interval schedules of reinforcement do
appear to evoke contrasting reactions—or at least different rates of behavior—in a
wide range of organizational settings.

One final point: while simple schedules do operate in many situations, there
are also numerous cases in which they are not present in "pure" form. Instead, they
are combined with each other to produce more complex sets of rules or contingen-

cies. For example, consider the promotion policies in effect in many companies. Often, these involve both the completion of a number of specific tasks (e.g., closing a number of deals; successful participation in several projects) *and* a minimum amount of time on the job. Only when both conditions have been met is promotion granted. In short, reinforcement (promotion) occurs only after the requirements of both a ratio and an interval schedule have been met. As you can well imagine, simple schedules of reinforcement can be combined in many other ways as well—far too many for us to consider in detail here. However, this fact should in no way interfere with your firm grasp of two basic principles. First, in many real-life situations, reinforcements do *not* follow every appropriate response; rather they occur only part of the time. Second, in such cases, the rules (or schedules) determining the delivery of positive or negative reinforcers can exert strong effects upon behavior.

Extinction and Punishment:
Unwanted Behaviors

So far in this discussion, we've focused on the manner in which individuals acquire new behavior, and key factors that influence the rate at which they perform them. Obviously, though, there must be another side of the coin. There must be some mechanism through which behaviors that are ineffective, or that yield undesirable consequences, are eliminated. If there were not, we would soon find ourselves performing many actions which serve no purpose, or which interfere with our major goals. Fortunately, two basic processes spare us from such a fate: **extinction** and **punishment.**

Extinction: Getting rid of "excess baggage."   Suppose that a manager at a large municipal bus system faces the following problem. In recent months, growing numbers of customers have called to complain about buses failing to pick them up. Apparently, the drivers involved have zipped right past regular stops, leaving customers to fume—and complain! A check of existing conditions soon explains this puzzling behavior. By passing their stops, drivers can get back to the terminal early where they can then participate in a spirited poker game that develops late each afternoon. In order to alter this situation, the manager calls a meeting and announces that such games can no longer take place on company property. The result: drivers grumble about this "unfair" treatment, but soon begin stopping for passengers once again. The reason for this change in their behavior is simple: there is no longer anything to gain by rushing back to the terminal; in fact, if they do arrive early, there's little or nothing to do until quitting time. (Steps are also taken to assure that no one can leave early.) In short, by eliminating the reinforcement for inappropriate behavior (failing to pick up waiting passengers) the manager has succeeded in greatly reducing its occurrence.

This incident provides a clear example of the process of *extinction*. Briefly, this term refers to the fact that when behaviors that previously yielded reinforcement no longer do so, they gradually decrease in frequency or strength, and may totally disappear. One effective means of eliminating undesirable behavior within an organization (or elsewhere), then, is that of applying this basic principle. Of course, identifying and then eliminating various sources of reinforcement for objectionable behavior is often a complex task. If these steps can be successfully implemented, however, extinction of the behavior in question is almost certain to occur.

Extinction and the partial reinforcement effect: When "less is more."   Consider the following question: which behaviors would be more resistant to extinction—ones that have previously been reinforced every time they were performed, or ones that were reinforced only part of the time, perhaps in accordance with one of the schedules described above? Common sense probably leads you to reply, "Behaviors that have always been reinforced—they'll be stronger." This is one of those cases in which common sense leads us astray, however. A large body of research evidence indicates that, in fact, it is behaviors acquired under conditions of partial reinforcement that are more resistant to extinction. This surprising phenomenon is usually termed the **partial reinforcement effect,** and can be observed in operation in a wide variety of situations.

For example, consider two secretaries. Each asks her boss several times each month if she can leave early. One is always rewarded for such requests: her boss is soft-hearted and always agrees. The other is rewarded only part of the time: sometimes her boss consents, and sometimes she does not. Now, imagine that the company adopts a new policy that specifically forbids any manager from allowing his or her secretary to leave early. In other words, reinforcement for such requests is no longer possible, so extinction has begun. Which secretary would stop asking to leave early sooner? The answer is clear: the one whose boss previously said "yes" every time (see Figure 2.5, page 50).

This example is also useful for illustrating one possible explanation for the occurrence of the partial reinforcement effect. For which secretary would the shift to extinction be more noticeable or abrupt? Again, the answer is clear: the one whose boss had always said "yes." Thus, it may be that behaviors acquired under partial reinforcement are more resistant to extinction than ones acquired under continuous reinforcement because conditions during acquisition and extinction are more similar for the former than for the latter. Regardless of the basis for the partial reinforcement effect, however, it has intriguing implications for human behavior. Specifically, it helps explain why individuals often persist in performing actions that no longer work—ones that no longer yield desired reinforcers. When it is realized that most behaviors are acquired under conditions of partial reinforcement, such persistence becomes less puzzling. Indeed, it becomes clear that actions often viewed as a sign of human stubbornness or inflexibility may actually reflect the operation of basic principles of operant conditioning.

Punishment: Effective (perhaps) but tricky.   Suppose that you conducted a survey of one hundred managers, chosen at random from a wide range of organizations. In your survey, you asked these people to indicate what tactics they use in dealing with undesirable behavior among their employees. What would you find? Probably, most make heavy use of *punishment*. That is, many would report that they attempt to deal with such problems as tardiness, repeated absence, or violations of company policy by subjecting the persons involved to some kind of punishment. If these were the results of your survey, they would be quite accurate, for

CONDITIONS DURING
ACQUISITION

RESULTS DURING EXTINCTION
(After new company policy is put into effect)

Secretary A:

**Continuous
reinforcement**
Every time she asks to
leave early, her boss agrees

**Rapid
extinction**
She quickly stops asking
for permission
to leave

The partial
reinforcement effect

Secretary B:

Partial reinforcement
Sometimes her boss agrees
to let her leave early, but
sometimes she refuses

Slower extinction
She continues to ask for permission
to leave for several weeks

FIGURE 2.5 *The Partial Reinforcement Effect: A Concrete Example.*
Every time Secretary A asks her boss if she can leave early, she agrees. In contrast, Secretary
B's boss agrees to her requests only part of the time. The result: when a new company policy
forbids managers from allowing their subordinates to leave early, Secretary A gives up sooner
on such requests than Secretary B. In other words, her tendency to ask permission to leave
early extinguishes more quickly. This is known as the *partial reinforcement effect.*

punishment *is* widely used by practicing managers.[6] There are several reasons why
this is the case.

First, many managers—especially those at lower levels of the organization—
feel that they really don't have much of a choice in this matter. Since they exert little
if any control over important positive reinforcers (e.g., raises, promotions) they
conclude that they must fall back upon the only tactics that *are* at their disposal—
certain kinds of punishment (e.g., raking offenders "over the coals"). Similarly, the
impact of punishment, when it works, appears to be immediate. For this reason, it
seems suitable in cases where actions by employees are too dangerous or costly to be
allowed to continue (e.g., failure to wear protective gear around dangerous chemicals; flagrant violations of safety standards in working with machinery). Whatever
the reasons for its widespread use, however, the key question with respect to punishment is this: does it really work? Is it effective in producing lasting, desirable
changes in individuals' behavior?

Interestingly, the pendulum of scientific opinion has swung back and forth on
this issue over the course of several decades.[7] At present, though, most experts agree
that punishment *can* succeed in permanently changing behavior. They also agree,
however, that this will be the case only when it is used in accordance with certain
key principles. First, to be most effective, punishment should be immediate. If it is

delayed, its impact may be greatly reduced. Second, it should be quite intense. Mild punishments, or ones individuals do not really find objectionable, will have little lasting effect upon behavior. Fourth, individuals receiving punishment must be provided with acceptable alternative forms of behavior. If they are not, the punished behaviors will tend to reappear. Finally, undesirable behaviors should *not* be rewarded after punishment has been delivered. For example, after criticizing a subordinate for poor work, it is an error to "make up" with this person a few hours later by treating him or her to lunch. In that case, any potential benefits of the prior punishment may be totally eliminated.

Unfortunately, stating these principles is one thing; putting them to systematic use in the complex world of organizations is quite another. For example, sometimes it is difficult, if not impossible, to deliver punishment immediately; an appropriate opportunity may simply not exist. Similarly, it may be difficult to come up with a form of punishment truly aversive to the recipients; the range of options open to a manager may be restricted by company policies or a union contract. And of course the guilt or sympathy a manager often feels after the delivery of punishment to a subordinate make it difficult to avoid being extra nice to this person later that day—perhaps totally counteracting any benefits produced. These are not the only problems connected with the use of punishment, however. In addition, punishment itself often generates undesirable "side-effects" that operate to reduce its success. One of these is the arousal of strong emotional reactions among recipients (e.g., feelings of anger or resentment). Obviously, such feelings can damage working relationships, and exert adverse effects upon individuals and their organization. A second side-effect of punishment is that persons who receive it frequently tend to adopt a pattern of inhibited activity. They "play it safe" by doing as little as possible and this, in turn, can prevent them from offering their maximum contribution to a work group or organization.

In view of these complexities and problems, it is clear that the use of punishment is indeed tricky, as suggested by the section heading above. In order to succeed, it must be used in an orderly, rational manner—not, as is too often the case, as a handy outlet for a manager's anger or frustration. If used with skill, and concern for human dignity, it *can* be useful. When used inappropriately, however, it may backfire and generate more problems than it solves. (For a concrete example of the ineffective use of punishment, see the **Case in Point** insert on page 52.)

MODELING: LEARNING BY OBSERVING

There can be little doubt that operant conditioning plays a central role in human behavior. Over time, most persons do indeed learn to engage in actions that yield positive consequences, or ones that permit them to avoid unpleasant outcomes. Yet it is equally clear that this is not the only way we learn. If you have ever watched another person perform some action (anything from a fancy new dance step to operating a complex piece of machinery) and then tried to do this yourself, you are

"Who's Punishing Whom, Anyway?"

Ellie Mulvaney is upset, and it shows. In fact, her feelings are so obvious that Bob Chen departs from his usual reserve and stops her in the hall.

"Gee, Ellie," he comments, "you look terrible. What's wrong?"

"Oh, just the usual," Ellie replies. "Another round with Fran."

At this, Bob nods his head knowingly. Fran is Ellie's secretary, and their encounters are getting to be something of a legend in the department. "So what was it this time?" Bob asks.

"Phone messages. If I've asked her once, I've asked her a hundred times to be sure to take them carefully. But does she listen? No! She gives me slips with first names only, no area codes, no message about why they called—It makes me furious!"

"I know, I know," Bob says soothingly. "But screaming at her and getting yourself all worked up doesn't help matters."

"No, it doesn't," Ellie agrees. "But what else can I do? She gets me so mad. I've tried reasoning with her, but it does no good. We just don't seem to get along."

"Well, I don't mean to butt in," Bob replies, "but I don't think you're going about this the right way. When she makes the same mistake over and over, you have to tell her, sure. But when you wait until you've lost your temper, you ruin the effect."

"What do you mean?" Ellie asks, a puzzled expression on her face.

"When you shout at her like that, what does she do?" Bob asks in reply.

Ellie thinks for a moment. "Hm . . . she kind of looks hurt, like she's almost in tears. Then she looks at the other secretaries as if to say 'See what I have to endure—Isn't she terrible?' And for the rest of the day she calls me 'Ms. Mulvaney' instead of Ellie."

"Exactly!" Bob says with considerable feeling. "And then later, how do you feel?"

"Pretty rotten. You know I don't want that kind of trouble. And I sure don't want a reputation for being difficult . . ."

"So then you try to make it up to her by letting her leave early, or visit with her friends for hours."

At this remark, Ellie looks embarrassed. "Yes, that's what happens all right," she admits. "I tend to be really easy on her for a while after losing my temper."

"And that ruins the whole thing. In fact, what you end up doing is teaching her that she can really control *you*. All she has to do is act hurt, play the martyr, and you cave in. Looking at it from the outside, it's really hard to tell who's punishing whom!"

Now Ellie really looks thoughtful. "You know, Bob, I think you've really got something there. I'm *not* handling this right at all, am I? Well, I'm going to think this through. I'm sure I can do better—a *lot* better!"

Questions

(1) What errors in Ellie's use of punishment did Bob point out? Is she making others as well?

(2) Suppose Fran continues to make the same errors; how would you recommend that Ellie respond?

(3) Could Ellie handle this situation through positive reinforcement rather than punishment? If she did, do you think it would be more effective?

---

familiar with a second major type of learning: **modeling.** Briefly, this term refers to our ability to acquire new behaviors, or absorb pertinent information, merely through observing the actions of others and the consequences they experience.[8] In short, it calls attention to the fact that we can profit from vicarious as well as direct experience with the world around us.

Countless instances of modeling exist in virtually every sphere of life. For example, this process seems to play a major role in the transmission of cultural values and beliefs from one generation to the next. Similarly, it accounts, in large measure, for the impact of media violence upon viewers of all ages.[9] It helps explain the rapid spread of new styles of speech, dress, and grooming. And it may even account for the occurrence of grisly "copy-cat" crimes. That modeling also plays a role in several important forms of organizational behavior is also apparent. First, it contributes to both formal and informal programs of *job training*, helping new employees acquire the skills and knowledge they need to perform effectively.[10] Second, it contributes to *organizational socialization*—the process through which individuals acquire the norms, values, and procedures of their organizations, and so become fully integrated in them. Third, it is central to **mentorship**—an important process in which older, experienced individuals "adopt" younger ones and actively contribute to their careers, and it also plays a role in *peer relationships*— mutually beneficial associations between persons at roughly the same level in an organization.[11] We will return to concrete examples of the role of modeling in each of these processes below. For the present, however, we simply wish to emphasize the following points: (1) modeling is a basic form of learning with important implications for a wide range of human behavior; (2) it helps account for our ability to acquire new behaviors or information even without the process of trial-and-error usually required by operant conditioning.

Modeling: A Closer Look

As we have already noted, modeling is a common and widespread process. Yet, even a moment's reflection suggests that it is far from random in nature. First, we do not attempt to learn from the actions of everyone around us. On the contrary, we usually select the persons we will emulate with care. Second, modeling itself is far from an "all-or-none" process. Sometimes it occurs rapidly and efficiently, while on other occasions it proceeds more slowly. Together, these points have led researchers to examine modeling more closely. The results of their investigations point to the conclusions that it is affected by four key factors.

The first of these is *attention*. Unless we focus carefully on others' behavior we cannot hope to reproduce their actions. For this reason, any characteristics of other persons that attract and hold our attention—for example high status, physical beauty, expertise—tend to facilitate the modeling process. The second factor is *retention*. Unless we can somehow retain an internal representation of others' actions (e.g., a verbal description or visual image of them), modeling cannot take place. A third factor involves our ability to *reproduce* others' behavior. Finally, *motivation*, too, plays a key role. Modeling will simply not occur unless we have some reason for paying attention to others and emulating their actions. For example, an accountant who works at the next desk to a marketing executive would probably not acquire much knowledge of her neighbor's field through simple observation. Only if she were contemplating a career change would such modeling be likely to take place. In sum, observational learning, like operant conditioning, appears to be affected by several factors which determine whether and to what extent it will take place.

Modeling and Social Learning

This discussion of modeling would be sadly incomplete if it did not contain mention of one additional fact. Modeling, important as it is, is only part of a broader framework for understanding human learning known as **social learning.**[12] This approach differs from operant conditioning in several ways. Since all of these have implications for our understanding of organizational behavior, they are worth considering here.

First, as we have already noted, social learning theory takes account of the fact that human beings can acquire new behaviors (or information) through observation. Second, and perhaps even more important, it emphasizes the role of cognitive processes in many learning situations. Specifically, social learning theory notes that external conditions in the world around us (including positive and negative reinforcers) do not usually influence behavior in a direct or simple way. Rather, they produce their effects largely through their impact on intervening cognitive processes. Put very simply, social learning theory takes account of the fact that people think about (or actively process) their experiences. Thus, the impact of these stimuli and events is filtered through a complex web of interpretation and memory. Finally, social learning theory also emphasizes the fact that individuals are capable of regulating their own behavior. People usually monitor and evaluate their own actions in a fairly continuous manner. Moreover, they often compare their behavior to internal standards and values, administering self-reinforcement when these are met ("Not bad, if I say so myself") but self-criticism when they are not ("Come on, you can do better than that!"). For example, an individual writing a report may edit and re-edit his words until he feels they are both logical and clear. Similarly, an architect planning a building will alter her sketches over and over again until she attains the effect she wants. In these and countless other situations, individuals show an impressive capacity to control or regulate their own behavior. Social learning theory takes full note of these abilities, and underscores their important role in many situations.

In sum, social learning theory suggests that to fully understand human behavior and its modification through learning, we must take careful account of the complex interplay between external events, cognitive processes, and the internal as well as external effects of behavior. Applying this framework to organizational behavior, social learning theory suggests that we must focus on the conditions and events within an organization, the cognitive processes that underlie individuals' interpretation of these stimuli, and the nature and consequences of their overt actions. Moreover, as shown in Figure 2.6, it suggests that we must recognize the reciprocal, two-way relationships existing between all of these factors.[13]

A final word of caution: social learning theory does not seek to refute operant conditioning, nor to deny the validity of its basic principles. On the contrary, it takes

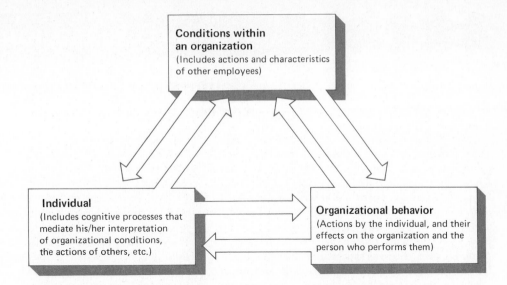

FIGURE 2.6 *Organizational Behavior: A Social Learning Perspective.*
According to the *social learning approach*, full understanding of organizational behavior must involve careful attention to the conditions existing in an organization, the characteristics and cognitive processes of individuals, and both the internal and external effects of their behavior. Moreover, it suggests that the relationships existing between all of these factors are reciprocal (two-way) in nature.

full account of the important role of positive and negative reinforcers. What it *does* do is attempt to expand this earlier approach and enhance its sophistication by considering processes (e.g., modeling, the self-regulation of behavior) that operant conditioning largely ignores. From this perspective, then, these two views of human learning are complementary rather than contradictory. (Please see the **Focus** insert on page 56 for a discussion of *mentorship*—an organizational process in which modeling plays a major role.)

LEARNING AND ORGANIZATIONAL BEHAVIOR: PRACTICAL APPLICATIONS

Over the years, we have often heard students make the following remarks: "All this is pretty interesting—but what can I *do* with it? Does it really have any practical value?" Where knowledge about human learning is concerned, our answer is "Yes, yes, a thousand times yes!" In fact, information about operant conditioning and social learning has already been applied to the solution of a wide range of practical problems. For example, it has been used to help educate retarded persons, to treat several forms of mental illness, to assist children in overcoming social isolation, and to help adults cope with many personal problems, including smoking, obesity, and excessive shyness.[17] Such work, of course, is not directly relevant to organizational

Mentorship: Modeling and Career Development

Master and apprentice, teacher and student, physician and intern. These are familiar pairings, used throughout recorded history. All involve a basic relationship in which an older, more experienced person (a *mentor*) takes a younger, less knowledgeable one (a *protégé*) under his or her wing, and so helps this person toward a successful career. Clearly, modeling plays a key role in this process. Within mentor-protégé pairs, the protégé learns much from observing his or her mentor. Moreover, protégés usually attempt to emulate mentors' traits and actions. Indeed, they may go so far as to imitate their mannerisms or style of dress—efforts that can sometimes have amusing results.

In general, we tend to think of *mentorship* in connection with such fields as medicine, the arts, or science. However, recent findings indicate that it is quite common in organizations as well. Thus, one study found that most presidents of major corporations report having had a mentor at some point during their career.[14] As you might guess, however, mentor–protégé pairs do *not* form at random. Instead, such relationships tend to develop among persons possessing certain characteristics that suit them for their respective roles.[15] Mentors are usually older than their protégés—often by eight to fifteen years. In addition, they tend to be persons with considerable power and status within their companies. For this reason, they are quite secure, and are not readily threatened by the rapid progress often achieved by their protégés. Protégés, in contrast, tend to be younger than mentors, and are generally lower in status and power. They are selected by mentors because of good initial performance, because they possess the "right" social background, or because they make a positive first impression.

At first glance, it is tempting to assume that most of the benefits in mentor–protégé relationships go to the protégés. And of course, such persons *do* gain substantially from such arrangements. They learn a great deal from their mentors—including techniques for avoiding dangerous pitfalls and useful shortcuts to success. They receive the protection and support of their powerful allies. Their visibility is greatly en-

hanced simply by being associated with these persons. However, mentors, too, gain important rewards. They often receive approval and recognition from their organization for helping to nurture "young talent." They can bask in the reflected glory of any success attained by their young protégés. And they often gain personal satisfaction from serving as a model and guide for bright young persons. Organizations, too, may profit from the development of mentor–protégé relationships, for recent findings indicate that persons who have once been protégés are more satisfied with their jobs, less likely to seek employment elsewhere, and more knowledgeable about their organizations than persons who have not been protégés. Further, older employees are often rejuvenated by the experience of serving as a mentor, and this, too, can be a plus.

Most human relationships develop over time, and mentorship is no exception to this general rule. In fact, it appears to pass through several distinct stages.[16] The first, known as *initiation*, occurs during the first six months to a year, and represents the period during which the relationship gets started and takes on importance for both parties. The second, known as *cultivation*, may last from two to five years. During this time, the bond between the mentor and protégé deepens, and the younger individual may make rapid strides because of the assistance he or she is receiving. The third stage—*separation*—begins when the protégé feels it is time to assert independence and strike out on his own, or when there is some externally produced change in the role relationship between the protégé and mentor (e.g., the protégé is promoted and no longer works under the direct supervision of the mentor). It can also occur if the mentor feels unable to continue providing support and guidance to the protégé (e.g., if the mentor is experiencing a mid-life or career crisis). This phase can be quite stressful in cases where the mentor resents the protégé's growing independence, or in instances where the protégé feels that the mentor has withdrawn support and guidance before he or she is ready to stand alone (see Figure 2.7). If separation is successfully negotiated, the relationship may enter a final stage termed *redefinition*. Here, both persons perceive their bond primarily as

"You, sir, were my hero—until I became my own hero."

FIGURE 2.7   *Mentorship: The Separation Stage.*
As shown here, the growing independence of protégés can sometimes be quite unsettling for mentors. (Source: Drawing by Wm. Hamilton; © 1981 The New Yorker Magazine Inc.)

one of friendship. They come to treat one another as peers, and the roles of mentor and protégé may completely fade away.

In many cases, individuals who have been involved in a mentor–protégé relationship look back upon it with considerable nostalgia, and strong positive feelings. Further, they often report that it was of major benefit both to their careers and to their personal growth. When these benefits to individuals coupled with the gains mentorship often provides to organizations, an obvious conclusion is suggested: steps designed to encourage the formation of such relationships may often prove worthwhile.

behavior, except from the point of view of employee health and wellbeing. We mention it here, however, to call your attention to the breadth of practical problems that have been addressed—and partially solved—through techniques based on learning principles.

Not surprisingly, the success of such tactics in other fields has led to efforts to apply similar procedures to key aspects of organizational behavior.[18] Thus, in recent years, principles of operant conditioning and modeling have been employed to increase attendance, enhance productivity, and reduce errors.[19, 20] Moreover, such principles have been adapted for use in settings as varied as large department stores, factories, and busy hospitals. In general, the results of such projects have been quite encouraging: they suggest that principles of learning, when properly applied, can indeed produce desirable changes in many forms of organizational behavior. To provide you with some idea of the specific procedures useful in this regard, we will describe a few examples of this intriguing work.

Operant Conditioning and the Encouragement of Safe Work Practices

According to one old saying, "Accidents happen." What this implies is that accidents are often the result of chance factors or unknown forces beyond human control. Certainly this is true in some instances. In many others, however, accidents result from dangerous or foolhardy actions by the persons involved. By ignoring safety precautions, they virtually invite the disasters that soon follow. Can anything be done to modify such behaviors, and so reduce the frequency of industrial accidents? The results of a series of investigations carried out by Komaki and her colleagues offer a positive reply.[21,22]

For example, in one of these investigations, efforts were made to encourage good safety practices among employees in the vehicle maintenance facility of a large city. In an initial step, various unsafe practices were identified, and their frequency among employees was recorded by trained raters. These observations continued over a period of several months. Next, employees underwent special training designed to call attention to these unsafe practices. This involved attendance at a session in which they viewed slides of unsafe behaviors, discussed such hazards, and then viewed slides showing how these dangers could be avoided. Following training, employee behavior was again observed for several weeks. After this, the next phase of the study was begun. During this part, employees underwent further training in safety rules. In addition, their supervisor posted a graph designed to show how well they were doing in adopting proper safety practices. Entries were made on this graph several times a week, thus providing employees with continuing *feedback* about their progress. Again, trained raters made careful observations of their behavior throughout the period. In two additional phases of the study, each lasting approximately ten weeks, supervisors first stopped making entries on the charts (i.e., feedback was eliminated), and then began providing such information once again. These procedures were followed in order to determine if continued feedback was necessary to maintain any changes in safety behavior or, alternatively, if training in such practices would be sufficient to produce lasting effects.

As you can see in Figure 2.8, results were impressive. Safety practices were relatively rare during the initial baseline period (prior to training or feedback). They rose slightly following safety training, but then increased much more when direct feedback on performance was provided. Interestingly, safety practices declined when feedback was removed, but then rose once again when it was restored. These findings indicate that training in safety practices alone is not sufficient to produce major shifts in such behavior; only when training is combined with feedback do lasting changes occur. Further support for this conclusion is provided by the results of a recent study conducted by Reber and Wallin.[23] These investigators

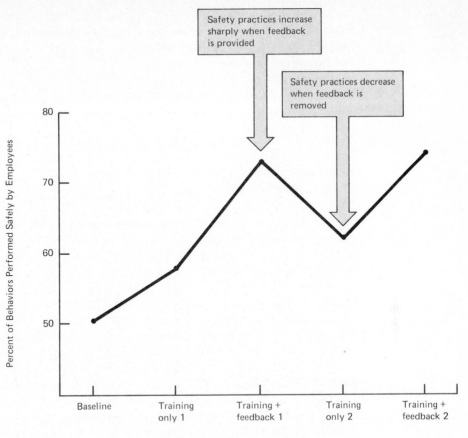

Safety practices increase sharply when feedback is provided

Safety practices decrease when feedback is removed

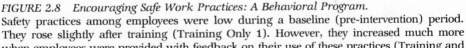

FIGURE 2.8   *Encouraging Safe Work Practices: A Behavioral Program.*
Safety practices among employees were low during a baseline (pre-intervention) period. They rose slightly after training (Training Only 1). However, they increased much more when employees were provided with feedback on their use of these practices (Training and Feedback 1). When feedback was stopped (Training Only 2), use of safety practices fell. However, they increased once again when feedback was restored (Training and Feedback 2.) (Source: Based on data from Komaki et al., 1980; see Notes 21 and 22.)

found that providing employees in a farm machinery plant with feedback about their safety behavior improved their performance in this respect over that produced by a combination of training and goal setting. Indeed, when feedback (knowledge of results) was provided, fully ten out of eleven participating departments actually exceeded the agreed-upon goal of 90 percent compliance with safety regulations by employees.

Together, the results reported by Komaki and her colleagues and by Reber and Wallin indicate that techniques based upon operant conditioning can be highly effective in producing beneficial shifts in employee behavior. In order to be successful, however, such procedures must be both planned and executed in a systematic manner. Specific steps for accomplishing these goals have recently been devised by

Luthans and his colleagues, in an approach known as **O.B. Mod.**[24] (short for *organizational behavior modification*). Positive results have already been obtained with this approach in several organizational settings (e.g., manufacturing companies, stores, hospitals). Thus, it seems likely that O.B. Mod. and related techniques will find increasing application in the years ahead. To the extent they do, basic knowledge about operant conditioning may well make a substantial contribution to the solution of many practical organizational problems.

Behavioral Modeling and the Enhancement of Managerial Effectiveness

Managers face many different problems in their jobs. Among the most common are those involving difficulties with their subordinates. For example, many supervisors are uncertain about how to motivate these persons when their output decreases, how to deal with their complaints, how to overcome their resistance to change, or how to provide recognition for good performance. This is hardly surprising, for most managers are trained in general business practices or in some technical specialty. Few receive direct instruction in tactics for handling or improving relations with subordinates. Is there any efficient way for them to improve their skills in this respect? Fortunately, there is. The findings of several recent studies indicate that managers can readily acquire improved interpersonal skills through *behavioral modeling*.[25] That, is they can learn improved ways of dealing with subordinates through procedures in which they observe examples of such behavior on the part of others. One especially impressive demonstration of such effects has been reported by Porras and Anderson.[26]

These investigators began by asking supervisors at a large forest-products company to identify the most difficult problems they faced in dealing with subordinates. Among the problems identified by these first-line managers were several listed above (e.g., motivating an employee who is experiencing a performance problem, handling employee complaints, overcoming resistance to change, improving attendance). Next, Porras and Anderson devised a training program designed to enhance interpersonal skills that might prove useful in dealing with these and many other manager-subordinate problems. These skills included the ability to clearly identify and describe specific problems to employees, improved ways of discussing the problems with them, actively involving employees in the formulation of solutions to the problems, and delivering positive reinforcement to them when progress is attained. In order to help managers develop these skills, Porras and Anderson conducted special workshops (one each week for six weeks) in which first-line managers from several of the company's plants observed concrete examples of these skills in actual practice. (Managers from other plants did not participate in the training, and constituted a no-treatment control group.) The examples were presented on videotapes in which a company supervisor successfully used a specific skill to solve a difficult interpersonal problem. During each workshop, such skills were first described and explained. Then modeled demonstrations of their use were presented. Next, managers rehearsed the skill under the workshop leader's supervision. They then received feedback on their performance. Finally, they formally committed themselves to the use of their newly acquired skills while on the job.

Several steps were taken to assess the effectiveness of these procedures. First, employees completed a questionnaire about their managers' behavior before training, after it was completed, and again six months later. Second, records of average daily production were gathered. Finally, several measures of company-employee relations (e.g., number of grievances reported, number of absences) were obtained. Results were clear: in virtually every instance, outcomes were more favorable for managers who had undergone modeling than for managers who had not. Specifically, managers who had attended the workshops showed improved interpersonal skills relative to those who had not. Average daily production in their plants was higher, and both the number of grievances and absences reported were lower. Moreover, these benefits seemed to persist; they were still visible even six months after the modeling workshops ended.

These results, and similar findings in several other studies, point to two conclusions. First, behavioral modeling can be highly effective in producing beneficial shifts in organizational behavior. Second, these procedures can often yield such benefits in a rapid and efficient manner. (Recall that in the study by Porras and Anderson, participants attended a mere handful of weekly sessions.) Given these two important "pluses," it seems likely that procedures based on modeling will find increasing application to organizational problems in the years ahead. (For some hints on how you can use operant conditioning and modeling yourself, please see the **Perspective** box on pages 62–63.)

LEARNING AND OTHER ASPECTS OF ORGANIZATIONAL BEHAVIOR: EMPLOYEE TRAINING AND ORGANIZATIONAL SOCIALIZATION

Learning has sometimes been described as the "key to survival." What this implies is that it is often our capacity to learn—to benefit from our experience—that permits us to cope with a complex and ever-changing world. Nowhere, perhaps, is this adaptive value of learning more apparent than in the situation faced by new employees. Persons entering an organization must acquire new skills, learn the rules and values of their company, adapt to new task demands, and form relationships with many persons. Little wonder, then, that entry into a new job can often be a traumatic experience! To illustrate the role of learning in such situations, we will briefly consider two topics: **employee training** and **organizational socialization.**

Employee Training: Learning the Skills

One of the major tasks faced by new employees is that of gaining the skills and knowledge needed to perform their jobs. Recognizing this fact, many organizations

FROM THE MANAGER'S PERSPECTIVE

Operant Conditioning and Behavioral Modeling: Some Hints on Their Practical Use

By now, we trust you are convinced of the potential benefits that can be obtained through careful application of techniques based on operant conditioning and modeling. When used with skill and care, such procedures do seem capable of producing valuable shifts in key forms of organizational behavior—changes that can benefit individuals as well as organizations. You may also have concluded, however, that putting such tactics to use requires a major investment of time and energy, as well as more expertise than you are likely to possess. To a certain extent, these conclusions are accurate. Systematic programs designed to change the behavior of large numbers of employees *are* often complex, and require the efforts and cooperation of many people. At the same time, though, there are several simple steps you can take as an individual to guide the actions of your own subordinates into more desirable channels. Several of these are outlined below. Please consider them carefully; together, they may save you much unnecessary trouble in the years ahead.

(1) *Establish clear contingencies:* One common gripe in many organizations is as follows: employees complain that they really don't know what behaviors will yield desired rewards. In short, they are uncertain about what actions on their part will bring raises, promotions, good work assignments, or other benefits. Faced with ambiguity, many become discouraged, and conclude that what they do really doesn't matter; rewards are distributed according to some obscure system they will never figure out. A key task for managers, therefore, is to avoid such conditions. Clear contingencies between organizational behavior and organizational rewards should be established, and these should be communicated to employees. When this is the case, motivation, performance, and commitment may all be enhanced.

(2) *Reward—don't punish—desirable behavior:* In many organizations, it is downright dangerous to have a totally clear desk or to be completely caught up with one's work. The reason for this is simple: individuals who demonstrate such efficiency are soon loaded down with extra tasks. In short, they are "rewarded" for their high levels of productivity by being asked to do even more. Clearly, this is a serious error. The persons involved quickly learn to slow down, or to adopt tactics that make them appear busier than they are. The moral for managers in such situations is obvious: always make certain that desirable behavior by subordinates is *rewarded*, not punished.

(3) *Tailor reinforcers to the people who will receive them:* Suppose that one of the people in your department resembles the man shown in Figure 2.9. Would it make sense to reward him for excellent performance by an extra week's vacation? Obviously, it would not. Since this individual seems to thrive on hard work, time away from the office would probably not constitute a positive experience for him. On the contrary, it might be viewed as a kind of cruel and unfair punishment! Similarly, imagine that one of your subordinates is extremely shy. Would it make any sense to reward her for a job well done by public praise delivered in front of the entire department? Again, the answer is "no." She would be embarrassed by such treatment, and might well find it painful. These situations call attention to a key principle managers often overlook: everyone does *not* seek the same rewards. Thus, in choosing reinforcers for subordinates, it is crucial to consider their preferences and personalities. Failure to do so can prove very costly.

(4) *When you must use punishment, do so with care:* As we noted earlier, punishment can be tricky—very tricky. If you find that you must use it to alter the actions of one of your subordinates, therefore, try to do so in accordance with the principles discussed earlier.

(5) *Remember that, usually, subordinates will do as you do, not as you say:* Managers often serve as role models for their subordinates, especially when

they possess high status, expertise, or power. Often, they are aware of this fact, and try to use it to encourage desirable actions by their employees. What they frequently fail to realize, however, is this: in most cases, these people will do as the managers *do*, not as they *say*. Unfortunately, many managers permit a substantial gap to open between what they recommend to their subordinates, and what they themselves do. For example, they may urge employees to be prompt—but then appear late for meetings (or for work in the morning) themselves. Similarly, they may pay lip service to staying at one's desk, but then disappear for two-hour lunches. Such gaps between verbal statements by managers and their own actions can have disastrous consequences on morale and productivity. Thus, it is important to avoid their occurrence. The general rule to follow, then, is this: never urge actions or standards on your subordinates that you are not willing to follow yourself. Disparities between what you practice and what you preach can often prove fatal.

FIGURE 2.9 *Different People Seek Different Reinforcers*
The person shown here would probably *not* view extra vacation time as a positive reinforcer. Thus, providing him with this "reward" for excellent performance would make little sense. (Source: Drawing by M. Stevens; © 1982 The New Yorker Magazine, Inc.)

establish special programs of *employee training* (see Figure 2.10, page 64). The goal of these programs, of course, is that of helping new employees master job-related skills and behaviors as quickly and easily as possible.[27] But how, precisely, can this task be accomplished? Basic knowledge about human learning provides some useful clues.

First, conditions in the training environment itself can be arranged to maximize learning. This requires taking careful account of such factors as amount of practice, the sequence with which new tasks are presented, and the manner in

FIGURE 2.10 Employee Training: A Key Task for Organizations.
Many organizations establish special programs to help new employees master job-related skills.

which feedback about progress is provided. For example, it is well known, from basic research on learning, that practice in new skills is often more effective when it occurs in several fairly short sessions rather than a single "massed" session. Similarly, providing clear and frequent feedback often seems to be a major plus to individuals attempting to master new tasks.[28] By directing careful attention to these and related factors, the success of training programs can be increased.

Second, conditions should be arranged so as to maximize the *transfer of training*—the extent to which skills mastered in a training program can be put to actual use on the job. Here, such factors as assuring that the skills learned during training are actually the ones needed for various jobs should be considered.

Third, attention can be directed to selecting individuals who are most likely to profit from training programs. This may involve choosing as emplyees persons high in motivation, intelligence, and certain characteristics (e.g., responsibility, independence).[29] The purpose is certainly *not* that of excluding all but a tiny elite; rather, it is that of assuring that persons who do enter training have a reasonable probability of succeeding in it.

Finally, of course, techniques based on operant conditioning and behavioral modeling, such as the ones described in the preceding section, can often be applied to improve training, and can help individuals acquire job-related skills in an efficient and rapid manner.

In sum, careful attention to basic principles of learning can aid in the development of effective programs for training new employees. This, in turn, can be of substantial benefit both to the individuals involved, and to organizations themselves.

Organizational Socialization: Learning the Ropes

Acquiring job-related skills and knowledge are certainly important tasks faced by newcomers to an organization. However, they are far from the total picture. In addition, persons joining an organization must learn much more. First, they must come to understand its *norms*—the formal or informal rules that tell organization members how to behave in various situations. Second, they must form a clear picture of role requirements, both their own and those of others. Third, they need an accurate grasp of the organization's internal *culture*—its major values, attitudes, and perspectives. Finally, they must understand how it really works: who holds power and who does not, which informal networks of communication are reliable and which are unreliable, and what political maneuvers they are likely to encounter in their department or unit. In short, if they wish to survive and prosper in their new work home, they must soom come to "know the ropes." The process through which such learning takes place is generally termed **organizational socialization,** and it can have important consequences.[30] Indeed, recent studies suggest that its outcome can affect employees' level of organizational commitment, the length of time they spend in their jobs, and even various aspects of their later career development.[31]

Many organizations are well aware of these important effects, and attempt to facilitate the socialization of new employees through special orientation programs. Many others, though, lack such programs and rely on informal means for the transmission of the required information to newcomers. Whichever approach is used, modeling almost certainly plays a key role in the process. That is, newcomers generally acquire much of their knowledge about the organization through observation of the actions of more experienced persons, or by listening to their advice. In some cases, this can take the form of *mentorship*—a topic we have already considered. In others, experienced employees simply act as guides for newcomers, helping them to acquire appropriate values and to avoid various pitfalls, in the absence of any deep emotional bonds between them.

The outcomes of the socialization process are affected by many different factors. For example, the past experience of new employees can play an important role. Many newcomers frequently remark, during their first few weeks or months on the job, that "we did things differently where I came from." To the extent the values and norms of their former organization conflict with those of their new one, the task of organizational socialization may be impeded. Similarly, the outcomes of this process can be strongly affected by various characteristics of the persons involved. Individuals who are fairly high in self-esteem or feelings of competence often find the task of adjusting easier than those who are fairly low on such dimensions.[32]

Such factors aside, it appears that socialization often proceeds through three distinct stages. In the first, or *entry stage*, newcomers concentrate on forming a basic understanding of the rules and procedures of their organization. Once this is accomplished, they enter the second, or *encounter stage*. Here, they focus on exploring their own roles within the organization, and means of developing their competence and careers. Finally, in the third or *appreciative stage*, they are fully integrated into the organization. Depending on their own background and events

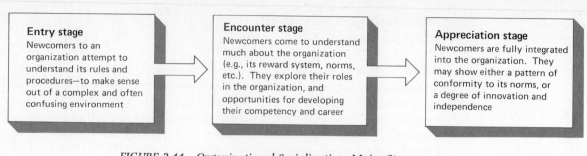

Entry stage
Newcomers to an organization attempt to understand its rules and procedures—to make sense out of a complex and often confusing environment

Encounter stage
Newcomers come to understand much about the organization (e.g., its reward system, norms, etc.). They explore their roles in the organization, and opportunities for developing their competency and career

Appreciation stage
Newcomers are fully integrated into the organization. They may show either a pattern of conformity to its norms, or a degree of innovation and independence

FIGURE 2.11   Organizational Socialization: Major Stages
Organizational socialization often proceeds through the stages summarized here. (Based on proposals offered by Jones, 1983; see Note 32.)

during the earlier stages, this may involve either a pattern of conformity to the organization's norms and culture, or a degree of innovation and independence. (Refer to Figure 2.11 for a summary of these stages.)

One final word: the process of organizational socialization always involves at least one built-in conflict or dilemma. On the one hand, it is important that newcomers accept the norms, roles, and culture or their organization. On the other, it is equally crucial that they maintain at least *some* ability to question or change these. If they do not, the organization will stagnate, and be unable to cope with shifting environmental or technological conditions. Thus, the ideal outcome of organizational socialization probably lies somewhere in between the twin dangers of total conformity at one extreme, and total independence (or anarchy) at the other.

SUMMARY

Learning refers to fairly permanent changes in behavior produced by experience. One basic form of learning is **operant conditioning.** In this process, individuals learn to perform actions that yield desirable outcomes, or actions that permit them to avoid or escape from undesirable ones. *Schedules of reinforcement*—rules that determine the timing and frequency of reinforcement—often exert powerful effects upon operant conditioning. When a given behavior is no longer followed by reinforcement, the tendency to perform it gradually diminishes; this is *extinction.* Undesirable behaviors may also be eliminated (or at least suppressed) through *punishment.* Here, performance of the behaviors in question is followed by negative outcomes.

A second major form of learning, **modeling,** involves our ability to acquire new responses or information merely through observing the actions of others. Modeling is given careful attention in *social learning theory,* a modern framework that emphasizes the importance of cognitive processes in human learning. Modeling plays an imortant role in *mentor-protégé relationships,* assisting younger and less experienced persons in learning from older, more experienced ones.

Principles of operant conditioning and modeling have been applied to a wide range of organizational problems. Thus they have been used to increase employee attendance, enhance productivity, encourage safety practices, and improve managers' interpersonal skills.

Basic forms of learning also play a key role in other organizational processes. Among the most important of these are programs of **employee training** and **organizational socialization.**

KEY TERMS

employee training: Special programs designed to help new employees master job-related knowledge and skills.

extinction: The process through which responses that are no longer followed by reinforcement gradually diminish in strength or frequency.

fixed interval schedule: A schedule of reinforcement in which after delivery of one reinforcement, a fixed interval of time must elapse before responding can yield another reinforcement.

fixed ratio schedule: A schedule of reinforcement in which a fixed number of responses must be performed before reinforcement is obtained.

mentorship: A close relationship between a more experienced individual (mentor) and a less experienced one (protégé), in which the former aids the career development of the latter.

modeling: A basic form of learning in which one individual acquires new forms of behavior or new information merely through observing the actions and outcomes of another person.

negative reinforcers: Stimuli that strengthen responses leading to their removal or termination.

O.B. Mod. (organizational behavior modification): Systematic procedures for modifying organizational behavior based on principles of operant conditioning.

operant conditioning: A basic form of learning in which responses that yield positive outcomes or eliminate negative ones are acquired or strengthened.

organizational socialization: The process through which new members learn the norms, role requirements, procedures, and culture of their organization.

partial reinforcement effect: Refers to the fact that responses acquired under conditions of partial reinforcement are usually more resistant to extinction than responses acquired under conditions of continuous reinforcement.

positive reinforcers: Stimuli that strengthen responses leading to their occurrence.

punishment: Conditions in which the delivery of unpleasant stimuli is contingent upon the performance of a specific form of behavior. By refraining from such behavior, individuals avoid unpleasant outcomes.

schedules of reinforcement: Rules governing the timing and frequency of reinforcement.

social learning theory: A modern perspective that calls attention to the importance of cognitive and self-regulatory processes in human learning.

variable interval schedule: A schedule of reinforcement in which after the delivery of one reinforcement, a variable interval of time must elapse before responding can yield another reinforcement.

variable ratio schedule: A schedule of reinforcement in which a variable number of responses must be performed before reinforcement is obtained.

NOTES

1. B. Schwartz (1984). *Psychology of learning and behavior*, 2nd ed. New York: Norton.

2. F. Luthans and R. Kreitner (1975). *Organizational behavior modification.* Glenview, Ill.: Scott-Foresman.

3. R. D. Pritchard, J. Hollenback, and P. J. DeLeo (1980). The effects of continuous and partial schedules of reinforcement on effort, performance, and satisfaction. *Organizational Behavior and Human Performance, 25,* 336–356.

4. C. B. Ferster and B. F. Skinner (1975). *Schedules of reinforcement.* New York: Appleton.

5. W. C. Hamner (1977). Reinforcement theory. In H. L. Tosi and W. C. Hamner (eds.), *Organizational behavior and management: A contingency approach.* Chicago: St. Clair.

6. See Note 2.

7. W. S. Sahakian (1984). *Introduction to the psychology of learning.* Itasca, Ill.: F. E. Peacock.

8. A. Bandura (1977). *Social learning theory.* Englewood Cliffs, N.J.: Prentice-Hall.

9. R. M. Liebert, J. N. Sprafkin, and E. S. Davidson (1982). *The early window: Effects of television on children and youth,* 2nd ed. New York: Pergamon.

10. K. N. Wexley (1984). Personnel training. *Annual Review of Psychology, 35,* 519–551.

11. K. E. Kram and L. A. Isabella (1985). Mentoring alternatives: The role of peer relationships in career development. *Academy of Management Journal, 28,* 110–137.

12. A. Bandura (1982). Self-efficacy mechanism in human agency. *American Psychologist, 37,* 122–147.

13. F. Luthans and T. R. V. Davis (1980). A social learning approach to organizational behavior. *Academy of Management Review, 5,* 281–290.

14. G. R. Roche (1979). Much ado about mentors. *Harvard Business Review, 57,* 17–28.

15. D. M. Hunt and C. Michael (1983). Mentorship: A career training and development tool. *Academy of Management Review, 8,* 475–485.

16. K. E. Kram (1983). Phases of the mentor relationship. *Academy of Management Journal, 26,* 608–625.

17. See Note 2.

18. W. R. Nord (1969). Beyond the teaching machine: The neglected area of operant conditioning in the theory and practice of management. *Organizational Behavior and Human Performance, 4,* 375–401.

19. F. Luthans, R. Paul, and D. Baker (1981). An experimental analysis of the impact of a contingent reinforcement intervention on salespersons' performance behaviors. *Journal of Applied Psychology, 66,* 314–323.

20. L. M. Saari and G. P. Latham (1982). Employee reactions to continuous and variable ratio reinforcement schedules involving monetary incentive. *Journal of Applied Psychology, 67,* 506–508.

21. J. Komaki, K. D. Barwick, and L. R. Scott (1978). A behavioral approach to occupational safety: Pinpointing and reinforcing safe performance in a food manufacturing plant. *Journal of Applied Psychology, 63,* 434–445.

22. J. Komaki, A. T. Heinzmann, and L. Lawson (1980). Effect of training and feedback: Component analysis of a behavioral safety program. *Journal of Applied Psychology, 63,* 434–445.

23. R. A. Reber and J. A. Wallin (1984). The effects of training, goal setting, and knowledge of results on safe behavior: A component analysis. *Academy of Management Journal, 27,* 544–560.

24. See Note 2.

25. P. J. Decker (1982). The enhancement of behavior modeling training of supervisory skills by the inclusion of retentional processes. *Personnel Psychology, 35,* 323–332.

26. J. I. Porras and B. Anderson (1981). Improving managerial effectiveness through modeling-based training. *Organizational Dynamics, 9,* 60–77.

27. See Note 10.

28. T. Matsui, A. Okada, and T. Kakuyama (1982). Influences of achievement need on goal setting, performance, and feedback effectiveness. *Journal of Applied Psychology, 67,* 645–648.

29. R. W. T. Gill (1982). A trainability concept for management potential and an empirical study of its relationship with intelligence for two managerial skills. *Journal of Occupational Psychology, 55,* 138–147.

30. J. Van Maanen and E. H. Schein (1979). Towards a theory of organizational socialization. In B. Staw (ed.), *Research in organizational behavior,* vol. 1. Greenwich, Conn.: JAI Press, 209–264.

31. J. P. Wanous (1980). *Organizational entry: Recruitment, selection, and socialization of newcomers.* Reading, Mass.: Addison-Wesley.

32. G. R. Jones (1983). Psychological orientation and the process of organizational socialization: An interactionist perspective. *Academy of Management Review, 8,* 464–474.

CHAPTER 3

Human Motivation in Organizations

As the lunch whistle sounded and members of Ziprin Fabricating's workforce streamed into the employee cafeteria, the conversations that could be heard left no doubt that today was Friday—another payday. Every week at this time Eric, Dave, and Tim received their paychecks, which seemed to trigger the same reactions over Friday's lunch.

"Why do I work so hard to just barely get by?" Eric grumbled. "I give this job everything I've got, and all they give me in return is enough pay to make ends meet. They don't seem to appreciate the work I do. After seven years at this company, I hoped to be more comfortable. But what they pay you around here makes it impossible to get ahead."

Tim was quick to pick up on Eric's lead. "Yeah," he piped in without hesitation, "I know just what you mean." Putting down his sandwich as he began to speak, Tim was prepared to take Eric's complaints even further. "The three of us went to the same trade school and we do the same work here at the plant—and good work, at that! I've been here at Ziprin two years longer than you guys and I hardly make any more money than you do. I don't know about you, but I've stopped working as hard as I used to. What's the point? The way I figure it, if they don't take care of me, I'm not gonna take care of them!"

"You paint a pretty gloomy picture of what I have to look forward to around here," Dave replied. "But, I think you've got the right idea, at least. Why should I work so hard without being recognized for it? There's no future in it!"

"Y'know, Dave," Eric added, "It's not just the low pay that shows they don't care about us, but management's whole approach to the workers. They never praise us, never make us feel good about what we do. When was the last time anyone ever told you you did a good job?"

Nobody responded to Eric's question. Their griping session had run its course, at least for this day. A few more bites of sandwich later the whistle sounded again, marking the time to return to work. Throughout the lunchroom could be heard the sound of closing lunchboxes and chairs pushing away from the tables. "Only four more hours of work," they collectively thought, "before the weekend!"

This gloomy picture we have painted of the complaints of employees in one hypothetical company comes close to capturing the common malaise among today's workers that is often sounded in the press.[1] Why are employees interested or not interested in working hard on their jobs? What kinds of things does management do to contribute to these negative feelings, and what can be done to help alleviate them? Some insight into these important questions may be derived from the topic considered in this chapter—**motivation**.

The scientific study of motivation in organizations is concerned with two different sets of issues. First, we are interested in understanding the process of motivation itself. Toward this end, several theories of work motivation have been developed. However, because the field of organizational behavior is also concerned with applying our knowledge of human behavior in organizations, we also are interested in developing practical techniques for enhancing worker motivation. This chapter will focus both on *theories of motivation*—understanding *what* motivates workers, and *why*—and on *practical application* of these theories—understanding *how* to motivate workers on the job (refer to Figure 3.1). Before discussing the theories and their application to organizational practice, we will first take a closer look at the general concept of motivation.

FIGURE 3.1   *Motivating Employees: A Key Task for Managers.*
Most managers want to motivate their employees—to increase their desire or willingness to work hard at their jobs. However, few would be pleased with the "success" illustrated here! (Source: King Features Syndicate, Inc.)

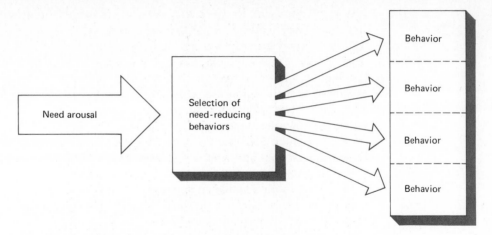

FIGURE 3.2   *Motivation: A General Framework.*
As shown here, the process of motivation involves not only the arousal of needs, but also the
selection of behaviors designed to gratify them.

THE NATURE OF HUMAN MOTIVATION
AT WORK

It should not be too surprising from the questions just raised that the topic of motivation is a central one in the field of organizational behavior. Indeed, concerns about motivational theory and practice have made it one of the most widely studied topics among organizational scientists.[2] So that we may better understand the current state of this knowledge, this section of the chapter will take a closer look at some basic issues about human motivation at work. As our first task, we need to define the concept of motivation and explain how it is applicable to understanding behavior in organizational settings.

Motivation: A Definition

In spite of the many different approaches that have been taken to the study of motivation, there is general agreement among scientists about what motivation is.[3] For our purposes, we will define **motivation** as *the set of processes that energize a person's behavior and direct it toward attaining some goal.* ie choices people make

Let's examine this definition more closely to understand precisely what is involved in the process of motivation. The diagram in Figure 3.2 will aid our presentation. Two very important aspects of motivation suggested by our definition are shown in the diagram. The first idea is that motivation is concerned with energizing behavior. For example, people may be motivated to seek food to reduce their hunger, or they may be motivated to seek companionship to reduce their

73

loneliness. Similarly, in organizations workers may be motivated to please their supervisors and leave a good impression on them.

The second important aspect of the definition is that it deals with the choices people make. For example, a hungry person may choose to eat a hamburger at a fast-food restaurant, a bologna sandwich at home, or a four-course meal at an expensive French restaurant. Similarly, a lonely person may decide to seek the company of one friend or another. The worker motivated to please his or her supervisor may decide to do a personal favor for the supervisor, or to work especially hard on an important project. The point is that motivation involves making intentional choices and selecting goals—not just directing people toward goals. Combining these two facets of our definition, motivation may be likened to the operation of an automobile engine and steering wheel: we are not only concerned with the needs that drive a person's behavior, but also the direction in which the person is steered to satisfy those needs.

Despite the apparent simplicity of our definition of motivation, it should be readily apparent that the concept of motivation is not really all that simple. One thing that makes motivation such a difficult concept to deal with is that it is a *hypothetical construct* and cannot be observed directly. Motives can only be inferred—usually on the basis of behavior. However, this is not to say that motivation and job performance are synonymous. On the contrary, many factors influence a worker's job performance—such as this person's levels of skill and ability, and working conditions—not just motivation.[4] It would be a mistake for a manager to assume that a subordinate's sagging productivity is necessarily the result of his or her poor motivation. Our point should be clear: although motivation is *a* determinant of work performance, it is not the *only* determinant, and motivation should not be viewed as synonymous with performance.

Studying motivation is also complicated by the fact that multiple motives may exist at once. Sometimes, motives may even conflict, making it difficult to predict how a person will behave in any given setting. For example, an employee who is motivated to please her supervisor may refrain from working at a considerably higher level than other workers if she believes that doing so would jeopardize her relationships with these individuals. Clearly, as suggested by this case, a behavior that satisfies one motive may conflict with the satisfaction of another motive. This may be especially problematic if the behaviors a worker is motivated to perform on the job conflict with the things he or she may be motivated to do for his or her career.[5]

These points about the complex nature of motivation help us appreciate some of the factors that must be incorporated into any usable theory of work motivation. Before we present these theories, however, let's further set the stage for understanding them by considering another very basic issue about the role of motivation in the workforce.

Are Employees Motivated to Work?

Much has been said lately about how uninterested American workers are in doing hard work—especially compared to employees in other countries, particularly Japan.[6] Claims such as these raise questions about the extent to which some workers, at least, care about work and are motivated to perform it. The implications of whether or not workers may be motivated by the work they do are quite important for developing both motivational theories and practical managerial techniques.

As we noted in Chapter 1, two opposing philosophies of human nature at work have been distinguished by management theorist Douglas McGregor.[7] The traditional set of managerial assumptions about workers is referred to as **Theory X**—an approach that takes an extremely pessimistic view of human motivation at work. Specifically, the *Theory X* philosphy of management assumes that workers are by nature lazy, lacking in ambition, selfish, and indifferent to organizational needs—in short, unmotivated to work. McGregor's argument is that managers who endorse the Theory X philosophy tend to treat workers in very coercive ways, thereby causing the very type of worker "withdrawal behaviors" (e.g., absenteeism and lateness) and lack of interest that managers hoped to minimize in the first place. As an alternative to this self-defeating strategy, McGregor proposes an approach called **Theory Y**. This more optimistic view of human nature assumes that workers are not passive and that they want to assume responsibilities and develop their skills in accord with their organization's needs. Of course, the accuracy of this assumption depends on the extent to which management creates policies and motivational systems that enable workers to develop their own potential. It also depends on the workers themselves—the attitude toward work they bring to their jobs.

It appears to be true that people in some of the world's cultures view work as a form of punishment that must be endured to satisfy one's basic life needs.[8] However, an opposite philosophy also exists, particularly in the United States, where prevailing views place a high value on work for its own good. As then President Richard M. Nixon said in a 1971 in Labor Day address, "Labor is good in itself. A man or woman at work . . . becomes a better person by virtue of the act of working."[9] As these observations clearly demonstrate, the motivation to work is a cherished value in American society.

The importance of this work value is suggested by survey results showing that the vast majority of Americans claim they would continue to work even if they didn't need the money—such as winners of large lottery prizes.[10] Managerial and professional workers report that having a challenging job is more important to them than the amount of their earnings. Even clerical and unskilled employees place a higher value on the work environment, both social and physical, than on the pay itself.[11] Recent surveys of Israeli workers show similar results: they too are more concerned with doing interesting work than with the pay they receive, suggesting that the motivation to perform interesting work is *not* uniquely American.[12]

Even today's assembly line workers are becoming more motivated by the work they do, and are less content than in the past merely to exchange hours of labor for pay. Commenting on this, the president of the United Automobile Workers local has been quoted as saying, "Five years ago, the union didn't even discuss it. But now they are, [because] for younger, better educated workers . . . pay is not sufficient for life spent on the line. They are still a minority, but their pressure does concern management."[13] Apparently, the high value placed on work among many of today's workers suggests that they may indeed be motivated to do their jobs—challenging jobs that provide opportunities to develop their potential. Management's task, then, becomes one of providing employees with jobs they are motivated to perform.

Keeping this discussion in mind, we think you will find it easy to see how these philosophies about worker motivation have been incorporated into the various theories and practices presented in the following sections of this chapter.

Theories of Motivation
I. Indl. motivational models
A. Need Theory - Maslow
B. Herzberg - (2 Factor Theory
C. McClelland's achievement - Motivation Theory

II. Complex models
A. Expectancy Theory - (VIE theory)
B. Equity theory (social comparison theory)
- Adams
C. Goal setting Theory - "Locke"

WORK MOTIVATION

...al views of work motivation have been proposed by organiza... ...r presentation of these theories will be limited to three of the ...—**need theory, equity theory,** and **valence-instrumentality-**... Although all three theoretical approaches deal with individual ...er with respect to the scope of their analysis. As will become ... discussion, the theories range from focusing exclusively on ...rough social comparison, to broader organization-wide per-... ...ntation of each of these theories will focus on not only what the ...on how the theory may be put to use in organizational practice.

The basic fact that human beings have various needs, some of which may be satisfied on their jobs, has not escaped the attention of organizational researchers and theorists. (Indeed, in Chapter 6 we will discuss their needs for achievement and power as important personality variables influencing organizational behavior.) Probably the best-known theory of human needs in organizations has been proposed by Abraham Maslow.[14] Although originally derived from observations in the 1940s and 1950s about the development of personality, Maslow's theory has been popularly applied to understanding human motivation in organizations.[15]

Description. Maslow has theorized that people have five different types of needs that operate in a *hierarchical* manner. According to this hierarchical arrangement, needs are activated in a specific order such that a lower-order need must be satisfied before the next higher-order one is activated. Once a need is satisfied, the stage is set for the next higher need in the hierarchy to be activated. The five major need categories in Maslow's hierarchy are listed in Table 3.1.

The lowest order of needs specified by Maslow are *physiological* needs. These refer to the need to satisfy one's basic biological drives such as the need for food, water, and sex. The second level of needs is know as *safety* needs. These refer to the need to be free from threats of physical or psychological harm. The third level of needs is *social*; these needs refer to the desire to be loved and accepted by other people. Taken together as a group, physiological needs, safety needs, and social needs are known as *deficiency* needs. Maslow's idea was that unless these needs are met, an individual will fail to develop into a healthy person, both physically and psychologically.

TABLE 3.1   *Need Theories: A Comparison.*
The three needs indentified in Alderfer's *ERG theory* correspond to the five needs indentified in Maslow's *need hierarchy theory*. Although Maslow's theory specifies that the needs are activated in order from the lowest to the highest, ERG theory allows for needs to be activated in any order.

Theory I Maslow's Need Hierarchy Theory	*Theory II* Alderfer's ERG Theory
highest order **Growth needs**	
5) Self-actualization needs	Growth needs
--	
4) Esteem needs	
Deficiency needs	
3) Social needs	Relatedness needs
2) Safety needs	
--	Existence needs
lowest order 1) Physiological needs	

In contrast, the two highest-order needs—the ones at the top of the hierarchy—are known as *growth* needs. Gratification of these needs is said to help a person grow and develop to his or her fullest potential. One such growth need, the fourth in Maslow's hierarchy, is *esteem* needs. These refer to a person's need to develop self-respect and to gain the approval of others. Finally, at the top of Maslow's hierarchy is *self-actualization* needs, which refer to the need to become all that one is capable of being, to develop to one's fullest potential.

It is important to appreciate the implications of the hierarchical nature of Maslow's theory. According to the theory, only after an individual's physiological needs are satisfied is it possible for his or her safety needs to be activated. Once these safety needs are gratified, the social needs are activated, and so on. In other words, the desire to fulfill a particular need will arise only after all needs falling below it in the hierarchy have been satisfied. Thus, when all three deficiency needs have been satisfied, a person will become interested in satisfying the high-order growth needs. Ultimately, a person who has satisfied the four lower level needs will strive to become self-actualized—the need at the top of the hierarchy.

Applying the theory.   The fact that Maslow's theory conceptualizes needs as being arranged in a hierarchical fashion has some very interesting implications for how managers might go about motivating workers. The main idea is that organizations should attempt to help satisfy employees' lower-order needs, clearing the way for them to become self-actualized. After all, an individual who is worried about where his or her next meal is coming from would be expected to have very little interest in striving to be as productive as possible on the job. In contrast, employees who are self-actualized work up to their creative potential, and can be considered valuable assets to their organizations.

With this in mind, let's consider some of the things done in organizations to satisfy the needs of employees. Providing an adequate salary helps ensure that workers' physiological and safety needs are satisfied by enabling them to afford adequate food and housing. Social needs are often satisfied in organizations by coordinating company-wide social gatherings, bowling teams, and even arranging country club memberships for top executives. Finally, through various forms of formal and informal recognition—such as giving awards at company banquets or the key to the executive washroom—organizations may help satisfy their members' esteem needs. According to Maslow's theory, once these needs have been met, such as through the examples given here, it is possible for workers to become self-actualized, and thereby to perform at the height of their potential—a maximally effective use of the organization's human resources.

Testing the theory—and an alternative.   From our description of how Maslow's theory may be applied to organizational settings, it should not be surprising that it has a great deal of appeal among managers, who find it useful in conceptualizing employees' motivation to work.[16] Indeed, the general ideas behind Maslow's theory seem to be supported, such as the distinction between deficiency needs and growth needs.

This distinction has been sucessfully tested in a recent study by Betz, who compared the needs of housewives to the needs of women working outside the home.[17] It was found that full-time homemakers had higher levels of deficiency needs than married women employed outside the home, presumably because they did not have a job through which these needs could be fulfilled. It was also found that the growth needs of working women were higher than those of full-time homemakers, presumably because their deficiency needs were already satisfied on the job. This evidence is consistent with Maslow's ideas about the satisfaction of deficiency needs prior to growth needs.

Despite this, however, the theory has not received a great deal of support with respect to the exact needs that exist and the order in which they are activated.[18] Specifically, many researchers have failed to confirm that there are only five basic categories of needs. Also, these needs don't appear to be activated in the exact order specified by Maslow. In response to these criticisms, an alternative formulation has been proposed by Clayton Alderfer.[19] This approach, known as **ERG theory**, is much simpler. Not only does Alderfer specify that there are only three types of needs instead of five, but he also specifies that these are not necessarily activated in a specific order.

The three needs specified by *ERG theory* are the needs for existence, relatedness, and growth. *Existence* needs correspond to Maslow's physiological needs and safety needs. *Relatedness* needs correspond to Maslow's social needs, the need for meaningful social relationships. Finally, *growth* needs correspond to the esteem needs and self-actualization needs in Maslow's conceptualization—the need for developing one's potential. A summary of Maslow's need hierarchy theory and the corresponding needs identified by Alderfer's ERG theory is shown in Table 3.1. Clearly, ERG theory is much less restrictive than Maslow's need hierarchy theory. Its advantage is that it fits better with research evidence suggesting that, although basic categories of needs do exist, they are not exactly as specified by Maslow.[20]

Despite the fact that need theorists are not in complete agreement about the exact number of needs that exist and the relationships between them, they do seem to agree that human needs are important in motivating behavior on the job.

Equity Theory

In contrast to this focus on individual needs, equity theory views motivation from the perspective of the social comparisons workers make between themselves and others. J. Stacy Adams, the originator of equity theory, asserted that workers are motivated to maintain fair, or "equitable," relationships between themselves and to change those relationships that are unfair, or "inequitable."[21] The ways in which employees do this has been a topic of considerable interest in the field of organizational behavior.[22]

Description.   Equity theory is considered a theory of organizational motivation because it is concerned with people's drives to escape the negative feelings that result from being treated unfairly on their jobs. Such feelings may result when workers engage in the process of *social comparison*—that is, when they compare themselves to other people.

Equity theory proposes that workers make social comparisons between themselves and other people in two areas: **outcomes**—what workers believe they and others get out of their jobs, and **inputs**—the contributions they believe they and others make to their jobs. A worker's *outcomes* may include such benefits as pay, fringe benefits, or the prestige one receives on the job. *Inputs* may include such contributions as the amount of time worked, the amount of effort expended, the number of units produced, or the qualifications one brings to the job. It is important to note that equity theory is concerned with outcomes and inputs as they are *perceived* by the people involved, *not* necessarily how they actually are. It shouldn't be surprising, therefore, that workers may disagree about what constitutes equity and inequity.[23]

Equity theory states that people compare their outcomes and inputs to those of others in the form of a ratio. Specifically, they compare the ratio of their own outcomes/inputs to the ratio of outcomes/inputs of other people. As shown in Figure 3.3 (page 80), these comparisons can result in any of three states: *overpayment, underpayment,* or *equitable payment.* According to the theory, a person is said to experience **overpayment inequity** when his or her outcome/input ratio is *greater than* the corresponding ratio of another person with whom the person compares himself or herself. Overpaid workers are theorized to feel *guilty*. Someone is said to experience **underpayment inequity** when the ratio of his or her outcome/input ratio is *less than* the corresponding ratio of another with whom the person compares himself or herself. Underpaid workers are theorized to feel *angry*. Finally, a condition of **equitable payment** is said to exist when the outcome/input ratio of a person is *equal to* the corresponding ratio of another person with whom the individual compares himself or herself. Equitably paid workers are theorized to feel *satisfied*.

Let's assign some values to outcomes and inputs in a hypothetical example to clarify our description of equity theory thus far. Suppose that Steve and Howard work alongside each other on an assembly line, doing the same job. Both workers have the same degree of experience, training, and education (i.e., their inputs are identical), but Steve is paid $400/week compared to Howard's $300/week (i.e., Steve's outcomes are greater than Howard's). How will they feel when they talk to

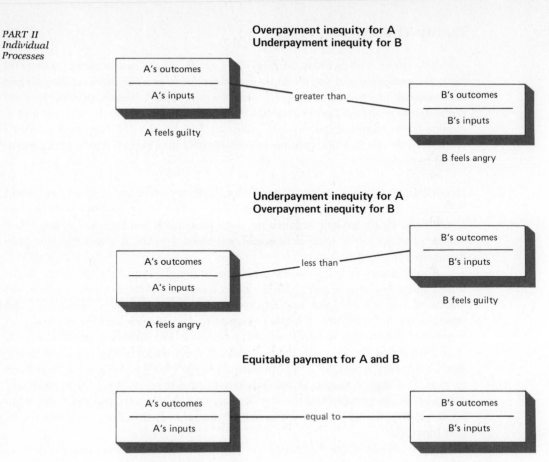

FIGURE 3.3 *Equity Theory: An Overview.*
By comparing their outcome/input ratios to the corresponding ratios of others, individuals judge the equity or inequity of their relationships. The resulting states and the associated emotional responses are shown here.

each other one day and learn of this situation? According to equity theory, Steve may be considered overpaid, and would be expected to feel guilty, while Howard may be considered underpaid, and would be expected to feel angry.

Equity theory suggests that people are motivated to escape these negative emotional states of anger and guilt. In our example, there are several things Steve and Howard could do to correct the inequity and feel better. Victims of inequity can redress it in several ways, turning their inequitable relationships into equitable ones. These fall into two categories—*behavioral* (taking some appropriate action) and *psychological* (changing how the situation is perceived). In Table 3.2 we have summarized some possible behavioral and psychological reactions that inequitably overpaid and underpaid persons may have.

A person who feels underpaid may seek to redress the inequity behaviorally by lowering his or her inputs. As an example, a salaried employee may work less hard, such as by arriving at work late, leaving early, taking longer breaks, doing less work, or performing lower quality work. A worker also can redress inequities behaviorally by attempting to raise his or her outcomes. An employee who feels underpaid and who asks the boss for a raise may be seen as attempting to follow this strategy. Similarly, we may view "borrowing" company property as a behavioral reaction to underpayment inequity. The employee who takes home from the office some company pens or paperclips may be seen as attempting to raise his or her outcomes. All these examples may be considered behavioral reactions to inequity because they represent things people can do to change their existing inputs or outcomes.

In addition to these behavioral reactions to underpayment inequity, there are also some likely psychological reactions. Given that many workers may feel uncomfortable stealing from their employers (as they should) or would be unwilling to restrict their productivity or to ask for a raise, they may resort to resolving the inequity *psychologically*—that is, by changing the way they think about the situation. Because equity theory deals with perceived inequities, it is reasonable to expect that inequitable states may be redressed effectively by merely thinking about the circumstances differently. For example, an underpaid worker may convince himself that another person who receives higher pay really *deserves* such outcomes. In this way, he or she can reduce or entirely avoid the distress stemming from inequity.

An analogous set of behavioral and psychological reactions can be identified for overpayment inequity. Specifically, a salaried worker who feels overpaid may raise his or her inputs, such as by working harder, or for longer hours. Similarly, workers who lower their own outcomes, such as by not taking advantage of company-provided fringe benefits may be seen as redressing an overpayment inequity. In addition, overpaid persons may readily convince themselves psychologically that they are really worth their higher outcomes by virtue of their superior inputs.

TABLE 3.2   *Inequity: Some Possible Reactions.*
The behavioral and psychological reactions listed here represent only a few of the many possible reactions workers may have to experiencing overpayment inequity and underpayment inequity. These reactions help redress the inequity and bring about an equitable state.

Type of reaction to inequity	Type of Inequity	
	Underpayment	Overpayment
Behavioral	Lower own inputs (reduce effort)	Raise own inputs (work harder or longer hours)
	Try to raise own outcomes (ask for a raise)	Try to lower own outcomes (don't accept a raise)
Psychological	Convince oneself that other's inputs are higher than one's own (rationalize that the comparison other really is more qualified)	Convince oneself that own outcomes are justified by higher inputs (rationalize that you really do more work than the other and deserve higher outcomes)

Workers who receive substantial pay raises may not feel too distressed about it at all because they already may have rationalized that the raise was warranted on the basis of their superior inputs, and therefore does not constitute an inequity.

As this discussion suggests, there are many ways employees can resolve inequitable situations, and there are likely to be some disagreements about what constitutes an inequitable situation at all. In fact, whether or not people believe they are equitably or inequitably treated will depend on who they choose for comparison. Not surprisingly, the perceptual nature of equity theory makes it possible for a worker and a manager to disagree about what worker's inputs and outcomes may be.[24] It is precisely because there is likely to be disagreement over what constitutes legitimate inputs and outcomes that controversies have arisen over what constitutes fair pay for various jobs. In particular, the current controversy over *comparable worth* is concerned with establishing the value of different job inputs so that pay equity can be created across various jobs in an organization. It would be equitable for people performing jobs of equal worth to their organizations to receive equal pay. (For a detailed description of some of the difficulties involved in establishing comparable worth, please see the **Case in Point** insert on page 83.)

Equity theory research.   In several decades of research, predictions about organizational behavior based on equity theory have received a great deal of support.[36] In one of the most ambitious tests of equity theory, Pritchard, Dunnette, and Jorgenson hired male clerical workers to work part-time over a two-week period.[37] In their simulated company, the experimenters manipulated the equity of their workers' pay. *Overpaid* workers were told the pay they received was higher than others doing the same work. *Underpaid* workers were told their pay was lower than that of others doing the same work. *Equitably paid* workers were told the pay they received was equal to that of others doing the same work. The results of the study were consistent with equity theory: overpaid workers were more productive than equitably paid workers, and underpaid workers were less productive than equitably paid workers. Moreover, both overpaid and underpaid workers reported being more dissatisfied with their jobs than the equitably paid workers. Thus, the subjects in this study behaved precisely as equity theory predicted.

A more recent test of equity theory by Greenberg and Ornstein examined the effects of adding inputs—in the form of additional responsibilities—and outcomes—such as a high status job title—to workers' jobs.[38] If we increase a person's inputs (such as by giving the person extra responsibilities) without increasing his or her outcomes, we have created an underpayment inequity. However, if we simultaneously compensate the person for those added inputs (such as by conferring a high status job title), then an equitable state would exist.

To test this reasoning, an experiment was devised in which undergraduate students were hired to do proofreading at a rate of pay they considered to be equitable—$3.85 per hour. After an initial work period, some of the subjects (those in the "title" condition) were singled out for their good performance and were given the title of "senior proofreader." This required them to stay for an additional hour to help check the other proofreaders' work. Although subjects did not expect to be paid extra from this work, they were compensated by being given this high status job title. The performance of these subjects was compared to another group who

CASE IN POINT

Comparable Worth: The Controversy Over Establishing Organizational Equity

Whose work is worth more, a public health nurse or a tree pruner? How about a historical researcher compared to a federal librarian? These are just some of the questions that courts in the United States and Canada have recently had to address.[25] These questions all center around the issue of **comparable worth**, the idea that persons performing jobs judged to be of equal worth or difficulty must be compensated equally. Although equity theory is content to recognize that people judge their work inputs subjectively, the law—such as the Equal Pay Act of 1963 or Title VII of the 1964 Civil Rights Act in the United States, or the Human Rights Act in Canada—has been charged with more objectively determining what constitutes comparable worth. Instigated by charges that women earn only a small fraction of what men earn for seemingly comparable jobs, the courts have had to consider the causes and consequences of such wage discrimination.[26]

Is it necessarily inequitable for men to be paid more than women? To the extent that cultural norms view "women's work" as being less valuable than "men's work," it should not be surprising that women tend to work in lower paying jobs than men.[27] Less valuable work would indeed warrant lower pay, according to equity theory. The real question of equity, of course, concerns *why* the jobs that women usually do tend to be viewed as less valuable ones (see Figure 3.4). Many would claim that the pay gap between men and women is perpetuated by societal values and labor market conditions that trap women in lower-paying, "traditionally female" occupations.[28]

As one solution, some legal scholars propose that the issue confronting personnel and organizational specialists is to establish objectively the value of each job performed (with respect to such factors as effort, skill, responsibility, and working conditions).[29] Then compensation decisions could be made on the basis of the worth of each job being performed. Doing this would establish comparable worth as defined under the Equal Pay Act of 1963. One popular way of establishing comparable worth is known as the *point method*.[30] This approach requires several representatives of an organization who are familiar with all the jobs to form a *compensation committee* charged with the responsibility for assigning point values to different

FIGURE 3.4   *Who Should Receive Higher Pay?*
Questions of comparable worth often arise when females in higher status jobs are paid less than males in lower status positions.

jobs based on its collective judgment of their worth to the company. By including a wide range of members on the committee (e.g., males and females, union and nonunion employees, management and nonmanagement personnel), it is possible to take into account the opinions of many different organization members in reaching a consensus over the worth of various jobs. For example, in one case in the state of Washington, the job of truck driver was given 97 points, licensed practical nurse, 173 points, and physician, 861 points.[31] One reason why the concern over comparable worth is so great is that such wage evaluation studies often find that people working in many highly valued jobs—particularly those that are predominantly held by females—tend to be paid less than people in less valuable positions. For example, in 1980 maintenance carpenters in Washington (only 2.3 percent of whom were women) were paid an average of $1707 per month, whereas secretaries (98.5 percent of whom were women) were paid only $1122 per month despite the fact that both jobs were evaluated at 197 points. In part because of such evidence of sex discrimination, in December 1983 a U.S. District Court judge ordered the state of Washington to pay an estimated one billion dollars in back pay and wage increases to 15,000 people in female-dominated professions who were paid less than employees in male-dominated jobs of comparable value.[32]

Although using the point method to establish comparable worth would seem to be a step in the right direction, it is not without problems.[33] For example, it may be difficult to compare the worth of different jobs because different criteria may be important for different ones. Also, even for identical jobs, individual employers may value different things, resulting in different evaluations of the same job in different organizations. Obviously, the problem of evaluating the worth of jobs remains a very complex one.

Unfortunately, there appears to be no simple answer to the important question of how to establish comparable worth. Indeed, the findings of a recent study by Madigan suggest that all of the methods now in common use (the point method plus several others) suffer from serious drawbacks.[34] Little wonder, then, that the courts have been disturbingly inconsistent in their decisions about comparability. Recall the opening questions in this insert. In these cases, the courts found that: tree pruners *were* worth more than public health nurses, but historical researchers *were not* worth as much as federal librarians. In deciding this latter case, the Human Rights Commission of Canada ordered back-payment amounting to $2.3 million to 470 librarians.[35] Because the current legal forces toward establishing comparable worth can make it quite costly for organizations to redress past inequities, it is not surprising to find strong resistance to these rulings on the part of most business organizations. As a result, we believe that debate over the question of comparable worth will continue to fill the pages of our newspapers in the years to come.

---

also were asked to stay after the experiment was over to help check others' work, but who were not compensated with a high status job title (the "no-title" condition). Did the subjects who were not compensated for their added inputs respond by lowering their inputs as equity theory would predict?

The results, shown in Figure 3.5, support predictions derived from equity theory. Subjects not given a title—those asked to do the extra work (increase their inputs) without receiving any higher outcomes (without getting the title), responded by lowering their inputs. Because their inputs were increased but not their outcomes, they reported feeling underpaid. In contrast, subjects who experienced an increase in both their outcomes and inputs (those given the title) believed they were equitably treated and maintained their high level of performance. Their increased inputs were apparently offset by their increased outcomes they received in the form of a high status job title.

The studies by Pritchard, Dunnette, and Jorgensen, and by Greenberg and Ornstein, and others, indicate that equity theory can make good predictions about how people respond to perceived unfairness. It is also important to note that equity theory takes account of the fact that managers may be interested in striving to create equity among their workers. This may take the form of managers attempting to pay their workers in proportion to their relative contributions so as to avoid conflict and dissension among the members of the workforce.[39] Concerns about inequity not only motivate workers to escape inequitable situations, but concerns about equity also motivate managers to attempt to create equitable relationships between themselves and employees.

Valence-Instrumentality-Expectancy theory

Valence-instrumentality-expectancy theory—referred to as **VIE theory**—is the broadest in scope of the three theories presented in this chapter. Instead of narrowly focusing on individual needs or on social comparisons as the previously

FIGURE 3.5   *Reacting to Inequity: An Experimental Demonstration.*
An experiment showed that giving workers a high status job title equitably compensated them for the added responsibilities associated with it. However, giving workers the same extra responsibilities without granting the title created underpayment inequity, causing them to lower their performance. (Source: Based on data in Greenberg and Ornstein, 1983; see Note 38.)

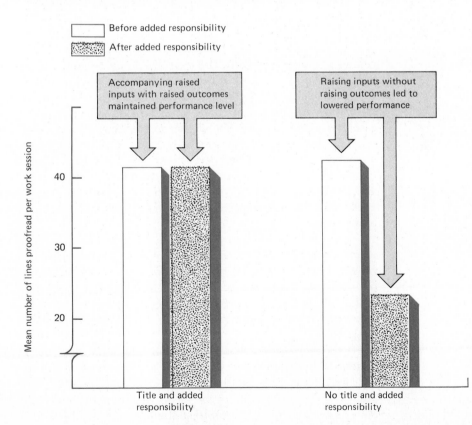

described theories have done, VIE theory looks at the role motivation plays in the overall work environment. In essence, the theory asserts that people are motivated to work when they expect they will be able to achieve the things they want from their jobs. VIE theory characterizes workers as rational beings who think about what they have to do to get rewarded and how much the reward means to them before they perform their jobs. But the theory doesn't just focus on what people think—it also recognizes that these thoughts combine with other aspects of the organizational environment to influence job performance.

Before we get more specific in our description of VIE theory, we should note that it has been presented in many different forms—including the important pioneering work of Vroom, and of Porter and Lawler.[40,41] However, the differences between the various versions of VIE theory need not concern us; we will describe the theory in its most general form.

Description of VIE theory.   VIE theory specifies that motivation is the result of three different types of beliefs that people have. These are:

(1) The belief that a person's effort will result in performance, referred to as **expectancy**,
(2) The belief that a person's performance will be rewarded, referred to as **instrumentality**, and
(3) The perceived value of the rewards to the people receiving them, referred to as **valence**.

Sometimes, workers believe that putting forth a great deal of effort will result in getting a lot accomplished. However, there are certainly occasions in which how hard one works will have little bearing on how much gets done. For example, an employee operating a faulty piece of machinery may be expected to have a very low *expectancy* that his or her efforts will lead to high levels of performance. In such a case, we wouldn't expect the worker to continue to exert much effort.

It is also possible that even if one works hard and performs at a high level, motivation may falter if that performance is not suitably rewarded by the organization—that is, if the performance is not perceived as being *instrumental* in bringing about the rewards. So, for example, an individual may be unwilling to put much effort into her job if she perceives that no one will notice, let alone reward, improved performance.

Finally, even if employees receive rewards based on their performance, we would expect them to be poorly motivated if those so-called "rewards" have a low *valence* to them. A worker who doesn't care about the rewards offerred by the organization would not be motivated to attempt to attain them. For example, a millionaire would be expected to be poorly motivated to obtain a reward of $100, whereas a poor person might be expected to perceive that reward as being quite valuable.

VIE theory claims that motivation is a multiplicative function of all three components. This means that higher levels of motivation will result when valence, instrumentality, and expectancy are all high than when they are all low. The multiplicative assumption of the theory also implies that if any one of the components is zero, then the overall level of motivation will be zero. So, even if a worker

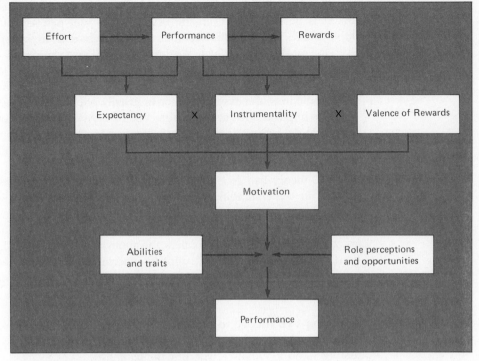

FIGURE 3.6   VIE Theory: An Overview.
VIE theory defines motivation as the product of expectancy, instrumentality, and valence. It also recognizes that motivation is only one of several determinants of work performance.

believes that her effort will result in performance, which will result in reward, motivation may be zero if the valence of the reward received is zero. Figure 3.6 summarizes the definitions of the components of VIE theory and shows the interrelationships between these components.

As you can also see from Figure 3.6, VIE theory assumes that motivation is not equivalent to job performance, but that it is just one of several determinants of job performance. In particular, the theory assumes that *skills and abilities* also contribute to a person's job performance. It is no secret that some people are better suited to perform their jobs than others by virtue of their unique characteristics and special skills. For example, a tall, well-coordinated person is likely to make a better professional basketball player than a very short, poorly-coordinated person, even if the shorter person is more highly motivated to succeed.

VIE theory also recognizes that job performance will be influenced by an individual's *role perceptions*. How well people perform their jobs will depend, in part, on what they believe is expected of them. An assistant manager, for example, may believe his or her primary job responsibility is to train employees. But, if the manager believes the assistant manager should be doing the paperwork instead, he or she may be seen as a poor performer. Of course, this seeming poor performance results *not* necessarily from poor motivation, but from misunderstandings concerning the role one is expected to play in the organization.

Finally, VIE theory also recognizes the role of *opportunities* to perform one's job. It is possible that even the best workers will perform at low levels if their opportunities are limited. A good example may be seen in the work of salespersons. Even the most highly motivated salesperson will perform poorly if opportunities are restricted—if the available stock for sale is very low (as is sometimes the case among certain popular cars), or if the customers are unable to afford the product (as is sometimes the case in territories heavily populated by unemployed persons).

It is important to recognize that VIE theory views motivation as being just one of several determinants of job performance. Motivation combines with a person's skills and abilities, role perceptions, and opportunities to influence job performance.

VIE theory has generated a great deal of research and has been successfully applied to understanding behavior in many different organizational settings.[42] However, although some specific aspects of the theory have been supported (particularly the impact of expectancy and instrumentality on motivation), others have not (such as the contribution of valence to motivation and the multiplicative assumption).[43,44] Despite this mixed support, expectancy theory has been a dominant approach to the field of organizational motivation.[45] This appears to be due, in part, to the theory's important implications for organizational practice.

Applying VIE theory to organizational practice.   Let's now consider some of the suggestions made by VIE theory about how to motivate workers.[46] What might managers do to enhance workers' motivation?

1) One important suggestion would be to *clarify workers' expectancies that their effort will lead to performance.* Workers' motivation may be enhanced by training them to do their jobs more efficiently, thereby achieving higher levels of performance from their efforts. It may also be possible for effort-performance expectancies to be enhanced by following workers' suggestions about ways to change their jobs. To the extent that employees are aware of problems in their jobs that interfere with their performance, then attempting to alleviate these problems may help them perform more efficiently. In essence, what we are saying is: *Make the desired performance attainable.* It is important to make it clear to people what is expected of them *and* to make it possible for them to attain that level of performance. Obviously, what is needed to make these suggestions possible is two-way communication between subordinates and their supervisors. During periodic performance appraisal sessions, supervisors need to pay attention to their employees' suggestions concerning ways of making their jobs more efficient, and workers need to pay attention to managers' suggestions for ways of improving their productive efficiency.[47]

2) A second practical suggestion from VIE theory is to *clearly link valued rewards and performance.* Using the terminology of VIE theory, managers should attempt to enhance workers' beliefs about instrumentality—that is, make it clear to them exactly what job behaviors will lead to what rewards. To the extent that it is possible for employees to be paid in ways that are directly linked to their performance—such as through piece-rate incentive systems, or sales commission plans—VIE theory specifies that it would be effective to do so because this will enhance beliefs about instrumentality. One note of caution is in order here: not only should workers be led to believe that their performance will be rewarded in a certain way,

it is also important for there to be an accurate follow-up—that is, for them actually to be paid in the stated way. It may be considered effective to enhance instrumentality beliefs only insofar as these beliefs are borne out in actual practice.

3) Finally, one of the most obvious practical suggestions from VIE theory is to *administer rewards that are positively valent to employees*. The carrot at the end of the stick must be a tasty one, according to the theory, for it to have potential as a motivator. At present when the composition of the workforce is changing, with increasing numbers of unmarried parents and single people working, it would be a mistake to assume that all employees care about the same rewards made available to them by their companies. Some may recognize the incentive value of a pay raise, while others may prefer additional vacation days, improved insurance benefits, or day care facilities for children. With this in mind, more and more companies are instituting *cafeteria-style pay plans*—incentive systems through which employees select their compensation package from a menu of available alternatives. The success of these plans suggests that making highly valent rewards available to employees may be an effective motivational technique.[48]

TECHNIQUES FOR ENHANCING WORKER MOTIVATION

Now that we have covered the basics of the concept of motivation and have examined some of the major theories about it, we are prepared to put some of this information to practical use. Our presentation of techniques for improving worker motivation will focus on two different approaches: *goal setting*, an approach in which individuals strive to meet specified performance goals; and *job design*, an approach in which jobs are changed or created so as to build in more of what motivates workers. Both approaches have been shown to be effective ways of enhancing motivation on the job.[49]

Motivating by Setting Performance Goals

The idea that worker motivation and performance may be enhanced by setting performance goals is an important part of the dominant management philosophy today in organizations in the United States and Canda. In view of the vast amount of research applying **goal setting** procedures to organizational practice, it is possible for us to point out several well-established principles of goal setting.[50] (We will also have more to say about goal setting in Chapter 16, when we consider the topic of *management by objectives*.)

Assign specific goals. Probably the best established finding of studies on goal setting is that workers will perform at a higher level when given a specific goal than when simply asked to "do your best."[51]

A particularly dramatic demonstration of this principle can be seen in research conducted at Parkdale Mills, Inc. Before the goal setting program began the employees in this organization had an average attendance rate of 86 percent. As part of the goal-setting program, they agreed to raise their average attendance rate to 93 percent. Each day an attendance chart was kept so workers could be kept informed of their progress toward meeting their goal. As you can see from Figure 3.7, setting the specific goal was very successful. Not only did workers achieve their goal within four weeks of setting it, but they surpassed it—averaging 94.3 percent attendance for the nine weeks following the goal setting![52]

It is important to note that the beneficial effects of setting specific performance goals appear to be long-lasting. In one study, loggers who worked to meet the goal of loading trucks to 94 percent of capacity were found to sustain their high level of performance as long as seven years later.[53] Of course, it is not sufficient for performance goals merely to be specific—it is also important to consider the difficulty level of these goals.

2 **Assign difficult—but acceptable—performance goals.** The study at Parkdale Mills described above demonstrated the effectiveness of assigning specific goals. But note also that the goal set in that organization was a difficult one. A goal must be difficult and challenging, as well as specific, for it to raise performance. A specific, yet very easy to achieve goal may even lower performance. Several studies have found that performance levels can be raised when workers attempt to meet

FIGURE 3.7 *Goal Setting: A Demonstration of Its Effectiveness.*
Setting the specific, difficult goal of attaining 93 percent attendance was effective in raising the attendance rate in one company soon after the goal was set. (Source: Based on data in Miller, 1978; see Note 52.)

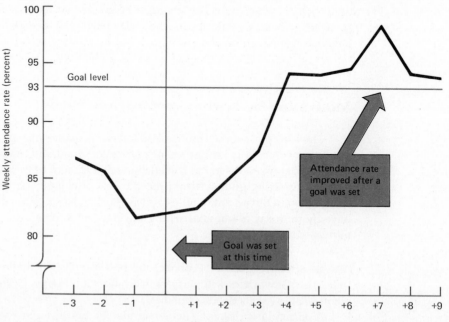

specific difficult goals. At the same time, however, it is important that the goals are not so difficult that they are rejected by the workers.

The effects of setting difficult goals has been demonstrated in a recent study by Garland.[54] The subjects in this experiment were undergraduate students hired to perform a creative task—listing as many objects as they could that could be described by a given adjective (e.g., items that are "soft," such as a pillow or cotton). Before any goals were set, subjects listed an average of about 7.5 objects. In one condition in which an easy goal was set (four objects—fewer than they were capable of doing) performance dropped to just over six objects. However, when a difficult goal of fourteen objects was set, performance levels increased to just short of nine objects.

Although this study shows that assigning difficult goals may raise productivity levels, it may not be a good idea to set goals so high that they are not accepted. The detrimental effects of setting unacceptably high goals also has been demonstrated experimentally. In a recent study Erez and Zidon had a group of engineers and technicians perform a perceptual speed test requiring them to match the number of characters appearing in two lines of text.[55] Although performance levels improved with increasingly difficult goals, they did so only up to a point. As the goals became *too* difficult, the subjects reported not accepting the goals and their performance dropped.

With these findings in mind, an important question needs to be raised about how to arrive at a difficult, but acceptable, goal level. One obvious way of enhancing goal acceptance is that of *involving employees in the goal-setting process*. Research on this topic has shown that performance is enhanced only when the persons involved actually show increased acceptance of the goals as a result of their participation. Those who accept the goals prior to the goal-setting process do not demonstrate similar improvements in performance.[56] Because it is not always practical to involve workers in goal-setting, other techniques may be used to enhance goal acceptance. One such approach involves *psychological contracts*—public commitments by employees to attaining specific goals. Such commitment appears to increase acceptance of the stated goals, and so the likelihood that they will be reached.

Provide feedback concerning goal acceptance. The final principle of goal setting we will mention is an obvious one. Just as golfers need to see where their ball goes when they hit it if they are to improve their swing, workers need feedback concerning how closely they are approaching their performance goal in order to meet it.

The importance of combining feedback and goal setting has been shown in a recent field study examining the effects of goal setting on occupational safety.[57] The subjects were employees working in various shops of a manufacturing plant. Before and after safety goals were set, observations were made of various employee behaviors from which judgements were made of the percentage of employees performing their jobs in a completely safe manner. As shown in Figure 3.8 (page 92), about 65 percent of the workers performed their jobs safely during the ten weeks before goal setting. However, after a difficult but attainable goal of 95 percent safe behavior was set, the safety rate rose to over 80 percent—an improvement, but a rate still shy of the goal. As you can see, the goal was met only after the goal setting was accompanied by feedback about safety.

These findings about the effectiveness of incorporating feedback into goal set-

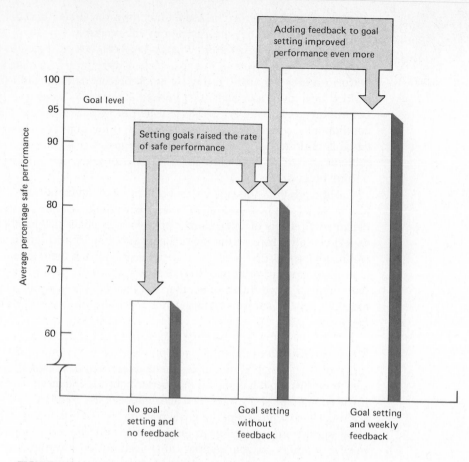

FIGURE 3.8   *Using Feedback Enhances Responses to Goal Setting.*
Research in one manufacturing firm showed that accompanying specific goals with feedback was more effective in raising the rate of safe behavior than goal setting alone. (Source: Based on data in Chhokar and Wallin, 1984; see Note 57.)

ting programs are further clarified by additional recent findings concerning the *kinds* of feedback that are particularly effective. One thing we know is that it is not always sufficient simply to inform workers about the outcome of their effort. Providing them with information about *how* and *why* their performance is enhanced by doing certain things (a procedure known as *cognitive feedback*) is also helpful.[58] Moreover, research has shown that gains in performance result from adding information about specific successful behaviors to information about performance outcomes.[59] Apparently, the gains to be had by providing performance feedback may be enhanced further by supplementing this feedback with information about the causes of its effectiveness and the specific behaviors that led to its effectiveness.

Despite these impressive findings, it would be erroneous to assume that using goal setting to motivate workers is a simple matter. Indeed, there are a number of pitfalls and shortcomings of goal setting that need to be noted. Please refer to our discussion of these in the **Perspective** insert on page 93.

Avoiding Pitfalls in Goal Setting

Like most managerial programs, putting goal setting plans into practice in organizations has not proven to be an easy task to accomplish. Although the principles of goal setting we have described are well supported, this is not to imply that they are always successful. In fact, the vast majority of companies using goal setting have reported that their effectiveness is mixed at best.[60] Learning from the problems that some organizations have had in implementing goal setting programs, let's consider some of the pitfalls to be avoided and the limitations of goal setting.

First, we should note that *goal setting cannot easily be implemented for all jobs.* For many positions, particularly high-level managerial ones, it is very difficult to set objectively quantifiable goals. Merely being objective in setting goals may be counterproductive if it diverts workers' attention from the jobs they really need to be doing just so they can meet less important—but objectifiable—"targets."[61] We should also note that it would be difficult to institute and fairly implement goal setting plans in jobs whose outcomes are dependent on the simultaneous efforts of several workers. For example, imagine the difficulty that would be involved in assessing the success of an individual baseball infielder in increasing the rate of double-plays made. When one worker's performance depends on others' efforts—such as the work of members of teams—it would be questionable to judge an individual worker's goal attainment by the group's outcomes, and it is also difficult to assess an individual worker's contribution to a group product.[62]

Another common problem with implementing goal setting programs in organizations is that they frequently suffer from *limited managerial support.* Managers are often impatient with the paperwork burden placed on them by having to implement goal-setting plans. They sometimes also force workers to accept goals, thereby undermining the spirit and effectiveness of goal setting techniques. Acceptance of goals by workers must be genuine and managers must be committed to carrying out goal setting programs carefully if they are to succeed.[63]

As part of the same idea, we are led to a final problem—*limited worker acceptance.* We have emphasized the importance of worker acceptance of performance goals in effectively implementing goal setting. However, it sometimes happens that with intense pressure to meet goals, goal attainment becomes an end in itself—even at the expense of ultimate job performance. In fact, one survey of over two hundred American business executives found that more than 64 percent agreed with the statement that "managers today feel under pressure to compromise personal standards to achieve company goals."[64] Not only are personal ethics being sacrificed in the name of goal attainment, but so too are organizational ethics, with many companys falsifying records to appear to meet organizational goals.[65] Such practices are ethically questionable, and also of limited benefit to the company, whose best interests are ultimately served by maintaining accurate records.

In sum, managers attempting to implement goal setting programs are cautioned about some of their inherent pitfalls. Goal setting can be an effective managerial tool, but its use should be restricted to jobs for which meaningful goals can be set, and to circumstances in which managers and employees are mutually committed to making it succeed.

Job Design: Motivating by Changing the Work

In addition to enhancing motivation by setting goals, another popular approach to motivation involves designing (or redesigning) jobs so as to make them more appealing to workers. The roots of this idea can be traced back to the early part of this century, when Fredrick W. Taylor attempted to stimulate productivity by analyzing the specific motions involved in work tasks to discover the most efficient ways of performing them, and rewarded employees for working in those ways.[66] This approach, know as **scientific management**, made work highly efficient. (We have already commented on scientific management in Chapter 1 and will have more to say about it in Chapter 14.) Unfortunately, however, it also made many jobs highly routine and monotonous. The problem with this, of course, is that workers who are bored with their jobs tend to be absent and to quit.[67] As a result, motivational practitioners have sought ways of designing jobs that are simultaneously efficient and pleasant for those who do them.

Several modern approaches to task design have been advocated that seek to motivate workers in more humane—and effective—ways than scientific management. These approaches tend to motivate employees by designing jobs so they are more involving for the persons performing them. The rationale is that jobs should be made more *intrinsically* rewarding—benefits derived from the work itself, such as feelings of accomplishment and personal growth. By contrast, scientific management focused more on *extrinsic* rewards—the benefits associated with doing the job (such as pay and fringe benefits) rather than the work itself. Our discussion will focus on two approaches to job design popular in the 1950s and 1960s—*job enlargement* and *job enrichment*, as well as an approach developed in the 1970s and 1980s—the *job characteristics model*.

Job enlargement and job enrichment.   One of the first modern ways of motivating workers in organizations was to redesign jobs according to principles of **job enlargement**. Job enlargement refers to the practice of expanding the content of a job by increasing the number and variety of tasks performed at the same level. If a worker on an automobile assembly line normally has the job of tightening the lugs on the left rear wheel of the car as it rolls down the line, that job may be enlarged by requiring the worker to both tighten the lugs and install the wheel cover. Please note that the worker now performs a wider variety of tasks, but these are all at the same level. Because of this, the enlargement process is said to have increased the *horizontal job loading* of the job. That is, the worker now performs more tasks at the same level of difficulty.

In contrast to job enlargement, **job enrichment** not only gives workers more jobs to do, but gives them more tasks to perform at a higher level. Job enrichment refers to the practice of giving workers the opportunity to have greater responsibility for their work and to take greater control over how to do their jobs. Because workers performing enriched jobs have increased opportunities to perform work at higher levels, the job enrichment process is said to increase the job's *vertical job loading*. (Incidently, we should note that the idea of job enrichment was developed by Fredrick Herzberg. However, because Herzberg's theory focuses heavily on the determinants of job satisfaction, we have reserved discussion of it until Chapter 5.) For a summary of these differences between job enlargement and job enrichment, please refer to Figure 3.9.

Job enlargement and job enrichment programs have been used at some of the largest companies in the United States, including IBM, AT&T, General Foods, Proctor & Gamble, and others.[67] The important question, of course, is: Do they work? The support for job enlargement is mostly anecdotal. There are more case

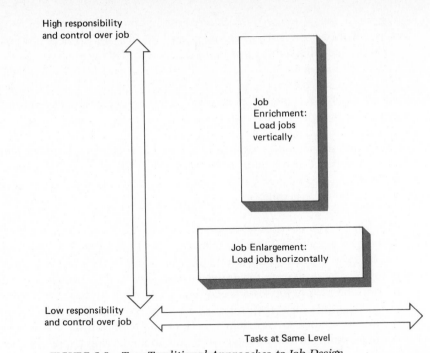

High responsibility
and control over job

Job
Enrichment:
Load jobs
vertically

Job Enlargement:
Load jobs horizontally

Low responsibility
and control over job

Tasks at Same Level

FIGURE 3.9   *Two Traditional Approaches to Job Design.*
Designing jobs by adding more tasks at the same level (horizontal loading) is referred to as
job enlargement. Designing jobs by increasing the level of responsibility and control (vertical
loading) is referred to as *job enrichment.*

studies than good empirical investigations that support the effectiveness of job
enlargement programs. Job enrichment has been the subject of more rigorous
empirical investigations, but here, too, critics have found evidence suggesting that
its effectiveness is questionable.[69] In other words, although it is often reported that
enlargement and enrichment programs are effective, existing scientific evidence is
not all that compelling.

Without going into detail about the specific problems with studies on job
enlargement and enrichment programs, let's review some of the complexities involved in putting such programs to use. One obvious problem lies in the *difficulty of
implementation.* Clearly, it would be expensive to redesign existing physical plants
so as to enrich jobs. Not only that, but the technology required to perform many jobs
makes it difficult if not impossible for them to be performed in a different manner. It
is perhaps for these reasons that formal job enrichment plans remain still quite
atypical in the United States. In one survey of 125 industrial firms, it was reported
that only 5 had attempted to institute formal job enrichment programs.[70]

Another problem is that job enlargement or enrichment programs *may not be
accepted by all employees.* Workers do not always want the added responsibility
that goes along with performing enriched jobs. This fact is demonstrated nicely in
one study in which six auto workers from Detroit worked in Sweden as engine
assemblers in a Saab plant. In Sweden, enriched jobs are typical, and the workers in

the Saab plant exercised a great deal of freedom and responsibility about how to perform their jobs. After a month five out of the six workers reported preferring their traditional assembly line jobs. To quote one of the workers, "If I've got to bust my a–– to be meaningful, forget it; I'd rather be monotonous."[71] Clearly, enriched jobs might not be for everyone. But, which employees respond most positively to enriched jobs? Steers and Spencer found that workers who were particularly interested in striving to be successful in their lives (a personality trait known as *need for achievement* that is discussed in Chapter 6), worked harder at enriched jobs because they provide more opportunities to achieve success. However, employees who were less concerned about achieving success found enriched jobs a frustrating, dissatisfying experience.[72] In sum, job enlargement and job enrichment programs may not be for everyone.

The job characteristics model.   One problem with the job enrichment approach as we have presented it thus far is that it fails to specify *how* to enrich a job. In other words, exactly *what* elements of a job need to be enriched for job enrichment to be effective? The answer to this important question is provided by a recent attempt to expand the idea of job enrichment known as the **job characteristics model**.

This approach assumes that jobs can be redesigned so as to "help individuals regain the chance to experience the kick that comes from doing a job well, and . . . once again *care* about their work and about developing the competence to do it even better."[73] The job characteristics model specifies that there are certain elements of jobs that need to be enriched because these are effective in altering workers' psychological states in a manner that enhances their work effectiveness.[74]

Specifically, the model indentifies five *core job dimensions* that help create three *critical psychological states* that, in turn, lead to several beneficial outcomes for workers and their organizations. The model is presented in Figure 3.10. As shown in that diagram, there are three job dimensions—skill variety, task indentity, and task significance—that contribute to a task's experienced meaningfulness. *Skill variety* refers to the extent to which a job requires the use of several of the worker's different skills and talents. *Task identity* refers to the extent to which a job requires completing a whole piece of work from beginning to end. And finally, *task significance* refers to the degree of impact the job is believed to have on other people. These three factors are said to contribute to a task's *experienced meaningfulness*. According to the model, a task is considered meaningful if it is experienced as important, valuable and worthwhile.

Autonomy is identified as another basic job dimension. It refers to the extent to which a worker has a great deal of freedom and discretion to carry out the job as desired. Autonomous jobs are said to make individuals feel personally responsible and accountable for the work they perform.

A final job characteristic—*feedback*—contributes to a worker's knowledge of results about the job performed. When a job is designed so that it provides workers with information about the effects of their work, they will be better able to develop an understanding of how effectively they have performed.

The job characteristics model specifies that the three critical psychological states—experienced meaningfulness, responsibility for outcomes, and knowledge of results—influence workers' feelings of motivation, the quality of work performed, satisfaction with work, and absenteeism and turnover. Specifically, the higher the

experienced meaningfulness of work, responsibility for work outcomes, and knowledge of results, the more positive these outcomes are theorized to be.

We should also note that the model is theorized to be especially effective in
describing the behavior of individuals who are high in *growth need strength*—that
is, workers who have a high need for personal growth and development. Employees
who are not particularly interested in personal growth and development are not
expected to experience the theorized psychological reactions to the core job dimensions, nor consequently, to enjoy the beneficial personal and work outcomes predicted by the model. By including this variable in the model, Hackman and Oldham
recognize the important limitation of job enrichment noted in the previous section:
Not everyone wants or benefits from enriched jobs.

Based on the proposed relationship between core job dimensions and their
associated psychological reactions, the model proposes that job motivation would
be highest when jobs are performed that are high on the various dimensions. To

FIGURE 3.10   *The Job Characteristics Model.*
The job characteristics model suggests that certain core *job dimensions* create certain critical
psychological states, which lead to certain positive *personal* and *organizational outcomes*.
(Source: Adapted from a figure in Hackman and Oldman, *Work Redesign*; © 1980 by
Addison-Wesley Publishing Company. Used by permission.)

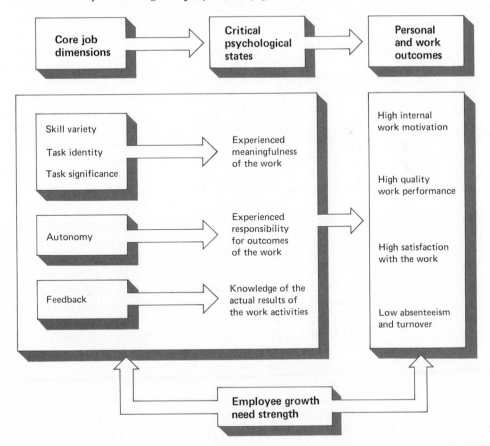

assess this idea, a questionnaire known as the *Job Diagnostic Survey* (JDS) has been developed to measure the degree to which various job characteristics are present in a particular job.[75] Based on responses to the JDS it is possible to make predictions about the degree to which a job is motivating to the people who perform it. This is done using an index known as the *motivating potential score* (MPS). It is computed as follows:

$$MPS = \left[\frac{skill\ variety\ +\ task\ identity\ +\ task\ significance}{3}\right] \times autonomy \times feedback$$

The higher the MPS for any given job, the greater will be the likelihood of experiencing the beneficial personal and work outcomes specified by the job characteristics model.

Despite the relative newness of the job characteristics model, it has been the focus of many empirical tests.[76] Given the complex nature of the model, it should not be particularly surprising that support for the model has been mixed, but at least mildly encouraging.[77] Thus, to date, there have been several convincing demonstrations of the model's ability to suggest effective ways of enriching jobs. One study conducted among a group of South African clerical workers found pariicularly strong support for many aspects of the model.[78] The employees in some of the offices in this organization had their jobs enriched in accordance with the suggestions of the job characteristics model. Specifically, they could: (a) choose what kinds of tasks they would perform (skill variety), (b) perform the entire job (task identity), (c) receive instructions regarding how their job fit into the organization as a whole (task significance), (d) freely set their own schedules and inspect their own work (autonomy), and (e) keep records of their daily productivity (feedback). Another group of workers, who were equivalent in all respects except that their jobs were not enriched, served as a control condition.

After workers performed the newly designed jobs for six months, comparisons were made between them and their counterparts in the control group who performed the traditional jobs. With respect to most of the outcomes specified by the model, those performing the redesigned jobs showed superior results. Questionnaire measures showed them to feel more internally motivated and more satisfied with their jobs. Furthermore, objective measures found lower rates of absenteeism and turnover among workers performing the enriched jobs. The only outcome predicted by the model that was not found involved actual work performance; performance quality was *not* significantly higher for workers performing the enriched jobs compared to those performing the traditional jobs. This result is typical of those found in many other studies. Enriching jobs appears to have much greater impact on workers' job attitudes and beliefs than on their actual job performance.[79] Considering the many factors that enter into determining job performance, this finding should not be too surprising. (We will discuss the relationship between job attitudes and performance more thoroughly in Chapter 5.)

Implementing job enrichment programs is not an easy thing to do, despite the specific suggestions offerred by the job characteristics model. In Table 3.3 we have listed some ways of enriching jobs inspired by the job characteristics model. In examining these, it should be clear that there may be several obstacles to overcome and limitations to consider in carrying out any job enrichment program.[80] First, the *technology* of the work process often makes it difficult to enrich jobs. For example,

TABLE 3.3   *Enriching Jobs: Some Suggestions.*
The job characteristics model suggests some specific ways in which jobs can be redesigned so as to enhance motivation and job performance. A few are listed here. (Source: Based on information in Hackman, 1976; see Note 73.)

Suggestion for enriching job	Core job dimensions affected
1. Redistribute jobs so that an individual worker may take credit for it.	Task identity Task significance
2. Combine tasks to enable workers to perform the entire job.	Skill variety Task identity
3. Allow workers to establish contact with clients of their services and ultimate users of their products.	Autonomy Feedback
4. Open feedback channels, giving workers knowledge of the results of their work.	Feedback

assembly line jobs, or jobs requiring the extensive use of machinery, are considered impractical to enrich. Second, the ability to change jobs is often limited by *personnel systems*—by long-standing traditions and formal agreements concerning the ways of doing work. A third barrier lies in the threat to existing *control systems*, such as accounting systems or quality control arrangements. Naturally, employees in certain segments of the organization may feel threatened by changes in jobs that minimize the extent of their jurisdiction in the organization. Although these limitations are severe, they do *not* imply that jobs cannot be enriched. Rather, they should be taken as useful advice to be considered in making the implementation of job enrichment programs more effective.

SUMMARY

Many people in today's workforce are motivated to perform interesting work. **Need theory** focuses on the nature of human needs and the extent to which workers' needs are fulfilled on their jobs. A broader theoretical conceptualization of work motivation is taken by **equity theory**. It asserts that workers are motivated to maintain fair relationships between themselves and others in their organizations. **VIE theory** proposes that individuals are motivated by their beliefs concerning the extent to which the organization can offer them meaningful rewards for the effort they put forth. It also recognizes that motivation is just one of several determinants of job performance.

There are several ways of motivating workers. One of the most effective is by **goal setting.** Research has shown that workers will improve their performance when given specific, difficult goals that they consider acceptable. Motivation can also be enhanced at the organizational level, by designing or redesigning jobs. *Job design* techniques include **job enlargement** (giving workers more tasks to perform at the same level) and **job enrichment** (giving workers greater control over how they do their jobs). The **job characteristics model** is a current approach to job enrichment that considers how certain core job dimensions produce psychological states that lead to beneficial outcomes for both individuals and organizations.

KEY TERMS

equity: The state in which one worker's outcome/input ratio is equivalent to that of another worker with whom this person compares himself or herself.

equity theory: A theory suggesting that workers strive to maintain ratios of their own outcomes (rewards) to their own inputs (contributions) that are equal to the outcome/input ratios of other workers with whom they compare themselves.

ERG theory: An alternative proposed by Alderfer to Maslow's need hierarchy theory, asserting that there are three basic human needs: existence relatedness, and growth.

expectancy: The belief that a worker has about the extent to which his or her efforts will influence his or her performance.

goal setting: The process of determining specific levels of performance for workers to attain.

inequity: The undesirable condition in which a worker's outcome/input ratio is not equal to that of another person who is used for comparison. If this inequity favors a person, the result is *overpayment inequity*, which leads to feelings of guilt. If this inequity is to a person's disadvantage, the result is *underpayment inequity*, which leads to feelings of anger.

inputs: Workers' contributions to their jobs, such as their experience, qualifications, or the amount of time worked.

instrumentality: A worker's belief about the likelihood of being rewarded in accord with his or her level of performance.

job characteristics model: An approach to job enrichment which specifies that five core job dimensions (skill variety, task identity, task significance, autonomy, and job feedback) produce critical psychological states that then lead to beneficial outcomes for the worker (e.g., high job satisfaction) and the organization (e.g., high performance).

job enlargement: The practice of expanding the content of a job so as to include more and varied tasks at the same level.

job enrichment: The practice of giving workers a high degree of control over their work, from planning and organization through implementing the job and evaluating the results.

motivating potential score (MPS): A mathematical index describing the degree to which a job is designed so as to motivate workers, as suggested by the job characteristics model. It is computed on the basis of responses to a questionnaire known as the *job diagnostic survey (JDS)*.

motivation: The set of processes that energize a person's behavior and that direct it toward attaining some goal.

need hierarchy theory: Maslow's theory that there are five human needs (physiological, safety, social, esteem, and self-actualization) and that these are arranged in such a way that lower, more basic needs must be satisfied before higher-level needs become activated.

outcomes: The rewards a worker receives from his or her job, such as salary and recognition.

overpayment inequity: The condition, resultings in feelings of guilt, under which the ratio of one's outcomes/inputs is greater than the corresponding ratio of another person against whom the person compares himself or herself.

scientific management: An older approach to motivation through which jobs are redesigned to make them simpler and more efficient, although highly routine and monotonous.

self-actualization: The need to find out who we really are and to develop to our fullest potential.

Theory X: A traditional view of behavior in work settings, holding that most persons are lazy and irresponsible. According to this view, the major task of managers is that of providing employees with direction and enforcing discipline.

Theory Y: A view of behavior in work settings suggesting that under appropriate circumstances employees are fully capable of working productively and accepting responsibility.

underpayment inequity: The condition, resulting in feelings of anger, under which the ratio of one's outcomes/inputs is less than the corresponding ratio of another person against whom the person compares himself or herself.

valence: The value a person places on the rewards he or she expects to receive from the organization.

valence-instrumentality-expectancy (VIE) theory: The theory which asserts that workers' motivation is based on their beliefs about the probability that effort will lead to performance (*expectancy*), multiplied by the probability that performance will lead to reward (*instrumentality*), multiplied by the perceived value (*valence*) of the reward.

NOTES

1. Staff (1983). The disenchantment of the middle class. *Business Week*, April 25, pp. 82–83, 86.

2. T. R. Mitchell (1983). Motivation: New directions for theory, research, and practice. *Academy of Management Review*, 7, 80–88.

3. C. C. Pinder (1984). *Work motivation: Theory, issues, and applications.* Glenview, Ill.: Scott, Foresman.

4. B. M. Staw (1984). Organizational behavior: A review and reformulation of the field's outcome variables. *Annual Review of Psychology, 35,* 627–666.

5. M. London (1983). Toward a theory of career motivation. *Academy of Management Review, 8,* 620–630.

6. E. Schein (1982). Does Japanese management style have a message for American workers? *Sloan Management Review, 23,* 55–68.

7. D. M. McGregor (1960). *The human side of enterprise.* New York: McGraw-Hill.

8. L. Dumont (1970). *Homo hierarchus.* Chicago: University of Chicago Press.

9. *Newsweek* (1971). October 18, p. 31.

10. *Los Angeles Times* (1981). Work still a labor of love. As reported in *Columbus Dispatch,* April 20, p. 1.

11. G. W. Hofstede (1972). The colors of collars. *Columbia Journal of World Business, 7,* 72–79.

12. D. Elizur (1984). Facets of work values: A structural analysis of work outcomes. *Journal of Applied Psychology, 69,* 379–389.

13. *Life* (1972). Boredom spells trouble on the line. September 1, pp. 30–38.

14. A. H. Maslow (1970). *Motivation and personality,* 2nd ed. New York: Harper & Row.

15. H. S. Schwartz (1983). Maslow and the hierarchical enactment of organizational reality. *Human Relations, 36,* 933–956.

16. F. Tuzzolino, and B. R. Armandi (1981). A need-hierarchy framework for assessing corporate social responsibility. *Academy of Management Review, 6,* 21–28.

17. E. L. Betz (1982). Need fulfillment in the career development of women. *Journal of Vocational Behavior, 20,* 53–66.

18. M. A. Wahba and L. G. Bridwell (1976). Maslow reconsidered: A review of research on the need hierarchy theory. *Organizational Behavior and Human Performance, 15,* 212–240.

19. C. Alderfer (1972). *Existence, relatedness, and growth.* New York: Free Press.

20. G. R. Salancik and J. Pfeffer (1977). An examination of need-satisfaction models of job satisfaction. *Administrative Science Quarterly, 22,* 427–456.

21. J. S. Adams (1965). Inequity in social exchange. In L. Berkowitz (ed.), *Advances in experimental social psychology*, vol. 2. New York: Academic Press.

22. R. P. Vecchio (1982). Predicting worker performance in inequitable settings. *Academy of Management Review, 7,* 103–110.

23. R. A. Cosier and D. R. Dalton (1983). Equity theory and time: A reformulation. *Academy of Management Review, 8,* 311–319.

24. R. P. Vecchio (1981). An individual-differences interpretation of the conflicting predictions generated by equity theory and expectancy theory. *Journal of Applied Psychology, 66,* 470–481.

25. D. Thomsen (1981). Compensation and benefits. *Personnel Journal, 60,* 258–259.

26. M. J. Wallace, Jr. (1983). Methodology, research practice, and progress in personnel and industrial relations. *Academy of Management Review, 8,* 6–13.

27. P. England, and S. D. McLaughlin (1979). Sex segregation of jobs and male-female income differentials. In R. Alverez and K. G. Lutterman (eds.), *Discrimination in organizations.* San Francisco: Jossey-Bass.

28. M. J. Wallace, Jr. and C. H. Fay (1981). Job evaluation and comparable worth: Compensation theory basis for modeling job worth. *Proceedings of the Academy of Management,* 296–300.

29. R. E. Williams and D. M. McDowell (1980). The legal framework. In R. E. Livernash (ed.), *Comparable worth: Issues and alternatives.* Washington, D.C.: Equal Employment Advisory Council.

30. L. R. Burgess (1984). *Wage and salary administration.* Columbus: Charles E. Merrill.

31. A. O. Bellak (1984). Comparable worth: A practitioner's view. In *Linking employee attitudes and corporate culture to corporate growth and profitability.* Philadelphia: Hay Management Consultants.

32. M. Curtin (1985). Celeste wants $9 million for pay equity. *Columbus Dispatch,* January 29, p. 1.

33. T. A. Mahoney (1983). Approaches to the definition of comparable worth. *Academy of Management Review, 8,* 14–22, 30.

34. R. M. Madigan (1985). Comparable worth judgments: A measurement properties analysis. *Journal of Applied Psychology, 70,* 137–147.

35. See note 25.

36. J. Greenberg (1982). Approaching equity and avoiding inequity in groups and organizations. In J. Greenberg and R. L. Cohen (eds.), *Equity and justice in social behavior.* New York: Academic Press.

37. R. D. Pritchard, M. D. Dunnette, and D. O. Jorgenson (1972). Effects of perceptions of equity and inequity on worker performance and satisfaction. *Journal of Applied Psychology, 56,* 75–94.

38. J. Greenberg and S. Ornstein (1983). High status job title as compensation for underpayment: A test of equity theory. *Journal of Applied Psychology, 68,* 285–297.

39. S. M. Freedman and J. R. Montanari (1980). An integrative model of managerial reward allocation. *Academy of Management Review, 5,* 381–390.

40. V. H. Vroom (1964). *Work and motivation.* New York: John Wiley.

41. L. W. Porter and E. E. Lawler (1968). *Managerial attitudes and performance.* Homewood, Ill.: Irwin.

42. L. R. Walker and K. W. Thomas (1982). Beyond expectancy theory: An integrative motivational model from health care. *Academy of Management Review, 7,* 187–194.

43. H. Garland (1984). Relation of effort-performance expectancy to performance in goal-setting experiments. *Journal of Applied Psychology, 69,* 79–84.

44. O. Behling, J. F. Dillard, and W. E. Gifford (1979). A test of expectancy theory predictions of effort: A simulation study of comparing simple and complex models. *Journal of Business Research, 7,* 331–347.

45. T. Connolly (1976). Some conceptual and methodological issues in expectancy models of work performance motivation. *Academy of Management Review, 1,* 37–47.

46. D. A. Nadler and E. E. Lawler, III (1977). Motivation: A diagnostic approach. In J. R. Hackman, E. E. Lawler and L. W. Porter (eds.), *Perspectives on behavior in organizations.* New York: McGraw-Hill.

47. H. J. Bernardin and R. W. Beatty (1984). *Performance appraisal: Assessing human behavior at work.* Boston: Kent.

48. R. Folger and J. Greenberg (1985). Procedural justice: An interpretive analysis of personnel systems. In K. Rowland and G. Ferris (eds.), *Research in personnel and human resources management,* vol. 3. Greenwich, Conn.: JAI Press.

49. D. D. Umstot, C. H. Bell, and T. R. Mitchell (1976). Effects of job enrichment and task goals on satisfaction and productivity: Implications for job design. *Journal of Applied Psychology, 61,* 379–394.

50. E. A. Locke and G. P. Latham (1984). *Goal setting: A motivational technique that works!* Englewood Cliffs, N.J.: Prentice-Hall.

51. E. A. Locke, K. N. Shaw, L. M. Saari, and G. P. Latham (1981). Goal-setting and task performance: 1969–1980. *Psychological Bulletin, 90,* 125–152.

52. L. Miller (1978). *Behavior management: The new science of managing people at work.* New York: John Wiley.

53. G. P. Latham and E. A. Locke (1979). Goal setting: A motivational technique that works. *Organizational dynamics, 8*(2), 68–80.

54. H. Garland (1982). Goal levels and task performance: A compelling replication of some compelling results. *Journal of Applied Psychology, 67,* 245–248.

55. M. Erez and I. Zidon (1984). Effect of goal acceptance on the relationship of goal difficulty to performance. *Journal of Applied Psychology, 69,* 69–78.

56. M. Erez and F. H. Kanfer (1983). The role of goal acceptance in goal setting and task performance. *Academy of Management Review, 8,* 454–463.

57. J. S. Chhokar and J. A. Wallin (1984). A field study of the effect of feedback frequency on performance. *Journal of Applied Psychology, 68,* 524–530.

58. J. Jacoby, D. Mazursky, T. Troutman, and A. Kuss (1984). When feedback is ignored: Disutility of outcome feedback. *Journal of Applied Psychology, 69,* 531–545.

59. J. S. Kim (1984). Effect of behavior plus outcome goal setting and feedback on employee satisfaction and performance. *Academy of Management Journal, 27,* 139–149.

60. C. D. Pringle and J. G. Longenecker (1982). The ethics of MBO. *Academy of Management Review, 7,* 305–312.

61. C. I. Stein (1979). Objective management systems: Two to five years after implementation. *Personnel Journal, 54,* 525–528.

62. R. Likert and M. S. Fisher (1977). MBGO: Putting some team spirit into MBO. *Personnel, 54,* 40–47.

63. M. L. McConkie (1979). A clarification of the goal setting and appraisal process in MBO. *Academy of Management Review, 4,* 29–40.

64. A. B. Carroll (1975). Managerial ethics: A post-Watergate view. *Business Horizons, 18*(2), 75–80.

65. G. Getschow (1979). Some middle managers cut corners to achieve high corporate goals. *Wall Street Journal,* November 8, pp. 1, 26.

66. F. W. Taylor (1911). *The principles of scientific management.* New York: Harper & Brothers.

67. R. W. Griffin (1982). *Task design: An integrative approach.* Glenview, Ill.: Scott, Foresman.

68. R. J. Aldag and A. P. Brief (1979). *Task design and employee motivation.* Glenview, Ill.: Scott, Foresman.

69. M. Fein (1974). Job enrichment: A reevaluation. *Sloan Management Review,* Winter, 69–88.

70. F. Luthans and W. E. Reif (1974). Job enrichment: Long on theory, short on practice. *Organizational Dynamics, 2,* 30–43.

71. R. B. Goldman (1976). *A work experiment: Six Americans in a Swedish plant.* New York: Ford Foundation.

72. R. M. Steers and D. G. Spencer (1977). The role of achievement motivation in job design. *Journal of Applied Psychology, 62,* 472–479.

73. J. R. Hackman (1976). Work design. In J. R. Hackman and J. L. Suttle (eds.), *Improving life at work.* Santa Monica, Calif.: Goodyear, p. 103.

74. J. R. Hackman and G. R. Oldham (1980). *Work redesign.* Reading, Mass.: Addison-Wesley.

75. J. R. Hackman and G. R. Oldham (1976). Motivation through the design of work: Test of a theory. *Organizational Behavior and Human Performance, 16,* 250–279.

76. K. H. Roberts and W. Glick (1981). The job characteristics approach to task design: A critical review. *Journal of Applied Psychology, 66,* 193–217.

77. B. T. Loher, R. A. Noe, N. L. Moeller, and M. P. Fitzgerald (1985). A meta-analysis of the relation of job characteristics to job satisfaction. *Journal of Applied Psychology, 70,* 280–289.

78. C. Orpen (1979). The effects of job enrichment on employee satisfaction, motivation, involvement, and performance: A field experiment. *Human Relations, 32,* 189–217.

79. R. W. Griffin, A. Welsh, and G. Moorehead (1981). Received task characteristics and employee performance: A literature review. *Academy of Management Review, 6,* 655–664.

80. G. R. Oldham and J. R. Hackman (1980). Work design in the organizational context. In B. M. Staw and L. L. Cummings (eds.), *Research in organizational behavior,* vol. 2. Greenwich, Conn.: JAI Press.

CHAPTER 4

Perception: Understanding the World Around Us

For the past three weeks, Helen Talbot and Tom O'Connor, Director and Associate Director of Graphics at Elco Engineering, have been trying to choose the right person for a job in their department. The position in question is that of Senior Designer, so it's quite important. After going over the records of more than forty applicants, they picked the top five. Then, they interviewed each of these people in detail and narrowed the field to only two. Today, they are meeting to try to choose between them. Their conversation goes something like this:

"Well, I think Faye Henderson is the right choice," Helen begins. "She's got a solid background in design and has already worked on a lot of projects similar to the ones we have here. Also, she really impressed me as being a steady performer—someone we can count on even when the pressure gets high."

Tom responds to this comment with considerable surprise. "Steady? Are you kidding? Didn't you notice that she's changed jobs four times in the past three years? *You* may call that steady, but I don't."

Helen seems a bit confused at this remark. "Hmmm . . . now that you mention it, I *did* notice that. But I don't think it means much. I think she's moved around just because she didn't want to miss out on good opportunities. Heck, you can't blame her for *that.*"

"I don't agree," Tom responds. "I got the impression that she moved so much because she just doesn't like to stay in one spot too long. Restless, that's how I'd describe her."

Now it's Helen's turn to get angry. "I don't think you're being fair, Tom. You're letting her appearance influence you. All willowy blondes aren't dumb, you know!"

Tom is stunned, but answers quickly. "Hey, take it easy. I'm not reacting to her looks. It's just that this other applicant, Santini, seems so much better. He's experienced too, and he really seemed sharp during my interview with him—a quick thinker if ever I saw one. You have to be pretty fast on your feet for this job, you know."

Helen is shaking her head even before Tom stops talking. "Sharp? Who did *you* interview, anyway. I thought he was downright dull! Just listen to this (she reads from one of Bill Santini's recommendations): 'Mr. Santini is a solid, cooperative employee. In general, though, he's much better at performing routine tasks than in handling anything out of the ordinary . . .' Does that sound like someone who's quick on his feet?"

Now Tom is the one who looks confused. "Gee, I don't remember that letter at all. I must have missed it—But anyway, he graduated from Carter College. My first assistant was from there and she was first-rate."

"Aha!" Helen exclaims. "A Carter alumnus. No wonder he wore that creepy tie. You know what we used to say about men from Carter when I was at State U?"

"Please don't tell me!" Tom exclaims. "I can't take another 'How many blanks does it take to change a light bulb' joke right now!"

At this remark, the tension is broken, and both Helen and Tom laugh. But more than an hour has passed since they began, and it is growing all too clear that they will not manage to resolve matters today. Recognizing this fact, they agree to study the files once more, and to meet again tomorrow. Perhaps then they'll see eye-to-eye. . .

There's an old saying that states: "Everyone sees the world through different eyes," and incidents such as the one above suggest that this is true. Even when exposed to the same situation, information, or events, different persons often report sharply contrasting reactions. Further, like the characters in the opening story, each tends to assume that her or his view is the correct one (see Figure 4.1). Such differences, which can be large, point to a key fact: contrary to what common sense may suggest, we do *not* know the world around us in a simple or direct manner.[1] On the contrary, we construct a "picture" of it through an active, complex process. This is known as **perception,** and is often defined as follows: *perception is the process through which we actively select, organize, and interpret information brought to us by our senses in order to understand the complex world around us.*

As you might already guess, perception plays a key role in human behavior. Indeed, how people act is often largely a function of how they interpret their current surroundings, both physical and social. For example, imagine the following situation. You are scheduled to meet with one of your subordinates at 2:00 P.M. Much to your irritation, he does not show up until 2:45 P.M. How do you react? Obviously, it depends on your interpretation of the reasons behind his tardiness. If he enters in a slightly tipsy state, just back from a three-martini lunch, you may be very angry. After all, this is a poor reason for keeping you waiting. If, instead, he rushes in out

"*Now, I'm a reasonable fellow, but it seems to me that in case after case and time after time in these labor disputes the fairer, more enlightened position has always been held by management.*"

FIGURE 4.1   *Perception: Seeing the World Through Different Eyes.*
As suggested by this cartoon, individuals tend to perceive the world through different eyes. Further, each assumes that her or his view is the correct one. (Source: Drawing by Stan Hunt; © 1982 The New Yorker Magazine, Inc.)

of breath, explaining that his plane was delayed, or that he encountered a mammoth traffic jam on the way from the airport, your reaction will be quite different. In this and countless other situations, our behavior is strongly determined by the process of perception, and the interpretation of physical or social reality it yields.

Unfortunately, as we noted above, perception is a very private process. Thus, when faced with the same external events or stimuli, different persons often construct contrasting pictures or interpretations of them. A good example of this potential source of difficulties was provided by the opening story. In that incident, Helen and Tom interviewed the same candidates, and examined the same information about them in their application folders. Yet, they formed radically different impressions of these persons. On the basis of these contrasting perceptions each then reached opposite conclusions about who should be hired. In short, their interpretations of various stimuli, events (or in this case, persons) led them to different actions—ones with potentially important consequences.

Given the central role of perception in many aspects of organizational behavior, it is important for you to gain a basic grasp of this process—to understand how it operates, and how it can affect a wide range of key organizational processes. To provide you with such information, our discussion will proceed as follows.

First, we will describe some basic aspects of perception—built-in features of this process that help us with the vast (and potentially overwhelming) array of information brought to us by our senses. Next, we will turn to **social perception,** the process through which we come to understand other persons—their motives and characteristics. Third, we will consider several common *errors* in perception—biases or "tilts" in this basic process that often lead us astray. Finally, we will examine the impact of perception on a very central organizational process: **performance appraisal.**

PERCEPTION: SOME BASIC ASPECTS

At any given time, we are literally flooded with input from our various senses. Our eyes respond to many wavelengths of light, our ears react to sounds of many pitches, and so on. Yet, we do not perceive the world around us as a random collection of sensations—far from it. Instead, we recognize specific objects, and orderly patterns of events (e.g., cause and effect). The basic reason for this orderliness lies in perception, and the fact that it imposes order and meaning on what otherwise might be a hopeless jumble. Several aspects of perception contribute to this beneficial outcome, but by far the most important concerns the fact that perception is *selective.*

Attention: Selectivity in Perception

If you've ever attended a noisy party, you are already familiar with the fact that perception is highly selective in nature. As such times, you can easily decide to screen out all the voices around you except that of the person with whom you are conversing. While the words of this individual stand out and make sense, those of all the others tend to blend into a single background buzz. If for some reason you decide that you wish to listen to what someone else is saying, though, you can readily shift your attention to *this* person. Indeed, you can even do this while continuing to look the first person in the eye—thus convincing him that he is still the center of your interest! In such cases, attention is obviously a conscious process: we decide where to direct it and then do so.[2] In many others, however, attention seems to follow a course of its own. Indeed, on some occasions (e.g., during a dull meeting) we cannot seem to force our attention to remain where we want even for a few minutes! What factors influence attention at such times? In short, what factors cause us to notice some aspects of our surroundings while totally ignoring others? Systematic research has revealed that many different variables play a role in this regard. Most of these, though, fall into one of two major categories: *personal* influences relating to our internal states, and *external* influences pertaining to various properties of objects or stimuli.

Personal influences on attention: Motives, attitudes, and past experience. One personal factor that strongly affects our tendency to notice certain aspects of our immediate surroundings is our current motives. The impact of these internal states can be readily illustrated. Imagine that you are attending a business meeting. What stimuli or events in it will you notice? To a large extent, this depends on your current motivational state. If it is close to lunch time and you are hungry, you may focus on the delicious smell of food entering the room from a nearby restaurant, or the sound of the snack cart as it rolls down the hall. If, instead, you are deeply concerned about your upcoming performance appraisal, you may direct your attention to the reactions of your supervisor to all of your ideas and reports. In short, what you notice will be strongly affected by your current needs or motives. The same principle holds true in many other situations as well: often, where we direct our attention—and thus what we perceive—is strongly affected by our current motives.

A second personal factor that often exerts a strong impact upon attention is our *attitudes* or *values.* Typically, we notice stimuli about which we have clear positive or negative feelings (strong attitudes) much more readily than ones toward which we are neutral. Thus, an individual who is strongly opposed to some plan of action would be highly sensitive to even indirect references to it during a meeting; another person who has no strong views on this matter would probably be less likely to pay attention to such comments. Similarly, a manager who really likes one of her subordinates (perhaps she has entered into a *mentor-protégé* relationship with this person) will probably be more likely to notice his performance than that of other subordinates toward whom she has weaker personal feelings.

Third, the selective nature of perception is often affected by our past experience. In a word, we tend to notice those aspects of the world around us that are familiar, or that fit with cognitive frameworks established through past experience.[3] For example, imagine that two individuals, an engineer and a marketing expert, examine a new product just released by a major competitor. What will they notice about this item? Probably, very different things. The engineer's attention may be drawn to the advanced technology it incorporates, or the quality of its construction. In contrast, the marketing expert may focus on its potential appeal to customers, or ways it will compete with her own company's line of products. Thus, both will look at the same object, but each will "see" different things.

Unfortunately, such differences in perspective can sometimes lead to major problems of communication. Since persons trained in different fields and holding different jobs tend to perceive the same events, objects, or situations differently, they often find it difficult to "get through" to one another. It is partly for this reason that the members of one department or organizational unit are often heard to grumble or complain about "those people" in some other unit or department. Obviously, an important task for managers is that of noticing such differences, and assuring that they do not result in unnecessary and potentially harmful friction.

External influences on attention. In addition to the internal factors mentioned above, attention is often affected by external ones as well—various aspects of stimuli themselves. Specifically, certain features of objects, persons, or events determine whether they are more or less likely to be noticed. One of the most important of these is *salience*—the extent to which a stimulus stands out from the others around it. The greater its salience, the more it tends to be noticed. For example, you would probably be much more likely to notice a nude bather on a beach where all other persons are wearing swimsuits than on a beach where every other person present is also nude.

More generally, salience—and attention—is enhanced by *intensity, size, contrast, motion,* or *novelty.* To the extent stimuli possess these characteristics, they tend to attract—and hold—our attention. Advertisers are well aware of these principles, and often use them in planning ads, commercials, and roadside signs. Examples of such use are shown in Figure 4.2. As you can readily see, ignoring these stimuli would probably be a difficult task!

Attention: A word on its effects. Attention, of course, is the crucial first step in perception. Unless a stimulus is noticed, it cannot be perceived and interpreted. Thus, attention acts as a kind of filter with respect to perception: only what passes

FIGURE 4.2   *Attention: Its Role in Advertising.*
Experts in advertising are well aware of the fact that stimuli high in *salience* are much more likely to be noticed than stimuli low in salience. Thus, they often attempt to build this characteristic into their ads and commercials.

through can have any impact on our interpretation of the world around us. Several factors influencing the kinds of information that manage to penetrate this filter have just been considered. At this point, we simply wish to add that attention has other effects as well. In many cases, stimuli that succeed in capturing our attention tend to be viewed as more important than ones that do not. For example, they are more likely to be interpreted as the cause of later events.[4] In a similar manner, people we notice most in a group tend to be viewed as being the most influential, and therefore, as the most capable of leadership.[5] In short, stimuli that capture our attention often become "larger than life" in several key ways. In this respect, attention is indeed a crucial process, and one with more general implications than you might at first suspect.

SOCIAL PERCEPTION: PERCEIVING—AND UNDERSTANDING—OTHER PERSONS

Why do people act the way they do? What are their major traits? Goals? Motives? Are they responsible for their own actions, or do their actions stem from factors beyond their control? These are only a few of the questions we ask about the persons around us.[6] Our interest in such issues is far from surprising. After all, other persons—bosses, co-workers, subordinates, friends, relatives, lovers—have a profound impact on our lives. Thus, efforts to understand them, and so, perhaps, render them more predictable, make eminent good sense. The importance of this task, however, by no means guarantees its simplicity—far from it! Other persons are—and often remain—one of the major puzzles of life. Yet, in general, we *do* succeed in obtaining at least partial answers to all of the questions mentioned above. How do we accomplish this difficult task? The answer is: through an active process of **social perception.** Briefly, we actively attempt to combine, integrate, and interpret information about other persons and in this way, to form useful "pictures" of them—a basic grasp of what they are like and what, essentially, makes them "tick." Since human beings are extremely complex, social perception, too, is a complicated affair. For this reason, we could not possibly consider all of its major features here. What we can do, though, is focus on two key aspects of such perception: **attribution**—the process through which we seek to understand the causes behind others' behavior, and **impression formation**—the manner in which we combine varied information about other persons into a unified, overall impression of them. (In the section that follows, we will turn to several sources of error in social perception—tendencies that often lead us to false conclusions about others.)

Attribution: Understanding the Causes of Others' Behavior

In our efforts to understand other persons, we actually focus on several different issues.[7] Two of the most important of these involve attempts on our part to identify their major traits or characteristics, and efforts to determine whether their actions stem mainly from internal or external causes.

From acts to dispositions: Using others' behavior as a guide to their major traits.   Having a basic grasp of others' major traits can often be very useful. For example, knowing that your boss is ambitious and self-disciplined may help you to act in ways that please her. Similarly, knowing that some member of your department has a bad temper and is easily irritated can assist you in avoiding several kinds of trouble with this person. But how, precisely, do we go about identifying the major traits possessed by the persons around us? The answer offered by a large body of research findings is as follows: in general, we attempt to obtain a working knowledge of others' major traits by observing their overt actions and then using this information to *infer* these characteristics.[8]

At first glance, this might seem to be an easy task. Other people are always doing *something,* so we have a rich source of evidence on which to draw. Unfortunately, however, there are certain complications in this process. Perhaps the most important of these lies in the fact that most individuals attempt to conceal or disguise at least some of their major traits. For example, if they are lazy, unprincipled, or manipulative, they try to hide these facts as best they can. Similarly, if they are bent on taking away our job, or jumping over us on their way up the organizational hierarchy, they do not want us to be aware of these motives. For this basic reason, it is often tricky to infer others' major traits from their overt actions.

The fact that this task is more difficult than at first meets the eye, however, does not suggest that it is impossible. In fact, there are several techniques we can use to help cut through these efforts at concealment or deception. First, we can focus on actions by others that are low in *social desirability*—actions that are not widely approved of in a given situation, and that most persons would not choose to perform. For example, imagine that while someone in your company is delivering a report, one of the people in the audience shouts at the speaker, criticizes him strongly, and laughs out loud at his remarks. Clearly such behavior is unusual and many would view it as inappropriate; because it is, it provides important clues about the true characteristics of the individual performing them. Second, we can pay careful attention to actions by others that produce what are termed *noncommon effects*—outcomes that would not be produced by other, different actions. Since such behaviors produce highly distinctive effects, they often tell us much about the motives of the persons involved. For instance, imagine that you learned that the young assistant to one of the top executives in your organization had just resigned suddenly to take a job with another company. Further, according to the "grapevine," everything about his new job is much worse than his old one except for one fact: his salary has nearly doubled. Would this incident tell you anything about the assistant's major traits? It would. From his behavior, you could infer (and probably accurately) that he is fairly mercenary—money is more important to him than good working conditions, an interesting job, a pleasant place to live, and so on. Finally, in our efforts to understand others' major traits, we also tend to focus on behaviors that they have freely chosen to perform. Ones that were somehow forced upon them by role obligations of their job, by unshakable company rules, or by circumstances beyond their control, are relatively uninformative.

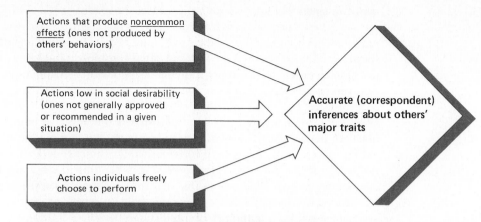

FIGURE 4.3   *Inferring Others' Traits from Their Behavior.*
In our efforts to infer others' major traits from their behavior, we often focus on (1) actions that produce noncommon effects, (2) actions that are low in social desirability, and (3) actions that these persons freely chose to perform. (Source: Based on suggestions by Jones and Davis, 1965; see Note 8.)

In sum, by focusing on certain aspects of others' behavior we often *can* form an accurate picture of their major traits and motives. And as we noted earlier, such knowledge is often useful in many different ways. (Please refer to Figure 4.3 for a summary of this process.)

Causal attribution: How we answer the question "Why?"   Imagine that you observe the following scene: a clerk at a large company is working furiously—as hard as she can. In fact, the flow of paper across her desk is something to behold. Does this necessarily mean that she is a highly motivated person, well deserving of a raise or promotion? The answer is "no." It may simply be the case that her supervisor is standing just out of view, carefully watching the clerk's every move. Further, he may have just warned this person that she is on dangerously thin ice, and will be looking for another job if her performance does not improve greatly and at once. There is an important message in this and many similar incidents: to the extent an individual's behavior stems from *external* factors, it tells us little about his or her motives or traits. After all, under other conditions, the clerk just described might strongly prefer to goof off by visiting his friends, or reading a novel. A major task we face in our efforts to understand others, then, is that of determining whether their actions stem from internal causes, such as their own traits, motives, and goals, or external causes beyond their control. How do we choose between these possibilities? In short, how do we answer the question "Why?" with respect to others' behavior? Most experts on this topic—generally known as **causal attribution**—currently agree that the answer goes something like this.[9]

    In order to determine whether another person has acted in some manner because of internal causes, we focus mainly on three basic factors. First, we consider the extent to which others behave in the same manner as the person in question (*consensus.*) Second, we consider the extent to which this person acts in the same manner on other occasions (*consistency*). Third, we consider the extent to which this person behaves in the same manner in other situations (*distinctiveness*). Information about these three factors is then combined, and forms the basis for our decision as to whether another individual's behavior stems mainly from internal or external causes. Specifically, if consensus and distinctiveness are high (other persons also act this way, and the person in question has acted diffferently in other situations), but consistency is low (he also acts differently at other times), we often attribute his actions to *external* conditions (something about the situation the individual confronts). In contrast, if consensus and distinctiveness are low (other people do not act in the same way; this person acts like this in other situations too), and consistency is high (he behaves this way at other times as well), we often attribute his actions to *internal* causes—his own traits, motives, or characteristics. (Please see Figure 4.4 for a summary of these suggestions.)

Admittedly, our comments about causal attribution so far have been somewhat abstract. To clarify the nature of this process, and to set the stage for understanding its important role in organizational behavior, we will now turn to a concrete example. Imagine that during a meeting with an important customer, a member of your sales group loses her temper, makes angry remarks to the customer, and storms out of the room. Why does she act this way? In short, is her behavior due to internal or external causes? The answer depends largely on the three factors outlined above. To see why this is so, consider two possible sets of circumstances. First, assume that (1) no other sales representative has ever acted in this manner while dealing with this customer (consensus is low); (2) you have seen this salesperson lose her temper during other meetings (consistency is high); and (3) you have also seen her lose her temper in other situations, such as in restaurants, if her food was not cooked as she requested (distinctiveness is low). Under these circumstances, you would probably conclude that her behavior at the meeting stems largely from internal causes: she is a person with a "low boiling point" who often loses her temper.

Now, in contrast, assume that the following conditions exist instead: (1) other salespersons, too, have gotten into arguments with this customer (consensus is high), (2) you have never seen your co-worker lose her temper during other meetings (consistency is low), and (3) you have rarely seen her lose her temper in other situations (distinctiveness is high). Here, you would probably decide that her actions stem mainly from external causes. For example, you might conclude that there is something about this particular customer that makes many people angry (perhaps he is abrasive or condescending).

A great deal of evidence indicates that in many cases, we do in fact decide whether another's behavior has stemmed from internal or external causes by considering consensus, consistency, and distinctiveness.[10] As noted recently by Lord and Smith, however, we do not always operate in this fashion.[11] Sometimes, we proceed in a simpler manner and merely assume that whatever potential cause is *salient*—most noticeable or obvious—is the one behind another person's behavior. In short, we act as "cognitive misers," doing as little mental (cognitive) work as possible. However we reach our conclusions about the causes behind others' behavior, though, these decisions have important implications for organizational processes and organizational behavior. For example, in evaluating a subordinate's

114

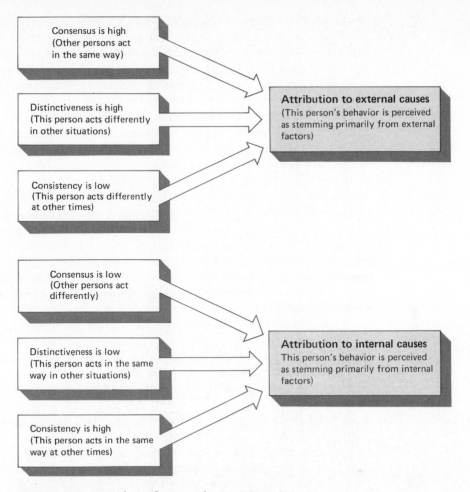

FIGURE 4.4 *Causal Attribution: The Key Dimensions.*
In determining whether others' behavior stems mainly from internal or external causes, we focus on three forms of information: *consensus, distinctiveness,* and *consistency.*

performance it is crucial to know whether it stems mainly from internal factors (e.g., this person's ability or effort) or from external causes (e.g., good or bad luck, the difficulty of the tasks he or she was assigned). Similarly, in deciding how to improve group or individual output, it is important to determine whether current performance is largely a function of internal or external causes. Until this basic question is answered, it may be difficult to know exactly how to proceed.[12]

We will return to the role of causal attributions in these and other organizational processes below. For the moment, though, we simply wish to emphasize the following point: how we answer the question "Why?" is central to understanding others' behavior in many different settings, and organizations are definitely no exception to this general rule.

Attribution and organizational behavior: Concrete applications. Throughout this discussion of attribution, we have attempted to emphasize the relevance of this process to key aspects of organizational behavior. Thus, we have already hinted at its role in performance appraisals, its potential impact on effective relations between subordinates and their supervisors, and its possible role in efforts to improve work group performance.[13] Since our comments in this respect so far have been fairly general, it may be useful to conclude this section with a concrete example of how attribution principles can be applied to understanding actual behavior within an operating organization. Many projects of this type have been conducted in recent years. Indeed, attribution has been applied to organizational processes as varied in nature as the formation of decision-making coalitions in large banks,[14] the nature of feedback provided by supervisors to their subordinates,[15] and even perceptions of leader behavior or performance.[16] As an example of this research, however, we will consider an investigation by Norris and Niebuhr, concerned with the link between job performance and job satisfaction.[17]

These investigators reasoned that the strength of this key relationship might be strongly mediated by certain attributional "styles." Specifically, they suggested that the link between job performance and job satisfaction might be stronger among persons who generally attribute their own performance to internal causes (e.g., their ability or effort) than among persons who typically attribute their performance to external factors (e.g., luck, various aspects of the tasks they perform). According to Norris and Niebuhr, this might be the case for the following reasons. Persons who attribute their performance to internal causes can take credit for success. They can "pat themselves on the back" for a job well done. As a result, the better their performance, the higher their job satisfaction. In contrast, persons who attribute their performance to external causes cannot enjoy such self-administered rewards. After all, if they do happen to succeed, they view these positive outcomes as stemming largely from factors beyond their control. Thus, the link between their performance and their reported job satisfaction may be weaker.

In order to investigate this hypothesis, Norris and Niebuhr asked technical employees in a medium-sized industrial company to complete both a measure of job satisfaction (the *Job Description Index;* see Chapter 5), and a measure of their tendency to attribute their performance to internal or external causes (the *Locus of Control* scale; see Chapter 6). Persons who score low on this scale generally attribute their outcomes to internal causes; those who score high generally attribute them to external factors. In addition, ratings of the job performance of all participants in the study were obtained from their supervisors. As you can see from Figure 4.5, results were both clear and impressive. Among persons who typically attribute their performance to internal causes (Internals), the better the subjects' job performance, the higher their reported job satisfaction. In contrast, among persons who typically attribute their own performance to external causes (Externals), there was no clear link between performance and reported satisfaction. In fact, if anything, the better such persons did at their jobs, the *less* satisfied they reported being.

These results, and those of many related studies, suggest that attributions, whether applied to explaining our own actions or those of other persons, can often play a key role in organizational behavior. Thus, this aspect of social perception is well worth the attention of managers or anyone else who must deal with people in organizational settings. (For another example of the practical application of attribution principles, please see the **Focus** insert on page 118.)

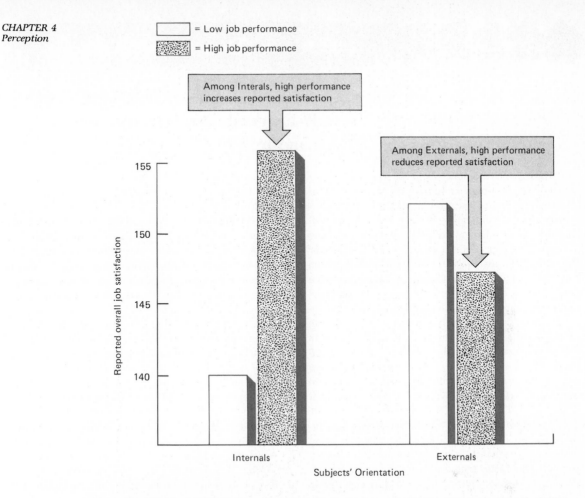

FIGURE 4.5 *Job Performance and Job Satisfaction: The Mediating Role of Attributions.*
Among *Internals* (individuals who typically attribute their outcomes to internal causes), high
job performance led to higher reported job satisfaction than low performance. Among
Externals (individuals who typically attribute their outcomes to external causes), the opposite was true. (Source: Based on data from Norris and Niebuhr, 1984; see Note 17.)

Forming Impressions of Others: Integrating Social Information

First impressions, it is widely believed, are quite important. Presumably, initial
reactions to others tend to persist over long periods of time, and remain largely
unchanged even in the face of later, contradictory input. In this instance, common
sense appears to be correct. A large body of research evidence suggests that first
impressions *do* matter greatly.[20] This fact, in turn, has important implications for
the field of organizational behavior. For example, it underscores the importance of
"coming across" favorably during interviews. Similarly, it calls attention to the fact

Overcoming the Effects of Low Self-Esteem: An Attributional Approach

Think, for a moment, about all your current acquaintances—people you know at work, at school, or elsewhere. Among these, are there any who are sadly lacking in self-confidence—persons who seem to evaluate their own traits and abilities negatively, and who generally hold an unfavorable view of themselves? Probably there are, for such individuals are far from rare. Generally, they are described as suffering from *low self-esteem;* and the term "suffering" is really accurate. Research findings show that in addition to being relatively unhappy, such individuals often perform more poorly on the job and in many other aspects of life than persons who are relatively high in self-esteem.[18] Thus, in a sense, all the worst fears of low self-esteem persons are confirmed: they expect to do badly, and they do. Can anything be done to help such individuals? Fortunately, the answer seems to be "yes." Moreover, assisting them does *not* seem to require years of therapy or counseling. Instead, growing evidence suggests that their problems can be alleviated through short-term techniques based upon attributions. To understand how such procedures operate, it is first necessary to grasp two facts.

First, low self-esteem individuals tend to attribute their failures to *internal* causes (e.g., their own weaknesses or shortcomings). This is not surprising, for such persons do, after all, entertain strong doubts about their own self-worth. The second fact, however, is more unsettling: low self-esteem individuals also tend to attribute successes to *external* causes. Thus, if by some chance they manage to succeed, they explain such positive outcomes away. "I got lucky," they seem to reason, "it probably won't happen again." Together, these facts suggest an interesting possibility: perhaps the harmful effects of low self-esteem can be partly overcome by somehow inducing such persons to reverse these attributions. That is, the negative effects of low self-esteem may be reduced by getting these individuals to attribute their failures to external causes (factors beyond their control), and their successes to internal causes (their own abilities or traits). That

such shifts can readily be produced is indicated by the findings of a study conducted by Brockner and Guare.[19]

In this investigation, college students previously found to be either low or high in self-esteem first worked on an insoluble concept formation task. (Participants were told that some stimuli they examined all shared a common characteristic, and were asked to identify it. In fact, the stimuli did *not* share a characteristic.) After this failure experience, they worked on an anagrams tasks that *was* solvable. At this time, some individuals were provided with information suggesting that their previous poor performance stemmed from *external* causes (they were led to believe that the task was very hard). In contrast, others were provided with information suggesting that their previous failure stemmed largely from *internal* causes (they were led to believe that the task was quite easy and that they were responsible for their poor performance). Subjects in another condition received no information designed to affect their attributions. It was predicted that among low self-esteem subjects, those who attributed their past failure to external causes would now do better on the anagrams task than those who attributed it to internal causes, or who were given no attribution-shaping information. Since high self-esteem subjects would tend to attribute failure to external causes regardless of what information they received, however, no such effects were predicted among this group. As shown in Figure 4.6, results offered support for both of these predictions.

These findings suggest that both performance and underlying self-esteem can be enhanced by inducing individuals to interpret failure as stemming from external causes. Of course, in order for such shifts to be of practical value, they must be general in nature rather than restricted to one specific task. Also, it would certainly not be wise to induce low self-esteem persons to attribute *all* of their failures to external causes. On some occasions, poor outcomes do indeed derive from internal causes. Often, though, getting

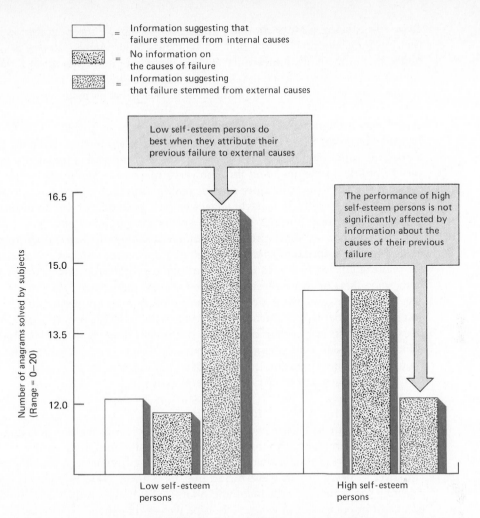

Legend:

☐ = Information suggesting that failure stemmed from internal causes

▨ = No information on the causes of failure

▨ = Information suggesting that failure stemmed from external causes

Low self-esteem persons do best when they attribute their previous failure to external causes

The performance of high self-esteem persons is not significantly affected by information about the causes of their previous failure

Y-axis: Number of anagrams solved by subjects (Range = 0–20)

16.5
15.0
13.5
12.0

Low self-esteem persons

High self-esteem persons

FIGURE 4.6 *Countering the Effects of Low Self-Esteem: An Attributional Approach.*
When low self-esteem individuals were induced to attribute failure on one task to external causes, they did much better on a second task. In contrast, information on the causes of their failure had little impact upon the performance of high self-esteem persons. (Source: Based on data from Brockner and Guare, 1983; see Note 19.)

such persons to change their attributions about the causes of their performance and outcomes may be a useful strategy—one that can help them escape from the vicious, self-fulfilling circle produced by their negative self-concept.

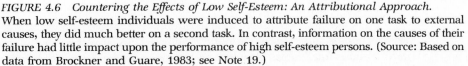

that initial meetings between new supervisors and their subordinates can shape their future relations in lasting ways. Given the existence of such effects, it is probably useful for you to know something about this complex process. Thus, we will now comment briefly on how first impressions are formed, what factors seem to affect them, and how they can be "managed" so as to be as favorable as possible.

First impressions: How they are formed.   When we meet another person for the first time, we are literally flooded with new information. Almost at once we notice this individual's appearance, style of dress, apparent status, and manner of speech. Further, as we listen to what he or she has to say, and observe the things he or she does, we begin to form some idea of this person's major traits or motives through the attribution process described above. As you know from your own experience, though, we do not merely gather these separate pieces of information. Instead, we go further and combine them into a unified picture. In short, we form an overall impression of each person we meet—an impression that can range from very favorable on the one hand through very unfavorable on the other. How do we perform this difficult task? How do we combine so much varied information with such lightning speed? The answer suggested by a great deal of careful research is as follows: we perform this task through a special type of averaging.[21]

Put very simply, our impressions of others seem to represent a *weighted average* of all available information about them. Such impressions reflect a process in which all information about others currently at our disposal is averaged together—but with some facts or input receiving greater weight than others. As you can readily see, this makes good sense. For example, in forming an impression of a new boss you would probably be influenced to a greater extent by this person's apparent level of expertise than by the color of his eyes, or the style of her suit. The fact that not all information about other persons affects our impressions of them to the same degree, though, raises an important question: just what kinds of input receive the greatest weight? Again, research offers some useful answers.

First impressions: What input matters most?   In forming impressions of others, we seem to take account of many kinds of information. The importance assigned to each type varies from situation to situation and from context to context. (For example, you might attach little importance to the correctness of a potential employee's speech if you were hiring him for a production line job. If you were selecting someone to handle incoming phone calls, however, this factor would take on added importance.) In general, though, we seem to attach greatest weight to five distinct types of information.

First, we pay more attention to information relating to others' lasting traits than to information about more temporary factors. Thus, if you notice that a new assistant is highly intelligent, this will have a stronger and more permanent impact upon your impression of her than noticing that she is somewhat tired and run-down. The former trait is lasting and hard to change; the latter can presumably be rectified by a few extra hours of sleep. Second, information about others that we acquire first (e.g., during an initial meeting) often seems to exert a stronger impact on our impressions than information we receive later. Such *primacy effects,* as they are often termed, help explain why it is indeed often hard to alter first impressions. Once they are formed, they *do* tend to persist. Third, when we receive information about others "second-hand," rather than from a direct face-to-face meeting with them, we are much more strongly affected by such input when it derives from a source we view as credible or reliable than when it comes from a source whose reliability we doubt. Thus, rumors spread by the office gossip may be largely discounted in forming an impression of another person. Statements about this person made by one of your good, trusted friends may weigh more heavily in the balance. Fourth, we seem to assign much greater weight to negative information about others than to positive information about them.[22] And finally, we attach greater importance to information relating to extreme or unusual behavior by others (either very positive or very negative) than to information about more moderate actions. For example, if during a conversation, a new member of your work group remarks that he left his last job after suing his former boss for failing to promote him, you may begin to form a very clear impression of this individual. If, instead, he mentions that he left his last job because he moved and could no longer easily commute to it, your impression would probably be affected to a lesser degree.

In sum, existing evidence suggests that in forming overall impressions of others, we are *not* influenced to an equal degree by all types of information. Rather, certain kinds of input, derived from certain kinds of sources, carry extra weight, and exert maximum impact upon the process.

Impression management: The fine art of "looking good." Given that first impressions are important and exert lasting effects on social perception, it is only reasonable to expect individuals to engage in attempts to make them as favorable as possible. In fact, such efforts at **impression management** are very common.[23] Almost everyone seeks to project a positive "image" at one time or another—to convince other persons that they possess desirable characteristics or traits. As you probably already know from personal experience, a number of different tactics can be used for this purpose.

First, individuals wishing to create a favorable first impression often engage in attempts at *ingratiation.* That is, they flatter the target persons, hang on their every word, indicate that they share their opinions, and in general, communicate high positive feelings toward the persons who use them. Occasionally, though, they may backfire, especially if they are used too frequently (or with too much enthusiasm) and become obvious to the individuals toward whom they are directed.

Second, persons attempting to produce favorable impressions can seek to demonstrate their competence and expertise. These traits are highly valued, especially in organizational contexts, and can contribute to positive reactions toward persons who seem to possess them. Several techniques can be used to project a favorable image in these respects. However, recent findings suggest that the possession of good *verbal skills* can be especially valuable in this regard. For example, in one recent study, Rasmussen found that a job applicant was rated as being significantly more qualified for a position as personnel trainee when he answered an interviewer's questions appropriately (with relevant and informative replies) than when he answered in an inappropriate manner (with irrelevant and uninformative replies).[24] Similarly, Parsons and Liden found that the better job applicants' speech (e.g., the more correct their grammar), the higher their ratings along a dimension ranging from "not qualified" to "highly qualified."[25] Thus, in job interviews—one organizational context where first impressions are clearly important—the possession of effective verbal skills can be a major plus.

A third tactic often used by persons wishing to create good first impressions involves personal grooming. Most individuals realize that all too often, they are judged on the basis of their personal appearance. Aware of this central fact, many attempt to "dress for success," and to adopt a style of personal grooming that will contribute to their appeal.[26] Unfortunately, a growing body of research evidence indicates that such factors *do* play a role in many settings, and that organizations are no exception to this general rule. For example, in one recent study, photos of women were shown to male and female managers at a large number of different companies.[27] These executives were asked to rate these individuals on several career-related dimensions (e.g., competence, potential for future success, and so on). In some cases, the persons shown in the photos were dressed in a traditionally feminine manner (they wore dangling earrings, frilly blouses, and the like). In others, they were dressed in a much more professional fashion (they wore tailored suits, plain and understated jewelery, etc.). As you can probably guess, the ratings assigned to the women were higher when they "dressed for success" than when they wore more traditional (and sex-stereotyped) clothing. (The same women served as models in both conditions; only their style of dress was varied.) Additional studies indicate that physical attractiveness and various grooming aids, as well as style of dress, can also strongly affect first impressions in business settings. In general, attractive, well-groomed persons receive higher ratings during interviews and are evaluated more favorably in other situations than unattractive or poorly groomed ones.[28] (We should note, though, that attraction can sometimes boomerang for women, *lowering* rather than raising their evaluations.[29]) Obviously, then, these factors should be given careful attention by individuals wishing to enhance the impressions they make upon others. (Please refer to Figure 4.7 for a summary of major techniques of impression management.)

FIGURE 4.7   *Impression Management: Some Basic Techniques.*
At one time or another, most persons engage in *impression management:* they attempt to project a favorable image to others. Several techniques widely used for this purpose are summarized here.

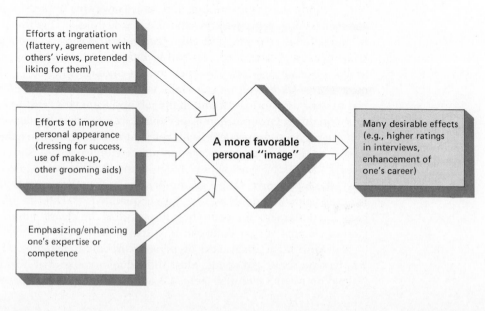

To conclude: because they realize that first impressions are important, and can exert strong effects upon their later outcomes, many persons engage in attempts to enhance this aspect of social perception. In short, they take active steps to project the most favorable image they can to the persons around them. Unfortunately, of course, there is often a large gap between these images and the underlying reality. For this reason, it is important for managers and others who must deal with people at work to be aware of these tactics, and of the false impressions they can sometimes create.

WHEN SOCIAL PERCEPTION FAILS: COMMON ERRORS IN OUR EFFORTS TO UNDERSTAND OTHER PERSONS

Have you ever "seen" what appears to be water on the road in front of you on a hot day, only to discover that the ground is perfectly dry when you arrive there? If so, you are already familiar with the fact that our perception of the physical world often goes astray. In such cases, we seem to process the information brought to us by our senses incorrectly, and so arrive at false conclusions concerning the world around us. If perception can encounter such difficulties with respect to physical stimuli, it is not surprising to learn that it can fail—and fail badly—with respect to other persons. In fact, there are many ways in which social perception can err, and lead us to false conclusions about others. Since many of these have important implications for organizations and key processes within them, we will describe several of the most common here.

Halo Effects: When Overall Impressions Shape Specific Judgments

One common type of error in social perception is suggested by the phrase "love is blind." What this saying implies, of course, is that when we are in love, we lose all ability to evaluate the object of our affection in an accurate, impartial manner. Unfortunately, one does not have to be in love to fall victim to such effects. Once we form an overall impression of another person, this global reaction often tends to exert powerful effects upon our judgments of his or her specific traits. These tendencies are known, collectively, as **halo effects,** and can be either positive or negative in nature. Thus, if our impression of another person is favorable, we tend to see everything he or she does or says in a positive light (a favorable halo). If, instead, our overall impression is unfavorable, we tend to perceive all of this person's words and actions in a negative manner (a "rusty halo" or "horns" effect; refer to Figure 4.8 on page 124). Both types of bias are common in organizations. For example, most companies possess one or more young "super stars"—individuals who have acquired a reputation for exceptional brilliance or talent. Once they have gained such a "halo," of course, everything these persons do is evaluated favorably. Ideas

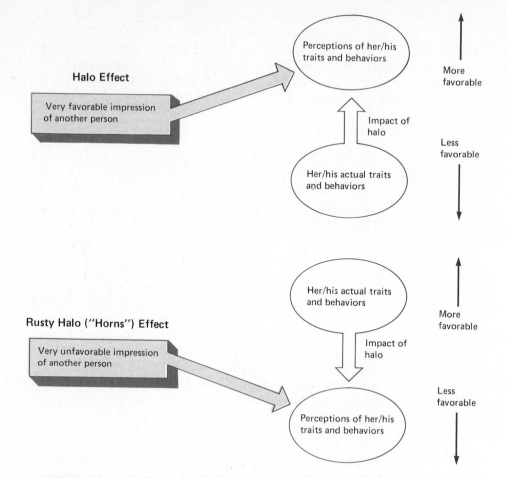

Halo Effect

Very favorable impression
of another person

Perceptions of her/his
traits and behaviors

More
favorable

Impact of
halo

Less
favorable

Her/his actual traits
and behaviors

Rusty Halo ("Horns") Effect

Very unfavorable impression
of another person

Her/his actual traits
and behaviors

More
favorable

Impact of
halo

Less
favorable

Perceptions of her/his
traits and behaviors

FIGURE 4.8   *Halo Effects: A Major Source of Error in Perceiving Others.*
Halo effects occur when our overall impression of another person influences our judgments of
his/her specific traits and behaviors. Such halos can be favorable, as in the upper diagram, or
unfavorable, as in the lower one.

that would be viewed as mediocre if suggested by others are seen as brilliant and
creative when offered by these persons. Actions that might be perceived as risky or
foolish if carried out by other, less admired individuals, are interpreted as daring
and inspired when performed by these "chosen" men and women. And when the
subject of raises, promotions, or other organizational rewards arises, you can guess
who is likely to be first in line to receive them! On the other side of the coin, some
people acquire a "rusty halo"—a reputation for being unable to do anything right.
Again, this global impression spills over onto everything they do so that even when
they perform in a competent manner, they receive little or no credit for such accomplishments.

As you can readily see, halo effects carry high costs. They may lead organizations to put too much faith in some persons, and not enough in many others.

124

Similarly, they may lead to an unfair distribution of available rewards, with all that this implies in terms of morale and employee commitment. Finally, such errors in social perception can lead some persons to develop an overblown view of their own merits or worth, while unnecessarily crushing the egos of others who are equally deserving. Given these potential negative outcomes, it is important for managers to recognize the existence of halo effects, and to take active steps to overcome them.

Contrast Effects: Why People Sometimes Look Better (or Worse) Than They Really Are

Imagine the following situation. An individual with moderately good qualifications applies for a job as an accountant with two different firms. At the first, she is interviewed by a personnel director who has just finished speaking with two other applicants. Both were at the top of their class, and possess all of the skills and training sought by the company. At the second, she is interviewed by a personnel director who has just seen two other applicants, neither of whom is at all suitable for the job in question. From which interviewer will our individual receive higher ratings? The answer is clear: from the second. The reason for this is also obvious: the applicant will "look" better in the second case, because she has better qualifications than the other two persons interviewed. In comparison to them, in short, she will shine. In contrast, when compared to the two outstanding people interviewed by the first company, she will appear to be quite ordinary, and only marginally qualified at best.

This incident illustrates the potential impact of **contrast effects,** another common source of error in social perception. Briefly, contrast effects refer to the fact that our reaction to a given stimulus (or person) is often influenced by other stimuli (people) we have recently encountered.[30] The impact of contrast effects is, perhaps, most apparent in the context of interviews, as suggested by the example above. However, they can also operate in many other organizational contexts as well. For example, if several individuals in succession give reports at a meeting, reactions to the performance of each will almost certainly be influenced by the quality of the presentations that preceded them. Thus, if the first individual does an outstanding job, the others may appear mediocre, even if they actually do quite well. Similarly, if the second presenter is terrible, the third may benefit from this fact and appear highly competent even if her performance is actually only average. In such cases, it is important to be aware of contrast effects and their potential impact. If they are ignored, the results can be quite serious.

Implicit Personality Theory: Unspoken Assumptions about "Human Nature"

Suppose that one day, you return early, and unexpectedly, from a business trip. It's late in the afternoon, but you decide to stop by your office to pick up some papers. As you round the corner, you spot one of your subordinates rushing out of the building. Glancing at your watch, you note that it's only 4:25 P.M.; thus, he's leaving more than a half hour before the official quitting time. How would you interpret this scene? One possibility is this: you'd assume that he's taking advantage of your absence, and is "goofing off." Another is as follows: you give him the benefit of the doubt, and assume that he must have some legitimate reason for leaving early (e.g., perhaps he has an important package to mail, and has missed the last pick-up at your building). Which of these interpretations would you be likely to accept? In short, how would you perceive your subordinate's behavior? The answer involves your own "theory" of human behavior—your own informal view of human nature. If you happen to subscribe to **Theory X,** the view that people are basically lazy and irresponsible, and must somehow be coerced into working, then you will probably accept the first, negative interpretation suggested above. In contrast, if you subscribe to **Theory Y,** a more optimistic view of human nature holding that most individuals are quite willing to work hard and accept responsibility if they view such effort as meaningful, you may well adopt the second perception, at least tentatively.[31] (As you may recall, we discussed these contrasting views in both chapters 1 and 3.)

At this point, we should add two facts. First, whether they realize it or not, everyone seems to hold implicit theories of human nature or personality. Second, research findings indicate that such views are often quite elaborate in nature. Thus, many persons appear to have clear-cut ideas about which traits or characteristics occur together.[32] For example, they may assume that ambitious people are also conscientious, that hostile people tend to be manipulative, and so on. As you might guess, some of these assumptions are valid, while others appear to be false. Regardless of the accuracy of any given individual's implicit theory of human nature, however, it is important to be aware of the fact that such views exist, and that they can strongly affect our perception of other persons. In this way, of course, they can also play a key role in several forms of organizational behavior.

The Self-Serving Bias:
An Attributional Error

Our earlier discussion of attribution may have suggested that it is a totally rational process—one in which we observe key aspects of others' behavior and then, on this basis, systematically infer the causes behind their actions. To a degree, this is true; attribution *is* quite logical in several respects. Like other aspects of social perception, though, it is subject to distortion and bias. A number of such errors exist, and can lead us to false conclusions about the traits and motives of other persons. Perhaps the most important of these from the point of view of organizations, however, is the **self-serving bias.** It refers to our tendency to take credit for positive outcomes or behaviors by attributing them largely to internal causes (e.g., our own ability or effort), but to deny responsibility for negative ones by attributing them largely to external factors (e.g., the actions of other persons, factors beyond our control).[33] The nature of this form of bias, as well as its common occurrence in organizations, can be readily illustrated.

Imagine that at some point, you write a report for your boss. After reading it, she informs you that she likes it very much, and is very pleased with your work. How would you account for this result? Probably, by assuming that it stemmed largely from such actions as your own hard work, high level of intelligence, and good judgment. In short, you would attribute it mainly to internal causes relating to you as a person. Now, in contrast, imagine that after reading your report, your boss criticizes it harshly, and labels it "unacceptable." How would you explain *this* result? The chances are good that you would view it as stemming primarily from external causes—her unreasonably high standards, a lack of clear instructions, an unexpectedly busy schedule that prevented you from devoting as much time to this project as you would have liked. In this and many other situations, we seem to be all too ready to take full credit for success by attributing it to our own "sterling" qualities, but equally willing to explain away failure by attributing it to external causes outside our control.

Recent research findings suggest that there are two basic reasons behind the occurrence of the self-serving bias.[34] First, this "tilt" in the attribution process allows us to protect or enhance our self-esteem. After all, if we are responsible for positive outcomes, but are not to blame for bad ones, our feelings about our own worth as a person may soon be improved. Second, the self-serving bias permits us to improve our public image—to "look good" in the eyes of others. Regardless of its precise

FIGURE 4.9 *The Self-serving Bias: Summary of Its Harmful Effects.*
When individuals work together on a task, each tends to attribute good outcomes or success to his/her own contributions, but any failure or negative outcomes to the shortcomings of others. Both of these tendencies (which reflect the *self-serving attributional bias*) can generate conflict, and reduce the likelihood of future cooperation.

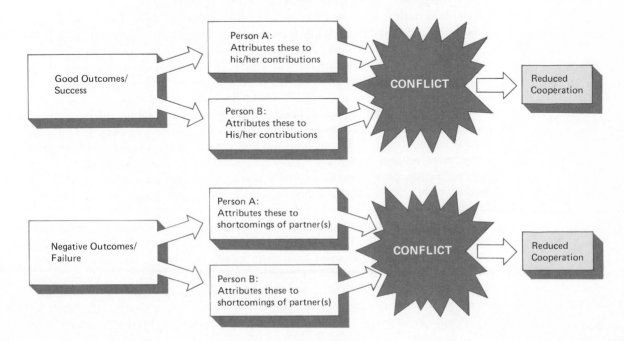

basis, however, this common attributional error can be the cause of much friction and trouble within organizations. Imagine, for a moment, what occurs when two or more persons work on a task together—a common situation in work settings. Because of the self-serving bias, each may perceive any success attained by their joint efforts as stemming mainly from his or her own contributions. In contrast, each may perceive failures as primarily the fault of the others. Clearly, such reactions can prove deadly to future cooperation (see Figure 4.9, page 127, for a graphic illustration of this process.)

Stereotypes: Perceiving Others as All Alike

The final type of error in social perception we will consider is, in some respects, the most unsettling. It involves the belief that all members of certain groups are very much alike, possessing the same traits and showing similar patterns of behavior.[35] Such beliefs are known as **stereotypes,** and can exert powerful effects upon perceptions of others. For example, an individual who believes that all bankers are hard-hearted and unfeeling may perceive any member of the banking profession she happens to meet as confirming these stereotypes, even if they actually possess different characteristics. Similarly, a person who believes that all individuals of Mexican descent are lazy and irresponsible will often perceive such tendencies in the actions of these persons, even if they are not really present.

Unfortunately, stereotypes are very widespread. Thus, they exist for ethnic and racial minorities, the two sexes, various religious groups, older persons, different political persuasions (e.g., liberals, conservatives), members of various occupations and professions, and even for specific jobs.[36] In some cases, stereotypes can be favorable in nature. For example, many Americans hold positive stereotyped beliefs about the characteristics of people from England. Usually, though, stereotypes have a distinct negative tinge; most of the traits or behaviors they attribute to the members of various groups are quite unflattering. That such views can exert important effects upon key aspects of organizational behavior is suggested by the results of a recent investigation by Kraiger and Ford.[37] These researchers examined the findings of almost one hundred previous studies in which black and white raters assigned ratings to black and white ratees. Results indicated that across these varied projects (which involved close to twenty thousand participants and several kinds of ratings), white raters assigned higher scores to white than to black ratees, while black raters showed the opposite pattern. One interpretation of these findings is that racial stereotypes held by members of both groups introduced an important form of bias into the rating process.

Perhaps even more disturbing, stereotypes appear to have a powerful self-fulfilling impact.[38] When individuals perceive that all members of a given group possess specific traits, they may treat them in certain ways. Then, in response to such treatment, the targets of the stereotype may actually begin to act in a manner that confirms its accuracy. For example, many managers hold an unfavorable stereotype of older employees (e.g., persons in their fifties or sixties). They believe that people in this age bracket are lacking in energy, can't learn or adapt very quickly, and are likely to suffer from poor health. On the basis of these beliefs, managers engage in such actions as assigning older employees only easy tasks, refusing to consider them for promotion, and showing surprise when they perform well or maintain good records of attendance. Confronted with such treatment, older workers soon realize that they are not expected to perform as well as younger employees. Since it is only reasonable for them to assume that there must be *some* basis for this belief, they soon begin to doubt their own abilities, and experience mounting concern over their capacity for keeping up with their younger colleagues. These anxieties and doubts, in turn, may interfere with their actual performance. The result: a stereotype that is largely false gains added confirmation. We will return to stereotypes in more detail in Chapter 5, when we consider prejudice and other negative work-related attitudes. At present, though, we will close with these two points. First, stereotypes, because of their implications for prejudice and bigotry, represent an especially damaging type of error in social perception. Second, they go beyond the other forms of error we have already considered for in contrast to these other sources of distortion, they can sometimes actively *shape* reality as well as merely reflect it. (For a concrete example of stereotypes in action, see the **Case in Point** insert on page 130.)

SOCIAL PERCEPTION AND PERFORMANCE APPRAISAL

As noted throughout this chapter, perception exerts powerful effects upon several aspects of organizational behavior. Perhaps the single most important process it influences, however, is **performance appraisal.** Briefly, this refers to efforts by organizations to assess or evaluate the performance of individual employees.[39] Such appraisals are serious business; after all, they often determine who receives raises, promotions, bonuses, and other valued rewards. At one time, it was assumed that performance appraisals could be carried out accurately and fairly by anyone who seriously sought such goals—by anyone who honestly wanted to be fair and impartial. This was a comforting thought, both for persons who found it necessary to conduct appraisals, and those whose careers depended upon them. Unfortunately, it turned out to be false. The task of appraising others' performance is actually highly complex, and is affected by many factors. Thus, even the best intentions are insufficient to guarantee accuracy or fairness. The major reason underlying this fact can be simply stated: performance appraisals involve a very large element of social perception. When one person attempts to evaluate the past job-related actions of another, processes such as attribution and impression formation play a major role. Further, all of the potential sources of error and distortion considered earlier can come into play, and affect the final outcome. As realization of these principles has grown in recent years, much attention has been devoted to two tasks: understanding the role of social perception in performance appraisal, and developing techniques for reducing sources of error in this process. We will now consider some key findings relating to both of these topics.

"You Know, They're Not Like I Thought at All . . ."

When top management at Harling, Inc. announced agreement to enter into joint operations with Tanaka, Ltd., a large and successful Japanese company, there were mixed reactions among employees. Most realized that Harling was in trouble, and could use all the help it could get. At the same time, though, they were uneasy about the kind of changes the new venture would bring. Nearly everyone had read or heard about Japanese executives—their fanatical dedication to their companies, their incredible self-discipline, their ruthless competitiveness. Harling had always been a pleasant place in which to work, so there was a great deal of concern that all this would soon change. Now, though, the time for speculation was past. The first contingent of Japanese managers was scheduled to begin work at Harling today. Tom Borelli and Karen Edgefield are two of the people involved in this first phase of joint operations. They are to start working closely with two Japanese counterparts this very morning. Right now, both are sitting in Karen's office, waiting for their new colleagues to arrive.

"Well, we ought to be here early enough," Karen remarks. "I mean 7:30; when have we ever been here at *this* time?"

"I know, I can hardly keep my eyes open," Tom answers. "I was so nervous about this business last night that I couldn't sleep. Anyway, we want to start out right and make a good impression, so it's probably worth it."

"Right. You know what Japanese are like. I'm sure they'll be here any minute."

In fact, though, over an hour passes before Akio Isiwara and Masaru Narita, the new people, arrive. When they do, there is the usual exchange of pleasantries. Much to their surprise, Karen and Tom find their new colleagues to be friendly and humorous—not at all like the popular image of the grey, grim, driven Japanese executive. The morning passes quickly, and soon it is time for lunch. Believing that Akio and Masaru will want to waste as little time as possible on anything as mundane as food, Karen suggests that they

send out for sandwiches. Much to her surprise, her new associates seem disappointed.

"We will do whatever you wish," Akio states. "But we really had hoped to go to a restaurant. We want to see something of your beautiful city . . ."

Tom and Karen quickly agree and soon the four are seated in a pleasant nearby restaurant. During lunch, surprise follows surprise. Both Japanese order large steaks—the largest on the menu—explaining that in Japan, beef is a luxury they can rarely afford. Also, Masaru turns out to be something of an expert on French wine, and selects an outstanding Bordeaux to accompany the meal. Conversation becomes friendlier and more animated as the wine and food take effect, and all four persons are having a good time. But glancing at his watch, Tom has a shock: it's already 2:00 P.M.—they've been at lunch for two full hours!

"I guess we'd better get back," he exclaims. "It's really late."

"Oh, no hurry," Akio answers. "Work later. Now, we enjoy your company. This is first day!"

When they do finally get back to the office, no one feels much like doing anything serious, so the remainder of the afternoon is spent in a tour of the plant and the nearby area. At 5:00 P.M. Tom and Karen, who often commute together, depart, bidding a warm good evening to their new friends. As they pull away in Karen's car, they turn to each other and smile.

"Well, I don't think this is going to be bad at all," Tom remarks. "They seem like a couple of really nice people to me."

"Right!" Karen agrees. "They're real friendly, and easy to get along with. Working with them is going to be O.K."

"Yeah," Tom replies. "And how about that Masaru knowing so much about wine. I never would have guessed that Japanese liked it. I thought they all drank Saki, or Kirin beer."

"And that Akio—he's a card all right," Karen adds. "One joke after another. No, this isn't going to be half bad. They're regular fellows. And here I was worrying about whether they'd be human . . ."

"Yep. They're really not like I thought at all," Tom exclaims, a broad grin on his face.

Questions

(1) What stereotype of Japanese did Karen and Tom hold before meeting their new colleagues?

(2) Since neither had ever met anyone from Japan before, how did they acquire such beliefs?

(3) Do you think that one day's experience with Akio and Masaru is sufficient to overcome this stereotype? Or will it reappear on the next day?

(4) Do you think that Akio and Masaru also have a stereotype of Americans? If so, what is it probably like?

Attribution and Performance Appraisal: It's Not Just How You Perform That Counts—"Why" Matters, Too

Suppose that at some future time, you are faced with the task of evaluating the performance of two persons, both up for promotion. When you examine the records, you find that both are about equal. But you also know that they have attained these similar results in different ways. One individual is highly talented, but is coasting along, putting little effort into her work. The other is lower in ability, but has worked very hard to attain success. To whom would you assign the higher rating? Probably, to the hard worker of modest ability. In many cases, it seems, we assign greater "credit" to effort and commitment than to innate ability. Whatever your decision, though, it is likely that you would take account of the causes behind each person's behavior, as well as her or his actual performance. In short, attribution would play a major role.

That attributions strongly affect the process of performance appraisal in a wide range of organizational settings is indicated by the findings of many studies. Together, these projects indicate that attributions can affect (1) supervisors' ratings of their subordinates, (2) the kind of feedback they provide to these persons, (3) supervisors' conclusions regarding the causes behind poor performance, and (4) the specific steps they then take to correct such problems.[41] For example, consider an intriguing study by Mitchell and Wood.[42] Here, nursing supervisors read brief accounts of hypothetical errors committed by nurses. Each incident was accompanied by information about each nurse's past work history, and this was varied so as to suggest either that the error stemmed from internal causes (lack of effort or ability) or external causes (a negative, demanding work environment). After reading these materials, the supervisors were asked to indicate what kind of action they would take in the situation. That is, they were asked to rate the appropriateness of doing something to change the nurses' behavior or something to improve the work situation. It was predicted that they would rate actions directed toward the nurses as more appropriate when errors stemmed from internal rather than external causes. However, they would rate actions aimed at the work setting as more appropriate when errors stemmed from external rather than internal sources. As

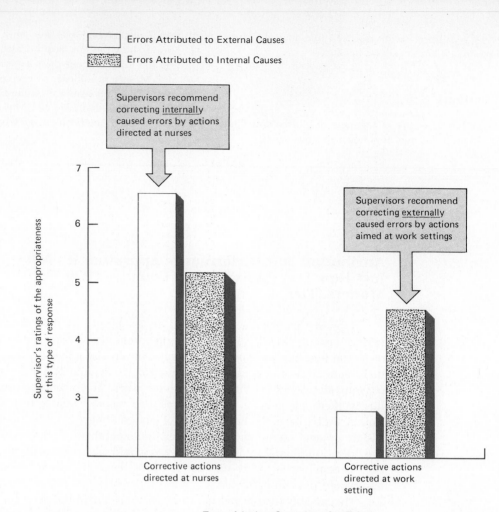

FIGURE 4.10 *Attributions: Their Role in Supervisors' Reactions to Poor Performance.*
Supervisors reported that it was more appropriate to direct corrective actions at nurses when
errors by these employees seemed to stem from internal rather than external causes. In
contrast, they reported that it was more appropriate to direct corrective actions at the work
environment when errors by nurses seemed to stem from external rather than internal
factors. (Source: Based on data from Mitchell and Wood, 1980; see Note 12.)

you can see from Figure 4.10, results offered support for these predictions. Thus, it
appeared that supervisors' causal attributions concerning the reasons behind subordinates' errors could strongly affect the strategies they chose for dealing with these
problems.

These findings, and those of many related studies, indicate that performance
appraisal is often strongly affected by attribution. Thus, full understanding of this
key organizational process must involve attention to attribution and other aspects of
social perception.

Perception-Based Errors in Performance Appraisal: Reducing Their Impact

If social perception were a totally accurate process, the fact that it plays an important role in performance appraisal would not be disturbing. As you already know, however, such perception is subject to a number of sources of error. Are such errors "imported" into the appraisal process, creating difficulties in this manner? Unfortunately, they are. Virtually every type of perceptual distortion described earlier, plus several others we have not yet considered, can influence—and distort— appraisals of others' performance. This poses a serious problem, for errors in appraisal can have disastrous consequences both for individuals and organizations. From the point of view of individuals, promising careers can be shattered by unfair or inaccurate assessments by a supervisor. Similarly, organizations can suffer if talented individuals go unrewarded, and so perhaps seek employment elsewhere, or if undeserving persons *do* receive important rewards, and so rise to positions they don't deserve and can't handle. Given such costs, the task of eliminating (or at least reducing) various sources of error in performance appraisals is an important one. Can it be accomplished? Fortunately, the answer suggested by recent studies is "yes." In particular, it appears that certain kinds of training can greatly assist evaluators in resisting the impact of several types of errors. An especially clear illustration of the benefits of such techniques has recently been provided by McIntyre, Smith, and Hassett.[43]

These investigators asked college students to evaluate the performance of graduate students, who were shown lecturing on videotape. Before watching the tapes and evaluating the instructors, subjects in three groups received different types of training, each designed to help improve the accuracy of their assessments. Individuals in one group (*rater error training*) received instruction in common rater errors. Thus, they were told about the nature of such errors as the halo effect and *leniency* (the tendency to assign higher ratings than are deserved to others). In contrast, subjects in a second group (*frame-of-reference training*) were exposed to procedures designed to assist them in developing useful standards for evaluating the effectiveness of lectures. This type of training involved the provision of information about the nature of lecturing, practice in rating performance on this task, and examples of specific behaviors noticed by experts when *they* evaluate lecturers. Subjects in a third condition received a combination of these two types of training, while those in a fourth (control) group, received no special training whatsoever.

In order to assess the accuracy of subjects' ratings, and their tendency to fall prey to various types of rating errors, the performance of the lecturers was independently assessed by a group of individuals with considerable experience in lecturing. It was assumed that to the extent subjects' ratings matched those of these experts, they could be viewed as being accurate in nature. On the basis of previous research findings, it was predicted that frame-of-reference training would lead to the most accurate assessments by subjects, but that error training might be more effective in reducing both leniency and halo errors. In fact, results indicated that frame-of-reference training was superior in both respects. Individuals who received this type of training were the most accurate of all in assessing the lecturers' performance, and

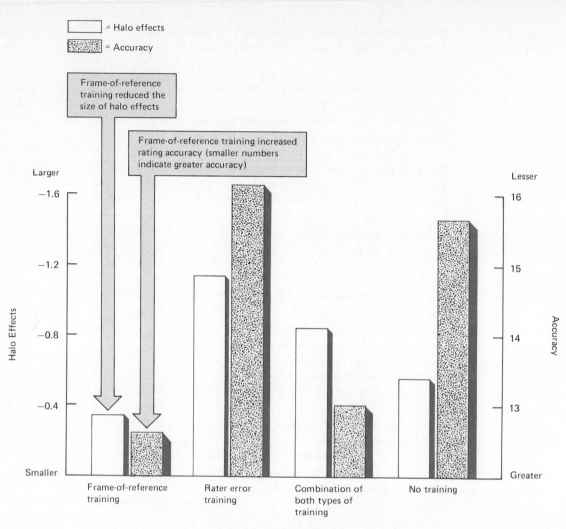

FIGURE 4.11   *Reducing Errors in Performance Appraisal: The Benefits of Special Training.*
Individuals given frame-of-reference training showed less tendency toward halo effects and
greater accuracy in assessing the performance of lecturers than individuals given rater error
training, a combination of both types of training, or no training at all. (Source: Based on data
from McIntyre, Smith, and Hassett, 1984; see Note 43.)

also showed less tendency to fall victim to halo effects than those who received
specific instruction in the nature of such errors (refer to Figure 4.11).

When it is noted that the training procedures employed in this study required
only a few minutes (typically, half an hour or less), these results are quite impressive. Together with the findings of other research they suggest that common and
potentially costly errors in performance appraisal *can* be overcome. Thus, there
appear to be some grounds for optimism. Evaluating others' performance *is* a

complex task. However, under appropriate conditions, it *can* be conducted fairly. An important task for managers, then, is assuring that such conditions prevail in their own organizations.

SUMMARY

We do not know the world around us directly. Rather, we actively construct a representation of it through the process of **perception.** Perception is highly selective in nature; thus, we notice (and process) only a portion of the information brought to us by our senses.

A key task we face in our efforts to make sense out of the external world is that of understanding other persons. This is accomplished through **social perception.** One important aspect of such perception is **attribution**—the process through which we attempt to infer others' major traits and the causes behind their behavior. Another is **impression formation.** Here, we combine diverse information about others into unified impressions of them. Individuals often attempt to produce favorable reactions in others through various tactics of **impression management.**

Social perception is subject to many forms of bias and distortion. These include *halo effects, contrast effects,* the impact of *stereotypes,* implicit assumptions about human nature (*implicit personality theory*), and various attributional errors such as the *self-serving bias.* Such errors, and social perception generally, play an important role in **performance appraisal.** Their impact can be reduced by special kinds of training.

KEY TERMS

attention: Refers to the active process through which some stimuli in the world around us are noticed, while others are ignored and do not enter our perceptual system.

attribution: The process through which we seek to understand others' major traits and the causes behind their behavior.

causal attribution: The process through which we seek to infer the causes of others' behavior, and to determine whether these are largely internal or external in nature.

contrast effects: The fact that our perceptions of a given stimulus are often influenced by other, related stimuli, that have preceded it.

halo effect: The tendency for our overall impressions of others to affect our evaluations of their specific traits or behaviors. Such effects can be positive (a favorable halo) or negative (a rusty halo) in nature.

implicit personality theory: Informal views about human nature held by individuals.

impression formation: The process through which we combine diverse information about others into unified impressions of them.

impression management: Efforts by individuals to project a favorable image to others, and so to create a positive first impression.

perception: The process through which we interpret information brought to us by our senses in order to understand the complex world around us.

performance appraisal: Refers to the process by which job-related performance is assessed or evaluated.

self-serving bias: An attributional error in which individuals tend to attribute success or favorable outcomes to internal causes (e.g., their own ability or effort), but failure and unfavorable outcomes to external causes (e.g., the shortcomings of others).

social perception: The complex process through which we attempt to understand other persons.

stereotypes: Beliefs suggesting that all members of a particular group (e.g., a racial, ethnic, occupational, religious, or political) share the same traits and behaviors.

Theory X: The view, still held by many managers, that most persons are lazy and irresponsible, and must be coerced into working.

Theory Y: A view of human nature suggesting that most persons are willing to accept responsibility and work hard, as long as they view such work as meaningful and worthwhile.

NOTES

1. M. W. Matlin (1983.) *Perception.* Boston: Allyn and Bacon.

2. S. T. Fiske and S. E. Taylor (1984). *Social cognition.* Reading, Mass.: Addison-Wesley.

3. See Note 1.

4. See Note 2.

5. S. E. Taylor and S. E. Fiske (1978). Salience, attention, and attribution: Top of the head phenomena. In L. Berkowitz (ed.), *Advances in experimental social psychology,* vol. 11. New York: Academic Press.

6. R. A. Baron and D. Byrne (1984). "Social Perception." Chapter 2 in *Social psychology: Understanding human interaction,* 4th ed. Boston: Allyn and Bacon.

7. R. G. Lord and J. E. Smith (1983). Theoretical, information processing, and situational factors affecting attribution theory models of organizational behavior. *Academy of Management Review, 8,* 50–60.

8. E. E. Jones and K. E. Davis (1965). From acts to dispositions: The attribution process in person perception. In L. Berkowitz (ed.), *Advances in experimental social psychology,* vol. 2. New York: Academic Press.

9. H. H. Kelley and J. L. Michela (1980). Attribution theory and research. *Annual Review of Psychology, 31,* 457–501.

10. J. H. Harvey and G. Weary (1981). *Perspectives on attributional processes.* Dubuque, Iowa: William C. Brown.

11. See Note 7.

12. T. R. Mitchell and R. E. Wood (1980). Supervisor's responses to subordinate poor performance: A test of an attribution model. *Organizational Behavior and Human Performance, 25,* 123–138.

13. K. A. Brown (1984). Explaining group poor performance: An attributional analysis. *Academy of Management Review, 9,* 54–63.

14. J. A. Pearce II and A. S. DeNisi (1983). Attribution theory and strategic decision making: An application to coalition formation. *Academy of Management Journal, 26,* 119–128.

15. D. R. Ilgen, T. R. Mitchell, and J. W. Fredrickson (1981). Poor performers: Supervisors' and subordinates' responses. *Organizational Behavior and Human Performance,* 386–410.

16. R. G. Lord, R. J. Foti, and J. S. Phillips (1982). A theory of leadership categorization. In J. G. Hunt, U. Sekaran, and C. Schriesheim (eds.), *Leadership: Beyond establishment views.* Carbondale: Southern Illinois University Press, pp. 104–121.

17. D. R. Norris and R. E. Niebuhr (1984). Attributional influences on the job performance-job satisfaction relationship. *Academy of Management Journal, 27,* 424–431.

18. A. Korman (1970). Toward an hypothesis of work behavior. *Journal of Applied Psychology, 54,* 31–41.

19. J. Brockner and J. Guare (1983). Improving the performance of low self-esteem individuals: An attributional approach. *Academy of Management Journal, 26,* 642–656.

20. B. R. Schlenker (1980). Impression management: The self-concept, social identity, and interpersonal relations. Monterey, Calif.: Brooks/Cole.

21. N. H. Anderson (1981). *Foundations of information integration theory*. New York: Academic Press.

22. S. T. Fiske (1980). Attention and weight in person perception: The impact of negative and extreme behavior. *Journal of Personality and Social Psychology, 38,* 889–906.

23. See Note 20.

24. K. G. Rasmussen, Jr. (1984). Nonverbal behavior, verbal behavior, resume credentials, and selection interview outcomes. *Journal of Applied Psychology, 69,* 441–556.

25. C. K. Parsons and R. C. Liden (1984). Interviewer perceptions of applicant qualifications: A multivariate field study of demographic characteristics and nonverbal cues. *Journal of Applied Psychology, 69,* 557–568.

26. J. T. Molloy (1975). *Dress for success.* New York: Warner.

27. T. F. Cash (1985). The impact of physical appearance on the evaluation of women in management. Unpublished manuscript, Old Dominion University.

28. R. A. Baron (1983). "Sweet smell of success?" The impact of pleasant artificial scents (perfume or cologne) on evaluations of job applicants. *Journal of Applied Psychology, 68,* 709–713.

29. M. E. Heilman and M. H. Stopeck (1985). Attractiveness and corporate success: Different causal attributions for males and females. *Journal of Applied Psychology, 70,* 379–388.

30. J. M. Ivancevich (1983). Contrast effects in performance evaluation and reward practices. *Academy of Management Journal, 26,* 464–476.

31. D. McGregor (1960). *The human side of enterprise.* New York: McGraw-Hill.

32. D. J. Schneider (1973). Implicit personality theory: A review. *Psychological Bulletin, 79,* 294–309.

33. D. T. Miller and M. Ross (1975). Self-serving biases in the attribution of causality: Fact or fiction? *Psychological Bulletin, 82,* 213–225.

34. J. Greenberg, T. Pyszcynski, and S. Solomon (1982). The self-serving attributional bias: Beyond self-presentation. *Journal of Experimental Social Psychology, 18,* 56–67.

35. D. L. Hamilton, P. M. Dugan, and T. K. Trolier (1985). The formation of stereotypic beliefs: Further evidence for distinctiveness-based illusory correlations. *Journal of Personality and Social Psychology, 48,* 5–17.

36. J. N. Cleveland and F. J. Landy (1983). The effects of person and job stereotypes on two personnel decisions. *Journal of Applied Psychology, 68,* 609–619.

37. K. Kraiger and J. K. Ford (1985). A meta-analysis of ratee race effects in performance ratings. *Journal of Applied Psychology, 70,* 56–65.

38. B. J. Skrypnek and M. Snyder (1982). On the self-perpetuating nature of stereotypes about women and men. *Journal of Experimental Social Psychology, 18,* 277–291.

39. F. J. Landy and J. L. Farr (1980). Performance rating. *Psychological Bulletin, 87,* 72–107.

40. J. M. Feldman (1981). Beyond attribution theory: Cognitive processes in performance appraisal. *Journal of Applied Psychology, 66,* 127–148.

41. T. R. Mitchell, S. G. Green, and R. E. Wood (1981). An attributional model of leadership and the poor performing subordinate: Development and validation. In B. Staw and L. Cummings (eds.), *Research in organizational behavior,* vol. 3. Greenwich, Conn.: JAI Press, pp. 197–234.

42. See Note 12.

43. R. M. McIntyre, D. E. Smith, and C. E. Hassett (1984). Accuracy of performance ratings as affected by rater training and perceived purpose of rating. *Journal of Applied Psychology, 69,* 147–156.

CHAPTER 5

Work-Related Attitudes: Job Satisfaction, Organizational Commitment, and Prejudice

Fran Williams, an Assistant Financial Analyst at Fidelity American Life, is bursting with excitement. In fact, she can hardly wait to tell Jim Evans, one of her good friends, what she's just discovered. Rushing into his office, she positively bubbles over.

"Jim, Jim, look what I found!" she practically shouts.

At the sight of her excitement, Jim chuckles. He's a much more laid-back type of person, and is often amused by Fran's enthusiasm. "Well, what is it this time? he asks, a slight grin on his face.

"I was going over this commission program, see, and I found what looks like a pretty important error. In fact, the way I figure it, it's costing the company at least $300,000 a year in extra payments to some of our independent agents. And it won't take much to correct. All we have to do is change this sub-routine here, see . . ."

"Now wait a minute," Jim says, pushing away the papers Fran has spread on his desk. "What you're saying is that you've found a mistake in favor of some of our agents? I can hardly believe it. Are you sure?"

"Absolutely. I've gone over the numbers three times, and they always come out the same. Isn't that great? I can't wait to tell Mr. Jenkins."

But Jim doesn't seem to share Fran's pleasure. In fact, the grin has vanished from his face, and has now been replaced by a slightly cynical expression. "What for?" he asks. "What's it to *you* anyway? Are you going to get the difference? Besides, doesn't this company make enough right now without your help? No, I don't think I'd bother."

Fran is dismayed. "But Jim," she murmurs in a surprised voice. "Why should we go on paying out money we don't have to? I don't understand."

"Yeah, you *wouldn't*," Jim replies. "For some reason, you actually seem to *like* it here. But I don't. To me, Fidelity is a terrible place to work. Always pushing you around, telling you what to do, letting you know how little you matter. Heck, if I had a choice, I'd leave in a minute. So what's it to *me* what happens to their profits? If you were smart, you'd feel the same way. I mean, what have they ever done for you that's so great?"

Now Fran is really disturbed. She knows that Jim isn't as happy at Fidelity as she is, but she hardly expected *this.*

"Well, I mean, I really do like my job here. It's exactly what I expected. And my supervisor, Ms. Lettinger, is really nice. I feel like she's behind me 100 percent and that I have a good future . . ."

"Sure, sure, that's O.K. for you—*you* haven't been passed over for a promotion a couple of times, *you* don't have to deal with Jack Thompson. *You* don't have to do the same dumb things over and over. So go ahead, save the company some dough. But don't expect me to get excited about it. I'm taking care of number one, and no one else."

The two people in this incident present a sharp and obvious contrast. One is enthusiastic about her job, likes her work, and is deeply committed to the welfare of her company. The other is bored, cynical, and perhaps even hostile toward his organization; its future and profitability mean little if anything to him. In short, these individuals differ sharply in terms of their *work-related attitudes.* Fran's are positive, while Jim's are mainly negative. If such attitudes existed in isolation, quite apart from on-the-job behavior, they would be of little practical importance. As the incident above suggests, however, this is far from the case. The views individuals hold about their jobs and organizations often exert powerful effects upon their performance and other aspects of organizational behavior (refer to Figure 5.1).

Because work-related attitudes often play a key role in shaping behavior in organizations, it is important for you to know something about them. Such knowledge will be useful in its own right, and will also enhance your understanding of the "people side" of several major organizational processes considered later in this book—processes such as cooperation and conflict. In order to provide you with a basic understanding of work-related attitudes, we will proceed as follows. First, we will comment on the nature of attitudes in general: what they are, and how they can be changed.[1] Second, we will turn to a central type of work-related attitude—**job satisfaction.** Here, we will examine factors contributing both to feelings of satisfaction and dissatisfaction with one's work, as well as the impact of such reactions on several aspects of organizational behavior.[2] Third, we will consider attitudes relating to entire organizations rather than on one's own work or job. These are often described by the term **organizational commitment,** and exert powerful effects upon both individuals and organizations themselves.[3] Finally, we will turn to a special type of work-related attitude: **prejudice.** This involves negative views about other organizational members (or potential members), especially ones belonging to specific groups or categories (e.g., women, older persons, the members of various minorities). Such attitudes can be very disruptive to effective organizational func-

FIGURE 5.1 *Work-related Attitudes: An Example of Their Effects.*
As shown here, when individuals hold negative attitudes about their work, the results can be disastrous. (Source: Drawing by Cheney; © 1984 The New Yorker Magazine, Inc.)

tioning and also have great significance for society as a whole. Thus, they, too, are fully deserving of our careful attention.

ATTITUDES: THEIR NATURE AND CHANGE

Consider the following list:

- your boss
- Michael Jackson
- pizza
- water skiing
- the telephone company
- Ronald Reagan
- the game of "Trivial Pursuit"

Do you have any reactions to each of these items? If you are like most people, you probably do. For example, you may like your boss and admire his technical knowledge. You may love pizza, but realize that it can be fattening. If you are a Republican you may like Ronald Reagan and approve of his political views; if you are a Democrat, you may feel the opposite. We could continue, but by now the main point should be obvious: in general, we are *not* totally neutral to the events, people, ideas, and objects we encounter in our daily lives. On the contrary, we usually have positive or negative *feelings* about many of these, hold various *beliefs* about them, and tend to *behave* (or at least intend to behave) in certain ways toward them. Further, such reactions are often quite stable over time. Thus, if you like water skiing today, you will probably also like it next week or next month. Similarly, if you dislike the telephone company now, and believe that it is unreasonable, such feelings may well persist in the months or years ahead. Together, it is these kinds of reactions that constitute attitudes. Specifically, experts on such reactions usually define them as follows: *attitudes are relatively lasting clusters of feelings, beliefs, and behavior tendencies directed toward specific persons, ideas, objects, or groups.*[4] Thus, when we say that an individual holds an attitude toward some aspect of the external world, we simply mean that this person has positive or negative feelings toward the attitude object, holds certain beliefs about it, and tends to behave in specific ways toward it. Put another way, attitudes are often assumed to involve three basic parts: an *affective* (feeling) component, a *cognitive* (belief) component, and a *behavioral tendency* or intention component.

Work-related attitudes, too, fit under this basic definition. They involve lasting feelings, beliefs, and behavior tendencies toward various aspects of work, work settings, or the people in them. Thus, such attitudes may focus on bosses, subordinates, customers, specific departments, company policies, the grapevine, new equipment and technology, performance appraisals, or even an entire organization—the list is practically endless. In short, individuals can—and usually do—hold well-developed attitudes toward virtually every aspect of their lives at work.

We have already mentioned the basic reason why attitudes are important to managers or anyone else wishing to understand behavior in organizational settings: often, they strongly shape overt actions. Usually (although not always) individuals act in ways that are consistent with their attitudes. For example, if they like their supervisor, they may put out more effort for this person than if they dislike her. Similarly, if they have positive feelings about their company, and believe it has their welfare at heart, they are more likely to behave responsibly and efficiently in their jobs than if they have negative feelings about it, and believe that it is out to exploit them. Thus, understanding others' attitudes is often a useful first step to understanding many aspects of their behavior at work. From the point of view of a manager, though, this is only part of the story. In addition to simply understanding employees' attitudes, effective managers often wish to *change* them. They want to replace negative feelings and beliefs with more positive ones—to shift employees from patterns of reactions like those shown by Jim (the cynical character in the opening story) to ones like those held by Fran (his more enthusiastic co-worker). In short, they wish to alter attitudes—not simply recognize them. How can this goal be attained? What techniques are effective in inducing other persons to change their views about various aspects of work settings? It is on this basic question that we will focus next.

Changing Attitudes: Some Basic Techniques

As you already know from your own experience, efforts to change our attitudes are extremely common. Each day we are exposed to countless advertisements urging us to buy various products, to vote for particular candidates, or contribute to various causes. Similarly, we are often on the receiving end of direct pressure from bosses, friends, relatives, and acquaintances—pressure designed to alter our views on a wide range of topics. And of course we do not sit idly by as the passive recipients of such attempts. We, in turn, often try to influence the views of others. In short, efforts to alter attitudes are a common part of daily life.

Because researchers have long recognized the practical importance of attitude change, this process has been the subject of careful study for several decades.[5] The findings of such investigations have uncovered many different tactics effective in changing existing attitudes. Among the most successful of these are approaches based on **persuasion** and on **dissonance.**

Persuasive messages: hearing—sometimes—is believing. Perhaps the most common technique for inducing attitude change involves the use of *persuasive messages*. These consist of written, spoken, televised, or videotaped communications seeking to alter attitudes through "logical" arguments and convincing "facts." As our quotation marks suggest, the arguments presented are often far from logical and the facts anything but accurate. Usually, though, these flaws are concealed and the messages maintain at least an outward appearance of reason and authority.

Many different factors influence the success of persuasive messages in altering attitudes—far more than we can examine here. The most important of these factors, though, seem to involve certain characteristics of the *communicator* (the person doing the persuading), the *communication* itself (its specific content), and the *recipients* (those who receive it).

With respect to communicator characteristics, three seem to be most central: *attractiveness, style,* and *credibility.* All things being equal, attractive communicators—ones we like—are more effective in altering attitudes than unattractive ones. Similarly, persons who present their message in a fluent, convincing style tend to be more persuasive than ones who stumble over their words, or who show signs of low self-confidence. Interestingly, considerable evidence suggests that communicators who speak at a faster-than-average pace are actually more persuasive than ones who present their messages more slowly.[6] Thus, the popular belief that fast-talkers are often mistrusted does not seem to be true.

The single most important characteristic determining a communicator's success at persuasion, however, appears to be this person's *credibility*—his or her trustworthiness or believability. The higher a communicator is on this dimension, the more attitude change he or she will produce. Our impressions of a communicator's credibility, in turn, seem to depend largely on this person's apparent *expertise* and the *motives* behind his or her behavior. Communicators who seem to know what they are talking about (i.e., ones high in expertise) and who have little to gain from changing our views are usually much more influential than ones lacking in expertise, and who have a definite "axe to grind"—they can gain substantially from changing our attitudes. For example, imagine that one of your subordinates comes to see you, complaining about the performance of another member of your department. If she is an inexperienced employee still learning the ropes, and is in direct competition with the other person for a merit raise, you may well doubt her words. After all, there is a good chance that she has ulterior motives for her report. In contrast, if she is an experienced, effective worker, not in direct competition with

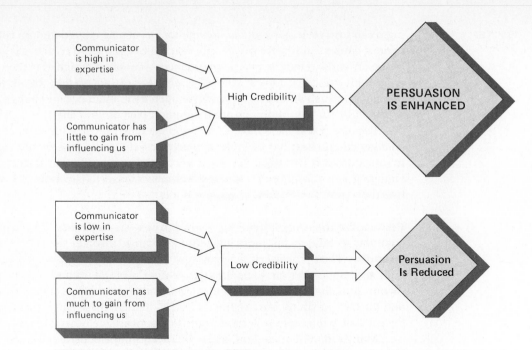

FIGURE 5.2 *Communicator Credibility and Persuasion.*
When a communicator possesses a high degree of expertise and has little to gain from influencing us, this person will be perceived as high in *credibility*. Then, persuasion is enhanced (upper panel). In contrast, when a communicator lacks expertise and has much to gain from influencing us, he or she will be viewed as low in credibility. Then, persuasion is reduced (lower panel).

the person she names, you are likely to attach greater importance to her remarks. (Please refer to Figure 5.2 for a summary of these effects.)

The *content* of a persuasive message, too, is important in determining its success in changing attitudes. First, the material it contains should be presented in a manner, and at a level, that is intelligible to the recipients. The reason for this is obvious: messages people cannot understand have little chance of affecting their views. Failure to take account of this basic fact is all too common in business settings. For example, engineers, scientists, attorneys, and others with technical knowledge often forget that people outside their fields do not share information that is second-nature to them (i.e., to scientists, engineers, or attorneys). As a result, they talk "over the heads" of their audience, and fail to get through to these people. Second, it is often useful to take the current attitudes of recipients into account. Research findings indicate that persuasive messages presenting views very different from the ones held by the persons who receive them tend to be rejected out of hand. They are perceived as extreme and unreasonable, and so have little chance of changing attitudes. In contrast, messages that present views only moderately divergent from the ones held by recipients are seen as more reasonable, and at least have a *chance* of altering attitudes.[7] Third, it appears that individuals can sometimes be frightened into changing their attitudes. Persuasive messages that vividly describe the negative outcomes that will follow if the communicator's recommendations are not adopted, and so manage to induce anxiety among recipients, are often effective in altering their views.[8] However, this is most likely to be the case if (1) the level of fear or anxiety induced is moderate rather than high, (2) recipients view the dangers described as realistic ones, and (3) they also believe that the recommendations presented by the communicator will actually help them to avoid such outcomes.

Finally, the success of persuasive messages in changing attitudes is also affected by certain characteristics of the persons who receive them. As you might guess, highly intelligent individuals are often less affected by such communications than those low in intelligence. Similarly, persons high in self-esteem and confidence are less likely to change their attitudes in response to such messages than those lower in self-esteem or confidence.[9] Finally, recent findings suggest, perhaps surprisingly, that people with good memories (especially for attitude-related beliefs) are less influenced by persuasive messages than persons with poor memories. [10] Apparently, this is the case because persons with good memories are able to remember more facts or beliefs supporting their own views during a persuasive message. Thus, they can argue against it internally while it is occurring, and so avoid being affected by it. People with poor memories, in contrast, are less capable of accomplishing this task.

To conclude: spoken, written, or taped messages designed to alter attitudes *can* often succeed in doing so. Indeed, the existence of a giant advertising industry, and the increasing use of such appeals in political campaigns, leaves little room for doubt on this score. In order to be maximally successful, though, such appeals must take careful account of the factors outlined above. If they do, considerable attitude change can result. If they do not, they may well be exercises in futility, and leave the views of recipients largely undisturbed. (How can managers make use of the principles discussed in this section to increase their impact on subordinates? For some concrete suggestions, see the **Perspective** box on page 146.)

Dissonance: When attitudes and behavior don't match.   Have you ever had to say something you didn't believe or had to act in a way contrary to your own views? Probably you have. Factors such as good manners, legal restrictions, the desire to further our career, or our wish to spare others' feelings often give us little choice in this respect. For example, imagine that at a staff meeting, your boss supports a specific policy—one with which you personally disagree. If he asks you to express your opinion about it in front of everyone else at the meeting, what will you do? It's hard to predict with certainty, but the chances are good that you will at least "waffle," and adopt some compromise position between his and your own.

But what happens in such situations? Are our attitudes affected in any manner? According to the theory of **cognitive dissonance,** they may be.[12] This theory argues that human beings dislike inconsistency. Specifically, it suggests that we dislike inconsistency between two or more of our own attitudes, or between our attitudes and behavior. When such conditions arise, we experience an unpleasant state known as *dissonance*. Then, under certain circumstances, our attempts to reduce such feelings can result in considerable attitude change. To see why this is so, let's return to the example mentioned above.

Imagine that at the meeting in question, you hesitate, but then give in: you state that you are in favor of the boss's view. What will be the result? According to

Applied Persuasion: Loading the Dice in Your Favor

It has often been said that a manager's central task is that of motivating his or her employees—somehow "building a fire" under these people so they perform in an effective, efficient manner. If this is indeed the case, then it is clear that persuasion is important. In fact, efforts to alter others' attitudes must constitute a basic tool in any manager's blueprint for building organizational effectiveness. Influencing subordinates, however, is only part of the total picture. Frequently, managers wish to change the views of other people too. Bosses, customers, suppliers, members of other departments—these are only a few of the many persons a manager may wish to influence. In sum, a working knowledge of persuasion—and being effective at it—are probably essential ingredients in managerial success. The next question, then is probably obvious: how can *you* improve your own skills in this regard? What steps can you take to maximize the impact of your own future efforts at persuasion? Fortunately, the research findings we have already described offer several concrete hints.

(1) *Build your personal attractiveness.* Attractive persuaders—ones who are liked by the persons they seek to influence—are usually more successful than unattractive persuaders. Thus, an initial task you should undertake is that of increasing your personal appeal. As we noted in our discussion of *impression management* in Chapter 4, many techniques for accomplishing this goal exist (e.g., flattering others, indicating that you share their views). Through careful use of these procedures, you can enhance your own attractiveness, and so increase your effectiveness as a persuader.

(2) *Enhance your credibility.* As we noted earlier, individuals who are high in credibility are often far more effective at persuasion than ones who are low on this dimension. Thus, it is crucial for you to maximize your own standing on this characteristic. This will involve doing your "homework" so that you really *do* know what you are talking about most of the time (high expertise), and also assuring that your actions seem to stem from the "right" motives. (For example,

make certain that your subordinates perceive that you have their interests at heart, and are *not* simply trying to further your own career at their expense.) All these efforts are well worth while, however, for high credibility is probably the best single step you can take on the road to being an effective persuader.

FIGURE 5.3 Repetition: Often, It Really Works.
Do you recognize this man? In all probability, you do, because advertisers often rely on *repetition* as a means of influencing our attitudes. Research findings suggest that, at least up to a point, this strategy may work. The more often we are exposed to a specific message or stimulus, the more favorable our reactions toward it tend to become. (Source: Courtesy of The Procter & Gamble Company.)

(3) *Make use of social pressure.* As we will see in more detail in Chapter 11, few persons like to stand out from the crowd—to be different from the people around them. This fact suggests a useful technique for changing attitudes. Often, it is helpful to convince the target persons that their views are *not* widely shared by others, while the attitudes or positions you recommend *are* quite popular. To the extent they accept this assessment, considerable degrees of attitude change may soon follow, for no one likes to stick out like the proverbial "sore thumb."

(4) *Design your appeals with care.* Obviously, people can't be influenced by messages they don't understand. Thus, if you want to change others' attitudes, it is essential that you take their intelligence, technical skill, and background into account when planning your remarks. If you don't, you stand little chance of altering their views. Similarly, remember that most persons tend to ignore statements or recommendations they perceive as too different from their own attitudes. This fact, too, should be taken into careful account. In short, where persuasion is concerned, moderation—not shocking extremity—is usually the best policy.

(5) *Familiarity breeds content: why repetition can often help.* How many times have you seen Mr. Whipple and his famous product? (Refer to Figure 5.3). Probably, on more occasions than you can count. This fact suggests that advertisers—accomplished masters at persuasion—often rely on repetition as a means of getting their message across. Will the same tactic work for you? Surprisingly, the answer is "yes." Research findings indicate that the more times individuals are exposed to persuasive appeals, other persons, or almost any object, the more positive their reactions to it become.[11] Thus, while repeating your recommendations over and over again may slightly annoy some persons, the impact on their attitudes may more than offset such reactions.

---

dissonance theory, you will notice the large gap between your underlying attitudes (remember: you are actually opposed to this policy), and your behavior—what you have just said. The result: you will experience uncomfortable feelings of dissonance. Will such feelings then produce shifts in your own views? The answer is: it depends. And what it depends upon, primarily, is the *magnitude* of dissonance produced. If this is great, the pressure for attitude change will be intense, and your views may well change. If it is small, the pressure will be much less and little attitude change will follow. The magnitude of dissonance, in turn, depends on several factors. One of the most important of these, though, involves your reasons for engaging in such attitude-discrepant behavior—for saying something you don't really believe. If you have many good reasons for endorsing your boss's position (e.g., the last member of your group to contradict him was quickly fired!) dissonance will be low. In contrast, if you have very few or weak reasons for taking this stand (e.g., you just don't like to disagree with others under any conditions, you're tired from a late date the night before and just don't want to invest the energy necessary for disagreeing), dissonance will be higher. In sum, the more good reasons you have for saying something you don't believe, the less dissonance you will experience, and the smaller the pressure to change your views. Conversely, the fewer your reasons for engaging in such actions, the greater the dissonance, and the greater the likelihood that your underlying views will change (refer to Figure 5.4, page 148).

This relationship between the reasons behind attitude-discrepant behavior and magnitude of dissonance leads to an intriguing prediction. If you wish to produce changes in other's attitudes by somehow getting them to voice support for views they don't hold, try to provide them with just barely enough inducement for doing so. If

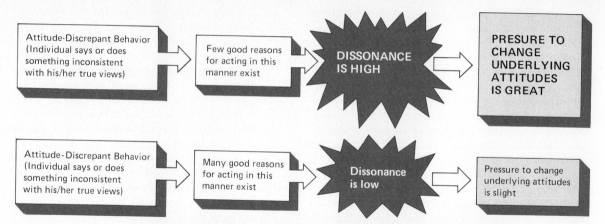

FIGURE 5.4   *Attitude-Discrepant Behavior, Dissonance, and Attitude Change.*
If an individual says or does something inconsistent with his or her true attitudes, dissonance results. If there were few good reasons for acting in this manner, the magnitude of dissonance is high, and considerable pressure to change the attitudes in question occurs (upper panel). In contrast, if there were many good reasons for engaging in attitude-discrepant behavior, the magnitude of dissonance is low, and little pressure for attitude change results (lower panel).

you offer more than this minimum, you will arm them with good reasons for having acted in this manner; thus, dissonance will be reduced. If you offer them less, they may not engage in attitude-discrepant behavior at all. In short, where attitude change is concerned, "less" may sometimes lead to "more": smaller rewards or inducements may actually produce greater shifts in attitudes than larger ones!

Before concluding, we should mention one additional implication of dissonance theory for organizational behavior. Briefly, dissonance often results whenever individuals make choices or decisions. The reason for this is simple: when we select one of the options open to us, we must usually forego the others. Doing so is then inconsistent with all the attractive aspects of these rejected choices. But the process does not stop here. Since making decisions often generates dissonance, we must now cope with these unpleasant feelings. One effective way of doing so, it appears, is raising our evaluation of the options we selected, while lowering our evaluations of the ones we rejected. For example, once we choose a mate, a school, a career, or a specific job, we tend to emphasize the positive features of these selections, while at the same time magnifying the negative aspects of the ones we discarded. A very clear illustration of such effects is provided by a study conducted by Lawler and his colleagues.[13] In this investigation, accounting students about to graduate from college were asked to indicate how desirable it would be to work at various firms. (That is, they expressed their attitudes toward these firms.) Several months later, after they had chosen a job, they were asked to rate the same companies once again. Dissonance theory predicts that after selecting a job, the students would tend to raise their evaluations of the chosen company, but would lower those of the others. As you can see from Figure 5.5, results offered support for this hypothesis.

Similar effects seem to occur in many other contexts.[14] Indeed, given existing evidence, it seems reasonable to suggest that they come into operation in almost any

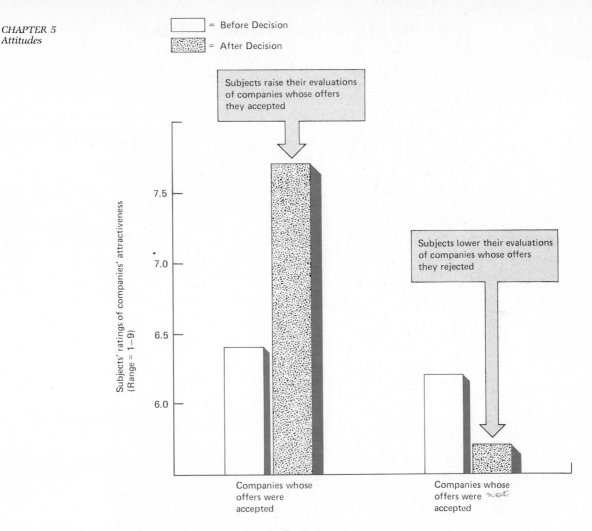

□ = Before Decision

▨ = After Decision

FIGURE 5.5 *Dissonance and Job Choice.*
After deciding to accept job offers from certain companies, students raised their evaluations of these firms. In contrast, they lowered their evaluations of companies whose offers they rejected. Both of these effects are predicted by dissonance theory. (Source: Based on data from Lawler et al., 1975; see Note 13).

situation where individuals make important decisions. The result of such efforts at dissonance reduction is certainly added comfort for decision-makers: they become more and more convinced of the wisdom of their choices. The danger, however, is that this will be the case even in the face of external evidence to the contrary. In short, where decisions are concerned, our strong desire to avoid uncomfortable dissonance may sometimes overwhelm our reason or judgment. To the extent it does, the consequences for persons making decisions, and for their organizations, can be disastrous.

149

JOB SATISFACTION: ATTITUDES TOWARD WORK

Like it or not, work plays a dominant role in our lives. It occupies more of our time than any other single activity. It provides the economic basis for our necessities, luxuries, and chosen lifestyle. Further, for most of us, it is central to our self-concept: we define ourselves, in part, through our careers, jobs, or professions. It seems only reasonable that anything of such central importance must evoke strong positive and negative reactions from us. In fact, this is definitely the case. When asked, most persons can readily report feelings, beliefs, and behavioral intentions relating to their jobs. In short, they report holding strong attitudes toward their work and specific aspects of it. Such attitudes are generally summarized by the term **job satisfaction,** and it is on this important topic that we focus in this section. Specifically, we will first comment on how such reactions are measured. Second, we will turn to several of the major causes of job satisfaction. Third, we will consider its prevalence—the extent to which people are generally satisfied with their jobs. Finally, we will examine some of the consequences of job satisfaction—ways it affects behavior in organizational settings.

The Measurement of Job Satisfaction: Assessing Reactions to Work

As you probably already know, most persons do *not* go about stating their attitudes to everyone they meet. On the contrary, they generally keep their views about politics, religion, and other matters largely to themselves. Attitudes about work are no exception to this general rule. In fact most persons express these views in an open manner only to a small group of friends or relatives—certainly not to their managers or supervisors. For this reason, measuring job satisfaction is somewhat more difficult than you might guess. Fortunately, though, several techniques for assessing this important aspect of work environments exist. Among the most useful of these are *rating scales* or *questionnaires, critical incidents*, and *interviews* or other forms of direct, face-to-face *meetings*.

Rating scales and questionnaires: Measuring job satisfaction through self-report. The most common approach to measuring job satisfaction involves the use of special rating scales or questionnaires. In this method, employees are asked to complete special forms on which they report their current reactions to their jobs. A number of scales have been developed for this purpose, and they vary greatly in scope. For example, one that is very popular, the **Job Descriptive Index (JDI),** presents individuals with lists of adjectives and asks them to indicate whether each one does or does not describe a particular aspect of their work.[15] They do so by placing a *Y* for "yes," an *N* for "no," or a *?* for "undecided" next to each adjective. Items similar to the ones included on the JDI are presented in Table 5.1. One interesting feature of this scale is that it measures reactions to five distinct aspects of jobs: the work itself, pay, promotional opportunities, supervision, and people (co-workers).

In another widely used measure of job satisfaction, the **Minnesota Satisfaction Questionnaire,** (MSQ), individuals rate the extent to which they are satisfied with various aspects of their present job (e.g., their degree of responsibility, opportunities for advancement, and pay).[16] Such ratings range from "not at all satisfied" through "extremely satisfied." Obviously, the higher the ratings individuals report, the greater their degree of satisfaction with various aspects of their job.

An important advantage of ratings scales such as the JDI or MSQ is that they can be completed quickly and efficiently by large numbers of persons. Another is that because they have already been administered to many thousands of individuals, average scores for persons in many kinds of jobs and many types of organizations are available. Thus, it is possible for any user to compare the scores of persons in his or her company with these, and obtain a measure of *relative* satisfaction—useful information in many cases. A key problem with such scales, however, should also be mentioned. As is true with all self-report measures, the accuracy of the results obtained depends on the willingness of individuals to be honest, as well as their ability to report accurately on their feelings. Obviously, to the extent these factors are absent, the findings obtained can be misleading.

Critical incidents as a key to job satisfaction. A second technique for assessing job satisfaction is the **critical incident procedure.** Here, individuals describe incidents relating to their work that they found especially satisfying or dissatisfying. Their replies are then carefully examined to uncover underlying themes and reactions.[17] For example, if many employees mention situations in which managers failed to take account of their input as especially upsetting, an important role of this factor in work-related attitudes would be suggested.

Interviews and other face-to-face meetings. Additional techniques for assessing job satisfaction involve interviews with employees, and what have sometimes been termed *confrontation meetings*. Interviews permit a more detailed exploration of employees' attitudes than questionnaires, and are sometimes useful for this reason. Unfortunately, of course, they are often costly and time-consuming. An alternative is group (confrontation) sessions in which employees are invited to "lay it on the line," and discuss their major complaints and concerns. If such sessions are conducted with skill, problems that adversely affect job satisfaction, but that might

TABLE 5.1 *Items Similar to Those on the JDI.*
The items shown here are similar to ones appearing on a popular measure of job satisfaction—the *Job Descriptive Index.* Persons completing this scale indicate whether each of the adjectives listed does or does not describe some aspect of their work.

Place a *Y* (for yes), an *N* (for no), or a *?* (for undecided) next to each word to indicate whether it does or does not describe your job:

Work		Pay	
_____	Complex	_____	More than I deserve
_____	Interesting	_____	Related to my performance
_____	Useful	_____	Appropriate for my level of skill
_____	Unpleasant	_____	Fair
_____	Tiring	_____	Adequate for my current life-style

otherwise remain hidden, can be brought out into the open. Then, steps to correct or eliminate them can be developed.

Assessing job satisfaction: A concluding comment. All the methods described above can be useful. As you probably already realize, though, none is perfect. Thus, the choice among them must depend upon the specifics of a given situation. In any case, while they can't answer all our questions about how people view their jobs, they *can* provide a general picture of these reactions. In this way, at least, they can get us off to a good start.

Job Satisfaction: Some Major Causes

Job satisfaction varies greatly from individual to individual and also from organization to organization. While some persons report mainly positive feelings about their work, others offer endless gripes about real or imagined problems. Why, precisely, is this so? In short, what factors contribute to job satisfaction and dissatisfaction? Attempts to answer this question have taken two basic forms. First, some scholars have sought to develop comprehensive theories of job satisfaction—frameworks for understanding not only *which* factors influence such attitudes, but also *why* this is the case. We will examine one such theory—**Herzberg's motivator-hygiene approach**—here.[18] Second, other investigators have adopted a more empirical approach, focusing primarily on the task of identifying variables responsible for positive or negative reactions toward work. Key findings of this research, too, will be summarized below.

Herzberg's motivator-hygiene theory. Do job satisfaction and dissatisfaction stem from the same conditions? Or are they actually the result of different sets of factors? Common sense suggests that both reactions probably derive from common causes. That is, certain factors produce job satisfaction when they are present, but feelings of dissatisfaction when they are absent. A theory proposed some years ago by Frederick Herzberg, however, offers a different conclusion. It suggests that job satisfaction and job dissatisfaction actually spring from different sources. Since this is a surprising conclusion, you may find it interesting to learn how Herzberg first reached it.

He began by conducting a study in which more than two hundred engineers and accountants were asked to describe times when they felt especially satisfied or dissatisfied with their jobs. (This is the *critical incident* technique described earlier.) Careful analysis of their answers then yielded the following pattern of results. When describing incidents in which they felt dissatisfied, many persons mentioned conditions surrounding their jobs rather than the work itself. For instance, they commented on such factors as physical working conditions, pay, security, the quality of supervision they received, company policies, and their social relations with others. To the extent these conditions were positive, feelings of dissatisfaction were prevented. Given their role in preventing such negative reactions, Herzberg termed these factors *hygienes* or *maintenance factors*. In contrast, when describing incidents in which they felt especially satisfied or happy with their jobs, subjects often mentioned factors relating more directly to the work they performed. For example, they spoke about the nature of their jobs and daily tasks, achievement in them, promotion opportunities, recognition from management, increased responsibility, and the chance for personal growth. Because such factors contributed to job satisfaction, Herzberg decided to label them *motivators*. (Please refer to Figure 5.6 for a summary of both motivators and hygienes.)

FIGURE 5.6   *Herzberg's Motivator-Hygiene Theory.*
According to a theory proposed by Herzberg, job satisfaction stems from the presence of one set of factors (*motivators*), while dissatisfaction stems mainly from the absence of another set of factors (*hygienes* or *maintenance factors*). Evidence concerning the accuracy of these suggestions is mixed.

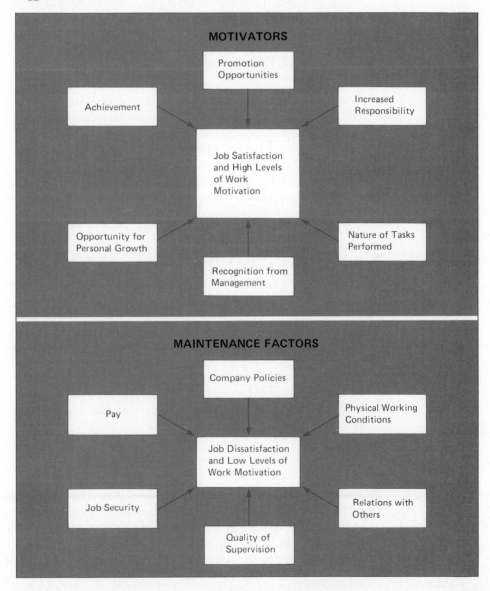

These interesting suggestions were soon investigated in several separate studies. Unfortunately, we must report that generally, this work failed to offer clear support for the theory's accuracy. While some studies did yield findings similar to those reported by Herzberg, many others reported sharply different results. Specifically, it was often found that factors labeled as hygienes and motivators exerted powerful effects on *both* satisfaction and dissatisfaction.[19] Needless to add, such findings are contrary to the theory's basic assertion that these positive and negative reactions stem from distinct clusters of variables.

In view of this negative evidence, Herzberg's theory should not be accepted as a fully adequate framework for understanding job satisfaction. This is not to say, however, that it has been of little value. On the contrary, the theory has called attention to the importance of such factors as the opportunity for personal growth, recognition, and increased responsibility as basic conditions for lasting job satisfaction. Attention to such factors, in turn, has stimulated much work on **job design** and **job enrichment**—topics discussed in Chapter 3. In this way, it has contributed much to the field of organizational behavior, despite the lack of clear support for some of it's key predictions.

Major causes of job satisfaction: Some consistent empirical findings.   As we have just seen, efforts to formulate comprehensive theories of job satisfaction have met with mixed success. In contrast, research designed to simply identify those factors influencing such reactions has attained much progress. Many of the conditions that lead individuals to hold positive or negative feelings toward their work have been established. As you might expect, these are highly varied in nature. Most, though, fall into three major categories: factors relating to (1) *work settings,* (2) *specific aspects of jobs,* and (3) the *persons* who perform them.

Work settings and job satisfaction.   With respect to work settings, the most important factors appear to be *reward systems*—how an organization distributes rewards such as pay and promotions, and certain *procedures* and *policies.* Satisfaction is enhanced by reward systems that employees view as fair and reasonable, but is reduced by systems they view as unfair and unreasonable. Similarly, job satisfaction is increased by such policies as permitting employees to participate in decisions that involve them, and ones that spread responsibility and authority throughout the organization rather than concentrating it in a few positions. Another factor that should be mentioned is *perceived quality of supervision.* When employees approve of the style adopted by their supervisors, perceive these persons as fair, and believe they have the ability to help them with their jobs or within the organization generally, satisfaction tends to be high. When, in contrast, they dislike their supervisors' approach to management, view them as incompetent, or believe they have little influence within the organization, satisfaction tends to be low.[20]

Work itself and job satisfaction.   Turning to jobs themselves, several consistent findings have been reported. First, most persons tend to prefer work that is mentally challenging, varied, and interesting, but not too stressful or exhausting. In short, there seems to be a "happy medium" where effort in one's work is concerned. Second, general work conditions, too are important. A work environment that is

154

comfortable and that facilitates the attainment of work goals will usually produce higher levels of satisfaction than one that is uncomfortable, chaotic, and unpredictable. Third, most persons strongly prefer to know just what is expected of them at work. Thus, ambiguity concerning their responsibilities or goals often reduces job satisfaction. Clarity with respect to these matters can enhance it.

3) *Individuals and job satisfaction.* Individuals play an important role in job satisfaction in two different ways. First, their personal characteristics can affect their feelings about their work. For example, it appears that persons high in self-esteem and ones who believe that their outcomes are under their own control (Internals) are often more satisfied with their jobs than persons who are low in self-esteem or who feel that they have little impact on their outcomes (Externals). Second, their relations with others play a key role in this regard. Research findings indicate that individuals generally express higher job satisfaction when they enjoy positive, friendly relations with co-workers and supervisors than when they do not. In fact, positive social relations appear to be a major source of reward for many individuals. Such positive relations, in turn, are facilitated when employees feel that the persons around them share their major beliefs and values. When, in contrast, they perceive that they must work with people holding different views from their own, satisfaction may decrease.

Finally, we should add that *expectations* about one's job are also important. Often, when recruiting new employees, organizations tend to paint an overly rosy picture of their internal conditions. When individuals then join the company, they find that their expectations about their jobs are not met. As a result, they may become dissatisfied, and seek employment elsewhere. To avoid such reactions, Wanous and other researchers recommend the use of *realistic job previews*— procedures in which applicants are provided with accurate descriptions of the jobs they will perform.[21] Presumably, under these conditions, their expectations are more realistic, and have a better chance of actually being met. In addition, knowing what problems to expect may prepare them for these, and so help them to cope with these difficulties more effectively. The results of several studies suggest that realistic job previews may indeed contribute to later job satisfaction.[22] However, as noted recently by Breaugh, this may only be the case under certain conditions (e.g., when individuals can afford to be selective about accepting a given job, when they would otherwise hold unrealistic expectations about it).[23] Whatever the precise boundary conditions for beneficial effects of realistic job previews, however, one fact is certainly clear: individuals' expectations about their jobs—what they will be like, what problems and rewards they will offer—can exert powerful effects upon their attitudes toward them.

The Prevalence of Job Satisfaction: Do People Like Their Work?

Suppose you approached a large sample of persons doing many different jobs in many locations and asked them to rate their satisfaction with their work. What would you find? Would most report a reasonable degree of satisfaction? Judging from images of the world of work contained in recent movies and magazine articles, you might predict the latter outcome (see Figure 5.7) That is, you might expect to uncover huge pools of anger and discontent. Surprisingly, though, large-scale surveys of job satisfaction do not support this gloomy picture. On the contrary, most point to the conclusion that a large majority of persons are relatively satisfied with their jobs. For example, one survey that has continued for more than twenty years indicates that between 81 percent and 92 percent of employees are relatively happy with their jobs.[24] And other investigations stretching across even longer periods of time have obtained similar findings.[25] Thus, it appears that most persons are quite satisfied with their work.

The findings just described paint a comforting picture of conditions in work settings. But how do they square with such facts as rising absenteeism and turnover

FIGURE 5.7   *The World of Work: One Common View.*
In recent years, many films have represented employees as being bored and unhappy with their jobs. Actually, though, most surveys indicate that a large majority of individuals are quite satisfied with their work.

in many businesses, and major declines in productivity (which have only recently begun to be reversed)? If most persons are so happy with their jobs, why do such conditions exist? The answer, it appears, is this: the actual situation is far more complex than at first meets the eye.

First, while job satisfaction *is* generally high, these positive attitudes are not uniformly distributed across all aspects of work and work settings. For example, satisfaction with pay is generally lower than satisfaction with quality of supervision or with such factors as having enough time, help, and equipment to get one's job done properly. Thus, when we ask "How satisfied are employees generally?" we may overlook important aspects of this issue.

Second, job satisfaction varies greatly across different groups of employees. As you might expect, managers, technical and professional workers, and self-employed persons generally report higher satisfaction than blue-collar personnel.[26] Similarly, older workers, or ones who have held their jobs for long periods of time and feel secure in them, often report greater satisfaction than younger ones, or those lacking the benefits of seniority. Members of minority groups tend to indicate lower overall levels of satisfaction than do others. Finally, there appear to be certain differences between males and females in this regard (although, we should add, the pattern here seems to be in the midst of important change). In the past, it was often found that men reported higher job satisfaction than women. Recent investigations indicate, however, that such differences may be declining, perhaps because of the removal of many barriers to female advancement. Yet, some differences continue to exist. For example, in one study on this topic, Varca, Shaffer, and McCauley measured job satisfaction among four-hundred college graduates (half male, half female).[27] Intriguing differences between the sexes were uncovered, at least with respect to satisfaction with pay and opportunities for promotion. Among persons holding relatively high-level jobs (e.g., marketing manager), males reported greater satisfaction than females. In contrast, among those holding low-level jobs (e.g., waiter or waitress), the pattern was reversed. Here, females reported greater satisfaction with their current jobs than males (refer to Figure 5.8 on page 158).

One possible explanation for these results involves the specific *reference groups* chosen by males and females—the groups with whom they compare themselves to determine how well they are doing in their jobs. Females holding low-level jobs may compare their pay and promotion opportunities only with those of other women holding the same kind of position. As a result, they are relatively satisfied with their outcomes. In contrast, males holding such jobs may compare themselves with persons holding higher level positions, and so become dissatisfied. Similarly, females in higher level occupations may compare their pay and promotion opportunities with those of males holding similar jobs. Since there may well be a disparity in this regard in favor of the men, they may then experience reduced satisfaction. We should hasten to add that this interpretation is only tentative in nature, and should *not* be viewed as conclusive. What is clear, however, is this: important differences in job satisfaction continue to exist among different groups of employees, and should not be overlooked.

A third point to keep in mind concerning the high levels of job satisfaction uncovered in many surveys is this: in one sense, such findings may be more apparent than real. In fact, they may stem as much from the way in which job satisfaction

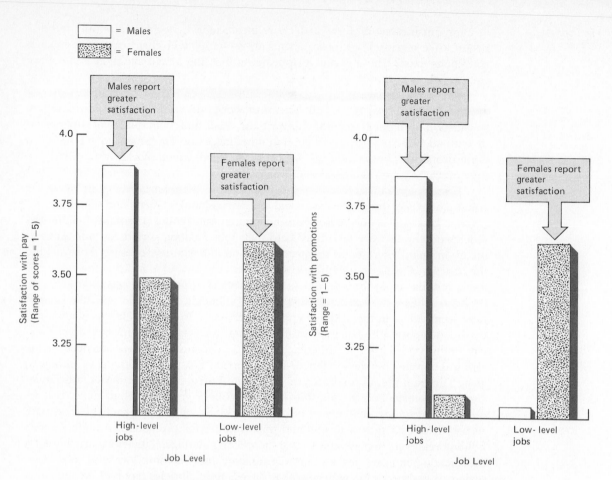

FIGURE 5.8 *Sex Differences in Job Satisfaction: Some Intriguing Findings.*
In one recent study, intriguing differences between the two sexes with respect to job satisfaction were uncovered. Among persons holding high-level jobs, males reported greater satisfaction with both pay and promotion opportunities than females. Among individuals holding low-level jobs, however, the opposite was true. These differences may stem from the adoption of different *reference groups* by males and females. (Source: Based on data from Varca, Shaffer, and McCauley, 1983; see Note 27.)

is measured as from high levels of positive attitudes among employees. That this is the case is suggested by the following fact: when asked if they would choose the same work again (assuming they could start over), many persons answer "No!" For example, more than half of white-collar employees indicate that they would select some other job or career. Among blue-collar persons, the figure is even higher, with fully three-quarters reporting that they would prefer other jobs.[28] Clearly, then, many people are not nearly as happy with their work as standard surveys of job satisfaction seem to suggest.

If this is so, you may be wondering, why do they also report that they are quite satisfied with their current jobs? One possibility is suggested by the theory of *cogni-*

tive dissonance, discussed earlier. Most persons realize that they will probably have to stay in the job they now hold, or one quite similar to it—economic conditions rarely permit the luxury of great job-to-job mobility. Thus, if they report being dissatisfied with their present work, considerable dissonance may result. After all, stating that one dislikes one's job is inconsistent with the knowledge that holding it is a fairly permanent (and necessary) fact of life. In order to avoid such inconsistency, therefore, many persons choose both to describe and to perceive their work in relatively favorable terms. At the moment, no direct evidence for the contribution of dissonance to high reported levels of job satisfaction exists. However, a large body of research evidence does support the impact of dissonance on many other types of attitudes. Thus, the possibility that it affects individuals' ratings of job satisfaction, too, seems quite feasible.

Job Satisfaction: Its Major Effects

Throughout this discussion of job satisfaction, we have made an important assumption: attitudes exert strong effects on overt behavior. Probably, you find this suggestion reasonable. We should note, however, that for years, a heated debate concerning the accuracy of this assertion persisted. Some findings indicated that the link between attitudes and behavior is relatively weak, while others suggested that it is quite strong. Fortunately, this issue has now been resolved. Growing evidence suggests that attitudes *do* affect behavior. Indeed, recent findings indicate that they are often the direct cause of a wide range of actions. This is not to say that attitudes *always* translate into overt behavior in a direct or immediate manner—far from it. But there is now enough positive evidence to conclude that certain kinds of attitudes—especially ones that are strong and clearly formed, specific rather than general in nature, and directly relevant to an individual's life—do influence many forms of behavior.[29]

To the extent this is true, it is only reasonable to expect job satisfaction to play a role in several aspects of organizational behavior. In fact, this appears to be the case. Some of its major effects will now be reviewed.

Job satisfaction, absenteeism, and turnover.   Consider two employees, both of whom hate to get up in the morning and dislike fighting their way through the rush hour to work. One likes her job very much, while the other dislikes it. Which one is more likely to call in sick or miss work for other reasons? The answer is obvious: the one who dislikes her job. That job satisfaction does affect absence from work in this manner is indicated by the findings of many different studies. In general, these investigations report that the lower an individual's satisfaction with his or her job, the more likely is that person to be absent from work.[30]

Similar findings have been obtained with respect to voluntary turnover. The lower an individual's level of satisfaction with his or her job, the more likely is this person to resign and seek other opportunities. Again, though, the strength of this relationship is modest.[31] The reason why the links between job satisfaction on the one hand and both absenteeism and turnover on the other are not even stronger is this: both of these behaviors are affected by many different factors, and job satisfaction is only one of them. For example, absence from work is probably affected by such variables as weather, traffic conditions, personal health, and family responsibilities as well by attitudes toward work. Similarly, recent studies indicate that the decision to leave one's job is actually the result of a complex **withdrawal process** involving thoughts about leaving, intentions to search for another position, actual search, and intentions to quit.[32] Further, many factors (e.g., general economic conditions, current demand for persons with specific skills) play a role in employees' decisions to resign from one job and seek another. Given the fact that many different variables affect both absenteeism and turnover, it is only reasonable that the links between these behaviors and job satisfaction are modest. Indeed, it would be more surprising if they were far stronger than they are.

Job satisfaction and performance: The "missing link"?   It has often been assumed that happy workers are productive workers, and at first glance, this assertion makes good sense. Won't persons who are pleased with their jobs work harder than those who are unhappy and dissatisfied? Such arguments sound convincing, and even today many managers accept them as valid. Actually, though, there is little support for their accuracy. Most studies designed to examine the possibility of a link between job satisfaction and performance have yielded weak or negative results.[33] Thus, contrary to what common sense suggests, productivity does *not* seem to rise with increased satisfaction. At first glance, this finding seems puzzling. However, several facts help account for it.

First, in many work settings, there is little room for large changes in performance. Jobs are structured so that the persons holding them must attain at least some minimum level of performance. If they do not, they cannot retain their position. In addition, there is often little leeway for *exceeding* this baseline. Even if an individual speeds up her own output, this may be to no avail if the persons around her continue to work at the same pace. Given the close interdependence of employees in most businesses, the individual investing maximum effort in her work may soon find that she has little to do. Essential work materials may not be available, and other employees may put pressure on her to slow down. In such cases, even high levels of job satisfaction can do little to raise productivity.

Second, it may actually be the case that job satisfaction and productivity are not directly linked. Rather, any apparent relationship between them may stem from the fact that both are related to a third factor—receipt of various rewards. As suggested by Porter and Lawler, the situation may go something like this.[34] Past levels of performance lead to the receipt of both extrinsic rewards (e.g., pay, promotions) and intrinsic rewards (e.g., feelings of accomplishment). If these rewards are judged to be fair by employees, they may come to perceive a contingency between their performance and these outcomes. This, in turn, may have two effects. First, it may encourage high levels of effort and so good performance. Second, it may lead to a high level of job satisfaction. In short, high productivity and high satisfaction may both stem from the same conditions. These two factors themselves, however, are not directly linked (please refer to Figure 5.9 for a summary of these suggestions).

For these and other reasons, job satisfaction may not be directly related to performance in many situations. We should note, however, that this conclusion may hold true only with respect to what might be described as "standard" measures of

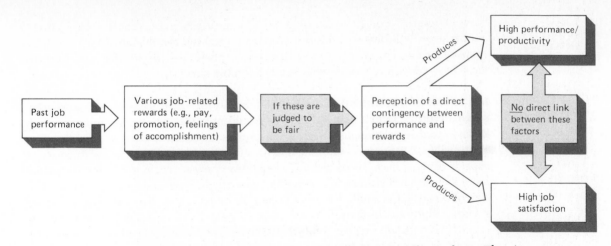

FIGURE 5.9 *Job Satisfaction and Job Performance: Why, Perhaps, They Are Not Directly Linked.*
According to a model proposed by Porter and Lawler, job satisfaction and performance are not directly linked. Instead, both stem from individuals' perception that there is a contingency between their output and the rewards they receive. (Source: Based on suggestions by Porter and Lawler, 1968; see Note 34.)

performance. It may indeed be the case that employees' level of job satisfaction does not strongly affect the quantity or even the quality of their output. Yet, at the same time, it may well influence other aspects of their on-the-job behavior. For example, it may affect what have been termed **citizenship behaviors.** These are actions by individuals that "lubricate the social machinery" of their organizations. They include helping co-workers with their jobs, accepting orders in a willing manner, promoting a positive work climate, protecting or conserving the organization's resources, cheerfully tolerating temporary inconveniences, and similar actions. In short, such actions contribute to the smooth and effective functioning of an organization, without showing up directly in weekly summaries of output or sales. Presumably, the higher individuals' satisfaction with their jobs, the more likely they will be to engage in such actions. (This possibility is suggested by the fact that when individuals experience positive feelings, they are often more willing to engage in helpful, generous behaviors than when they experience more negative reactions.[35]) Is this actually the case? A recent study by Bateman and Organ indicates that it is.[36]

These investigators had the supervisors of administrative employees at a large university rate their subordinates in terms of their tendency to engage in the type of citizenship behaviors mentioned above. At the same time, these employees reported on their own level of job satisfaction by completing the Job Descriptive Index. These procedures were repeated on two occasions, five to seven weeks apart. Results were clear: at both times, there was a moderately strong, positive relationship between job satisfaction and citizenship behaviors. Thus, the higher subjects' reported job satisfaction, the higher were the citizenship ratings they received from their supervisors.

These findings suggest that in answer to the question "Are job satisfaction and performance related?" we must first respond "What kind of performance do you have in mind?" For many traditional indices of job performance (e.g., output, quality), the link between positive work attitudes and performance appears to be weak or nonexistent. For other aspects of performance—ones harder to quantify or measure—however, it may well be considerably stronger.

Job satisfaction and other aspects of behavior: Life satisfaction and personal health. Before concluding, we should note that job satisfaction influences behavior outside as well as within work settings. First, there is some indication that it affects *life satisfaction*—the extent to which individuals are pleased with personal aspects of their lives. In particular, a "spillover" effect seems to occur, so that the more satisfied individuals are with their jobs, the happier they are in general. The size of this effect is small, but does appear to be real. Moreover, at least one study suggests that job satisfaction has a greater impact upon life satisfaction than vice versa.[37] Second, job satisfaction also influences personal health—both physical and mental. The greater individuals' satisfaction with their work, the healthier they seem to be in both of these respects.[38]

Together, these findings indicate that the benefits of holding positive attitudes toward one's work go beyond simple economics. If organizations needed further inducement for seeking to generate such reactions among their employees, this evidence should provide it! (What specific actions do individuals take when they experience strong dissatisfaction with their jobs? For the answer provided by recent research, please see the **Focus on Behavior** insert on page 163.)

ORGANIZATIONAL COMMITMENT: ATTITUDES TOWARD ORGANIZATIONS

Have you ever known anyone who loved her work, but hated the company that employed her? Conversely, have you ever met a person who hated his job, but felt strong loyalty toward his organization? If you have encountered individuals of either type, you are already aware of an important fact: positive or negative feelings about one's job are only part of the total picture where work-related attitudes are concerned. In addition to holding such views, individuals often also possess positive or negative attitudes toward their entire organization. Such attitudes are usually termed **organizational commitment,** and reflect the extent to which an individual identifies with and is involved with his or her organization.[41] Specifically, a high degree of organizational commitment is associated with (1) strong acceptance of the organization's goals and values, (2) willingness to exert effort on its behalf, and (3) a strong desire to remain within the organization. In contrast to job satisfaction, which can change rapidly in response to shifting work conditions, organizational commitment is a more stable attitude—one that remains consistent over long periods of time.

Interest in organizational commitment has increased greatly in recent years, perhaps in response to mounting concern over sharp drops in productivity and what many perceive to be a society-wide decline in such commitment. Much of this research has been concerned with the causes of organizational commitment, and its effects upon work-related behavior. Consistent with this emphasis, the present discussion will also address both of these topics.

Exit, Voice, Loyalty, or Neglect? *EVLN Model* Potential Reactions to Job Dissatisfaction

So far in this discussion, we have focused mainly on the causes and impact of job satisfaction—positive attitudes toward one's work. Except for a few indirect references, we have left the question of how individuals respond to strong feelings of dissatisfaction largely unexplored. At this point, therefore, we will turn to this issue.

One useful framework for understanding how people react to job dissatisfaction is provided by what has been termed the *EVLN model*.[39] Briefly, this theory suggests that when faced with strong feelings of job dissatisfaction, individuals often adopt one of four distinct strategies. First, they may choose to leave their job or firm, a reaction known as *exit*. Second, they may engage in attempts to change or eliminate the causes of their negative feelings—an approach known as *voice*, since in it, individuals often state their grievances. Third, they may demonstrate *loyalty*, sticking to their guns and hoping that the situation will soon improve. Finally, they can become demoralized, lower their effort, and demonstrate lax, irresponsible behavior—a pattern termed *neglect*. That these are in fact the major reactions to job dissatisfaction is suggested by the findings of an intriguing study by Farrell.[40]

In this investigation three concrete instances each of exit, voice, loyalty, and neglect reactions were first prepared. (For example, an instance of exit was "deciding to quit the company"; an instance of voice was "putting a note in the suggestion box.") These statements were then placed on cards and given to seven experts in organizational behavior and human resource management. Their task was that of sorting the twelve examples into as many separate piles of related items as they wished. It was predicted that these experts would tend to sort the examples into four piles representative of exit, voice, loyalty, and neglect. The same twelve cards were also given to 185 students enrolled in graduate business courses. They were asked to rate how similar each of the statements were to each other. It was expected that they would view the statements representing a given pattern as more similar to each other than to one representing other patterns. (For example, the three statements illustrating exit would be rated as more similar to one another than to statements representing loyalty or neglect.) Results offered support for both of these suggestions.

The findings obtained by Farrell, and those uncovered in other investigations, point to an important conclusion. Although specific reactions to job dissatisfaction can be quite diverse, most fit under four major headings. This knowledge is useful in its own right, for it helps clarify the key dimensions underlying such varied reactions as absenteeism, lateness, grievances, and general "goofing off." In addition, it brings the next crucial question sharply into focus: What factors lead individuals to choose one of these patterns over the others? When further research provides an answer to this puzzle, we will be much closer to a full understanding of the impact of work-related attitudes.

Organizational Commitment: Its Major Causes

Like job satisfaction, organizational commitment seems to stem from many different factors. First, it is affected by several aspects of jobs themselves. In general, the higher the level of responsibility and autonomy connected with a given job, and the more interesting and varied it is, the higher the level of commitment associated with it. On the other hand, the greater the tension and ambiguity associated with a job, the lower the level of commitment it produces.

163

Second, organizational commitment is affected by the existence of other employment opportunities. The greater the perceived chances of finding another job, and the greater the desirability of such alternatives, the lower an individual's commitment tends to be.[42]

Third, organizational commitment is also affected by several personal characteristics. As you might expect, older individuals, those with tenure or seniority in their positions, and those who are satisfied with their own level of work performance tend to evidence higher levels of commitment than others. In the past, it was often suggested that women demonstrate lower levels of commitment than men. However, recent findings indicate that this is *not* the case. In fact, one study which examined the organizational commitment of almost six hundred persons working for many different organizations found no differences whatsoever between males and females on this dimension.[43] (Surprisingly, and also contrary to popular belief, Japanese and Korean employees do not report higher levels of organizational commitment than their American counterparts.[44])

Finally, organizational commitment is strongly affected by several factors relating to work settings generally. For example, the more satisfied individuals are with their supervisors, with the fairness of performance appraisals, and the more they feel their organization cares about their welfare, the higher their level of commitment. In sum, feelings of identification with and commitment toward one's organization are influenced by many different factors. (Please refer to Figure 5.10 for a summary of these variables.)

Organizational Commitment: Its Major Effects

It seems only reasonable to predict that persons who feel deeply committed to their organization will often behave differently in it than persons who do not share such loyalty, and can hardly wait to leave. In fact, growing evidence suggests that this is the case. Organizational commitment appears to exert powerful effects on several aspects of work behavior.

First, as you might expect, the higher individuals' feelings of commitment, the lower their rates of absenteeism and turnover. Second, the higher such commitment, the less likely are individuals to engage in an active search for another position. Organizational commitment also appears to be related to both effort and performance. The higher employees' commitment toward their company, the greater the effort they are willing to invest on its behalf and so, in many cases, the better their performance.

None of these results are surprising; indeed, they seem to follow logically from the nature of organizational commitment itself. Somewhat more unexpected, however, is the following fact: strong feelings of organizational commitment may also *produce* rather than simply stem from high levels of job satisfaction. At first glance, this almost seems backward. Wouldn't it be more reasonable to expect that job satisfaction produces feelings of commitment rather than vice versa? At least one recent and carefully conducted investigation, however, indicates that in some cases, it may in fact be commitment that causes satisfaction.

FACTORS TENDING TO INCREASE ORGANIZATIONAL COMMITMENT

| Motivating potential of specific job | High level of responsibility | High level of autonomy | Satisfaction with own level of work performance | Seniority/ tenure | High quality of supervision | Fair appraisals |

Level of organizational commitment

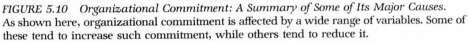

| Role ambiguity | Job tension | Availability of other employment opportunities | Belief that company does not care about employees | Use of punishment by supervisors |

FACTORS TENDING TO REDUCE ORGANIZATIONAL COMMITMENT

FIGURE 5.10 *Organizational Commitment: A Summary of Some of Its Major Causes.*
As shown here, organizational commitment is affected by a wide range of variables. Some of these tend to increase such commitment, while others tend to reduce it.

In this study, carried out by Bateman and Strasser, nurses at four large hospitals completed questionnaires designed to assess their level of organizational commitment, their level of job satisfaction, plus several other factors that might influence both of these attitudes (e.g., level of job tension, the perceived availability of other jobs, the behavior of their supervisors).[45] Because the nurses answered the questionnaires on two separate occasions some five months apart, it was possible to determine the nature of any causal links between these variables. Results in this respect were clear: job satisfaction appeared to *stem from* rather than *cause* organizational commitment. In addition, it appeared that such commitment itself was affected by several different factors, such as certain aspects of supervisors' behavior and the availability of other jobs.

One possible explanation for these results is as follows.[46] In some cases, individuals may develop an initial level of commitment to an organization at the time they seek, and then accept, a job with it. This level of commitment may then influence the way in which they perceive many aspects of their jobs. In this way, it may shape their subsequent feelings of satisfaction or dissatisfaction with their work. Persons who begin with a high initial level of commitment tend to see their organization through the proverbial "rose-colored glasses." Thus, they develop high levels of job satisfaction. In contrast, those who begin with a low initial level of commitment (e.g., they view the organization as a temporary location en route to greener pastures), tend to focus on negative factors, and so develop low job satisfaction. In short, by shaping expectations, initial levels of commitment may affect employees perceptions, and so their overall levels of job satisfaction. Of course, further research is necessary to determine whether this interpretation is valid. Regardless of the outcome of such investigations, however, one fact is already clear: employees' level of commitment to their organization can exert important effects on several aspects of their behavior.[47] For this reason, efforts by managers to enhance such commitment through attention to the factors discussed above appear to be fully worthwhile.

PREJUDICE: NEGATIVE ATTITUDES TOWARD OTHER ORGANIZATION MEMBERS

Most people would agree that the phrase "don't jump to conclusions" offers good advice. Yet somehow, where other persons are concerned, we often seem to lose sight of it. In many cases, we *do* jump to conclusions about others. Moreover, these usually rest on the flimsiest type of foundation imaginable: their membership in some group or category. Thus, we often form judgments about others solely on the basis of their ethnic background, race, sex, or age. Even worse, these judgments are often negative in nature. We assume that another person possesses undesirable traits or is inferior in some manner simply because he or she belongs to a specific group. Such reactions are usually termed **prejudice.** To be more precise, prejudice can be defined as *a negative attitude toward the members of some group based solely on their membership in that group.*[48]

As we're sure you already realize, prejudice has important implications for society as a whole. Indeed, recent decades have been marked by an effort, in many nations, to eliminate the lingering, harmful effects of such attitudes. What you may not realize as clearly, however, is that prejudice has important implications for organizations and organizational behavior, too.

First, where such reactions persist, they may be the cause of friction or conflict within an organization. If specific persons dislike one another simply because of differences in their personal backgrounds, it may be difficult for them to work together. This can have devastating effects on cooperation and efficiency. Second, prejudice may have an adverse impact on the careers of persons who are the target of such attitudes. These individuals may encounter discrimination with respect to hiring, promotion, pay, and evaluation of their work. Third, organizations themselves may suffer greatly from such practices. If individuals are overlooked or passed over simply because of their membership in certain groups, the organizations involved may experience a loss of precious human resources. This is an outcome few companies can afford.

For these and other reasons, prejudice is indeed a type of attitude with great relevance to work and work settings. In order to illustrate some of its major effects, we will now focus on one form that has recently been the subject of a great deal of political, legislative, and research interest: prejudice based on sex.

166

Prejudice Toward Females: A Special, Timely Case

Females constitute a majority of the world's population. Yet, despite this fact, they have been treated like a minority in most cultures. They have been largely excluded from economic and political power. They have been the object of pronounced negative stereotyping (beliefs suggesting that all women are much alike, and that the traits they share are undesirable in nature). Finally, they have often experienced overt discrimination in many spheres of life (e.g., exclusion from certain jobs, kinds of training, social organizations). Fortunately, such practices seem to be decreasing. Yet females still seem to be concentrated in low-level jobs in many organizations. As noted recently by Steinberg and Shapiro, "Women populate corporations but they rarely run them."[49] Why is this the case? Research findings suggest that it derives from several subtle, but powerful, forces that continue to operate against the advancement of women in work settings.

First, even today, members of both sexes tend to perceive males as being better leaders than females.[50] Apparently, such tendencies stem from persistent *stereotypes* about the supposed characteristics of men and women (refer to our earlier discussion in Chapter 4). According to these beliefs, men are dominant, assertive, and self-assured, while women are passive, submissive, and emotionally unstable. Given such assumptions, it is not surprising that many people tend to perceive males as more effective in leadership roles than females. Of course, as you may already know, recent evidence suggests that these stereotypes are largely false: males and females do *not* differ as consistently nor to as large a degree as these traditional conceptions suggest.[51] Yet such beliefs persist, and continue to distort perceptions of leadership performance.

Second, there seems to be a tendency on the part of many persons to attribute good, successful performance by males to internal causes, such as their own ability or effort, but similar performance by females to external causes such as good luck or an easy task.[52] As we noted in Chapter 4, to the extent good performance is attributed to external causes, individuals receive less credit for it. The result of this attributional bias, then, is that when a male and female perform at the same level, the male is often seen as more deserving of praise, promotion, or other rewards. Needless to state, this tendency—which, again, seems to exist among *both* males and females—operates against the advancement of women in organizational settings. (Fortunately, the tendency to downgrade the performance of females in this manner seems to be on the wane. For evidence that it is, please see the **Focus** box on page 169.)

Third, women seem to hold lower expectations about their careers than men. For example, in one recent study, conducted by Major and Konar, male and female business students were asked to indicate how much money they thought they would earn during their first year on the job (starting salary) and during the year they would earn the most (peak salary).[53] As shown in Figure 5.11 (page 168), females reported substantially lower figures in both categories. Several factors probably contribute to such differences (e.g., the fact that females tend to specialize in lower paying areas than do males; their tendency to base their estimates of future earnings on the current earnings of women, who *do* receive less.) Whatever the basis, however, the lower expectations held by females can exert a powerful, self-confirming impact, and so help to perpetuate their "second-class" status in many organizations.

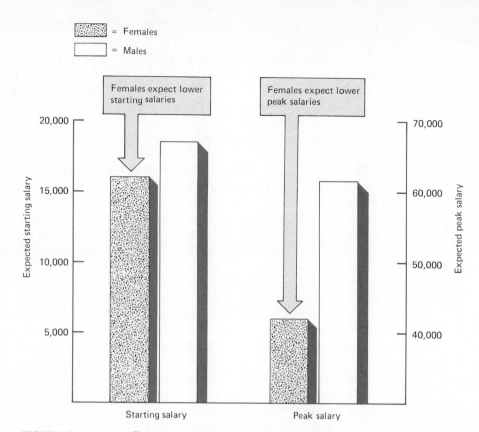

FIGURE 5.11 *Sex Differences in Expectations of Future Pay.*
Female business students (both B.A. and M.B.A.) reported lower expectations concerning their future starting and peak salaries than did male business students. These lower expectations, in turn, may be one factor contributing to the lower outcomes of females in many organizations. (Source: Based on data from Major and Konar, 1984; see Note 53.)

Together, these and related forces (e.g., internal conflicts stemming from the belief that they have been selected for a job simply because they are a woman) contribute to the fact that females are overrepresented at lower rungs of the organizational ladder, but underrepresented near the top.[54]

Women as Managers: Do They Really Differ?

As we have already noted, cultural stereotypes suggest that males and females differ greatly with respect to many key traits. If such stereotypes are correct—even to a small degree—we might expect men and women also to differ sharply when serving as managers. That is, once they succeed in overcoming the barriers mentioned above and attain managerial rank, females might still behave differently than males in comparable positions. Is this actually the case? Do male and female

Sex Bias in Performance Appraisals: Going, Going—?

As we noted in Chapter 2, performance appraisals are a key organizational process. Important rewards, such as promotions, merit raises, and the like are often determined by the ratings individuals receive from their supervisors. Thus, if bias based on sex existed in this respect, it would be serious indeed. Is there evidence for such effects? Fortunately, the answer seems to be "no." While such discrimination may well have been present in the past, the findings of several studies indicate that it has largely vanished at present. For example, consider a well-conducted investigation by Peters and his colleagues.[55]

FIGURE 5.12   *Sex Bias: Does It Influence Performance Appraisals?*
Contrary to what might be predicted on the basis of sex bias, female managers did *not* receive lower ratings from their supervisors than male managers. In fact, they actually received *higher* ratings from both male and female supervisors. (Source: Based on data from Peters et al., 1984; see Note 55.)

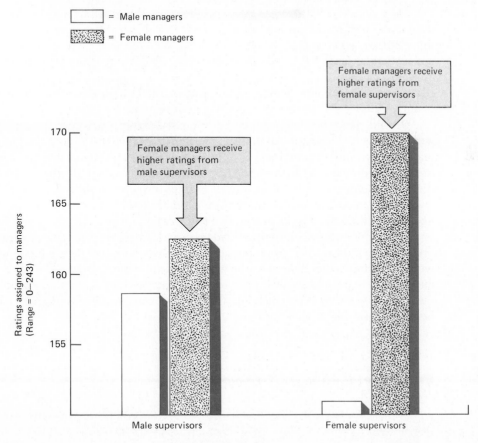

□ = Male managers

▨ = Female managers

Female managers receive higher ratings from female supervisors

Female managers receive higher ratings from male supervisors

Ratings assigned to managers
(Range = 0–243)

170

165

160

155

Male supervisors   Female supervisors

Sex of Supervisor

In this project, the performance of more than six hundred store managers was evaluated by their immediate supervisors. Ratings involved key job-related tasks such as store maintenance, ordering merchandise, customer service, and employee supervision. All possible combinations of sex of manager and sex of supervisor were included (i.e., male supervisor–female manager, female supervisor–male manager, male supervisor–male manager, female supervisor–female manager). If sex bias influenced the ratings assigned to managers, it would be predicted that females would receive lower ratings than males, and that this would especially be likely to be true in cases where male supervisors evaluated female managers.

In fact, results showed no evidence for such effects. As shown in Figure 5.12 (page 169), the only significant finding was that female managers received *higher,* not lower, ratings from both male and female supervisors.

Of course, these findings do not provide conclusive evidence for the absence of bias toward females. It is possible that the woman managers deserved even higher ratings than they received. Still, these results, and those in related studies, suggest that such bias, even if it exists, does not prevent females from obtaining relatively high appraisals.[56] Thus, there do seem to be grounds for at least a limited degree of optimism with respect to this important aspect of organizational functioning.

managers really differ in the ways that cultural expectations predict? The answer provided by many recent studies is, again, "no."

First, consider the traits of male and female managers. Existing evidence indicates that contrary to cultural expectations, few if any differences exist between these groups. When compared on a number of key traits (e.g., assertiveness, conscientiousness, practicality, self-assuredness), male and female managers do *not* differ appreciably. Moreover, when they do, it is not in the ways predicted by widely held stereotypes. For example, females actually appear to be *higher* not lower than males in such traits as self-assuredness and venturesomeness.[57]

Second, male and female managers do not differ in terms of actual on-the-job performance. For example, in one large-scale study involving almost two thousand managers, virtually no differences appeared between males and females with respect to key dimensions such as managerial philosophy, skill in dealing with subordinates, managerial style, or approach to motivating one's subordinates.[58] (Male and female managers in this study were carefully matched in terms of age, rank, and type of organization in which they worked.)

When added to the findings already reviewed, these results make any traces of prejudice against women in organizational settings even less defensible than they would be if important differences between the sexes really existed. After all, if male and female managers show virtually identical patterns of behavior, why should the question of their sex even enter into the picture? Our answer—and yours too, we believe—is simple: it shouldn't!

Prejudice: A Note on Its Generality

In the preceding discussion, we have focused on prejudice based on sex. Before concluding, we should note, again, that this is only one aspect of a more general problem—the tip of a large and dangerous iceberg, so to speak. Many other forms of prejudice exist in organizational contexts, and exert harmful effects upon individuals, groups, and organizations themselves. As we noted earlier, such negative reactions can involve race, ethnic background, religion, and many other characteristics. One additional form of prejudice worthy of special note, though, is that based on age.

Growing evidence points to the existence of strong forms of bias against older employees. Such persons are often viewed as lower than young individuals in capacity for work and in potential for future development. Further, they frequently receive the "short end of the stick" where promotion and similar organizational decisions are involved.[59,60] Unfortunately, the impact of prejudice based on age may actually increase in the decades ahead, as the average age of the working population (and the population in general) increases. Eliminating this form of bias, as well as several others, constitutes an important task for organizations in the late 1980s.

SUMMARY

Attitudes are lasting clusters of feelings, beliefs, and behavior tendencies directed toward some person, object, or group in the world around us. *Work-related attitudes,* which focus on various aspects of work and work settings, play a key role in many forms of organizational behavior.

Individuals usually hold strong positive or negative attitudes toward their work. These are known as **job satisfaction,** and are affected by many different factors (e.g., ones relating to the work itself, conditions existing in work settings). Job satisfaction influences absenteeism and turnover, but is not directly related to standard measures of job performance. However, recent evidence indicates that it may affect *citizenship behaviors*—actions by employees that help to smooth the operation of their organizations.

In addition to holding attitudes toward their jobs, individuals often have more general reactions toward their organization as a whole. These fall under the general heading of **organizational commitment.** Like job satisfaction, such attitudes stem from a number of different factors, and can affect several aspects of organizational behavior (e.g., turnover, performance).

Prejudice involves negative attitudes toward others based solely on their membership in certain groups. Such reactions can exert harmful effects on individuals, interfering with their careers, and on organizations, reducing coordination and wasting precious human resources. One form of prejudice that has received a great deal of attention in recent years is prejudice based on sex. Such reactions appear to be on the wane, but continue to interfere with the advancement of females in some work settings.

KEY TERMS

attitudes: Enduring clusters of feelings, beliefs, and behavioral intentions directed toward specific persons, groups, ideas, or objects in the world around us.

citizenship behaviors: Actions by individuals that facilitate the smooth and effective functioning of their organizations, but which are not part of their formal job description. These include helping others with their jobs, accepting orders willingly, and promoting a positive work climate.

cognitive dissonance: An unpleasant state that occurs when individuals become aware of inconsistencies between their attitudes, or between their attitudes and their behavior.

critical incident procedure: A method for measuring job satisfaction or dissatisfaction in which employees are asked to describe incidents relating to their work that they have found especially satisfying or dissatisfying.

Herzberg's motivator-hygiene theory: A theory of job satisfaction proposing that satisfaction and dissatisfaction stem from different groups of variables (*motivators* and *hygienes,* respectively).

Job Descriptive Index (JDI): A rating scale for assessing job satisfaction. Individuals respond to this questionnaire by indicating whether various adjectives describe certain aspects of their work.

job design: Refers to efforts to design jobs so that they can be performed as efficiently as possible, and are also satisfying for employees.

job enrichment: Efforts to make jobs more satisfying by providing the persons who perform them with greater autonomy and a more varied range of activities.

job satisfaction: Positive and negative attitudes held by individuals toward their jobs.

Minnesota Satisfaction Questionnaire (MSQ). A rating scale for the assessment of job satisfaction. Individuals completing this scale indicate the extent to which they are satisfied with various aspects of their jobs.

organizational commitment: The attitudes held by individuals toward their entire organization. The more favorable these are, the greater their acceptance of the organization's goals, and the greater their willingness to expend effort on its behalf.

persuasion: Refers to efforts by one or more individuals to change the attitudes of one or more others through written, spoken, or filmed messages.

prejudice: Negative attitudes toward the members of some specific group.

withdrawal process: The complex process through which individuals form intentions to leave their present jobs, search for alternative positions, and then actually move to them.

NOTES

1. D. W. Rajecki (1982). *Attitudes: Themes and advances.* Sunderland, Mass.: Sinauer Associates.

2. E. A. Locke (1976). The nature and causes of job satisfaction. In M. Dunnette (ed.), *Handbook of industrial and organizational psychology.* Chicago: Rand McNally.

3. R. T. Mowday, L. W. Porter, and R. M. Steers (1982). *Organizational linkages.* New York: Academic Press.

4. R. A. Baron and D. Byrne (1984). *Social Psychology: Understanding human interaction,* 4th ed. Boston: Allyn and Bacon.

5. See Note 1.

6. W. Apple, L. A. Streeter, and R. B. Krauss (1979). Effects of pitch and speech rate on personal attributions. *Journal of Personality and Social Psychology, 37,* 715–727.

7. See Note 4.

8. See Note 1.

9. M. Zellner (1970). Self-esteem, reception, and influenceability. *Journal of Personality and Social Psychology, 15,* 87–93.

10. W. Wood (1982). Retrieval of attitude-relevant information from memory: Effects on susceptibility to persuasion and on intrinsic motivation. *Journal of Personality and Social Psychology, 42,* 798–810.

11. R. B. Zajonc (1968). Attitudinal effects of mere exposure. *Journal of Personality and Social Psychology Monograph Supplement, 9,* 1–27.

12. R. A. Wicklund and J. W. Brehm (1976). *Perspectives on cognitive dissonance.* Hillsdale, N.J.: Erlbaum.

13. E. E. Lawler, III, W. J. Kuleck, Jr., J. G. Rhode, and J. E. Sorensen (1975). Job choice and post-decision dissonance. *Organizational Behavior and Human Performance, 13,* 133–145.

14. J. C. Younger, L. Walker, and A. J. Arrowood (1977). Post-decision dissonance at the fair. *Personality and Social Psychology Bulletin, 3,* 284–287.

15. P. C. Smith, L. M. Kendall, and C. L. Hulin (1969). *The measurement of satisfaction in work and retirement.* Chicago: Rand McNally.

16. L. Lofquist and R. V. Dawis (1969). *Adjustment to work.* New York: Appleton.

17. See Note 2.

18. F. Herzberg, B. Mausner, and B. Snyderman (1959). *The motivation to work.* New York: Wiley.

19. J. Schneider and E. A. Locke (1971). A critique of Herzberg's incident classification system and a suggested revision. *Organizational Behavior and Human Performance, 6,* 441–457.

20. J. Trempe, A. J. Rigny, and R. R. Haccoun (1985). Subordinate satisfaction with male and female managers: Role of perceived supervisory influence. *Journal of Applied Psychology, 70,* 44–47.

21. J. P. Wanous (1980). *Organizational entry: Recruitment, selection, and socialization of new-comers.* Reading, Mass.: Addison-Wesley.

22. B. L. Dugoni and D. R. Ilgen (1981). Realistic job previews and the adjustment of new employees. *Academy of Management Journal, 24,* 579–591.

23. J. A. Breaugh (1983). Realistic job previews: A critical appraisal and future research directions. *Academy of Management Review, 8,* 612–619.

24. R. P. Quinn and G. L. Staines (1979). *The 1977 quality of employment survey.* Ann Arbor: Institute for Social Research.

25. G. H. Gallup (1972). *The Gallup poll.* New York: Random House.

26. C. N. Weaver (1980). Job satisfaction in the United States in the 1970s. *Journal of Applied Psychology, 65,* 364–367.

27. P. E. Varca, G. S. Shaffer, and C. D. McCauley (1983). Sex differences in job satisfaction revisited. *Academy of Management Journal, 26,* 348–353.

28. R. L. Kahn (1972). The meaning of work: Interpretations and proposals for measurement. In A. A. Campbell and P. E. Converse (eds.), *The human meaning of social change.* New York: Basic Books.

29. J. Sivacek and W. D. Crano (1982). Vested interest as a moderator of attitude-behavior consistency. *Journal of Personality and Social Psychology, 43,* 210–221.

30. L. W. Porter and R. M. Steers (1973). Organizational work, and personal factors in employee turnover and absenteeism. *Psychological Bulletin, 80,* 151–176.

31. R. T. Mowday, C. S. Koberg, and A. W. McArthur (1984). The psychology of the withdrawal process: A cross-validational test of Mobley's intermediate linkages model of turnover in two samples. *Academy of Management Journal, 27,* 79–94.

32. S. R. Rhodes and M. Doering (1983). An integrated model of career change. *Academy of Management Review, 8,* 631–639.

33. See Note 2.

34. L. W. Porter and E. E. Lawler, III (1968). *Managerial attitudes and performance.* Homewood, Ill.: Dorsey Press.

35. A. M. Isen (1984). Toward understanding the role of affect in cognition. In R. S. Wyer, Jr. and T. K. Srull (eds.), *Handbook of social cognition.* Hillsdale, N.J.: Erlbaum.

36. T. S. Bateman and D. W. Organ (1983). Job satisfaction and the Good Soldier: The relationship between affect and employee "citizenship." *Academy of Management Journal, 26,* 587–595.

37. T. I. Chacko (1983). Job and life satisfactions: A causal analysis of their relationships. *Academy of Management Journal, 26,* 163–169.

38. A. W. Kornhauser (1965). *Mental health of the industrial worker: A Detroit study.* New York: Wiley.

39. A. O. Hirschman (1970). *Exit, voice, and loyalty: Responses to decline in firms, organizations, and states.* Cambridge: Harvard University Press.

40. D. Farrell (1983). Exit, voice, loyalty, and neglect as responses to job dissatisfaction: A multidimensional scaling study. *Academy of Management Journal, 26,* 596–607.

41. See Note 3.

42. T. S. Bateman and S. Strasser (1984). A longitudinal analysis of the antecedents of organizational commitment. *Academy of Management Journal, 27,* 95–112.

43. N. A. Bruning and R. A. Snyder (1983). Sex and position as predictors of organizational commitment. *Academy of Management Journal, 26,* 485–491.

44. F. Luthans, H. S. McCaul, and N. G. Dodd (1985). Organizational commitment: A comparison of American, Japanese, and Korean employees. *Academy of Management Journal, 28,* 213–219.

45. See Note 42.

46. See Note 42.

47. S. A. Stumpf and K. Hartman (1984). Individual exploration to organizational commitment or withdrawal. *Academy of Management Journal, 27,* 308–329.

48. See Note 4.

49. R. Steinberg and S. Shapiro (1982). Sex differences in personality traits of female and male master of business administration students. *Journal of Applied Psychology, 67,* 306–310.

50. G. S. Sanders and T. Schmidt (1980). Behavioral discrimination against women. *Personality and Social Psychology Bulletin, 6,* 484–488.

51. S. A. Basow (1981). *Sex role stereotypes: Traditions and alternatives.* Monterey, Calif.: Brooks/Cole.

52. G. E. Stevens and A. S. DeNisi (1980). Attitudes and attributions for performance by men and women. *Academy of Management Journal, 23,* 355–361.

53. B. Major and E. Konar (1984). An investigation of sex differences in pay expectations and their possible causes. *Academy of Management Journal, 27,* 777–792.

54. T. I. Chacko (1982). Women and equal employment opportunity: Some unintended effects. *Journal of Applied Psychology, 67,* 119–123.

55. L. H. Peters, E. J. O'Connor, J. Weekley, A. Pooyan, B. Frank, and B. Erenkrantz (1984). Sex bias and managerial evaluations: A replication and extension. *Journal of Applied Psychology, 69,* 349–352.

56. R. Grams and D. P. Schwab (1985). An investigation of systematic gender-related error in job evaluation. *Academy of Management Journal, 28,* 279–290.

57. R. Steinberg and S. Shapiro (1982). Sex differences in personality traits of female and male master of business administration students. *Journal of Applied Psychology, 67,* 306–310.

58. S. M. Donnell and J. Hall (1980). Men and women as managers: A significant case of no significant difference. *Organizational Dynamics,* 60–77.

59. B. Rosen and T. H. Jerdee (1979). Influence of employee age, sex, and job status on managerial recommendations for retirement. *Academy of Management Journal, 22,* 169–173.

60. J. C. Crew (1984). Age stereotypes as a function of race. *Academy of Management Journal, 27,* 431–435.

CHAPTER 6

PERSONALITY: Its Basic Nature

PERSONALITY: Its Impact in Work Settings
The Type A Behavior Pattern: Who Succeeds—and Who Survives?
Machiavellianism: Manipulating Others as a Way of Life   Locus of Control:
Are You—or Others—Master of Your Fate?   Self-Esteem: Why
Self-Evaluations Are Important   Work-Related Motives: Achievement and
Power

MEASURING PERSONALITY: Some Basic Methods
Inventories and Questionnaires   Projective Techniques   Assessment Centers:
Identifying Management Potential   Using Knowledge about Personality: Some
Words of Caution

SPECIAL INSERTS
FOCUS ON BEHAVIOR   Boundary Spanning in Organizations: When High
  Self-Monitoring Can Help
CASE IN POINT   "You're Your Own Worst Enemy!"

Personality: The Nature and Impact of Individual Differences

Cal Fiske, Marilyn Jennings, and Dave Osborne, three young employees at Intercom Systems, Inc., are having lunch at a restaurant near company headquarters. Up until a month ago, they had worked in the same department. Because of a reorganization at Intercom, though, their old unit was dissolved, and they found themselves transferred to different departments. Right now, they are comparing notes on their new jobs, with special emphasis on their new supervisors.

"Well, I guess I can get along with Randy Peters O.K., " Marilyn comments. "He's an up-front sort of guy, so you always know where you stand. That's a definite plus. But I wish he'd slow down a little. Rush, rush, rush! With him, everything has to be done yesterday. And he's *so* competitive—whew! One of these days he's just bound to keel over with a heart attack, the way he drives himself."

"Yeah, I've heard he's like that," Cal replies, nodding his head. "A work-addict if ever there was one. I don't think I'd like taking orders from him. Now Fran Jackson, *my* supervisor—she's a different type. Low-key, laid back. In fact, in some ways, she's just the opposite of Connors. She likes to think things through, weigh everything carefully. Never makes a snap decision. But she does have one problem . . ."

"What's that?" Dave asks, pausing with his knife in mid-air.

"Maybe the best way to put it is to say that she's not a team player. From what I've seen, she likes to do everything her own way. That may work out in the short run, but I think it's going to cost her eventually. In fact, I doubt that she'll ever make it to Level 4. She's just too much of a maverick for the powers-that-be."

"You're probably right," Marilyn agrees. "The higher up you go, the more they want you to stick to the rules and follow company policy. That's definitely going to count against her."

There's a brief pause as all three diners munch their food, and contemplate the dangers of seeking too much independence. Then, putting down his glass, Dave continues:

"Hmm . . . I think I've landed in a situation different from both of yours. In fact, I'm afraid that I've fallen into the clutches of a real manipulator.

"What do you mean, Dave?" Cal asks. "I've heard some good things about your boss—Denise Rochambeau, isn't it?"

"I'm not surprised," Dave answers. "At first glance, she *does* seem real nice—concerned with her people, loyal to them, and all that. But after you've been around her a while, you begin to wonder whether it isn't just an act. Every so often, she says or does something that makes me think she really doesn't care about anything but herself. I could be wrong, but it sure worries me."

"Well," Marilyn remarks, a concerned look on her face, "don't let it get you down. That type always gets what they deserve in the end."

"Maybe so," Dave agrees, "but they can do a lot of damage before people get wise to them. Oh well, one thing's for sure: we've really come up with a mixed bag, haven't we? Oh, for the good old days when we all worked together!"

"Variety," it is often said, "is the spice of life." If this is true, then other people certainly provide us with a lot of spice! They differ from one another in a seemingly countless number of ways. Moreover, as our opening story suggests, such differences often count—and count heavily—in work settings. To mention just a few examples, they often play a key role in determining who will succeed and who will fail, who will make an effective leader and who an ineffective one, and who will enjoy good relations with the people around them, and who bad ones (refer to Figure 6.1).

Many kinds of differences between individuals contribute to such outcomes. Among the most important, however, are ones relating to **personality**—differences among individuals in terms of their lasting *traits* or characteristics. It is on such differences that we focus in the present chapter. Specifically, we will begin by defining personality, and explaining its relevance to organizational behavior. Next, we will consider several specific traits that have important implications for behavior in organizational settings. These include the **Type A behavior pattern, Machiavellianism, locus of control,** and several differences in *personal motives* (e.g., motivation for achievement, power, and independence). Finally, we will turn to methods for measuring or assessing personality. Such techniques are necessary if we wish to compare individuals in this regard, and then put such knowledge to practical use.

PERSONALITY: ITS BASIC NATURE

Our own experience seems to tell us two things about human beings. First, they are all unique. Each possesses a pattern of traits and characteristics not totally duplicated in any other person. Second, these traits are fairly stable over time. Thus, if one of your friends is bright, courteous, and ambitious today, she will probably also show the same characteristics next month, next year, and perhaps throughout her life. These observations concerning *uniqueness* and *consistency* form the core of many modern definitions of personality. Specifically, personality is usually defined as *the unique but stable set of characteristics that sets each individual apart from*

FIGURE 6.1 *Personality: An Important Factor in Organizational Behavior.*
The young man shown here is exceptionally high on one trait that can strongly affect his future career: self-confidence! (Source: Drawing by Stan Hunt; © 1984 The New Yorker Magazine, Inc.)

"If I should come to work for you, Mr. Hysop, I could transform this organization overnight."

others.[1] In short, it refers to the lasting ways in which a given person is different from others.

In all probability, you find this definition quite reasonable. Most of us believe that all human beings (including ourselves) possess important traits, and that these strongly affect their feelings, thoughts, and actions. You may be surprised to learn, therefore, that until quite recently, a heated controversy concerning the accuracy of these suggestions existed. On one side of this debate were scientists who contended that, in fact, people do *not* possess lasting traits.[2] Rather, according to these researchers, their behavior is shaped largely by external factors and conditions. As a result, we should not expect much consistency in human behavior; indeed, the same person may well act very differently across situations, and at different times.[3] On the other side of the controversy were scientists who held, equally strongly, that stable traits *do* exist. According to these scholars, people demonstrate a considerable degree of stability in their behavior, and do often act in ways consistent with—and reflective of—their underlying traits.[4] Which of these opposing views has triumphed? As you can probably guess from the inclusion of this chapter in our text, the latter one. At present, the weight of scientific opinion has swung strongly toward the existence of important, stable traits. This is not to say that the controversy outlined above is totally resolved—far from it. But at present, there is a growing consensus among experts that people often show a high degree of consistency in their actions across situations and over time, and that this is best explained through reference to lasting, underlying traits.[5] Several lines of evidence have contributed to growing confidence in this conclusion, but here, we will mention only two.

First, in a number of major studies, the behavior of individuals has been carefully studied over extended periods of time (several weeks or even months), and across a wide range of situations. This is in sharp contrast to earlier investigations in which samples of behavior in only one or two situations, and over only a few hours, were obtained. Results have been clear: in such studies, considerable evidence for consistency is present.[6] For example, in one such project, individuals' energy level was rated by their friends and acquaintances. Then, several behaviors that might relate to this characteristic (e.g., their walking speed, the presence of an alert or slumped posture during a lecture) were observed on a number of different occasions. A correlation of fully +.70 between peer ratings of energy level and these overt behaviors was obtained, thus suggesting that subjects *did* in fact behave in a manner consistent with this underlying trait.

Second, growing evidence suggests that just as individuals differ greatly with respect to many specific traits, they also vary considerably in the extent to which their behavior reflects either their personal characteristics, or, alternatively, external (situational) factors.[7] At one end of this dimension are persons whose actions stem from, and are guided by, their underlying traits. As you might expect, such persons show a high degree of consistency across situations and over time. At the other extreme are persons who are primarily responsive to ever-changing external conditions and who, accordingly, demonstrate little consistency in their behavior.

Recognition of this important dimension (often termed **self-monitoring** since it involves the degree to which individuals monitor and adjust their own behavior), points to two conclusions directly relevant to the situations-versus-traits debate mentioned earlier. First, although everyone appears to possess underlying traits, it is naive to expect all persons to behave in ways consistent with them. Large individual differences in this characteristic, too, exist. Second, because this is the case, instances in which persons fail to demonstrate consistency over time or across situations are *not* necessarily evidence against the existence of underlying traits. Indeed, such inconsistency itself may merely reflect a key dimension of personality, self-monitoring. (For a concrete illustration of the relevance of self-monitoring to organizational behavior, please refer to the **Focus** insert on page 182.)

One final point: the fact that traits exist and exert strong effects upon the behavior of at least some persons does *not* imply that the impact of situational factors is weak or unimportant. On the contrary, most experts on personality—and most practitioners of organizational behavior—believe that human behavior actually stems from a complex interplay between situational and personal factors. Thus, in order to understand it fully, we must take careful account of both types of factors. We have already encountered several instances of this type of *person-by-situation interaction* in earlier chapters (e.g., our comment, in Chapter 3, that the job characteristics model applies primarily to people high in growth needs), and we will meet it again in later units. You should recognize, then, that it is this sophisticated view, *not* the suggestion that traits or personality are unimportant, that currently constitutes the mainstream perspective within our field.[8]

PERSONALITY: ITS IMPACT IN WORK SETTINGS

During the course of your career, you will encounter hundreds of different persons. These individuals will vary along an almost countless number of dimensions—every one you can imagine now, plus others that are certain to take you by surprise. Many of these differences will be of interest in their own right, but they will have little bearing on organizational behavior. In contrast, others will play a key role in this respect. It is on several of the most important of these work- and organization-related characteristics that we focus now.

The Type A Behavior Pattern: Who Succeeds—and Who Survives?

Think back over all the persons you have known. Can you recall any who always seemed to work under great pressure, were hard-driving and super-competitive, and who were both impatient and aggressive? Now, in contrast, try to remember people who showed the opposite pattern—individuals who were generally relaxed and easy-going, sociable, and not very competitive. The persons you now have in mind in each of these categories represent contrasting patterns of behavior labeled, respectively, **Type A** and **Type B.** While these are clearly extremes on a continuous dimension, it appears that most people actually do fall into

Boundary Spanning in Organizations: When High Self-Monitoring Can Help

In almost every organization, some persons face the task of transmitting information across internal or external boundaries. That is, they find themselves at the interface between departments or divisions, or at the boundary between their organization and people or groups outside it (e.g., suppliers, customers). As you can readily guess, serving this *boundary spanning* function can be difficult. The persons involved must deal with several different groups—groups that often speak different languages, and have sharply different perspectives. What kind of individuals would best be able to fulfill this role? One possibility is as follows: persons who are flexible, and can readily adjust to different situations and conditions. In short, it seems possible that success as a boundary spanner might be related to the dimension of *self-monitoring*, considered previously. To be more precise, persons high on this dimension, who are sensitive to social cues, and can readily adapt their own behavior to meet the requirements of different situations, may be more effective in this role than persons who are low in self-monitoring, and so less flexible in these respects (refer to Figure 6.2). That this is actually the case is indicated by the findings of a study conducted by Caldwell and O'Reilly.[9]

The subjects in this investigation were field representatives for a large franchise organization. Their duties included explaining company positions to franchise-holders, mediating disputes between these persons and the company, and referring franchise-holders to sources of information or suppliers. In short, they definitely served as boundary spanners, moving information back and forth between the home office and franchisees. Caldwell and O'Reilly asked these field representatives to complete a questionnaire designed to measure individual differences in self-monitoring. In addition, they obtained performance ratings of the representatives, previously supplied by their supervisors. When these variables were then subjected to careful analysis, evidence for the hypothesis mentioned above was obtained: the higher individuals' self-monitoring score, the higher their performance ratings. Interestingly, this relationship appeared to be much stronger during employees' first few months on the job than later on, perhaps because persons low in self-monitoring soon discover that they

---

one group or the other. Specifically, about 40 percent of the population is Type A and 60 percent is Type B.[10]

Obviously, the differences between Type A and Type B persons have important implications for behavior in work settings. For example, hard-driving, competitive individuals would be expected to act in very different ways from their more relaxed counterparts (refer to Figure 6.3 on page 184). As we shall soon see, this is in fact the case. But Type A and Type B persons also differ in other key respects that are, perhaps, less apparent. The most important of these involve personal health and social relations.

The Type A pattern and health. Common sense suggests that highly competitive, driven persons are more likely to expire prematurely than calm and relaxed ones. It is for this reason that friends and relatives often plead with such hyperactive individuals to "slow down and live longer." In this case, common sense seems to be

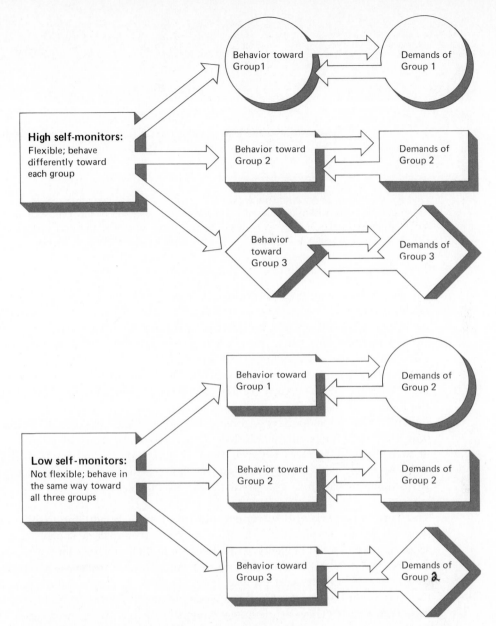

FIGURE 6.2 *Self-monitoring and Boundary Spanning.*
Because they can readily adjust their behavior so as to meet the requirements of different groups, *high self-monitors* may be quite successful in *boundary-spanning* roles. In contrast, *low self-monitors,* who are less flexible, may encounter more difficulties in such positions.

are not successful in this role, and seek employment elsewhere. In any case, whatever the explanation for this latter finding, it appears that self-monitoring can play a key role in the successful performance of at least one important type of job. This, in turn, is only the first illustration of a fact we will meet on several more occasions in this chapter: where organizational behavior is concerned, individual differences *can* often make a difference.

FIGURE 6.3 *A Type A Person in Action.*
This person's driven, work-centered behavior is characteristic of the Type A behavior pattern. As you can see, it doesn't endear him to his co-workers! (Source: Copyright, 1981, Universal Press Syndicate. Reprinted with permission. All rights reserved.)

correct. Research findings indicate that Type A persons are more than twice as likely as Type Bs to experience serious heart disease.[11] Further, they are more likely to suffer a second heart attack if the first one is not fatal. In this respect, certainly, Type A persons pay a high price for their hard-driving, overstimulated lifestyle. (Refer to our discussion of stress in Chapter 7.)

Recent evidence helps explain precisely why Type As are so much more at risk than Type Bs in this regard. Briefly, they seem to respond to stress with more pronounced physiological reactions than Type Bs. When performing stressful, difficult tasks, Type As have significantly higher blood pressure and pulse rates than Type Bs.[12] Interestingly, this does *not* seem to be the case when they are at rest; at such times, differences between Type As and Type Bs are minimal. But since Type As rarely slow down, they subject their cardiovascular systems to greater stress much of the time, with predictable consequences.

The Type A pattern and interpersonal relations. In addition to differences in personal health, Type A and Type B persons also demonstrate sharply contrasting styles of interpersonal behavior. First, because of their constant time-urgency (they always seem to feel that they are running out of time), Type As tend to be more impatient with others, and grow angry with them if people delay them in any manner. Second, when given a choice, Type As prefer to work by themselves rather than with others. They are definitely "loners" rather than "team players." Third, Type As are more irritable and aggressive than Type Bs. They lose their tempers more frequently, and are more likely to lash out at others for even slight provocations.[13] The other side of the coin, of course, is that the super-competitive, always-in-a-hurry style of Type As often irritates or annoys persons with whom they work. (Such reactions were illustrated in Figure 6.3.) Clearly, then, several characteristics shown by Type A individuals can get them into personal difficulties in work settings.

The Type A pattern and performance. Given their competitiveness and hyperactivity, it seems reasonable to expect that Type As will often work harder on various tasks than other persons, and will perform at higher levels. In fact, however, the situation turns out to be more complex. On the one hand, Type As *do* tend to work faster on many tasks than Type Bs, even when no pressure or deadline is involved. Similarly, they complain less about hard work and describe themselves as feeling less tired when it is completed than do Type Bs.[14] In addition, they tend to seek more challenge in their work and daily lives than Type Bs. This latter fact is clearly demonstrated by the findings of a recent study conducted by Ortega and Pipal.[15]

In this investigation, male subjects previously identified as being either Type A or Type B (on the basis of their responses to a standard inventory designed to measure these patterns), were asked to choose problems on which they would later work. These varied greatly in difficulty. Thus, subjects' preference for varying degrees of challenge could be assessed from their choices. Another feature of the study involved the activities subjects were asked to perform immediately prior to choosing among the problems. Some engaged in procedures designed to induce feelings of relaxation, others merely sat quietly during this period, and the remainder worked on a simple task designed to raise their level of activation. These procedures were included to determine whether, as has sometimes been suggested, the harder Type As work (and therefore the more activated they become), the greater the degree of effort and challenge they then seek. Results offered support for this hypothesis, and also for the view that Type As do tend to prefer greater challenge in their work than Type Bs. Specifically, Type As chose more difficult problems than Type Bs, and the magnitude of this difference increased as subjects' level of activation rose (refer to Figure 6.4, page 186). As noted by Ortega and Pipal, these findings suggest that Type As are often true "workaholics." Indeed, they seem to develop a kind of tolerance for work, so that the more effort they expend, the more they feel the need for even greater challenge. Given their tendency to get trapped in this dangerous type of spiral, it is little wonder that Type As sometimes work themselves right into the ground!

While all the evidence we have reviewed so far seems to support the view that Type As will usually, if not always, perform better than Type Bs, there appear to be situations in which the reverse is true. For example, Type As frequently do poorly on tasks requiring patience or careful, considered judgment. They are simply in too much of a hurry to complete such work in an effective manner.[16] More important, surveys reveal that most members of *top* management are Type B, not Type A. (Note our emphasis on the word "top"; at lower levels of organizational hierarchies, Type As may indeed outnumber Type Bs.) Several factors probably contribute to this somewhat surprising finding. First, it is possible that Type As simply don't last long enough to rise to the highest management levels—the health risks outlined above tend to remove them from contention at an early age![17] Second, the impatient, always-in-a-hurry style of Type A is probably incompatible with the decision-making role of top-level executives. Finally, the impatient, hostile style of Type As may lead them to make many enemies—a factor that can count heavily against them when the possibility of promotion arises.

In sum, available evidence suggests that Type As tend to do better than Type Bs on some tasks—especially ones involving time pressure or solitary work. However, they may actually do *worse* than Type Bs on tasks involving complex judgment, accuracy rather than speed, and working as part of a team. Thus, neither pattern

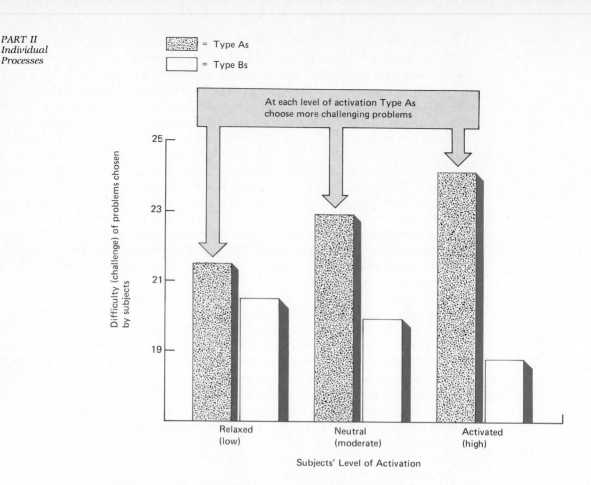

FIGURE 6.4   *Type As: Often, They Seek Greater Challenge.*
Type As chose more difficult (and therefore more challenging) problems than Type Bs. Moreover, the higher subjects' level of activation at the time of such choices, the larger the difference in this respect between Type As and Type Bs. (Source: Based on data from Ortega and Pipal, 1984; see Note 15.)

appears to have an overall edge over the other. Rather, it is the nature of the tasks being performed that will usually determine whether Type As or Type Bs tend to excel. This is an important point for organizations to consider when choosing which of these two types of persons to place in specific jobs.

Machiavellianism: Manipulating Others as a Way of Life

In 1513 the Italian philosopher Niccolo Machiavelli published *The Prince.* In it, he outlined a ruthless strategy for seizing and holding political power. The basic idea behind his approach was simple: other persons can be readily manipulated or used for our own purposes if we remember to stick to a few basic rules. Among the guiding principles he recommended were these: (1) never show humility—arrogance is far more effective when dealing with others; (2) morality and ethics are for the weak—powerful persons should feel free to lie, cheat, and deceive whenever this suits their purpose; (3) it is much better to be feared than loved. In more general terms, Machiavelli urged those who desired power to adopt a totally pragmatic approach to life. Let others be swayed by considerations of friendship, loyalty or fair play, he suggested; a truly successful leader should always be above such influences. In a word, he or she should be willing to do *whatever it takes to get his or her way.*

Machiavelli and the princes he advised have long since vanished. Yet, the basic ideas he developed are still very much with us. In fact, they are readily visible in several books that have made their way onto the best-seller lists in recent years—volumes such as Korda's *Power: How to Use It* and Ringer's *Winning Through Intimidation.* The popularity of such books suggest that people are as fascinated by features of Machiavelli's approach today as they were almost five hundred years ago. Of course, it is one thing to be intrigued by such tactics, and quite another to put them to actual use. Are there really individuals who choose to live by the ruthless, self-serving creed proposed by Machiavelli? The answer appears to be "yes." When large numbers of persons complete a test designed to measure acceptance of a Machiavellian approach to life (the *Mach Scale*), many receive very high scores.[18] Thus, persons with a Machiavellian orientation (*High Machs* as they are often termed) are far from rare. Indeed, you are almost certain to encounter them on many occasions during your own career. Since this is the case, it is probably useful for you to know two things about them: (1) how they operate—how they attempt to manipulate others for their own gain, and (2) how you can defend yourself against them.

High Machs: How they operate.   As we noted in Chapter 5, we all seek to influence others; this is a basic part of life both within organizations and elsewhere. Yet, few persons manage to bend others to their will quite as effectively as High Machs. What accounts for their success in this endeavor? Several factors seem to play a role. First, High Machs are true *pragmatists*. As far as they are concerned, any means is justified, so long as it helps them attain their ends. Thus, they are perfectly willing to lie, cheat, play "dirty tricks," or engage in virtually any other actions that will help them reach their goals. Needless to say, this often gives them a large advantage over opponents who *are* guided, at least in part, by principles of morality. Second, High Machs often possess many characteristics associated with success at persuasion. In many cases they are confident, eloquent, and competent. When these traits are combined with their pure pragmatism, the combination can be very difficult to resist! Third, High Machs are often very adept at choosing situations in which their favorite tactics are most likely to work. Such situations are ones in which they can interact with their intended victims in a face-to-face manner (and so make use of their persuasive skills), in which there are few firm rules (this leaves High Machs considerable room for maneuver), and in which others' emotions are running high. Since High Machs themselves never let their "hearts rule their heads," they can take full advantage of the fact that others' emotions make them especially vulnerable to manipulation.[19] Finally, High-Machs are also skilled at forming coalitions or alliances with others—alliances that usually work to their advantage. For example, in one well-known demonstration of this fact, ten $1.00 bills were placed on a table in front of groups of three individuals: one High Mach, one Low Mach, and one person who fell in between these extremes.[20] They were told that the money would belong to any two of them who agreed on how to divide it; the third individual would be totally "cut out." As you can see from Figure 6.5, the High Machs did exceedingly well in this situation. They usually managed to lure one of the other players into a coalition in which *they* received the lion's share of the money.

High Machs: Defending yourself against them.   Now that you know something about how High Machs operate, we can turn to a practical question: What steps can you take to protect yourself against them? Fortunately, there are several tactics you can use to blunt their self-serving strategies. Several of these are outlined below.

(1) *Expose them to others.*   One reason why High Machs often get away with breaking their promises, lying to others, and so on is that in many cases of this type,

FIGURE 6.5   *High Machs: A Demonstration of Their Skills.*
In one study demonstrating the persuasive skills of High Mach persons, ten $1.00 bills were placed in front of groups of three subjects (one High Mach, one Low Mach, and one individual in between). The money would belong to any two who could agree on how to divide it. As shown here, High Machs did much better in this situation than their opponents—they walked off with a larger share of the money. (Source: Based on data from Christie and Geis, 1970; see Note 18.)

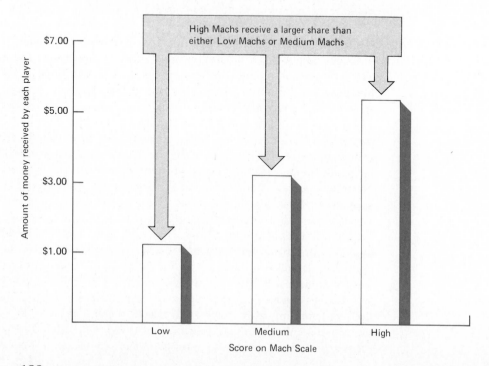

their victims choose to remain silent. This is hardly surprising; when one has been "had," this in itself is punishing enough. Informing the world about such treatment compounds the damage to one's ego. While remaining silent in such cases is understandable, though, it plays directly into the hands of High Mach persons. Thus, the moral is clear: if you have been treated unfairly by someone else, and suspect that he or she is an unprincipled High Mach, tell other members of your organization about it. The costs to your self-image may be high, but the costs of failing to do so may ultimately be much greater.

(2) *Pay attention to what others do—not simply what they say.* As we noted previously, High Machs are often masters at deception. They frequently succeed in convincing others that they have their best interests at heart, just while they are busy cutting the ground from beneath them. While it is often difficult to see through such maneuvers, useful steps in this direction can often be taken by focusing on what others do rather than on what they say. If their actions suggest that they are cold-bloodedly manipulating the persons around them, don't be fooled by statements to the contrary. You are probably face to face with a High Mach, and should avoid becoming one of his or her victims.

(3) *Avoid situations that give High Machs an edge.* In order to assure their success, High Machs prefer to operate in certain types of situations—ones in which others' are emotionally aroused or uncertain about how to behave. The reason for this preference is simple: they realize that under such circumstances, many persons will be distracted, and less likely to recognize the use of various manipulative techniques. It is usually wise, therefore, to be on guard in such situations, or to stay out of them altogether. And if this is not possible, at least avoid making important decisions or commitments in them. Such precautions may assist you in staying *out* of the clutches of dangerous manipulators.

(4) *Beware of one-sided alliances.* A favorite tactic of High Machs is that of luring others into coalitions in which they reap most of the benefits. They accomplish such maneuvers in many ways, but one of the most common is that of "playing both ends against the middle." Briefly, they try to convince the other persons involved that they will join with someone else if their current offer is not quickly accepted. While such bluffs are easy to spot at times when people are cool and collected, they may be more effective when used in situations involving high levels of emotional arousal—a favorite stamping ground of High Machs. If you wish to avoid such traps, therefore, refrain from making such decisions until you have explored all the options—all the potential coalitions open to you. And above all, be very suspicious of offers involving threats (veiled or otherwise) and other types of pressure.

Locus of Control: Are You—Or Others—Master of Your Fate?

Before proceeding, turn to Table 6.1 and follow the directions it contains.

How did you respond? If you chose (a) for most items, you probably believe that there is a direct link between the way you behave and the outcomes you experience. In short, you feel that, by and large, you can control your own fate. In contrast, if you selected (b) in most cases, you probably feel that there is little relationship between how you behave and the outcomes you experience. Rather, it is forces beyond your control (e.g., luck, chance, the actions of others) that tend to shape these results.

The items in Table 6.1 are quite similar to ones on a test designed to measure another important aspect of personality—**locus of control**.[21] At one end of this dimension are *Internals*—persons who feel that their outcomes stem mainly from internal factors (e.g., their own effort, ability, decisions), and so are directly under their own control. At the other extreme are *Externals*—individuals who believe that their outcomes are determined largely by external causes (e.g., fate, luck, the actions of others). Most persons, of course, fall somewhere in between these extremes. However, large individual differences with respect to locus of control exist, so you are likely to encounter many persons who can readily be classified as primarily Internal or External in orientation during the course of your career.

Some scientists believe that a given person's location on the locus of control dimension is determined early in life by certain conditions existing in his or her home environment. Specifically, individuals raised in families in which effort and accomplishment are systematically rewarded tend to become Internals. In contrast, ones raised in families in which rewards seem to occur in a random manner tend to develop as Externals. Whatever the origins of these orientations, however, they have important implications for organizations and organizational behavior.

First, as you might expect, Internals perceive stronger and more direct links between (1) their effort and their performance, and (2) their performance and the kinds of rewards they will receive than do Externals.[22] As we noted in Chapter 3, such expectancies, in turn, often play a key role in motivation. Thus, such differences can exert a powerful effect on actual job performance. Second, and closely related to the points just made, Internals tend to be more successful than Externals. They hold higher level jobs, advance more quickly in their careers, and earn more money.[23] In addition, and to add icing to the cake, they are also more satisfied with

TABLE 6.1 *Locus of Control: An Important Factor in Organizational Behavior.*
Items similar to those used to measure one important aspect of personality.

For each of the items below, indicate whether you feel that choice (a) or choice (b) is closer to your own beliefs.

1. (a) I am the master of my fate.
   (b) A great deal of what happens to me is probably a matter of chance.
2. (a) Promotions are earned through hard work and persistence.
   (b) Making a lot of money is largely a matter of getting the right breaks.
3. (a) People like me can change the course of world affairs if we make ourselves heard.
   (b) It is only wishful thinking to believe that we can really influence what happens in society at large.
4. (a) In my experience, I have noticed that there is usually a direct connection between how hard I study and the grades I get.
   (b) Many times the reactions of teachers seem haphazard to me.
5. (a) Getting along with people is a skill that must be practiced.
   (b) It is almost impossible to figure out how to please some people.

---

their work than are Externals. Finally, Internals seem better able than Externals to cope with several types of work-related stress.[24] Taking all these findings into account, it seems clear that from the point of view of an organization, Internals often make better employees than Externals. Thus, this may be one factor worth considering when decisions relating to hiring or promotion must be made. We should hasten to note, however, that an individual's position along the Internal-External dimension is definitely *not* set in stone. If organizations establish conditions under which good performance is quickly recognized and rewarded, even persons holding strong External beliefs can be induced to shift toward a more Internal orientation. This appears to be one case, then, in which good management—and careful attention to establishing effective reward systems—can make an important difference.

Self-Esteem: Why Self-Evaluations Are Important

Consider two people working for the same company. Both possess similar traits and similar job-related skills. However, one has a positive view of himself—he believes that he is a talented person with many excellent qualities. In short he possesses high **self-esteem.** In contrast, the other holds a very negative view of his own traits. He feels that he is sadly lacking in talent, and that he has many characteristics other persons find unattractive. In a word, he has low self-esteem. Which of these persons will do better work? While it's impossible to say for certain, a good guess is *the first*. A substantial body of research findings indicate that persons high in self-esteem often demonstrate higher levels of job satisfaction, motivation, and actual productivity than persons low on this dimension.[25] There are several mechanisms that may account for these findings. For example, persons high in self-esteem generally possess better social skills than those low in self-esteem. As a result, they make better impressions on others, and get along with them more effectively. This can contribute to their high morale and good performance. Second, low self-esteem is often accompanied by feelings of depression and helplessness. Such reactions can seriously interfere with performance on many different tasks. For these and other reasons (refer to Figure 6.6 on page 192), individuals' self-esteem may have important implications for their behavior in work settings.

Unfortunately, however, even this is not the entire picture. Low self-esteem seems to exact other costs as well. One of the most important of these involves the ability to conduct an adequate job search, and then obtain a suitable job. Research findings suggest that persons suffering from low self-esteem are far less effective in this crucial task than those possessing high self-esteem. Clear evidence pointing to these conclusions has recently been reported by Ellis and Taylor.[26]

These researchers asked business school seniors to complete several questionnaires. Some of these forms provided measures of their self-esteem, while others provided information on the nature and success of subject's job search (e.g., the sources of information about jobs they used; the number of job offers they received). In addition, ratings of participants by organizational recruiters who had interviewed them were also gathered. It was predicted that low self-esteem individuals

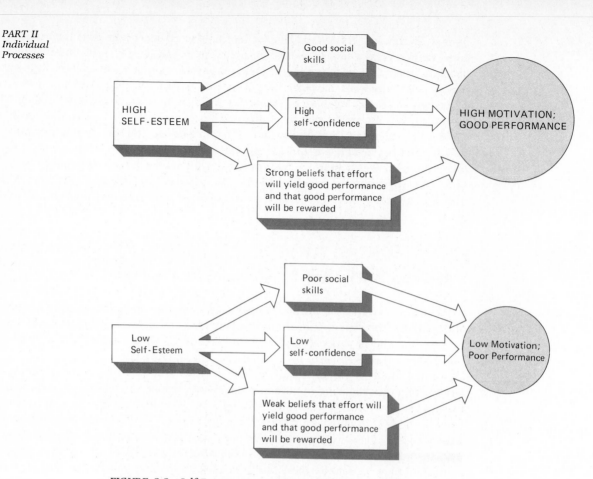

FIGURE 6.6   *Self-Esteem: Its Impact on Behavior at Work.*
As shown here, individuals high in self-esteem (upper panel) possess several characteristics that may contribute to high levels of motivation and performance. In contrast, persons low in self-esteem (lower panel) possess characteristics that may interfere with effective organizational behavior.

would generally conduct a less adequate job search, and attain less favorable results in this process, than persons high in self-esteem. Specifically, it was expected that the lower subjects' self-esteem, the less likely they would be to use informal sources of information (e.g., friends, relatives), the fewer offers they would receive, and the lower the ratings they would get from interviewers. Results offered support for all of these hypotheses. Thus, low self-esteem appeared to be costly indeed for these young individuals about to launch their careers.

While our comments so far may seem somewhat discouraging, there are grounds for concluding this discussion on a positive note. Low self-esteem, it appears, is not necessarily a permanent state of affairs. On the contrary, several practical techniques for enhancing the self-concepts of such persons exist. We have already examined one of these in Chapter 4, where we noted that inducing low self-esteem persons to attribute their failures to *external* rather than *internal* causes can help improve their confidence, and so their subsequent performance.[27] Other techniques include exposing such persons to positive feedback or success, and helping them to overcome the feelings of depression and hopelessness from which they often suffer. Through these and related procedures, the harmful effects of a negative self-image can be countered, and self-esteem itself may be enhanced. The results of such changes can be of major benefit both to the individuals involved, and to the organizations in which they work. (For a concrete illustration of the devastating effects of low self-esteem, see the **Case in Point** insert on page 194.)

Work-Related Motives: Achievement and Power

At several points in this book, we have called your attention to a basic fact about people: often, they possess sharply contrasting motives or patterns of motives. While some are ambitious and burn for success, others are largely lacking in such desire; while some prefer to be in charge and exert power, others are happy to receive rather than exert influence; and while some view friendship and good relations with others as necessary to their happiness, other persons have little interest in these matters. Do such differences in individual motivation affect organizational behavior? The answer is simple: they do. In fact, differences with respect to several basic motives can affect the course of individuals' careers, their performance on many tasks, their ability to serve as leaders, and many other work-related outcomes. Research findings suggest that many different motives are relevant to organizational behavior and organizational processes. Among the most important, however are the **need for achievement,** and the **need for power.**

As its name suggests, the **need for achievement** relates to the strength of individuals' desire to excel—to do something better than others do it. Research by McClelland and his colleagues indicates that persons high on this dimension show several consistent tendencies.[28] First, they are task-oriented in outlook. Their major concern is getting things done and accomplishing concrete goals. Other considerations, such as good relations with others, are of much less concern to them. Second, they tend to prefer situations involving moderate levels of risk or difficulty—ones in which the odds are strongly in their favor. Third, persons high in need for achievement strongly desire feedback on their performance. This allows them to adjust their goals in terms of current conditions, and to know just when—and to what degree—they have succeeded. Finally, such persons prefer situations in which they can take personal responsibility for outcomes. One in which external factors control results have little appeal for them.

At first glance, it seems reasonable to expect that persons high in need for achievement will tend to attain greater success in their careers than persons low in this motive. To some extent, this seems to be true. For example, high need-achievers tend to gain promotions more rapidly than low need-achievers, at least at lower levels of organizational hierarchies.[29] However, contrary to what you might predict, persons high in need for achievement do not always make better managers than

"You're Your Own Worst Enemy!"

Jerry Zodek is nervous. In fact, he squirms in his chair, licks his lips, fidgets with his tie, and shows all the classic symptoms of anxiety. The reason for his discomfort is simple: he's about to have his first semi-annual appraisal session with Jeanne Burt, his immediate supervisor. At this meeting, she'll give him formal feedback on his performance with the company so far, and discuss areas where there's room for improvement. As he waits, Jerry's thoughts race wildly, adding to his growing panic.

"Why doesn't she call me in already?" he wonders to himself. "I just can't stand this waiting. I'd rather get it over with. I know what's going to happen—it's going to be a disaster. Why can't I ever do anything right? If only . . ." At this point, Jerry's thoughts are interrupted by Jeanne's secretary, who tells him that she's ready for him, and that he can go in. Trembling visibly, and on unsteady legs, Jerry enters Jeanne's office.

"Hi, Jerry," Jeanne begins. "Take a seat and we'll begin right away."

"O.K.," Jerry murmurs weakly. "But please be merciful. Give me the bad news as soon as possible."

At this, Jeanne raises her eyebrows and frowns slightly, but she makes no comment. Instead, she launches into delivery of the appraisal.

"Well, first, let's go through the checklist. As you see, I've rated your performance over the past six months on each of these dimensions. Overall, the pattern is pretty encouraging. Not bad at all. See, I've given you high scores on motivation and effort, as well as on cooperative attitude and willingness to listen to advice. The only area where I think you could do a little better is here, in terms of initiative and confidence. Lots of times I get the impression that you don't really trust your own judgment as much as you could."

Jerry looks stunned. This is much better than he expected. How could *he* be getting such positive feedback when he's such a boob? Maybe Jeanne is just being kind; she does seem to be a soft-hearted person. But she's really put her finger on it with her remarks about his lack of confidence.

"Well, um, you're, um, right" Jerry stammers. "I guess I'm really not too sure of myself. But when you're

a blunderer like me, that's not surprising. I mean, I've always known that I'm not really much of a person—you know, the kind who's lucky to just get by. But anyway, I'm glad you can tell I'm trying—I know I don't have much going for me, but I do give it my best . . ."

"Oh, I can tell you're trying, all right. But really, why do you want to sell yourself short all the time? You've got plenty of good points, from what I can tell. No one's perfect, you know."

"I know that," Jerry answers, growing redder in the face by the minute. "But some people come a lot closer than others. Besides, things just don't seem to work out too well for me. Remember that problem with the Sherwood account? I should have caught that before it made trouble for Bud. But that's me all the way; I always fold just when I'm needed most."

"Now wait a minute," Jeanne says with some feeling. "That wasn't *your* fault. It was Jane's responsibility to spot it. You have other things to keep you busy. Why do you want to take the blame?"

"Well, I don't, but I just feel that lots of times, I don't hold up my end, so when things go wrong, it's probably my fault—if only I could have a success once in a while."

"But you *do*, Jerry. I think you handled the people at Pensalco really well. You got things straightened out as well as anyone could."

"Yeah, it did work out. But I think that was just blind luck. It wasn't anything special I did. Anyone could have gotten the same result."

"I don't agree, Jerry. I think *you* deserve the credit." Then, pausing, Jeanne shakes her head. "Honestly, I don't know what I'm going to do with you. I think you have real potential—that you could be one of our better people. But you'll never reach it if you don't stop seeing yourself in such a negative light. The way things are, *you're your own worst enemy!*"

Questions

(1) How would you describe Jerry's current level of self-esteem?

(2) What specific aspects of his behavior are most revealing of these feelings about himself?

(3) Do you think Jeanne's comments, and her appraisals of Jerry's work, will affect his self-esteem? If so, how?

(4) What steps could Jeanne take to raise Jerry's level of self-esteem? If these succeeded, how do you think it would affect his performance?

---

ones lower in such motivation. In fact, often, they are worse.[30] This seems to be due to two factors. First, high need-achievers want to do everything themselves—an approach that is frowned upon in many organizations. Second, as noted above, they desire immediate feedback on their work. Often, this is unavailable, and its absence can exert adverse effects upon the efficiency of high need-achievers.

A second motive closely related to behavior in organizational settings is the *need for power*. Persons high on this dimension have a strong desire to exert influence over others and to control their behavior. Initially, you might expect that persons high in such power motivation will tend to rise to positions of leadership and influence within their organizations. Once again, however, research findings indicate that the relationship is somewhat more complex than common sense suggests. Specifically, it appears that high need for power *is* associated with leadership and actual power, but only when it occurs in combination with certain other factors. This fact is clearly demonstrated in a longitudinal study conducted by McClelland and Boyatzis.[31]

In this investigation, the success of several hundred managers at AT&T in attaining promotions over a sixteen-year period was related to their possession of what has been termed the **leadership motive pattern** (LMP). Briefly, this pattern consists of a moderately high need for power, coupled with high self-control, and relatively low need for affiliation (the need for warm, friendly relations with others). Persons possessing this pattern are expected to be more successful as managers than persons lacking it for the following reasons. Their high need for power permits them to focus on gaining influence over others, while at the same time, their low need for affiliation permits them to make difficult decisions without worrying much about being disliked by subordinates. Their high level of self-control, in turn, helps them to follow orderly procedures, and work within existing organizational systems.

In order to assess the role of this pattern in managerial success, McClelland and Boyatzis scored managers' responses to the *Thematic Apperception Test* for need for power, need for affiliation, and self-control. On the basis of these scores, they then classified subjects into two groups: those showing the leadership motive pattern and those not possessing it. (Managers were also divided into two additional categories—technical and nontechnical—depending on the nature of their job.) Next, the researchers obtained information on subjects' job level both eight and sixteen years later. As you can see from Figure 6.7 (page 196), results offered clear support for the role of the leadership motive pattern in managerial success, at least in the case of nontechnical managers. For this group, persons possessing this pattern of motives were much more likely to be promoted to higher-level jobs than persons not possessing it. Additional evidence indicated that the reason such findings were not obtained for managers holding technical jobs was that for such persons, promotion depended mainly on technical competence, *not* the possession of leadership qualities.

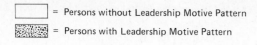

= Persons without Leadership Motive Pattern

= Persons with Leadership Motive Pattern

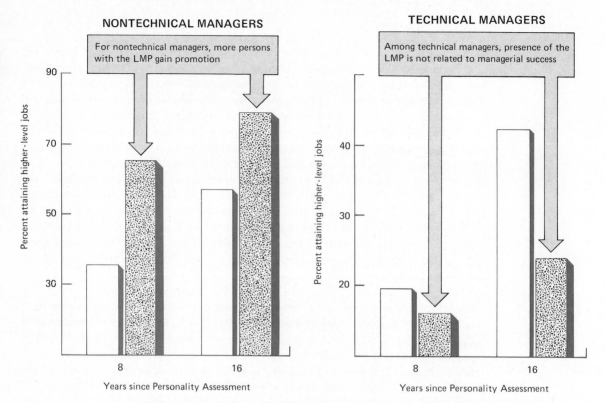

NONTECHNICAL MANAGERS

For nontechnical managers, more persons with the LMP gain promotion

TECHNICAL MANAGERS

Among technical managers, presence of the LMP is not related to managerial success

Percent attaining higher-level jobs

Years since Personality Assessment

Percent attaining higher-level jobs

Years since Personality Assessment

FIGURE 6.7   *The Leadership Motive Pattern: Its Role in Managerial Success.*
Among nontechnical managers, possession of the leadership motive pattern (LMP) was associated with success: a greater proportion of persons with than without this pattern attained promotion to higher level jobs. Among technical managers, in contrast, possession of the LMP did not seem to influence such success. (Source: Based on data from McClelland and Boyatzis, 1982; see Note 31.)

While these results have not been confirmed in all subsequent studies, there do seem to be sufficient grounds for concluding that several motives (and individual differences in these) are closely linked to key aspects of organizational behavior.[32] The nature of this relationship, however, is far from simple. In order to understand how individuals' motives influence their job performance or careers, we must take account not only of the motives themselves, but also of the combinations or patterns in which they occur, the specific jobs being performed, and the general organizational context in which these motives operate. Only when the complex interplay of such factors is given full consideration can knowledge about individuals' motives provide us with useful insights into both their present and future organizational behavior.

196

MEASURING PERSONALITY: SOME BASIC METHODS

Physical traits such as height and weight can be measured directly. Various aspects of personality, however, cannot be assessed in a similar manner. There are no rulers for measuring ambition, no thermometers for determining self-confidence. How, then, can we hope to quantify these often-hidden characteristics or traits? Fortunately, several methods for accomplishing this task exist. Three of these are *self-report inventories or questionnaires*, special *projective techniques*, and complex procedures known as **assessment centers.**

Inventories and Questionnaires

Perhaps the most widely used method for assessing personality involves the use of *inventories* or *questionnaires*. These consist of a series of questions or statements to which individuals respond in various ways. For example, they may be asked to indicate which statements are true of themselves, or to indicate whether, or how often, they experience certain feelings. Their answers to these items are then scored in accordance with special keys. The numbers obtained in this manner are then compared with those obtained for hundreds or even thousands of other persons who have previously completed the same inventory. In this way, a specific person's *relative standing* on the trait or traits of interest can be determined. For example, it might be found that an applicant for a job as a loan officer at a bank has scored higher than 90 percent of recent college graduates on a measure of willingness to take risks. Obviously, this information could have a direct bearing on the decision to hire this person. Similarly, it might be found that an individual seeking a job in which she will have to handle complaints from irate customers scores lower than most persons on a measure of assertiveness. Again, this could be useful in the personnel officer's decision. Because a great deal is known about the best ways to construct psychological tests, and to assess their **validity**—the extent to which they measure what they purport to measure—many experts view inventories and questionnaires as among the best measures of personality currently available. (For an example of one such inventory, see Table 6.2 on page 198.)

Projective Techniques

A markedly different approach to the measurement of personality, **projective techniques,** is based on an intriguing assumption. If we expose individuals to ambiguous stimuli and then ask them to tell us what they see, each person will "read" different meanings into these stimuli. Then, the pattern of their responses will tell us much about aspects of their personalities that would otherwise be hidden from view.

We have already mentioned one projective technique used extensively by both

TABLE 6.2   *Personality Questionnaires: An Example.*
The items shown here are similar to ones from a personality questionnaire designed to measure individual differences in *sensation-seeking:* the tendency to seek new experiences, excitement, and high levels of risk.

For each item below, circle the letter of the choice (a or b) that best describes your preferences or the way you feel.

1. (a) I often wish I could be a mountain climber.
   (b) I can't understand people who risk their necks climbing mountains.
2. (a) A sensible person avoids activities that are dangerous.
   (b) I sometimes like to do things that are a little frightening.
3. (a) I would like to take up the sport of water-skiing.
   (b) I would not like to take up water-skiing.
4. (a) I would not like to learn to fly an airplane.
   (b) I would like to learn to fly an airplane.
5. (a) I enjoy spending time in the familiar surroundings of home.
   (b) I get very restless if I have to stay around home for any length of time.

---

researchers and practitioners in connection with organizational behavior: the *Thematic Apperception Test* (*TAT*). This test consists of a series of ambiguous drawings, and people taking it are asked to make up a story about each. These are carefully analyzed for certain basic themes, in accordance with highly specific scoring procedures. The TAT is often used to measure various aspects of individuals' motivation, such as their need for achievement, need for power, and need for affiliation. As we have already seen, such motives are closely related to several aspects of organizational behavior. (Please note, by the way, that the task of scoring and interpreting projective tests is complex. Thus, it should only be performed by individuals who have had special training in such procedures.)

Assessment Centers: Identifying Management Potential

A major task faced by organizations is identifying talented persons—ones suited for management or leadership roles. Many techniques for accomplishing this task have been developed, but among the most successful of these to date are **assessment centers.**[33] The rationale behind these procedures can be simply stated: it is assumed that certain traits or characteristics are closely related to success as a manager. Thus, careful assessment of these characteristics should prove useful in predicting individuals' potential for this role.

Assessment centers are much more elaborate in scope than the other techniques for measuring personality and related individual characteristics we have considered so far. Typically, they occupy two or three days rather than one or two hours of an individual's time. During this period, the persons being assessed are asked to perform a wide range of tasks designed to simulate conditions and activities they might well encounter in their actual (or future) jobs. For example, one assessment center, run for many years by AT&T, requires two days of testing, and includes an "in-basket" exercise (in which individuals must deal with and integrate a number of memos and other sources of information), leaderless group discussions, simulated interviews, paper-and-pencil tests, and various management games or simulations. Another key aspect of assessment centers is their emphasis on a number of different characteristics. Information relating to administrative skills, work motivation, interpersonal skills, creativity, social dominance, maturity, independence, and many other characteristics is gathered. In some cases, the individuals who carry out these assessments are specially trained professionals (e.g., psychologists). In other cases, they are people highly experienced in the tasks and jobs involved (e.g., managers). Further, in some uses of assessment centers, the raters discuss their reactions to the persons being evaluated until they reach a consensus. In others, individual ratings by each assessor are maintained, and no consensus is sought. Regardless of such differences, however, all uses of assessment centers involve efforts to measure a number of work-related characteristics through a wide range of tasks, and careful observations by several assessors (i.e., raters).

That assessment centers are in fact successful in their major task—predicting management potential—is suggested by the findings of many different studies.[34] As an example of this work, we will briefly consider an investigation conducted by Ritchie and Moses.[35] In this project, more than 1,600 female managers employed by the Bell System participated in two-day assessment. These assessments took place during 1973 and 1974. As a result of their performance on many different tasks, each participant was assigned an overall rating of future management potential. These ranged from "more than acceptable" through "acceptable," "questionable," and "not acceptable." In order to determine if these ratings were useful in predicting future management success, records of participants' management level on December 31, 1980, were obtained. (More than 1,000 members of the original sample were still employed by Bell at that time.) Results were quite encouraging: the ratings assigned to individuals approximately seven years earlier correlated positively, and significantly, with their current management position (+ .47). Further, managers who, on the basis of the assessment center, were identified as having potential for advancement to higher-level jobs scored higher on several key dimensions than managers who were identified as *not* having such potential for advancement. These included oral and written communication, leadership, energy level, inner work standards, and resistance to stress. These findings, and similar results in other studies with male participants, suggest that assessment centers can be a useful tool, yielding important practical benefits. Further, as noted recently by Lifton, they can also contribute to our knowledge of many traits, and to our basic understanding of human personality itself.[36] Thus, despite certain drawbacks (e.g., they are costly in terms of time and effort; negative ratings in them can sometimes devastate individual careers) assessment centers appear to represent a potentially valuable technique for gaining added insight into the ways in which individuals differ.

Using Knowledge about Personality:
Some Words of Caution

Personality is clearly a fascinating topic. We are all interested in other people, and insights into their uniqueness are certainly intriguing. Further, as we have already seen, many personality traits appear to have important implications for various aspects of organizational behavior. Given these facts, it is hardly surprising that managers (and others) have often sought to use such information for several purposes: employee selection, placement, and even performance appraisal. While we fully understand the temptation to do so, there are several reasons for exercising caution in this regard, and we wish to call these to your attention.

First, many measures of personality are of doubtful *reliability* and *validity*. That is, they do not yield the same scores when applied to the same persons on different occasions, and may not always measure what they claim to measure. To the extent this is so, it is unwise to base important decisions about employees on them. Further, it is actually *illegal* to do so; laws in the United States and several other nations require that procedures used in placement and selection be valid (i.e., predictive of actual on-the-job performance). If they are not, their use is forbidden. Second, even when measures of personality are both reliable and valid, relationships between the traits they assess and organizational behavior are often complex. Thus, considerable caution must be adopted in the interpretation and use of such measures. Third, when using information about personality, it is all too easy to fall into the trap of viewing human beings as mere collections of traits. Doing so may lead to a lack of attention to the impact of situational factors, and so to the important (and often complex) person-by-situation interactions mentioned earlier.

For all these reasons, it is important to exercise caution in the use of information about employees' personality. Such information can indeed be revealing and useful in many contexts. It should be employed, however, only when three conditions prevail: (1) the information itself is to be trusted (it is reliable and valid), (2) it has direct bearing on performance and other key aspects of organizational behavior, and (3) the persons charged with its interpretation possess sufficient knowledge to perform this task successfully. If uncertainty exists with respect to any one of these conditions, our advice is simple: proceed with care; or better yet, don't proceed at all!

SUMMARY

Personality refers to the unique set of stable traits and characteristics possessed by individuals. Contrary to a view popular in the past, such traits do seem to exist, and to exert strong effects upon behavior in many different contexts. However, individuals also differ with respect to a characteristic known as *self-monitoring*. Persons high on this dimension adjust their behavior to changing external conditions, and so show little stability across situations. In contrast, persons low on this dimension generally behave in accordance with their own lasting traits, and so demonstrate considerable stability.

Many different traits have direct implications for various aspects of organizational behavior. These include the *Type A behavior pattern*, *Machiavellianism*, *locus of control*, *self-esteem*, and several motives (e.g., *need for achievement*, *need for power*). Individual differences on these dimensions have been found to be related to performance on various tasks, personal health, success as a manager, interpersonal relations, effectiveness of job search, and many other work-related outcomes. Thus, attention to these and other dimensions of personality may be of considerable practical value both to individuals and to organizations.

Several techniques for measuring personality exist. These include *question-naires* or *inventories,* and *projective techniques.* The most comprehensive procedure for measuring personality involves the use of *assessment centers.* Here, individuals perform a wide range of tasks designed to yield information on many different traits, over a two- or three-day period. Information obtained through assessment centers has important uses in the selection and placement of employees, and has been found to predict managerial success.

KEY TERMS

assessment centers: A technique for measuring various personality traits in which individuals perform a wide variety of tasks during a two- to three-day period.

leadership motive pattern (LMP):   A pattern consisting of high need for power, low need for affiliation, and a high degree of self-control. This pattern of motives is associated with success as a manager.

locus of control: Refers to the extent to which individuals believe that their outcomes stem from internal causes, and so are under their own control, or from external causes, and so are beyond their personal influence.

Machiavellianism: A personality trait involving willingness to manipulate or use others for one's own purposes.

need for achievement: The need to excel—to do something better than others do it.

need for power: The need to exert influence over others or control their behavior.

personality: The unique but stable set of characteristics possessed by a specific individual.

projective techniques: Methods for measuring personality in which ambiguous stimuli are presented to individuals. Their reactions to these stimuli then provide information on their major traits.

self-esteem: An individual's characteristic evaluation of himself or herself.

self-monitoring: The extent to which individuals adjust their behavior to external, situational factors, or, instead, act in ways consistent with their traits and values. Persons high on this dimension behave differently in different situations, while those low in self-monitoring show higher levels of consistency.

Type A behavior pattern: A pattern of behavior involving impatience, competitiveness, hostility, and a tendency to seek high levels of challenge in one's work.

Type B behavior pattern: A pattern of behavior involving a relaxed, easy-going, noncompetitive lifestyle.

validity: In the context of personality, refers to the extent to which a test designed to assess some trait or characteristic actually measures that trait.

NOTES

1. S. Feshbach and B. Weiner (1982). *Personality.* Lexington, Mass.: D.C. Heath.

2. W. Mischel (1977). The interaction of person and situation. In D. Magnusson and N. S. Endler (eds.), *Personality at the crossroads: Current issues in interactional psychology.* Hillsdale, N.J.: Erlbaum.

3. R. A. Schweder (1975). How relevant is an individual difference theory of personality? *Journal of Personality, 43*, 455–484.

4. S. Epstein (1980). The stability of behavior: II. Implications for psychological research. *American Psychologist, 35*, 790–806.

5. D. Byrne and K. Kelley (1981). *An introduction to personality.* Englewood Cliffs, N.J.: Prentice-Hall.

6. S. Epstein (1979). The stability of behavior: I. On predicting most of the people much of the time. *Journal of Personality and Social Psychology, 37*, 1097–1126.

7. M. Snyder (1979). Self-monitoring processes. In L. Berkowitz (ed.), *Advances in experimental social psychology*, vol. 12. New York: Academic Press.

8. H. M. Weiss and S. Adler (1984). Personality and organizational behavior. In B. M. Staw and L. L. Cummings (eds.), *Research in organizational behavior*, vol. 6. New York: JAI Press, pp. 1–50.

9. D. F. Caldwell and C. A. O'Reilly III (1982). Boundary spanning and individual performance: The impact of self-monitoring. *Journal of Applied Psychology, 67*, 124–127.

10. D. C. Glass (1977). *Behavior patterns, stress, and coronary disease.* Hillsdale, N.J.: Erlbaum.

11. R. H. Rosenman, R. J. Brank, C. D. Jenkins, M. Friedman, and M. Wurm (1975). Coronary heart disease in the Western Collaborative Group study: Final follow-up experience of 8.5 years. *Journal of the American Medical Association, 223*, 872–877.

12. D. S. Holmes, B. M. McGilley, and B. K. Houston (1984). Task-related arousal of Type A and Type B persons: Level of challenge and response specificity. *Journal of Personality and Social Psychology, 46*, 1322–1327.

13. D. S. Holmes and M. J. Will (1985). Expression of interpersonal aggression by angered and nonangered persons with the Type A and Type B behavior patterns. *Journal of Personality and Social Psychology, 48*, 723–727.

14. C. S. Carver, A. E. Coleman, and D. C. Glass (1976). The coronary-prone behavior pattern and the suppression of fatigue on a treadmill test. *Journal of Personality and Social Psychology, 33*, 460–466.

15. D. F. Ortega and J. E. Pipal (1984). Challenge seeking and the Type A coronary-prone behavior pattern. *Journal of Personality and Social Psychology, 46*, 1328–1334.

16. D. C. Glass, M. L. Snyder, and J. Hollis (1974). Time urgency and the Type A coronary-prone behavior pattern. *Journal of Applied Social Psychology, 4*, 125–140.

17. M. Friedman and R. H. Rosenman (1974). *Type A behavior and your heart.* New York: Knopf.

18. R. Christie and F. L. Geis, eds. (1970). *Studies in Machiavellianism.* New York: Academic Press.

19. See Note 18.

20. R. Christie and F. L. Geis (1970). The ten dollar game. In R. Christie and F. L. Geis (eds.), *Studies in Machiavellianism.* New York: Academic Press.

21. J. B. Rotter (1975). Some problems and misconceptions related to the consruct of internal versus external control of reinforcement. *Journal of Consulting and Clinical Psychology, 43*, 56–67.

22. A. D. Szilagyi, Jr. and H. P. Sims, Jr. (1975). Locus of control and expectancies across multiple organizational levels. *Journal of Applied Psychology, 60*, 638–640.

23. P. J. Andrisani and C. Nesetl. (1976). Internal-external control as a contributor to and outcome of work experience. *Journal of Applied Psychology, 61*, 156–165.

24. C. R. Anderson (1977). Locus of control, coping behaviors, and performance in a stress setting: A longitudinal study. *Journal of Applied Psychology, 62*, 446–451.

25. P. Tharenou (1979). Employee self-esteem: A review of the literature. *Journal of Vocational Behavior, 15*, 316–346.

26. R. A. Ellis and M. S. Taylor (1983). Role of self-esteem within the job search process. *Journal of Applied Psychology, 68*, 632–640.

27. J. Brockner and J. Guare. Improving the performance of low self-esteem individuals: An attributional approach. *Academy of Management Journal, 36*, 642–656.

28. D. C. McClelland (1977). Entrepreneurship and management in the years ahead. In C. A. Bramlette, Jr. (ed.), *The individual and the future of organizations.* Atlanta: Georgia State University, College of Business Administration.

29. J. D. W. Andrews (1967). The achievement motive and advancement in two types of organization. *Journal of Personality and Social Psychology, 6*, 163–168.

30. D. C. McClelland and D. H. Burnham (1976). Power is the great motivator. *Harvard Business Review*, March/April, 100–110.

31. D. C. McClelland and R. E. Boyatzis (1982). Leadership motive pattern and long-term success in management. *Journal of Applied Psychology, 67*, 737–743.

32. E. T. Cornelius III and F. B. Lane (1984). The power motive and managerial success in a professionally oriented service industry organization. *Journal of Applied Psychology, 69*, 32–39.

33. G. C. Thornton III and W. C. Byham (1982). *Assessment centers and managerial performance.* New York: Academic Press.

34. See Note 33.

35. R. J. Ritchie and J. L. Moses (1983). Assessment center correlates of women's advancement into middle management: A 7-year longitudinal analysis. *Journal of Applied Psychology, 68,* 227–231.

36. P. D. Lifton (1983). Assessment centers: The AT&T and IPAR models. *Journal of Personality Assessment, 47,* 443–445.

CHAPTER 7

STRESS: Its Major Causes

Organizational Causes of Stress   Personal Factors and Stress

STRESS: Its Major Effects

Stress and Health: The Silent Killer   Stress and Mental States   Stress and
Behavior at Work   Alcohol, Drugs, and Stress   Burnout: When Stress
Consumes

MANAGING STRESS: Some Useful Techniques

Personal Tactics for Managing Stress   Organizational Strategies for Managing
Stress

SPECIAL INSERTS

FOCUS ON BEHAVIOR   Unemployment, Commitment to Work, and Stress
FOCUS ON BEHAVIOR   Managing Stress: Long-Term Benefits from Short-Term
  Interventions

Stress at Work: Its Causes, Impact, and Management

As he approaches the door to his office, Ron Jackson feels a knot begin to form deep within the pit of his stomach. Actually, "form" is the wrong word. These days, the knot is always there: it's just bigger and more noticeable at some times than others. And the start of a new day is definitely one of those times. "Funny," Ron thinks to himself as he turns the handle and walks inside, "I didn't always feel this way. I used to actually *enjoy* coming to work. How things change!" Catching sight of the photo on his desk, his thoughts take a different turn. "Gee," he muses, "if only Joan and I hadn't had that fight last night—I feel real bad about it. I know I'm partly to blame. I *did* get home very late, and I guess I wasn't much fun over dinner—but really, it's her fault too. When is she going to understand that my work has to come first? We've got all those bills for Kirsten's school . . . and this is definitely no time to be out looking for another job . . ."

If Ron was feeling upset before entering his office, however, this was just the warm-up. A glance at another part of his desk sends shivers up and down his spine. It's only a few minutes after nine, but already his In-box is filled to overflowing. "Oh no," he groans out loud. "Where did all *this* stuff come from? I mean, I was here until after eight last night. How will I ever get through it all before that meeting? And I wanted some time to go over my presentation. What'll I do?" To stop himself from panicing, Ron begins to sort through the pile on his desk. Fortunately, some of the items aren't urgent, and can be put on the back burner, at least temporarily. Others, though, require immediate attention. One item, especially, stands out from all the rest, and causes Ron's unhappy expression to turn even more glum. It's an angry memo from Sue Clark, his supervisor. He and Sue haven't been getting along lately, and her words have the sharp, sarcastic edge he's learned to dread. "Why can't she ever see things my way?" he wonders. "Life would sure be a lot easier around here if I felt that I could count on her support even once in a while. But no, we just have to go at it all the time. What a rotten break for me—and that annual appraisal is coming up soon." At this last thought, Ron breaks into a cold sweat, and begins to feel as though someone is tightening a vice directly over his temples.

But he doesn't have long to dwell on even *these* problems. At this moment, his intercom buzzes loudly. "Hal Preston's on line 3," his secretary Shirley announces. "And by the way, you're already late for your ten o'clock meeting. You'd better get going." Now the panic Ron managed to avoid before really catches up with him—and with a vengeance. This is an important meeting, and Jack McKenzie, the head of his division, hates to be kept waiting. Making a wild grab for his papers, he rushes off toward the elevator—only to see it close seconds before he can reach it. Taking the stairs two at a time, he is soon badly out of breath. "What a life," he pants as he pauses briefly between floors. "It's like living in a pressure-cooker, and I don't know how much more of it I can stand!"

Have you ever faced conditions like those confronting Ron Jackson? We hope not. Even if you have never had to deal with a similar set of circumstances, though, you probably *have* encountered situations which caused you to experience emotions very similar to Ron's: the growing feeling that you were in imminent danger of being overwhelmed. In short, you undoubtedly have had your own first-hand encounters with **stress.**

Actually, the term *stress* is used in two distinct ways. First, it is often applied to conditions in the world around us that induce feelings of discomfort and tension. In this context, the term *stress* refers to the presence of various **stressors**—external sources of pressure. Second, it is also applied to the internal reactions induced by such stressors—the unpleasant feelings we all label "stress." Both of these perspectives are useful, and will be employed throughout this chapter. The essence of stress, however, seems to lie mainly in our feelings of being one short step away from "the edge." As stated by McGrath, a noted expert on this topic: ". . . there is a potential for stress when an environmental situation is perceived as presenting a demand which threatens to exceed the person's capabilities and resources for meeting it."[1]

As you probably know from your own experience, reactions to stress vary greatly—from shaking knees through feelings of hopelessness and despair. Most, however, fall under three major categories. First, we respond *physiologically*. Our heart rate, blood pressure, and respiration all increase, and the flow of blood to our skeletal muscles (the ones used in "fight" or "flight" reactions) rises sharply. As noted by Hans Selye, a scientist who has studied stress for several decades, these reactions help us cope with threat or danger.[2]

Second, we respond *psychologically*. We experience feelings such as fear, anxiety, and tension. And we actively seek to evaluate or *appraise* the current situation, to determine just how dangerous or threatening it really is. Finally, we respond to stress overtly, with a variety of *coping behaviors*—everything from attempts to deal

FIGURE 7.1   Stress: A Fact of Modern Life.
As suggested by this cartoon, stress derives from many sources and is an all-too-common part of modern life. (Source: Drawing by Cheney; © 1983 The New Yorker Magazine, Inc.)

directly with sources of stress, through actions designed simply to make us feel better (e.g., retreating into an alcohol-induced haze; convincing ourselves that there really isn't much danger).

Unfortunately, stress is far from rare in organizations, or in modern life generally (see Figure 7.1). Moreover, when it occurs, it often exerts far-reaching effects upon the persons involved, and upon their companies. For these reasons, it is an important topic, fully deserving of careful attention within this book. In the discussion that follows, we will focus upon several key aspects of this complex process. First, we consider major *causes* of stress—factors leading to its occurrence. These involve many aspects of organizations, as well as the traits and experiences of particular individuals. Second, we turn to key *effects* of stress—its impact on personal health, performance, and other work-related behaviors. Our discussion here will include attention to **burnout**, a disastrous syndrome that sometimes results from prolonged exposure to intense stress. Finally, we will examine several techniques for *managing stress*—tactics for reducing or countering its harmful impact on both individuals and organizations.

STRESS: ITS MAJOR CAUSES

Stress and work. Somehow, the two words seem to go together. The reason for this pairing in our minds is obvious: most of us experience at least some degree of stress in our jobs. In fact, like Ron, the character in the story on page 205, we are exposed to many different events and conditions that cause us to feel pressured or in danger of being pushed beyond our personal limits. Many different factors contributes to stress in organizational settings, and these vary greatly in both their nature and scope. Most, though, seem to fall into two major categories: factors relating to organizations or jobs themselves, and factors relating to the traits and experiences of specific individuals.

Organizational Causes of Stress

What aspects of jobs or organizations contribute to stress and *strain* (the physical and psychological damage resulting from such pressure)? Unfortunately, the list is long—too long for us to do it full justice here. However, several of the most important of these factors are described below.

Occupational demands: Some jobs are more stressful than others.   Consider the following jobs: production manager, librarian, emergency room physician, farmer, firefighter, college professor, airline pilot. Do you think that they vary in stressfulness? The answer is fairly obvious: they do. Some, such as emergency room physician, firefighter, and airline pilot, subject the persons who hold them to very high levels of stress. Others, such as college professor, farmer, and librarian, do not. This basic fact—that some jobs are much more stressful than others—is confirmed by the results of a careful survey involving more than 130 different occupations.[3] Results indicate that several jobs (e.g., physician, office manager, foreman, waitress or waiter) are quite high in stress. In contrast, others (e.g., maid, craft worker, farm laborer) are much lower in this regard. Additional reasearch, reported recently by Shaw and Riskind, takes these findings one step further, revealing just what aspects of various jobs tend to make them either low or high in stressfulness.[4] These investigators began with a careful review of existing information about the levels of stress experienced by persons holding a wide range of jobs—from executive and architect on the one hand through secretary and pulp mill worker on the other. Then, they related this information about apparent stressfulness to various aspects of the jobs in question. Results indicated that several features of jobs are indeed linked to the levels of stress they produce among persons holding them. For example, the greater the extent to which specific jobs require decisions, the constant monitoring of devices or materials, repeated exchange of information with others, or threatening physical conditions, the more stressful they tend to be (refer to Table 7.1). Further—and this is the key point—such relationships were found to be quite general in nature. That is, the greater the extent to which *any* job possesses these characteristics, the more stressful it tends to be, regardless of the specific work it involves.

TABLE 7.1 *Job Characteristics That Contribute to Stress.*
The greater the extent to which a specific job requires the activities listed here, the more stressful it tends to be for persons holding it. (Source: Based on data from Shaw and Riskind, 1983; see Note 4.)

Making decisions
Monitoring devices or information
Performing complex manual activities
Exchanging job-related information with others
Being in a stressful environment
Being in a hazardous job situation
Engaging in general personal contact
Performing unstructured versus structured work
Being alert to changing conditions

These findings and related evidence in other studies indicate that one major source of stress at work involves the nature and demands of various jobs. For this reason, it is probably wise to take two factors into account when considering a career in some field, or a job with some organization: the level of stress it will involve, and your ability to handle such pressure. Given the powerful impact of stress upon our physical and mental wellbeing (effects we will soon review), this is probably one case where it really pays to look before you leap!

Role conflict: Stress from conflicting demands.   Imagine the following situation. Because she has done such an excellent job in negotiating contracts with local suppliers, a young manager is promoted and becomes one of her company's chief negotiators. Her new job involves a great deal of travel, since she must now fly all over the country (and even outside it), in order to represent her organization at many different meetings. Her supervisor is pleased with her work, and continues to give her more and more assignments. Her husband and two children, though, have very different reactions to her growing success. They miss her very much, and put increasing pressure on her to give up her new job and stay at home. Is this a stress-inducing situation for the woman concerned? Absolutely! She finds herself being pulled in opposite directions by the needs and expectations of different groups: her family and her organization. Moreover, there is no simple or easy way to reconcile these conflicting demands. The result: she experiences a considerable degree of **role conflict**.[5] That is, the demands of her role as a rising young executive conflict sharply with the demands of her roles as wife and mother.

Unfortunately, such conflict is far from rare. Since most people play several different roles in their lives, and must deal with groups of persons holding contrasting expectations about their behavior both at work and elsewhere, role conflict is all too common. Thus, it is often an important source of stress both on and off the job.[6] Moreover, as might be anticipated, such conflict seems to increase in magnitude as individuals marry and then have children. For this and other reasons, it tends to rise over the course of many persons' careers. We should hasten to add, however, that the total picture concerning the clash between family and work demands is not entirely negative. Some findings indicate that although growing family commitments do contribute to role conflict (and so to stress), they may also be beneficial in other ways. For example, in one recent study, Cooke and Rousseau found that while growing family obligations did tend to conflict with work demands among a large group of teachers, they also helped reduce signs of physical strain among these persons.[7] Specifically, individuals with a spouse, or with a spouse and children, reported fewer symptoms of such strain (e.g., headaches, loss of sleep) than persons who were single. These results suggest that family ties are something of a "two-edged sword." On the one hand they do often conflict with demands from one's job, and so contribute to role conflict and subsequent stress. At the same time, though, they provide individuals with important sources of comfort and support, and so assist them in overcoming at least some of the harmful effects associated with stress. We will have more to say about the important role of social support in reactions to stress in a later section.

Role ambiguity: Stress from uncertainty.   Even if an individual manages to avoid the strain associated with role conflict, she or he may still encounter an even more common source of job-related stress: **role ambiguity**. This occurs when individuals are uncertain about several matters relating to their jobs: the scope of their responsibilities, the limits of their authority, specific production requirements, the criteria used in evaluating their work, and so on. Most persons dislike such uncertainty, and find it quite stressful. Unfortunately, though, few possess complete or totally satisfactory knowledge about such matters. The result: role ambiguity is quite common. In fact, from 35 to 60 percent of employees surveyed report experiencing it to some degree.[8] Clearly, then, it is one major cause of stress at work.

Overload and underload: Doing too much or doing too little. When the phrase "job stress" is mentioned, most people envision scenes like the ones shown in Figure 7.2. That is, they imagine either a harried executive attempting to dictate a letter, talk on two phones, and conduct an interview all at once, or a production worker frantically trying to keep up with a rapidly moving assembly line that threatens to get ahead of him. In short, they conjure up an image of someone caught in the trap of trying to do too much in too little time. In this case, common belief is not far off the mark, for overload is in fact a major cause of stress at work. Actually, though, a distinction is often made between **quantitative overload**—situations in which an individual is asked to do more work than can be completed in a given period of time, and **qualitative overload**—feelings, on the part of an individual, that he or she lacks the required skills or abilities needed to perform a given job. Both types of overload are unpleasant, and research findings suggest that both can lead to high levels of stress.[9]

Qualitative deals with skills

But overload is only part of the total picture. While being asked to do too much on one's job can be stressful, so too, is the opposite—being asked to do too little. In fact, there seems to be a considerable grain of truth in the following saying: "The hardest job in the world is doing nothing—you can't take a break." Such *underload* (or under-utilization) leads to boredom and monotony, and since these reactions are unpleasant, it can be quite stressful. Again, a distinction between **quantitative underload** and **qualitative underload** is often drawn. Quantitative underload refers to the boredom that results when employees have so little to do that they find themselves sitting around much of the time. In contrast, qualitative underload refers to the lack of mental stimulation that accompanies many routine, repetitive jobs. As you can readily guess, both sets of conditions are aversive for most persons.

In sum, it appears that with respect to the amount of work or effort demanded from individuals by their jobs, the middle course is best. The most desirable—and least stressful—jobs seem to be ones that keep the persons in them busy, but do not overtax their abilities or cause them to feel that they will soon be unable to cope.

Responsibility for others: A heavy burden. In any organization there is a division of responsibility. Some persons deal primarily with the physical side of the business (e.g., procuring supplies, overseeing production, maintaining equipment), others focus mainly on financial matters (e.g., budgets, taxes, accounting), and still others—usually supervisors or managers—must deal primarily with people. Are there any differences in the level of stress associated with these contrasting types of positions? Research findings suggest there are. In general, individuals who are responsible for other people—ones who must motivate them, reward or punish them, and make decisions about them—experience higher levels of stress than

FIGURE 7.2 Overload: Two Examples
Overload—being asked to do too much in a limited amount of time—is often a major cause of work-related stress

persons who handle other organizational functions.[10] Such persons are more likely to report feelings of tension and anxiety, and are actually more likely to show overt symptoms of stress such as ulcers or hypertension than their counterparts in finance or supply. The reasons behind this difference are complex, but we can mention two of the most important here. First, it is such managers who must, ultimately, confront the human costs of organizational decisions. For example, it is they who must witness the distress of persons who receive negative feedback, are passed over for promotion, are laid off, or who are fired. Second, it is their task to deal with the many frictions that are a normal part of human relations at work. This involves listening to endless complaints, mediating disputes between employees, promoting cooperation, and exercising leadership. Needless to say, all of these tasks are highly demanding, and can contribute to the total burden of stress experienced by such managers.

Lack of social support: The costs of isolation. There is an old saying which suggests that "Misery loves company." In the context of stress, this statement implies the following: if we have to face stressful conditions, it's better to do so along with others (and with their support) rather than alone. As you probably know from your own experience, many people accept this view as correct. When confronted with stress (e.g., an important exam, an anxiety-provoking presentation in front of an important audience) they do seek support and comfort from others. Does this strategy actually work? In short, do people who can count on a high degree of support from others actually cope with stress more effectively than ones who are lacking in this type of backing? The answer provided by many different studies seems to be "yes."

Actually, there are two distinct ways in which **social support** (which is usually defined as helpful activities by other organization members, coupled with the belief that they have one's welfare at heart) might produce positive effects. First, it may be the case that stress is less disruptive in the presence of such support. In short, social support may act as a *buffer*, reducing the strain produced by stressful conditions.[11] Second, social support might actually serve as a *coping strategy*—one technique individuals use when exposed to stress. In short, when suddenly confronted with stressful conditions, many persons may actively seek closer ties with others as a means of handling this situation.[12] The results of recent investigations suggest that both these proposals may be valid. For example, Kobasa and Puccetti found that managers in a large public utility who were experiencing high levels of stress but felt that they had the support of their immediate boss reported fewer physical symptoms associated with stress than managers who did not feel that they had such support.[13] These findings lend support to the *buffer hypothesis* mentioned earlier.

Similarly, in a related project involving employees in a large government agency, Seers, McGee, Serey, and Graen found that for individuals reporting high levels of stress, the greater social support they had from co-workers or their branch chief, the higher their satisfaction with various aspects of their jobs (e.g., work, supervision, pay).[14] In contrast, among individuals reporting low levels of stress, there was no link between social support and such satisfaction. Since the *coping hypothesis* suggests that individuals will be more likely to seek social support when confronted with high levels than with low levels of stress, these findings can be viewed as offering support for its accuracy.

Whatever the precise mechanisms involved, it seems clear that social support from others can often help individuals cope more effectively with stress. In contrast, if they fail to develop good, friendly relations with other organization members (e.g., co-workers, their boss, subordinates), such persons may find themselves cut off from these valuable social resources at just those times when they need them most. In this respect, as well as others, then, the costs of remaining aloof or isolated from others can be high indeed.

Lack of participation in decisions: Helplessness strikes again.   As we have noted on several occasions, most persons want to feel that they have at least some control over their own fate. The opposite belief—that were are helpless pawns tossed aimlessly about by forces beyond our control—is quite disturbing: Unfortunately, one factor contributing to such feelings is common in work settings: lack of participation by employees in decisions affecting their jobs. Most persons feel that they know quite a lot about their work. Thus, when they are prevented from offering

FIGURE 7.3   *Participation in Decision-making and the Reduction of Job-related Stress.* Employees at an outpatient hospital facility who were given increased opportunities for participation in decisions relating to their jobs reported lower levels of emotional strain than employees not given such opportunities. Moreover, this was true both six and nine months after these procedures were instituted. (Source: Based on data from Jackson, 1983; see Note 15.)

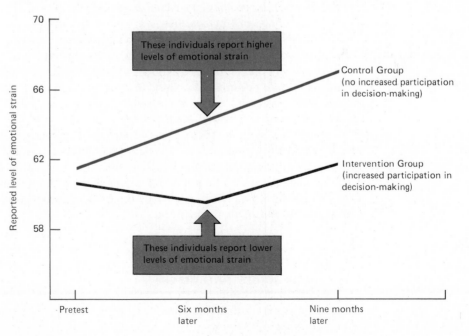

input into decisions relating to them, they feel left out, and unable to control their own outcomes. The result: they may experience considerable stress.

Clear evidence for the existence of a link between lack of participation in decision-making and job-related stress is provided by the result of a study conducted by Jackson.[15] In this project, some employees in an outpatient hospital facility were provided with increased opportunities for input into decisions affecting their jobs. The frequency of staff meetings in their units was increased, and their supervisors received special training in encouraging worker input. In contrast, other persons in the same facility did not experience such changes. When all employees completed various questionnaires six and nine months later, the beneficial impact of increased input into decision-making became clear. Individuals in the group receiving enhanced opportunities for such input reported lower levels of emotional strain (symptoms resulting from stress) than those in the no-change control group (refer to Figure 7.3, page 213). In addition, they also reported lower levels of role conflict, and higher job satisfaction. These results suggest that permitting employees to participate in decisions affecting their jobs may be quite beneficial. Not only does it enhance their attitudes toward their work; it helps counter an important source of work-related stress as well.

Other organizational sources of stress: Appraisals, working conditions, and change.   The factors described above appear to be among the most important sources of stress within organizations. However, several others exist too, and should be briefly mentioned. One of these involves the process of **performance appraisal.** Being evaluated by others is a stressful experience, especially when the results of such appraisal have important effects upon one's career. For this reason, as well as several others, it is crucial that such evaluations be conducted in as fair a manner as possible. Second, *working conditions* are often an important source of stress. Unpleasant environmental conditions (e.g., extreme heat or cold, loud noise, crowding), swing-shifts, and even flexible work hours can all act as stressors and exert negative effects upon employees exposed to them.[16] Third, stress often derives from *change* within an organization. Shifts in company policy, reorganizations in internal structure, mergers, and major changes in management can all generate high levels of stress among employees.

A summary of all the organizational sources of stress considered in this discussion is provided in Figure 7.4. As this figure and our remarks so far suggest, sources of stress literally *abound* in the modern world of work. Little wonder, then, that coping with such conditions is a major task faced by most persons in the mid-1980s. (For discussion of another major cause of stress—unemployment—please see the **Focus** box on page 217.)

Personal Factors and Stress

In Chapter 6 we called attention to a key fact about people: they differ greatly along an almost infinite number of dimensions. As you can probably guess, reactions to stress are no exception to this general rule. While some persons are capable of dealing with even intense levels of strain or pressure, others seem to fall apart at

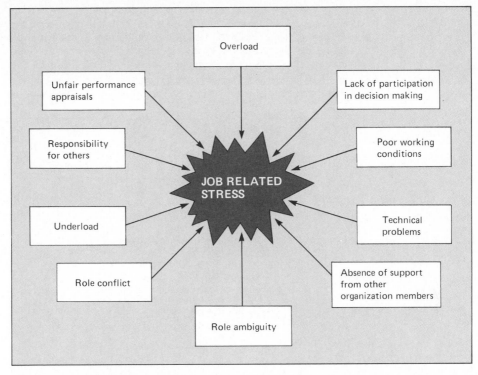

FIGURE 7.4 *Organizational Causes of Stress: A Summary.*
As shown here, job-related stress stems from a wide range of organizational factors.

even the slightest sign of stress. Because of such differences, it is impossible to fully grasp the nature of stress in work settings without attention to personal as well as organization-based factors. That is, we must consider the current lifestyles, attitudes, and traits of individuals as well as various features of jobs and work settings. Several of these personal factors will now be examined.

Life events and stress.   Movies and plays often suggest that there is an important link between certain events in one's life and personal health. Specifically, they often show individuals who have recently experienced traumatic events (e.g., the death of a loved one, divorce) pining away until they become seriously ill or even die. This suggestion of a link between stressful life events and health has important implications for organizational behavior. After all, employees who are suffering from ill health or deep depression are unlikely to be very productive. Is this idea accurate? The answer seems to be "yes." Many studies indicate that when individuals undergo stressful changes in their lives, their personal health does indeed suffer.[19] Some of the events that seem to produce such effects are listed in Table 7.2 (page 216), along with numbers reflecting their relative stressfulness.[20] Ones near the top of the table (which receive many points) are highly stressful; those farther down are less upsetting or traumatic. Research findings indicate that the greater the number and intensity of stressful life events endured by individuals in a given period of time, the greater their likelihood of developing serious illness. For example, persons who

TABLE 7.2   *Stressful Life Events.*
Events near the top of this list are highly stressful, and often seem to produce adverse effects upon health. Those near the bottom are only mildly stressful, and have less impact upon personal health. (Numbers to the right provide an index of relative stressfulness; 100 = maximum stress.) (Source: Adapted from Holmes and Rahe, 1967; see Note 20.)

Life Events	Scale Value (Range = 1–100)
Death of a spouse	100
Divorce	73
Separation (Marital)	65
Death of close family member	63
Major personal injury or illness	53
Marriage	50
Fired from job	47
Retirement	45
Death of close friend	37
Foreclosure of mortgage or loan	30
Trouble with in-laws	29
Wife begins or stops work	26
Trouble with boss	23
Change in residence	20
Change in sleeping habits	15
Change in eating habits	15
Vacation	13
Christmas	12
Minor violations of the law	11

report life events totaling 150 to 300 points during one year have a 50 percent chance of becoming seriously ill during the next twelve months. Those who experience events totaling more than 300 points have a 70 percent chance of such outcomes.

Additional research findings, however, indicate that people differ greatly in their susceptibility to such effects. Some readily succumb to the stress produced by traumatic life events, while others are quite resistant to this factor and continue to function effectively in the face of one personal disaster after another. What characteristics distinguish these two types of individuals? Three seem to be most important: *commitment, control,* and *challenge. Commitment* refers to a sense of purpose and meaningfulness. Persons who are resistant to the trauma of stressful life events perceive more purpose and meaning in their lives than ones who are less capable of dealing with such events. Similarly, *control* involves individuals' beliefs that they can influence their own lives and outcomes. As you might expect, persons able to cope effectively with stress (who are often described as being high in **hardiness**) are higher on this dimension than persons less able to adjust. Finally, *challenge* refers to the extent to which individuals perceive change as an opportunity for development rather than as a threatening burden. Hardy, stress-resistant persons are more likely to hold the first of these views than non-hardy, stress-susceptible persons.

That persons high in hardiness are in fact more stress-resistant than those lower on this dimension is indicated by the findings of several studies. For example, in one investigation, Kobasa and Pucetti asked executives at a large utility to com-

FOCUS ON BEHAVIOR

Unemployment, Commitment to Work, and Stress

By now, the following fact should be clear: few jobs are totally free from stress. On the contrary, most expose the persons who hold them to at least moderate degrees of stress on at least some occasions. Despite this fact however, there are millions of persons around the world who would gladly trade their current state for even high levels of pressure; these are the unemployed. Growing evidence suggests that unemployment itself is highly stressful. Indeed, it has been linked to such negative outcomes as reduced life satisfaction, feelings of anxiety, lowered self-esteem, and an increased incidence of psychiatric disorders.[17] Thus, while work can be stressful, its absence, too, can produce such effects.

While unemployment is an unpleasant state for most persons, recent findings suggest that its impact is often moderated by another important factor: *commitment to work*. The stronger the desire of unemployed persons to be engaged in paid employment, the greater the level of stress they experience as a result of finding themselves without a job. This fact is illustrated clearly by the results of an investigation carried out by Jackson, Stafford, Banks, and Warr.[18]

Participants in this study were young men and women in England who had recently left school to seek employment. These persons were interviewed and asked to complete various questionnaires on three different occasions: seven, fifteen, and thirty months

FIGURE 7.5 *Shifts in Employment: Their Impact on Psychological Distress.*
When young persons moved from being unemployed to being employed, they experienced reductions in psychological distress. In contrast, when they shifted from being employed to being unemployed, such distress increased. (Source: Based on data from Jackson et al., 1983; see Note 18.)

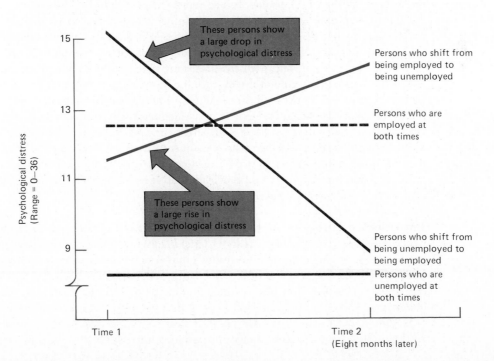

after leaving school. During these sessions they reported on their current employment status, and responded to questionnaires designed to measure their level of psychological distress, and their current employment commitment (i.e., the extent to which they desired paid employment). These data were then used to test several predictions. First, it was expected that among persons who were unemployed, the higher their commitment to work, the higher would be their psychological distress, but that among persons who were employed, the higher their commitment to work, the lower would be their distress. Both these hypotheses were confirmed. Second, it was predicted that changes in employment status would be reflected in shifts in psychological distress. Specifically, persons moving from unemployment to employment should show reductions in such distress, while individuals moving from employment to unemployment should show increments in distress. As shown in Figure 7.5,

this pattern of results was in fact obtained. Finally, it was expected that shifts in level of psychological distress brought about by changes in employment status should be larger for persons high in employment commitment than persons low in employment commitment. This complex hypothesis, too, was confirmed.

Considered in the context of other research on the impact of unemployment, the findings reported by Jackson and colleagues point to the following basic conclusions. First, unemployment *is* quite stressful for many persons. Second, the magnitude of such stress depends, to an important degree, on the strength of individuals' commitment to work: the greater this commitment, the greater the distress produced. For this reason, efforts to fully understand the impact of unemployment on specific individuals must consider the attitudes and traits of such persons, as well as the more general economic and stress-inducing nature of lack of work itself.

plete questionnaires designed to provide information on their current health, their level of hardiness, and the number of stressful life events they had recently experienced.[21] It was predicted that executives high in hardiness would report fewer symptoms of ill health than those low in hardiness both in the context of high and low levels of stress. Results offered strong support for this prediction. Another interesting finding of the project is also worthy of mention. In addition to completing the questionnaires mentioned above, subjects also reported on the amount of social support they received from their families. When these data were examined, it was found that for persons high in hardiness, such support made little difference: they were able to cope well in all cases. Among persons low in hardiness, however, a more surprising pattern was uncovered: the more support they enjoyed, the worse their personal health! These findings suggest that support from one's family is not a totally unmixed blessing. Indeed, it may encourage persons low in hardiness to "give up" in their efforts to cope with stress, and so actually reduce their limited abilities in this respect even further. Of course, further research is needed to confirm these findings, and fully explain their occurrence. Since many persons turn to their families for support and comfort in times of stress, however, these results have important implications well worth investigating.

Individual differences in tension discharge rate (TDR). Nearly everyone experiences some degree of pressure or tension at work—this is a basic fact of life in modern organizations. Individuals differ greatly, however, in terms of what they do with such feelings at the end of the day. Some seem capable of leaving them in the office when they head for home. Others carry them along as excess psychological "baggage." It seems reasonable to suggest that persons in the first of these groups will suffer fewer ill-effects from stress than those in the second category, and in fact, recent findings suggest that this is so. In an intriguing study on this topic, Matteson

218

and Ivancevich had several hundred medical technologists complete two question-naires.[22] One measured what has been termed their **tension discharge rate (TDR)**—the rate at which individuals dissipate job-related tensions at the end of the day. The second measured several aspects of personal health (e.g., the total number of health problems subjects had experienced during the past six months; the number of visits they had made to a physician; their use of aspirin, tranquilizers, cigarettes, and alcohol). It was predicted that persons low in the ability to dissipate job-related tension would report poorer health than persons high in this ability. As you can see from Figure 7.6, results offered clear support for this hypothesis. On all measures except those for the use of cigarettes and alcohol, differences between the low and high TDR groups were in the predicted direction.

These findings suggest that learning to "leave your worries behind you" at the

FIGURE 7.6   *Tension Discharge Rate and Personal Health.*
Individuals high in the ability to discharge job-related tension (i.e., the ability to leave such stress at the office) show better personal health than persons low in this ability. (Source: Based on data from Matteson and Ivancevich, 1983; see Note 22.)

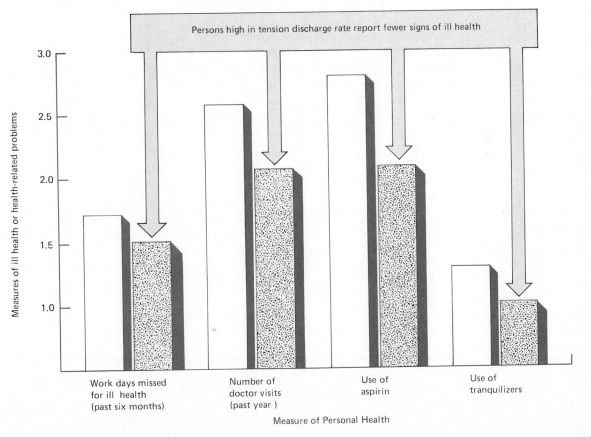

□ = Persons low in tension discharge rate

▨ = Persons high in tension discharge rate

end of the day can be a very beneficial strategy. Indeed, it can enhance your personal health, and so your ability to cope with further stress. Fortunately, there are several concrete steps people can take to help master this skill. For example, they can make it a rule to leave work at the office rather than bringing it home with them. Similarly, they can cultivate hobbies and other leisure-time activities that will distract them from re-living the day once it is over. Through these and related steps, individuals can help assure that they will have at least *some* time away from the cares and woes of their jobs—a period during which they can rest and recuperate. The advantages of establishing such "islands of tranquility" in a busy life are too obvious to require further comment.

The Type A behavior pattern and stress: Compounding the costs.   In Chapter 6, we noted that Type A persons often pay a high price for their hard-driving, competitive lifestyle: they are more than twice as likely as Type B persons to suffer serious heart attacks. One key reason for this difference in health seems to derive, at least in part, from the ways in which Type As and Type Bs handle stress. First, when exposed to stressful conditions, Type As often show larger increases in physiological arousal (e.g., heart rate, blood pressure) than Type Bs.[23] Second, Type As seem more likely than Type Bs to give up and feel helpless when confronted with certain types of stress—especially stress they cannot readily control.[24] Perhaps even more important, Type As seem to employ different strategies for coping with stress than Type Bs. When faced with stressful events, Type As seem to exhibit *denial* and *projection* to a much greater degree than Type Bs. That is, they tend to deny that they are upset by the stress, and often project their own feelings of tension and anxiety onto others. The result of such strategies is clear: because they avoid coming to grips with their own reactions to stress, Type As often expose themselves to more of it, for longer periods to time, than Type Bs. In view of all these tendencies in their reactions to stress, it is hardly surprising that Type As are often outlasted by calmer and less competitive Type Bs.

STRESS: ITS MAJOR EFFECTS

By now, you are probably convinced that stress derives from many sources, and is quite common in organizational settings. What you may still not fully grasp, though, is just how powerful and far-reaching its effects can be. Systematic research on this topic has revealed that stress influences our physical and psychological wellbeing, our personal adjustment, the course of our careers, and many aspects of our behavior—both at work and elsewhere. Several of these effects are described in some detail below.

Stress and Health: The Silent Killer

At present, most people realize that prolonged exposure to stress can be harmful to their health. In this respect, they are definitely correct, for growing evidence indicates that stress plays a role in a wide range of common ailments (e.g., headaches and stomachaches).[25] Medical experts, however, have gone far beyond this simple generalization. In fact, many now believe that from 50 to 70 percent of all physical illnesses are at least partly caused by stress![26] Moreover, included among these stress-related ailments are some of the most serious—and fatal—ones known to medical science. We have already called attention to evidence linking stress to heart disease. However, this is only a small part of the total picture. In addition, stress appears to play a role in the following major health problems: high blood pressure, hardening of the arteries, ulcers, and diabetes. Please note: this in no way implies that stress is the only cause, or even simply the most important cause, of such ailments. On the contrary, these complex conditions stem from many different factors (e.g., genetic predispositions, diet, variations in lifestyle). However, growing evidence suggests that stress contributes to these diseases, and may intensify the physical harm they produce. From this perspective, it clearly plays an important role in human health.

Stress and Mental States

Few scientists currently doubt that mind and body are closely related. That is, events and conditions affecting one often affect the other as well. Given this fact, it is far from surprising to learn that as stress affects our basic bodily processes, it also influences our psychological states. Several such effects have been discovered. First, exposure to stress often induces negative shifts in moods and emotions. Persons experiencing stess frequently report such feelings as anxiety, depression, irritation, and fatigue. Second, exposure to stress—especially stess relating to one's job—can result in lowered self-esteem. This seems to stem from the fact that persons experiencing stress often feel unable to cope with their jobs. This, in turn, affects feelings of competence and self-worth that often play a key role in self-esteem. Third, and perhaps most important, stress is often associated with reductions in job satisfaction. Given the strong impact of such attitudes upon key forms of organizational behavior (refer to our discussion in Chapter 5), the role of stress in this regard has important practical implications.

Stress and Behavior at Work

Any factor that exerts powerful effects upon physical wellbeing and psychological states would also logically be expected to influence overt behavior, too. With respect to stress, this is definitely the case. Exposure to strong or prolonged stress exerts many effects upon behavior in work settings.

First, there can be little doubt that stress affects performance on many different tasks. While this general conclusion is widely accepted, however, we must note that the precise nature of such effects remains to be established. In the past, it was often assumed that the relationship between stress and performance took the form of an upside-down letter U, as shown in Figure 7.7 (page 222). That is, at very low levels,

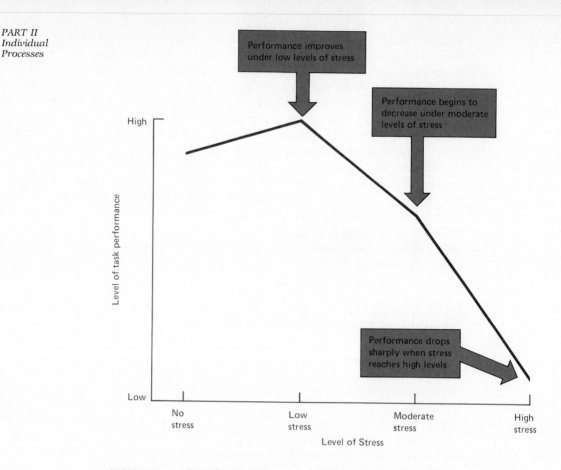

FIGURE 7.7 *The Relationship between Stress and Task Performance: One Possibility.*
In the past, it was widely assumed that as stress rises from very low to low or moderate levels,
performance improves, but that beyond this level, further increments in stress lead to actual
drops in performance. However, recent evidence indicates that the relationship between
stress and performance is probably somewhat more complex in nature.

stress has little impact upon performance. As it rises to low to moderate levels, it
serves as a source of activation, and so actually enhances performance on many
tasks. Beyond some level, however, it begins to produce the negative effects described previously (e.g., fatigue, anxiety, breakdowns in health), and so interferes
with work-related performance.

While these suggestions appear to make good sense, recent findings have called
this fairly simple picture into question. It now appears that the relationship between
stress and performance is much more complex. For example, it is affected by such
variables as the difficulty of the task being performed, the specific stressors involved,
and a wide range of personal and situational factors.[27] For this reason, we cannot
offer a simple description of the overall relationship between stress and task performance; indeed, no single description of this type may be possible. However, two

general conclusions do seem warranted: (1) performance on many tasks *is* in fact affected by stress, and (2) such performance does usually drop off sharply when stress rises to high levels.

Task performance is not the only aspect of work behavior influenced by stress, however. In addition, it is modestly related to both absenteeism and turnover: the higher the levels of stress encountered by individuals in their jobs, the higher the incidence of these actions seems to be. Finally, high levels of job stress are also linked to two problems that are so important in many organizations at the present time that they deserve separate treatment: *alcoholism* and *drug abuse*.

Alcohol, Drugs, and Stress

Stress, especially when it rises to high levels, is unpleasant. For this reason, most persons seek to reduce or avoid it whenever possible. For a large majority of individuals, this involves efforts to actively cope with the causes of stress—problems they face at home or at work. Some, however, adopt a sharply different strategy. Instead of attempting to deal directly with stress, they seek to withdraw or escape from it. One of the major tactics such persons use for accomplishing this goal is simple: they retreat into an alcohol or drug-induced haze.

Unfortunately, this strategy has become alarmingly common in organizational settings in recent years. At the present time, nearly ten million persons (more than 5 percent of the total labor force!) can be classified as alcoholic in the United States alone. Drug abuse, too, is far from rare. Marijuana, cocaine, tranquilizers, amphetamines, and even heroin are all in widespread use and can be encountered everywhere from the factory floor and loading dock, up to and including the executive offices. We should hasten to note that individuals use (and abuse) these substances for many reasons; efforts to escape from stress are only part of the story. Yet, when asked why they turned to alcohol or drugs in the first place, many persons mention intense boredom, role conflicts, anxiety, and other factors closely linked to stress.

Whatever the specific reasons behind the growing problems of alcoholism and drug abuse, though, there can be little doubt that they exact serious costs from both individuals and organizations alike. From the point of view of individuals, such costs are all too obvious. Abuse of alcohol and drugs can affect personal health, destroy promising careers, wreck good marriages, and shatter happy families. The costs for organizations, too, are staggering. For example, alcoholic employees are absent from work and experience accidents several times more frequently than other workers. The toll due to drug abuse may be even higher. Persons who abuse such substances show sharply reduced productivity, and may account for a large share of company thefts.[28] One dramatic illustration of the costs associated with drug abuse at work is provided by a serious accident that took place in the United States during 1984. This accident involved a head-on collision between two Amtrak passenger trains moving through the crowded East-coast rail corridor. The collision occurred when an employee failed to throw a switch that would keep the trains on

FIGURE 7.8 *Drug Abuse at Work: Some Tragic Consequences.*
The tragic accident shown here took place when an employee failed to throw the switch that would put these two speeding trains on different tracks. Medical examination of the person responsible later showed that he was probably under the influence of several drugs at the time in question.

different tracks. Blood samples collected from this person shortly after the accident indicated that he was probably under the influence of several different drugs (including marijuana) at the time (see Figure 7.8). Tragedies such as this suggest that alcoholism and drug abuse among persons at work can sometimes involve costs most individuals would find totally unacceptable.

In the past, alcoholism or drug abuse by employees was viewed by management in most companies as a cause for immediate dismissal. More recently, though, public attitudes have shifted, and such behaviors have come to be seen as serious but treatable illnesses. As this new perspective has gained support, and also as many organizations have recognized the huge costs associated with alcoholism and drug abuse among their employees, a growing number have established special programs designed to aid affected persons. These **Employee Assistance Programs** either provide employees with counseling and treatment, or direct them to various agencies specializing in such assistance. Since recognizing a problem is usually the first step toward its solution, these developments, preliminary as they are, provide some basis for optimism. Nevertheless, alcoholism and drug abuse remain serious problems in many organizations—ones for which there are no simple or obvious solutions. Thus, they must be included on any list of the damaging effects of stress.

Burnout: When Stress Consumes

Most persons are exposed to some degree of stress in their work. Yet, despite this fact, most manage to cope. Somehow (often with the aid of techniques we will consider in a later section), they continue to function. Further, they avoid total panic, feelings of helplessness, and despair. A few individuals, however, are not so lucky. They are gradually worn down (or out!) by stress, and the physical and psychological strain it produces. Over time they become exhausted (both emotionally and physically), grow cynical, and develop negative attitudes toward their work, other persons, and life in general. In a word, they become victims of **burnout**.[29] It is on this disturbing syndrome that we will now focus.

Burnout: Its nature and effects.   In a sense, we have already outlined the major components of burnout above. Briefly, it can be defined as *a syndrome of emotional, physical, and mental exhaustion resulting from prolonged exposure to intense stress.*

The *physical* aspect of burnout is often easy to spot. Persons suffering from this reaction have low energy, and are always tired. In addition, they often report many symptoms of physical strain, such as frequent headaches, nausea, back pain, sleep disturbances, and changes in eating habits. In contrast, the *emotional exhaustion* experienced by victims of burnout centers around feelings of depression, hopelessness, and entrapment. Such persons are constantly "down." Further, they frequently feel that they need all of the emotional energy remaining to them just to keep going—merely to get through the motions of their jobs or lives. Needless to say, this leaves them little room for interest in or concern with others. In addition, many feel trapped by their careers, and see little hope for change in the future. Finally, victims of burnout also suffer from *mental exhaustion*. They become cynical about others, hold negative attitudes toward them, and disparage themselves, their jobs, and life in general. To put it simply, they come to view the world around them through dark gray rather than rose-colored lenses. (Please refer to Figure 7.9 on page 226 for a summary of the major components of burnout.)

In sum, burnout represents what may best be described as an erosion of the human spirit. People suffering from this syndrome feel incapable of accomplishing anything, have little concern for others, lack interest in virtually everything (including their own lives), and frequently feel fatigued, irritable, and depressed. Little wonder, then, that they are usually carefully avoided by other organization members!

Burnout: Some contributing factors.   As we noted earlier, the key cause of burnout seems to involve prolonged exposure to intense stress. Thus, it is much more common in some fields (e.g., the helping professions) than others. Recent studies indicate, though, that a number of other variables also play a role in its

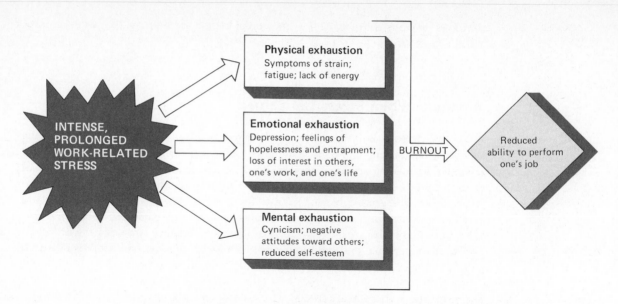

FIGURE 7.9 *Burnout: Its Major Components.*
When individuals are exposed to intense stress over long periods of time, they may experience *burnout*. This syndrome involves intense physical, emotional, and mental exhaustion. Persons suffering from it usually show sharp drops in their ability to perform their jobs adequately.

occurrence. An especially revealing investigation in this respect has been conducted by Gaines and Jermier.[30]

These researchers had members of a city police department complete questionnaires designed to yield information on several factors that might, potentially, be related to emotional exhaustion—a central component of burnout. These included personal variables (e.g., marital status), task-related factors (e.g., the motivating potential of various jobs; refer to Chapter 3), organizational factors (pay equity, promotion opportunities, rule inflexibility), and contextual variables (the specific unit or department in which persons work). Information on all of these factors was then related to subjects' responses to a measure of emotional exhaustion. Results indicated that many different factors contributed to such feelings. For example, women reported greater exhaustion than men. Similarly, individuals working in the patrol department reported greater exhaustion than those working on clerical tasks at headquarters. Interestingly, the strongest effects were obtained for promotion opportunities: the lower these were perceived to be, the greater the emotional exhaustion reported by subjects. Several other factors, too, seemed to affect such exhaustion (e.g., the more inflexible subjects perceived the rules in their organization to be, the greater exhaustion they reported; the more interesting and motivating they found their jobs to be, the lower their reported exhaustion). Taken as a whole, these complex findings point to the following conclusion: while stress is undoubtedly the major cause of emotional exhaustion and other aspects of burnout, many other factors, too, play a role in this regard. Thus, these must be taken into account if the nature of this damaging syndrome is to be fully understood.

226

Burnout: Its effects on organizations.   The costs of burnout to its victims are obvious, and require no added discussion here. But what about its impact on organizations? How does the occurrence of burnout among employees influence an organization's effectiveness and functioning? The answer depends, to a large extent, on just what happens to persons after they have been ravaged by this syndrome.

First, and perhaps best from the point of view of an organization, burnout victims may choose to quit their jobs and withdraw from their present careers. In short, they may conclude that they have had quite enough of marketing, engineering, sales, law, or whatever field they are in, and simply "drop out." Obviously, the departure of burned-out individuals from the organization can have positive effects on its productivity and morale. Further, the persons involved, too, may benefit: they escape from what has become, for them, an unbearable situation. Yet, the loss to society in terms of expertise, training, and talent can be great, and should be weighed in the balance along with these potential gains.

Second, individuals suffering from burnout may simply decide to change jobs, without leaving their career or field. Sometimes this is helpful, for a new work environment may permit them to recapture a portion of their earlier enthusiasm and energy. The danger, however, is that they will bring their cynicism, exhaustion, and despair with them to a new organization, and so disrupt its effective functioning.

Third, the victims of burnout may choose to move from the jobs and careers for which they were trained into purely administrative roles. In this way they escape from work activities they now find intolerable, and can minimize their contacts with their former field. Indeed, if they find the right spot, they can disappear behind a mountain of papers, forms, and red tape, never to be seen again in the active portions of the company's business. The danger here, of course, is that their fatigue, negative views, and lack of interest in their work will be transmitted to other members of the organization, with obvious negative effects.

Finally, individuals experiencing burnout may choose to remain on their jobs and mark time until retirement. In short, they may become "dead wood"—totally nonproductive members of the organization who draw on valuable resources, but offer no contribution in return. Needless to add, to the extent any organization acquires sizable numbers of such persons, it may soon find itself in serious trouble.

Burnout: Countering its effects: Admittedly, our discussion of burnout up to this point has been somewhat depressing. We have focused on the negative nature of this syndrome, its many causes, and its potentially devastating effects upon both individuals and organizations. Fortunately, though, we can conclude on a more positive note. While burnout does often mark the end of productive careers, this is not necessarily the case. If its victims recognize its presence and take appropriate steps to counter its influence, it *can* be reversed. In short, recovery from burnout is possible. Since this syndrome stems primarily from prolonged exposure to high levels of stress, a central technique for dealing with it involves efforts to reduce such pressure, or at least give individuals some respite from it. However, other steps, too, can prove useful.[31] Several of these are summarized in Table 7.3 (page 228). Please examine them carefully, for the chances are fairly high that you or someone you know will find them useful at some point in the years ahead.

TABLE 7.3   Burnout: Countering Its Impact.
The steps outlined here can all prove useful in countering the harmful effects of burnout.

Step	Value in Countering Burnout
Admit that there is a problem	Unless individuals are aware that they are suffering from burnout, they will fail to take any actions to overcome it
Reorder priorities and goals	Individuals should recognize that they can't do everything, and should scale down their goals accordingly
Establish a network of social support	Friends who appreciate one's work and understand one's problems can be helpful in overcoming negative feelings about oneself and one's work
Divide life into work and nonwork segments	By learning to leave problems at the office, individuals can gain the time needed to recover from stress
Cultivate hobbies and outside interests	Such activities can help individuals avoid going stale, and prevent them from becoming totally wrapped up in their work

MANAGING STRESS: SOME USEFUL TECHNIQUES

Because stress stems from many different sources, it is probably impossible to totally eliminate it from work settings. While it can't be completely removed, though, it *can* be managed. That is, steps can be taken to hold it to acceptable levels, and to minimize its harmful effects. Several different techniques for attaining these valuable goals exist. Most, however, seem to fall under two major headings: procedures individuals can apply themselves, and techniques that require changes in or interventions by organizations.

Personal Tactics for Managing Stress

What steps can individuals take to protect themselves against the adverse effects of stress? Fortunately, several useful ones seem to exist. First, and perhaps foremost, persons concerned with enhancing their own "stress tolerance" can focus on increasing their physical fitness. A large and growing body of evidence indicates that individuals who exercise regularly, and avoid gaining weight, are much less likely to suffer from several types of stress-related illness (e.g., heart disease, high blood pressure) than those who do not engage in such activity or who permit themselves to pick up extra pounds.[32] Further, it doesn't seem to matter how physical fitness is attained; jogging, swimming, aerobic dancing, participation in team sports—all seem equally effective.

Improving their physical fitness is not the only thing individuals can do to increase their resistance to stress, however. Several other techniques exist as well.

228

For example, they can participate in what is known as *coping skills training*—special procedures which help them recognize situations that cause them to experience anxiety or feelings of being overwhelmed, and specific tactics for dealing with such situations.[33] Many techniques for managing stress, however, center around the following common theme: teaching individuals special methods for replacing feelings of strain and tension with relaxation. One of the most popular of these is **relaxation training.** Here, individuals learn how to relax their muscles in a systematic manner (e.g., starting with their feet and moving upward toward the head). Such relaxation seems effective in reducing emotional tension. Another precedure for attaining similar effects is known as *meditation.* Individuals using this technique assume a comfortable position, close their eyes, and attempt to clear all disturbing thoughts from their minds. Then, they silently repeat a single syllable or *mantra* over and over again. Although it remains somewhat controversial, many persons report that meditation helps them feel relaxed. Further, some research findings indicate that it affects basic bodily functions in a manner suggestive of relaxation (e.g., it reduces oxygen consumption, produces brain-wave patterns indicative of a calm mental state).[34]

Additional tactics for managing stress that can be used effectively by individuals include developing hobbies or other outside interests that help distract them from the pressures of their jobs, taking short vacations in order to "unwind," and learning to structure work and personal lives so that these do not consist of a perpetual struggle to meet important deadlines. Through these steps, and the ones outlined above, individuals can enhance their ability to meet—and cope with—the unavoidable stress connected with their work. (For evidence concerning the effectiveness of such techniques, please see the **Focus** box on page 230.)

Organizational Strategies for Managing Stress

While individuals can increase their own resistance to stress, they cannot, by themselves, eliminate many of its causes from their work environments. For this reason organizations, too, can play a key role in stress management. Specifically, they can adopt changes in their own structure and procedures, or alter the nature of jobs so as to reduce stress among their employees.

Changes in organizational structure and function. Several changes in organizational policy and function appear to be useful in reducing job-related stress. First, such benefits can sometimes be produced by *decentralization*—a process in which authority is spread more widely throughout an organization. This seems to reduce feelings of helplessness among employees, and so reduce their overall level of stress. Second, employees can be afforded greater participation in decisions, especially ones involving their jobs. As we noted earlier, the lack of opportunities for such input can be highly upsetting to many persons. Third, steps can be taken to assure that both performance appraisals and the distribution of organizational rewards are as fair as possible. To the extent individuals perceive that these matters are being handled in a reasonable manner, the stress related to them can be greatly

Managing Stress: Long-Term Benefits from Short-Term Interventions

As recognition of the harmful effects of stress has grown, many organizations have encouraged their employees to participate in various *stress management programs*. Research concerned with the effectiveness of these procedures has been encouraging. For example, many individuals demonstrate lower levels of anxiety over their ability to cope with their jobs at the conclusion of such programs than at their start.[35] Thus, there seems to be little doubt that they can yield short-term gains. The question of whether such programs also produce benefits of longer duration, however, has remained more open. Do individ-

FIGURE 7.10   *Managing Stress: Encouraging Results.*
After participating in a relatively brief stress management intervention, individuals showed reduced levels of two kinds of anxiety. (Feelings of anxiety are often one effect of exposure to stressful conditions.) Further, they maintained these lowered levels of anxiety during a subsequent stress-inducing event (mid-term examinations). (Source: Based on data from Rose and Veiga, 1984; see Note 36.)

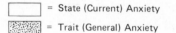

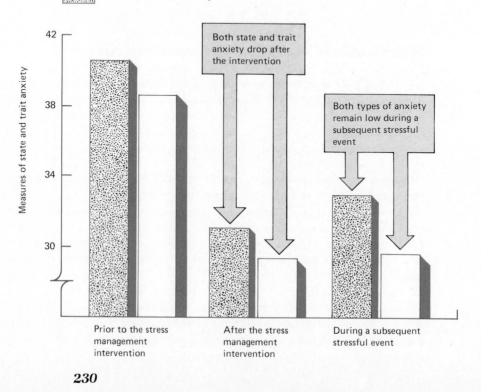

uals carry an enhanced ability to cope with stress back to their jobs and organizations? Or do these gains quickly fade in the face of the pressures of normal work activities? Until recently, little evidence on this crucial issue was available. An interesting study performed by Rose and Veiga, however, now provides at least a partial—and mainly positive—answer.[36]

In this investigation, business students at a large university first completed scales designed to measure both their current levels of anxiety (state anxiety) and their tendency to react to many situations in an anxious manner (trait anxiety). Subjects then took part in a stress management intervention involving several of the procedures described earlier (e.g., training in relaxation, specific coping skills). This intervention involved six two-hour sessions, spaced over a three-week period. At the conclusion of these procedures, subjects completed the anxiety questionnaires once again. Then, to assess the longer-term impact of the interven-

tion program, they completed the same scales one month later, during a highly stressful event: mid-term examinations. As you can see from Figure 7.10, results were highly encouraging. Both state (current) and trait anxiety dropped sharply after participation in the stress management program. Further, both remained at these reduced levels even during the stress of mid-term exams.

The findings reported by Rose and Veiga help answer the question raised above. Apparently, participation in appropriate stress management programs *can* yield lasting benefits. Indeed, they seem capable of arming individuals with skills they can use in dealing with the pressures and strains of their everyday lives. When it is realized that these gains were obtained through an intervention occupying only a few hours, an additional, important conclusion is suggested: efforts to help individuals cope with stress can be efficient as well as effective.

---

lessened. Fourth, efforts can be made to enhance *communication* within the organization. The smoother and more rapid the flow of information along such channels, the lower the likelihood of role ambiguity, and so the lower the level of stress present.

Changes in the nature of specific jobs. In addition to the type of changes just outlined, stress can also often be reduced through careful attention to the nature of specific jobs. For example, the stress resulting from boring, repetitive tasks can be lessened through *job enlargement*—efforts to broaden the scope of the activities they involve. Second, stress deriving from feelings of helplessness or lack of control can be reduced by *job enrichment*—procedures in which employees are provided with more responsibility for planning and directing their own work. (Please refer to our discussion of these topics in Chapter 3.) Third, the stressfulness of specific jobs can be reduced through such steps as limiting unnecessary travel or geographic relocations. These activities often expose individuals to high levels of strain. Finally, important causes of stress can be removed through the elimination of hazardous or unpleasant working conditions.

Through attention to these and related matters, organizations can greatly reduce the level of stress faced by their employees, and so help to make their lives at work more satisfying and fulfilling. Since these outcomes, in turn, may then serve to enhance morale, raise motivation, and increase performance, efforts to manage stress represent more than mere attempts at improving the quality of working life. In addition, they may well contribute to the survival and effectiveness of organizations themselves.

SUMMARY

Stress occurs when individuals perceive that their ability to cope in a specific situation may soon be overwhelmed. Such reactions stem from many different causes. Among the more important *organizational causes* of stress are the demands of a given job, role conflict, overload or underload, lack of social support, role ambiguity, and the absence of opportunities to participate in decisions concerning one's job. *Personal factors*, too, play a key role in stress, and reactions to it. These include stressful events in individuals' lives which can adversely affect their health, and several personal traits or characteristics that mediate reactions to stress (e.g., *hardiness, tension discharge rate*, and the *Type A behavior pattern*).

Stress exerts many effects upon individuals and organizations. First, it can lead to several forms of illness (e.g., heart disease, high blood pressure). Second, it produces negative shifts in moods, depression, reduced self-esteem, and lowered job satisfaction. The relationship between stress and performance appears to be complex. However, in some cases, performance may be enhanced by low to moderate levels of stress, but reduced by higher levels of this factor. Prolonged exposure to strong emotional stress can lead to **burnout.** Persons suffering from this syndrome generally show signs of physical, emotional, and mental exhaustion. To the extent an organization numbers many victims of burnout among its employees, its overall effectiveness may be sharply reduced.

Many techniques for managing stress exist. Individuals can enhance their own capacity for resisting the impact of stress by improving their physical fitness, learning specific coping skills, and mastering techniques that allow them to substitute relaxation for tension. Organizations can help lower the level of stress faced by their employees by decentralizing authority, improving lines of communication, enlarging or enriching jobs, and by eliminating unnecessary travel and transfers.

KEY TERMS

burnout: Physical, emotional, and mental exhaustion resulting from prolonged exposure to intense emotional stress.

hardiness: A characteristic that enables individuals to resist the adverse effects of stressful life events. Hardiness primarily involves a sense of purpose in one's life (commitment), the belief that one can control one's own outcomes (control), and a tendency to view change as an opportunity for growth rather than a threat (challenge).

performance appraisal: The process through which individuals' performance in their jobs is evaluated.

qualitative overload: The belief, on the part of employees, that they lack the skills or abilities required to perform a specific job.

qualitative underload: The lack of mental stimulation that accompanies many routine, repetitive jobs.

quantitative overload: Occurs in situations where individuals are required to do more work than they can actually complete in a given period of time.

quantitative underload: Occurs in situations where individuals have so little to do that they find themselves sitting around doing nothing much of the time.

relaxation training: Procedures through which individuals learn to relax in the face of anxiety or tension.

role ambiguity: Refers to uncertainty, on the part of employees, about key requirements of their jobs, and about how they are expected to behave in them. Such ambiguity often generates high levels of stress.

role conflict: Occurs when different groups or persons with whom an individual must interact (e.g., family, members of one's work group) hold conflicting expectations about his or her behavior. Such conflict is often responsible for high levels of stress.

social support: Refers to the level of help or support individuals receive from others. In some situations, social support can help individuals cope with even high levels of work-related stress.

stress: The physical, psychological, and behavioral reactions experienced by individuals in situations where they feel that their ability to cope may soon be overwhelmed.

stressors: Various aspects of the physical or social world that contribute to stress.

tension discharge rate (TDR): The rate at which individuals rid themselves of work-related tension at the end of the day. Persons who are able to dissipate such tensions quickly show better health than those who bring such pressures home with them.

NOTES

1. J. E. McGrath (1976). Stress and behavior in organizations. In M. D. Dunnette (ed.), *Handbook of industrial and organizational psychology.* Chicago: Rand McNally.

2. H. Selye (1976). *Stress in health and disease.* Boston: Butterworths.

3. National Institute for Occupational Safety and Health, Department of Health, Education, and Welfare (1978). Washington, D.C.: Government Printing Office.

4. J. B. Shaw and J. H. Riskind (1983). Predicting job stress using data from the position analysis questionnaire. *Journal of Applied Psychology, 68,* 253–261.

5. D. Katz and R. Kahn (1978). *The social psychology of organizations,* 2nd ed. New York: John Wiley.

6. E. R. Kemery, A. G. Bedeian, K. W. Mossholder, and J. Touliatos (1985). Outcomes of role stress: A multisample constructive replication. *Academy of Management Journal, 28,* 363–375.

7. R. A. Cooke and D. M. Rousseau (1984). Stress and strain from family roles and work-role expectations. *Journal of Applied Psychology, 69,* 252–260.

8. See Note 1.

9. J. R. P. French and R. D. Caplan (1972). Organizational stress and individual strain. In A. J. Morrow (ed.), *The failure of success.* New York: Amacom.

10. A. A. McLean (1980). *Work stess.* Reading, Mass.: Addison-Wesley.

11. R. O. Caplan, S. Cobb, J. R. P. French, R. Van Harrison, and S. R. Pinneau (1975). *Job demands and worker health: Main effects and occupational differences.* Washington, D.C.: Government Printing Office.

12. N. Lin, W. M. Ensel, R. S. Simeone, and W. Kuo (1979). Social support, stressful life events, and illness: A model and an empirical test. *Journal of Health and Social Behavior, 20,* 108–119.

13. S. C. Ouellette Kobasa and M. C. Puccetti (1983). Personality and social resources in stress resistance. *Journal of Personality and Social Psychology, 45,* 839–850.

14. A. Seers, G. W. McGee, T. T. Serey, and G. B. Graen (1983). The interaction of job stress and social support: A strong inference investigation. *Academy of Management Journal, 26,* 273–284.

15. S. E. Jackson (1983). Participation in decision making as a strategy for reducing job-related strain. *Journal of Applied Psychology, 68,* 3–19.

16. B. J. Fine and J. L. Kobrick (1978). Effects of altitude and heat on complex cognitive tasks. *Human Factors, 20,* 115–122.

17. A. Campbell, P. E. Converse, and W. L. Rodgers (1976). *The quality of American life.* New York: Russell Sage.

18. P. R. Jackson, E. M. Stafford, M. H. Banks, and P. B. Warr (1983). Unemployment and psychological distress in young people: The moderating role of employment commitment. *Journal of Applied Psychology, 68,* 525–535.

19. R. J. Ganellen and P. H. Blaney (1984). Hardiness and social support as moderators of the effects of life stress. *Journal of Personality and Social Psychology, 47*, 56–63.

20. T. H. Holmes and R. H. Rahe (1967). Social readjustment rating scale. *Journal of Psychosomatic Research, 11*, 213–218.

21. See Note 13.

22. M. T. Matteson and J. M. Ivancevich (1983). Note on tension discharge rate as an employee health status predictor. *Academy of Management Journal 26*,(5) 540–545.

23. M. S. Pittner, B. K. Houston, and G. Spiridigliozzi (1983). Control over stress, Type A behavior pattern, and response to stress. *Journal of Personality and Social Psychology, 44*, 627–636.

24. B. I. Brunson and K. A. Matthews (1981). The Type A coronary-prone behavior pattern and reactions to uncontrollable stress: An analysis of performance strategies, affect, and attribution during failure. *Journal of Personality and Social Psychology, 40*, 906–918.

25. M. Frese (1985). Stress at work and psychosomatic complaints: A causal interpretation. *Journal of Applied Psychology, 70*, 314–328.

26. See Note 10.

27. T. A. Beehr and J. E. Newman (1978). Job stress, employee health, and organizational effectiveness: A facet analysis, model, and literature review. *Personnel Psychology, 31*, 665–699.

28. R. C. Hollinger and J. P. Clark (1983). *Theft by employees.* Lexington, Mass.: Lexington Books.

29. C. Maslach (1982). Understanding burnout: Definitional issues in analyzing a complex phenomenon. In W. S. Paine (ed.), *Job stress and burnout: Research, theory, and intervention perspectives.* Beverly Hills: Sage.

30. J. Gaines and J. M. Jermier (1983). Emotional exhaustion in a high stress organization. *Academy of Management Journal, 26*, 567–586.

31. A. M. Pines, E. Aronson, and D. Kafry (1981). *Burnout: From tedium to personal growth.* New York: Free Press.

32. See Note 10.

33. R. M. Suinn and F. Richardson (1971). Anxiety management training: A non-specific behavior therapy program for anxiety control. *Behavior Therapy, 4*, 498–511.

34. R. K. Wallace and H. Benson (1972). The physiology of meditation. *Scientific American, 226*, 84–90.

35. R. Roskies, M. Spevack, A. Surkis, C. Cohen, and S. Gilman (1978). Changing the coronary-prone behavior pattern (Type A) in a nonclinical population. *Journal of Behavioral Medicine, 13*, 201–216.

36. R. L. Rose and J. F. Veiga (1984). Assessing the sustained effects of a stress management intervention on anxiety and locus of control. *Academy of Management Journal, 27*, 190–198.

PART III

GROUP PROCESSES

CHAPTER 8

Group Dynamics: Understanding Groups at Work

Gary Lewis knew that his company, Lewis Microbits, wasn't number one. Although it wasn't even close to being in the same league as the "big guys," Gary knew his young company—like all others—had to start someplace. He firmly believed his newly developed microprocessor, the KZ-32 chip, would revolutionize the microcomputer business. Now, all he needed was a team around him, a group of experts who shared his vision and could help transform the dream into reality. Lewis Microbits, Inc. was created to do just that.

The first thing Gary did was to combine his interests with a small group of experts in production and marketing, and meet with them to try to get the business off the ground. "Gentlemen," he began, "we are on the verge of a revolution in computer technology, and with your help, the KZ-32 will lead that revolution." These grandiose thoughts were hardly in keeping with the modest surroundings within which they were expressed. Yet, the two other principals in Lewis Microbits, Craig Sternoff and Leslie Fisher, listened intently to their guru as they shared their mutual beliefs in their prospects for success.

"With your design, Gary, it should be easy to manufacture the KZ-32 at very low cost," Craig said.

"That's good," replied Leslie, "but we still have to decide whether to sell the chip to computer manufacturers or to build our own computers around that chip."

Gary Lewis was a gifted engineer, but his naivete about marketing problems showed as he replied to Leslie. "I never thought about that," Gary said, in an uncertain tone. "Les, you'll have to handle that decision. That's why you're here."

"I'd like to," Leslie replied, "but I'll need to hire some market researchers to conduct a feasibility study to see what our best chances are for short-term *and* long-term success." Scratching his head, Gary remarked, "I guess it's not as easy as I thought."

At this point Craig interjected. "Exactly how we produce the chip will depend on whether we manufacture it for ourselves or for other companies." "After all," he added, "the industry's too young to see much standardization, and we'd have to meet different manufacturing specifications depending on our market."

Leaning back in his chair, Gary Lewis was more perplexed than ever. "Things are more complicated than I imagined," he said. "I built a better mousetrap. I'm sure of it. Now we've just got to get the world to beat a path to our door."

"That's why we're all here," Leslie and Craig chimed in.

"How complicated the group was making it all seem!" Gary thought to himself. "I really need these people to get all the work done." It was clear that coming up with the invention was only the first step toward creating a marketable product. Sharing his thoughts, Gary said, "As long as we can work together as a team, I'm sure we can make our dream a reality."

As this scene at Lewis Microbits unfolds, one important fact emerges: running an organization requires a group effort. The three characters in our story all add something to the company and will have to work together to achieve success. Already we can see the social dynamics at work. The group members are each performing their specific individual tasks, but they have to coordinate their efforts. What factors will help keep the group together or break it apart? Will the group members work better because of each other, or would they be better off working alone? These questions all are basic ones in the field of **group dynamics**—an important topic in organizational behavior, and the focus of this chapter.

Our presentation will examine the functioning of work groups in organizational settings. We will consider how groups are structured and then turn to some of the factors influencing work group behavior, such as the presence of other individuals, and the type of task performed. Before proceeding with these topics, however, we will begin by considering some basic questions about groups themselves.

GROUPS AT WORK: SOME BASIC ISSUES

Probably the most basic question confronting us is: What is a group? The term is often used, yet it is not always clear what it implies. After defining what we mean by the word *group*, we will review some of the ways groups are involved in organizational behavior.

What Is a Group?

Imagine three people waiting in line at a supermarket checkout counter. Now, compare them to Gary, Craig, and Leslie, the three characters in our opening story. Clearly these "groups" are not the same. But how are they different? Which collection of people would you consider to be a group? We may refer to the people waiting in the supermarket checkout line as a "group," yet we don't think of them as being one in the same sense as our three characters at Lewis Microbits. Obviously, a group is more that just a collection of people, but what exactly makes a group a group?

A precise definition of the term **group** is clearly needed. Our definition will be based on some of the key characteristics of groups noted by many different social scientists. We will first review some of the characteristics of groups and then combine these to form our definition.[1] These elements are summarized in Figure 8.1.

One obvious characteristic of a group is that it is composed of *two or more individuals engaged in social interaction.* People interact by mutually influencing each other. Interaction can take the form of verbal communication (such as sharing corporate plans at a stockholders' meeting), or nonverbal communication (such as two workers who exchange smiles as they pass each other in the hall). People must influence each other in some way to be considered a group. We would not consider individuals who are isolated from each other and incapable of influencing each other as constituting a group.

Social interaction is not the only characteristic needed to form a group. Groups must also have some *structure,* some stable relationships between members. Later in this chapter we will identify the stabilizing rules used by groups to organize the interaction between members. For now, suffice it so say that groups must have some

FIGURE 8.1 *What Is a Group? Some Defining Characteristics.*
The four major characteristics of a group are summarized here. As shown, a group consists of two or more people in social interaction who have some stable, structured relationships, share common goals, and perceive themselves as being a group.

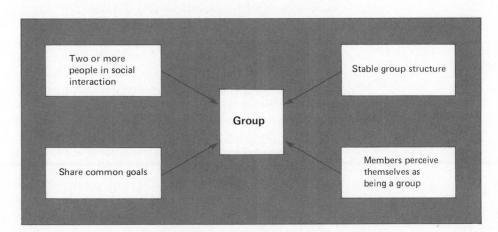

lasting structure to exist. Just as the human body requires a skeleton, so too must a group have a structure.

A third characteristic of social groups is that they *share common goals.* Groups form for some reason; their members come together to achieve some goal that they might not be able to realize individually. It is this unifying interest that helps sustain the group.

A final characteristic of groups is that their *members perceive themselves as a group.* People must recognize each other as similar in some way, as sharing some common fate. Shoppers in a checkout line probably don't recognize themselves as a group. Other than being close to each other at the same time, they have little in common. It is a critical characteristic of any group that its members recognize each other and be able to differentiate who is and who is not part of the group.

Based on these characteristics, we may define a group as *a collection of two or more interacting individuals with a stable pattern of relationships between them who share common goals and who perceive themselves as being a group.* (Refer to Figure 8.1, page 239.) The various aspects of this definition will, no doubt, become clearer as we begin to discuss the behavior of groups in this chapter.

Now that we have defined what we mean by a group, we are in a better position to understand the importance of group behavior in organizations.

The Importance of Groups in Organizations: Some Early Demonstrations

The study of group behavior has a long tradition among social scientists in many disciplines. In fact, it has been said that the study of social groups "does not 'belong' to any one of the recognized social sciences alone. It is the common property of all."[2] The field of management has been among those most interested in studying group behavior.

Beginning in the late 1920's, administrators became aware of the need to understand how the relationships between group members influenced work behavior. When pioneering organizational scientists attempted to improve work performance by changing working conditions, they soon discovered that such performance was determined more by the influence of informal groups than by formal managerial policies. For example, in one of the first large-scale studies to interview workers (discussed in Chapter 1), Elton Mayo found that groups of workers at a large manufacturing plant informally agreed to limit production levels.[3] Despite management's attempts to raise productivity by financially rewarding workers for improving their performance, employees found the social pressures imposed by their colleagues provided an even greater incentive to restrict their performance. Mayo and his colleagues learned that the risks of social rejection by one's fellow workers had a profound influence on workers.

In view of some of the potent effects of group influence, it should not be surprising that groups have been found to be effective sources of social change. One of the first experimental tests of this effect was conducted by Kurt Lewin, a founder of the field of group dynamics.[4] Lewin's research was performed at the request of the Food Habits Committee of the National Research Council, whose members were interested in getting homemakers to change their eating habits in the face of a beef shortage during World War II. Lewin's task was to convince the homemakers to substitute certain readily available, but less desirable meat products (e.g., sweet-breads, kidneys, and hearts) for beef. Two different approaches were compared. In one, the homemakers listened to a persuasive lecture emphasizing the nutritive value of the new foods and the patriotic benefits of serving them. In the other approach, the same information was discussed by a group of homemakers who were asked to reach a consensus about eating these foods. In a follow-up question-naire of eating habits, it was found that 32 percent of the homemakers who partici-pated in the group discussion served at least one meal using less desirable foods, compared to only 3 percent of those who heard the lecture. Findings such as these suggest that it may be easier to change people's opinions by dealing with them as members of a group than as individuals.

Not surprisingly, it has been reported that employees are likely to be more accepting of changes in their organization when they meet as a group to discuss those changes than when no such group meetings take place. Coch and French clearly demonstrated this effect in the late 1940s in a classic study at a pajama manufacturing plant of the Harwood Manufacturing Corporation.[5] The workers at Harwood were unhappy about the frequent changes in production methods that resulted from engineering advances and product alterations. Some of the Harwood workers were given a verbal explanation for the changes (control group subjects) and others met in groups to discuss and reach a consensus about the need for change at Harwood (experimental group subjects). As in Lewin's study, Coch and French found that changing a group's opinion was more effective than changing the opinions of individual workers. Within forty days after implementing the changes at Harwood, 17 percent of the control group subjects quit their jobs, compared to none who did so in the experimental group. These findings make the point that groups are very influential in affecting organizational change.

One reason for this would seem to be the natural attraction group members have for each other. We have already discussed the basic needs of people to gain respect and admiration from others (recall our discussion of Maslow's need hierar-chy theory in Chapter 3). Being part of a desirable work group can help promote job satisfaction. Van Zelst showed this in a study of carpenters and bricklayers working on a housing development.[6] During the first five months of the job, the men got to learn all about each other by being assigned many different co-workers by their supervisors. Then they were allowed to work in groups with those they liked best. This new arrangement resulted in a greatly reduced rate of turnover and a drop in the cost of building the housing development. Among the greatest benefits were surely the personal gains experienced by the workers themselves. To quote one of the workers, "The work is a lot more interesting when you've got a buddy working with you. You certainly like it a lot better anyway."[7]

We may summarize this section by noting that work groups have a profound influence on behavior. Groups have been found to improve organizational perfor-mance or to restrict it in very important ways. With this background, we will now take a closer look at the process of group dynamics in work settings.

THE STRUCTURE OF WORK
GROUPS

One of the defining characteristics of groups, as we have noted, is that they have a stable structure. By the term **group structure,** we are referring to the interrelationships between the individuals comprising a group, the guidelines to group behavior that make group functioning orderly and predictable.[8] The structure of a group has been likened to the interrelationship between the planets in our solar system.[9] Just as we may learn about the solar system by studying the relationships between the planets, we may learn about groups by studying the relationships between the people comprising them. In this section we will describe three different aspects of group structure: group *cohesiveness*, group *norms*, and the *roles* played by group members.

Cohesiveness: Getting the "Team Spirit"

One obvious determinant of any group's structure is its **cohesiveness.** We may define *cohesiveness* as the pressures group members face to remain part of their groups. Highly cohesive work groups are ones in which the members are attracted to each other, accept the group's goals, and help work toward meeting them. In very uncohesive groups, the members dislike each other and may even work at cross-purposes.[10] In essence, cohesiveness refers to a "we-feeling," an *esprit de corps*, a sense of belonging to one's group.

Although we often hear about the benefits of highly cohesive groups, the consequences of cohesiveness are not always positive. In fact, research has shown both positive and negative effects of this factor. On the positive side, it is known that people enjoy belonging to highly cohesive groups. Members of closely knit work groups participate more fully in their groups' activities, more readily accept their group's goals, and are absent less often than members of less cohesive groups.[11] However, the tendency for members of highly cohesive groups to go along with their fellow members' wishes may sometimes have negative consequences on the ultimate group product. Consider, for example, the actions of the highly cohesive Committee to Re-elect President Nixon preceding the 1972 presidential election. The Watergate conspirators were a highly cohesive group—so cohesive, in fact, that they were blinded to the possibility that they were committing illegal and unethical acts. These poor decisions that result from too high a level of cohesiveness describe the phenomenon known as *groupthink*.[12] Groupthink occurs when a group is so cohesive it potentially loses sight of its ultimate goals. Because of the negative impact of groupthink on the quality of group decisions, we will discuss this phenomenon in greater detail in our chapter on decision making (Chapter 13). (For a dramatic example of the potentially negative consequences of too much group cohesion, please refer to the **Case in Point** on page 243.)

Group cohesion can influence productivity in many additional ways. It makes sense that after a group experiences success, its members will feel more committed

Violence on the Picket Line: The Deindividuating Effects of Groups

The strike at Farrington Steel was in its third week and things were tough all around. The company was losing revenue and falling desperately behind on its orders. The workers, having missed three consecutive paychecks, were getting deeper in debt. The talks at the bargaining table were stalled and, not surprisingly, tension between Farrington management and its workforce was high.

Malcolm Everett had worked for Farrington for ten years. He was a quiet, unassuming man who was well liked by his fellow workers and never got into trouble. In fact, his loyalty to the company was marked only three months earlier with a gold ring—a coveted award for a decade of service to the company.

When Farrington's management brought a group of "scabs" through the picket line, the workers revolted, and Malcolm was among them. This was the last straw! "They're not gonna get away with this," one of the picketers screamed. Soon some of the workers formed a human barricade in front of the company's main gate. Others rocked the buses carrying the new people brought in to replace the strikers. As tempers flared, violence erupted.

Screaming, "Down with the scabs," Malcolm and his colleagues successfully blocked the buses from entering Farrington's gates. This didn't end the incident, though, as the strikers picked up rocks and hurled them through the bus windows. As one Farrington employee began throwing rocks, others quickly followed suit, including Malcolm. The more glass that shattered, the more the picketers pummeled the bus with debris. Rock after rock left Malcolm's hand—the hand of this usually quiet, loyal employee. Later that evening Malcolm spoke to his wife about the incident. "I don't know why I did it," he said, "I'm not a violent person." Remorsefully, he added, "Everyone else did it, and it just felt right. I guess I just got carried away with the heat of the moment."

Unfortunately, scenes such as this one are not uncommon. Indeed, people often get "carried away" in social groups and do things they would never dream of doing alone. If you have ever witnessed violent outbreaks at professional hockey games or the behavior of people at wild parties, you may recognize the spontaneous acts of the Farrington strikers as falling into the same category. Often, the presence of other people tends to weaken our restraints against acting in impulsive, antisocial ways (see Figure 8.2). The pro-

FIGURE 8.2   *Deindividuation: Some Serious Consequences.*
The tendency for people to feel anonymous in groups sometimes lowers their restraints against acting in antisocial ways—a process known as *deindividuation*. These photos show some situations in which deindividuation appears to have occurred.

cess through which these unsettling group influences occur is known as **deindividuation.** Many forms of violence and vandalism, such as in the above case, have been explained in terms of the deindividuating effects of groups.[13]

Scientists have noted that the state of deindividuation is one in which people become less aware of themselves and distort their perceptions of reality. When they are part of a cohesive group, it is easy to think about the group instead of oneself, become anonymous, and get carried away with what the group does. As a result, a person in a deindividuated state may act in a less rational manner and be less resistant to acting impulsively than someone who is not deindividuated.[14] It should not be surprising, therefore, that studies have shown vandalism to be more likely to occur in large anonymous groups, where people are anonymous, than in small groups, where members know each other well.[15]

Questions

(1) What could have been done to counter the deindividuating conditions on the picket line that led to the violence at Farrington?
(2) Can you identify some additional organizational situations in which the negative effects of deindividuation may be expected to occur?

---

to each other. Similarly, we might expect a cohesive group to work well together and to achieve a high level of success. However, just because members of a work group are strongly committed to each other does not mean the group will perform well in organizations.[16] For example, if a group's goals are contrary to the organization's goals, a highly cohesive group may actually do a great deal of harm to an organization. Highly cohesive workers who conspire to sabotage their employees are a good example. Obviously, there is no simple relationship between group cohesiveness and task performance.

One of the first studies to examine the relationship between group cohesion and organizational productivity was conducted over thirty years ago by Stanley Seashore.[17] The participants in this experiment were employees of a manufacturing plant who formed over two hundred small work groups. These persons completed questionnaires measuring the degree of cohesiveness of their work groups, which were then compared with job performance over a three-month period. It was found that high cohesiveness was associated with high productivity when group members felt that management supported them, but low productivity when management threatened them. This implies that a cohesive work group may only be successful if what it is doing goes along with management's wishes.

More recently, in a study conducted at a public utility, it was found that in highly cohesive groups a supportive managerial style was related to higher performance, but not so in weakly cohesive groups.[18] A similar tendency for high performance levels to be associated with highly cohesive groups operating under a supportive managerial atmosphere has also been found in a study of Israeli soldiers.[19] It appears, then, that there is no simple relationship between group cohesion and job performance. A summary of these studies in Figure 8.3 shows that a cohesive group *can* enhance productivity, but *only* when the manager's style supports the group's efforts. If a group of workers band together but finds that its efforts are not supported by the company's management, it will be likely to perform poorly. Cohesion can aid productivity only as long as workers and managers are not operating in opposition to each other.

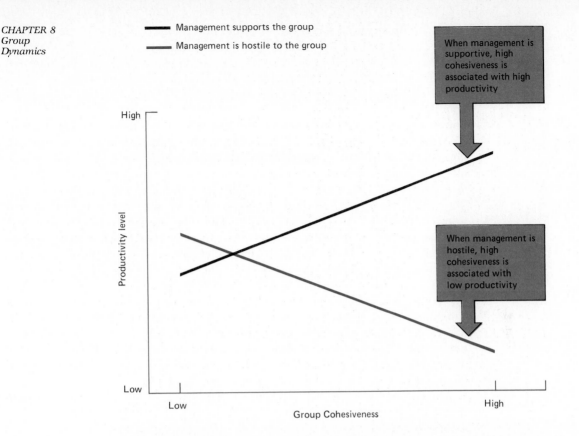

Management supports the group

Management is hostile to the group

When management is supportive, high cohesiveness is associated with high productivity

When management is hostile, high cohesiveness is associated with low productivity

High

Productivity level

Low

Low

High

Group Cohesiveness

FIGURE 8.3   *Group Cohesion and Productivity: It Depends on Management.*
Several studies have shown that the relationship between group performance and group cohesiveness depends on the level of managerial support for the group. Greater cohesion is associated with greater productivity when management is supportive of the group, and less productivity when management is hostile to the group.

Norms: A Group's Unspoken Rules

One element of group life that enhances its orderly structure is group **norms.** We define *norms* as generally agreed upon informal rules that guide group members' behavior.[20] Norms differ from organizational rules in that they are *not* formal and written. In fact, group members may not even be aware of the subtle group standards that exist and regulate their behavior. Norms can be either *prescriptive*— dictating behaviors that should be performed, or *proscriptive*—dictating behaviors that should be avoided. For example, work groups may develop prescriptive norms to follow their leader, to attain a given level of performance, or to pitch in and help a group member who needs assistance.[21] They may also develop proscriptive norms not to work much harder than other group members, or to refrain from tattling on each other.

The question of how group norms develop has been one of considerable interest to organizational researchers. (We will have more to say about the power of groups to get members to accept norms in Chapter 11.) Feldman has recently proposed four ways in which group norms may develop.[22] These are summarized in Table 8.1. First, we can say that norms develop due to *precedents set over time.* Whatever behaviors emerge at a first group meeting will usually set the standard for how that group is to operate. Initial group patterns of behavior frequently become normative, such as where people sit, and how formal or informal the meeting is to be. Such routines help establish a predictable, orderly interaction pattern. Similarly, norms develop because of *carryovers from other situations.* Group members usually draw from their previous experiences to guide their behavior in new situations. The norms governing professional behavior apply here. For example, the norm for a physician to behave ethically and to exercise a pleasant bedside manner carries over from one hospital to another, so that a doctor changing hospitals can expect the same norms of professionalism to preside in the new setting. Such carryover norms can help make interaction easier in new social situations. Carryover norms mean there may be fewer new norms to learn, thereby enhancing the ease of social interaction.

Sometimes norms also develop in response to an *explicit statement by a superior or a co-worker.* Newcomers to groups quickly "learn the ropes" when one of their co-workers tells them "that's the way we do it around here." The explanation is an explicit statement of the norms—it describes what one should do or avoid doing to be accepted by the group. Sometimes the explicit statement of group norms represents the accepted desires of a powerful group member, such as a supervisor. If a supervisor wants reports to be prepared in a certain way, or expects a certain degree of formality or informality in addressing others, norms may develop to adapt to these standards. The socialization of new group members frequently requires the learning of group norms by listening to more experienced group members.[23]

Finally, group norms may develop out of *critical events in the group's history.* If an employee releases an important organizational secret to a competitor, causing a loss to the company, a norm to maintain secrecy may develop out of this incident. In a similar manner, a professional group that decides to censure the inappropriate behavior of one of its members may be seen as acting to reaffirm its commitment to the violated norm, for example, a member of congress who accepts a bribe, or a physician who harms a patient because of poor medical judgment. Both incidents represent critical events that helped either establish or reaffirm a group norm.

Roles: The Hats We Wear

In addition to norms, group structure is also enhanced by the fact that members tend to play specific roles in group interaction. Social scientists use the term *role* in much the same way as a director of a play would refer to a particular character in the script of a play. Indeed, the part one plays in the overall group structure is what we mean by a role. More formally, we may define a **role** as the typical behaviors that characterize a person in a social context.[24] For example, the President of the United States makes foreign policy decisions, attempts to improve the American economy, and so on—all behaviors expected of the person occupying

TABLE 8.1   *Norms: How Do They Develop?*
This table summarizes four ways group norms can develop. (Source: Based on Feldman, 1984; see Note 21.)

Basis of norm development	Example
1. Precedents set over time	Seating location of each group member around a table
2. Carryovers from other situations	Professional standards of conduct
3. Explicit statements from others	Working a certain way because you are told "that's how we do it around here"
4. Critical events in group history	After the organization suffers a loss due to one person's divulging company secrets, a norm develops to maintain secrecy

the office, or playing that role. Such a person referred to as a *role incumbent*. When a new president takes office, that person assumes the same role and has the same powers as the former officeholder, and the same behaviors are expected of this person as well. Although the specific behaviors of individual presidents may vary, certain behaviors (referred to as *role expectations*) are expected of all role incumbents. The fact that each role incumbent recognizes the expectations of his or her role helps avoid the social disorganization that would surely result if clear role expectations did not exist.

Role differentiation: Specialized parts.   As work groups and social groups develop, the various group members come to play different roles in the social structure—a process referred to as **role differentiation.** The emergence of different roles in groups is a naturally occurring process. Think of committees to which you may have belonged. Was there one member who joked and made people feel better, and another member who worked hard to get the group to focus on the issue at hand? These examples of differentiated roles are, in fact, typical of role behaviors that emerge in groups. Researchers long ago found that there emerges in groups one person who—more than others—helps the group reach its goal. Such a person is said to play the *task-specialist* role. In addition, another group member may emerge who is quite supportive and nurturant, someone who makes everyone else feel good. Such a person is said to play a *socio-emotional* role.

There are many specific role behaviors that can fall into either the task-oriented or the socio-emotional categories. Some specific sub-roles of these categories are listed in Table 8.2 (page 248).[25] Although this simple distinction helps us to understand some of the roles one may find in work groups, we should note that more complex conceptualizations have been proposed, including one that identifies as many as twenty-six different roles.[26] These efforts at understanding role differentiation, regardless of how simple or complex the distinctions may be, help make the point that similarities between groups may be recognized by the common roles played by members.

Role conflict: Competing demands from the roles we play.   There is a great deal of interest in the field of organizational behavior in the concept of **role con-**

TABLE 8.2   The Many Roles Played by Group Members.
The *task-specialist* and *socio-emotional* roles played by group members are composed of several sub-roles, many of which are listed here. (Source: Based on Benne and Sheats, 1948; see Note 25.)

Task-Specialist Roles	Socio-Emotional Roles
Initiator-contributor: Recommends new solutions to group problems	*Harmonizer:* Mediates group conflicts
Information seeker: Attempts to obtain the necessary facts	*Compromiser:* Shifts own opinion to create group harmony
Opinion giver: Shares own opinions with others	*Encourager:* Praises and encourages others
Coordinator: Relates various ideas to the problem at hand	*Follower:* Goes along with the ideas of group members
Energizer: Stimulates the group into action when interest drops	*Expediter:* Suggests ways the group can operate more smoothly

flict—the idea that the appropriate behaviors for enacting a role may be inconsistent with the appropriate behaviors for enacting another role or other requirements of the same role. It shouldn't be too surprising that various role requirements may conflict given the many roles that a person plays—employee, friend, and family member, just to name a few (refer to our discussion in Chapter 7).

Although there are many types of role conflicts, the two most common varieties are *interrole* conflict and *intrarole* conflict.[27] These are summarized in Figure 8.4. **Interrole** conflict refers to the incompatible demands of two or more different roles played by the same person. A common example is when a supervisor becomes friendly with his or her subordinates. What a supervisor may be expected to do as a boss (e.g., "be tough") may conflict with the more congenial behaviors expected as a friend. As a result, it is difficult to fulfill the demands of both roles simultaneously. Individuals may also experience **intrarole** conflict, in which there are contradictory demands within a single role as viewed by different members of the group (referred to as *role senders*). A good example may be seen in the dual set of expectations faced by supervisors who are also members of their work groups. These supervisors are expected to be loyal to their fellow group members, which may be difficult given that upper management may expect them to be loyal to corporate interests instead. Intrarole conflict can also stem from ambiguities inherent in the positions held by role incumbents.[28] If it isn't clear what a person occupying a given role is expected to do, it would not be surprising to find that different people would expect different things of a role incumbent, thereby creating intrarole conflict.

Research has revealed the negative consequences of role conflict, including job dissatisfaction, poor group performance, and the rejection of other group members.[29] One recent study of interrole conflict found that the more managers and employees disagreed about the employee's role expectations, the more employees experienced work-related stress and felt uncertain about the possibility of promotion (see Chapter 7).[30] A particularly important focus of recent research on role conflict has been the conflicts caused by the demands made on workers by their jobs and their families, a common problem faced by members of today's dual-career families. In one study, Cooke and Rousseau examined the role conflicts experienced by two hundred teachers.[31] The researchers found that the more teachers experienced conflicts between their roles as teachers and family members (such as by taking home extra work to do), the more they reported feeling work overload (difficulty having enough time to get their work done) and high role conflict (interference between job demands and free-time activities), the more they showed symptoms of physical and psychological strain. These findings support the idea that role conflicts can have a severe negative impact on workers' job performance and their personal well being. (Recall our discussion of this topic in Chapter 7.)

INDIVIDUAL PRODUCTIVITY IN GROUPS: WORKING IN THE PRESENCE OF OTHERS

Imagine that you have been studying drama for three years and you are now ready for your first acting audition in front of some Hollywood producers. You have been rehearsing diligently for several months, getting ready for the part. Now, you are no longer alone at home with your script in front of you. Your name is announced and silence fills the auditorium as you walk to the front of the stage. How will you perform now that you are in front of an audience? Will you freeze, forgetting the lines you studied so intensely when you practiced alone? Or will the audience spur you on to your best performance yet? In other words, what impact would the presence of the audience have on your behavior (see Figure 8.5, p. 250)?

Approximately ninety years ago this same question was asked by a bicycling enthusiast named Norman Triplett who put his skills as a social scientist to work to find an answer.[32] Triplett noticed that cyclists invariably achieved faster times when they raced against others than when they raced alone, against the clock. Intrigued

FIGURE 8.4 *Role Conflict: Two Sources.*
Two major sources of role conflict are summarized here. In *interrole* conflict, there are different sets of expectations on a person playing more than one role. In *intrarole* conflict, there are different sets of expectations sent from different persons to a person playing one role.

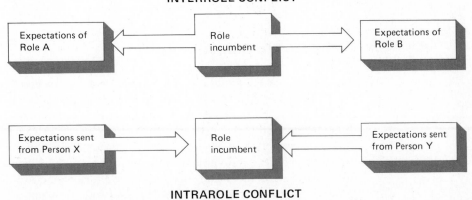

INTERROLE CONFLICT

INTRAROLE CONFLICT

FIGURE 8.5 *Working Alone or with Another: Which Is Better?*
Would the mother in this cartoon have done a better job of prying had she been alone? The question of whether people work better alone or in the presence of others is an important one for organizational scientists. (Source: Copyright, 1984, Universal Press Syndicate. Reprinted with permission. All rights reserved.)

by these observations, he conducted a laboratory experiment requiring children, either alone or in pairs, to play a game in which they were required to turn a fishing reel as fast as possible. Just as he had observed at the bicycle track, Triplett found that the children performed the task better when they were in the presence of another person than when they were alone.

As other scientists began studying the effects of the presence of an audience or *coactors* (people working on the same task at the same time) on individual performance, it was not always found that performance improved, as Triplett noted. In fact, sometimes it was found that people did *worse* when performing a task in the presence of others than when alone. This tendency for the presence of others sometimes to enhance an individual's performance and sometimes to impair it became known as **social facilitation.** For many years, scientists were confused about the effects of others' presence on task performance. Then, in the mid 1960s, Robert Zajonc proposed a model that accounted for the apparent inconsistency in the findings regarding social facilitation.[33] Zajonc's model offered a simple, yet elegant explanation of when others' presence would help and when it would hinder performance.

Social Facilitation: A Model

Zajonc reasoned that social facilitation was the result of the heightened emotional arousal (e.g., feelings of tension and excitement) people experience when in the presence of others. (Wouldn't you feel more tension playing the piano in front of an audience than alone?) When people are aroused, they tend to perform the most *dominant response*—their most likely behavior in that setting. (It may be considered an example of a dominant act to return the smile of a smiling coworker; it is a very well-learned act to smile at someone when he or she smiles at you.) If someone is performing a very well-learned act, the dominant response would be a correct

250

one (such as speaking the right lines in an acting audition). However, if the behavior in question is relatively novel, the dominant response would be expected to be incorrect (such as speaking the wrong lines during an audition). Together, these ideas are known as Zajonc's **drive theory of social facilitation.** According to this theory, the presence of others increases arousal, which increases the tendency to perform the most dominant responses. If these responses are correct, the resulting performance will be enhanced; if they are incorrect, the performance will be impaired. (For a summary, please refer to Figure 8.6.)

According to Zajonc's drive theory of social facilitation, one may be expected to perform better on a task in the presence of others if that task is very well-learned, but poorer if that task is not well-learned. Reasoning that dressing in one's own clothes is a well-learned task, but that putting on new, unusual clothes is not well-learned, Hazel Markus conducted an experiment in which she tested social facilitation effects.[34] She compared the amount of time it took subjects to put on and take off novel clothes—such as a pair of large shoes and socks—and more familiar clothes—such as their own shoes and socks. Consistent with the drive theory of social facilitation, it took subjects more time to don and remove the unusual clothes (i.e., to perform the nondominant response) but less time to don and remove their own clothes (i.e., to perform the dominant response) when in the presence of others than when alone. In other words, the presence of others facilitated the performance of well-learned responses, but hampered the performance of unfamiliar responses.

FIGURE 8.6   *Social Facilitation: A Drive Theory Approach.*
The *drive theory* of social facilitation states that the presence of others is arousing. Such increased arousal enhances the tendency to perform dominant (strong) responses. If these are correct in a given situation, performance is improved. If they are incorrect, performance is impaired.

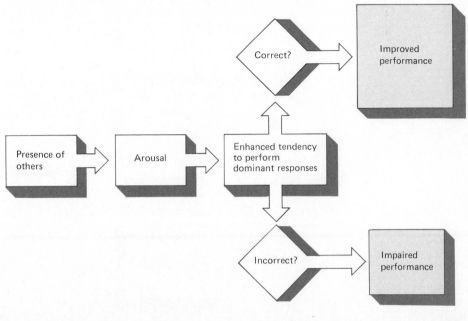

Social Facilitation: Why Are Others Arousing?

Although it is well established that dominant responses (be they correct or incorrect) are enhanced by the presence of others, there is considerable disagreement about exactly *why* these effects occur. Three different perspectives have been offered that we will describe here (please refer to the summary of these positions shown in Figure 8.7).

As we have already explained, Zajonc proposed that the presence of others makes people feel aroused. According to Zajonc, this arousal results just because the others are there, what he calls their "mere presence." He uses the term **compresence** to refer to the presence of others and the innately arousing effects that it has.[35] Modifying Zajonc's approach, Cottrell has claimed that the arousal resulting from others' presence is not due to the fact that others are simply there, but that these others can potentially evaluate the person.[36] Cottrell's position is that the drive resulting from others' presence is a response to having learned, from previous experiences, that other people can be the source of either positive of negative evaluations. As such, it is referred to as **learned drive theory.** The major idea of this theory is that social facilitation results from **evaluation apprehension**—the fear of being evaluated, or judged by another person. Cottrell theorized that people are aroused by performing a task in the presence of others because of their concern over what those others might think of them.

FIGURE 8.7 *Why Are Others Arousing? Three Explanations.*
There are three major explanations of the arousal caused by the presence of others. These are the *compresence* explanation (based on the drive theory of social facilitation), the *evaluation apprehension* explanation (based on the learned drive theory of social facilitation), and the explanation based on the *distraction-conflict* theory of social facilitation.

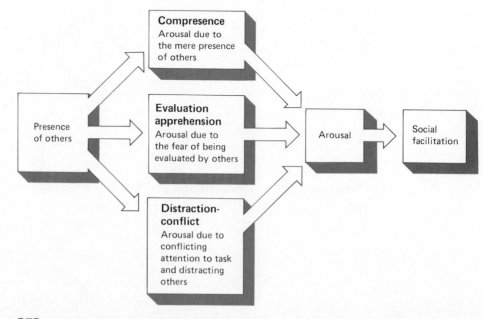

Does social facilitation occur just because other people are present, or because those others can evaluate our performance? The evidence bearing on this question is confusing, and some support is found for each possibility. For example, the presence of others in Markus's study of people getting dressed produced social facilitation effects although the threat of evaluation over how one puts on one's shoes and socks would be minimal. Moreover, Markus found no more social facilitation when the members of the audience attentively watched the subjects than when they had their backs to the subjects. However, other studies have found that social facilitation effects occur *only* when members of the audience can evaluate the performer.[37] A new approach to social facilitation known as **distraction-conflict theory** offers a promising resolution to this dilemma.

The basic idea of *distraction-conflict theory* is that the presence of an audience or coactors creates a conflict in attention among people performing a task.[38] People are directed toward the demands of the task while, at the same time, the other persons present provide a source of distraction. If the others are coactors, people may wish to look at them to see how well they are doing relative to themselves (as in the case of the lead runner in a race who looks back at the field to see how nearby the next closest competitor is). If the others comprise an audience, people may try to assess their approval or disapproval, or they may simply desire to look at the audience out of curiosity. In either case, these conflicts are arousing, and (as Zajonc hypothesized) this arousal leads to the tendency to perform the dominant response.

Distraction-conflict theory recognizes that task performance can be impaired both because the presence of others arouses so much concern that it lessens attention to the task at hand and because those others divert our attention away from our work, even if we are unconcerned about what they think of us. As such, the theory reconciles the inconsistent findings of Zajonc's compresence explanation and Cottrell's evaluation apprehension explanation of social facilitation. In short, distraction-conflict theory recognizes that the presence of others can impair performance both when these persons represent a source of evaluation and when they do not.

Some support for distraction-conflict theory is provided by a recent study by Ferris and Rowland.[39] The subjects in this experiment were student workers performing a proofreading task under one of three conditions. They either worked *alone,* alongside three others (the *coaction* condition), or alongside three others against whom they expected to compare their work later on (the *coaction with expected evaluation* condition). Of interest to the experimenter was the effects of these conditions on performance quality—how accurately the workers performed the proofreading task. The results, summarized in Figure 8.8 (page 254), show that performance quality was lowest in the *coaction* condition. These findings were taken as support for the distraction-conflict theory because of the following reasoning. Subjects working alone obviously were not distracted because no others were present. Subjects who coacted with others with whom they later expected to compare their work were only minimally distracted because they knew an opportunity for evaluation was forthcoming. However, subjects in the coaction condition performed the poorest on the task because they knew this was their only chance to compare themselves to their coworkers, and as a result were most distracted by them.

To summarize, scientists have proposed that social facilitation occurs as a

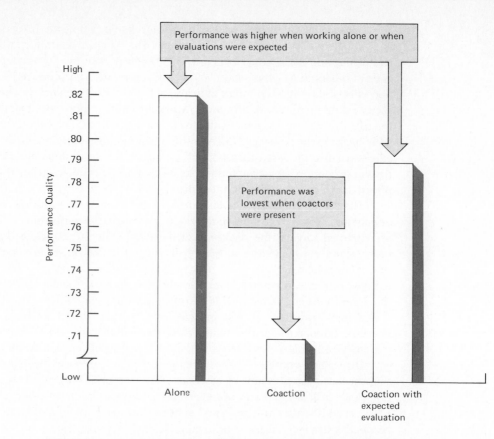

Performance was higher when working alone or when evaluations were expected

Performance was lowest when coactors were present

High

.82
.81
.80
.79
.78
.77
.76
.75
.74
.73
.72
.71

Low

Performance Quality

Alone   Coaction   Coaction with
                                  expected
                                  evaluation

FIGURE 8.8   *Social Facilitation Effects: Some Experimental Evidence.*
Subjects in one recent experiment performed a proofreading task either alone, with coactors
present, or with coactors with whom they later expected to compare their work. Performance
was lowest in the coaction condition, suggesting that the presence of coactors distracted
subjects. Less distraction (and higher performance) resulted when subjects expected to
compare their work with coactors later on. (Source: Based on data reported in Ferris and
Rowland, 1983; see Note 39.)

result of either the mere physical presence of others, the fact that these others can
evaluate the person, or the tendency for others to provide a source of distraction. At
this time there appears to be no one best explanation of why social facilitation
occurs. However, recent findings seem to suggest that the third (distraction-conflict
theory) may be the most comprehensive and useful in this respect.[40]

GROUP PERFORMANCE: WORKING WITH OTHERS

Thus far, our discussion of group performance has focused on tasks in which
people work in the presence of others to produce an individual result. Although

there are many such tasks performed in organizations (e.g., typists working in a typing pool), not all tasks fall into this category. There are many other jobs done in organizations in which group members interact with each other to produce a group product. Clearly, such tasks are more complex in nature. (For some suggestions as to how to facilitate performance in one common type or interactive group setting—the meeting—please refer to the **Perspective** insert on page 256.)

In order to better understand the effectiveness of work groups in performing interacting tasks, we will begin by identifying the different types of tasks on which group members may interact.

Varieties of Group Tasks

Most of the jobs work groups perform, especially the most complex ones, can be seen as being made up of many smaller tasks. As such, we would consider the overall job to be one that is **divisible**—capable of being divided into smaller subtasks. Any one musician cannot play a symphony alone; other musicians are required. Each musician's job, however, is such that it cannot be divided into separate tasks to be performed by several persons. Only one musician is needed to play a single violin at a time. We would consider such a task to be unitary, in that only one person is required to perform it. An important question for organizational scientists is: How can individual (unitary) tasks be combined to form a group product? Steiner has identified four different kinds of group tasks that we will describe in this section. [48,49] These are summarized in Table 8.3.

Additive tasks.   Probably the most obvious way of combining individual inputs to form a group product is by adding them all together. Tasks in which the individ-

Table 8.3   Group Tasks: A Typology.
Four different types of group tasks are summarized here. Each represents a different way of combining the unitary output of group members performing a divisible task. (Source: Based on Steiner, 1976; see Note 48.)

Type of task	Description	Example
Additive	Taking the sum of individual contributions as the group's product	Several people shoveling snow off a driveway
Compensatory	Taking the average of several individual contributions as the group's product	Averaging the judgments of several committee members about how to allocate funds on a project
Disjunctive	Taking one group member's input (hopefully, the best) as the group's product	Selecting one group member's solution to a problem as its answer
Conjunctive	Taking the performance of the poorest group member as the group's product	Slowing the speed of a mountain climbing expedition to that of the slowest member

FROM THE MANAGER'S PERSPECTIVE

Conducting an Effective Group Meeting: Some Guidelines

One of the most common settings for group interaction in work organizations is the meeting. Surveys have shown that corporate executives spend an average of over three hours a week in formally scheduled meetings and almost ten hours in informal conferences. In fact, the amount of time spent in meetings appears to increase the higher an executive's position is in the organizational hierarchy.[41] Although meetings are a major part of organizational life, their effectiveness often suffers from wasted time, boring presentations, and poor organization. With this in mind, we will outline some suggestions for improving the efficiency of group meetings.

1. Create a supportive atmosphere. A frequently occuring problem in many meetings is that group members are reluctant to talk. This is often due, in part, to the insecurities that some people may have about being evaluated for their contribution.[42] If an entire group is composed of members afraid to talk, not much will result from the meeting. In an attempt to avoid this pitfall, management theorist Rensis Likert urges leaders of group meetings to create a "supportive atmosphere."[43] This may be accomplished by showing respect for all points of view and offering comments and criticisms with a helpful orientation. Not only should group leaders follow these guidelines, but they should also encourage other members of the group to do so, too.

2. Be prepared. Few things waste more time than meetings run by and attended by persons who are unprepared. The person calling the meeting should make sure that all in attendance are given the agenda well in advance so that they can prepare their contributions. Moreover, the agenda should not be so long that it makes it impossible to get to all items on it.

Obviously, it would be frustrating to find that an agenda item that one is prepared to address never gets considered due to lack of time. Group leaders should carefully plan an agenda with this in mind. Likewise, group members should be encouraged to carefully prepare their points in advance. All presentation materials should be clearly organized to enhance the effectiveness of the communication.[44]

3. Structure the meeting and monitor its process. Most formal business meetings are traditionally conducted following *Robert's Rules of Order*.[45] First published in 1876, Army engineer Henry Robert developed a system of organizing and conducting meetings that strictly structures the group's interaction. The system is closely patterned after that used in the U.S. House of Representatives. Although these rules help avoid chaos in large groups, there are some potential problems with using them.

In particular, these rules (such as rules for "obtaining the floor," "seconding a motion," and the like) may so restrain group dynamics that there is little room for group development and openness. Accordingly, it has been suggested that these guidelines sometimes be abandoned in favor of more open discussions.[46] This is not to imply that group leaders should let a free-for-all atmosphere prevail. A good leader of a meeting should help keep the discussion moving along by soliciting everyone's opinions and not letting one person run away with control. Clear time constraints may help discourage monopolization of the discussion. Moreover, effective group leaders try to synthesize the group members' points in an attempt to come to consensus and move on to the next point.[47]

With practice in following these guidelines, almost anyone can learn to conduct a more effective meeting.

ual, coordinated contributions of several persons are combined and taken as the group's product are referred to as **additive.** Any one person can shovel snow or stuff envelopes for a political campaign, but tasks such as these may be considered additive because any one person's contribution can be added to the others' to yield a group's total accomplishment. A group's success on an additive task requires some degree of coordination. For example, one snow shoveler should not push the snow into the path of a fellow shoveler, and one envelope stuffer should not insert the same materials into the envelopes already stuffed by another. So long as group members can coordinate their efforts, the more work each individual member contributes, the higher will be the group's output.

Compensatory tasks. A second way of combining individual inputs to form a group product is by taking the average of individual contributions. A task in which this is done is considered a **compensatory task.** Compensatory tasks are usually ones involving the judgments made by several group members. For example, if a committee of managers is charged with the responsibility of deciding how much money to spend on a special organizational project, the group's decision might be taken as the average judgment of all the members.

Disjunctive tasks. Imagine a group of executives attempting to decide whether or not their company should buy out another, smaller company. In the case of such a task, a compromise is out of the question; the acquisition is either attempted or not. One person's decision—someone who is either for the merger or someone who is against it—will be taken as the group's decision. Such a task is considered **disjunctive** in that it is "either-or" in nature—the group can act on only one position. In a disjunctive task, several persons may make a contribution to the group, but only one of these will be taken as the group's product; the others will be discarded. Ideally, groups will benefit if they select as the group's product the work of the most qualified member. But, as we shall see, this is not always the case.

Conjunctive tasks. Instead of taking the performance of the one best group member as the group's product, sometimes groups are limited by the performance of its weakest members. For example, a group of mountain climbers can move no faster than the speed of the slowest-moving member of the expedition. Teachers often complain that the level of their class is brought down by their attempts to teach the slowest students. Tasks of this type are considered **conjunctive** because all members must work in unison. When a group's task is conjunctive, its performance may be summarized by the old adage, "a chain is only as strong as its weakest link."

The Productivity of Working Groups

Each of the four different types of tasks just described requires that groups operate in different ways to be successful. Let's now review the productivity of work groups on each of the different types of tasks.

Additive tasks: When "social loafing" occurs.   You may recall that an additive task is one in which the individual contributions of the group members are added together to form the group's product. When people know that their work will be combined with that of others, an interesting thing often happens: they stop working as hard as they did as individuals, appearing to let others do their work for them—going on a "free ride."

As suggested by the old saying, "many hands make light the work," a group of people would be expected to be more productive than any one individual. Five people raking leaves would get more work done than only one person, as you might expect, but generally *not* five times more. This effect was first noted by a German scientist named Ringlemann, who compared the amount of force exerted by different size groups of people pulling on a rope. Specifically, he found that one person pulling on a rope alone exerted an average of 63 kilograms of force. However, in groups of three, the per-person force dropped to 53 kilograms, and in groups of eight it was reduced to only 31 kilograms per person—less than half the effort exerted by people working alone! In short, the greater the number of people working together on the task, the less effort each one puts forth—a phenomenon known as **social loafing.**

The phenomenon of social loafing has been studied extensively in recent years by Latané and his associates. In one of their earliest experiments, groups of subjects were asked to perform a very simple additive task—to clap and cheer as loudly as they could.[50] It was explained to subjects that the experimenter was interested in seeing how much noise people could make in social settings. Comparisons were made between the amount of noise produced by one person relative to groups of two, four, and six persons. Although more people made more noise, the amount made per person dropped dramatically as group size increased (see Figure 8.9).

These results may be explained by **social impact theory.**[51] According to this theory, the impact of any social force acting on a group is divided equally among its members. The larger the size of the group, the less is the impact of the force on any one member. In this case, the subjects faced external pressure to make as much noise as possible. With more people present, the less pressure each person faced to create noise. That is, the responsibility for making noise was diffused over more people when the size of the group increased. As a result, each group member felt less responsible for behaving appropriately, and social loafing occurred.

Obviously, the tendency for people to "goof off" when working with others can be a serious problem in organizations. Fortunately, some research has shown that the tendency for social loafing to occur can be overcome. The antidote seems to be: *make each performer identifiable.* It may be reasoned that social loafing occurs under conditions in which people feel they can get away with taking it easy—namely, when each worker's inputs are not identified. Identifying each person's performance has been shown to be an effective way of countering social loafing in another experiment by Latané and his associates.[52] In this study it was found that male swimmers swam 100 meters faster alone than as members of a relay team—a social loafing effect—but only when their names and times were *not* announced individually. However, this decrement was completely reduced when each swimmer's name and time were announced. Apparently, with some attempt at identifying the contributions of individual performers to an additive task, social loafing can be overcome. We are not likely to loaf if we believe we may get caught loafing!

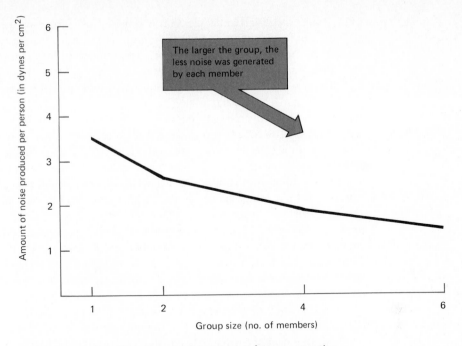

FIGURE 8.9   *Social Loafing: An Experimental Demonstration.*
Research on *social loafing* has found that the amount of effort exerted by any one person decreases as the size of his or her group increases. In the research findings summarized here, subjects clapping and cheering made the most noise per person when working alone but progressively less noise per person as the group size increased from two to four to six members. (Source: Based on data reported in Latané, Williams, and Harkins, 1979; see Note 50.)

Compensatory tasks: The benefits of compromise.   On some tasks the inputs of all members are averaged together to create a single group outcome. The resulting compromise solution is referred to as *compensatory* because one person's judgments may compensate for another's. Imagine that a group of people are attempting to judge the temperature of the room they are in. As you might expect, the judgments made by some group members that are incorrect in one direction (i.e., too high) may be offset by the judgments of others that are incorrect in the other direction (i.e., too low). As a result, more accurate decisions would be made by averaging the decisions of everyone in the group than by most individual members. Several studies have found that on compensatory tasks groups *do* tend to make more accurate judgments than those of many individual group members.[53]

Disjunctive tasks: When "the truth" wins out.   On a disjunctive task the members of a group cannot compromise; they must select a solution offered by one of the members of the group. Suppose a group of people are given the following car-trading problem to solve:

> A used car salesman bought a car from one customer for $3,000 and then sold it to another customer for $4,000. He then bought it back for $5,000 and resold it for $6,000. How much money did the salesman make?

Each group member comes up with his or her own answer, but only one solution can be accepted. Whether or not the group will perform better on such a task than any single individual will depend, of course, on whether or not (a) anyone in the group comes up with the right answer, *and* (b) the group accepts that answer.

Because the odds of any one coming up with the right answer are higher in larger groups, it is not surprising to find that larger groups out-perform smaller groups on disjunctive tasks.[54] However, just because someone in the group has the right answer does not always mean it will be recognized as correct by the members of the group. On some tasks with obvious correct answers (referred to as *Eureka* tasks), as soon as the correct answer is given, it is immediately recognized and accepted by the group (Eureka, that's it!). On other tasks, however, such as our car-trading problem, the correct answer is not immediately obvious and needs to be explained before the group is likely to accept it. This is known as the **truth supported wins rule.**[55] For the correct answer to be taken as the group's answer, that answer not only has to be obtained; it then has to be supported by the group. On a Eureka task the truth usually wins out, giving the advantage to the group over most individuals. However, on the other, less obvious tasks, any potential group advantage is less certain.

(Oh yes, the answer to our car-trading problem—the dealer made $2,000.)

Conjunctive tasks: Slowed down by the "weakest link." It should be readily apparent that most individuals will do better than a group on a conjunctive task. Imagine a group of people filling sandbags and passing them to each other in a line, attempting to secure a crumbling retaining wall. If any one person consistently drops the bags or otherwise falters, the group will be probably far *less* effective with this person than without this person. In such a situation, the group is forced to adjust its performance downward to the level of the poorest worker.

In some cases, such as an expedition of mountain climbers whose pace accommodates the slowest climber, the lower performance of conjunctive groups is not problematic. However, most work organizations can hardly afford to be slowed down by an ineffective team member. If any one individual proves so inept that his or her group suffers, that person may be expected to be fired, or to face so much social pressure from group members that he or she resigns.[56] As an example, the final assembly of an automobile can be no faster than the speed at which the various subassemblies are manufactured. It is therefore not surprising to find that some auto manufacturing plants are closed when technical problems or labor stoppages plague other plants. Similarly, it is often found that the construction of an entire building must come to a halt when one of the construction unions goes on strike.

Group performance: Some final considerations. In Figure 8.10 we have summarized the likely effects of task type on group performance that we have been describing here. On some tasks (e.g., additive tasks) groups may be expected to out-perform individual group members, although on others (e.g., conjunctive tasks), the average individual would out-perform the group.

Of course, the picture is far more complex than suggested by the diagram in Figure 8.10. As we have noted, although groups performing additive tasks do better than a single person, there is an important loss of efficiency for each individual—

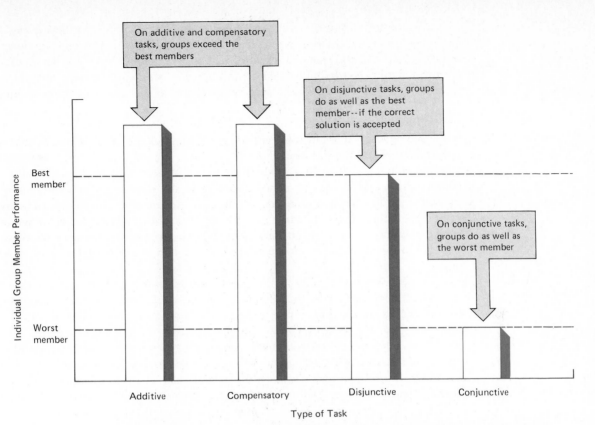

FIGURE 8.10   Group Productivity: The Influence of Task Type.
As summarized here, how effectively groups perform tasks relative to individual members depends on the type of task performed. (Source: Based on Steiner, 1976; see Note 48.)

the social loafing effect. Also, whether or not the group's decision on a disjunctive task is as good as the best individual judgment depends on the group's willingness to accept that answer. Obviously, the question of group performance is a very complex one. Indeed, we have only begun to scratch the surface of this topic in this chapter. You will find that questions of group productivity will arise elsewhere in this book, particularly in our discussions of leadership (Chapter 9), social influence (Chapter 11), decision-making (Chapter 13), and communication (Chapter 10).

SUMMARY

A **group** is a collection of two or more interacting individuals with a stable pattern of relationships between them who share common goals and who perceive themselves as being a group. Work groups have been found to have a major impact on the functioning of organizations.

The stable pattern of interrelationships between members of a group is referred to as its *structure*. A group's structure is determined, in part, by its *cohesiveness*—the pressures members face to remain in their groups. Contrary to popular belief, highly cohesive groups sometimes can be less effective than less cohesive groups. Group structure is also influenced by the informal rules that operate in groups, referred to as *norms*. The development of norms in groups helps make groups function smoothly. Finally, a group's structure is also determined by the many *roles* played by group members. Sometimes the demands of several roles are inconsistent with each other resulting in *role conflict*, a condition that has negative consequences for employees and their organizations.

Individual productivity is influenced by the presence of other group members. Sometimes, a person's performance improves in the presence of others (such as when the job they do is well-learned), and sometimes performance declines in the presence of others (such as when the job is novel). This phenomenon is known as *social facilitation*. These effects have been attributed to the *mere presence* of others, the *evaluation apprehension* caused by others, and the *distraction* caused by others.

Group productivity is affected by the type of task performed. On *additive* tasks, where each member's individual contributions are combined, it is found that *social loafing* occurs. According to this phenomenon, the more people who work on a task, the less each group member contributes to it. On *compensatory* tasks, the judgments made by the group members are averaged together, and groups tend to do better than the average individual group member. On *disjunctive* tasks, one solution to a problem must be accepted. So long as one group member comes up with the correct answer and convinces others of its accuracy, the group will do as well as the best individual. On *conjunctive* tasks the group can do no better than the poorest group member. As a result, groups tend to perform worse than the average individual group member.

KEY TERMS

additive tasks: Type of group tasks in which the individual coordinated efforts of several persons are added together to form the group's product.

cohesiveness: The pressures on group members to remain a part of their group.

compensatory tasks: Type of group tasks in which the average of member's contributions is taken as the group's product.

compresence: The innately arousing effects of the mere presence of others.

conjunctive tasks: Type of group tasks in which the performance of the poorest member is taken as the group's product.

deindividation: The processes through which the presence of other people weakens our restraints against acting in an impulsive, irrational manner.

disjunctive tasks: Type of group tasks in which only one member's judgment is taken as the group's product.

distraction-conflict theory: The theory that attempts to explain social facilitation in terms of the distractions caused by the presence of other people that may conflict with task performance.

divisible tasks: Tasks that are capable of being divided into smaller parts.

drive theory: The theory of social facilitation suggesting that the presence of others increases arousal, which increases people's tendencies to perform the dominant response. If that response is well-learned, performance will improve, but if it is novel, performance will be impaired.

evaluation apprehension: The fear of being evaluated or judged by another person.

group: A collection of two or more interacting individuals with a stable pattern of relationships between them, who share common goals and who perceive themselves as being a group.

group structure: The pattern of interrelationships between the individuals comprising a group; the guidelines of group behavior that make group functioning orderly and predictable.

interrole conflict: The incompatible demands made on someone playing two or more different roles.

intrarole conflict: The contradictory demands made on one person by virtue of the different sets of expectations imposed on that person by others.

learned drive theory: The theory that social facilitation occurs as a result of the arousal resulting from concern over being evaluated by others (see *evaluation apprehension*).

norms: Generally agreed upon informal rules that guide group members' behavior.

role: The typical behaviors that characterize a person in a specific social context.

role conflict: A condition that results when the appropriate behaviors for enacting one role are inconsistent with the appropriate behaviors for enacting another role (see *interrole conflict*) or other requirements of the same role (see *intrarole conflict*).

role differentiation: The tendency for various specialized roles to emerge as groups develop (see *task-specialist role* and *socio-emotional role*).

social facilitation: The tendency for the presence of others sometimes to enhance an individual's performance and sometimes to impair it.

social impact theory: The theory that explains social loafing in terms of the diffusion of responsibility for doing what is expected of each member of a group. The larger the size of a group, the less each member is influenced by the social forces acting on the group.

social loafing: The tendency for group members to exert less individual effort on an additive task the larger the size of the group.

task-specialist role: The role in which a group member acts so as to help the group achieve its goals.

truth supported wins rule: The tendency for groups to accept as their answer to a problem the correct solution of one of their members so long as the group perceives that answer as correct.

unitary task: A task that cannot be divided into smaller parts, and as such, requires only one person to perform it.

NOTES

1. D. L. Forsyth (1983). *An introduction to group dynamics.* Monterey, Calif.: Brooks/Cole.

2. A. P. Hare, E. F. Borgatta, and R. F. Bales (1955). *Small groups: Studies in social interaction.* New York: Knopf, p. vi.

3. E. Mayo (1933). *The social problems of an industrial civilization.* Cambridge: Harvard University Press.

4. K. Lewin (1943). Forces behind food habits and methods of change. *Bulletin of the National Research Council, 108,* 35–65.

5. L. Coch and J. R. P. French (1948). Overcoming resistance to change. *Human Relations, 1,* 512–532.

6. R. H. Van Zelst (1952). Sociometrically selected work teams increase production. *Personnel Psychology, 5,* 175–185.

7. See Note 6, p. 183.

8. A. Zander (1979). The psychology of group processes. *Annual Review of Psychology, 30,* 417–451.

9. See Note 1.

10. A. P. Hare (1976). *Handbook of small group research,* 2nd ed. New York: Free Press.

11. D. Cartwright (1968). The nature of group cohesiveness. In D. Cartwright and A. Zander (eds.), *Group dynamics: Research and theory,* 3rd ed. New York: Harper & Row.

12. I. L. Janis (1982). *Groupthink: Psychological studies of policy decisions and fiascos,* 2nd ed. Boston: Houghton Mifflin.

13. R. W. Rogers and S. Prentice-Dunn (1983). Deindividuation and anger-mediated interracial aggression: Unmasking regressive racism. *Journal of Personality and Social Psychology, 35,* 677–688.

14. E. Diener (1980). Deindividuation: The absence of self-awareness and self-regulation in group members. In P. B. Paulus (ed.), *The psychology of group influence.* Hillsdale, N.J. Erlbaum.

15. G. Maruyama, S. C. Fraser, and N. Miller (1982). Personal responsibility and altruism in children. *Journal of Personality and Social Psychology, 42,* 658–654.

16. T. Douglas (1983). *Groups: Understanding people gathered together.* New York: Tavistock.

17. S. E. Seashore (1954). *Group cohesiveness in the industrial work group.* Ann Arbor: Institute for Social Research.

18. J. F. Schriescheim (1980). The social context of leader subordinate relations: An investigation of the effects of group cohesiveness. *Journal of Applied Psychology, 65,* 183–194.

19. A. Tziner and Y. Vardi (1982). Effects of command style and group cohesiveness on the performance effectiveness of self-selected tank crews. *Journal of Applied Psychology, 67,* 769–775.

20. J. R. Hackman (1976). Group influences on individuals. In M. Dunnette (ed.), *Handbook of industrial and organizational psychology.* Chicago: Rand McNally.

21. T. R. Mitchell, M. Rothman, and R. C. Liden (1985). Effects of normative information on task performance. *Journal of Applied Psychology, 70,* 48–55.

22. D. C. Feldman (1984). The development and enforcement of group norms. *Academy of Management Review, 9,* 47–53.

23. G. R. Jones (1983). Psychological orientation and the process of organizational socialization: An interactionist perspective. *Academy of Management Review, 8,* 464–474.

24. B. J. Biddle (1979). *Role theory: Expectations, identities, and behavior.* New York: Academic Press.

25. K. D. Benne and P. Sheats (1948). Functional roles of group members. *Journal of Social Issues, 4,* 41–49.

26. R. F. Bales (1980). *SYMLOG case study kit.* New York: Free Press.

27. D. Katz and R. L. Kahn (1978). *The social psychology of organizations,* 2nd ed. New York: Wiley.

28. J. L. Pearce (1981). Bringing some clarity to role ambiguity research. *Academy of Management Review, 6,* 665–674.

29. M. Van Sell, A. P. Brief, and R. S. Schuler (1981). Role conflict and role ambiguity: Integration of the literature and directions for future research. *Human Relations, 34,* 43–71.

30. V. Berger-Gross and A. I. Kraut (1984). "Great expectations": A no-conflict explanation of role conflict. *Journal of Applied Psychology, 69,* 261–271.

31. R. A. Cooke and D. M. Rousseau (1984). Stress and strain from family roles and work-role expectations. *Journal of Applied Psychology, 69,* 252–260.

32. N. Triplett (1898). The dynamogenic factor in pacemaking and competition. *American Journal of Psychology, 9,* 507–533.

33. R. B. Zajonc (1965). Social facilitation. *Science, 149,* 269–274.

34. H. Markus (1978). The effect of mere presence on social facilitation: An unobtrusive test. *Journal of Personality and Social Psychology, 14,* 389–397.

35. R. B. Zajonc (1980). Compresence. In P. B. Paulus (ed.), *Psychology of group influence.* Hillsdale, N. J.: Erlbaum.

36. N. B. Cottrell (1972). Social facilitation. In C. G. McClintock (ed.), *Experimental social psychology.* New York: Holt, Rinehart & Winston.

37. R. G. Geen (1980). The effects of being observed on performance. In P. B. Paulus (ed.), *Psychology of group influence.* Hillsdale, N.J.: Erlbaum.

38. R. S. Baron, D. L. Moore, and G. S. Sanders (1978). Distraction as a source of drive in social facilitation research. *Journal of Personality and Social Psychology, 36,* 816–824.

39. G. Ferris and K. Rowland (1983). Social facilitation effects on behavioral and perceptual task performance measures. *Group and Organization Studies, 8,* 421–438.

264

40. G. R. Ferris, T. A. Beehr, and D. C. Gilmore (1978). Social facilitation: A review and alternative conceptual model. *Academy of Management Review, 3,* 338–347.

41. R. Tillman Jr. (1960). Problems in review: committees on trial. *Harvard Business Review, 38,* 162–172.

42. A. Zander (1977). *Groups at work.* San Francisco: Jossey-Bass.

43. R. Likert (1961). *New patterns of management.* New York: McGraw-Hill.

44. R. W. Lord (1981). *Running conventions, conferences, and meetings.* New York: AMACOM.

45. H. M. Robert (1876). *Robert's rules of order.* Glenview, Ill.: Scott, Foresman, 1970.

46. See Note 1.

47. L. Nadler and Z. Nadler (1980). *The conference book.* New York: Gulf.

48. I. D. Steiner (1976). Task-performing groups. In J. W. Thibaut, J. T. Spence, and R. C. Carson (eds.), *Contemporary topics in social psychology.* Morristown, N.J.: General Learning.

49. I. D. Steiner (1972). *Group process and productivity.* New York: Academic Press.

50. B. Latané, K. Williams, and S. Harkins (1979). Many hands make light the work: The causes and consequences of social loafing. *Journal of Personality and Social Psychology, 37,* 822–832.

51. B. Latané and S. Wolf (1981). The social impact of majorities and minorities. *Psychological Review, 88,* 438–453.

52. B. Latané, S. G. Harkins, and K. Williams (1980). *Many hands make light the work: Social loafing as a social disease.* Unpublished manuscript, Ohio State University.

53. See Note 48.

54. R. M. Bray, N. L. Kerr, and R. S. Arkin (1978). Effects of group size, problem difficulty, and sex on group performance. *Journal of Personality and Social Psychology, 36,* 1224–1240.

55. P. R. Laughlin (1980). Social combination processes of cooperative problem solving groups on verbal intellective tasks. In M. Fishbein (ed.), *Progress in social psychology.* Hillsdale, N.J.: Erlbaum.

56. J. B. Miner and J. F. Brewer (1976). The management of ineffective performance. In M. D. Dunnette (ed.), *Handbook of industrial and organizational psychology.* Chicago: Rand McNally.

CHAPTER 9

LEADERSHIP: A Brief Historical Perspective

The Trait Approach: Leadership and Personal Characteristics   The Situational Approach: Leaders and Situations   The Transactional Approach: Leaders, Situations, and Followers

LEADER BEHAVIOR: Some Key Dimensions

Participative versus Autocratic Leaders: Contrasting Styles, Contrasting Effects   Person-Oriented versus Production-Oriented Leaders: Showing Consideration or Initiating Structure

MAJOR THEORIES OF LEADERSHIP: The Contingency Model, Normative Theory, and Path-Goal Theory

Contingency Theory: Matching Leaders and Tasks   Normative Theory: Decision Making and Leader Effectiveness   Path-Goal Theory: Leaders as Guides to Valued Goals

TWO RECENT ADVANCES: The Vertical Dyad Linkage Model and Substitutes for Leadership

The VDL Model: Focus on Leader-Member Pairs   Substitutes for Leadership: When Technology, Organizational Structure, and Subordinate Characteristics Make Leaders Superfluous

SPECIAL INSERTS

FOCUS ON BEHAVIOR   Male and Female Leaders: The Same or Different?
FROM THE MANAGER'S PERSPECTIVE   Becoming a More Effective Leader: Some Useful Steps

Leadership in Organizations

Randi Clark and Phil Stolkowski, two top people at Volex Air (a new but highly successful entry into the overnight delivery business) are puzzled. The reason for their confusion is easy to recognize—if hard to penetrate. Six months ago, Volex opened two new regional centers designed to speed processing of its growing volume of business. Great care had been exercised in choosing the people to head them. The two persons finally selected—Martin Blake and Lee Kahana—were widely recognized as being among the brightest young managers in the entire organization. Yet, despite this fact, the outcome to date has not been encouraging. One for two—that seems to be the score at the moment. Blake is off to a great start. Volume at his Southeast Regional Center is already ahead of projections. Morale among employees is high, and on-time deliveries (a key index of performance for the company) is already above average for similar operations. The picture at Lee Kahana's Southwestern unit, unfortunately, is not nearly as rosy. Business there has been consistently below projections. Market penetration is practically nil. And perhaps worst of all (at least from the point of view of management), employees are so dissatisfied that support for unionization is gaining ground at a rapid pace. It is to consider these problems, and perhaps find a solution to them, that Randi and Phil are meeting today. Shaking her head in disbelief as she examines the latest figures, Randi begins.

"Just look at this stuff," she mutters. "I can hardly believe it. What the heck's going on down there? I mean, Lee is one of our best people!"

"Well, I sure used to *think* she was," Phil replies. "But you've seen the numbers. It's a disaster."

"I can't argue you with you there. It looks like she's letting us down in a big way. But what I can't figure out is just *why* she's bombing out like this. What's Lee doing so wrong and Blake so right?"

"Well, I think I'm beginning to get an idea," Phil replies. "The problem with Lee sure isn't motivation—she's working as hard as any two people I've ever seen right now. But to put it bluntly, I just don't think she knows much about handling people."

"What do you mean? Be precise!" Randi urges.

"O.K, O.K. Well, one thing she does is to go around acting like she's everyone's friend, real warm and cozy like, if you know what I mean."

"But Blake does that too, doesn't he? He's got the same style."

"Yeah, but with one major difference: he also lets people know that he really cares about efficiency, too. With Lee, that part of the message seems to get lost. And another thing—the way she makes decisions—whew!

"What does she do?" Randi asks.

"Just sort of closes her door, thinks things through, and decides by herself. Then she announces the outcome as if it came direct from above, with divine guidance! I can tell you, lots of people don't like that. They think they should at least be consulted. And that's just what our friend Martin Blake does. He asks people for their views. After they've said their piece, he makes up his own mind. But at least they feel they've had a chance to have some input."

"Anything else?"

"Hmm. Well, one thing. I don't know how to put it, exactly, but it seems to me that Lee just isn't good at reading people—or situations either, for that matter. She doesn't seem to have a feel for what'll work and what won't. So she ends up stepping on one toe after another. She's probably managed to get more people mad at her in a shorter period of time than anyone else I've ever seen."

"Stop, stop! I've heard enough!" Randi practically shouts. "Just what we *don't* need in a new operation. Honestly, Phil, everything you've said makes sense. And there's really no way we could have known about all these problems from her performance here at headquarters—it's an entirely different situation out there. But where does it all leave us? We've got to do something, and soon. I don't want to hurt Lee—I *like* her. But there's too much at stake here to let personal feelings get in the way. We've got to get someone in there who can handle the job."

During the course of your life, you have belonged to many different groups—formal ones such as social clubs, professional associations, or departments within an organization; and informal ones ranging from play groups of neighborhood children through unofficial alliances and "grapevines" at the office. Think back over some of these groups now. For each, can you recall one member who was more influential than the others? In all likelihood, you can, for almost every group contains one person who wields more power or control than all the rest. Such individuals are usually labeled **leaders;** the process through which they exert influence over others is known, appropriately, as **leadership.**

As you probably already realize, the impact of leaders upon the groups they

FIGURE 9.1   Leaders: Examples of Their Powerful Effect.
Leaders often exert powerful effects upon their followers. Indeed, they can often induce them to perform actions they would never choose in the absence of influence from the leader.

head can be profound. Such persons often strongly affect the attitudes, behavior, and even perceptions of their followers. Indeed, in extreme cases, they may induce their subordinates to accept views that make little sense to others, and cause them to engage in actions they would otherwise never perform (refer to Figure 9.1). Of course, in work settings, such total submission to the will (or whims) of leaders is rare. Yet, even in organizational contexts, strong, effective leaders can exert powerful effects upon their subordinates. The basis for such influence is easy to understand; after all, it is leaders who usually control the distribution of available rewards and punishments, who assign duties and responsibilities to specific persons, and who select various goals. Given this authority, there can be little wonder that other group members often orient toward and readily accept influence from leaders.

Because leaders play such an important role in the functioning of organizations, it is important for you to gain a basic grasp of their impact—to know something about who leaders are, how they operate, and the kind of effects they produce. To provide you with such knowledge, we will focus on several major topics. First, we will present a brief *historical perspective*, describing early views of leadership and how they evolved into the sophisticated, modern perspective. Second, we will focus on *leader behavior*, especially the contrasting styles such persons adopt in dealing with their subordinates. Third, we will turn to several modern *theories of leadership*, systematic efforts to explain the dynamics of leadership within complex organizational settings. Finally, we will touch briefly on recent advances in the study of leadership—new perspectives that promise to add to our overall understanding of this key organizational process.

LEADERSHIP: A BRIEF HISTORICAL PERSPECTIVE

At some time or other, almost everyone has dreamed of being a leader. To take charge, direct others, alter events or even history—these are all common daydreams. In fact, however, only a very small number of individuals manage to live these fantasies by becoming actual leaders. Most spend their lives in obscurity, taking rather than giving orders. Why is this the case? In other words, why do some individuals, but not others, rise to positions of power and authority? Contrasting answers to this question have been offered at different points in history, as the basic conception of leadership itself has altered. We will consider three of these perspectives here.

The Trait Approach: Leadership and Personal Characteristics

Are some people born to lead? Common sense seems to suggest that this is so. Great leaders of the past such as Queen Elizabeth I, Alexander the Great, and George Washington do seem to differ from ordinary human beings in several ways (e.g., they appear to possess unusually high levels of energy, a will of iron, unshakable self-confidence). To a lesser degree, even leaders lacking such worldwide fame seem different from their followers. Top executives, many politicians, and even sports heroes or heroines often seem "larger than life," and possess an aura that sets them apart from other persons. On the basis of such observations, early researchers interested in leadership formulated a view known as the **great man/great woman theory.** According to this approach, great leaders possess key traits that set them apart from most other persons. Further, the theory also contends that these traits remain stable across time and across groups. Thus, all great leaders are assumed to share such characteristics regardless of when and where they live, or the precise role history has prepared for them.

These are intriguing suggestions, and ones that seem to fit well with our own personal experience. You may be surprised to learn, therefore, that they have *not* been strongly confirmed. Decades of active research (most conducted prior to 1950) failed to yield a short, agreed-upon list of "key" traits shared by all leaders.[1] A few consistent findings emerged (e.g., leaders tend to be slightly taller and more intelligent than their followers) but these were hardly dramatic either in nature or scope.[2] Indeed, so disappointing were overall results that most investigators reached the following conclusion: leaders simply do not differ from followers in clear and consistent ways. (Refer to Figure 9.2 for an illustration of this view.)

While this conclusion continues to hold sway at the present time, we should note that there has recently been a reawakening of interest in the possibility that

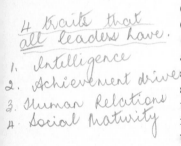

4 traits that
all leaders have.

1. Intelligence
2. Achievement drive
3. Human Relations
4. Social Maturity

(Official Government Photo)

Nov. 28 (UPI)—At his office in the capital city, the world's most powerful dictator greets the world's funniest standup comic.

FIGURE 9.2   *Leaders and Followers: How Much Do They Differ?*
Do great leaders possess a small set of traits that set them apart from other persons? As suggested by this cartoon, little evidence for this view exists. (Source: Drawing by Ziegler; © 1978 The New Yorker Magazine, Inc.)

leaders and followers *do* differ in some respects. Several types of evidence have contributed to this trend. First, research studies indicate that persons possessing certain patterns of motives (e.g., a high need for power coupled with a high degree of self-control) tend to be more successful as managers than persons showing other patterns.[3] Similarly, political leaders do appear to differ from nonleaders in ways we might expect (e.g., they are higher in self-confidence, need for achievement, and dominance).[4] Finally, a recent investigation by Kenny and Zaccaro suggests that stable characteristics may well play a major role in determining who becomes a leader in a wide range of different contexts.[5] These researchers carefully re-examined the data from an earlier study concerned with the stability of leadership potential—the extent to which specific individuals tend to become leaders in different groups performing different tasks. Results indicated an impressive degree of stability in this regard—a much higher level than had previously been reported. In short, as an approach emphasizing traits suggests, persons possessing certain characteristics *do* tend to rise to positions of authority in a wide range of settings. As noted by Kenny and Zaccaro, however, the stable characteristics that play a role in this regard may consist primarily of the ability to recognize and respond to changing conditions, *not* traditional personality traits.

Please don't misunderstand: none of these findings indicate that all leaders share certain traits, or that the possession of these characteristics is required for leadership at all times and in all places. Rather, they merely suggest that personal characteristics *can* play a role in leadership in at least some cases, and should not be totally ignored.

The Situational Approach: Leaders and Situations

By now, you may be a bit puzzled. If leadership is not largely a function of the traits and characteristics of leaders, what, precisely, *does* it involve? One intriguing answer is provided by a second major perspective known as the **situational ap-**

proach. Central to this view, which emerged as researchers grudgingly surrendered their search for a short list of "key" leadership traits, is the following crucial fact: often, different situations call for different kinds of leaders. For example, consider a young company fighting for its life against a giant competitor. What kind of person does it need as its CEO? Probably, one who is highly competitive, assertive, and decisive. In contrast, consider an organization involved in delicate merger discussions with another. What type of individual should it choose to lead its team of negotiators? The answer is obvious: one who possesses many interpersonal skills (e.g., an individual who is persuasive, charming, and so on).

According to the situational approach, then, full understanding of leadership involves careful attention *both* to characteristics of leaders (e.g., their abilities, traits, skills) *and* to situations (e.g., the tasks being performed, the availability of needed resources, etc.).[6] Selection of a leader, therefore, should involve a process of *matching*—one in which an individual whose particular mix of skills and characteristics is closely aligned with the requirements faced by the group is chosen. To the extent such matching succeeds, both the group and the leader will benefit; to the extent it fails, both sides will suffer.

In addition, the situational approach implies that when one individual occupies a leadership position for an extended period of time, this person must adapt his or her behavior to shifts in situational factors. Leaders, in short, must be *flexible,* and respond to changes both within and outside their organizations (e.g., trends in employee motivation, new technology, changing patterns of competition).

The situational perspective represented a clear advance over the earlier trait approach. By taking account of a wealth of situational factors—ones largely ignored by the "great man/woman" perspective—it more accurately reflects the complexities faced by actual organizations. However, it, too, suffers from a major drawback: it devotes little or no attention to the role and impact of *followers.* Largely because of this weakness, it has recently been replaced by a third, and even more sophisticated view: the **transactional approach.**

The Transactional Approach: Leaders, Situations, and Followers   *& The Reciprocal Determinism Approach*

That leaders influence their subordinates is obvious. Indeed, as we noted earlier, the exercise of such authority is a basic test for determining whether a given individual should be viewed as a leader. A related fact, however, may be less obvious: leaders, in turn, are also influenced by their followers. Contrary to what many persons seem to believe, leaders do not operate in a social vacuum. Rather, they are often strongly affected by the attitudes, perceptions, and values of their subordinates. This fact is clearly recognized by the modern *transactional approach.*[7] This perspective argues that leadership should be viewed as a complex social relationship, one in which leaders and followers each gain various benefits, and in which influence flows reciprocally (although not equally) between them. According to the transactional view, full understanding of leadership can be attained only through careful attention to three major factors: leaders (their characteristics, motives, skills, legitimacy), situations (the demands they place on groups, the tasks being performed within them), and followers (their traits, motives, perceptions, and expectations. A summary of these suggestions is presented in Figure 9.3.

Support for the accuracy of this view has been obtained in a growing number of investigations. For example, in one recent study, Sims and Manz arranged for MBA students to play the role of supervisors, and discuss both past and future performance with several subordinates.[8] In reality, these subordinates were accomplices, specially trained to present information indicating either that they had previously performed very well or very poorly, and that their performance was improving at a rate lower than, equal to, or higher than that of other workers. One major purpose of the study was that of determining whether these different patterns would evoke contrasting reactions from the supervisors. In fact, they did. For example, subjects were much more likely to deliver positive rewards (e.g., "Your performance that time was really good") when their subordinate's performance was high and improving rapidly than when it was low and improving only slowly. Conversely, supervisors were less likely to make requests for information about how accomplices were performing their current tasks when their past record was good than when it was poor. In sum, the subject-supervisors behaved very differently toward their subordinates, depending on the past performance of these people. Thus, their "style of management," if you will, was strongly affected by the behavior of their followers. This is precisely the type of pattern predicted by the transactional (or *reciprocal determinism*) perspective.

To conclude: because it emphasizes the social nature of leadership, and directs attention to leaders, situations, *and* followers, the transactional approach is more complex than the earlier perspectives it has replaced. Such complexity seems well justified, however, for the transactional view also seems to provide a more adequate representation of this key organizational process. For this reason, several of its basic assumptions are reflected in the modern theories of leadership we will soon consider. Before turning to these theories, however, we will pause to examine another basic aspect of leadership: key dimensions in *leader behavior* or *style*.

FIGURE 9.3   *Leadership: The Transactional Approach.*
The *transactional approach* suggests that in order to fully comprehend the nature of leadership, we must take careful account of leaders, followers, and the situations in which interactions between them occur.

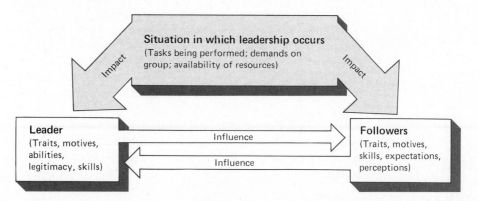

LEADER BEHAVIOR: SOME KEY DIMENSIONS

As we noted earlier, leaders do not appear to differ from other persons with respect to a small number of central traits. Yet they certainly *do* differ from one another. Various leaders possess contrasting motives and seek sharply different goals. In addition, they employ different techniques for exerting influence over others and directing their activities. In a word, they demonstrate contrasting *styles*. While there are probably as many unique styles of leadership as there are individual leaders, several decades of research suggest that two underlying dimensions are most important. The first of these involves the extent to which a leader is willing to allow subordinates a voice in the way things are run—a piece of the action, so to speak. It ranges from a fully **participative** style at one extreme, through a totally **autocratic** (directive) style at the other. The second dimension involves the degree to which a given leader is primarily concerned with *production* or with *people* and relations between them.

Participative versus Autocratic Leaders: Contrasting Styles, Contrasting Effects

Think about different bosses you have had. Can you remember one who wanted to control virtually everything—someone who made all the decisions, and who generally left no room for doubt about who was in charge and who ran the show? In contrast, can you recall a boss or supervisor who allowed employees greater freedom and responsibility—one who invited input before making decisions (and paid attention to it), who was always open to suggestions, and who preferred the "velvet glove" to the "iron fist"? If you can bring such persons to mind, you have already had first-hand experience with two sharply contrasting styles of leadership: *autocratic* and *participative*.

Of course, the pictures presented above represent extreme cases. In organizational settings, most leaders fall somewhere in between these two end-points, and you are unlikely to encounter a "pure" example of either one. Yet, it does appear that many managers are more comfortable with one of these styles than the other, and tend to adopt one in their dealings with subordinates.

But given that leaders can often be classified as relatively autocratic or relatively participative in style, does either approach have a clear-cut edge? The answer is complex. Both styles of leadership appear to have advantages, and both involve disadvantages. For example, an autocratic approach often yields high levels of productivity, especially when a group finds itself facing stressful conditions (e.g., high time pressure, poor relations between its members).[9] Further, recent evidence suggests such benefits are enhanced if a directive leadership style is combined with at least a minimum level of friendliness or warmth.[10] While it increases productivity, though, an autocratic leadership style may sometimes lower morale or work satisfaction, largely because people value their freedom and object strongly to having someone "boss them around." Turning to a participative approach, growing evidence indicates that it often produces positive effects upon morale, and increases employees' commitment to the organization.[11] Further, individuals seem to prefer this style even under conditions where favorable reactions to autocratic leadership might be expected (e.g., when the problem is clearly structured and the leader has all the information needed to make a good decision).[12] Offsetting these benefits, however, are certain costs. First, a participative style may lead subordinates to question the leader's competence (e.g., "If he's the boss, why does he have to ask *me* what to do?"). Second, a participative style of leadership often slows things down. In Japan, where many corporations reach decisions through consensus, only after *everyone* involved has had a chance to offer input, the process often takes several times longer than in United States and Canadian companies.

In sum, both approaches represent something of a "mixed bag," and which one is most effective depends on many different factors. (Please refer to Table 9.1 for a summary of the advantages and disadvantages associated with each style.) Having said this, however, we feel compelled to insert at least a mild "plug" for a participative approach. As we noted in Chapter 7, lack of opportunity to participate in decisions concerning one's job is often a major source of work-related stress. When this factor is added into the equation, it seems to tip the balance in favor of affording subordinates at least *some* opportunity for input into key decisions. Please note: this does *not* imply that their suggestions or views should always be followed (i.e., adoption of a "pure" participative style). On the contrary, it merely suggests that prior to important decisions directly affecting them, subordinates should at least be given a chance to express their views. In short, our recommendation is for a *consultative style* in which final authority is retained by the leader, but in which subordinates do not feel left out or totally ignored. Existing evidence indicates that this approach may prove useful in a wide range of contexts.[13] However, further research is needed to determine the precise conditions under which it will be most and least successful.

TABLE 9.1 *Participative versus Autocratic Leadership Styles: Advantages and Disadvantages.*
Both autocratic and participative leadership styles offer potential benefits and potential costs. Thus, there is no simple basis for choosing between them.

	Leadership Style	
	Participative	*Autocratic*
Advantages	Enhances job satisfaction	Enhances productivity
	Increases organizational commitment	Especially helpful in high-pressure situations
	Strongly preferred by most subordinates	Speeds decisions
Disadvantages	Raises doubts about the leader's competence	Can reduce employee satisfaction
	Slows the decision process	Fails to fully utilize skills and knowledge of subordinates

Person-Oriented versus Production-Oriented Leaders: Showing Consideration or Initiating Structure

Have you ever seen a film version of Dickens's *A Christmas Carol?* If so, you are already familiar with two other extremes in terms of leadership style. Prior to his night with the spirits, Scrooge was interested primarily in one thing: production. He focused totally on carrying out his business in the most efficient and profitable manner. Friendly relations with his subordinates, their welfare, or their job satisfaction were of little interest to him. After visits from the ghosts of Christmas Past, Present, and Future, though, Scrooge underwent a dramatic change. His major concern became helping his loyal and long-suffering clerk, Bob Cratchett. Efficiency and profits receded in importance and took a back seat to friendly human relations.

While few people ever experience such radical shifts in leadership style, a great deal of evidence (much of it collected at the University of Michigan by Likert and his colleagues[14] and at Ohio State University by Stogdill and his associates[15]) suggests that leaders do differ greatly along these dimensions. Some are highly concerned with production and focus mainly on getting the job done. Thus, they engage in such actions as organizing work, inducing subordinates to follow rules, setting goals, and making leader and subordinate roles explicit. In contrast, other leaders are lower on this dimension, and show less tendency to engage in these actions. Turning to the second dimension, some leaders are strongly concerned with establishing good relations with their subordinates and with being liked by those persons. They engage in such actions as doing favors for subordinates, explaining things to them, and assuring their welfare. Others, in contrast, are low on this dimension, and don't really care much about how they get along with these persons. At first glance, you might assume that these two dimensions (often termed **initiating structure** and **showing consideration)** are closely linked. That is, you might guess that persons high on one must, necessarily, be low on the other. In fact, this is not the case. The two dimensions actually seem to be largely independent.[16] Thus, it is possible for a leader to be high on both concern with production and concern for people, high on one of these dimensions and low on the other, moderate on one and high on the other, and so on. This, in turn, leads to a basic and practical question: which of these patterns, if any, is best?

Actually, this turns out to be a complex issue. As was the case with participative and autocratic leadership styles, task-oriented and people-oriented approaches both involve a mixed pattern of "pluses" and "minuses." With respect to showing consideration (high concern with people and relations between them) the major benefits center around improved group atmosphere and morale.[17] However, since leaders high on this dimension are reluctant to provide specific directions to their subordinates, and often shy away from presenting them with negative feedback, productivity can sometimes suffer. Turning to initiating structure (high concern with production), efficiency and performance are indeed sometimes enhanced by this type of leadership style.[18] If leaders focus *entirely* on production, though, employees may soon conclude that no one cares about them or their interests. Then, both job satisfaction and organizational commitment may suffer greatly.

On the basis of our comments so far, you may now be ready to conclude that

Male and Female Leaders: The Same or Different?

Who makes better leaders: males or females? Twenty, or perhaps even ten years ago, many members of both sexes would have answered this question without hesitation: males. The past decade, however, has brought growing awareness of the fact that sex-role stereotypes (beliefs about the supposed traits of men and women, or the differences between them) are quite inaccurate.[21] Thus, at present, most people would at least think twice before replying. But what does systematic research tell us about this issue? Are there any differences between men and women in their performance of leadership roles? Actually, we have already provided a partial reply in our discussion of male and female managers (see Chapter 5). At that time, we noted that recent studies have failed to uncover important differences between these groups, either in their traits or in their on-the-job behavior. Thus, where such leaders are concerned, sex appears to be largely irrelevant. Is this true of leaders in other contexts as well? Growing evidence suggests that it is. Perhaps the most dramatic evidence in favor of such a "no difference" conclusion is provided by a large-scale investigation conducted by Rice, Instone, and Adams.[22]

The subjects in this study were two groups of male and female cadets at West Point, the U.S. Military Academy. One group was studied after participating in a six-week training program for incoming freshmen. During this program, they were divided into squads of ten to twelve persons, each led by a junior or senior cadet. The second group of subjects was studied after taking part in a six-week summer training program for sophomores. Here, they were divided into different "details," again led by junior or senior cadets. In both cases some of the subjects in each unit were males and some were females. Further, some leaders were male and others female. After completing the training programs, subjects responded to a questionnaire aimed at assessing their views on the effectiveness of their leaders, as well as various aspects of the leadership process (e.g., the content and quality of downward communication from the leader, the kind of influence tactics he or she used, the extent to which rewards and punishments by the leader were contingent upon follower behavior). The major purpose of the study, or course, was that of determining whether subjects reacted differently to male and female leaders. On the basis of widely held stereotypes concerning the traits of males and females, it was predicted that males would be perceived as more successful in this role than females, and that other differences between male and female leaders consistent with such stereotypes would also be reported (e.g., females would be perceived as using more indirect influence tactics than males; female leaders would be seen as more accessible to upward communication from subordinates than male leaders). In fact, *virtually no support for any of these predictions was obtained.* Only a few differences in subjects' ratings of male and female leaders were observed, and even these were not consistent across the two settings (the training program for freshmen and the summer program for sophomores). Further, the few significant findings obtained were *not* generally consistent with the simple prediction that male leaders would always have an advantage. For example, it was found that female subjects described female leaders as being less likely to reward excellent performance than male leaders; however, a similar pattern was *not* observed among males.

In sum, the findings reported by Rice and his colleagues are fully consistent with earlier results pointing to a lack of important differences between male and female managers. Apparently, when men and women serve as the leaders of real groups (ones that persist over substantial periods of time) there are few, if any, differences in their behavior. Of course, this does not imply that *no* differences of this type exist. Even today, women seem to be somewhat reluctant to "take charge" and assume leadership when interacting with males.[23] Once such barriers are overcome, though, they appear to be just as effective in wielding influence, exercising authority, and aiding their groups as their male counterparts.

there is no single best style for leaders to adopt relative to these dimensions. In one sense, this is true: as we noted earlier, and will soon see in more detail, a given leader's effectiveness is determined by many different factors—so many that there can be no simple, unitary tactics for guaranteeing such success. However, evidence does suggest that, with respect to showing consideration and initiating structure, one specific pattern may indeed have an edge. This is one in which a leader's style and behavior demonstrate high concern with *both* people and production.[19] A clear

FIGURE 9.4 *The Benefits of High Concern with Production Coupled with High Concern for People.*
When leaders showed high concern for productivity but still demonstrated personal warmth, subordinates worked hardest on a subsequent task. In contrast, subordinates exerted least effort when their leaders showed little concern for production coupled with personal warmth. These findings offer support for the view that a leadership style involving high levels of concern with *both* production and people is often most effective. (Source: Based on data from Tjosvold, 1984; see Note 10.)

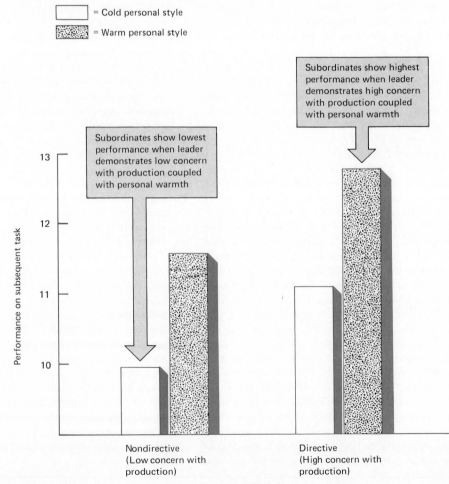

illustration of the potential benefits of this pattern is provided by an intriguing study carried out by Tjosvold.[20]

In this experiment, male and female students first worked on a problem (rank ordering the survival value of items available after a plane crash) along with another person. Subjects played the role of a subordinate, while another individual—actually an accomplice—served as their manager. During this period, the accomplice either behaved in a manner indicative of high concern with productivity (e.g., he or she told the subject precisely what to do; praised and criticized the subject's performance), or evidenced low concern with productivity. In addition, the accomplice either demonstrated personal warmth (e.g., showed a friendly facial expression, maintained a high level of eye contact) or showed personal coldness. Following completion of the first task, the accomplice asked the subject to work on a second task and then left the room, explaining that he or she had other work to perform at this time. It was predicted that both variations in the accomplice's behavior would influence subjects' performance on this second task (which involved arithmetic and word problems). Specifically, it was hypothesized that subjects would work hardest when the leader was both warm and showed high concern with productivity, but that they would exert least effort when the leader was warm and showed low concern with productivity. As you can see from Figure 9.4, both predictions were confirmed. In addition, it was found that subjects generally had more favorable impressions of the leader when this person acted in a warm and friendly manner than when he or she behaved in a cold and aloof fashion. That is, they liked the leader more, and expressed greater willingness to work with this person again in the "warm" than in the "cold" condition.

These findings, and similar results in related research, point to several important conclusions. First, they indicate that leaders who are high on both consideration and initiating structure are more effective than leaders who are high on only one of these dimensions. Second, they suggest that leaders should usually avoid a style involving high concern with people but obvious lack of interest in productivity. The costs produced by such a pattern do not appear to be offset by potential gains in group atmosphere or morale. Finally, the results reported by Tjosvold call attention to the fact that high concern with productivity and high concern with people are *not* mutually exclusive. Indeed, skillful leaders can often combine these orientations in their overall style. To the extent they do, both they and the groups they lead may benefit greatly. (Do male and female leaders differ in their style or approach to leadership? For a discussion of this timely topic, please see the **Focus on Behavior** insert on page 277).

MAJOR THEORIES OF LEADERSHIP: THE CONTINGENCY MODEL, NORMATIVE THEORY, AND PATH-GOAL THEORY

By now, you should be convinced of the following fact: leadership is an extremely complex process. It is affected by a wide range of factors, and can be exercised in an almost infinite number of styles. As a result, the task of unraveling the mysteries of this phenomenon is clearly a formidable one. Why, then, should we set about it? Why should we attempt to understand the nature and complexities of leadership? The answer should be obvious: leadership is a central (perhaps *the* central) organizational process. More precisely, effective leadership is essential for the success of most organizations, in most environments, much of the time. Recognition of this fact lies at the heart of several modern theories of leadership—systematic frameworks for understanding this process in a comprehensive and adequate manner. As will soon become apparent, these theories differ sharply from one another in terms of both content and scope. Yet, they are linked by at least one common theme: all are concerned, to some degree, with *leader effectiveness.* In other words, all attempt to specify the conditions and factors that determine whether, and to what extent, leaders will enhance the performance and satisfaction of their groups. A number of such theories have been proposed, but three have received by far the most attention: Fiedler's **contingency theory,** Vroom and Yetton's **normative theory,** and House's **path-goal theory.** It is on these important views that we will focus here.

Contingency Theory:
Matching Leaders and Tasks

Leadership, we have repeatedly noted, does *not* occur in a social or environmental vacuum. Rather, leaders attempt to exert their influence on group members within the context of specific situations. Given that these can vary greatly along a countless number of different dimensions, it seems reasonable to expect that no single style or approach to leading others will always be best. Rather, the most effective strategy will vary from one situation to another.

Acceptance of this basic fact lies at the core of a theory of leader effectiveness developed by Fred Fiedler.[24] Fiedler describes his model as a *contingency* approach, and this term seems apt, for the basic assumption behind the theory is this: a leader's contribution to successful performance by his or her group is determined both by the leader's traits and by various features of the situation in which the group operates. To fully understand leader effectiveness, the theory contends, both types of factors must be taken into account.

With respect to characteristics possessed by leaders, Fiedler has identified *esteem for least preferred co-worker* (or *LPC* for short) as most important. This refers to leaders' tendencies to evaluate the person with whom they find it most difficult to work in a favorable or unfavorable manner. Leaders who perceive this person in negative terms (*low LPC leaders*) seem primarily motivated to attain successful task performance. In short, they are primarily task or production-oriented. In contrast, leaders who perceive their least preferred co-worker in a positive light (*high LPC leaders*) seem concerned mainly with establishing good relations with their subordinates; they are primarily relations-oriented in outlook. Which of these types of leaders is more effective? Fiedler's answer is: it depends. And what it depends upon is several situational factors.

Specifically, Fiedler suggests that whether low LPC or high LPC leaders prove more effective depends on the degree to which the situation is favorable to the leader, or provides this person with *control* over other group members. This, in

Leader/member relations	Good				Poor			
Task structure	High		Low		High		Low	
Position power	Strong	Weak	Strong	Weak	Strong	Weak	Strong	Weak

Very High   Intermediate   Very Low

◄———— Degree of Situational Control (favorability to leader) ————►

FIGURE 9.5   Leader's Situational Control: A Key Factor in the Contingency Model.
According to Fiedler's contingency model, a leader's degree of situational control over his or her group (and hence, the favorability of the situation to the leader) can range from very low through very high. As shown here, several factors determine where any given situation falls along this dimension.

turn, is determined largely by three factors: (1) the nature of the leader's *relations with group members* (the extent to which he enjoys their support and loyalty), (2) the degree of *structure* in the task being performed (the extent to which task goals and roles are clearly defined), and (3) the leader's *position power* (her or his ability to enforce compliance by subordinates). Combining these three factors, the leader's situational control can range from very high (positive relations with group members, a highly structured task, high position power) to very low (negative relations with members, an unstructured task, low position power; refer to Figure 9.5).

Now that we have examined both the leader characteristics and situational factors emphasized by Fiedler's model, we can return to the central question: when are different types of leaders most effective? The answer it suggests is somewhat complex. Briefly, the theory indicates that low LPC leaders (ones who are task-oriented) are superior to high LPC leaders (ones who are people-oriented) when situational control is either low or high. In contrast, high LPC leaders have an edge when situational control falls within the moderate range. The reasoning behind these predictions is as follows.

Under conditions of *low* situational control, groups need considerable guidance and direction to accomplish their tasks. Since low LPC leaders, with their focus on task performance, are more likely to provide such structure than high LPC leaders, they will usually be superior in such cases. Similarly, low LPC leaders also have an edge in situations that offer the leader a *high* degree of situational control. Here, low LPC leaders realize that because conditions are good (e.g., the task is well structured, group members enjoy good relations), task-related goals are likely to be met. As a result, they may relax and adopt a "hands-off" style—one that is appreciated by their subordinates in this context. In contrast, high LPC leaders, feeling that they already enjoy good relations with their subordinates, may focus their attention on task performance. The efforts at guidance and encouragement they then provide may be perceived as needless meddling by their group, and can, in fact, actually interfere with productivity.

Turning to situations offering the leader *moderate* control, a different set of circumstances prevails. Here, conditions are mixed, and attention to good interpersonal relations is needed to "smooth ruffled feathers" and assure good performance. High LPC leaders, with their interest in and concern with people, often have an important advantage in such cases. In contrast, low LPC leaders, who remain concerned about task performance under such conditions may adopt an autocratic, directive style. and so induce negative reactions among subordinates.

To summarize, Fiedler's theory predicts that low LPC leaders will prove more effective than high LPC leaders under conditions of either low or high situational control. In contrast, high LPC leaders will have a major edge under conditions where such control is moderate. (Please refer to Figure 9.6 for a graphic illustration of these predictions.)

FIGURE 9.6   *The Contingency Theory: Some Key Predictions.*
According to Fiedler's *contingency theory,* low LPC leaders (who are primarily task-oriented) are more effective than high LPC leaders (ones who are mainly relations-oriented) when situational control is *either* very low or very high. However, the opposite is true when situational control is moderate.

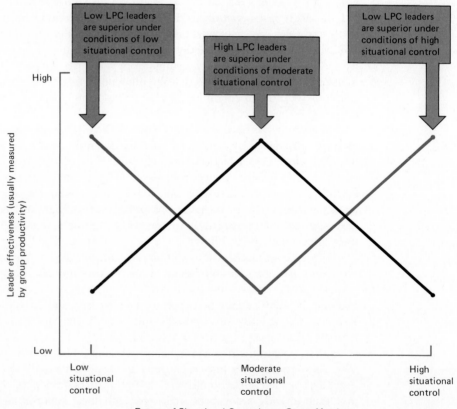

The contingency theory: Its current status. In several ways, the contingency theory is quite sophisticated. Moreover, because it directs attention to characteristics of leaders, situational factors, and even the reactions of subordinates, it is consistent with the modern view of leadership presented earlier in this chapter. Where any scientific theory is concerned, however, the ultimate question must be: how does it fare when put to actual test? For the contingency theory, the answer appears to be "moderately well." One review of more than 170 studies undertaken to test various aspects of Fiedler's framework indicates that most obtained positive results—ones in agreement with predictions derived from the theory.[25] However, a more recent analysis of such evidence suggests that while laboratory studies have tended to support the theory, field investigations (ones carried out with existing groups operating in a wide range of contexts) have not been as favorable.[26] Indeed, such investigations have sometimes yielded results directly contrary to what contingency theory would predict.

In addition, we should note that some features of the theory remain controversial. For example, a degree of ambiguity persists with respect to classifying specific situations along the dimension of favorability to the leader or situational control. Unless situations can be accurately classified as very low, low, moderate, and so on in this regard, predictions concerning leader effectiveness are impossible to make. Second, some critics have questioned the adequacy of the questionnaire used to assess leaders' standing on the LPC characteristic. In particular, they have noted that the reliability of this measure is not as high as might be preferred.[27]

Taking both these criticisms and the findings summarized above into account, it appears that contingency theory can benefit from further development and refinement (e.g., the inclusion of additional variables it does not presently consider). However, there can be little doubt that even in its present form, it contributes to our understanding of leadership and leader effectiveness, and in these respects, constitutes an important contribution to the field.

Normative Theory: Decision Making and Leader Effectiveness

One of the major tasks performed by leaders is that of making decisions. Indeed, one defining characteristic of leadership positions is that they are ones where "the buck comes to rest," and concrete actions must be taken. Since the decisions reached by leaders often have far-reaching effects upon their groups, the following fact is clear: one major determinant of leader success or effectiveness is the adequacy with which they perform this central task. Obviously, leaders who make good decisions will be more effective, in the long run, than leaders who make bad or foolish ones. We will consider various strategies leaders can employ to help them choose the best options in Chapter 13. For the moment, however, we wish to focus on a different, but equally important issue: in reaching decisions, how should leaders behave, vis-à-vis their subordinates? Specifically, how much participation should they invite from these persons? As we noted earlier, participation in decision making is an important organizational variable, with implications for job satisfaction, stress, and productivity. Thus, the manner in which leaders handle this sensitive issue has major implications for their effectiveness.

We have already described two extremes with respect to this process. On the one hand, leaders can simply gather appropriate information and make their decisions alone, without any input from subordinates. On the other, they can invite participation by followers, discuss problems with them, and then reach a decision through consensus. Which approach is better? Research designed to answer this question points to the following conclusion: just as there is no single best style of leadership, so, too, there is no single best strategy for making decisions. Rather, a host of situational factors determines which specific approach will yield the best results.[28] Valuable insight into the nature of these factors, and into leader decision making generally, is provided by the *normative model* developed by Vroom and Yetton.[29]

After careful study, these investigators concluded that leaders often employ one of five distinct methods in reaching their decisions. As you can see from the brief descriptions presented in Table 9.2, they cover the entire range from decisions made solely by the leader without any subordinate input, through ones that are fully participative in nature. Consistent with our comments above, Vroom and Yetton note that none of these strategies represents an "unmixed blessing." For example, decisions reached through participative means stand a better chance of gaining support and acceptance among subordinates. At the same time, though, reaching decisions this way may take a lot of time—more time than the leader or organization can afford. In contrast, decisions reached autocratically by the leader alone can be made rapidly and efficiently. However, such an approach may generate feelings of anger and resentment among followers. According to Vroom and Yetton, then, the major task faced by leaders is that of selecting the specific decision-making strategy that will maximize potential benefits, but hold potential costs to a minimum. How can this be done? Vroom and Yetton offer specific suggestions.

They propose that leaders should attempt to zero in on the best approach (or at least identify ones that are feasible) by answering several basic questions about the situation (questions relating to key attributes of the problem they face) and specific rules based upon them. As shown in Table 9.3, these questions relate to both the *quality* of the decision (e.g., is a high-quality decision required in this situation?

TABLE 9.2 *How Leaders Make Decisions: Five Potential Strategies.*
According to Vroom and Yetton, leaders often adopt one of the five strategies shown here in making decisions.

Decision Strategy	Description
AI (Autocratic)	Leader solves problem or makes decision alone, using information available to him or her at the time
AII (Autocratic)	Leader obtains necessary information from subordinates but then makes decision alone
CI (Consultative)	Leader shares the problem with subordinates individually, but then makes decision alone
CII (Consultative)	Leader shares problem with subordinates in a group meeting but then makes decision alone
GII (Group Decision)	Leader shares problem with subordinates in a group meeting; decision is reached through discussion to consensus

TABLE 9.3 *Selecting the Best Decision Making Strategy: Some Key Questions.*
According to Vroom and Yetton's *normative model,* leaders can select the most appropriate decision-making strategy in a given situation through careful attention to these questions, and to specific rules based upon them.

Questions Relating to the *Quality* of a Decision:
A. Is a high-quality decision required?
B. Do I have enough information to make such a decision?
C. Is the problem well structured?

Questions Relating to *Subordinate Acceptance* of a Decision:
D. Is it crucial for effective implementation that subordinates accept the decision?
E. If I make the decision by myself, is it likely to be accepted by my subordinates?
F. Do subordinates share the organizational goals that will be reached through solution of this problem?
G. Do subordinates disagree about appropriate methods for attaining organizational goals, so that conflict will result from the decision?

does the leader possess sufficient information or expertise to reach the decision alone?) and to its *acceptance* by subordinates (e.g., is acceptance crucial for successful implementation of the decision? do subordinates disagree about appropriate methods for reaching organizational goals?). According to the normative model, as a leader answers each of these questions, and applies specific rules based upon them, some of the potential approaches to reaching the decision summarized in Table 9.2 will be eliminated. Those that remain constitute a *feasible set* that can, potentially, be used to reach the necessary decision.

In order to simplify this process, Vroom and Yetton recommend use of a decision tree such as the one shown in Figure 9.7 (page 286). To apply this diagram, a manager begins on the left side, and responds to each of the questions listed in Table 9.3. (These questions are represented by the letters *A* through *F* above the decision tree.) As the manager replies to each of these questions, the set of feasible approaches to making the particular decision narrows. For example, imagine that the manager's answers are as follows:

Question A: *Yes*—a high-quality decision is needed.
Question B: *No*—the leader does not have sufficient information to make a high-quality decision alone.
Question C: *No*—the problem is not structured.
Question D: *Yes*—acceptance by subordinates is crucial to implementation.
Question E: *No*—if the leader makes the decision alone, it may not be accepted by subordinates.
Question F: *No*—subordinates do not share organizational goals.
Question G: *Yes*—conflict among subordinates is likely to result from the decision.

As you can readily see, these replies lead to the conclusion that only one decision-making approach is feasible: full participation by group members. The path leading to this conclusion is shown in color in Figure 9.7. Of course, different answers to any of the seven key questions would have led to different conclusions. Regardless of the specific outcome, though, this technique for applying the Vroom and Yetton model seems to be a helpful one.

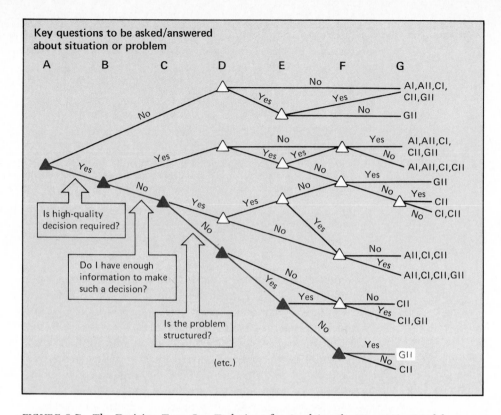

Key questions to be asked/answered about situation or problem

A B C D E F G

Is high-quality decision required?

Do I have enough information to make such a decision?

Is the problem structured?

(etc.)

FIGURE 9.7 *The Decision Tree: One Technique for Applying the Normative Model.*
By answering seven key questions and tracing a path through the type of *decision tree* shown here, managers (leaders) can identify those approaches to decision making that are feasible in a given situation. Such approaches are shown at the end of each potential path. Note: the path suggested by the answers to questions A–G provided on page 285 is shown in *colored ink.* Source: Adapted from V. H. Vroom (1976). Leadership. In M. D. Dunnette (ed.), *Handbook of industrial and organizational psychology* (Chicago: Rand McNally).

In several respects, the Vroom and Yetton model is highly appealing. It takes full account of the importance of subordinate participation in decisions, and offers clear guidance to leaders with respect to choosing among various methods for reaching decisions. As with any model or theory, though, the key question remains: is it valid? That is, does it accurately predict how leaders make decisions under various conditions, the quality or effectiveness of such decisions, and how they are perceived by followers? The results of several studies designed to test the model have been encouraging in all these respects.

First, it has been found that practicing managers rate their own past decisions as more successful when they were based on procedures falling within the set of feasible options identified by the model than when they fell outside this set of methods.[30] Second, when small groups of subjects reach decisions through methods falling within the feasible set identified by the model, these decisions are judged to be more effective by outside raters than when they are made through other methods.[31] Finally, it even appears that store managers who make their decisions in accordance with the basic principles of the model (even without formal training in its use) run more profitable operations than managers who do not seem to function in this manner.

Together, these findings suggest that the Vroom and Yetton model offers important insights into a key aspect of leader effectiveness. We should note, however, that not all research based on this model has yielded positive results. Indeed, an investigation conducted by Heilman, Hornstein, Cage, and Herschlag suggests that certain changes may be required.[32] In this study, individuals were stopped at many locations in New York City and asked to read four written stories involving decisions by leaders. In two of these stories, conditions were such that according to the Vroom

FIGURE 9.8 *The Vroom and Yetton Model: A Recent Test.*
When subjects adopted the perspective of a *leader*, they rated the decision process followed by an imaginary manager more favorably when it was consistent with recommendations derived from the Vroom and Yetton model than when it was not (left panel). However, when they adopted the perspective of a *subordinate* (right panel), they rated a participative decision process more favorably than an autocratic one regardless of what the Vroom-Yetton model predicted. (Source: Based on data from Heilman, Hornstein, Cage, and Herschlag, 1984; see Note 12.)

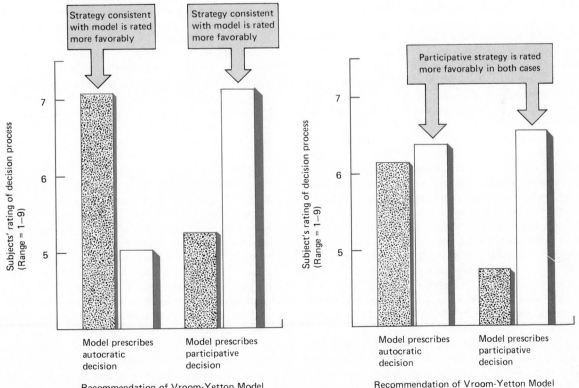

Becoming a More Effective Leader: Some Useful Steps

Nearly everyone who serves as a leader wants to be successful in this role. (The only major exception to this rule we can think of involves persons who have no wish to remain in positions of authority, and hope to escape from them by "gumming up the works.") We are certain, then, that if *you* ever become a leader, you will want to do the best job possible. Wanting to be a good leader and actually succeeding as one, though, are two different things. Even persons with a strong desire to serve their groups, advance their own careers, and assist their organizations often find that the task is more than they can handle. Are there any steps you can take to "load the dice" in your favor when you find yourself in authority over others? Fortunately, there are. Although it is impossible for us to arm you with a magic, no-fail formula for success, we *can* call your attention to several principles that may prove useful in many contexts. None of these in any way guarantees that you will be an effective leader. Together, though, they can at least point you in the right directions, and help you avoid important pitfalls.

(1) *Cultivate Your Sensitivity Quotient.* What characteristics set successful leaders off from ineffective ones? As we noted previously, the answer does not appear to involve a short list of well-known personality traits. Instead, it may center around a special type of *sensitivity.* Successful leaders, it appears, are often highly adept at "reading" both the needs of their followers and changing situational conditions that affect their organizations. Because they are in tune with such factors, good leaders can readily adapt their own behavior and strategies to them. The result: they usually find themselves riding the crest of waves of change rather than falling underneath them. So, be sure to develop your sensitivity in these directions; doing so can be a big help. (Please see our discussion of social perception in Chapter 4 and our discussion of nonverbal communication in Chapter 10 for further information.)

(2) *Show High Concern with People* **and** *High Concern with Production.* Is it necessary to choose between good relations with one's subordinates and a high level of productivity? At one time, many man-

agers believed that this was true: one could either be liked, *or* get the job done. Recent evidence indicates that this is simply not true. In fact, leaders who combine these two orientations—who demonstrate their concern with both people and production—tend to get the best of both worlds. When you serve as a leader, then, try to adopt this double-sided approach. The chances are quite good that your results will be better than if you choose to focus on only one or the other of these contrasting approaches.

(3) *Choose the Most Appropriate Means for Making Decisions.* One of the key tasks performed by leaders is making decisions. In this respect, it is important to keep two major goals firmly in mind. First, the decisions you reach should be as accurate and effective as possible. (We will consider techniques for maximizing such outcomes in Chapter 13.) Second, the process through which decisions are made should be carefully matched to existing conditions. If these suggest the need for participation by subordinates, this should be allowed or invited. If, instead, present conditions suggest the need for a relatively autocratic approach, *this* should adopted. Keep one additional point in mind, though: in general, subordinates prefer a participative approach. Thus, if you must err, do so in this direction. The costs will probably be small relative to those incurred by a leadership style subordinates find too autocratic.

(4) *Always Remember That Leadership Is a Two-Way Street.* One common error on the part of many leaders involves their failure to grasp a simple fact: while they exert considerable influence over their subordinates, these individuals, in turn, influence them. A leader's behavior is often shaped by the actions of his or her followers. Similarly, a leader can be effective only to the extent that he or she has the confidence and support of subordinates. In dealing with other members of your group, therefore, always remember that your relations with them are complex and reciprocal—*not* a simple one-way arrangement in which you exert all of the influence. Keeping this fact in mind will enhance your insight into the causes behind your own actions, and also help you to under-

stand the motives, needs, and attitudes of your subordinates.

(5) *Above All, Be Flexible.* If modern theories of leadership tell us anything, it is this: *flexibility*, at least with respect to leadership style, is a virtue. No single approach or strategy is best, so the guiding principle for leaders should be: adapt your methods to the specific situation. Doing so may prove highly beneficial, for in the complex world of organizations, the best leaders are often the most adaptable ones.

---

and Yetton model, an autocratic approach was best. In two others, conditions were such that a participative approach to the decision would be preferred. The leaders described in the stories either behaved in accordance with what the model would recommend, or in an opposite fashion. A final variable of interest was the perspective taken by subjects. Half were told to imagine that they were the leader while reading the stories, and half to imagine that they were the subordinates.

After reading the four stories, subjects evaluated the decision process used by the leader, and rated this person's attributes (e.g., his or her likability and competence). It was predicted that if individuals do indeed implicitly accept the Vroom-Yetton model, then their ratings of the decision process and of the leader's traits would be higher when the leader behaved in a manner consistent with this model than when he or she did not. As shown in Figure 9.8 (page 287), results offered only partial support for this prediction, and so for the Vroom and Yetton model. With respect to ratings of the decision process, subjects did indeed respond more favorably when the leader acted in accordance with the model, but only when they were asked to take the leader's perspective (i.e., to imagine they themselves were the boss). Under these conditions, autocratic behavior by the leader was rated more favorably than participative behavior when the model called for an autocratic approach, and the reverse was true when the model indicated the need for a more participative approach (refer to Figure 9.7, page 286). However, when subjects imagined that they were the subordinates in the stories, they *never* rated autocratic behavior by the leader more favorably than participative behavior—even when it was identified as more appropriate by the model. Turning to ratings of the leader's traits, results offered little support for predictions based on the Vroom-Yetton theory. Instead, leaders who demonstrated participative behavior were liked more and viewed as having a more favorable impact upon their subordinates than ones who were autocratic, regardless of what the model predicted.

The findings uncovered by Heilman and her colleagues suggest the need for two modifications in the Vroom-Yetton model. First, it appears that a participative approach to decision making generates favorable reactions among subordinates. For this reason, it may sometimes be effective even in situations where the model recommends a more autocratic approach. Second, differences in the perspective of leaders and subordinates are important, and should be taken into account. While leaders may view decision methods consistent with the model very favorably, subordinates may disagree—especially when these involve use of an autocratic method. Through added attention to these factors, the Vroom-Yetton model may be further strengthened, and so come to provide us with an even better understanding of leader decision making (and its role in leader effectiveness) than is true at present. (How can *you* become a more effective leader? For some practical hints, see the **Perspective** box on page 288.)

Path-Goal Theory: Leaders as Guides to Valued Goals

Suppose that you conducted an informal survey in which you asked fifty people to indicate just what they expect from their leaders. What kind of answers would you receive? Obviously, these would vary greatly. One common theme you might uncover, though, would go something like this: "Well, I expect my leader to *help*— to assist me in reaching goals I feel are important." In short, many people would report that they expect their leaders (or at least *good* leaders) to aid them in attaining valued goals.

This basic idea plays a central role in House's path-goal theory of leadership.[33] In very general terms, this theory contends that subordinates will react favorably to a leader's behavior only to the extent that they perceive it as helping them progress toward various goals by clarifying actual paths to these rewards. More specifically, the theory offers two basic proposals (see Figure 9.9 for a summary of these suggestions):

(1) A leader's behavior will be *acceptable* and *satisfying* to subordinates only to the extent that they perceive it as providing immediate rewards, or as instrumental to the attainment of future ones;

(2) A leader's behavior will be *motivating* to subordinates only to the extent that it makes subordinate rewards contingent upon effective performance and provides something not already offered by the work situation (e.g., additional guidance, clarification).

But how, precisely, can leaders best meet these requirements? The answer, as in other modern views of leadership, is: *it depends*. And what it depends upon is a complex interaction between key aspects of *leader behavior* and certain *contingency* factors. With respect to leader behavior, path-goal theory suggests that leaders can adopt four basic styles:

- *instrumental* (directive): an approach focused on providing specific guidance, establishing work schedules and rules;
- *supportive:* a style focused on the establishment of good relations with other group members and the needs and wellbeing of subordinates;
- *participative:* a pattern in which the leader consults with subordinates, permits them to participate in decisions;
- *achievement-oriented:* an approach in which the leader sets challenging goals and seeks improvements in performance.

Note, by the way, that these styles are not mutually exclusive; in fact, the same leader (manager) can adopt them at different times and in different situations.

Which of these contrasting styles is best from the point of view of maximizing follower satisfaction and motivation? This depends on the contingency factors mentioned above. First, the style of choice is strongly affected by several *subordinate characteristics.* For example, if followers are high in ability, an instrumental style of leadership may be unnecessary; instead, a less structured, supportive one may be preferable. On the other hand, if subordinates are low in ability, the opposite may

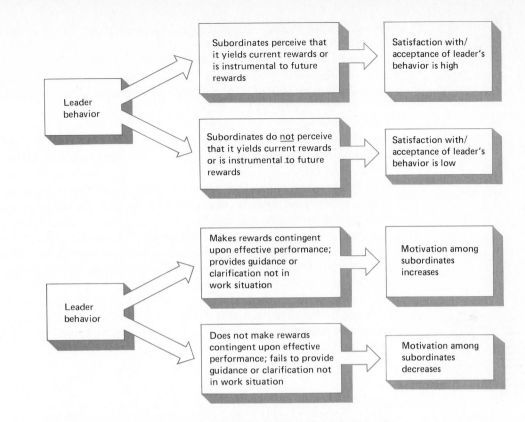

FIGURE 9.9   *The Path-Goal Theory of Leadership: Basic Proposals.*
According to *path-goal* theory, a leader's behavior will be acceptable and/or satisfying to subordinates only if it is perceived as providing immediate rewards, or as instrumental to future ones. Similarly, a leader's behavior will be motivating to subordinates only if it makes rewards contingent upon effective performance *and* provides guidance or clarification not already present in the work situation.

be true, for such persons need considerable guidance to help them attain their goals. Similarly, *externals*—persons who feel that they have little influence over their own outcomes—may prefer a directive style; *internals*—ones who feel they largely shape their own outcomes—may prefer a more participative one. Finally, the motives of subordinates, too, are important. Persons high in need for achievement may prefer an achievement-oriented leader; those lower in this motive may prefer another.

Second, the most effective leadership style also depends on several aspects of *work environments*. For example, path-goal theory predicts that when tasks are unstructured and nonroutine, an instrumental approach by the leader may be best; much clarification and guidance is needed. However, when tasks are structured and highly routine, such leadership may actually get in the way of good performance, and may be resented by subordinates who view the leader as engaging in unnecessary meddling.

Although path-goal theory is relatively new, it has already been investigated in several studies.[34] For example, in one project, carried out by Schriesheim and DeNisi, employees at a bank and a manufacturing concern rated their supervisors' behavior and their own job satisfaction.[35] In addition, they also completed a questionnaire designed to determine the extent to which their jobs were varied or routine. On the basis of path-goal theory, it was predicted that when individuals perceived their jobs as varied, their satisfaction would *increase* as the level of instrumental behavior by their supervisors rose. That is, persons performing such unstructured jobs would find planning and guidance by their leader useful, and would react favorably to it. In contrast, when individuals perceived their jobs as routine, the opposite pattern would hold. Here, reported job satisfaction would actually *decrease* as the level of instrumental behavior by supervisors rose. This would be the case because employees would perceive directive actions by their leaders as unnecessary. Results offered clear support for these hypotheses. Thus, as suggested by path-goal theory, employees did *not* prefer a specific style of leader behavior. Rather, they reacted most favorably to leaders whose style seemed likely to provide something not already present in the situation, and to assist them toward their goals.

To conclude: path-goal theory indicates that leaders will be perceived most favorably by their subordinates, and succeed in exerting most influence over them, when they behave in ways that closely match (1) the needs and values of subordinates, and (2) the requirements of a specific work situation.

TWO RECENT ADVANCES: THE VERTICAL DYAD LINKAGE MODEL AND SUBSTITUTES FOR LEADERSHIP

Leadership is clearly a central process in organizations—some would say *the* central process. Because of this fact, dozens of articles and many books dealing with this topic are published each year. Given the volume of such work, we could not possibly summarize all of it here. What we *can* do, however, is touch briefly on a few of the advances in our understanding of leadership made in recent years. Among the most intriguing (and potentially important) of these are two perspectives known as the **VDL model** and **substitutes for leadership.**

Vertical Dyad Linkage Model

The VDL Model: Focus on Leader-Member Pairs

Do leaders treat all their subordinates in the same manner? Many theories of leadership seem to assume that they do. Thus, they comment on leadership style or behavior as if this were constant across all subordinates. In fact, however, leaders often act very differently toward different followers, and develop contrasting kinds of relationships with them. These basic facts are given full recognition by an approach to leadership developed by Dansereau, Graen, and Haga.[36]

Briefly, this perspective, known as the **vertical dyad linkage** model (or *VDL* for short), suggests that leaders form distinct exchange relationships with each of their subordinates. In these relationships, leaders offer valued outcomes such as greater job latitude, input into decisions, and open communication, while followers can reciprocate with increased commitment to the organization or unit. While leaders form such relationships with all of their subordinates, however, the nature of these dyads can differ sharply. At one extreme, the leader holds positive views about a subordinate, and this person, in turn, feels that the leader understands his or her problems, appreciates his or her potential, and would offer help and support when needed. At the other end of the continuum, the leader holds negative views about the subordinate, and this individual has little faith or confidence in the leader. According to the VDL model, such differences in the quality of leader-member relations can have powerful effects upon productivity, job satisfaction, and other organizational processes.

To the extent this is true (and a growing body of research evidence suggests that it is), the next question is obvious: can any steps be undertaken to improve individual leader-member relations? Fortunately, a recent investigation conducted by Scandura and Graen provides a positive reply.[37] Participants in this study were supervisors and employees working in a large government unit. These individuals completed a series of questionnaires on two occasions: before their supervisors underwent special training designed to enhance leader-member relations, and again several weeks after this training had been completed. The questionnaires were designed to measure (1) subjects' perceptions of the quality of their relationships with their leader, (2) their satisfaction with their manager's leadership, (3) the level of support they felt they received from this person, and (4) their overall job satisfaction. (The interval between the first and second administration of these questionnaires was twenty-six weeks.) In addition, measures of participants' actual productivity (the number of cases they completed processing each week) were obtained over the course of the project. The training undergone by leaders involved their attendance at six two-hour sessions, spaced over a period of six weeks. During these sessions leaders received instruction in such skills as active listening and the effective exchange of expectations with subordinates. The overall goal of these procedures was that of increasing the level of understanding and mutual helpfulness between leaders and their followers. (For participants in a control condition, supervisors also attended special sessions, but did not receive the training described above.)

On the basis of certain aspects of the VDL model, it was predicted that these procedures would be especially helpful for subordinates whose initial relations with the leader were negative. To test this prediction, leader-member dyads were divided into three groups: low, medium, and high initial relations. As you can see from Figure 9.10 (page 294), results offered strong support for this hypothesis. Individuals whose relations with their supervisors were initially negative showed substantial gains in productivity, job satisfaction, satisfaction with their leader, and confidence in his or her support. In contrast, persons whose relations with their supervisors were initially favorable showed smaller gains in these respects.

The findings obtained by Scandura and Graen suggest that attention to dyadic relations between leaders and specific followers can often be very useful. Indeed, in

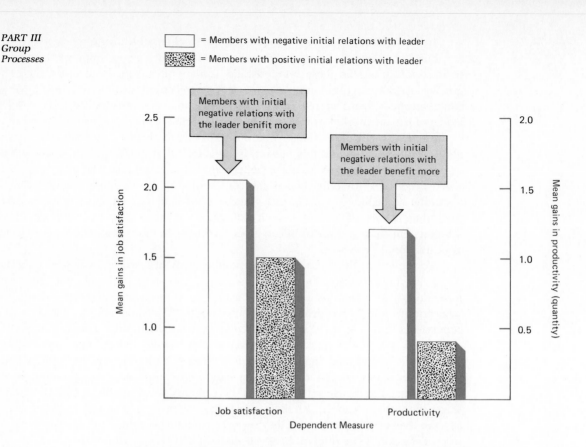

= Members with negative initial relations with leader

= Members with positive initial relations with leader

FIGURE 9.10   Enhanced Leader-member Relations: Who Benefits Most?
After their leaders underwent special training, subordinates whose initial relations with the
leader were negative experienced larger gains in both productivity and job satisfaction than
subordinates whose initial relations with their leader were positive. (Source: Based on data
from Scandura and Graen, 1984; see Note 37.)

this particular study, the leader-training intervention resulted in a 19 percent gain
in employee productivity—an outcome estimated to save the organization more
than $5 million each year! Given such practical benefits, and the important new
insights into leadership it provides, the VDL model seems to represent a promising
advance, fully deserving of further careful attention.

Substitutes for Leadership: When Technology, Organizational Structure, and Subordinate Characteristics Make Leaders Superfluous

Throughout this chapter, we have emphasized the following point: leaders are
important. Their style, their actions, and their degree of effectiveness all exert major
effects upon subordinates and, ultimately, upon organizations themselves. In many

cases, this is certainly true. Yet, almost everyone has observed or been part of groups in which the designated leaders actually had little influence—ones in which these persons were mere "figureheads," with little impact on subordinates. One explanation for such situations may lie in the characteristics of the leaders in question: perhaps they are weak and unsuited for their jobs. Another, though, has more general implications for our understanding of leadership: in some contexts, other factors may *substitute* for the leader's influence, and make it superfluous. According to a framework developed by Kerr and Jermier, many different variables can exert such effects.[38] First, a high level of knowledge, commitment, or experience on the part of subordinates may make it unnecessary for anyone to tell them what to do or how to proceed. Second, jobs themselves may be structured in ways that make direction and influence from a leader redundant. Third, work norms and strong feelings of cohesion among employees may directly affect job performance, and render the presence of a leader unnecessary. Fourth, the technology associated with certain jobs may strongly determine the decisions and actions of individuals performing them, and so leave little room for input from a leader. Finally, the administrative climate of the organization (e.g., the extent to which it focuses on status, task completion, or good human relations) may directly influence job performance, and so reduce the potential impact of supervisors.

Evidence for these assertions has been obtained in several recent studies.[39] For example, in an investigation involving hospital nurses, Sheridan, Vredenburgh, and Abelson examined the impact of several factors that might serve as substitutes for influence from a leader, as well as factors that might tend to reduce or neutralize such impact.[40] Participants in this project (both nurses and their supervisors) completed questionnaires designed to assess their formal education, commitment to nursing, the structure of their work units, the design of their jobs, and the administrative climate present in their hospital. In addition, the nurses rated the frequency with which their supervisors (head nurses) demonstrated specific leadership activities (e.g., decision making, asserting formal power). The head nurses, in turn, rated the performance of each of their subordinates.

Results indicated that job performance was indeed directly and indirectly affected by many of the factors that, potentially, might serve as substitutes for leadership. Thus, performance was influenced by the nurses' education, by certain features of each hospital's administrative climate, group norms concerning the quality of care, and the type of technology available. The only aspect of the head nurses' behavior that exerted similar effects was their level of assertiveness, and even the impact of this factor was mediated by organizational conditions. Specifically, a high level of assertiveness on the part of the head nurse enhanced job performance in hospitals where the administration was perceived as setting clear goals and providing rewards linked to individual accomplishments, but reduced performance in hospitals where less favorable conditions prevailed.

These findings, and those obtained in other research, suggest that the centrality of leaders to their groups may vary considerably. If subordinates are unskilled or inexperienced, if tasks are unstructured, and if administrative climate is unfavorable in any of several ways, leaders may be crucial. If, in contrast, employees are skilled or committed, if tasks are structured, if technology dictates certain actions, and if the administrative climate is fair and supportive, leaders may be viewed by their subordinates as largely superfluous. In sum, leaders *are* often important both to followers and to their organizations. However, as noted by Jermier and Kerr, their necessity should never be taken for granted; rather, it should be considered in the light of conditions prevailing in given organizational contexts.

SUMMARY

Leadership refers to the fact that in most groups, one individual wields greater influence or authority than the others. Such persons are known as **leaders,** and they often exert profound effects upon their subordinates. Several contrasting perspectives on leadership exist. One (the *great man/great woman theory*) holds that leaders possess special traits that set them apart from other persons. Another (the *situational approach*) contends that leaders rise to positions of authority because they possess the abilities or skills needed by their groups in certain situations. A third view (known as the *transactional approach,* or *reciprocal determinism*) suggests that the flow of influence between leaders and their groups is very much a "two-way street." Thus, successful leaders are individuals who adapt their own behavior to the needs and values of subordinates.

Leaders differ greatly with respect to their style or approach to leadership. Some are *autocratic* and wish to be totally in control of the groups they direct. In contrast, others show a more *participative* style, and share authority and decisions with subordinates. Another key dimension of leader style involves the extent to which such persons focus on task completion (*initiating structure*) or on good relations with subordinates (*showing consideration*). Differences between leaders on both of these dimensions can strongly affect the performance and satisfaction of followers.

Several major theories attempt to shed light on the causes of leader effectiveness. The **contingency theory,** developed by Fiedler, indicates that both a leader's characteristics and situational factors are crucial in this respect. Task-oriented leaders are more effective than person-oriented ones under conditions where the leader has either high or low control over the group. In contrast, person-oriented leaders are more effective under conditions where the leader has moderate control over the group. A second theory, Vroom and Yetton's **normative model,** focuses on decision making as a key determinant of leader effectiveness. According to this theory, different situations call for different styles of decision making (e.g., autocratic, consultative, participative) by leaders. To the extent they adopt an appropriate strategy, their effectiveness will be enhanced. A third major theory of leadership, **path-goal theory,** suggests that leaders' behavior will be accepted by subordinates, and will enhance their motivation, to the extent it helps them progress toward valued goals, and provides guidance or clarification not already present in work situations.

Two new perspectives on leadership are the *vertical dyad linkage (VDL) model* and *substitutes for leadership.* The VDL model calls attention to the fact that a leader may have very different relationships with different subordinates. Further, it notes that the nature of these dyadic relations may strongly affect subordinates' productivity, satisfaction, and perceptions of their leader. The substitutes for leadership approach takes account of the fact that under some conditions (e.g., when subordinates are highly skilled or committed), directives or guidance from a leader may be superfluous. Thus, it emphasizes the fact that leaders are not always essential to the effective functioning of groups or organizations.

KEY TERMS

autocratic leadership style: An approach in which the leader attempts to control virtually every aspect of group functioning (e.g., work activities, decision making).

contingency theory: A theory suggesting that leader effectiveness is determined both by characteristics of the leader and the level of situational control this person can exert over subordinates.

great man/great woman theory: A theory suggesting that leaders possess special traits that set them apart from others, and that it is these traits that cause them to rise to positions of power and authority.

initiating structure (task orientation): Activities by a leader designed to enhance productivity or task accomplishment. Leaders who focus primarily on such goals are often described as demonstrating a task-oriented style.

leader match: A training program for leaders in which they learn techniques for attaining a closer match between their personal style and the situational conditions they confront.

leaders: Individuals within groups or organizations who wield the most influence over others.

leadership: The process through which leaders influence the actions, attitudes, and values of other group members.

normative model: A theory of leader effectiveness focused primarily on means for choosing the most appropriate strategies for making decisions.

participative leadership style: An approach in which the leader shares authority and responsibility with subordinates. Thus, he or she invites their participation in decisions, and permits them a considerable degree of autonomy with respect to routine work activities.

path-goal theory: A theory of leadership suggesting that subordinates will find a leader's behavior satisfying and/or motivating only to the extent they perceive it as instrumental to reaching valued goals and as providing something not already present in their work environment (e.g., guidance, clarification).

reciprocal determinism: The view that leadership is very much a "two-way street" in which leaders influence their subordinates and are affected, in turn, by these persons.

showing consideration: Actions by a leader directed toward the goal of producing or maintaining good relations with subordinates. Leaders who focus primarily on this task are often described as demonstrating a "person-oriented" style.

situational approach: A theory suggesting that leaders are often those individuals whose traits, abilities, and characteristics most closely match the requirements of current situational factors.

substitutes for leadership: The view that under certain conditions, high levels of skill among subordinates, or certain features of technology and organizational structure, can render influence or guidance from a leader superfluous.

transactional approach: The view that full understanding of leadership must involve careful attention to characteristics of leaders, aspects of the situation in which leadership occurs, and characteristics of followers.

vertical dyad linkage model: A theory suggesting that leaders often form different kinds of relationships with various subordinates, and that the nature of such dyads may strongly affect subordinates' productivity and satisfaction.

NOTES

1. J. G. Geier (1969). A trait approach to the study of leadership in small groups. *Journal of Communication, 17,* 316–323.

2. R. Stogdill (1974). *Handbook of leadership.* New York: Free Press.

3. D. C. McClelland and R. E. Boyatzis (1982). Leadership motive pattern and long-term success in management. *Journal of Applied Psychology, 67,* 737–743.

4. E. Costantini and K. H. Craik (1980). Personality and politicians: California party leaders, 1960–1976. *Journal of Personality and Social Psychology, 38,* 641–661.

5. D. A. Kenny and S. J. Zaccaro (1983). An estimate of variance due to traits in leadership. *Journal of Applied Psychology, 68,* 678–685.

6. B. M. Bass (1981). *Stogdill's handbook of leadership: A survey of theory and research.* New York: Free Press.

7. E. P. Hollander (1978). *Leadership dynamics.* New York: Free Press.

8. H. P. Sims, Jr. and C. C. Manz. (1984). Observing leader verbal behavior: Toward reciprocal determinism in leadership theory. *Journal of Applied Psychology, 69,* 222–232.

9. E. M. Fodor (1976). Group stress, authoritarian style of control, and use of power. *Journal of Applied Psychology, 61,* 313–318.

10. D. Tjosvold (1984). Effects of leader warmth and directiveness on subordinate performance on a subsequent task. *Journal of Applied Psychology, 69,* 422–427.

11. E. A. Fleishman (1973). Twenty years of consideration and structure. In E. A. Fleishman and J. G. Hunt (eds.), *Current developments in the study of leadership.* Carbondale: Southern Illinois University Press.

12. M. E. Heilman, H. A. Hornstein, J. H. Cage, and J. K. Herschlag (1984). Reactions to prescribed leader behavior as a function of role perspective: The case of the Vroom-Yetton model. *Journal of Applied Psychology, 69,* 50–60.

13. See Note 12.

14. R. Likert (1961). *New patterns in management.* New York: McGraw Hill.

15. See Note 2.

16. P. Weissenberg and M. H. Kavanagh (1972). The independence of initiating structure and consideration: A review of the evidence. *Personnel Psychology, 25,* 119–130.

17. V. H. Vroom (1976). Leadership. In M. D. Dunnette (ed.), *Handbook of industrial and organizational psychology.* Chicago: Rand McNally.

18. D. Katz, N. Maccoby, and N. C. Morse (1951). *Productivity, supervision, and morale in an office situation.* Ann Arbor: University of Michigan, Institute for Social Research.

19. R. Blake and J. Mouton (1978). *The new managerial grid.* Houston: Gulf.

20. See Note 10.

21. S. A. Basow (1981). *Sex role stereotypes: Traditions and alternatives.* Monterey, Calif.: Brooks/Cole.

22. R. W. Rice, D. Instone, and J. Adams (1984). Leader sex, leader success, and leadership process: Two field studies. *Journal of Applied Psychology, 69,* 12–31.

23. J. L. Carbonell (1984). Sex roles and leadership revisited. *Journal of Applied Psychology, 69,* 44–49.

24. F. E. Fiedler (1978). Contingency model and the leadership process. In L. Berkowitz (ed.), *Advances in experimental social psychology,* vol. 11. New York: Academic Press.

25. M. J. Strube and J. E. Garcia (1981). A meta-analytic investigation of Fiedler's contingency model of leadership effectiveness. *Psychological Bulletin, 90,* 307–321.

26. L. H. Peters, D. D. Hartke, and J. T. Pohlmann (1985). Fiedler's contingency theory of leadership: An application of the meta-analysis procedures of Schmidt and Hunter. *Psychological Bulletin, 97,* 274–285.

27. A. S. Ashour (1973). The contingency model of leadership effectiveness: An evaluation. *Organizational Behavior and Human Performance, 9,* 339–355.

28. M. T. Wood (1973). Power relationships and group decisionmaking in organizations. *Psychological Bulletin, 79,* 280–293.

29. V. H. Vroom and P. W. Yetton (1973). *Leadership and decision-making.* Pittsburgh: University of Pittsburgh Press.

30. V. H. Vroom and A. G. Jago (1978). On the validity of the Vroom-Yetton model. *Journal of Applied Psychology, 63,* 151–162.

31. R. H. George Field (1982). A test of the Vroom-Yetton normative model of leadership. *Journal of Applied Psychology, 67,* 523–532.

32. See Note 12.

33. R. J. House (1971). A path-goal theory of leader effectiveness. *Administrative Science Quarterly, 16,* 321–33.

34. R. J. House and M. L. Baetz (1979). Leadership: Some generalizations and new research directions. In B. M. Staw (ed.), *Research in organizational behavior.* Greenwich, Conn.: JAI Press.

35. C. A. Schriesheim and A. S. DeNisi (1981). Task dimensions as moderators of the effects of instrumental leadership: A two-sample replicated test of path-goal leadership theory. *Journal of Applied Psychology, 66,* 589–597.

36. F. Dansereau, G. Graen, and B. Haga (1975). A vertical dyad linkage approach to leadership within formal organizations: A longitudinal investigation of the role making process. *Organizational Behavior and Human Performance, 13,* 45–78.

37. T. A. Scandura and G. B. Graen (1984). Moderating effects of initial leader-member exchange status on the effects of a leadership intervention. *Journal of Applied Psychology, 69,* 428–436.

38. S. Kerr and J. M. Jermier (1978). Substitutes for leadership: Their meaning and measurement. *Organizational Behavior and Human Performance, 22,* 375–403.

39. See Note 37.

40. J. E. Sheridan, D. J. Vredenburgh, and M. A. Abelson (1984). Contextual model of leadership influence in hospital units. *Academy of Management Journal, 27,* 57–78.

CHAPTER 10

COMMUNICATION: A Working Definition and a Model

INDIVIDUAL INFLUENCES ON COMMUNICATION: Why Some People Are Better at Communicating Than Others

Personal Style and Communication: Some Key Characteristics   Nonverbal Communication: Messages without Words

ORGANIZATIONAL INFLUENCES ON COMMUNICATION: Structure, Networks, and the Grapevine

Communication Networks: Their Impact on Performance and Satisfaction Organizational Structure and the Flow of Information: Up, Down, and Horizontal   Informal Channels of Communication in Organizations: The Grapevine and Rumors

ENHANCING ORGANIZATIONAL COMMUNICATION: Some Concrete Steps

Improving Communication: Individual Strategies   Improving Communication: Organizational Strategies

SPECIAL INSERTS

CASE IN POINT   "You Don't Really Notice Much, Do You?"
FOCUS ON BEHAVIOR   Organizational Communication and Organizational
   Performance: Evidence for a Link

Communication in Organizations: Enhancing the Flow of Information

". . . So in conclusion, let's all get out there and make this year the greatest yet for Continental. We've got the product, we've got the opportunity, and with you people behind us, I know we can really do it!" With these words, and the applause that follows, Marshal Andros, the C.E.O. of Continental Fidelity Insurance, leaves the podium, and turns the meeting back to Sara Granger, who's running this year's gathering for agents. After a few closing activities, the session breaks up and Curt Sorenson, Mimi Jones, and Dick Scheidt drift off together for a cup of coffee. Unfortunately, confusion is apparent on all their faces.

"Inspirational, just inspirational," Mimi comments as they settle into a comfortable booth in the hotel restaurant. "Why, I can hardly control myself. Let me at 'em, let me at 'em!" and she half-rises as if to launch her personal sales effort at once. At these remarks, her two companions chuckle, for their C.E.O. is well known for his corny, almost ministerial style. "But you know, I really don't get it," Mimi continues. "What's the overall message? Are we supposed to go for volume, or is the by-word this year quality? And what about the new umbrella package;—are we supposed to push it hard, or only when nothing else fits?"

"Who knows!" Curt answers. "*I* can't figure it out. Andros always talks in circles, as far as I'm concerned."

"He sure does," Dick agrees. "First he says one thing, and then another. Altogether, it's just too much. Pure overload. I always lose him after the first twenty minutes."

"And what *does* get through is so muddled. I mean, at one level he seemed to be saying 'From here on in, we want only preferred risk clients.' But on another, I got the feeling that this year, sheer volume is the name of the game. I mean, there really didn't seem to be much conviction in his voice when he made those comments about concentrating on preferred risks."

"Hmmph!" Curt exclaims. "If only he'd get his act together *before* he gives these talks. Ah, phoo, I can *never* make any sense out of these accounting types myself. They're just too darn cool for me."

At this, everyone laughs again, for Curt is well known for his expansive, pat-'em-on-the-back style. Also, the personality gap between the finance/accounting people in the home office and the company's agents is legendary at Continental.

"Well, maybe we can get the word from Sara. She usually knows what's up," Mimi comments.

"If you can ever get in touch with her," Dick responds. "That new assistant of hers is something else. Whew—you practically need a legal document to get past him! Talk about holding down the flow!"

"Oh well," Mimi says, smiling. "We'll get it straightened out before the meetings are over—we always do. And even if we don't, the old grapevine'll come through for us in the end. By the time we get back home we'll know just where we stand and just where the bonus points are this season. But you know, it sure would make life a lot simpler if these top people would learn to say what they mean once in a while . . ."

What one thing is most crucial to organizations—their very "lifeblood," so to speak? One potential answer, and probably the one you think of first is "money" or "profits." But think again: many organizations are nonprofit in nature (e.g., educational institutions, government agencies). And for others, the rate of return on investment is strictly regulated by law or special commissions (e.g., utilities, various financial institutions). Thus, while is it obviously important, money may not be the best or most general answer to our question. A better one, we believe, is simply *information.* In order to function, adjust to ever-changing external conditions, and attain their major goals, modern organizations require the free and orderly flow of information. And the movement of such information, in turn, requires some form of **communication**. It is on this central process that we fill focus in the present chapter.

The importance of communication in organizational settings is suggested by the following fact: practicing managers actually spend more of their time engaging in this process than in any other single activity. Indeed, some findings suggest that speaking to others, listening to them, or reading words they have written occupies up to 80 percent of their entire day![1] The central importance of communication is also indicated by the events that follow when something goes wrong with this process—when the flow of information within an organization is interrupted, faulty, or inadequate. Some idea of the nature of these negative outcomes is provided by the story on page 301. In that incident, failure of a top executive to effectively get his message across led to considerable confusion among employees. Further, restrictions on communication within the company made it unlikely that the persons involved could get the information they required quickly through the formal chan-

FIGURE 10.1   *Communication in Organizations: Far from Perfect.*
As shown here, communication in organizational settings is subject to many sources of inaccuracy. (Source: Drawing by Ziegler; © 1982 The New Yorker Magazine, Inc.)

nels (e.g., from Sara Granger, the head of their unit). As a result, they found it necessary to rely on informal—and perhaps less accurate—sources of information, such as the "grapevine."

As will soon be apparent, communication is a complex process, affected by a wide range of factors. Further, as suggested by Figure 10.1, it is subject to all-too-many sources of error, inaccuracy, and distortion. Since communication plays a vital role in virtually every aspect of organizational functioning, though, it is essential for you to know something about it. To provide you with such knowledge, we will touch on several topics. First, we will present a basic *model of communication*—a simple framework for understanding what it involves, and what it seeks to accomplish. Second, we will examine several *individual* influences on communication. These are factors that seem to determine why some persons are so much more effective at this process than others. Third, we will turn to *organizational* influences on communication—aspects of organizations themselves that shape the nature and direction of information flow within them. Finally, we will examine several techniques for *enhancing* communication—tactics individuals or organizations can employ to improve its accuracy and value.

COMMUNICATION: A WORKING DEFINITION AND A MODEL

A supervisor praises good work by one of her subordinates. A new employee reads a booklet outlining company procedures and policies relating to his job. A foreman directs the actions of a work crew who can't hear his words because of a high level of noise by means of a series of hand signals. A financial analyst prepares a written report summarizing the potential costs and benefits of entering a new market; after it is finished, she distributes it to several members of her department.

The incidents we have just described are highly varied in nature. Yet, you will probably agree that all involve some form of communication. In short, all represent instances in which one or more persons transmit some type of information to one or more others. This statement, simple as it may seem, actually constitutes a useful working definition of communication. Briefly (but a bit more formally) we can define it as *the process through which one person or group* (known as the **sender**) *transmits some type of information to another person or group* (known as the **receiver**).[2]

This working definition of communication, in turn, implies a simple model of the process—a basic framework for understanding just what steps it involves. Within this model (which is summarized in Figure 10.2), communication begins when two conditions exist: (1) some individual or group has an idea or concept, and (2) this person or group wishes to make such information known to someone else. Why is this the case? In short, what are the specific motives behind communication? The answer is: as many as you can imagine. Within organizations, specific persons may wish to communicate with others to influence them, to assist them with their work, to obtain imput they need for performing their *own* jobs, to affect decisions, to correct others' past mistakes, to dazzle or impress them with their vast knowledge—the list is almost endless.[3] In any case, regardless of the specific reason behind the desire to communicate, the process next moves to an important, initial step: **encoding**. Briefly, the concept or idea to be transmitted must be put into a

FIGURE 10.2 *Communication: A Basic Model.*
In its most basic form, communication consists of the steps shown here. First, an individual or group (the sender) has an idea or concept it wishes to make known to someone else. This information is then *encoded*—converted into a form that can be transmitted. Third, the information is actually sent to the intended audience over some channel of communication. The recipients must then *decode* it—convert it back into an idea or concept they can understand. Finally, information may be returned to the sender in the form of feedback.

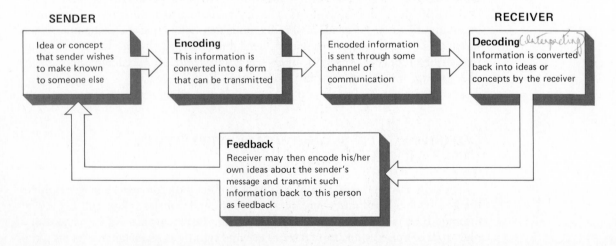

form that can be sent to the reciever. This is necessary because, contrary to popular beliefs about the existence of ESP (extra-sensory perception), most persons *cannot* read the minds of others! Thus, they can learn what the people around them are thinking only if this information is rendered observable in some way. For communication to occur, ideas and concepts must be converted either into spoken words, some type of written communication, or observable actions that convey a specific meaning (e.g., gestures and signals; facial expressions). It should be noted, by the way, that our ability to encode ideas, thoughts, and especially feelings, is far from perfect. If you have ever had difficulty describing the way you feel or a complex concept to another person, you are already familiar with this fact.

Once encoding is accomplished, another issue quickly arises: how can this information be transmitted to the receiver? The answer depends, in part, on how the message has been encoded. If it has been placed in the form of a written report, it can be transmitted by mail or messenger. If it has been entered into storage in a computer, it can be sent directly to another computer over phone lines or by satellite. If it is expressed in words, it can be presented directly in a face-to-face meeting, over the phone, or even by tape. Whatever means are chosen, though, the message must be transmitted in such a way that the receiver can actually obtain it.

Now, assume that the receiver has somehow gotten the intended message. What happens next? The answer is obvious: this person or group must *interpret* the information received. In short, the message must be **decoded**—converted back into an idea or concept that the recipient can understand. Once again, it is important to note that our abilities to accomplish this key task are limited. If you have ever experienced problems in understanding what another person is saying, or difficulties in making sense out of something you have read (hopefully, not this discussion of communication!), you are well acquainted with the frustrations that can stem from such restrictions.

Finally, after decoding has occurred, the receiver may reverse the process and transmit information back to the original sender. Such *feedback* is an essential part of communication in many settings. It is especially valuable in organizations where, as we will soon see, much communication sems to flow "downward"—from supervisors and managers to subordinates. Providing such persons with an opportunity to offer feedback yields several benefits. For example, it can enhance their belief that their views really count, and so increase their commitment to the organization. Similarly, it permits them to participate in decision making and other organizational processes; as we noted earlier, such participation can be beneficial from the point of view of work-related attitudes. The benefits of feedback are not in any sense restricted to receivers, however. Such information can also aid senders (e.g., managers) by keeping them informed as to whether their message has been understood, by providing them with evaluation of their ideas, and by enhancing their understanding of the perceptions of their subordinates.

To summarize: communication involves a process in which one or more persons transmits information to one or more others who, after efforts to interpret this message, often return information to the sender. As will soon become clear in this and later chapters, it is this two-way flow of facts, ideas, concepts, and knowledge that serves as the basis for most if not all activities carried out in organizational settings.

INDIVIDUAL INFLUENCES ON COMMUNICATION: WHY SOME PEOPLE ARE BETTER AT COMMUNICATING THAN OTHERS

Have you ever read a report that was so poorly written or obscure that trying to understand it made your head ache? Similarly, have you ever listened to a speaker who was so boring or confused that trying to follow his or her words made you feel numb? In contrast, have you ever encountered a report that was so clear and well-organized that reading it was almost a pleasure, or a speaker whose style was so entertaining that you wished this person would never stop? In all probability, you have had each of these experiences. The fact that you have underscores an important point about communication: where this central process is concerned, all individuals are definitely *not* created equal. Some find the task of transmitting their ideas and thoughts to others trivially easy; they are eloquent, organized, and easy to follow. Others, unfortunately, find the same process all but impossible. Try as they may, they simply cannot come up with the right words or techniques for getting their message across. Why is this the case? What factors account for these huge differences in communication skill? And from a very practical perspective, can anything be done to assist persons for whom communicating with others is a threatening and discouraging ordeal? It is on these and related issues that we will focus next.

Personal Style and Communication: Some Key Characteristics

In our discussion of leadership (Chapter 9), we called attention to the fact that power and influence are certainly *not* distributed equally within groups or organizations. On the contrary, some persons possess more of these valued commodities than others. The same principle applies to communication. In most organizations, some persons play a much more central and active role in this process than others.[4] Given this fact, one potential strategy for identifying the personal characteristics important in organizational communication follows logically: why not simply compare these two groups of persons? That is, why not compare effective and ineffective communicators, in order to determine just how they differ? This straightforward approach has been employed in several recent studies, with very revealing results. As an example of this research, and of the findings it has yielded, we will consider an investigation by Keller and Holland.[5]

Participants in this project were professional employees at several research and development organizations. These individuals completed questionnaires designed to yield information on a wide range of personal, demographic, and organizational factors (e.g., their self-esteem, need for clarity, age, job level, centrality to communication networks within their organizations). In addition, they also nominated up to four coworkers from whom they regularly received information; the more nominations a given person received, the higher his or her score as a communicator. On the basis of such nominations, participants in the study were divided into three groups: high, medium, and low in communication skills. Then, persons falling into these

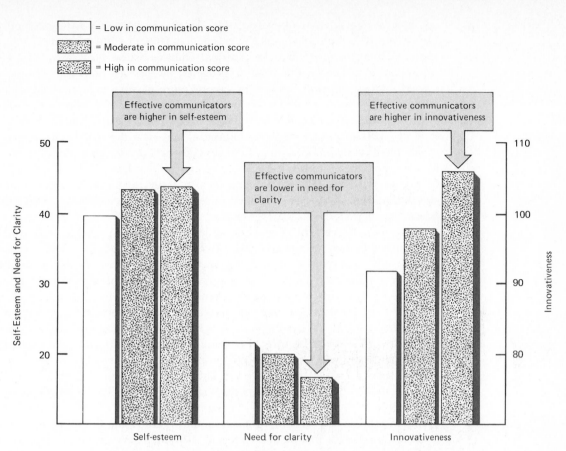

FIGURE 10.3 *Effective and Ineffective Communicators: How They Differ.*
Individuals perceived to be effective communicators by their co-workers were higher in self-esteem, higher in willingness to adopt innovations, and lower in the need for clarity than persons perceived to be less effective as communicators. (Source: Based on data from Keller and Holland, 1983; see Note 4.)

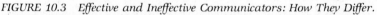

categories were compared in order to determine whether they differed with respect to the various personal, demographic, and organizational factors measured. As shown in Figure 10.3, several intriguing findings emerged. Specifically, persons viewed as being effective communicators by their colleagues were found to be higher in self-esteem, higher in willingness to adopt innovations, and lower in their need for clarity (the need to perceive situations in clear and simple terms) than persons viewed as being somewhat lower in communication ability. Further, those with high communication scores were also found to be more central to the communication networks within their organizations than those with lower scores. (We will return to such networks in more detail in a later section.)

These findings, and the results of similar studies carried out by other researchers, have added substantially to our knowledge of factors that distinguish effective from ineffective communicators. However, investigations of this type are not the only source of information about the personal characteristics relevant in this regard. Additional evidence on this issue is provided by the vast body of literature concerned with *persuasion*—efforts by one or more persons to change the views or attitudes of one or more others. We have already considered this process in Chapter 5. At that time, we noted that several personal characteristics, such as individuals' level of *credibility*, their apparent expertise, and even the speed with which they speak, all affect their success in influencing others. Since we have already examined the impact of these factors, we will not return to them here. Instead, we will focus on another variable relevant to persuasion *not* covered in our earlier comments: communicators' ability to keep their messages from exceeding the information-processing capacities of their audience.

The importance of this factor is readily illustrated. Suppose that at some time in the future, you have to listen to two members of your organization present verbal reports. The first person speaks in short, clear sentences consisting mainly of everyday language. The second offers involved thoughts, presented in lengthy sentences liberally sprinkled with jargon. Which will you prefer? The answer is obvious: the first. Most persons strongly prefer written or spoken messages that are short, simple, and to the point. Because of this fact, it is usually wise to adopt the well-known **K.I.S.S. principle** when attempting to communicate with others: *Keep It Short and Simple.*[6] While our preference for such simplicity is obvious, however, the important reasons behind it are not. Thus, they are worth a brief comment here.

Essentially, our positive reactions to simplicity and negative reactions to complexity (especially in the context of communication) stem from a basic fact: our ability to process new, incoming information (to understand it, to integrate it with existing knowledge) is limited. As a result, if we are exposed to more facts, ideas, or concepts than we can comfortably handle at any given time, much of this information is lost. In addition, the experience of having one's "cognitive circuits" overloaded in this manner is quite unpleasant. For these reasons, communicators who present too much (either in their words or written comments) run the dual risks of failing to get their message across *and* annoying or irritating their audience. The message in these facts for persons wishing to communicate with others in organizational contexts is clear: avoid cramming too much information into written or verbal messages; doing so can be disastrous. Of course, it is one thing to state this general principle, and quite another to adopt it. As you already know from your own experience, individuals differ greatly in terms of their ability to monitor their own communications. Thus, while some seem to be quite sensitive to the amount of information the people around them can absorb, others appear oblivious to such limits, and continue to pile fact upon fact and argument upon argument—well beyond the point at which their audience is totally numb. Needless to add, persons in the former, "sensitive" category are usually much more effective as communicators than those in the latter, "insensitive" one. For this reason, learning to recognize signs of information-overload in one's audience is a valuable skill, useful to communicators in many organizational contexts. (For further information on "reading" these and other reactions on the part of an audience, please see the next section of this chapter.)

Nonverbal Communication: Messages without Words

Memos, letters, reports—these are the items we think of when we encounter the phrase "organizational communication." Yet, even a moment's reflection suggests that much communication in organizations takes place in a more personal and direct manner. Supervisors provide feedback to their subordinates; work groups coordinate their activities to accomplish various tasks; managers meet to reach decisions and formulate general strategy; members of various departments discuss the division of available resources. In these and many other cases, communication involves face-to-face contact between individuals. When it does, an important fact becomes clear: information can be transmitted *nonverbally*, through an unspoken language of gazes, facial expressions, and body movements, as well as verbally, through written or spoken words.[7] Moreover, in many situations, such *nonverbal cues* seem to provide more accurate information about others' thoughts and feelings than their overt statements (refer to Figure 10.4). Because such **nonverbal communication** is very common, and transmits important kinds of information, no discussion of communication in organizations would be complete without some attention to it. In this section, therefore, we will focus on two major issues. First, we will describe some major ways in which human beings communicate nonverbally. Second, we will examine the role of such communication in several important organizational processes.

The major channels: How people communicate nonverbally.   Suppose that at a meeting of your department, you decide to "go for broke," and propose a strategic plan on which you've worked for several weeks. As you describe it, you eagerly search for feedback from the other persons present—and especially from your supervisor. As bad luck would have it, though, everyone remains noncommittal; they say very little as you proceed. Would you still be able to gauge their reactions,

FIGURE 10.4   *Nonverbal Cues: A Revealing Source of Information about Others.*
Sometimes, cues provided by other persons' facial expressions or body language provide more accurate information about their true feelings than their words. (Source: King Features Syndicate, Inc.)

in spite of this silence? Probably you would. Through careful attention to a whole series of nonverbal cues, you might gain at least *some* idea of how they are reacting—whether your plan is beginning to generate enthusiasm and interest, or whether it is going over like the proverbial lead balloon. The most useful of these cues will now be considered.

First, you might acquire such information from your audience's facial expressions. While most people don't display clear expressions of joy, sorrow, or anger during business meetings (at least, not most of the time), they *do* often permit more subtle and fleeting signs of their inner feelings to appear on their face. By noticing such **microexpressions** you could begin to gain some idea of how your plan is being received.

Second, you can gain valuable information from the pattern of their *eye-contact* with you. For example, if they avoid your gaze while you speak, or look away, your plan is probably in trouble: such reactions are often indicative of negative feelings.[9] If, in contrast, they seek your gaze, and watch closely as you speak, you can assume they are at least interested. Another important clue to their reactions might be provided by a pattern known as **staring**. Here, individuals lock your gaze with their own and do not look away no matter what you do or say. As the expression "a cold stare" suggests, this type of reaction usually reflects anger, annoyance, or hostility.[10] If you receive if from one or more of the individuals present, then, the chances are good that you have made some serious error, and should consider beating a retreat.

A third source of clues to the reactions of your audience is provided by what has been termed **body language**—movements in their body parts or changes in their posture. If several people fidget during your presentation, or slump down in their chairs, these are signs that you are failing to hold their interest. In contrast, if they sit up straight and adopt an alert posture, their reactions are probably more favorable. In a similar manner, if members of the audience nod their heads in approval, your plan is on the right track; if, instead, they shake their heads in confusion or disbelief, it is probably on the way to total oblivion.

By now, the main point of this example should be clear: in many cases, we can learn much about others' attitudes and feelings through careful attention to appropriate nonverbal cues. Moreover, the ability to "read" such messages is very useful for the following reason: often, other persons attempt to conceal their true reactions from us. During negotiations, in situations involving conflict, and in instances where issues of power, politics, and influence are at stake, they prefer to keep their feelings very much to themselves. Research findings indicate that even in such cases, however, their underlying feelings or attitudes frequently "leak" through in their expressions, gestures, and body movements.[11] Thus, skill at recognizing the information provided by such cues can provide a valuable edge in many contexts, and is definitely worth cultivating.

The other side of the coin, of course, is that it is also useful to be able to transmit clear and "readable" nonverbal messages. Persons whose facial expressions, body language, and other nonverbal cues are easy to decode stand less chance of getting into misunderstandings with others than persons who are harder to "read" in this respect. Further, they are often viewed as more effective communicators generally. Thus, being an effective sender as well as interpreter of nonverbal cues can be a useful skill.

The fact that individuals often communicate through facial expressions, ges-

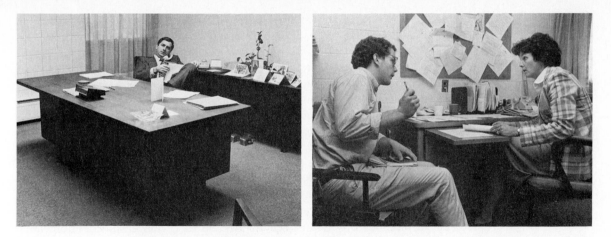

FIGURE 10.5 *Office Design: Communication through the Use of Physical Space.*
What would you conclude about the persons occupying these two offices? If you are like most
people, you might view individuals who arrange their offices like the one on the right (an
open design) as friendlier and more helpful than individuals who arrange their offices like
the one on the left (a *closed* design). Recent findings indicate that these perceptions may well
be accurate. Persons who select these contrasting office layouts do indeed differ with respect
to various traits (e.g., extroversion).

tures, eye contact, and body language is hardly surprising. All of us have experienced this unspoken language. Perhaps more unexpected is the fact that individuals
(and organizations) also transmit discrete messages through *physical objects* and
their use of *physical space*. For example, businesses often employ furnishings,
carpeting, brass plaques, painted titles on walls and doors, and similar items to
indicate status. Obviously, the plusher all of these are, the higher the level of status
communicated to visitors.[12] Similarly, organizations often strive for a particular
"image" in their physical surroundings—one that communicates the nature of the
organization and its values. For example, banks, insurance companies and other
financial institutions tend to prefer paneled walls, conservative decor, and impressive marble exteriors to reflect their presumed financial stability. In contrast, high-
tech companies may adopt a totally modern design in their buildings and offices to
reflect their place on the cutting edge of progress.

Turning to the use of physical space, this, too, can be a guide to status. The
larger an individual's office, and the greater the number of windows it possesses,
the higher the prestige of its occupant. Another, and perhaps even more intriguing
use of physical space as a means of communication pertains to *office design*. In
planning the layout of their offices, some persons choose a **closed** arrangement.
Their desk faces the door, and serves as a barrier between themselves and visitors.
Similarly, chairs for visitors are one side of the desk, while the office occupant sits on
the other. In contrast, other individuals select an **open** arrangement. Their desk
faces the wall, and chairs for visitors are next to their own, without any formal
barrier between them (see Figure 10.5). What messages do these contrasting layouts
convey? Recent studies report that most persons feel more welcome and comfortable
in offices with an open arrangement than in ones with a closed layout. Also, they
tend to view the occupants of open offices as friendlier and more helpful than those

of closed ones.[13] Additional findings, reported recently by McElroy, Morrow, and Ackerman indicate that such impressions may actually be justified.[14] These researchers found that persons who adopted an open arrangement in their offices were actually more outgoing, had stronger beliefs that they could control their own outcomes, and were more interested in good relations with others than persons who chose a more closed arrangement. These findings suggest that the ways in which individuals use physical space in their offices does in fact reflect several of their underlying traits and characteristics.

Nonverbal communication: Its role in organizations.   By now, you are probably convinced that individuals *do* communicate with one another through nonverbal cues. What you may still be wondering about, however, is this: does this language without words have any practical implications? As we have tried to indicate throughout this discussion, it does. In fact, nonverbal communication seems to play an important role in several forms of organizational behavior and several organizational processes. We will mention two of these here.

First, consider the following fact: in many cases, there is a sizable gap between what people say and the information conveyed by their expressions, tone of voice, posture, and other nonverbal cues. For example, when asked by her boss to stay late, a secretary may answer "Sure, O.K.," but then sigh and look unhappy. Similarly, during negotiations, a buyer may at first seem pleased with the latest offer from the seller, but then quickly recover, and remark that the asking price is still too high. In such cases, which source of information—verbal or nonverbal—should take precedence? The findings of a large body of research leave little room for doubt: nonverbal. The reason behind this conclusion is as follows. While most persons find it fairly easy to regulate what they say, they find it far more difficult to exert precise control over their nonverbal cues. Thus, their true feelings, reactions, and beliefs are more likely to be visible in the latter than the former.[15] Because of this fact, nonverbal communication can often be useful in enhancing understanding between individuals, and avoiding unnecessary conflict between them. In the first example above, the manager (if she is sensitive to nonverbal cues) may reconsider her request for overtime. And in the second, the seller's realization that further concessions are not needed may increase the likelihood of an agreement satisfactory to both sides. In short, careful attention to nonverbal cues can enhance communication generally; this, of course, is a desirable outcome, with many potential benefits.

A second practical application of nonverbal communication concerns its role in interviews. Recent studies suggest that persons who transmit positive nonverbal cues to an interviewer often receive higher ratings than those who do not. Moreover, this is the case across a wide range of subjects and interview settings.[16] For example, in one recent investigation, male and female subjects were asked by the investigator to play the role of a professional interviewer, and to conduct a brief job interview with another person who played the role of an applicant for an entry-level management job.[17] In fact, the applicant was an accomplice, specially trained to behave in one of two ways. In one condition, she emitted many positive nonverbal cues (e.g., she leaned forward toward the subject, smiled on many occasions, and maintained a high level of eye-contact with him or her). In a second condition, in contrast, she refrained from demonstrating such behaviors. Instead, she maintained a neutral manner throughout the session. After the interview, subjects rated the applicant on several dimensions relating to both her qualifications for the job in question (e.g., her apparent competence, motivation, potential for success) and her personal traits (e.g., her friendliness, likability, intelligence). Not surprisingly, results indicated that the accomplice received much higher ratings on most of these traits when she emitted many positive nonverbal cues than when she demonstrated more neutral behavior.

We could go on to consider additional implications of nonverbal communication for organizational processes. By now, however, the main point should be clear: the information individuals transmit through this silent language can often be just as useful and important as that they transmit through written and spoken words. It is the unwary manager, then, who chooses to ignore it. (For a concrete illustration of some of the problems that can arise from a lack of sensitivity to nonverbal cues, please see the **Case in Point** insert on page 314.)

ORGANIZATIONAL INFLUENCES ON COMMUNICATION: STRUCTURE, NETWORKS, AND THE GRAPEVINE

It is a rare person who can perform his or her job in total isolation from others. Thus, everyone (or nearly everyone) communicates in organizations—this is a basic fact of life at work. Just as clearly, though, everyone does *not* communicate with everyone else. Production employees do not generally meet with the company president. Similarly, people in different departments usually have direct contact with one another only on relatively rare occasions. In short, communication within most organizations (at least at the formal level) is far from random in nature. Why is this the case? One important answer involves the fact that most possess a specific internal *structure*. That is, they are put together in certain ways, and these internal arrangements of departments, divisions, units, and work groups often dictate the paths through which information flows, or is supposed to flow. Since we will deal with organizational structure at some length in Chapters 14 and 15, we will not attempt to cover this complex topic here. Instead, we will focus on two issues directly related to the present discussion: (1) how do specific patterns of contact between persons working within an organization affect their performance and satisfaction? and (2) how does the overall structure of an organization shape the direction and nature of communication in it? In addition, since **formal channels of communication** (ones specified by the organizational chart or company policy) are only part of the total picture, the nature and operation of **informal networks**, too, will be considered.

Communication Networks: Their Impact on Performance and Satisfaction

Consider the following groups: a regional sales manager and the four sales representatives working under her direction; the members of a standing grievance committee in a large corporation; the management staff of a single department in a manufacturing firm, consisting of an assistant director of product development, a

"You Don't Really Notice Much, Do You?"

"Oh no," Phil Magruder thinks to himself, as he hears Dan Elsner's heavy tread coming toward his office, "here it comes—whew! If only I could disappear somehow . . ." Phil is right, for when Dan opens the door and walks inside, he is far from the picture of calm and contentment. In fact, the little red spots on his cheeks indicate that he's on a slow boil—or maybe a fast one!

"Well, kiddo," Dan begins, "you really did it to us *this* time. Just what were you trying to pull in there? Who the heck are you working for anyway!"

"Take it easy, Dan, take it easy!" Phil interrupts. (He's learned from past experience that the only way to avoid a real explosion by his supervisor is to break into these escalating monologues. If he just sits there quietly, Dan will simply get angrier and angrier, until he loses all control.)

"Just tell me what I did," Phil continues in a pleading voice. "I mean, I tried to follow your instructions. I prepared until I could say it all in my sleep. And I really thought that it was going pretty well there for a while."

"Well! You thought it was going well!" Dan practically screams. "Where were *you* when Shapiro started to get that 'Now we've got them' look on his face and to scribble in his little book. Couldn't you see you were headed for trouble?"

"No . . . what look? I didn't notice anything." Phil answers weakly. "I just kept my mind on the points I was trying to get across—I didn't pay much attention to Sam at all."

"Sam or anyone else for that matter," Dan interjects. "Couldn't you tell he was getting ready to nail you on those cost figures? Umph! I tried to wave you off a dozen times. But did you pay any attention? No! And didn't you notice Halverson start to fiddle with his tie? You know what *that* means—he's bored. And when he's bored, you're through. Not that I can say I blame him, the way you just droned on and on. How did you think anyone would be able to make sense of all that stuff? No, I guess you really *don't* notice much, do you?"

By now Phil is really upset; the seriousness of his blunders is beginning to dawn on him, and he can see all the hard work he put into preparing for this session floating drearily down the drain. "Gee, Dan, I don't know what to say," is all he can murmur. And then he puts his head down on his desk and just groans. At this, Dan relents a bit.

"Well, O.K., O.K. It's not the end of the world. But you've got a lot to learn about dealing with people, my young friend. And unless you start making up for lost time, I don't see where you're going to go from here in *this* company!"

Questions

(1) What specific types of nonverbal cues did Phil miss during his presentation?
(2) Why do you think he is so poor at recognizing, and responding to, such cues?
(3) Do you think that just becoming aware of the fact that he's missing a lot during his attempts to communicate with others will help him overcome this problem?
(4) If you were Dan, Phil's supervisor, what steps would you take to avoid similar problems in the future? Would you be willing to give Phil another chance?

---

director of product development, the head of product development, and the vice president for corporate planning and development.

Obviously, these groups differ from one another in many ways. One of the most important, however, involves the *pattern* of communication links between their members. In the sales team, information will tend to flow to and from the regional

manager; indeed, the individual sales representatives will probably not communicate directly with one another on a regular basis. In the grievance committee, in
contrast, all members can communicate with all other members, at least while the
committee is in session. Finally, within the product development unit, information
will tend to flow up and (mostly) down the hierarchy: from the vice president for
development to the head of product development; from this person to the director of
product development; and from there to the assistant director. In short, within each
group, there are specific guidelines about who should communicate with whom—
rules indicating which individuals are supposed to be in direct contact with which
others. As you can probably guess (and as our examples suggest), many such
patterns are possible (please refer to Figure 10.6). Indeed, the number of specific
communication networks that might be established within a sizable organization is practically limitless. But do such arrangements matter? Does the pattern of
linkages between specific organization members exert any impact upon their behavior, or upon organizational functioning in general? The answer appears to be
"yes." A large body of evidence indicates that the nature of the communication
networks existing within a group or organization can strongly influence both the
performance and satisfaction of its members.[18]

Turning first to performance, the key question is as follows: are any of the
patterns shown in Figure 10.6 clearly superior to the others? In order to answer this
question, we must first consider differences between the various networks with
respect to a key feature: their degree of **centralization**. Briefly, this refers to the
extent to which information must flow through one specific member. As you can see
from Figure 10.6, such patterns as the Y and the *wheel* are centralized in nature; in
each, there is one person who is at the "crossroads" of information flow, and
receives input from several others. In contrast, other patterns (e.g., the circle and

FIGURE 10.6   Communication Networks: Some Basic Types.
Communication networks can vary greatly in form. A few of the more common types are
shown here. Both the *wheel* and the *Y* are highly centralized—informtation is channeled to a
single central member. In contrast, the *circle* and *comcon* patterns are decentralized; there is
no single person at the "crossroads" of all information flow. (Note: all the networks shown
here involve five members, but the same basic principles seem to apply to networks consisting
of more or fewer persons.)

◄── = Direction of information flow
● = Central member
○ = Peripheral member

Centralized network
(Information flows to a central member)

Decentralized networks
(There is no central member)

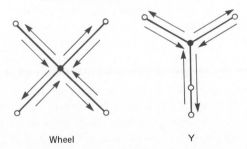

Wheel   Y

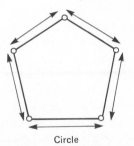

Circle

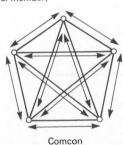

Comcon

comcon) are low in centralization. Here, information is *not* channeled through one person; rather, it can flow in many directions, and to many different people. But given that communication networks differ with respect to centralization, is one end of this dimension better than the other where task performance is concerned? The answer provided by research findings is somewhat complex. It appears that when the tasks being performed by a group are simple, *centralized* networks are more efficient—they solve problems faster, and make fewer errors, than decentralized networks.[19] However, when the tasks faced by the group are more involved, the opposite may be true: *decentralized* networks outperform centralized ones. What factors account for this puzzling pattern? The answer seems to lie in the information-processing capacities of the key or central member. When the tasks being performed by a group are simple, even a large flow of input from other members does not overload this person; he or she can continue to process incoming messages in an efficient manner. Thus, under these conditions, centralized networks have an edge, since the key member can readily integrate available information to solve current problems or reach needed decisions. When the tasks being performed by a group are complex, however, the flow of information to the central member may quickly exceed his or her capacity to deal with it. **Information saturation** may then occur, with the result that performance drops sharply—to levels below those attained by less centralized groups. (Please refer to Figure 10.7 for a summary of these suggestions.) In short, centralization is a two-edged sword. On the one hand, it provides one group member with a wealth of input and information—everything he or she needs to get the job done. On the other, it may sometimes result in overload for this person, and so bring performance to a virtual halt.

While findings concerning the impact of communication networks on group performance are mixed, evidence relating to their influence on member satisfaction is more straightforward. Generally, it has been found that individuals report higher levels of satisfaction in decentralized than in centralized networks. The reasons for such reactions are as follows. First, when part of a centralized network, individuals often feel powerless or "left out." This is hardly surprising, for all they do is funnel information to the key member; he or she combines this input to reach decisions or solve current problems. As we have noted repeatedly, most persons find a lack of participation in these processes unpleasant and stressful. Second, there are often clear status differences associated with various positions in centralized groups. The closer individuals are to the key member, the higher their status; conversely, the further away they are (as measured by communication links), the lower their status. Even worse, such differences are repeatedly emphasized by the direction and flow of information. In less centralized networks, in contrast, such contrasts are less pronounced, and are not called to members' attention as frequently or forcefully. Little wonder, then, that except for persons at or near the core of centralized groups, member satisfaction in such arrangements tends to be relatively low.

In sum, it appears that the *pattern* of communication within a group or organization, as well as the content of the information actually transmitted, can strongly shape its effectiveness. Clearly, this is an important way in which organizational structure influences organizational function. Before concluding, though, we should insert two notes of caution. First, much of the research dealing with the impact of communication networks has focused upon short-lived groups—ones specially created for purposes of investigation. As a result, it is not certain that the

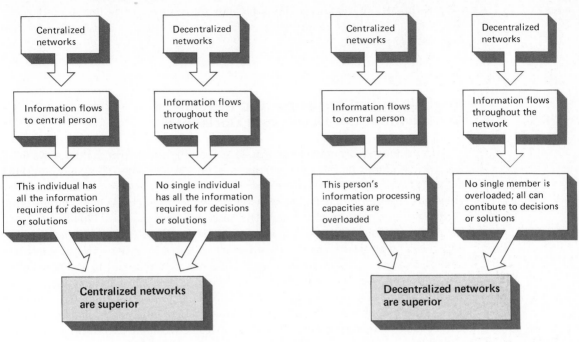

SIMPLE TASK		COMPLEX TASK	
Centralized networks	Decentralized networks	Centralized networks	Decentralized networks
Information flows to central person	Information flows throughout the network	Information flows to central person	Information flows throughout the network
This individual has all the information required for decisions or solutions	No single individual has all the information required for decisions or solutions	This person's information processing capacities are overloaded	No single member is overloaded; all can contibute to decisions or solutions
Centralized networks are superior		**Decentralized networks are superior**	

FIGURE 10.7   *Communication Networks and Task Complexity.*
When groups work on *simple* tasks, centralized networks are more efficient than decentralized networks. This is because information flows to the central member who can then make a decision or solve current problems (left panel). When groups work on *complex* tasks, however, decentralized networks are superior. This is due to the fact that when tasks are complex, the flow of information to the central person may exceed his or her information-processing capacity, and so reduce performance (right panel).

findings of such projects can readily be extended to groups remaining in existence for longer periods of time (i.e. as in most organizational settings). In fact, the findings of at least one major project concerned with this issue indicate that while centralized groups *are* initially faster than decentralized ones at performing simple tasks, this advantage tends to disappear with the passage of time.[20] These results suggest that the specific pattern of communication permitted within a group may be more important in the period immediately following its formation than is true later on. Second, as we will soon note in more detail, most organizations contain *informal* as well as formal channels of communication. In many cases, these can supplement or even replace the links established by formal networks. To the extent they do, the impact of these patterns may well be lessened. For example, to mention just one possibility, informal channels of communication may permit direct contact between individuals who, ostensibly, should communicate only through a central person. Such contacts may then serve to reduce the peripheral members' feelings of being "left out." In short, it may well be the establishment of informal linkages between group members that accounts for the reduced impact of formal networks over time.

Despite these limitations, however, it is clear that communication networks do play an important role in many organizational processes. Thus, they should always be taken into account when efforts to enhance performance, satisfaction, or effectiveness are planned.

Organizational Structure and the Flow of Information: Up, Down, and Horizontal

Consider two organizations. One is a small high-tech firm that employs fewer than one hundred people and that operates on the very edge of expanding knowledge. The other is a giant, mature business, with thousands of employees, and many divisions, each manufacturing a wide array of products. Will communication within these two companies differ? The answer is obvious: in all likelihood, it will. In the small, high-tech firm it may often be informal (occurring between any individuals who need to share information), will involve face-to-face contacts, and will often occur in a spontaneous, spur-of-the-moment manner. In the giant corporation, in contrast, it may well be more formal, may often involve written memos and reports, and will probably be subject to many rules governing who communicates with whom. Several factors contribute to these contrasting patterns of communication—everything from sheer differences between the two companies in size, through contrasting traits and perspectives on the part of their top executives. One of the most important of these, however, involves their sharply contrasting *internal structures*.

The small high-tech firm is likely to have few departments. Similarly, it probably possesses what is termed a *flat organizational structure*—few levels separate top people in the company from those working on production. In contrast, the mature corporation probably has many divisions, departments, and other subunits. Further, it may show a much *taller* organizational structure—one in which many levels separate top executives from people on the factory floor. Other contrasts, too, would exist, but we will leave these for our discussion of organizational structure in Chapter 14. Instead, we will focus on another key difference between these two organizations with respect to communication: the relative frequency of **upward, downward**, and **horizontal** communication within them. Before describing this difference, let us first examine the nature of these three contrasting forms of organizational communication.

Actually, there is little mystery here, for they operate in the manner suggested by their labels. Thus, *downward* communication involves the flow of messages and information from supervisors to their subordinates; *upward* communication involves the transmission of information from lower levels of the organization to higher ones; and *horizontal* communication consists of an exchange of information between individuals at the same level of the organization (although, perhaps, in different department or units). These three types of communication do not differ merely with respect to their direction, however. In addition, there are often sharp contrasts between them in terms of the kind of information they contain. As you can probably guess, downward communication often consists of instructions, directions and orders. In short, such messages are designed to tell subordinates what they should be doing and how they should behave. In addition, downward communication often provides formal feedback on past performance (e.g., standardized performance appraisals). In contrast, upward communication consists largely of various types of information required by managers to perform their job. Thus, such communication may contain reports on the status of various operations (e.g., sales figures, production schedules), and feedback on the implementation or success of past decisions or recently adopted policies. Upward communication, in short, is designed to keep managers in touch with what is happening throughout the organization, and often occurs in response to their requests for such input. Finally, horizontal communication typically serves the purpose of enhancing *coordination* within the organization. For example, within a given department or unit, it may help individuals integrate their efforts or align their work schedules. Similarly, it can also operate *between* different departments, helping them to work cooperatively, rather than at odds with one another. Thus, to mention just one specific instance, effective communication between production and marketing can help avoid situations in which large orders can't be filled because the required merchandise is simply not available, or the equally costly outcome of the wrong product "mix" in the company's total output. The basic nature and functions of upward, downward, and horizontal communication are summarized in Figure 10.8.

Now that we have considered these three types of organizational communication, we can return to our comparison between the two companies described on page 318. Will the patterns of upward, downward, and horizontal communication differ in these two organizations? Again, the chances are good that they may. Turning first to the small high-tech firm, communication will probably be very much a two-way street. While managers will communicate orders and directives

FIGURE 10.8 *Upward, Downward, and Horizontal Communication: An Overview.*
As shown here, *upward, downward*, and *horizontal communication* within organizations differ both with respect to direction and major function.

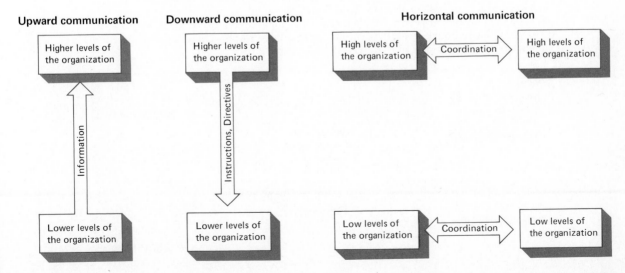

Organizational Communication and Organizational Performance: Evidence for a Link

A theme implicit in many of our comments so far, is this: good communication is essential to a high level of organizational effectiveness. At first glance—and also at second—this suggestion seems to make eminent sense. After all, how can an organization be efficient or productive unless information vital to its major functions moves smoothly between individuals or departments? That organizations themselves accept this principle is indicated by the fact that each year, many spend large sums of money on efforts to improve such communication. It is somewhat surprising to learn, therefore, that until quite recently, little direct evidence was available concerning the proposed link between organizational communication and organizational performance.[25] Several studies of the impact of communication on individual performance existed, but virtually no research focused on the potential link between communication and overall organizational effectiveness had been conducted.[26] Fortunately, this situation has now been at least partially rectified by a well-planned investigation carried out by Snyder and Morris.[27]

Participants in this project were more than five hundred employees at various district offices of a large state social services agency. These individuals completed questionnaires designed to measure several aspects of communication within their organizations (e.g., the skill of their supervisors as communicators; the extent to which job-related information was shared within work groups; the adequacy of communication about organizational policies and procedures). Subjects' responses to these questions were then related to several objective indices of overall organizational effectiveness. These included the total cost of running each district office, the cost per employee, and the cost of serving each client. Results offered clear support for the view that the more effective certain kinds of communication within an organization are, the more efficient or productive it will be. Specifically, it was found that the more skillful supervisors were as communicators, and the more effectively work groups shared information, the more cost-effective were the organizations studied (refer to Figure 10.9).

FIGURE 10.9   *Effective Communication: A Definite Plus for Organizational Effectiveness.* As shown here, two basic features of organizational communication (good communication skills on the part of supervisors, efficient sharing of information among work group members) contributed to high levels of performance by a large social agency. (Source: Based on findings reported by Snyder and Morris. 1984; see Note 25.)

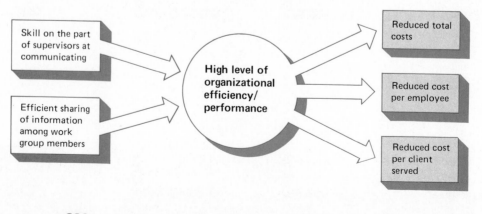

These findings indicate that current widespread faith in the benefits of effective communication is indeed justified. When individuals receive clear and informative input from their supervisors, and can readily share needed information with co-workers, the overall performance of their organizations can be greatly enhanced. If managers needed further inducement for devoting careful attention to this key organizational process, these potential benefits should certainly provide it.

---

downward to subordinates, their closeness to these people (both physically and psychologically) will assure that a good deal of information and feedback moves upward as well. Similarly, horizontal communication, too, may be encouraged. Marketing, production, development, and finance people will probably speak directly to one another on a regular basis, with the result that coordination between these crucial functions will be enhanced. In contrast, the pattern of communication in the large corporation may (but not necessarily so) be very different. Here, communication will be predominantly downward, with a steady stream of memos, directives, and instructions flowing from higher levels of the organization to lower ones. Upward communication, when it occurs, will consist almost entirely of supervisor-requested information, and reports on current operations. Little feedback on decisions and policies will be forthcoming, and when it is, it may well be viewed as inappropriate. Horizontal communication, too, may be impeded, with each department jealously guarding its own "perks," and no direct links between them available. Instead, the coordination of vital functions may rest almost entirely with senior-level people, who receive input from—and issue directives to—a number of different units. In short, communication in this large organization may be largely a one-way street. As a result, high-ranking executives within the company may gradually become isolated from the day-to-day realities of their business—a trend that may prove damaging indeed. That such isolation actually occurs in many companies is indicated by the following fact: in actual surveys, fully 95 percent of high-ranking managers report that they have a good grasp of their employees' problems. In contrast, only 30 percent of the employees agree that this is so![21]

Unfortunately, a lack of effective communication is not the only difficulty confronting many large organizations. Another has to do with the type of information that *is* ultimately transmitted to top management. As you probably know, most individuals are reluctant to deliver negative messages to others. One reason behind this reluctance is their realization that the "bearers of ill tidings" are often disliked or evaluated negatively by the persons to whom they carry the negative messages.[22] This reluctance to transmit negative information upward, often termed the **MUM effect** (short for keeping Mum about Undesirable Messages), is especially strong with respect to one's supervisors. Thus, it can sometimes badly distort the flow of feedback reaching top managers. Such persons tend to hear only positive reports and favorable evaluations. As a result, it is sometimes possible for them to bask in the glow of uniformly encouraging news from their subordinates while their company actually teeters on the edge of disaster! Needless to say, such circumstances pose a serious threat to the future of almost any organization, and are to be avoided at all costs.

Looking back over our comments so far, it may appear that we have painted a disturbingly bleak picture of communication in large organizations, and an overly "rosy" one of this process as it occurs in smaller companies. At this point, therefore, we should hasten to add that "big" does *not* necessarily mean "worse" where communication is concerned. The companies described above are imaginary ones, specifically chosen to contrast with one another, and to illustrate important points about communication in work settings. In reality, there is no clear-cut or necessary link between size and the effectiveness with which vital information gets transmitted in organizations. Further, even giant corporations can—and often do—undertake specific steps to avoid problems such as the ones outlined above, and to enhance the quality of communication at all levels. As you might suspect, however, this is especially true in the case of companies which are outstandingly successful in their field. Thus, in their recent and widely cited study of such organizations, Peters and Waterman found that many of these corporations had adopted specific steps to increase—and improve—communication among key employees.[24] For example, some strove for an informal, campus-like atmosphere at their headquarters—conditions that made it easier for individuals to get together for face-to-face discussions. Others took such steps as including many small conference rooms in their new buildings, scattering blackboards everywhere, and placing large tables, with seats for many persons, in company diningrooms. In short, they literally built a high level of communication between employees into their facilities. We will return to these and other techniques for enhancing communication in a later section. For the moment, though, we simply wish to emphasize the fact that even in the largest of multinational companies there are no compelling reasons why costly communication gaps and distortions must be allowed to develop. (Does effective communication within an organization actually contribute to a high level of productivity or performance? For convincing evidence that it does, please see the **Focus** box on page 320.)

Informal Channels of Communication in Organizations: The Grapevine and Rumors

So far in this discussion, we have emphasized *formal* channels of communication: the transmission of information through links or mechanisms specified by the company chart or official policies. Is this how individuals actually communicate in operating organizations? While it would be comforting to answer "yes," such a reply would be wrong—in some cases, dead wrong. While individuals *do* obtain much information through formal channels, they often receive more through informal ones. In short, they learn more about what's happening in their company, and what changes lie ahead, from friends and casual conversations than from official memos and announcements (refer to Figure 10.10). Such informal networks of communication are generally known as the **grapevine**, and they are present—and highly active—in virtually every organization.

The factors underlying development of the grapevine are fairly obvious. First, they develop in a natural way out of the friendly social relations that usually occur between persons who have regular contact at work. Exchanging the latest news or gossip with one's friends provides a pleasant break from work activities. In fact,

FIGURE 10.10   *The Grapevine: A Major Source of Information in Organizations.*
Individuals often acquire more information from the "grapevine" and other informal networks than from the formal communication channels in their organization.

checking the grapevine in this manner is one of the high points of the day for many persons. Second, the grapevine stems, in part, from the basic need to make sense out of the world around us. We all wish to understand events that affect our lives, and to exert some control over them if we can. Thus, gathering as much information as possible can be a useful course of action. Finally, the grapevine often serves as a kind of "safety valve," allowing individuals to express their concerns and anxieties, and to attain reassurance from others.

Given these important benefits, it is hardly surprising that active grapevines exist in almost all organizations. Somewhat more surprising, though, is the fact that the information they transmit is often quite accurate. For example, in one well-known study, approximately 80 percent of the information carried by the grapevine was found to be accurate.[28] It is important to note, however, that those remaining few percent (of *in*accurate information) can lead to serious trouble. As you may already know from your own experience, a story can be mainly true but still be quite misleading because one essential fact is omitted or distorted. For example, the grapevine may report that one person has been promoted over another who seems more deserving of this reward. This has obvious implications for employee perceptions about the fairness of company policies. What it may fail to report, however, is the fact that the first person let it be known that he would reject the promotion because it would require that he move to a distant city, something he is not willing to do. In cases like this, the grapevine can be mainly correct, but still be highly misleading.

While the grapevine can lead to serious errors in the way we have just described, this is not the main reason why it suffers from a bad reputation. The skepticism many people express about it frequently stems from the fact that all too often it transmits information for which there is practically no basis—**rumor**. Typically, rumors are based on speculation, imagination, or wishful thinking rather than on hard facts. And all too often, rumors circulate through the grapevine with breathtaking speed. Unfortunately, no one has yet devised a totally effective way of preventing rumors: they, too, arise out of the human need to know and understand, and so are probably unavoidable. While they can't be prevented, though, some steps seem useful in at least holding them in check.

First, rumors can often be stopped "cold" through the release of accurate information. Providing individuals with hard facts eliminates the need for speculation, and can terminate rumors before they do substantial damage. Second, once they have begun, efforts can be made to discredit their source. As we noted in Chapter 5, when the *credibility* of the source of a communication is low, the impact of this message is largely dissipated. Third, recent evidence suggests that the most effective means for countering the impact of rumors may not be that of attempting directly to refute them. Instead, a more indirect approach, in which individuals are somehow induced to recall facts or experiences counter to the rumor may be more successful.[29] For example, if a current rumor indicates that the company is about to reorganize several of its departments and eliminate a number of jobs, steps could be taken to remind employees that past reorganizations have been announced months in advance, and have *never* resulted in a reduction in work force. Through these and other steps, the negative effects sometimes produced by rumors and the grapevine can be reduced. Then, the positive impact of these informal channels of communication on both individuals and the entire organization can predominate.

ENHANCING ORGANIZATIONAL COMMUNICATION: SOME CONCRETE STEPS

If the present chapter has a major theme, it is this: communication is an essential process in organizations. Indeed, as some experts have noted, it plays an important role in virtually every aspect of their functioning, and is a key determinant of organizational effectiveness.[30] Together, these facts point to an obvious conclusion: efforts to enhance communication—to improve its accuracy and adequacy— are highly desirable. In this final section we will examine several steps that may prove useful in attaining such goals. Specifically, we will consider measures that can be taken both by individuals and organizations to enhance the quality of communication.

Improving Communication: Individual Strategies

Communication, ultimately, involves individuals. No matter how structured the content of a message, or how formal the channels over which it is transmitted, it must still be prepared (encoded) by one or more persons and understood (decoded) by one or more others. Given these basic facts, it stands to reason that there may be active steps individuals can take to enhance their performance both as senders and as receivers of information. In fact, there are, and a few of these will now be outlined.

The benefits of redundancy: To get it across, say it again—but in a different way. Try to recall the clearest and then the most obscure instructors you have had in college courses. What made persons in the first group so easy to follow, but those in the second virtually impossible to decipher? Many factors probably contributed to this difference, but among the most important of these is differences in their use of *redundancy*. The instructors you found easy to understand almost certainly repeated difficult concepts and principles several times during each lecture. In contrast, those you found hard to follow did not. Please note: this does not mean that the successful instructors merely stated the same words over and over again. As you can readily see, this would be boring or even distracting. Rather, what they did was to make the same points, but in different words, and perhaps with slightly different examples. In the context of communication, then, *redundancy* implies transmitting a message several times in slightly different ways.

This basic principle does not apply solely to communication involving face-to-face contact with others. On the contrary, it is equally valid in other contexts, too. For example, a manager who communicates with a potential client on the phone one day, might follow up this contact with a letter, and then with a written report about his product, or perhaps testimonials from satisfied customers. Similarly, advertisers and political candidates are well aware of the potential benefits of presenting the same basic message in different forms, through various media (e.g., in magazines and newspapers, over the radio, on television). Of course, in all these situations, it is important to avoid mere repetition—going beyond the point where persons on the receiving end become bored or annoyed. Within broad limits, though, redundancy can often be a valuable aid to effective communication.

Timing, if not everything, is important. Consider the following scene: it's 4:00 P.M. on the Friday afternoon before a three-day weekend, and most employees in the offices of Vende, Pitch, and Hawke, a large advertising firm, are clearing their desks. At this moment, Herman Vende, the firm's CEO, decides to call a special meeting to discuss strategy for landing a major account. How useful do you think it will be? And how effective do you think communication will be at this gathering? The answer is clear: low on both counts. The reason for these discouraging predictions, too, is clear: if ever there was a *wrong* time for such a meeting, this is it! Communication and other key processes at it are likely to suffer, as those present think about the upcoming weekend and repeatedly look at their watches. The moral in this example is simple: when attempting to communicate with others, try to choose a time when their minds are likely to be on what you have to say, *not* one when they will be distracted by other factors, or overwhelmed with other messages. Keeping these points in focus can definitely help you get through to others more effectively.

Listening: The other side of the coin. Most of us have had the following experience: we are introduced to someone at a meeting or party, and hold a brief conversation with him or her. A few minutes later, another person walks up, and waits to be introduced. Unfortunately, at this point, we realize that we have already forgotten our new acquaintance's name! Why do such events occur? It would be comforting to blame them on the limits of human memory, but in fact, this would not be accurate. The true explanation for such incidents is simply this: often, we just don't listen.[31] Instead of paying careful attention to what others say, we allow our minds to wander. We daydream, we think about what we are going to say when it is *our* turn to talk, or we mentally argue with the points being made by the speaker, and so lose his or her train of thought. Obviously, if we don't listen carefully to what other persons say, communication is bound to suffer. In fact, in extreme cases, it may cease altogether. For this reason, learning to be a good listener is essential to being an effective communicator. Fortunately, in this respect, a few simple guidelines can be of some help.

First, try hard to concentrate on what other persons say. Attention, as we noted in Chapter 4, is the first, crucial step in perception. Second, be an *active* listener. Ask questions, occasionally try to put the speaker's comments in your own words. Such steps will help you stay alert, and will facilitate your processing of the information presented. Third, avoid jumping to conclusions or making evaluations. Try to hear the other person out before deciding whether you agree or disagree. Finally, listen for the main points. Many people tend to wander when communicating, so it is often *not* important to try to understand or remember everything they say. Rather, try to identify the main points and keep these in mind. Developing such listening skills is far from easy, for most persons have had many years of practice in making the kind of errors mentioned above. Doing so is well worth the effort, however, for being an effective listener is an important key to communicating successfully with others.

Improving Communication: Organizational Strategies

While communication ultimately takes place between individuals, it does *not* occur in an organizational vacuum. As we have already seen, key elements of organizational structure and policy can strongly determine who communicates with whom, in what form, and with what effect. For this reason, organizations, too, can take steps to facilitate this central process. Several of these involve efforts to improve the content of communications themselves, while others focus on the establishment of an organizational climate favorable to the free exchange of information among employees.

The content of communications. Two complaints frequently voiced by employees in many organizations are these: (1) they don't know just what is expected of them on their jobs, and (2) they don't know how well (or poorly) they are doing. Obviously, both these complaints represent pleas for improved *downward communication*—for more explicit information on specific job requirements, and for better feedback about past performance. An organization than can fill these needs, therefore, is one well on the road to improved communication between manage-

FIGURE 10.11   *Informal Communication: An Important Ingredient in Organizational Success.*
Many successful companies take active steps to encourage high levels of informal communication among their employees. These include providing locations for spur-of-the-moment conversations (top photo), and efforts to attain at least moderate levels of informality (lower photo).

ment and employees. Thus, steps such as the development of clear and explicit job descriptions, and methods for the delivery of informative performance feedback can prove beneficial indeed.

While employees often complain about uncertainty, or a lack of relevant information, managers frequently grumble about the opposite problem—receiving *more* information from subordinates than they need or can possibly use. Such difficulties can be reduced by various types of *screening*—mechanisms for removing excessive detail or unnecessary input from messages before they are transmitted to the next higher level. When such screening is sucessful, it can improve the quality of *upward communication*, and help protect managers from overload and the many problems it entails.

Establishing a favorable organizational climate.   At Walt Disney Productions, all managers—everyone from the president on down—wear tags containing only their first names at all company functions. At IBM, which now employs more than 350,000 people, the chairman himself continues to handle complaints from any employee, at any level. Hewlett Packard and United Airlines, to name just two corporations, are committed to a policy they label "Management By Wandering Around." The purpose: to get managers out of their offices, and into direct contact with others. When Corning Glass constructed a new building for its engineering division, it installed escalators, not elevators, in order to increase the likelihood of face-to-face encounters. We could go on to describe other examples, but by now the main point should be obvious: many highly successful companies (all of those mentioned here are leaders in their fields), take active steps to encourage informal, direct communication between their employees (refer to Figure 10.11 on page 327). They do this because of the belief that such communication, in turn, plays a vital role in innovation. As one executive put it: "We're really not sure exactly how the innovative process works. But there's one thing we do know: the easy communications, the absence of barriers to talking to one another are essential. Whatever we do, whatever structure we adopt, whatever systems we try, that's the cornerstone—we won't do anything to jeopardize it."[32]

As the examples above suggest, many different procedures can be employed to reach these goals. They include (1) getting people out of their offices and into proximity with one another, (2) encouraging a degree of informality, (3) providing appropriate places for people to congregate, especially on a spur-of-the-moment basis, (4) conducting meetings with flexible (or largely nonexistent) agendas, and (5) establishing true "open-door" policies, in which not only do top executives listen to complaints and feedback from lower levels, but where they also *walk out* of their offices in order to see precisely what's going on within the company. Through such procedures, a very rich and intense level of communication can be fostered throughout an entire organization. Of course, this in itself is not sufficient to guarantee a high level of organizational success; many factors obviously contribute to such outcomes.[33] As the impressive accomplishments of many companies that have adopted this general strategy suggest, however, it can often be a major step in the right direction.

SUMMARY

Communication is the process through which one person or group (the *sender*) transmits information to another person or group (the *receiver*). It involves the *encoding* of ideas or concepts by the sender, and the *decoding* of this information by the receiver.

Many *individual factors* determine the extent to which communicators are successful in getting their message across. One of the most important of these involves the ability to keep communications simple, so they do not exceed the information processing capacities of their audience. Others relate to the apparent credibility and personal style of communicators. While much communication in organizations involves written or spoken words, a considerable amount of information is also transmitted *nonverbally*, through facial expressions, eye contact, and body movements. Both organizations and individuals also communicate specific messages through their use of physical objects (e.g., furniture, carpeting) and physical space (e.g., office design).

Certain features of organizations shape communication within them. *Communication networks*—patterns of contact between specific individuals—affect both task performance and satisfaction. Overall *organizational structure*, too, can exert powerful effects upon the nature, content, and direction of communication. *Downward* communication flows from higher to lower levels and often contains instructions or directives. *Upward* communication flows from lower to higher levels and often provides managers with required information. *Horizontal* communication occurs at a given level within an organization, and plays a key role in coordination. Recent findings indicate that effective communication enhances overall organizational performance.

Individuals can improve communication through the use of *redundancy*, through careful attention to timing in the delivery of messages, and by learning to listen effectively. Organizations can enhance communication among their employees through specific steps designed to bring people into face-to-face contact, and through the adoption of genuine open-door policies in which managers make special efforts to stay in close personal touch with key operations of their companies.

KEY TERMS

body language: Information transmitted by body position, posture, and movement.

centralization: The extent to which information transmitted through a communication network must flow to, and be processed by, one central member.

closed office: One in which the desk faces the door, and serves as a barrier between the office occupant and visitor.

communication: The process through which one person or group transmits information to another person or group.

communication networks: Patterns determining which individuals within a group or organization can communicate with which others.

decoding: The process through which information received through communication is converted back into ideas or concepts.

downward communication: Communication that flows from higher levels to lower ones within an organization.

encoding: The process through which ideas or concepts are converted into a form that can be transmitted to others.

formal channels of communication: The mechanisms and networks within an organization dictating who can (or should) communicate with whom.

grapevine: The informal channels of communication within an organization, based mainly on friendship or acquaintance.

horizontal communication: Communication between individuals or units at the same level of the organizational hierarchy.

informal networks: Channels of communication within an organization based largely on friendship or acquaintance. (The *grapevine* is one such network.)

information saturation: Conditions under which the information-processing capacities of a central member within a communication network are overloaded.

K.I.S.S. principle: A basic principle of communication indicating that messages should be kept as short and simple as possible (short for Keep It Short and Simple).

microexpressions: Fleeting facial expressions that often provide clues to the true feelings of others.

MUM effect: The reluctance of most individuals to transmit nagative information to others.

nonverbal communication: The transmission of information through an unspoken language involving facial expressions, eye contact, body language, and the use of physical space.

open office: An office in which the desk faces the wall and chairs for visitors are placed next to (or at least near) the occupant's seat.

receiver: The individual or group to whom communication is directed.

rumor: Information transmitted through informal channels within an organization that has little basis in fact.

sender: The individual or group who initiates communication.

staring: Continuous eye contact maintained by the starer regardless of what the recipient says or does.

upward communication: Communication that flows from lower to higher levels within an organization.

NOTES

1. H. Mintzberg (1973). *The nature of managerial work.* New York: Harper & Row.

2. J. J. Cribbin (1972). *Effective managerial leadership.* New York: American Management Association.

3. W. G. Scott and T. R. Mitchell (1976). *Organizational theory: A structural and behavioral analysis.* Homewood, Ill.: Irwin.

4. R. T. Keller and W. E. Holland (1983). Communicators and innovators in research and development organizations. *Academy of Management Journal, 26,* 742–749.

5. See Note 4.

6. E. Borman (1982). *Interpersonal communication in the modern organization,* 2nd ed. Englewood Cliffs, N.J.: Prentice-Hall.

7. R. Buck (1984). *Nonverbal behavior and the communication of affect.* New York: Guilford Press.

8. P. Ekman and W. V. Friesen (1975). *Unmasking the face.* Englewood Cliffs, N.J.: Prentice-Hall.

9. C. L. Kleinke, F. B. Meeker, and C. LaFong (1974). Effects of gaze, touch, and use of name on evaluation of "engaged" couples. *Journal of Research in Personality, 7,* 368–373.

10. J. C. Strom and R. W. Buck (1979). Staring and participants' sex: Physiological and subjective reactions. *Personality and Social Psychology Bulletin, 5,* 114–117.

11. M. Zuckerman, R. Koestner, M. J. Colella, and A. O. Alton (1984). Anchoring in the detection of deception and leakage. *Journal of Personality and Social Psychology, 47,* 301–311.

12. T. R. V. Davis (1984). The influence of the physical environment in offices. *Academy of Management Review, 9,* 271–283.

13. P. C. Morrow and J. C. McElroy (1981). Interior office design and visitor response: A constructive replication. *Journal of Applied Psychology, 66,* 646–650.

14. J. C. McElroy, P. C. Morrow, and R. J. Ackerman (1983). Personality and interior office design: Exploring the accuracy of visitor attributions. *Journal of Applied Psychology*, 68, 541–544.

15. B. M. DePaulo, J. I. Stone, and G. D. Lassiter (1985). Deceiving and detecting deceit. In B. R. Schlenker (ed.), *The self and social life.* New York: McGraw-Hill.

16. A. S. Imada and M. D. Hakel (1971). Influences of nonverbal communication and rater proximity on impressions and decisions in simulated employment interviews. *Journal of Applied Psychology*, 62, 295–300.

17. R. A. Baron (1985). Self-presentation in job interviews: When there can be "too much of a good thing." *Journal of Applied Social Psychology*, in press.

18. M. E. Shaw (1978). Communication networks fourteen years later. In L. Berkowitz (ed.), *Group processes.* New York: Academic Press.

19. D. R. Forsyth (1983). *An introduction to group dynamics.* Monterey Calif.: Brooks/Cole.

20. R. L. Burgess (1968). Communication networks: An experimental reevaluation. *Journal of Experimental Social Psychology*, 4, 324–337.

21. R. Likert (1959). Motivational approach to management development. *Harvard Business Review*, July–August, 75–82.

22. S. Rosen, R. J. Grandison, and J. E. Stewart, II. (1974). Discriminatory buckpassing: Delegating transmission of bad news. *Organizational Behavior and Human Performance*, 12, 249–263.

23. A. Tesser and S. Rosen (1975). The reluctance to transmit bad news. In L. Berkowitz (ed.), *Advances in experimental social psychology*, vol. 8. New York: Academic Press.

24. T. J. Peters and R. H. Waterman, Jr. (1982). *In search of excellence: Lessons from America's best-run companies.* New York: Warner Books.

25. R. A. Snyder and J. H. Morris (1984). Organizational communication and performance. *Journal of Applied Psychology*, 69, 461–465.

26. K. H. Roberts and C. A. O'Reilly (1979). Some correlates of communication roles in organizations. *Academy of Management Journal*, 22, 42–57.

27. See Note 25.

28. E. Walton (1961). How efficient is the grapevine? *Personnel*, 28, 45–49.

29. A. M. Tybout, B. J. Calder, and B. Sternthal (1981). Using information processing theory to design marketing strategies. *Journal of Marketing Research*, 18, 73–79.

30. L. W. Porter and K. H. Roberts (1976). Organizational communication. In M. Dunnette (ed.), *Handbook of industrial and organizational psychology.* Chicago: Rand-McNally, pp. 1553–1590.

31. P. V. Lewis (1980). *Organizational communication: The essence of effective management.* Columbus, Ohio: Grid Publishing.

32. See Note 24.

33. L. E. Penley and B. Hawkins (1985). Studying interpersonal communication in organizations: A leadership application. *Academy of Management Journal*, 28, 309–326.

CHAPTER 11

INFLUENCE, POWER, AND POLITICS: What They Are and How They Differ

INFLUENCE: Personal Tactics for Changing Others' Behavior

Pressure to Conform: How Groups Exert Influence   Tactics for Gaining Compliance: How Individuals Exert Influence

POWER: Beyond Influence or Persuasion

Individual Power: Its Major Bases   Group or Subunit Power: Its Structural Foundations   Power: Its Major Effects

ORGANIZATIONAL POLITICS: Power in Action

Organizational Politics: A Sample of Frequent Techniques   Organizational Politics: A Note on Its Ethics

SPECIAL INSERTS

FOCUS ON BEHAVIOR   Influence within Groups: Image and Reality
FROM THE MANAGER'S PERSPECTIVE   Power in Organizations: Using It Wisely

Influence, Power, and Politics

Gloom is in the air as several top people in the Comfort Conditioning Division of Multiplex Corporation gather for an afternoon meeting. The reason behind the general feeling of despair is obvious. Just two weeks ago, the word came down from headquarters that plans for a major program of expansion at the giant conglomerate were in the offing. However, no final decisions had yet been reached as to how the available resources would be allocated; this would be determined on the basis of input from the various operating units. At first, this announcement had produced great excitement. There was a general feeling that results in the division (which manufactures air conditioners and fans) had been good, and that "C.C." could make a strong case for a large share of the new funds. Ambitious plans for added staff and enlarged facilities were hastily prepared. Then, the "grapevine" brought discouraging news: the company's Control Systems division (which produces high-tech sensors and industrial robots) already had the inside track. In fact, according to rumor, the C.E.O. and several members of the board were leaning towards allocating fully *three-fourths* of the program to this one division. It is to discuss this disturbing state of affairs that today's meeting has been called.

"Well," begins Barney Lee, head of the Division, "You all know the situation. We've got to act, and act fast, or the game'll be over. Sue Sligo and her group have already outmaneuvered everyone else, and it looks pretty hopeless. But I don't want to go down without a fight, so let's see if there's anything we can do."

Art Nielsen, one of Barney's vice presidents, is the first to jump in. "How about using the personal approach? I know that Hamner is the toughest C.E.O. we've ever had, and that he's always favored Control. But there are a couple of people on the Board we might win over. Joe Stahl, Barb Cooper—they're good possibilities. Maybe we can get them to at least hold off until we have a chance to get our plan together."

"That *might* help," Anne Cheng, another vice president, comments, "but I've got my doubts about that kind of strategy. Sometimes it works and sometimes it doesn't. Besides, I think we've got *legitimate* claims on that money. Our earnings have been real good the past two years. And don't forget how important we are to the whole company. It's *our* "Frigid-King" trademark that most people think of when they think of Multiplex. And where would Fluids Handling or the Motor Division be without our supply and shipping networks? We've got a lot more power than some people think, and I, for one, feel we ought to use it."

"I'm with Anne," Gerald Nicholson agrees. "We *do* have a lot of power, and ought to use it. Whatever the Board says, they *need* our solid earnings for the total financial picture; without us, it's a mess. You all know how many shares they own because of that bonus plan! But it's going to take some time to get our message across. Meanwhile, I'm for a temporary alliance with the people in Electronics. They were hurt pretty bad by Control a few years back, when Sue and her troops moved in on 'em and squashed their hopes for a lab of their own, so they'll do almost anything to keep her from winning again. I think we can turn that to our advantage."

By this point, the atmosphere in the conference room has begun to change. Glum expressions have given way to hopeful ones, and there is a growing sense of excitement. Barney sums it all up as he remarks:

"Hm—so the situation *isn't* so hopeless after all. If we play our cards right, we may be able to come out of this O.K. Anyway, it sure would be nice to teach those arrogant jerks in Control a lesson!"

At one time or another, most of us have had the following daydream: somehow, we acquire the ability to control the thoughts and behavior of all the people around us. Through this mysterious power, we can get them to do or say anything we wish. Clearly, this is a provocative fantasy. If we could control others in this manner, we would soon be able to reach our every goal and satisfy our every whim. Of course, most of us realize this can never come true. Wish as we may, there simply *are* no magic formulas for exerting total control over others. They have minds of their own, and can usually be induced to do what we want only part of the time, at best.

While complete control over others seems beyond our grasp, however, the situation is far from hopeless. There are many tactics individuals and groups can use to "load the dice" in their favor—to increase the chances that other persons will think or behave as they wish. As you probably already realize (and as suggested by the story on page 333), such procedures are extremely common in organizations. Indeed, efforts by specific persons or units to alter the views, decisions, or actions of other individuals or units occur on what amounts, quite literally, to a non-stop schedule. For this reason, you will almost certainly serve as both the *target* and *user* of such procedures on countless occasions in the future. Given this fact, there can be little doubt that it is important for you to know something about this key organizational process. To provide you with knowledge about it, we will focus on three distinct, but closely related topics: **influence, power,** and **politics.**

INFLUENCE, POWER, AND POLITICS: WHAT THEY ARE AND HOW THEY DIFFER

Imagine the following incident. A young manager wants to add a highly productive member of her department to her own staff. Ostensibly, this transfer would be temporary, and last only during the course of a major project. The manager hopes, however, that once this person is on her team, she can keep him there permanently. To reach her goal, she goes to the productive employee's supervisor, *whom she outranks,* and asks permission to "borrow" his subordinate. Both persons realize, though, that this is merely a formality: the manager can simply transfer the person in question with or without his supervisor's permission.

Now, consider the same incident with one major change: the manager does *not* outrank the person whose subordinate she wants for her own staff. For this reason, she adopts a somewhat different tactic. Specifically, she approaches this person and through a combination of flattery, promises of future aid, and impassioned pleas, attempts to *persuade* him to agree to the transfer.

Finally, consider this incident once more, under the following conditions. Again, the manager does not outrank the person whose subordinate she wishes to transfer, so she can't simply order him to release this individual. Further, she knows from past experience that she won't be able to persuade him to agree to the transfer through personal efforts. With these facts in mind, she decides to "outmaneuver" her opponent. To do so, she forms an informal alliance with several other managers at her level, who promise to support the transfer when it is suggested at the next monthly staff meeting.

In each of these incidents, the major goal sought by the manager remained the same: adding a valuable person to her staff. Yet, because the conditions she faced differed sharply, she adopted contrasting tactics for reaching this outcome in each case. In the first incident, she outranked her opponent. As a result she simply asked this person for what she wanted, and fully expected to get it. In the second, in contrast, she did not outrank her adversary. Because of this fact, she adopted another approach—one based on personal appeals coupled with efforts to somehow convince this person to yield to her wishes. Finally, in the third case, she realized that efforts to win her opponent over voluntarily would probably fail. Knowing this, she chose yet another tactic—one in which she cut the ground out from under this person, and established conditions under which he would *have* to agree to her request.

Together, these three incidents represent the major ways in which we attempt to change others' behavior so that they act (or think) as we wish. The first provides an example of **power**—the ability to change or control others' behavior even against their will, and in the face of resistance from them.[1] As we will soon see in more detail, this capacity often stems from *structural sources* within an organization, such as an individual's position in its hierarchy, and his or her control over valuable resources (e.g., supplies, information). The second incident provides an illustration of a process known as **influence** (or sometimes, *social influence*).[2] In contrast to power, influence does *not* rest on status, centrality within an organization, or other external bases. Rather, it involves efforts by one person or group to change the attitudes or actions of another person or group through less formal means, such as persuasion, flattery, and repeated requests. In short, it is an approach individuals adopt when they have to "go it alone"—proceed on the basis of their own eloquence, wit, and interpersonal skills. Finally, the third incident offers an example of what is often known as **politics** (or **organizational politics**).[3] This refers to efforts by groups or individuals to enhance their power, control the actions of others, and attain desired goals through a wide range of relatively indirect tactics. For example, included among these are: forming coalitions or alliances with others (as in the example above), enlisting the aid of outside experts, and controlling access both to key persons and to important forms of information. The common thread running through all of these diverse strategies is simply this: persons engaging in politics attempt to arrange conditions so that their opponents find themselves with little or no choice—they literally *have to* behave as the "politicians" desire.

To recapitulate: power, influence, and politics represent three facets of the same basic process: efforts by individuals or groups to control the attitudes and actions of others. All are extremely common in organizational settings, and all play an important role in key forms of organizational behavior. Since they rest on different foundations, and make use of contrasting tactics, however, it seems reasonable to consider them separately. In the remaining sections of this chapter, therefore, we will focus on each in turn. (For a summary of the major characteristics of influence, power, and politics, as well as key differences between them, please refer to Table 11.1).

INFLUENCE: PERSONAL TACTICS FOR CHANGING OTHERS' BEHAVIOR

How can we induce others to act as we wish in situations where we have no direct authority over them, and don't control their outcomes in a direct manner? This is a key question often faced by groups and individuals in organizations. As

TABLE 11.1 *Influence, Power, and Politics: An Overview.*
As shown here, *influence, power,* and *politics* differ in terms of the specific tactics they employ, the foundations on which they rest, and some of the goals they seek.

	Tactics	Goals Sought	Basis for Impact
Influence	Persuasion, conformity pressure, ingratiation, compliance	Changes in others' attitudes or behavior	The eloquence, wit, or interpersonal skills of those exerting influence
Power	Direct orders, instructions, directives	Changes in others' attitudes or behavior	Formal authority, expertise, attractiveness, control over resources, centrality
Politics	Coalitions, control over access to information, "dirty tricks," etc.	Acquisition of power; changes in others' attitudes or behavior	Political skills of the persons or groups involved

you probably know from your own experience, many different tactics for accomplishing this task exist, and are put to frequent use. The most important of these, though, involve **persuasion, conformity pressure,** and various techniques for attaining **compliance.** Since we have already considered persuasion in some detail in Chapter 5, we will not return to it here. Please recall, however, that this process involves efforts to change others' attitudes (and hence their behavior) through written or spoken appeals (refer to pages 142–149).

Pressure to Conform: How Groups Exert Influence

Suppose that at some time in the future you accept a position in a large company. Your department holds monthly meetings, at which top-level people summarize recent operations, and describe new policies or procedures. At the first of these meetings you attend, one of the speakers pauses after her presentation, and asks if there are any comments. Being an outspoken person, you raise your hand. The result is totally unexpected: the speaker looks surprised, and does her best to ignore you. Even worse, everyone else in the room seems slightly embarrassed by what you have done. Realizing your mistake, you quickly drop your hand and pretend that you were simply reaching up to smooth your hair. Later, one of your co-workers clarifies matters for you: there is an unspoken—but nonetheless firm—rule that *no one* makes suggestions at these meetings, certainly not new employees such as yourself! You file this fact away for future reference, taking an oath that you'll keep it in mind at all future meetings.

This simple example illustrates the operation of one important source of influence in organizational settings: *conformity pressure.* Such pressure stems from the fact that most groups establish informal rules governing the behavior of their members. As we noted in Chapter 8, these are termed **norms,** and although they are often unstated (at least in an explicit form), individuals are expected to adhere closely to them. Persons who don't may be subject to criticism, isolation, and even expulsion from the group. For this reason, and also because they realize that adherence to established norms will enhance others' liking for them, most individuals find it difficult, if not impossible, to ignore the norms of groups to which they belong.[4] Instead, they usually accept these rules, and behave in ways consistent with them. In this sense, group-established norms often serve as an important source of influence in organizational settings: they induce individuals to behave in ways they would not choose in the absence of these rules.

As you may already know from your own experience in various groups, norms regulate a wide range of activities. Thus, in the kind of groups that exist in organizations (e.g., subunits, work teams, task forces) they can—and do—apply to everything from how much work should be performed during a given period of time and what specific tasks should be carried out by particular members, through rules governing who can interrupt whom during conversations, and who pays the bill at lunch. Clearly, then, norms exert profound effects upon many important organizational processes (e.g., communication, productivity, leadership). For this reason alone, it is important to take careful account of their existence.

At this point, we should note that norms do not develop in a random or haphazard manner. Rather, as suggested recently by Feldman (refer to Chapter 8), they seem to emerge—and to be enforced—in situations where their presence assists the groups that adopt them.[5] Thus, such rules often take shape in situations where there would otherwise be ambiguity over what behaviors are appropriate (e.g., what type of feedback should be offered during meetings? what degree of formality should managers demonstrate in dealing with subordinates?). Similarly, they frequently appear in contexts where groups need internal guidance to protect them from external rivals (e.g., rules about what information should be made public, and what information should be for "internal" consumption only). In these and many other ways, norms—and the *social pressure* to adhere to them—can make important contributions to group harmony, performance, and cohesion. Such benefits are not without their costs, however.

In some cases, the pressure to conform—to stick to the informal rules—can stifle creativity and produce an unquestioning acceptance of the status quo. Needless to say, such outcomes can be harmful both to the groups involved and to the organizations to which they belong. Similarly, in some instances the norms adopted by a particular group may clash with those of its parent organization. The results of such conflict are likely to be unfavorable for all concerned. Finally, informal norms often extend to areas of behavior that seem to have little if anything to do with group performance or other work-related activities. For example, unwritten rules about how one should dress, the kind of clubs to which one should belong, and even the political attitudes one should hold often emerge in various groups, despite the fact that they have little connection to major group functions. In such cases, conformity pressure can be viewed as an unnecessary or irrelevant restriction on personal freedom. (Please refer to Figure 11.1 for a summary of the potential costs and benefits of norms.)

One final point: in general, conformity pressure is a *group* tactic of influence—a mechanism through which groups seek to regulate or control the actions of their members. However, it can be used by individuals as well. Persons wishing to turn this force to their own benefit can do so in two ways. First, they can attempt to alter group norms, so that these now encourage the actions they desire. For example, a clerk more interested in goofing off than in doing her work might try to change the informal rules governing coffee breaks so that these are stretched from fifteen to thirty minutes. Second, individuals attempting to use conformity pressure for their own benefit can suggest to their intended targets that certain actions—the ones *they* desire—are strongly required by existing group norms. If they succeed in this tactic, they stand an excellent chance of encouraging the actions they want; after all, the full weight of the group will now seem to stand behind their requests!

Tactics for Gaining Compliance: How Individuals Exert Influence

As we have just seen, groups generally rely on conformity pressure to change the behavior of their members. Individuals, however, often make use of a different strategy, consisting of two major parts. First, they engage in preliminary actions designed to "soften up" the intended target of influence—to reduce his or her ability

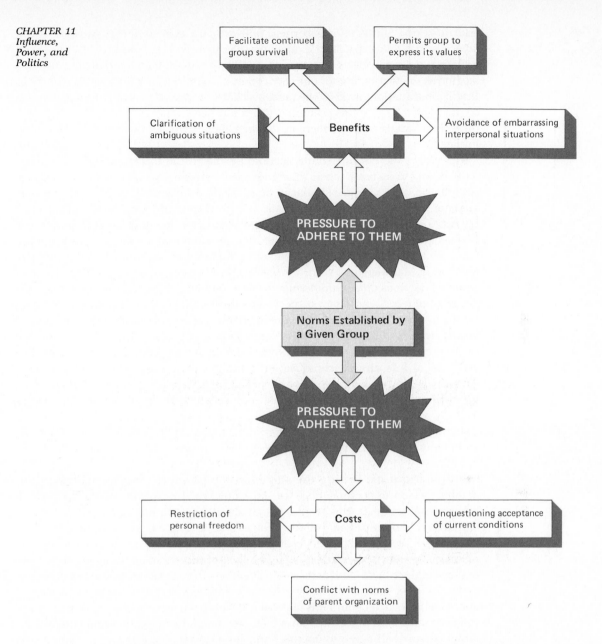

FIGURE 11.1 *Norms: Some Costs and Benefits.*
As shown here, norms can assist groups in several ways (e.g., by clarifying ambiguous situations, helping the group avoid embarrassing incidents). At the same, though, they can operate to restrict personal freedom, clash with the norms of the larger organization, and exact other costs. (Based on suggestions by Feldman, 1984; see Note 5.)

to resist. Second, they present this person (or group) with direct requests for some change in attitudes or behavior. In short, they seek to attain direct **compliance** with their wishes. Many variations on this general theme exist and are effective. Among the most common, though, are **ingratiation** and **multiple requests.**

339

Ingratiation: Flattery, sometimes, will get you everywhere. Most of us are aware of the following fact: if other persons like us, they will probably be more willing to do favors for us or carry out actions we request than if they dislike us. This fact forms the foundation for one very common technique of influence: *ingratiation*. Briefly, ingratiation involves one person's efforts to increase his or her appeal to one or more others. Once this preliminary task has been attained, attempts to influence these individuals—to get them to change their behavior in desired ways—are initiated.

Several different procedures seem to be effective in this regard. First, individuals seeking to increase others' liking for them can convince these persons that they share basic values, or are similar in other ways. A large body of research findings indicate that similarity often generates a high degree of interpersonal attraction.[6] Second, persons bent on the use of ingratiation can demonstrate outstanding job performance. Often, this contributes to high personal evaluations and positive reactions. By far the most common tactic of ingratiation, though, involves the communication of high personal regard to the intended targets of influence. This tactic— usually known as *other enhancement*—often takes the form of *flattery*, exaggerated praise of others.[7] And often, it succeeds: praising others *does* increase their liking for the flatterer. As you probably already realize, though, it is possible to go too far in this respect. If the recipients of flattery realize that it is being used to influence them, they may react with anger rather than enhanced liking for the flatterer. For this reason, less direct techniques for communicating positive feelings to others, such as hanging on their every word, encouraging them to talk about themselves, or the emission of positive nonverbal cues (see Chapter 10), are often more successful. Such tactics are common in many organizational settings, and you are certain to encounter them at some point or other in the future. When you do, try to recognize them for what they are: preliminary steps to the process of gaining your compliance.

Multiple requests: Setting the stage for compliance. Suppose that you want another person to do something for you—anything from giving you a big raise to buying your product. How would you go about reaching this goal? One possibility would simply be to present your request, and hope for the best. As we noted earlier, though, people attempting to exert influence over others rarely operate in this manner. Instead, they usually engage in preliminary actions designed to tip the balance in their favor—to increase the likelihood of compliance by the target person or group. One such tactic involves the presentation of several requests instead of one. The basic idea behind this approach is simple: in some cases, an initial request can serve as a kind of "set-up" for a later one. It can increase the likelihood that the target person will agree to another, and perhaps more important, demand. Two forms of this multiple-request approach in common use are (1) the foot-in-the-door, and (2) the door-in-the-face.

The Foot-in-the-Door: Small request first, large request second. There's an old saying that goes "Give them an inch and they'll take a mile." It refers to the fact that individuals seeking compliance from others often begin with a small or trivial request. Then, once this has been granted, they escalate to a larger or more important one. This tactic—known as the *foot-in-the-door* approach—can be observed in many different settings. For example, salespersons often begin by asking potential customers to accept a free sample or merely a brochure describing their products. Only later, after these small requests have been granted, do they try to close an order. Similarly, individuals seeking help with their work often start with requests for trivial amounts of aid (e.g., answer a simple question, give them a few minutes of your time). After these are granted, they shift to more effortful kinds of help.

Research findings indicate that this "start small but then escalate" approach often works.[8] Indeed, if applied with skill and care, it can markedly increase the likelihood that individuals will consent to very large requests they would almost certainly refuse if these were presented "cold," in the absence of smaller, preliminary ones. Additional findings suggest one possible explanation for the success of this tactic. Once individuals agree to a small initial request, they may undergo subtle shifts in their own self-perceptions. Specifically, they may come to see themselves as more helpful and cooperative than was true before. Since such shifts are flattering, they then experience internally-generated pressures to agree to later (and larger) requests; only by doing so can they maintain their improved self-image. Whatever the specific mechanisms underlying this tactic, however, it *is* often successful. Thus, it is one that is frequently used by individuals who have no direct authority over others, but who wish to change their behavior in some way.

The Door-in-the-Face: Large request first, small request second. While the technique of starting with a small request and then moving to a larger one can be quite effective, the opposite strategy, too, is often useful. In this approach, known as the *door-in-the-face* technique, individuals wishing to exert influence over others begin by asking for a large favor—one the target persons are almost certain to refuse. When this request is rejected, they shift to a smaller one—the request they really wanted all along. (Please see Figure 11.2 for a summary of both the foot-in-the-door and the door-in-the-face tactics.)

Evidence from several careful studies indicates that this "start big—shift small"

FIGURE 11.2   *The Foot-in-the-Door and the Door-in-the-Face: A Summary.*
Two useful techniques for attaining compliance from others are the *foot-in-the-door* and the *door-in-the-face.* Although they are opposite in nature, both appear to be effective.

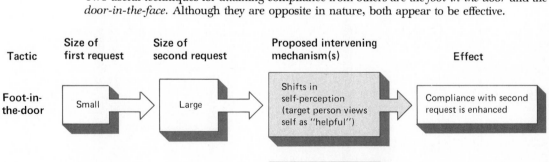

Influence within Groups: Image and Reality

In almost any group, some individuals are more influential than others. It is *their* views that are accepted, *their* recommendations that are followed, and *their* requests that are granted. An important key to understanding how groups function, therefore, lies in determining why, precisely, this is the case. In short, why are some members so much more influential than others? Many different factors seem to play a role in this regard (e.g., belonging to the "right" informal net-

works, occupying a central position in the unit or organization's workflow).[10,11] However, two variables that seem to be of major importance in this regard are *air time*—the sheer quantity of each participant's output, and *quality*—the accuracy of such contributions. Surprisingly, research designed to examine the impact of these factors has yielded inconsistent results. On the one hand, several investigations indicate that influence, in groups, may rest largely on air time (i.e.,

FIGURE 11.3 *Perceived and Actual Influence in Groups: Quantity or Quality?*
In small groups consisting of four to six persons, the *perceived* influence of each member was more closely related to "air time" (quantity of verbal contributions) than to expertise. In contrast, *actual* influence was more closely linked to expertise than to "air time." (Source: Based on data from Bottger, 1984; see Note 13.)

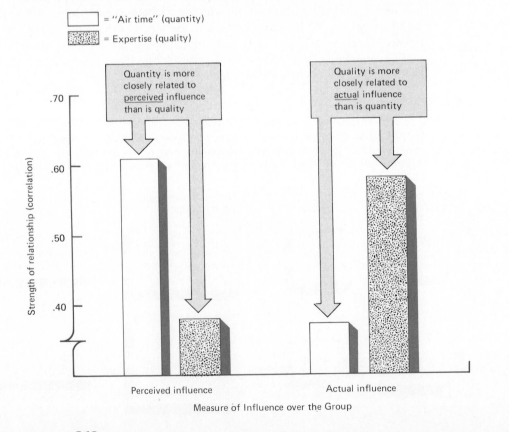

quantity). On the other hand, additional studies suggest that influence may stem primarily from expertise (i.e., quality).[12] Which of these conclusions is accurate? An excellent project, completed recently by Bottger, offers a convincing explanation.[13]

The basic idea behind this study was as follows: perhaps *perceived* influence in groups is largely a function of "air time," while *actual* influence is primarily a function of expertise. If this is the case, then the contradictory findings reported previously can be readily understood. In order to test this possibility, Bottger arranged for middle-level managers and graduate students in management to work on a complex problem in groups of from four to six members. The problem chosen was the NASA moon-survival test. In it, individuals are asked to imagine that they have crash-landed on the moon, and have only fifteen undamaged pieces of equipment remaining. Their task is that of ranking the survival value of each of these items. Groups were instructed to reach a team solution to the problem.

During group discussions, subjects' behavior was carefully observed by two trained observers; this provided an objective measure of each member's "air time." At the end of the session, all participants rated the other subjects in terms of their perceived expertise and influence on the group solution. An index of each subject's actual expertise or ability was obtained in the following way: prior to the group session, each person worked on the problem individually. His or her rankings of the equipment were then compared with the ranking provided by actual members of NASA. The closer the match between these two sets of numbers, the greater the subject's expertise was assumed to be. Finally, an index of each participant's actual influence on the group was obtained by comparing his or her initial ranking of the equipment with the ranking finally agreed upon by the group. The more similar these two sets of scores, the greater the influence a subject was assumed to have exerted.

When the data described above were carefully examined, clear support for Bottger's hypotheses was obtained. Specifically, *perceived* influence was more closely related to the quantity of each member's contributions (i.e., to "air time") than to expertise. However, *actual* influence was more closely related to expertise than to sheer quantity (refer to Figure 11.3).

These findings, and related results obtained in other studies, suggest that both "air time" and expertise are important with respect to influence in group settings.[14] The more an individual talks or participates, the more influential he or she will be perceived to be. And the higher the accuracy of these contributions, the more influence this person will actually exert. In sum, where influence in groups is concerned, both quantity and quality are important, and should be taken into account.

approach, too, really works. Indeed, after being exposed to a very large request and refusing to comply, many individuals are much more likely to consent to a second, smaller demand than would otherwise be the case.[9] Two factors seem to account for this success. First, when the would-be influencer scales down his or her initial request, the target person feels compelled to make a similar concession. Thus, he or she becomes more willing to comply with the next, more modest demand. Second, in the context of the first, huge request, the second seems quite reasonable. Thus, compliance is enhanced for this reason. Again, whatever the precise basis for its impact, the door-in-the-face strategy is widely used in organizations. For example, managers often begin by asking their subordinates to complete more work in a shorter period of time than they really want done. Then, when these persons protest, they scale down their request and "settle" for what they wanted all along. A similar tactic is often used in negotiations. Here, skilled bargainers often build considerable room for concessions into their initial positions. When these are rejected, they reduce their demands—but always to levels above their actual goal. The moral in these and many other instances is clear: if you ever find yourself in the position of dealing with someone who begins with huge and unreasonable demands, but then retreats to smaller ones, beware—he or she may well be "setting you up for the kill" via the door-in-the-face tactic. (Which individuals within groups are perceived as most influential by the other members? And which ones actually produce the greatest effects? For some intriguing evidence on these issues, see the **Focus** insert on page 342.)

POWER: BEYOND INFLUENCE OR PERSUASION

Imagine the following scene. One employee in the research department of a large company is trying to convince another to report for work on Saturday, so they can finish a major project. (She is up for promotion, and wants to establish as good a record as possible before the next appraisal.) The second person refuses, noting that he has many other things to do this weekend and can't spare the time. Because she has no direct authority over her co-worker, the first person resorts to influence: she reminds her co-worker of past favors she has done for him, praises his work, and stresses the importance of the job. All is to no avail; he still refuses to give up part of his weekend. Just then, their supervisor strolls by and asks what's happening. When the situation is explained, he turns to the reluctant employee and says: "Ashton, this job has to be finished. I want you to report for duty on Saturday." Remembering that this individual can hire or fire employees at will, the second employee answers: "Well, if you really need me, I guess I can make it."

This simple incident illustrates two key differences between *influence* and *power.* First, these processes rest on different foundations. Influence derives primarily from current relations between the persons who hope to use it and their intended targets. If would-be persuaders choose the right tactics and use them with skill, influence will succeed. If they select the wrong procedures and use them poorly, it will fail. In contrast, *power* derives from firmer and longer-lasting bases. In the example above, it stemmed mainly from formal **authority:** the supervisor had the right to request (or perhaps even to demand) extra hours of work from the reluctant person. As we will soon see, though, this is only one of several factors from which it can stem. The key point to remember, then is this: in many cases, power transcends the specific situation in which it is used, or current relations between those who

FIGURE 11.4   Power: A Goal Many Seek.
As suggested by this cartoon, *power* is one goal sought by many persons in organizations. (Source: King Features Syndicate, Inc.)

wield it and those who are affected by it. Second, influence and power differ in terms of degree. While influence involves the capacity to alter others' attitudes or behavior, power refers to the ability to do so regularly, strongly, and even in the face of concrete resistance.[15] Thus, in a sense, it can be viewed as influence carried to its ultimate extreme.

As you already know, power plays an important role in organizations. Indeed, it is one of the major goals many persons seek throughout their careers (refer to Figure 11.4). In the present section, therefore, we will delve into several aspects of this process. First, we will examine the bases of *individual power*—factors that provide specific persons with the capacity to alter the behavior of others. Next, we will turn to several bases of *group or subunit power*—structural aspects of organizations that afford power to specific groups within them. Finally, we will examine some of the major effects of power—its impact on both those who hold it and those who are subject to it.

Individual Power: Its Major Bases

Why are some individuals capable of changing the behavior of others, even in the face of strong resistance from them? In short, what factors provide particular persons with power over others, in organizations and elsewhere? According to an insightful framework proposed some years ago by French and Raven, the answer lies partly in the nature of the relationships between those with power and those without it, and partly in the characteristics often possessed by powerful persons.[16]

Reward power: Control over valued resources.   The first and in some ways most important source of power noted by French and Raven involves control over *valued resources*. Generally, persons able to determine who gets various rewards, in what form, and at what times acquire tremendous power over others. The reason for this is simple: only by doing what the resource-controller wants can persons hope to obtain wanted outcomes. In a key sense, then, they are entirely at the mercy of such power-wielders: either they must submit, and act as these people dictate, or they must forego any chance of obtaining desirable rewards.

The importance of gaining control of valued resources is well understood in all organizations. Indeed, it is recognition of this fact that often underlies the bitter political struggles so frequent in such settings. As we will see in more detail in a later section, many persons participate in such contests because they realize that if they succeed, and gain control over raises, promotions, information, supplies, or other resources, they will soon be able to do almost anything else they wish: after all, they will be the possessors of considerable power over others.

Coercive power: Control over punishments.   The other side of the coin from reward power, of course, is the ability to inflict punishments of various kinds on others—a capacity known as **coercive power.** Basically, this form of power rests primarily on fear. Individuals subject to it realize that if they do not behave as the power-holder wishes, they will be made to suffer unpleasant outcomes. For example, in organizations, persons holding coercive power can hold others up to humiliating public criticism, can assign them unpleasant tasks, and in some cases, can even demote or fire them. As you might suspect, the open use of coercive power is generally frowned upon in most work settings, and with good reason. Individuals exposed to such treatment—especially if they view it as harsh or abusive—often form grudges against the persons responsible, or against the entire company.[17] The effect of such reactions on satisfaction and morale can be devastating. Further, many experts agree that it is difficult for individuals to do their best work when they live in daily fear of harsh punishment or censure. For these reasons, coercive power is a form that should be used only cautiously in organizational settings.

Legitimate power: When right makes might.   Consider the following incident. In a busy hospital, a young medical student approaches one of the senior nurses and asks her to bring him some supplies from a distant storeroom. The nurse becomes angry, and simply walks off, totally ignoring the students' request. The next day, a senior physician on the staff makes a similar request. Without hesitation—and also without any visible resentment—the nurse hastens to follow his orders.

The reason for the nurse's contrasting reactions in these two incidents is obvious. In the first, she felt that she was receiving instructions from someone with no legitimate authority over her. In the second, she perceived the physician as someone with the right to tell her what to do on the job. Together, these examples illustrate the nature of a third major source of individual power: a belief by subordinates that the person exercising authority over them has a legitimate right to do so. Power stemming from this source is known as **legitimate power,** and usually derives from formal rank or position. For example, in most organizations, supervisors have the right to give instructions to their subordinates; this authority is accepted as appropriate by both sides. We should note, however, that legitimate power can sometimes spring from other sources as well. Thus, in several countries, persons belonging to an hereditary "royal family" are perceived as having the legitimate right to exercise authority over others. Similarly, the son or daughter of the founder of a company may acquire such power even if, on the formal organizational chart, he or she occupies a fairly minor post. One key advantage of power stemming from such legitimacy should be obvious: since it is accepted as fully appropriate by subordinates, its exercise is unlikely to generate the jealousy or resentment sometimes associated with other forms of power. Thus, it may be especially useful for this reason.

Referent power: Control based on attraction.   Have you ever had a hero or heroine—someone you admire and looked up to? If so, you are already familiar with another possible basis for power. When individuals like and respect another person, they are often willing to alter their behavior in accordance with his or her directives. Indeed, in some cases, they attempt to anticipate this person's wishes and respond to them even before they are expressed. Individuals fortunate enough to possess such attraction, therefore, gain considerable power over others. Dramatic examples of such **referent power** are provided by charismatic political leaders, sports heros and heroines, and stars in the entertainment field. However, such power can also be observed in organizations, where dynamic and popular managers sometimes inspire great respect—and willingness to serve—among their staffs. In many different settings, then, being liked or admired can often provide an important base for personal power.

Expert power: Control based on knowledge. A final source of power—that deriving from expertise—can be readily illustrated. Suppose that the owner of a medium-sized company is considering the purchase of expensive new equipment. After listening to the presentations of sales representatives from four potential suppliers, he tentatively makes up his mind. Then, just to be certain, he calls in one of his most senior production workers and asks his opinion. Much to his surprise, the employee recommends strongly against the equipment the owner has chosen, pointing out that he has had bad experiences with the service department of the company that produces it. What will the owner do? If he is a good manager, he will probably reconsider: after all, the experienced employee knows the equipment—and its manufacturer—in important ways he does not. Because of this knowledge, he possesses **expert power** even over the head of the company. In sum, expert power refers to the ability of individuals possessing high levels of knowledge or experience in a given area to affect the views or behavior or others with respect to such matters.

One final point: in most cases, such power *is* indeed restricted to the area of the expert's special knowledge. Thus, engineers are consulted about engineering matters, accountants are heeded with respect to taxes, and so on. Occasionally, though, it seems to spill over into additional areas, so that persons with expertise in one field use it as a base for exerting influence in another. This is common in advertisements, where athletes, movie stars, and other celebrities use their fame—and status—to endorse products or causes about which they probably have little special knowledge. Needless to add, it is wise to be on guard against such inappropriate uses of expert power. (The various sources of power proposed by French and Raven are summarized in Table 11.2. Please consider them carefully before proceeding.)

Bases of individual power: Independent or linked? Before concluding this discussion, we should touch briefly on one more point: are the various types of individual power independent or closely linked? The answer is clear: in many instances, they are highly interdependent. First, various sources of power tend to occur in combination. For example, individuals high in reward power are often high in coercive power as well. Similarly, those high in legitimate power are often admired, and so are also high in referent power. Second, the presence and use of

TABLE 11.2   Individual Power: Some Important Sources.
According to a framework proposed by French and Raven (see Note 16), individual power in organizations (and elsewhere) can stem from several different sources.

Type of Power	Description of Source
Reward	Derives from control over valued resources and rewards (e.g., raises, promotions, required information)
Coercive	Derives from control over various punishments (e.g., assignment to undesirable tasks, public criticism)
Legitimate	Derives from the belief, among subordinates, that certain individuals have the right to exercise authority over them
Referent	Derives from respect or admiration for the power-holder on the part of subordinates
Expert	Derives from the possession of expert knowledge in some area

one type of power often affects the others. To mention just two examples, use of coercive power can often reduce referent power, since most persons tend to dislike those who punish them. Similarly, a high degree of expert power often goes along with at least some legitimate power, since it is widely agreed that experts have the *right* (even duty) to offer advice in their fields. This interdependence between various sources of power has also been demonstrated in several investigations. For example, in one project, Greene and Podsakoff found that reductions in managers' reward power were accompanied by corresponding reductions in their referent and legitimate power.[18] These findings, and the facts outlined above, point to the following general conclusion: while individual power can stem from many different sources, in actual use, the different types tend to become closely linked.

Group or Subunit Power: Its Structural Foundations

So far in this discussion, we have concentrated on power as it is held and used by individuals. In organizations, though, power is also often wielded by groups or subunits. Certain groups (e.g., departments, divisions, informal alliances) can change the actions of other units, directing them into paths or patterns they desire. What are the sources of such power? How, in short, do certain groups or units gain the capacity to affect the actions of many others? Several factors seem to play a role in this regard, but among the most important are **resource control** and **network centrality.**[19]

Resource control.   From one perspective, a given organization can be viewed as consisting largely of a set of subunits engaged in a continuous process of exchange. Each unit both supplies certain outputs to others, and receives needed resources (inputs) in return. Thus, each is both *necessary* to and *dependent* upon the others. For example, through its operations, Sales provides financial resources, plus certain forms of information. Obviously, though, it cannot operate in the absence of sufficient output from Production. Production, in turn, cannot carry out its major functions without appropriate resources from Supply. Supply, of course, cannot purchase needed materials without funds from Finance—and so it continues, throughout the organization. Each unit is involved in a complex network of exchange relationships with others.[20] This perspective (sometimes known as the *resource-dependence view*) suggests that in a basic sense, each unit in an organization possesses power over the others. To the extent it controls resources they need, it can affect their actions. In addition, this perspective also pinpoints a major reason why some departments are much more powerful than others: they simply control more resources—or more important ones—than other units. In a word, groups or units within an organization often acquire power because of *asymmetries* in the pattern of resource dependencies. Those units with control over the most critical or valuable resources soon come to wield more power than ones with control over less critical or less valuable resources.[21] But what, precisely, are these central resources? In fact, this varies with the specific organization. Thus, in a high-tech company working at the edge of new technology, technical or scientific information would probably be

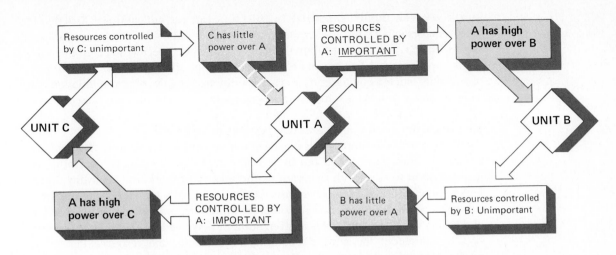

FIGURE 11.5   *Intraorganizational Power: The Resource-dependence View.*
According to the *resource-dependence* view of intraorganizational power, subunits within an organization acquire power to the extent that they control critical resources for other subunits. Thus, in the diagram shown here, Unit A has more power than both Units B and C because it controls more important resources than these other units.

critical. Groups or departments controlling such resources would acquire great power. In a firm that manufactures clothing, in contrast, adequate supplies of high-quality fabric and accurate information on current fashion trends may be crucial. In this organization, groups dealing with *these* matters would probably acquire power.

In sum, in answer to the question, "What units or departments in a particular organization wield power?" the resource-dependence model answers: the ones with most control over critical resources. (For a summary of this view, please refer to Figure 11.5)

Network centrality.   In our discussion of communication networks (Chapter 10) we noted that persons who occupy central positions—ones through which information must be channeled—often exert considerable influence over other persons in the network. In a similar manner, groups or subunits that occupy strategic positions in the *workflow network* of their organization can acquire considerable power.[22] In fact, if they are located at points where many different units interact or come into contact, they may become functionally indispensable: the organization simply cannot carry on its major functions without them.

Please note: such units acquire their power primarily from their location within the structure of their organization—*not* necessarily from their control over the information or resources that must flow through this position. Of course, as noted by Astley and Sachdeva, such control is often acquired by groups that occupy central positions.[23] However, it should be viewed as another potential source of power, over and above that conferred by network centrality itself.

The importance of centrality in intraorganizational power has been recognized by many researchers. Perhaps it is most clearly noted, however, in the **strategic**

contingencies theory proposed by Hickson and his colleagues.[24] Briefly, this theory suggests that subunits acquire power when the activities of other subunits are dependent (i.e., contingent) upon them in certain ways. Specifically, a given subunit gains in power when (1) it can help other units cope effectively with environmental uncertainty, such as changes in market conditions, or government regulations (see Chapter 15); (2) it is high in *workflow centrality*—its activities are linked to many other subunits, and strongly affect their performance; and (3) it is indispensable to the organization—no other unit can perform its activities.

Support for these proposals has been obtained in several studies. For example, in one investigation, carried out in several companies, the higher the ability of a given subunit to cope with uncertainty, the greater its workflow centrality and the lower the extent to which other units could perform its functions, the higher the subunit's power within the organization.[25] Moreover, only when all three of these conditions were favorable was a given subunit perceived as dominant in power.

To conclude: the strategic contingencies theory, the resource dependence model, and related views all call attention to a crucial fact about power within organizations. Often, it stems from *structural factors*—the ways in which they are "put together," and the nature of the contingencies between their various units.

Power: Its Major Effects

Different people seek different goals—this is a basic fact of life. Yet, included somewhere on almost everyone's "personal list" is *power*. The reasons behind this popularity should be obvious: power, once gained, usually confers major benefits on those who hold it. Such persons can change the actions of many other people, thus approaching, if not actually attaining, the fantasy of total control over others mentioned at the start of this chapter. In addition, they often acquire high degrees of *status*, with all the respect, prestige, and "perks" this implies. Given such outcomes, it is hardly surprising that many people in organizations invest considerable time and energy in a perpetual quest for power. Indeed, it would be more surprising if they did not!

Because the effects of power just described are fairly obvious, we will not devote further attention to them here. Instead, we will focus on other, less apparent, results of this capacity. In particular we will consider some of the ways power affects the behavior of those who hold it, and the reactions of those who do not. In addition, to illustrate the subtle and often complex effects of power, we will briefly consider its impact on one key organizational process—*negotiation*.

Power in operation: Its effect on power holders: The mass media (e.g., movies, television) often present a clear image of how powerful persons are supposed to look and behave. According to these stereotypes, such persons are impressive in physical appearance, and demonstrate a number of specific traits (e.g., decisiveness, ambition; refer to Figure 11.6). Is there any truth to such views? Are powerful persons really recognizable at a glance? Research findings cast doubt on such assumptions. No evidence suggests, for example, that powerful persons really

FIGURE 11.6   Powerful Persons: Do They Look and Act Different from Others?
According to a stereotype fostered by the mass media (television, movies), powerful people look and act differently from others. Research findings cast doubt on the accuracy of this view, however.

are more attractive than less powerful ones. Only one consistent difference in physical appearance has been noted: persons with considerable power (e.g., Presidents or Presidential candidates; the CEOs of major corporations) tend to be above average in height.[26]

With respect to specific traits or patterns of behavior, again, some of the assumed differences seem to exist, while others do not. First, as we noted in Chapter 9, political leaders—persons who usually possess a considerable amount of power—do appear to be higher than others in self-confidence, the need to dominate others, and the need for achievement.[27] Second, in organizational settings, managers who possess a high level of power do seem to behave differently toward their subordinates than managers with less power. For example, high-power managers rate their subordinates less favorably on performance appraisals, are less willing to socialize with them, and send more instructions and messages to them than lower-power managers.[28]

Finally, persons high in power often differ from others with respect to various aspects of their nonverbal behavior.[29] In terms of eye contact or gazing, powerful persons tend to establish slightly higher levels of eye contact than others. Further, they often show somewhat different facial expressions during conversations. Specifically, high-power persons lower their eyebrows more and show fewer smiles than persons lower in power. In contrast, these latter individuals often raise their eyebrows—a sign of submission—and smile more frequently.[30] Perhaps the most dramatic differences between powerful and nonpowerful persons, however, relate to their use of physical space. First, powerful individuals generally have larger zones of *personal space* around them than do less powerful persons. That is, they expect others to "keep their distance" to a greater degree; close physical approach is by invitation only. The existence of this fact was noted by the present author while working in a large government agency. When the author (a person with relatively low power in that organization) went to visit the director of his division (a person with high power), he waited at the doorway until invited to enter and be seated. In contrast, when the division director visited the author, he simply walked in and sat down without hesitation. Second, and related to the above, powerful and nonpowerful persons differ in their use of touch. While powerful persons can touch others with impunity (e.g., put their hands their shoulders), they do not expect to be touched in return. Thus, subordinates report being much more likely to be touched by their boss than vice versa.[31] In sum, considerable evidence suggests that where organizational behavior is concerned, power *is* an important dimension. While the very clear-cut differences between high- and low-power persons suggested by Hollywood fail to emerge, persons falling into these two categories *do* differ in certain respects, and these can be readily observed in many organizational settings. (How do subordinates react to the exercise of power in organizations? And what steps can be taken to prevent resentment over its use? For some suggestions, please see the **Perspective** insert on page 353.)

Power: Its role in negotiations.   As we have just seen, power exerts strong effects upon those who hold it, and those over whom it is exercised. Yet, even these are only part of the total picture. In addition, power affects a wide range of key organizational processes. As an example of such influence, we will briefly consider its impact on one such process: negotiations.

The most obvious way in which power can affect negotiations, of course, is through differential possession of this capacity by opposing sides. To the extent one party to negotiations has an advantage in this respect, it can shape the course of the exchange, and obtain an agreement favorable to itself. Another and perhaps less obvious way in which power can affect negotiations concerns the relationship between negotiators and their constituents—the people they represent. If the persons representing an organization in a bargaining situation are low in power, they will have to answer for their actions during negotiations. As a result, they may feel constrained, and adopt a cautious or defensive strategy. In contrast, if negotiators are high in power, they will be protected from such censure and may feel free to choose a more flexible and open approach. The result: negotiations involving high-power representatives from both sides may be more successful, and more efficient, than negotiations between persons of lower power. This possibility has recently been investigated by Jackson and King in a well-conducted study.[33]

In this project, student volunteers were divided into teams of two persons. One of the members of each team was chosen to be its "Executive Director," and was given considerable power over the other (e.g., the Executive Director evaluated the performance of the second person, decided how much to pay him or her, and so on). Negotiations between pairs of teams over the exchange of resources (letters that could later be used in a word-formation task) then took place. In these negotiations,

Power in Organizations: Using It Wisely

It is well known that in the physical world, every action produces a reaction in the opposite direction. Does this principle apply to the world of organizations as well? Where the exercise of power is concerned, it certainly does. As you probably already realize, few persons like being told what to do, or being ordered to change their behavior from patterns they prefer to ones they dislike. Yet, this is precisely what happens when power is put to use. The result, of course, is that those on the "receiving end" often experience anger and resentment. Even worse, they sometimes demonstrate a phenomenon known as **reactance**—a strong tendency to do exactly the *opposite* of what is demanded of them.[32] The major motive behind such reactions seems to be that of asserting or maintaining personal freedom—a desire to avoid being ground underfoot by the "big guns" in one's organization. Whatever the precise reasons, however, the exercise of power does often generate resistance among subordinates. Usually, this takes subtle and hidden forms (e.g., they drag their feet on various tasks, implement new policies slowly if at all, and so on). In a few cases, though, it is more direct (e.g., formation of a union, strikes, industrial sabotage). Obviously, such reactions to the use of power can be deadly to both satisfaction and productivity. Thus, it is important that they be avoided. Can this goal be accomplished? The answer, we believe, is "yes." While totally eliminating negative reactions to the exercise of power is probably impossible, several steps may be useful in holding such responses to a minimum. A few of these are listed below.

(1) *"It is better to be liked than feared."* Machiavelli, whose ideas we considered in Chapter 6, felt that it was better for rulers to be feared than admired. We strongly disagree. Individuals may follow the commands of those who threaten them with punishment, but they usually do so reluctantly. In contrast, they often enjoy doing things for people they respect or admire. The general rule, then, is this: in most situations, *referent power* is preferable to *coercive power.*

Thus, managers who cultivate positive feelings among their subordinates will often be more effective than ones who seek compliance through discipline.

(2) *Always know what you're doing:* If there's one thing subordinates *don't* like in a manager, it's lack of expertise. This is only reasonable: who would enjoy taking orders from someone who knows less than they do? For this reason, it is crucial for persons wishing to exercise authority over others to establish a high level of expertise. To the extent they do, they will be operating on the basis of *expert power,* and this may enhance their performance.

(3) *Be legitimate: Don't overstep the bounds.* In most organizational settings, managers have *legitimate power* over their subordinates: their positions grant them the right to change subordinates' behavior in some ways. At the same time, though, there are definite limits to such power; managers can seek to alter *some* aspects of employees' actions, but not others. *It is very important that these boundaries not be overstepped.* If they are, the legitimacy of managers' power may be called into question, and their effectiveness sharply curtailed.

(4) *Style counts: Always use the velvet glove.* Many young managers are unsure about how to give directives to their subordinates—especially ones older than themselves. Because of such uncertainty, they adopt a formal style, in which they deliver curt, abrupt orders to these people. This can be a serious mistake. As we noted earlier, most people strongly dislike being told what to do; it makes them angry, and can evoke reactance. A better strategy, then, is one in which instructions to subordinates are phrased as requests rather than commands. The basic message remains the same, but this approach can prevent employees from feeling—quite unnecessarily—that their egos have just been squashed.

each team was represented by one member—either the high-power Executive Director or the low-power subordinate. Three different combinations of such persons were formed: two high-power negotiators, one high-power and one low-power negotiator, and two low-power negotiators. In accordance with the reasoning noted above, it was predicted that the negotiations between two high power representatives would be more successful and more efficient, and produce greater satisfaction with the final agreements, than negotiations involving at least one low-power person. As you can see from Figure 11.7, results offered at least partial support for this hypothesis. Specifically, negotiations between two high-power persons were in fact completed more efficiently (in less time) than those involving one or more low-power persons.

The moral of these findings for organizations seems clear: when time pressures are great, and a rapid settlement is needed, it is best to send high-ranking, powerful representatives to negotiations. The freedom of action such people enjoy may enable them to adopt a flexible approach, and so to reach agreements more quickly than their less powerful counterparts.

FIGURE 11.7   Power: Its Impact on Negotiations.
Negotiations between two high-power representatives took less time to complete than negotiations involving at least one low-power person. These findings suggest that when time pressures are great, organizations should send only high-ranking or high-power representatives to participate in bargaining. (Source: Based on data from Jackson and King, 1983; see Note 33.)

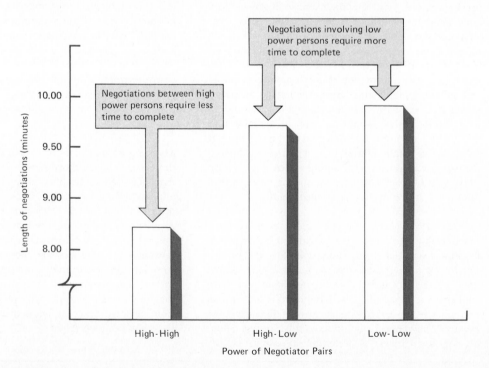

ORGANIZATIONAL POLITICS: POWER IN ACTION

Power, we have suggested, can be viewed as a force—the potential to affect events and people. If this is the case, then **politics** can be perceived as this force in action. As Pfeffer, a noted expert on this topic, has noted, it is "the exercise of power to get something accomplished."[34] And this "something," of course, is the outcome desired by the persons or groups engaging in politics. For purposes of this discussion, then, **organizational politics** can be defined as *any actions taken by individuals or groups to gain power and so secure goals and outcomes that they personally desire.* If this definition seems to smack a bit of selfishness—of putting one's personal interests above those of the organizaton—that is our intention. Politics often *is* selfish in its orientation. Indeed, this element of using or gaining power to further one's own self-interest is one of the major factors distinguishing politics from other, more legitimate uses of power. Stated slightly differently, power, as a force, is neutral: it can be used for a wide range of purposes. Politics, in contrast, implies its exploitation for personal gain.

But just how common is political maneuvering in modern organizations? As you probably already know, very common indeed. In fact, most organizations appear to be highly political environments, in which various persons, groups, and units are constantly jockeying for position and power. As a result, promotions, raises, and other rewards are not always distributed solely on the basis of merit. Major decisions are not always made on the basis of careful study of all available data. And the principles of fair play and rationality do *not* always serve as the guiding precepts. Instead, politics rules—and rules with a vengeance!

Given the highly political nature of most organizations, it is useful for you to know something about this complex process. In this final section we will first consider some of the specific tactics it involves. Then, we will comment briefly on the *ethics* of such procedures—whether, and when, they are morally justified.

Organizational Politics: A Sample of Frequent Techniques

How do people seek to gain and exercise power in organizations? The answer is: in many ways. Some of the most common (and perhaps effective) of these are described below.

(1) Coalitions: Forming the right alliances. One tactic that often proves useful from the point of view of gaining power and reaching one's goals is forming coalitions. When individuals or groups attain the right allies—others willing to support their positions or actions—they can often overcome even strong resistance. The word "right" should be emphasized, however. Joining forces with persons or groups who have something to contribute, and who can be relied upon is one thing; hooking up with ones who have little to offer, or who may desert at any moment is

quite another. Thus, considerable care is needed in implementing this general strategy.

(2) Choosing a powerful mentor.   As we noted in Chapter 2, having an experienced, powerful mentor can be highly beneficial to one's career. Thus, entering into such a relationship can be an effective tactic for acquiring power and reaching important goals. Since there are typically many more would-be protégés than there are openings for them, competition in this regard can be intense. However, given the substantial benefits yielded by the protection and guidance of a powerful mentor, efforts to establish such relationships are well worthwhile.

(3) Projecting the right image.   It is often said that "nothing succeeds like success," and where organizational politics is concerned, this principle appears to be highly accurate. Persons who demonstrate a high level of competence, who adopt a cooperative attitude, and who show many "good citizen" behaviors tend to acquire a positive "halo."[36] This, in turn, can confer a considerable degree of expert or referent power. For this reason, attempts to polish one's image can often yield valuable dividends where organizational politics are concerned.

(4) Establishing control over access to information.   One highly effective tactic for gaining power that can be used both by individuals and by groups, involves gaining control over vital information. As we noted in Chapter 10, information is the life-blood of organizations. Thus, anyone who can control its flow, or access to it, acquires considerable power. In some cases, of course, this is determined by structural factors within an organization (e.g., internal arrangements or rules that determine who reports to whom, and in what form). Often, though, persons or units wise in the ways of politics can alter the flow of information, or establish new channels for it, that pass directly through their hands. To the extent they succeed in such endeavors, power—and the capacity to attain their desired goals—is usually not far behind.

(5) Cooptation: Neutralizing opponents.   Another old saying relevant to organizational politics is "if you can't beat 'em, join em." Turning this around, groups bent on adding to their power often adopt the tactic of *cooptation*. That is, they bring people whose support is desired—and who, currently, stand in the group or unit's way—into the fold. Once they are made part of the group, they become subject to its norms, and often adopt its values and goals. Such cooptation can be accomplished formally through transfers, reassignments, or promotions. It can also be achieved informally by establishing friendly personal relations with such persons (e.g., asking them to join exclusive clubs, inviting them to various social functions). Whatever the specific strategy, the end result is much the same: important obstacles to the acquisition of greater power are removed.

(6) The use of reciprocity: Scattering IOUs.   A guiding principle in all human relations—whether between individuals or groups—seems to be *reciprocity*. In general, people treat others as they have been treated previously. Because of widespread adherence to this prinicple, another effective tactic for gaining and using power is one that might be termed "scattering IOUs." By doing favors for others,

assisting them with problems, or supporting them against opponents, it is possible to place them in one's debt. Then, at appropriate times (when their assistance is needed most), reciprocity can be invoked, and requests for repayment made. As you can probably guess, people or units effective at using this strategy are always careful to get more than they give: the favors they do for others are smaller, easier to perform, and less closely linked to the acquisition of power than the ones they receive.

(7) Politics in the extreme: The use of "dirty tricks." The final tactic—or group of tactics—we will mention are known, collectively, as "dirty tricks." These refer to strategies that most people view as deceitful, underhanded, and dishonest— ones that violate the ethical principles we will soon describe. Included among "dirty tricks" are such steps as (a) falsely attributing blame for negative outcomes to others (holding them responsible for events they did not produce); (b) announcing one agenda for meetings, but then following a totally different *hidden* one, thus preventing opponents from being adequately prepared (refer to Figure 11.8); (c) restricting the flow of information to others, or providing them with misleading "facts"; and (d) spreading false rumors about their personal lives, lack of commitment to the organization, or current behavior. As you can see, such tactics are highly objectionable, and seem to go far beyond the kind of political maneuvering most people would accept as a normal part of organizational life.[37] Unfortunately, though, they are also quite effective, and often help unscrupulous persons in their perpetual quest for power.

FIGURE 11.8   *Hidden Agendas: One Tactic of Organizational Politics.*
Hidden agendas are often used as a tactic of organizational politics. By introducing topics their opponents are not prepared to discuss, users of this strategy can gain an important advantage. (Source: Drawing by Ed Arno; © 1982 The New Yorker Magazine, Inc.)

*"We seem to have reached agreement on the agenda. Now
let's move on to the hidden agenda."*

Organizational Politics:
A Note on Its Ethics

Looking back over the tactics listed above, you may well have very mixed reactions. Some (e.g., forming coalitions) probably strike you as being quite reasonable; in fact, you might be willing to use them yourself. Others (especially "dirty tricks") probably seem questionable at best. They are manipulative, dishonest, and in some cases, perhaps, even illegal. Such reactions leave us facing an important question: when are efforts to acquire and use power through organizational politics justified, and when are they inappropriate? In other words, when are political actions *ethical* and when are they *unethical?* Obviously, no simple or clear-cut answer to this issue exists; it is far too complex to afford us such a luxury. As suggested by Cavanagh, Moberg, and Velasquez, however, there do appear to be some general guidelines or principles that can aid us in this task.[38]

First, whenever the use of political tactics is contemplated, the following question about their ultimate purpose should be addressed: are they designed to further purely selfish ends, or will they help to promote organizational goals and values as well? To the extent the former applies, the use of such tactics is unethical. At first glance, you might assume that politics are rarely, if ever, used to benefit an entire organization. However, this is not entirely true. There *are* instances in which political tactics are used to benefit persons other than the ones who use them. For example, consider a situation in which an entrenched group of power-holders is wedded to destructive policies, and refuses to change. Here, the use of political maneuvers to overcome their resistance may well be justified. Because of situations such as these, the ultimate goal of such strategies should be carefully considered in determining whether they are acceptable or objectionable.

Second, the impact of political behaviors upon the rights of individuals should be addressed. To the extent such tactics violate basic human rights, they are, or course, unacceptable. What rights may be at stake? Actually, quite a few. For example, some of the "dirty tricks" described above can violate the right to privacy; they may be used to obtain information about others they would rather keep concealed. Similarly, such tactics often violate several rights known, collectively, in Western society as *due process* (e.g., being informed of the charges against you; being provided with an opportunity to defend yourself against them). Finally, some political tactics violate the freedom of conscience: they more or less force individuals to go along with procedures they find abhorrent. Again, to the extent organizational politics produce such effects, they are unethical—and inexcusable.

Third, the relationship of political behaviors to principles of equity and fair play should be considered. Almost everyone likes to feel that they will be judged by their performance, and rewarded in accordance with their merit. Further, most persons like to believe that although all individuals won't finish together, they can at least begin from the same point, and run the same course. By their very nature, some political actions run counter to such views. Indeed, in an important sense, their ultimate aim is that of establishing two sets of rules: one for those with power, and another for those without it. To the extent political tactics operate in this manner, and directly conflict with principles of fairness or justice, they are unacceptable.

In sum, each time the use of political strategies is considered, their goals, effects, and potential outcomes must be evaluated. If these are consistent with the principles outlined above, they may be acceptable, at least in the present situation and under current conditions. If such tactics are inconsistent with these principles, however, persons contemplating their use should think again: some other means to the same desired ends would be preferable.

SUMMARY

Attempts to change others' attitudes or behavior are common in organizations. **Influence** involves efforts by one or more persons to affect others in the absence of any direct authority over them. Thus, it rests primarily upon the skill of would-be influencers. Among the techniques often employed for this purpose are persuasion, ingratiation, conformity pressure, and multiple requests (the foot-in-the-door; the door-in-the-face).

Power is the capacity to alter others' behavior even in the face of resistance from them. *Individual power* stems from many different sources (e.g., control over rewards or punishment, expertise, a belief on the part of subordinates that it is legitimate). *Group* or *subunit power* derives from several *structural factors* such as resource control and network centrality. Power affects the behavior of those who possess it, and influences key organizational processes such as negotiations.

Organizational politics involves efforts by individuals or groups to increase their power or attain desired outcomes. It includes such techniques as forming coalitions, gaining control over access to information, cooptation, and the use of "dirty tricks." Political behavior in organizations is ethical only when it furthers organizational as well as individual goals, when it does not violate individual rights, and when it is consistent with principles of equity, fair play, and justice.

KEY TERMS

authority: Refers to power based on the legitimate right to change others' behavior or tell them what to do.

coercive power: Individual power based on control over punishments.

compliance: The process through which one or more individuals attempts to induce one or more others to agree to various requests.

conformity pressure: The pressure, within groups, to adhere to norms.

cooptation: A tactic of organizational politics in which opposing individuals or groups are made part of the coopter's group. In this way, their opposition is overcome.

door-in-the-face: A technique for gaining compliance in which a large initial request is followed by a scaled-down, smaller one.

expert power: Individual power based on the possession of expert knowledge.

foot-in-the-door: A technique for gaining compliance in which an initial small request is followed by a larger one.

influence: Efforts by individuals or groups to change the attitudes or behavior of others in situations where they do not possess formal power or authority over their targets.

ingratiation: A tactic for gaining compliance based upon inducing a high level of liking by the target toward the person using ingratiation.

legitimate power: Individual power based upon the belief that the power-holder has a legitimate right to exert control over others.

network centrality: A source of group or subunit power deriving from the group or unit's central location in the workflow of the organization.

norms: Rules established by groups to govern the actions of their members.

organizational politics: Procedures for gaining power and using it to attain desired (and usually selfish) ends.

persuasion: Efforts to change others' attitudes or behavior through some form of communication with them.

politics: See *organizational politics*.

power: The capacity to change others' attitudes or behavior even in the face of resistance from them.

reactance: Negative reactions by individuals who feel that others are attempting to influence them unduly, or limit their personal freedom.

referent power: Individual power based on a high level of admiration or respect toward the power-holder.

resource control: A source of group or subunit power, deriving from the group or unit's control over valued resources within an organization.

strategic contingencies theory: A theory proposing that subunits within an organization gain power to the extent that they are central to the organization's work flow, reduce environmental uncertainty, and perform functions that cannot be carried out by any other unit.

NOTES

1. A. J. Grimes (1978). Authority, power, influence and social control: *Academy of Management Review, 3*, 724–735.

2. R. A. Baron and D. Byrne (1984). *Social psychology: Understanding human interaction*, 4th ed. Boston: Allyn and Bacon.

3. J. Pfeffer (1981). *Power in organizations*. Marshfield, Mass.: Pitman.

4. C. A. Insko, R. H. Smith, M. D. Alicke, J. Wade, and S. Taylor (1985). Conformity and group size: The concern with being right and the concern with being liked. *Personality and Social Psychology Bulletin, 11*, 41–50.

5. D. C. Feldman (1984). The development and enforcement of group norms. *Academy of Management Review, 9*, 47–54.

6. See Note 2.

7. C. B. Wortman and J. A. W. Linsenmeier (1977). Interpersonal attraction techniques of ingratiation in organizational settings. In B. M. Staw and G. R. Salancik (ed.), *New directions in organizational behavior*. Chicago: St. Clair Press.

8. R. B. Cialdini (1985). *Influence: Science and practice*. Glenview, Ill.: Scott, Foresman.

9. R. B. Cialdini, J. E. Vincent, S. K. Lewis, J. Catalan, D. Wheeler, and B. L. Darby (1975). Reciprocal concessions procedure for inducing compliance: The door-in-the-face technique. *Journal of Personality and Social Psychology, 31*, 206–215.

10. A. Zander (1979). The psychology of group processes. *Annual Review of Psychology, 30*, 417–451.

11. D. J. Brass (1985). Men's and women's networks: Study of interaction patterns and influence in an organization. *Academy of Management Journal, 28*, 327–343.

12. P. W. Yetton and P. C. Bottger (1982). Individual versus group problem solving: An empirical test of a best member strategy. *Organizational Behavior and Human Performance, 32*, 145–159.

13. P. C. Bottger (1984). Expertise and air time as bases of actual and perceived influence in problem-solving groups. *Journal of Applied Psychology, 69,* 214–221.

14. See Note 10.

15. See Note 1.

16. J. R. P. French and B. Raven (1959). The basis of social power. In D. Cartwright (ed.), *Studies in social power.* Ann Arbor: University of Michigan Press.

17. R. D. Arvey, G. A. Davis, and S. M. Nelson (1984). Use of discipline in organization: A field study. *Journal of Applied Psychology, 69,* 448–460.

18. C. N. Greene and P. M. Podsakoff (1981). Effects of withdrawal of a performance-contingent reward on supervisory influence and power. *Academy of Management Journal, 24,* 527–542.

19. W. G. Astley and P. S. Sachdeva (1984). Structural sources of intraorganizational power: A theoretical synthesis. *Academy of Management Review, 9,* 104–113.

20. J. Pfeffer and G. R. Salancik (1978). *The external control of organizations.* New York: Harper & Row.

21. G. R. Salancik and J. Pfeffer (1974). The bases and uses of power in organizational decision making: The case of a university. *Administrative Science Quarterly, 19,* 453–473.

22. N. M. Tichy and C. Fombrun (1979). Network analysis in organizational settings. *Human Relations, 32,* 923–965.

23. See Note 19.

24. D. J. Hickson, C. R. Hinings, C. A. Lee, R. E. Schneck, and J. M. Pennings (1971). A strategic contingencies theory of intraorganizational power. *Administrative Science Quarterly, 15,* 216–229.

25. C. R. Hinings, D. J. Hickson, J. M. Pennings, and R. E. Schneck (1974). Structural conditions of intraorganizational power. *Administrative Science Quarterly, 19,* 22–44.

26. S. Feldman (1971). The presentation of shortness in everyday life—Height and heightism in American society: Toward a sociology of status. Paper presented at the meetings of the American Sociological Association, Chicago, 1971.

27. E. Costatini & K. H. Craik (1980). Personality and politicians: California party leaders, 1960–1976. *Journal of Personality and Social Psychology, 38,* 641–661.

28. D. Kipnis (1972). "Does power corrupt?" *Journal of Personality and Social Psychology, 24,* 33–41.

29. J. A. Edinger and M. L. Patterson (1983). Nonverbal involvement and social control. *Psychological Bulletin, 93,* 30–56.

30. See Note 29.

31. N. M. Henley (1977). *Body politics: Power, sex, and nonverbal communication.* Englewood Cliffs, N.J.: Prentice-Hall.

32. F. Rhodewalt and J. Davison, Jr. (1983). Reactance and the coronary-prone behavior pattern: The role of self-attribution in responses to reduced behavioral freedom. *Journal of Personality and Social Psychology, 44,* 220–228.

33. C. N. Jackson and D. C. King (1983). The effects of representatives' power within their own organizations on the outcome of a negotiation. *Academy of Management Journal, 26,* 178–185.

34. See Note 3.

35. G. R. Ungson and R. M. Steers (1984). Motivation and politics in executive compensation. *Academy of Management Review, 9,* 313–323.

36. T. S. Bateman and D. W. Organ (1983). Job satisfaction and the Good Soldier: The relationship between affect and employee "citizenship." *Academy of Management Journal, 26,* 587–595.

37. G. F. Cavanagh, D. J. Moberg, and M. Velasquez (1981). The ethics of organizational politics. *Academy of Management Review, 6,* 363–374.

38. See Note 37.

CHAPTER 12

Cooperation, Competition, and Conflict

Consolidated Industries has a problem, and it can be summarized in just three words: *lack of coordination.* The company, a giant in its field, manufactures household appliances under several different brand names. Each is produced by an independent division and over the years, a tradition of competition among them has developed. For decades, this has served Consolidated well. Each division sought to outdo its rivals, and produce the best appliances possible. Recently, however, major cracks have begun to appear in this old, and once reliable, system. First, changing market conditions have led to a situation in which Consolidated's divisions find themselves competing more and more directly with each other, rather than with their external rivals. Second, inflation has raised the costs of duplication in research, administration, and marketing to levels that now seem intolerable. It is to discuss this general situation, and an especially glaring example of the waste it produces, that Ken McBride, C.E.O. of Consolidated, has called today's meeting. Just three days ago, he learned that two of the company's major units—its Cascade and Coolpoint divisions—have both been working on a new system for home washing machines. This system offers major benefits (e.g., it uses substantially less hot water), and promises great appeal to consumers. However, in accordance with Consolidated's traditional system of internal competition, each division has proceeded independently with development. The result: more than three million dollars have already been wasted on duplicated costs. No wonder Ken turned purple when Mary Kelley plunked a report describing the situation onto his desk.

"Well," Ken begins, "you all know why we're here. I'm *really* upset. Three million down the tubes—and at a time when we all have to tighten our belts. I won't stand for that kind of waste. *Something has to be done.*"

"I agree," Lynn Bellasco responds. "That old 'go-it-alone' attitude just doesn't cut it any more. The world is too complicated, and costs are too high. We've got to stop acting like our own worst enemy."

"I think we all see that," Bud Velasquez, a senior vice president comments, "but just what do we do about it? That's the question. We've operated this way for a long time, and change isn't going to be so simple."

"For one thing," Sharon Frankel, another vice president, replies, "we've got to start some new lines of communication between our divisions. I just can't believe this situation would have gone on as long as it did if it had come out into the open."

"Maybe not," Lynn agrees, "but you've got to consider our bonus system, too. The way it's set up right now, it's all-or-nothing. The division with the biggest jump in dollar volume gets the whole pie. It's hard for me to imagine a better way to make sure that they'll stay at each other's throats."

"Hmm," Ken comments, stroking his chin. "I think Lynn has a good point there. That's one thing we've definitely got to change. Set it up so that *everyone* who shows an increase gets something."

"Right," Bud agrees with enthusiasm. "Our bonus system *does* need revamping. But let's not overlook the personal factor too. We've got to get Dickinson and Gombert to bury the hatchet and patch things up. The way things are now, all they want to do is make each other look bad."

At this remark, there are nods all around the table. The feud between the heads of the Cascade and Coolpoint divisions is well known throughout the company, and inserts a note of tension into many meetings.

"Well," Ken adds thoughtfully, "it looks as though we've got our work cut out for us. We can make progress on this issue, and get coordination back into the company, but it's going to take some doing . . ."

Does the situation at Consolidated strike you as strange? In a key sense, it should. Ultimately, all the persons and units within an organization are *interdependent*: what happens to one affects what happens to the others. If the organization prospers, rewards will be available for everyone. (They may not be shared equally, but they will at least be there.) In contrast, if the organization does poorly, few if any of its groups, units, or members are likely to benefit on a long-term basis. Only its competitors will come out ahead. Given these basic facts, it seems only reasonable to assume that *coordination* should be the slogan in all work settings. Departments, divisions, units, and individuals should work together as closely and smoothly as possible to attain shared goals.

As you probably already realize, however, this ideal is not always attained. In many cases, individuals or groups largely ignore one another, and fail to coordinate their actions in essential ways. In other instances, such as the one described above, they may actually *compete*, with each group or person attempting to outdo the others. Finally, in even more extreme cases, open confrontation or *conflict* may

FIGURE 12.1 *Coordination: An Essential Ingredient in Organizational Success.*
When individuals, units, or groups within an organization fail to coordinate their actions, the
results can be costly. (Source: King Features Syndicate, Inc.)

develop, with all the negative feelings this implies. Needless to add, such departures
from optimal coordination can prove quite costly (refer to Figure 12.1). Indeed, they
can interfere with an organization's effectiveness, reduce its ability to perform vital
tasks, and sharply lower levels of satisfaction among its employees.

The fact that organizations often fail to attain levels of coordination which, to
an outside observer, would seem to be ideal, raises an important question: what
factors are responsible for this costly state of affairs? In short, what conditions
prevent the development of coordination even when it would clearly be of benefit to
all concerned? Similarly, but turning the question around, what factors tend to
enhance coordination—to encourage its development at the individual, group, or
subunit level? It is on these crucial issues that the present chapter focuses.
Specifically, our discussion of coordination in organizations will proceed as follows.
First, we will examine two contrasting patterns of relations between individuals or
groups—**cooperation** and **competition**. Our primary interest will be that of identifying factors (both ones involving individuals and ones involving organizations)
that tend to tip the balance toward one or the other of these two opposite patterns.
Second, we will turn to a process with even more disturbing implications for
organizations than the mere lack of coordination: open **conflict** between its members or units. Here, we will consider several of the major *causes* of conflict (factors
that seem to lead to its occurrence), the *effects* it produces, and specific techniques
for its effective *management* or control.

COOPERATION AND COMPETITION: WORKING
WITH—OR AGAINST—OTHERS

Is there such a thing as "pure altruism"—actions that benefit others but for
which the persons or groups performing them expect absolutely nothing in return?
Philosophers have debated this point since antiquity, and more recently, behavioral
scientists, too, have entered the discussion.[1] To date, however, no firm or simple

conclusions have been reached. There are so many subtle ways in which individuals can gain rewards for helping others (e.g., enhancement of their own self-image, positive feelings induced by the gratitude of the recipients) that the issue turns out to be extraordinarily complex. Regardless of whether "pure" altruism exists, however, there can be little doubt that on some occasions, people do engage in what appears to be *one-way* assistance. They offer aid to others without receiving anything obvious in return. While such one-way assistance (usually termed *helping* or *prosocial* behavior) clearly exists, however, another pattern—*cooperation*—is far more common. Here, two or more persons or groups work together in order to enhance the outcome received by each. In other words, assistance is *two-way* or reciprocal in nature. Cooperation is obviously a basic and common form of coordination in work settings. To mention just a few concrete examples, it occurs when several engineers work together to design a new piece of equipment, when employees on the loading dock pool their efforts to lift a heavy package, when key managers combine their expertise to reach an important decision, and when two departments come up with new procedures to streamline the flow of work and resources between them. In all these cases, the underlying principle is much the same: the persons, groups, or units involved coordinate their actions in order to reach goals or levels of performance they could not attain alone. Then, once the mutually desired goals are reached, the benefits are shared among the participants in some agreed upon manner. In sum, cooperation often pays—and pays quite handsomely—for all concerned.

The obvious benefits yielded by cooperation raise a basic question: why, if it is so useful, does it often fail to occur? Why don't people, groups, or units seeking the same (or at least compatible) goals always join forces? As we will soon see, several factors account for this puzzling lack of coordination. By far the most important, however, is this: *cooperation cannot develop in many situations because the goals sought by the person or groups involved* (or the rewards associated with them) *simply cannot be shared*. To the extent this is true, or course, it makes little sense for them to work together. For example, if two persons are seeking the same promotion, they cannot join forces to attain it—this prize can go to only one. Similarly, if, as in the example on page 363, several divisions within an organization are seeking a bonus for the greatest increase in sales, they cannot work together; only one will receive this reward. In such instances, cooperation is literally impossible, and an alternative form of behavior known as *competition* is likely to arise. Here, each person, group, or unit strives to maximize its individual gains, often at the expense of others. Because many valued goals in organizations (e.g., status, power, promotions, bonuses) are in short supply, and are sought by many more persons or units than can hope to attain them, competition, too, is very common in the world of work. In fact, it is a basic aspect of life in most organizations, at least part of the time (refer to Figure 12.2).

As we have just noted, in many cases, the choice between cooperation and competition is an obvious one; indeed, there may really be no choice at all. In others, however, the individuals or groups involved may find that they *do* have some room for maneuver. They can choose either to work with others toward mutually desired goals, or against others for their own gain. This fact, in turn, brings us back to the central question we wish to address: what conditions, specifically, serve to tip the balance toward one of the other of these contrasting patterns? In short, what

FIGURE 12.2   *Competition: A Fact of Life in Modern Organizations.*
When goals desired by several persons or groups can't be shared, *competition* between them
often develops.

conditions lead individuals, groups, or units to opt for cooperation, or, alternatively,
for competition? As we will now see, many factors play a role in this regard, and
they relate both to individuals and to certain aspects of organizations themselves.
(We should note, by the way, that tendencies to cooperate and compete often
coexist. For example, members of a work unit may wish to cooperate with one
another to secure mutually desired goals. At the same time, though, each individual
may wish to "outshine" the others, and so maximize his or her personal gains.)

Individual Factors and Cooperation

Several factors that affect the level of coordination within an organization seem
to operate primarily through their impact upon individuals. That is, they influence
the perceptions and reactions of specific persons, and in this manner shape their
decisions about cooperating or competing with others. Among the most important
of these variables are the principle of *reciprocity*, certain aspects of communication,
group size, and what might be termed *personal orientation* toward coordination
with others.

Reciprocity: Reacting to the behavior of others.　Throughout life, we are urged to "Do unto others as we would have others do unto us." Despite such recommendations, though, we usually behave in a somewhat different manner. Specifically, we tend to treat others not as we would prefer to be treated ourselves, but rather as *they* have treated *us*. In short, we follow the principle of **reciprocity**. This tendency to behave toward others as they have acted toward us is both general and strong. Thus, it can be observed in actions as diverse as attraction, where we tend to like others who express positive feelings toward us, through aggression, where "an eye for an eye and a tooth for a tooth" seem to prevail.[2] As you might suspect, our choice between cooperation and competition poses no exception to this powerful rule. When others act in a competitive manner toward us, we usually respond with mistrust and efforts to defeat them. In contrast, if they behave in a cooperative manner, we usually return high levels of coordination. Only one noteworthy exception to this general pattern seems to exist. If, for some reason, another person or group offers a high level of cooperation with absolutely "no strings attached"—with no requirement that it be returned—many persons yield to temptation and attempt to take unfair advantage of their opponent. That is, they respond to such unconditional cooperation with attempts at exploitation.[3] Needless to add, such conditions are quite rare in organizations. Few persons, groups, or units continue to offer cooperation in the face of exploitation—at least not for long! Thus, most individuals realize that they must reciprocate the cooperation they receive, or it will shortly be withdrawn.

In any case, the fact that cooperation is usually reciprocal in nature points to the following practical conclusion: the key task with respect to establishing coordination in organizations is often getting it started. Once individuals, groups, or units have begun to cooperate with one another, the process may be largely self-perpetuating. Managers wishing to encourage coordination, therefore, should do everything possible to get the process underway. From that point on, the obvious benefits cooperation confers, plus the principle of reciprocity, may well take care of the rest.

Communication: Its benefits and costs.　In many situations where cooperation could potentially develop but does not, its absence is blamed on a "failure to communicate." It is suggested that better or more frequent contact between the persons or groups involved might have facilitated such coordination (refer to Chapter 10). Is this suggestion correct? In one sense, it is. Some forms of communication do indeed seem to increase the likelihood of cooperation in many contexts. For example, an open exchange of views may convince all parties that working together is the best strategy. Similarly, unless some minimal level of communication exists, close coordination of work activities may be impossible. As noted by one of the characters in the opening story (page 363), then, adequate communication *can* often contribute to the development of cooperative patterns in organizations.

It is equally clear, however, that not all types of communication produce such beneficial effects. In fact, research findings indicate that at least one type of contact between persons or groups—the use of overt *threats*—can sometimes reduce rather than encourage cooperation.

Threats take many different forms, but they typically involve statements to the effect that (1) if the recipient does not behave in some manner, or (2) does not *refrain* from acting in some way, negative consequences will follow. For example, a manager may warn her subordinates that unless they attain certain goals, they will receive poor evaluations, smaller raises—or worse. Similarly, during negotiations, union officials may state that unless their demands are met, a costly strike will be called. As you can probably already see, such tactics produce mixed effects at best. Often, they merely stiffen the resolve of recipients to resist; as we noted previously, most persons react very strongly to efforts to limit their personal freedom. In other cases, however, threats do produce surrender: the persons or groups who receive them feel that they have no choice but to go along with those attempting to intimidate them. Even then, though, the ultimate effects may be negative. Having "lost face" through surrender to their opponents, such persons may harbor strong resentment against them. Accordingly, they will search long and hard for ways of "evening the score." The result: while coordination is increased in the present context, the chance for its development on future occasions are sharply reduced.[4] For these reasons, the use of threats as a means of establishing coordination between various persons, units, or groups in an organization should usually be avoided. While it may succeed in the short run, it can often leave a lingering negative residue that works against future cooperation.

Group size and cooperation: Why "bigger" is not always "better." One complaint often heard in organizations—especially in ones experiencing rapid growth—is this: "My department/unit/workgroup is getting so big that it's hard to coordinate." In short, many managers (and their subordinates, too), feel that as their organizations or subunits grow, coordination within them becomes harder and harder to achieve. Are these beliefs justified? Is cooperation harder to attain as group size increases? Research findings confirm that it is. As the number of individuals participating in almost any task-performing group rises, the level of cooperation or coordination within that group seems to drop.[5] Several factors contribute to this outcome.

First, the greater the number of persons present, the greater the likelihood that one will hold a totally selfish, exploitive orientation toward relations with others (see the discussion of such orientations below). Since coordination is reciprocal in nature, competitive or exploitive actions may then spread throughout the group. Second, as groups increase in size, communication among their members, as well as communication with other groups or units within the organization, may become more difficult. Finally, as the number of individuals in a group increases, **diffusion of responsibility**, in which each member feels less and less responsible for the group's performance, may develop.[6] Such a "pass-the-buck" attitude may sharply reduce overall coordination.

At first glance, these facts seem to suggest that as organizations (or units within them) grow in size, they must, necessarily, become less efficient and less pleasant places in which to work. This often seems to be true. However, growing evidence suggests that the negative effects of increasing size can be countered through application of a relatively simple principle: *division*. Specifically, as groups become larger and more unwieldy, they can be divided into several smaller subunits. That this strategy can succeed is indicated both by the results of systematic research, and by the outcome of practical programs in operating companies. With respect to research conducted under carefully controlled conditions, it has been found that cooperation is enhanced by dividing large groups into smaller ones. For example, in one recent study, it was observed that reducing the size of work groups by one-third increased the level of cooperation among group members by as much as 40 to 50 percent.[7] Turning to programs adopted by large organizations, a project carried out by Volvo, the Swedish auto manufacturer, seems noteworthy. When production-line employees in this company were assigned to relatively small work groups (of about fifteen to twenty-five members), both absenteeism and turnover dropped substantially.[8] Moreover, product quality (although not output) also rose. Of course, several other changes were instituted at the same time (e.g., alterations in the way work tasks were actually performed). Thus, these may also have contributed to the positive results. At the very least, though, these findings agree with the ones reported by systematic research studies. Thus, when combined, these two sources of evidence suggest that reducing the size of work groups may be one useful tactic for enhancing cooperation in even the largest of organizations.

Personal orientations and cooperation.   Think back over the persons you have known. Can you remember ones who were highly competitive—individuals who viewed every situation as one in which they had to defeat others or outdo them? Similarly, can you recall others who were almost always cooperative—persons who preferred to work with others, and who minimized differences between their outcomes and those obtained by their partners? Probably, you have little difficulty in bringing examples of both types to mind, for individuals differ greatly in their tendencies to cooperate and to compete. Such differences, in turn, seem to reflect contrasting underlying perspectives toward coordination with others.[9] Interestingly, most persons seem to fall into one of four categories in this respect.

First, there are **competitors.** These are persons whose primary motive is that of maximizing their own gains relative to those of others. They are mainly concerned with doing better than other people with whom they must deal. Indeed, they will even settle for negative results, as long as these exceed those of their opponents. Second, there are **cooperators.** Individuals of this type are primarily interested in maximizing joint gains—their own *and* those of others. They want all persons in their group, department, or unit to obtain positive outcomes, and will take active steps to assure that this is the case. Third, there are **individualists.** These are persons whose major concern is simply that of maximizing their own gains. Usually, they have little interest in the outcomes of others, and do not really care whether these persons do better or worse than themselves. Their major focus is simply that of doing as well as they can in every situation. Finally, some individuals can be described as **equalizers.** Their major goal is that of minimizing differences between their own outcomes and those of others. In short, such persons adhere closely to the principle of "share and share alike," and strive to assure that they and everyone else with whom they deal receive approximately equal results.

At this point we should note that while many persons seem to fall into one of these major categories or another, some demonstrate a mixture of such perspectives. For example, substantial numbers seem to combine an individualistic orientation with a competitive one: they want to do as well as they can, but are also interested in surpassing others. Similarly, some persons combine an individualistic orientation with a desire for equality: they want to do as well as they can, but don't want their outcomes to get *too* out of line with those of others.

By now, you are probably wondering just how common each of these patterns is. Are there more competitors or cooperators? Do the mixed patterns outnumber the "pure" ones? Valuable information on such issues has recently been provided by Knight and Dubro.[10] These investigators asked a large group of individuals (half male and half female) to complete several tasks designed to reveal their orientation toward coordination with others. Results indicated that substantial percentages of participants fell into each of the categories mentioned above. However, as shown in Figure 12.3, the patterns differed somewhat for men and women. Thus, among males, the single largest group was competitors; fully one-third showed this orientation. In contrast, among females, persons demonstrating a cooperative orientation (approximately 20 percent) were more numerous.

Not surprisingly, persons adopting different perspectives toward coordination tend to behave quite differently in their dealings with others.[11] Competitors frequently attempt to exploit other members of their group or unit, and will cooperate with them only when they see no other choice. In contrast, cooperators prefer

FIGURE 12.3 *Personal Orientations toward Coordination: Some Intriguing Sex Differences.* Males and females seem to differ somewhat in their orientations toward coordination with others. A higher proportion of males than females demonstrate a competitive approach, while a higher proportion of females than males demonstrate a cooperative orientation. (Source: Based on data from Knight and Dubro, 1984; see Note 10.)

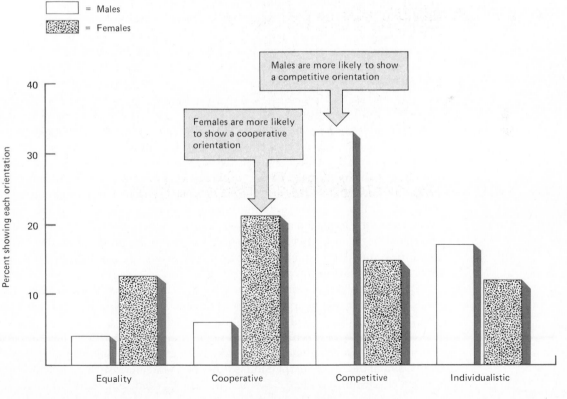

mutual coordination and will seek this pattern whenever feasible. Individuals are flexible—they choose whatever strategy will maximize their own outcomes in a given situation. Persons with a "mixed" orientation are somewhat harder to predict; they may oscillate, or adopt intermediate levels of coordination. In any case, managers can benefit substantially from taking careful account of such differences. For example, in situations where they can choose subordinates, it may often be better to select cooperators or individualists than pure competitors. (An exception: if a particular job or role, such as serving as a negotiator, requires a highly competitive individual, choosing someone with *this* orientation may be most appropriate.) Further, once managers are aware of their own underlying orientation, they can attempt to form alliances with others who share this orientation, and to avoid persons with sharply contrasting ones. Careful attention to such underlying perspectives, therefore, can yield important practical benefits.

Organizational Factors and Cooperation

That organizations differ greatly in terms of their levels of internal coordination is obvious. Some—typically, ones that are quite successful—demonstrate a high degree of integration between their various units, departments, or divisions.[12] Others—typically ones that are *not* highly successful—evidence a lower degree of coordination. All the parts are there, but somehow they just don't pull together into a unified whole. What accounts for such differences? We have already provided part of the answer: coordination within organizations is affected by several factors relating primarily to individuals (e.g., communication between them; their contrasting perspectives toward cooperation with others). At this point, we will complete the picture by focusing on *organizational* factors that influence coordination.

Organizational structure.   We have already hinted at one of the most important of these variables in the story on page 363. As you may recall, the fictional organization in that incident (Consolidated Industries) employed a structure consisting of several major divisions. Each of these divisions produced a similar array of products (but under a different brand name), and marketed them independently. Obviously, such conditions tended to foster at least a degree of competition between these units. The icing on the cake was a "winner-takes-all" bonus system in which only the division with the largest increase in sales and profits received extra organizational rewards. The result of this internal structure was quite predictable: the divisions ended up competing with each other as much as with external rivals, and wasted important resources in the process.

Clearly, this is an extreme example. Yet, it is reflective of conditions that sometimes exist in actual organizations. For example, many large companies adopt a structure involving independent product divisions. Each manufactures and sells different items, so in a sense, they do not compete directly. Yet, since important rewards are again distributed in accordance with gains in sales, market share, or profits, a high degree of competition is fostered. Please note: such competition is *not* necessarily harmful. In some cases, it can encourage efficiency and innovation. The important point, though, is that it can readily go too far, and generate duplication, waste, and other negative outcomes. (Please refer to Chapter 15 for additional discussion of organizational structure.)

Interdependence: When coordination is required. Imagine two organizations. In the first, the major tasks performed by employees are such that they can be completed alone; there is no necessity for individuals to work closely or continuously with others. In the second organization, in contrast, the tasks performed by employees cannot be completed alone; they must work together closely to do their jobs. In which organization will higher levels of coordination develop? The answer is obvious: in the second. The reason for this difference, too, should be apparent. The level of coordination attained is determined by the nature of the work performed. When employees are *interdependent* (they must work together on their jobs), coordination tends to be high. When employees are *independent* (they can complete their work alone), coordination tends to be low. Direct evidence for the existence of such a link between interdependence and coordination in organizations has recently been provided by a project conducted by Cheng.[13]

Participants in this investigation were persons working in research units in thirty-three different organizations in Belgium. (Both heads of units and their subordinates took part in the study.) These individuals indicated both the extent to which their groups were *interdependent* (i.e., the degree to which the tasks they performed required members to work closely together), and the extent to which they were in fact *coordinated* (i.e., the degree to which the research they performed was part of a coherent program). An index of each group's productivity was provided by the number of articles it had published during the past three years.

Results indicated that, as predicted, interdependence and coordination were positively linked. That is, the more interdependent members of the various units reported being, the greater the degree of coordination present in their work (refer to Figure 12.4 on page 374). In addition—and as might be expected—the greater the degree of coordination in these research units, the higher their level of performance. One additional finding is also worthy of note: the higher the level of interdependence in the various units, the stronger was the link between coordination and performance. Since coordination would be expected to facilitate performance only to the extent that it is necessary (i.e., only to the degree that employees are interdependent), this final result, too, would be predicted.

In sum, the findings obtained by Cheng, and those reported in related studies, indicate that coordination is closely associated with one basic organizational factor: the degree to which interdependence among employees is required by its major tasks.

Interorganizational coordination: A response to environmental change. So far in this discussion, we have focused on factors that affect coordination within a given organization. Before concluding, we should touch briefly on the fact that coordination can sometimes exist between separate organizations as well as within a single one. At first glance the existence of such **interorganizational coordination** might seem puzzling. Why, after all, should independent organizations join forces or coordinate their actions? Two basic answers exist.

First, they may engage in such coordination for the same reason specific individuals or subunits do: to attain mutually desired goals. For example, although the

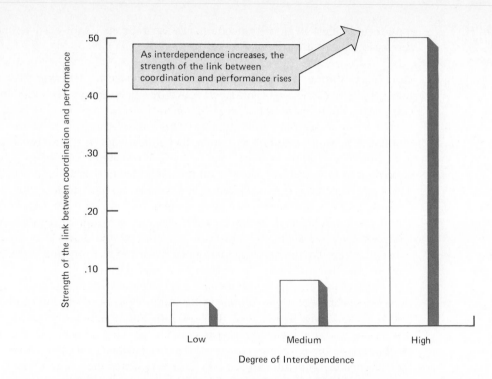

FIGURE 12.4   Interdependence, Coordination, and Performance.
The higher the level of interdependence between persons working in research units, the stronger the link between their degree of coordination and their level of performance. However, coordination strongly affected output only when interdependence was high. (Source: Based on data from Cheng, 1983; see Note 13.)

"big three" U.S. auto manufacturers are vigorous competitors, waging an endless battle for market share, they often work together when their interests coincide. Thus, they closed ranks when requesting import quotas on Japanese cars. Similarly, they coordinate their activities when attempting to defeat legislation they view as harmful to their interests. The most dramatic illustration of interorganizational coordination to attain shared goals in recent years, perhaps, is provided by the Organization of Petroleum Exporting Countries (OPEC). By coordinating their pricing policies, production, and related matters, this group of governments quickly seized control of world oil prices in the 1970s, and only changing patterns of energy use on a worldwide scale have recently weakened its iron grip. As this piece of history suggests, coordination among separate organizations can often yield huge benefits to the participants.

   A second, and perhaps less manipulative basis for interorganizational coordination lies in changing environmental conditions. It is sometimes the case that new patterns of trade, advances in technology, shifts in government policies, and other factors combine to create an environment in which independent organizations find it difficult, if not impossible, to exist in their traditional form. One response to such conditions is merger: surrendering independence and becoming part of a larger organization. Another is the information of *consortiums*—confederations in which organizations maintain their formal independence, but agree to coordinate their activities through a central *CMO*—consortium management organization. The costs associated with such actions are obvious: member organizations must surrender some portion of their independence (e.g., they must give up control over decisions and policies).[14] The gains in efficiency obtained, however, may be so great as to render this the only rational course of action.

A clear example of the type of conditions we have been discussing is provided by the hospital industry in the United States. Here, the growth of privately owned chains, the increasing complexity of medical treatment, the increasing size of government programs, and several other factors have put mounting pressure on independent, not-for-profit hospitals. Indeed, many have found it all but impossible to continue their traditional methods of operation. As a result, large numbers of such organizations have joined *multihospital consortia*. By doing so, they have been able to exert control over rising costs, provide a more optimal mix of medical services, avoid duplication of personnel and facilities, and improve several aspects of their performance. Given such benefits, it is far from surprising that this type of interorganizational coordination has shown a dramatic rise in recent years. And given the increasing complexity of the external environments in which many organizations must now operate (refer to Chapter 15), it seems reasonable to expect more, rather than less, of this type of cooperation in the decades ahead. (Does coordination always yield beneficial effects? For some surprising information on this issue, please see the **Focus** insert on page 376.)

CONFLICT: ITS CAUSES, EFFECTS, AND MANAGEMENT

For the tenth time this week, two workers in a large clothing factory get into an angry shouting match. They have to share certain tools in their jobs, and each feels that the other is monopolizing this equipment.

Friction between Operations and Maintenance at Bolex, a producer of high-quality optical equipment, has risen to new heights. People in Operations complain that those in Maintenance try to tell them what to do, and refuse to follow a reasonable system of priorities. On their side, Maintenance employees protest that their counterparts in Operations constantly meddle in *their* jobs, and do things that make their work harder. Relations between the two groups have gotten so bad, that there is now an open feud between them.

Unfortunately, situations such as these are far from rare in most organizations. Conflict between individuals, groups, or units occurs on an all too frequent basis. Indeed, the results of one well-known survey indicate that middle- and high-level managers spend up to *20 percent of their time* dealing with some form of conflict.[17] Clearly, then, it is an important process, with major implications for many aspects of organizational functioning.

But what, precisely, *is* conflict? Surprisingly, this is not as simple an issue as you might assume. On close examination, conflict turns out to be one of those

FOCUS ON BEHAVIOR

Cooperation and Performance: A Complex Link

At several points in this discussion, we have made an implicit assumption: cooperation (or, more generally, coordination), is good—it is a desirable goal for organizations to seek. In one sense, this suggestion *must* be true. When individuals, groups, or units work with rather than against one another, positive feelings often follow, and cohesiveness, satisfaction, and other work-related attitudes can all be enhanced. But what about performance; does cooperation yield positive results in this respect as well? The answer, it appears, is somewhat mixed. In general, cooperation does seem to enhance performance on a wide range of tasks, and in a wide range of settings. Indeed, a survey of more than 120 separate studies designed to compare productivity under cooperative, competitive, and individualistic condi-

FIGURE 12.5 *Reaching Complex Decisions: When Cooperation Is* Not *Always Superior.*
When groups working on a complex problem reached their decisions through consensus, those instructed to cooperate took less time to complete their work than those told to compete. When the groups reached their decisions through voting, however, such differences failed to appear. These findings indicate that cooperation does not facilitate performance under all conditions. (Source: Based on data from Tjosvold and Field, 1984; see Note 16.)

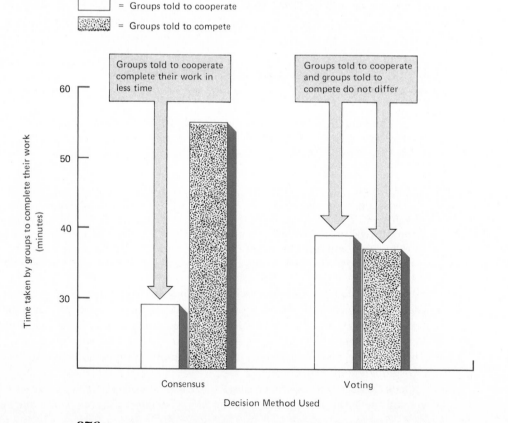

tions points to the following basic conclusions: cooperation generally has a significant edge.[15] It yields higher levels of performance than either of the other two approaches.

It is also important to note, however, that there appear to be definite limits on this generalization. First, as we noted earlier in our discussion of the study carried out by Cheng (see page 373), coordination seems to produce positive effects on performance only under conditions where the individuals or units involved are highly interdependent. When, in contrast, they can carry out their functions in an independent manner, it seems to have little impact upon performance.

Second, and related to the above, when individuals, groups, or units are largely independent, competition—not cooperation—may yield higher levels of performance. This is the case because it can provide a substantial boost to motivation, with all that this implies for both individual and group productivity.

Third, recent findings suggest that cooperation may sometimes fail to enhance one key organizational process: decision-making. This fact is illustrated clearly by an investigation carried out by Tjosvold and Field.[16] These researchers arranged for groups of four or five individuals to work on a complex problem (the NASA "lost on the moon" problem discussed earlier in Chapter 11) under either cooperative or competitive instructions. In the cooperative condition, participants were told to try to work together for mutual benefit. In the competitive condition, in contrast, they were instructed to try to win or to outdo the others. Another aspect of the study involved the manner in which the groups reached their final decision. For half of the subjects, this was accomplished through voting, in accordance with the "majority wins" rule. For the remainder, it involved reaching a shared consensus—a decision everyone could accept. Several measures of group performance were obtained (e.g., the accuracy of the decisions reached; the amount of time it took groups to reach their decisions). In addition, subjects rated the effectiveness of their group.

Results were complex, and open to several interpretations. However, one point seems clear: cooperation did *not* enhance performance on the problem solving task in all cases. As shown in Figure 12.5, groups instructed to cooperate took less time to complete their discussions than groups instructed to compete when the consensus decision method was used. However, they did not show a similar advantage when decisions were reached through voting. Further, while participants told to cooperate did rate their groups as more effective than those told to compete when the consensus method was employed, the opposite was true when voting procedures were followed.

In sum, existing evidence concerning the impact of cooperation on performance points to the following conclusions. Generally, a high level of coordination between the individuals, groups, or units within an organization contributes to improved productivity. However, there are some contexts in which this generalization does not hold true, and some circumstances under which competition may actually prove superior. Thus, while cooperation/coordination *is* often a plus, its value should be examined on a case-by-case and process-by-process basis. Only then can the level of coordination most appropriate for a specific organization be determined.

---

processes we can readily recognize (we know it when we see it), but find difficult to define (at least in highly precise terms). One definition that has proven very useful in the study of conflict, however, is as follows: *conflict involves direct confrontations between groups or individuals, usually arising in situations where each side perceives that the other is about to frustrate (or has already frustrated) its major interests.*[18] In short, the key elements in conflict seem to include (1) opposing interests between the persons or groups involved; (2) recognition of such opposition; and (3) the belief, by each side, that the other is out to thwart these essential concerns. Because conflict is so widespread in organizations, you are certain to encounter it yourself during your career. To help you understand this process more clearly, and perhaps to cope with it more effectively, we will consider several of its major aspects. First, we will examine several causes of conflict—factors that lead to its emergence in organizational settings. Second, we will turn to some of its important effects. These, you may be surprised to learn, can be beneficial as well as harmful. Finally, we will focus on several tactics for resolving or *managing* conflict—procedures for directing it into constructive rather than destructive pathways.

Conflict: Its Major Causes

As we noted above, conflict seems to center around the issue of opposing interests. While this is the basic ingredient in its occurrence, however, many other factors, too, play a role in its emergence. Several of these are outlined below.

Limited resources: "We've got to get our share."   No organization, no matter how successful, has unlimited resources. Space, money, equipment, materials, labor—all are in short supply relative to what most persons feel would be ideal. This basic fact, in turn, points to a key source of conflict: disagreement over how resources that *are* available should be divided. Because of the "self-serving bias" and related factors (refer to Chapter 4), each person or group tends to ask for more than the others feel is fair. The result: bitter disputes over this issue often erupt. Any list of the causes of organizational conflict, therefore, should begin with the struggle over limited resources firmly at the top.

Interdependence: "Why can't they do their job right?"   In most organizations, various units, groups, and individuals are highly interdependent. In fact, they cannot complete their work unless they receive appropriate input from others. For example, in a factory, all necessary supplies must be on hand for production to proceed; all parts must be available prior to final assembly; and assembly must be completed before products can be painted or tested. Such interdependence often serves as a major source of conflict. The reason for this is simple: each group or department requires input from others. When it is delayed, not provided, or supplied in an inadequate form, work in the affected units is disrupted. Such thwarting, in turn, initiates strong conflict. It is partly for this reason, of course, that coordination is so essential to organizations. When it fails, conflict is usually not far behind.

Ambiguity over responsibility: "That's not part of our job."   To illustrate a third major cause of organizational conflict, let's return to the second brief story on page 375—the one concerning friction between Operations and Maintenance. If members of these departments were questioned, statements such as these might be encountered. *Maintenance employee:* "They're never careful to keep scraps away from the filters. That clogs them up and makes a mess. If they'd only do that one thing, it would save us a heck of a lot of trouble." *Operations employee:* "They're always trying to get us to do their job. *They're* supposed to check on things around here, so why should we be bothered? We've got enough to do as it is."

As you can see, there is disagreement in this company about just what tasks members of the two departments are supposed to perform. This, in turn, stems from a degree of *ambiguity* over their basic responsibilities. Unfortunately, this kind of uncertainty is far from rare. "Gray areas" often form between departments—

regions in which neither is willing to accept responsibility. This is especially likely to occur in situations where new technology or procedures have recently been introduced, but it can develop in other settings as well. In any case, permitting such ambiguity to persist is usually a serious mistake. When it occurs, each side typically perceives the other as the one that should be performing unpleasant or demanding duties. The result: a continuing source of friction and conflict develops.

Group membership and identity: "Us versus them." Yet another potential source of organizational conflict—certain effects of *group membership*—is more subtle (but no less damaging) than the ones we have considered so far. It centers around the fact that once individuals become members of specific departments, units, or divisions, and accept the norms and values of these groups, their perceptions of other members of their organizations may be altered. They begin to view people outside their own unit as somehow different, less worthy, and less competent than those within it. Further, they tend to emphasize the positive attributes of their own group or unit, while ignoring its faults or weaknesses. The ultimate result of this process may be the initiation of costly conflicts.[19] After all, if individuals in each unit or group are fiercely loyal to their own "turf," they are likely to lose sight of shared organization-wide goals and to focus, instead, on pursuing their own narrow self-interests. Moreover, once conflict begins, these tendencies to divide the social world into "us" and "them" often strengthen, with the result that conflict, too, is intensified. Such reactions, then, can be a major factor in the initiation and persistence of costly conflicts.

Reward structures: "It's us or them." Suppose that in a given company, bonuses and raises are distributed to production employees on the basis of total output: the higher their overall production, the larger rewards they receive. In contrast, imagine that among service personnel (the people who must deal with customer complaints), rewards are linked to total costs: the lower these are during a given period, the larger their raises and bonuses. Is there a potential for conflict in this situation? Absolutely. From the point of view of production employees, faster is better—the more they produce, the higher their rewards. If the products they manufacture are of poor quality and likely to fail, who cares? It's not *their* problem. In contrast, from the point of view of service employees, quality is the key: the higher the standards, the larger their benefits. In a sense, therefore, some degree of conflict between these two groups is practically assured. The *reward system* adopted by their company pits the interests of one against those of the other. Obviously, this is an issue worth considering when such systems—or changes in them—are planned.

Interpersonal relations: "I'll remember that . . ." Most of the causes of conflict we have considered so far relate to aspects of organizations—their structure, resources, reward systems, and so on. Yet, in many cases, conflict occurs between individuals: it is *interpersonal* rather than *intergroup* in nature. This fact calls attention to another cause of conflict in work settings: faulty interpersonal relations between key individuals.

Sad to relate, many serious organizational conflicts seem to begin because two or more persons rub each other the wrong way, because each feels that *they* have

"Drop back soon, Benzinger. It's always nice besting you again."

FIGURE 12.6   *Faulty Interpersonal Relations: One Cause of Organizational Conflict.*
The "winner" in this situation obviously enjoys his victory. However, he is probably assuring
himself of future trouble: causing others to "lose face" is a dangerous, conflict-inducing tactic.
(Source: Drawing by Lorenz; © 1980 The New Yorker Magazine, Inc.)

the right to exert influence over others, because one has caused the other to look
foolish or "lose face" (see Figure 12.6), or because they have misunderstood the
others' motives.[20] The fact that such events can lie at the root of even serious
organizational conflicts probably strikes you as somewhat disturbing. After all, it is
comforting to believe that most individuals operate in a rational manner, and can
put their personal feelings out of the picture. Unfortunately, much evidence suggests
that they cannot.[21] Most persons find it difficult, if not impossible, to ignore their
feelings, emotions, and dislikes, or to prevent them from influencing their judgments and behavior. Indeed, such effects often occur even in the face of vigorous
efforts to hold them to a minimum. Thus, careful analysis indicates that many
organizational conflicts derive as much from hurt feelings, bruised egos, faulty
perceptions, and longstanding grudges as from directly opposing interests. In situations where a persistent or costly conflict cannot be readily explained in terms of the
organizational factors considered previously, therefore, it is useful to search for
them in this other arena. The chances are good that they will soon be identified.
(For a concrete example of the role of interpersonal factors in costly organizational
conflicts, please see the **Case in Point** insert on page 381.)

"I Never Forget My Enemies"

Melanie Williams is puzzled, and with good cause. For the past two hours she's done everything except stand on her head to convince Rex Breckman, the head of her department, to change his mind.

"Oh come on already, Rex," she mutters shaking her head. "Why are you being so stubborn? You *know* the plan's a good one, so why not accept it, be gracious, and win a few friends in the bargain?"

"No way," Rex answers. "If I've told you once, I've told you ten times: I don't like it, and I'm not going to get behind it."

Rex is referring to a new incentive pay plan devised by Frank Adams, head of Personnel. The plan has been well received throughout the company and Frank has done a good job of lobbying for it. Thus, if it weren't for Rex's resistance, it would probably have a good chance of being adopted. As things stand, though, few people are willing to risk the wrath of the highly-regarded head of Finance and Accounting; he simply has too much power in the company.

"Look, tell me once more why you feel it won't work," Melanie declares. "I want to get it straight so I can explain it to everyone downstairs. They don't know *what's* going on."

"Hmph!" Rex exclaims. "It seems perfectly simple to me. I just don't believe our people are going to put out more effort to get a piece of a pie that doesn't exist. They aren't built that way. And another thing: they'll *never* believe we're going to share extra profits with them. It just doesn't fit with our labor history."

"But Rex, that just isn't so. People down on the floor are pretty excited. I know—I've spoken to them. They *do* believe that it's going to be a new ball-game. I mean, they can read, they know what's happening in terms of international competition."

"I don't care, I'm still not for 'Adams' Folly,' and I never will be. It won't work, and that's all there is to it!" At this, Rex pounds his fist on the table, and begins to rise. Melanie motions for him to stop.

"You know, Rex, I've worked with you for—let me see—is it six years already? And in all that time I've always felt you were one of the most reasonable and level-headed people I'd met. But now, the way you're acting, I'm beginning to wonder. To be perfectly honest, I think there's more to it than you're letting on. Come on, you can tell *me*."

Rex pauses, thinks for a moment, and then responds. "O.K., I'll tell you something I've never told anyone else—I trust you that much. You want to know why I'm against this plan? I'll tell you: it's because Adams is behind it. I've been waiting a long time to get back at him and sink one of his pet projects. And now, finally, I can do it. He's really put his prestige on the line, and oh boy, am I ever going to crush it!"

"But what did he ever do to make you so angry?" Melanie asks. "You've always seemed to get along OK"

"It goes back a long way—long before your time. We were both at Ortex then, and I thought he was a real friend—someone I could count on. Well, he stabbed me in the back, that's what he did. We've both been a lot of places and held a lot of jobs since then, but it makes no difference. I'm going to nail him now for sure."

"It happened when you were at Ortex? That must be over fifteen years ago. You mean you've held a grudge that long?"

Rex looks at her with cold fire in his eyes. "Oh, fifteen years isn't so long," he answers in a steely voice. "And besides, *I never forget my enemies*."

Questions

(1) Do you think Frank Adams is aware of Rex's grudge toward him?

(2) Is there anything Adams could do to eliminate these old "hard feelings," and so possibly win Rex's support for his plan?

(3) Is Rex Breckman justified in trying to get even with his old enemy in the way he has chosen?

(4) If you were Melanie, what would you do in this situation?

Conflict: Its Major Effects

As used in everyday speech, the word *conflict* has a strongly negative tinge: it seems to imply negative emotions, destructive actions, and harmful outcomes. In fact, however, when it occurs in organizations, it operates like the proverbial "two-edged sword." Depending on why it develops, who it involves, and how it unfolds, conflict can yield beneficial as well as harmful results. Because both its positive and negative effects are quite varied in scope, we will consider them separately.

Conflict: The negative side of the coin.   Some of the negative effects produced by conflict are obvious, and require little comment. For example, it often generates strong negative feelings among the persons concerned, and can be quite stressful (refer to Chapter 7). It frequently interferes with communication between individuals, groups, or units, and in this way all but eliminates coordination between them. And it diverts needed energies from performance and the attainment of basic goals. In all these ways, it can seriously interfere with organizational effectiveness.

Other effects of conflict are somewhat more subtle, and can sometimes be overlooked. First, it has been found that conflict between groups often encourages their leaders to shift from participative to authoritarian styles.[22] The reason for this seems to be simple: groups experiencing stress require firm direction from their leaders. Recognizing this fact, these persons adopt more authoritarian tactics when conflict develops. As a result of such changes, groups experiencing conflict tend to be far less pleasant places in which to work than ones not faced with this form of stress.

Second, conflict increases the tendency of both sides to engage in *negative stereotyping*. As we noted earlier, the members of opposing groups or units tend to emphasize the differences between themselves and their opponents, and to view them in an increasingly negative light. "You know what Staff people are like." "How can you trust anyone in Marketing?" "No one back at headquarters cares a fig about us poor souls out in the boonies." Statements such as these capture the essence of this type of rigid "us versus them" thinking.

Finally, conflict leads each side to close ranks and emphasize loyalty to their own department or group. Anyone who suggests, even tentatively, that the other side's position has some merit is viewed as a traitor, and is severely criticized. As a result, it becomes increasingly difficult for opponents to take each other's perspective—a development that sharply reduces the likelihood of an effective compromise.

In sum, conflict within organizations produces many negative results, and can, as Blake and Mouton have recently noted, be costly indeed.[23]

Conflict: The positive side of the coin.   The picture is not entirely bleak, however. While conflict often exerts a disruptive impact upon organizations, it can, under appropriate circumstances, also yield important benefits. First, conflict often serves to bring problems that have previously been ignored out into the open. Since recognition of such difficulties is an essential first step to their solution, conflict can sometimes be useful in this respect.

Second, conflict often encourages the consideration of new ideas and approaches. In short, it facilitates innovation and change. This is so because once open conflict erupts, an organization *cannot* go on conducting business as usual. The need for new policies, new procedures, or a new structure is made clear, and appropriate change may follow.

Third, because conflict enhances group loyalty, it can increase motivation and performance within the groups or units involved. Each strives to attain even higher levels of excellence than before, both to confirm its own positive self-image, and to outdo its rival.

Finally, and related to the above, the opposing sides to a conflict may carefully monitor each other's performance, so that they will know just where they stand vis-à-vis their opponent. Such scrutiny, too, can enhance motivation and performance.[24]

In these ways, conflict can actually contribute to organizational effectiveness. It is important to note, however, that such benefits will occur only when conflict is carefully managed, and does not get out of control. If it is permitted to become extreme, rationality—and the possible gains just described—may both disappear. Assuming that such pitfalls are avoided, however, conflict *can* play a useful role. (Please refer to Figure 12.7 for a summary of both the potential costs and benefits of conflict.)

FIGURE 12.7   *Conflict: Its Potential Costs and Benefits.*
Contrary to popular belief, conflict can produce beneficial as well as harmful effects.

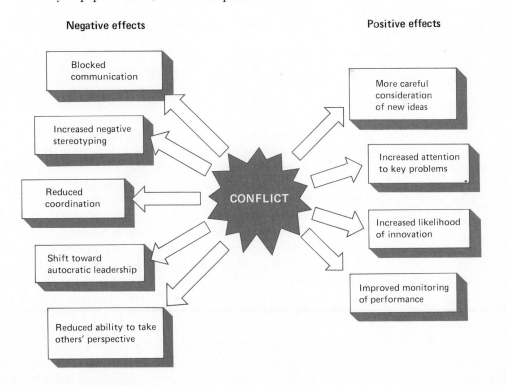

Conflict: Its Effective Management

As we have just pointed out, conflict can produce positive as well as negative effects. Yet, one fact about it is clear: if allowed to continue, it will, ultimately, exert a disruptive influence on organizational functioning. As conflicts persist, they drain more and more resources that would be better used for other purposes. Even worse, considerable evidence suggests that the longer a conflict continues, and so the more each side has invested in it, the harder it is to bring it to an end.[25] Previous losses must be justified in any agreement, and these soon become too large to permit much room for maneuver. Clearly, then, there are strong reasons for attempting to resolve conflicts in a rapid and efficient manner. Fortunately, a number of tactics for reaching this goal appear to exist.[26] Several that seem especially effective will now be described.

Bargaining: The attainment of integrative solutions. By far the most common tactic used for resolving organizational conflicts is **bargaining**—a process in which the opposing sides exchange offers, counteroffers, and concessions directly or through representatives. If the process is successful, a solution acceptable to both sides is reached, and the conflict is brought to a close. The catch, of course, is that often, the process is *not* successful. Negotiations deadlock, with the result that the conflict is intensified rather than ended. A key question about bargaining, then, is this: What factors either increase or reduce the likelihood of its success? Research findings point to some intriguing conclusions.

First, with respect to conditions that increase the chances of an agreement, several factors seem useful. For example, intervention by a third party (a mediator or arbitrator) can sometimes help. Moreover, the beneficial effects of such assistance seem to be greatest under just those conditions where they are needed most: when the conflict is both long-lasting and intense.[27] Similarly, as we noted in our discussion of cooperation, open and direct communication between the opposing sides, as long as it does not involve the use of threats or other "power plays," can be useful. Third, a willingness to make concessions—even very small ones—often facilitates agreement. The reason for this is clear: when one side to a conflict makes such a move, the rule of reciprocity dictates that the other should do likewise. The result: a path to further, mutual compromise is opened.[28]

Perhaps the single most important factor contributing to success in bargaining, however, involves participants' overall orientation toward this process. Growing evidence suggests that when persons or groups participating in negotiations perceive their task as that of attaining *integrative solutions*—ones that reconcile the underlying interests of both sides—the chances for agreement are greatly enhanced. If, in contrast, they perceive their task as that of defeating their opponent, and maximizing their own outcomes, the likelihood of a satisfactory resolution is sharply reduced.[29] Similarly, findings reported recently by Neale and Bazerman suggest that negotiators who view a situation largely in terms of potential gains are more likely to make concessions and obtain positive results than ones who view it largely in terms of potential losses.[30] It seems crucial, then, that bargainers approach this process from a constructive perspective.

In contrast, several additional factors tend to *reduce* the effectiveness of bargaining in resolving conflicts. First, if one or both sides believe that they have an "out"—some other option aside from reaching agreement with their opponent— they may refuse to grant concessions and so block movement toward agreement.[31] Second, as we noted in Chapter 11, when negotiators have low power vis-á-vis the persons they represent, they may adopt a relatively "tough" and inflexible stance and so reduce the chances of a satisfactory accord. Finally, as you might expect, when negotiators believe that they will have to deal with one another again on future occasions (as would be true in many organizations), they tend to seek more integrative agreements than if they do not anticipate further interactions with their opponents.[32]

To the extent that groups or their representatives take careful account of these and related factors, bargaining can yield positive results. When it does, it can be a highly effective technique for resolving even prolonged and bitter conflicts.

The induction of superordinate goals. At several points in this chapter, we have noted that individuals often tend to divide the world into two opposing camps: "them" and "us." Specifically, they perceive members of their own group as quite different from—and usually better than—people belonging to other groups. These dual tendencies to magnify the differences between one's own group and others and to disparage such "outsiders" appear to be very powerful, and are as common in organizations as in other settings.[33] Further, they seem to play a central role in many costly conflicts between various departments, divisions, and subunits.[34] How, then, can they be countered? One answer, suggested by research findings, is through the induction of **superordinate goals**—ones that tie the interests of the two sides together rather than drive them apart. The basic idea behind this approach is simple: by inducing the parties to a conflict both to focus on and to work toward common objectives, the barriers between them—ones that interfere with communication, coordination, and agreement—are weakened. As a result, the chances for cooperation, rather than conflict, are sharply enhanced.

One example of this process in operation is provided by events occurring in the U.S. automobile industry during the early 1980s. Faced with growing competition from foreign companies, labor and management—traditional opponents with a long-standing history of bitter conflicts—agreed to adopt a different strategy. They would join forces (at least temporarily), in order to attain a common goal: turning back the wave of imports that threatened their joint livelihood. Employees agreed to reductions in pay and other benefits, while management agreed to use such savings to retain as many jobs as possible. The results were dramatic: within a few years, the companies involved were generating record-setting profits instead of record-breaking losses. Of course, the total situation was much more complex than we have suggested here, and many others factors, too, played a role (e.g., government-established quotas on imports). However, there seems little doubt that the recognition of shared, superordinate goals made some contribution.

The benefits of superordinate goals have also been demonstrated in well-known research carried out by Sherif and his colleagues.[35] These investigators found that when opposing groups had to work together to achieve common goals their perceptions of each other improved, while conflict decreased. In sum, it appears that either reminding the parties of their shared goals (e.g., the overall success of their organization) or actually establishing such objectives can be one effective means for resolving conflict.

The interface conflict-solving model: A practical technique for resolving costly organizational conflicts. Another, and highly promising, approach to reducing organizational conflicts has recently been proposed by Blake and Mouton.[36] This technique, known an the **interface conflict-solving model**, focuses directly on disagreements between various departments or units. The basic rationale behind it is consistent with our comments about the role of group membership in many conflicts. Specifically, this model takes careful account of the fact that many confrontations between organizational units stem from the tendencies of each to (1) perceive itself more favorably than its opponent, (2) to emphasize group loyalty over the other considerations, and (3) to focus on group or unit goals while losing sight of broader organizational ones. In order to counteract such tendencies, the model recommends a process involving six specific steps.

First, representatives of each side meet individually and attempt to develop a description of what *ideal* relations between their units would be like. It is crucial that the people involved be ones who are influential in their groups—ones who can implement change if they decide this is useful. Second, the two sides then meet in an effort to integrate their views; they try to agree on a single description of what ideal relations between them should be like. In a third step, the two sides meet independently once again, to develop descriptions of their current, actual relations. The fourth task is that of integrating these often inconsistent pictures of the present situation. In a fifth step, the two sides work together to develop a detailed plan for change. Finally, times are selected for follow-up discussions designed to assess progress, and to plan further steps. (Please refer to Figure 12.8.)

The interface conflict-solving model has already been employed in a wide range of settings (e.g., conflicts between specific departments, union-management disputes, conflicts between parent and subsidiary organizations). In each case, it has produced lasting, beneficial results. Indeed, in some instances, it has been successful in resolving conflicts that have persisted for months or even years.[37] For

FIGURE 12.8   *The Interface Conflict-Solving Model: A Summary.*
As shown here, the *interface conflict-solving model* consists of six basic steps. (Source: Based on suggestions by Blake and Mouton, 1984; see Note 19.)

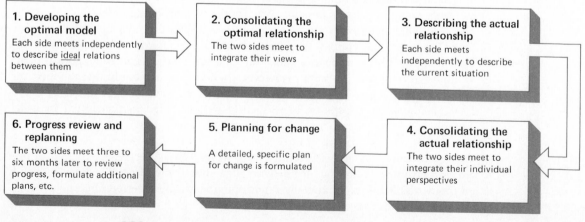

1. **Developing the optimal model**
Each side meets independently to describe <u>ideal</u> relations between them

2. **Consolidating the optimal relationship**
The two sides meet to integrate their views

3. **Describing the actual relationship**
Each side meets independently to describe the current situation

6. **Progress review and replanning**
The two sides meet three to six months later to review progress, formulate additional plans, etc.

5. **Planning for change**
A detailed, specific plan for change is formulated

4. **Consolidating the actual relationship**
The two sides meet to integrate their individual perspectives

27. J. M. Hiltrop and J. Z. Rubin (1982). Effects of intervention mode and conflict of interest in dispute resolution. *Journal of Personality and Social Psychology, 42*, 665–672.

28. See Note 4.

29. See Note 26.

30. M. A. Neale and M. H. Bazerman (1985). The effects of framing and negotiator overconfidence on bargaining behaviors and outcomes. *Academy of Management Journal, 28*, 34–49.

31. S. S. Komorita, C. W. Lapworth, and T. M. Tuomonis (1981). The effects of certain versus risky alternatives in bargaining. *Journal of Experimental Social Psychology, 17*, 525–544.

32. O. Ben-Yoav and D. G. Pruitt (1984). Resistance to yielding and the expectation of cooperative future interaction in negotiation. *Journal of Experimental Social Psychology, 20*, 323–335.

33. D. A. Wilder and J. E. Thompson (1980). Intergroup contact with independent manipulations of ingroup and out-group interaction. *Journal of Personality and Social Psychology, 38*, 589–603.

34. See Note 19.

35. M. Sherif, O. J. Harvey, B. J. White, W. E. Hood, and C. W. Sherif (1961). *Intergroup conflict and cooperation: The Robber's Cave experiment.* Norman: University of Oklahoma.

36. See Note 19.

37. See Note 19.

38. R. A. Baron (1985). Reducing organizational conflict: The role of attributions. *Journal of Applied Psychology, 70*, 434–441.

39. R. A. Baron (1984). Reducing organizational conflict: An incompatible response approach. *Journal of Applied Psychology, 69*, 272–279.

40. M. A. Rahim (1983). A measure of styles of handling interpersonal conflict. *Academy of Management Journal, 26*, 368–376.

41. P. Carnevale and A. M. Isen (1985). The influence of positive affect and visual access on the discovery of integrative solutions in bilateral negotiation. *Organizational Behavior and Human Decision Processes*, in press.

CHAPTER
13

AN OVERVIEW OF ORGANIZATIONAL DECISION MAKING

A General Model of Decision Making   Characteristics of Organizational Decisions

THE IMPERFECT NATURE OF INDIVIDUAL DECISIONS

The Rational-Economic Model: In Search of the Ideal Decision   The Administrative Model: Exploring the Limits of Human Rationality

GROUP DECISIONS: Do Too Many Cooks Spoil the Broth?

Comparing Group and Individual Decisions: When Are Two (or More) Heads Better Than One?   Improving the Effectiveness of Group Decisions: Some Techniques   The Riskiness of Group Decisions: A Case of Group Polarization

SPECIAL INSERTS

FOCUS ON BEHAVIOR   Commitment to Unsuccessful Decisions: Throwing Good Money after Bad?

FROM THE MANAGER'S PERSPECTIVE   Preventing Groupthink: Some Guidelines this reason, it seems to merit careful attention from any organization faced with persistent, harmful conflict.

Interpersonal approaches: Reducing anger and resentment. Earlier, we noted that conflict can stem from interpersonal as well as from organizational factors. Serious disputes often develop in situations where one person has angered another, has misunderstood the motives behind an opponent's behavior, or has caused this individual to lose face in some manner. The strong, negative emotions generated in such instances often make it difficult for the people involved to listen to reason. Indeed, in some cases, feelings may run so high that the parties to the conflict will endure actual losses if this assures that their opponent, too, is injured. Can anything be done to lessen such reactions, and so to avoid wasteful conflicts? Fortunately, the answer appears to be "yes." The results of recent studies suggest that several techniques are effective in lessening the feelings of anger that so often contribute to the initiation and persistence of costly conflicts. One such approach involves efforts to convince one or both sides that their opponent's position stems not from personal grudges or a desire to defeat them and make them look foolish, but rather from the sincere belief that it is reasonable.[38] Apparently, when individuals attribute a "tough" stance by an opponent to such sincerity, their willingness to compromise or collaborate is enhanced.

A second technique for reducing negative feelings in situations with the potential for conflict is based on a simple fact: it is extremely difficult, if not impossible, for individuals to experience two incompatible emotions at once. For this reason, it may often be possible to eliminate even strong feelings of resentment, and so to reduce the likelihood of conflict, by inducing positive feelings among the parties involved. Evidence in support of this **incompatible response strategy** has recently been reported in a study conducted by the author.[39]

In this project, male and female subjects played the role of executives in a large organization, and discussed two issues currently facing their company: should it move to the Sunbelt, and should it invest heavily in the manufacture of a new product. One of the persons present was actually an accomplice of the experimenter, specially trained to disagree with whatever views the real subject happened to adopt. The style in which he disagreed, however, was systematically varied. In one condition, the accomplice did so in a calm and reasonable fashion (e.g., "I can see why you feel that way, but I guess I disagree.") In another, in contrast, he disagreed in a highly condescending manner (e.g., "Oh come on, how could anyone *possibly* feel that way?") A second aspect of the investigation took place after discussion of both issues was complete. At this time, the experimenter left the room for a few moments, ostensibly to get some needed forms. During this period, the accomplice either sat quietly, or engaged in one of the three actions designed to induce positive feelings, incompatible with anger or annoyance, among subjects. Specifically, he either offered them a snack, explained that he was very tense because of several important exams, or asked them to help him choose the funniest of several cartoons for use in a class project. Previous findings suggested that these behaviors would induce feelings of gratitude, empathy, and amusement, respectively. Finally, when the experimenter returned, participants completed a questionnaire on which they rated the accomplice on several dimensions (e.g., his likability, pleasantness), and indicated how they would respond to future conflicts with him.[40]

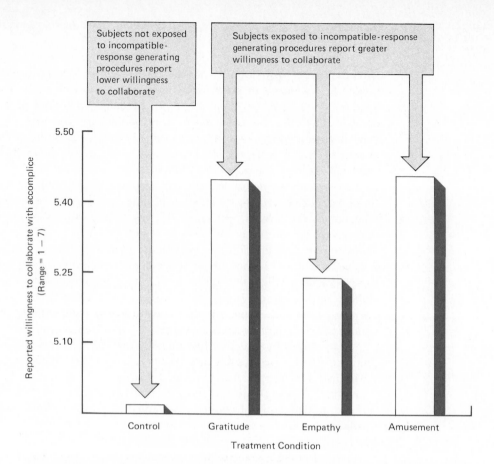

FIGURE 12.9   *The Incompatible Response Strategy: One Technique for Reducing Conflict.* Subjects exposed to procedures designed to induce positive emotional states incompatible with anger or resentment reported greater willingness to collaborate with an opponent than subjects not exposed to such procedures. These findings indicate that costly conflicts can sometimes be avoided through tactics focused on relations between the persons involved. (Source: Based on data from Baron, 1984; see Note 38.)

Results were both clear and encouraging. First, as you might expect, subjects assigned lower ratings to the accomplice, and reported a stronger likelihood of reacting negatively to him in future conflicts, when he had behaved in a condescending manner than in a reasonable one. Second, and of greater importance, they reported a greater willingness to collaborate with him when they had been exposed to the incompatible-response generating procedures than when they had not (refer to Figure 12.9).

These findings, and those of a related study indicating that negotiations are more successful when participants are in a pleasant than in a neutral mood, suggest that attention to the "emotional side" of conflict may be worth while.[41] Indeed, they point to the conclusion that eliminating the negative feelings that often accompany conflict may be an effective step toward eliminating this costly process itself.

SUMMARY

Coordination is essential for the effective functioning of most organizations. Yet, it is not always attained. Sometimes individuals or units *cooperate*, but on other occasions they fail to do so, or may even engage in open *competition*. Both individual and organizational factors determine which of these contrasting patterns develops. Individual factors important in this regard include reciprocity, communication, and group size. Organizational variables such as structure, and degree of interdependence are also important. Cooperation generally improves performance. Surprisingly, however, this is not always the case.

Conflict occurs when groups or individuals perceive that others are about to frustrate or have already frustrated their major interests. It stems from many factors including a struggle over limited resources, interdependence between units, and faulty interpersonal relations. Many of the effects produced by competition are negative in nature (e.g., it wastes valuable resources, interferes with effective communication). Sometimes, however, it can yield beneficial results. These include closer attention to important organizational problems, and enhanced openness to change. Several techniques for the management of conflict exist. Bargaining and the induction of superordinate goals are often effective. The *interface conflict-solving model* offers concrete suggestions for resolving costly organizational conflicts. Finally, several techniques that focus on the reduction of feelings of anger and resentment (e.g., the *incompatible response approach*) appear to be helpful.

KEY TERMS

bargaining: A process in which two or more sides exchange offers, counter-offers, and concessions in an effort to attain a mutually acceptable agreement.

competition: A process in which individuals or groups attempt to attain desired goals at the expense of others who also seek these goals.

competitors: Individuals who are primarily concerned with attaining better outcomes than others.

conflict: Confrontations between individuals or groups in situations where one or both sides perceives that the other has thwarted or is about to thwart its interests.

cooperation: A process in which individuals or groups work together to reach shared goals.

cooperators: Individuals who are primarily concerned with maximizing joint benefits—both their own outcomes and those of others.

diffusion of responsibility: The tendency of group members to feel less and less responsible for the group's performance or outcomes as group size increases.

equalizers: Individuals who wish to assure that they and others receive equal outcomes.

incompatible response strategy: A technique for reducing interpersonal conflict based on the induction of emotions incompatible with anger or resentment.

individualists: Persons who are primarily concerned with maximizing their own outcomes.

interface conflict-solving model: A set of procedures for eliminating costly conflicts between units or departments within an organization.

interorganizational coordination: Efforts by independent organizations to coordinate their activities or operations through a central management system.

reciprocity: The basic principle, followed by most individuals and groups, that others should be treated much in the way that *they* have acted.

superordinate goals: Goals shared by opposing groups. The establishment of such goals, or merely calling attention to their existence, is often helpful in reducing intergroup conflict.

NOTES

1. N. Eisenberg (ed.) (1982). *The development of prosocial behavior*. New York: Academic Press.

2. R. G. Geen and E. Donnerstein, eds. (1983). *Aggression: Theoretical and empirical reviews*. New York: Academic Press.

3. G. H. Shure, R. J. Meeker, and E. A. Hansford (1965). The effectiveness of pacifist strategies in bargaining games. *Journal of Conflict Resolution, 9,* 106–117.

4. D. G. Pruitt (1981). *Negotiation behavior*. New York: Academic Press.

5. S. S. Komorita and C. W. Lapworth (1982). Cooperative choice among individuals versus groups in an N-person dilemma situation. *Journal of Personality and Social Psychology, 42,* 487–496.

6. D. R. Forsyth (1983). *An introduction to group dynamics*. Monterey, Calif.: Brooks/Cole.

7. See Note 5.

8. P. G. Gyllenhammer (1977). *People at work*. Reading, Mass.: Addison-Wesley.

9. D. M. Kuhlman and D. L. Wimberley (1976). Expectations of choice behavior held by cooperators, competitors, and individualists across four classes of experimental games. *Journal of Personality and Social Psychology, 34,* 69–81.

10. G. P. Knight and A. F. Dubro (1984). Cooperative, competitive, and individualistic social values: An individualized regression and clustering approach. *Journal of Personality and Social Psychology, 46,* 98–105.

11. D. M. Kuhlman and A. F. J. Marshello (1975). Individual differences in game motivation as moderators of preprogrammed strategy effects in prisoner's dilemma. *Journal of Personality and Social Psychology, 32,* 922–932.

12. T. J. Peters and R. H. Waterman, Jr. (1982). *In search of excellence: Lessons from America's best-run companies*. New York: Warner Books.

13. J. L. Cheng (1983). Interdependence and coordination in organizations: A role-system analysis. *Academy of Management Journal, 26,* 156–162.

14. K. G. Provan (1984). Interorganizational cooperation and decision making autonomy in a consortium multihospital system. *Academy of Management Review, 9,* 494–504.

15. D. W. Johnson, G. Maruyama, R. Johnson, D. Nelson, and L. Skon (1981). Effects of cooperative, competitive, and individualistic goal structures on achievement: A meta-analysis. *Psychological Bulletin, 89,* 47–62.

16. D. Tjosvold and R. H. G. Field (1983). Effects of social context on consensus and majority vote decision making. *Academy of Management Journal, 26,* 500–506.

17. K. W. Thomas (1976). Conflict and conflict management. In M. Dunnette (ed.), *Handbook of industrial and organizational psychology*. Chicago: Rand McNally.

18. See Note 17.

19. R. R. Blake and J. S. Mouton (1984). *Solving costly organizational conflicts*. San Francisco: Jossey-Bass.

20. B. Kabanoff (1985). Potential influence structures as sources of interpersonal conflict in groups and organizations. *Organizational Behavior and Human Decision Processes, 36,* 113–141.

21. S. T. Fiske and S. E. Taylor (1984). *Social cognition*. Reading, Mass.: Addison-Wesley.

22. E. M. Fodor (1976). Group stress, authoritarian style of control and use of power. *Journal of Applied Psychology, 61,* 313–318.

23. See Note 19.

24. See Note 17.

25. J. Brockner, J. Z. Rubin, and E. Lang (1981). Face-saving and entrapment. *Journal of Experimental Social Psychology, 17,* 68–79.

26. D. G. Pruitt and P. Carnevale (1982). The development of integrative agreements. In V. Derlega and J. Grzelak (eds.), *Cooperation and helping behavior: Theories and research*. New York: Academic Press.

Decision Making in Organizations

(Pg. 409
to 418 only)

"It isn't going to be easy at the top," Graham Vivaldi thought to himself, "the important decisions made at the executive level really can be scary." The new thirty-seven year old vice president of Sunbelt Resorts was reflecting about the responsibility he had for making decisions involving millions of dollars and hundreds of people for one of the nation's fastest growing chains of hotels.

"For years as a hotel manager and assistant manager, I mostly carried out corporate decisions. Now, as a VP, I have to make those decisions myself." The decision that loomed so heavily this day was Graham's first big one. An option had arisen to acquire a small chain of resort hotels on the Gulf coast, and Sunbelt had a chance to take advantage of a potentially golden opportunity.

The price seemed right, and the units fit into Sunbelt's long-term growth plan. By acting now, a few years ahead of schedule, Sunbelt could take advantage of the savings from not having to build new units from the ground up. Renovation would be much less expensive, but still the purchase would put a huge drain on corporate finances. Cash flow was a problem, and with high interest rates, the cost of borrowing money would partially offset the bargain. Making things more difficult, Graham knew that if Sunbelt didn't purchase the chain, its closest competitor surely would.

The more Graham thought about the potential purchase, the more difficult he found the prospect of making a decision. There were just too many considerations, too many unknowns, and too many areas of expertise that he lacked to know what to do. After a few days of mulling it over the only thing Graham could decide was not to decide alone. So, this young VP assembled a group of Sunbelt's top corporate experts to help with the decision.

"Maybe a more seasoned executive would have taken a bold move by deciding for or against the acquisition alone," Graham thought to himself, "but this isn't the case." At this moment, Sunbelt's top accountants, real estate specialists, attorneys, and the other VPs filled the meeting room. Their job, Graham explained, would be to gather more complete information about the purchase to help make the decision. "Ladies and gentlemen," he said, "with your help, we will make this decision together."

Although this seemed like a good idea, it quickly became apparent that the group decision-making process wasn't going to be an easy one. Each executive saw the decision from his or her own special perspective. Not only did the accountants and the lawyers speak different languages, but they didn't get along. Those who were friendly toward each other were so close that they seemed more interested in covering each other's "corporate hides" than in making the best possible decision. Personality clashes and political battles now had to be contended with as well as the integrity of the decision itself.

It was 2:39 P.M., and little had been accomplished in over an hour's discussion. If nothing else, it became clear that drawing on the resources of the group would make getting anything done at all very difficult.

With good reason Graham began to have second thoughts about his group decision-making strategy. "Would I have been better off making the decision myself, or was using a group really the right thing?" These questions intrigued Graham as much as the decision regarding the acquisition itself. Deciding how to decide was going to be an important part of this young executive's entry into the corporate world.

Although you may not be a top executive accustomed to agonizing over the intricacies of an important corporate investment, you probably have no difficulty relating to Graham's dilemma. Anyone who has ever worked through a complex decision is doubtless aware of how difficult it is to consider *everything*. If you have ever been involved in committee work, you are probably only too familiar with how difficult it may be for a group of people, no matter how well-intentioned, to reach a decision. Thinking about the problems involved in making decisions in your own life may help you appreciate the importance of understanding **decision making** in organizations, where the stakes—both personal and financial—may be much greater.

This chapter will examine theories, research, and practical managerial techniques concerned with organizational decision making. Specifically, we will explore the ways individuals make decisions, and then look at the decision-making processes of groups. This will give us an opportunity to compare the quality of individual and group decisions on a variety of tasks and to present various methods of improving group decisions. Before we get to this, however, we will begin by taking a closer look at the general process of decision making and the varieties of decisions made in organizations.

AN OVERVIEW OF ORGANIZATIONAL DECISION MAKING

It is safe to begin our discussion with the statement that decision making is one of the most important—if not *the* most important—of all managerial activities.

FIGURE 13.1   Decision Making: A Common Job Role.
Making decisions—or in the case of this character, deciding to let others make decisions—is a primary managerial activity. (Source: King Features Syndicate.)

Management theorists and researchers agree that decision making represents one of the most common and most crucial work roles of the executive.[1] In fact, organizational scientist Herbert Simon, who won a Nobel Prize for his work on decision making, has gone so far as to describe decision making as *synonymous* with managing (see Figure 13.1).[2]

Given the central importance of decision making in organizational life, it makes sense to begin by highlighting some of the basics of the decision-making process and taking a look at the characteristics of organizational decisions.

A General Model of Decision Making

It is useful to conceptualize the decision-making process as a series of steps which groups or individuals take in solving problems. Although the various stages of the process may be difficult to identify in many situations, and the distinction between stages may be blurred in actual practice, a general model can help us appreciate the complex nature of organizational decision making.[3] With this in mind, we will present an eight-step model of the decision-making process in organizations (see Figure 13.2 on page 396).[4]

The first step in decision making is *problem identification*. In order to decide how to solve a problem, it must first be recognized and identified as existing. As an example, an executive may identify as a problem the fact that the company cannot meet its payroll obligations.

This step isn't always as easy as it sounds. You may recall from our discussion of social perception (see Chapter 4) that people do not always accurately perceive social situations. It is easy to imagine that someone may fail to recognize a problem if doing so makes him or her feel uncomfortable. Denying a problem may be the first impediment on the road to solving it!

After a problem is identified, the next step is to *define the objectives to be met in solving the problem*. It is important to conceive of problems so that possible solu-

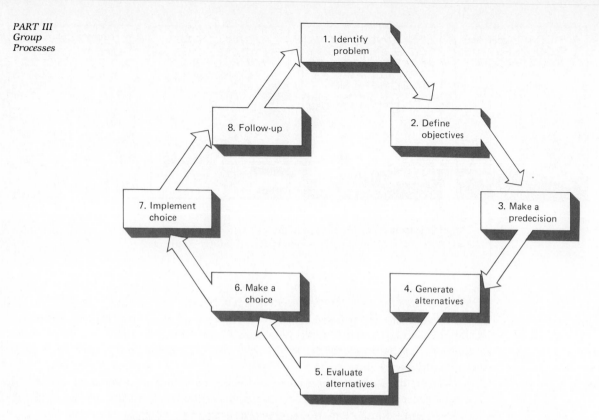

FIGURE 13.2 *The Decision-Making Process: A Basic Model.*
The decision-making process is concerned with identifying and solving problems as well as with generating and selecting alternative solutions. (Source: Based on information in Wedley and Field, 1984; see Note 4.)

tions can be identified. The problem identified in our example may be defined as not having enough money, or in business terms, "inadequate cash flow." By looking at the problem in this way, the objective becomes clear: increase available cash reserves. Any possible solution to the problem should be evaluated in light of reaching this objective. A good solution is one that attains it.

The third step in the decision-making process is to *make a* **predecision.** A predecision is a decision about how to make a decision. By assessing the type of problem in question, the style of the decision-maker, and other aspects of the situation, managers may decide to make a decision themselves, to delegate the decision to another, or to have the decision made by a group. Predecisions should be based on research findings about the nature of the decisions made under different circumstances—several of which will be reviewed later in this chapter. For many years managers have been relying on their own intuition, or better yet, on empirically-based information about organizational behavior (contained in books such as this) for the guidance needed to make predecisions. Recently, however, computer programs have been developed that summarize much of this information in a form that gives practicing managers ready access to a wealth of social science information that may help them decide how to decide.[5] We should note, of course, that such *decision support systems*, as they are called, can only be as good as the social science information that goes into them.

The fourth step in the process is *alternative generation*, the stage in which possible solutions to the problem are identified. In attempting to generate such solutions, people tend to rely on previously used approaches that might provide ready-made answers for them.[6] In our example, some possible ways of solving the revenue shortage problem would be to reduce the workforce, sell unnecessary equipment and material, increase sales, and so on. Because all these possibilities may not be equally feasible, the fifth step calls for *evaluating alternative solutions*. Which solution is best? What would be the most effective way of raising the revenue needed to meet the payroll? The various alternatives must be identified. Some may be more effective than others, and some may be more difficult to implement than others. For example, although increasing sales would help solve the problem, that is much easier said than done. It is a solution, but not an immediately practical one.

Next, in the sixth step, a *choice* is made. After several alternatives are evaluated, one that is considered acceptable is then chosen. As we will describe shortly, different models of decision making offer different views of how thoroughly people consider alternatives and how optimal their chosen alternatives are. The seventh step calls for *implementation of the chosen alternative*. That is, the chosen alternative is carried out.

The eighth and final step is *follow-up*. It is important to the success of organizations to monitor the effectiveness of the decisions they put into action. Does the problem still exist? Have any new problems been caused by implementing the solution? In other words, it is important to try to find out whether any attempted solution actually worked. For this reason, the decision-making process is presented as a circular one in Figure 13.2. If the solution works, the problem may be considered solved. If not, a new solution may have to be attempted.

This model makes it clear that decision making involves more than just making choices (step 6). By conceiving of the process in this broader way, our attention is directed to many important aspects of the organizational environment we might otherwise neglect if we focused solely on the choice-making phase of decision making.

Characteristics of Organizational Decisions

As you can readily see, there are many different types of decisions made in organizations. Some decisions may have far-reaching consequences (such as Sunbelt Resort's possible acquisition of new properties in our story on page 393), and others are more mundane and inconsequential (such as the decision to reorder office supplies). Organizations sometimes make decisions in situations in which the likely outcomes are well known (e.g., the decision to underwrite life insurance on the basis of actuarial tables), and sometimes in situations where the outcomes are much more uncertain (e.g., the decision to underwrite an insurance policy on a telecommunications satellite). These various examples are reflective of the two major characteristics of organizational decisions that we will describe: how structured or unstructured is the situation? and how much certainty or risk is involved in the decision?

Programmed versus non-programmed decisions: How well structured is the decision setting?   Think of a decision that is made repeatedly, according to a pre-established set of alternatives. For example, a word processing operator may decide to make a back-up diskette of the day's work, or a manager of a fast-food restaurant may decide to order more hamburger buns as the supply starts to get low. Decisions such as these are known as **programmed decisions**—they are routine decisions that rely on pre-determined courses of action.

By contrast, we may identify **non-programmed decisions** as ones for which there are no ready-made solutions. The decision-maker confronts a unique situation in which the solutions are novel. The research scientist attempting to find a cure for a rare disease faces a problem that is poorly structured. Unlike the order clerk whose course of action is clear, the scientist in this example must rely on creativity rather than pre-existing answers to solve the problem at hand.

In Table 13.1 we summarize the differences between programmed and non-programmed decisions with respect to three important questions. First, *what type of tasks* are involved? Programmed decisions are made on tasks that are common and routine, whereas non-programmed decisions are made on unique and novel tasks. Second, *how much reliance is there on organizational policies?* In making programmed decisions, the decision-maker can count on guidance from statements of organizational policy and procedure. However, non-programmed decisions require the use of creative solutions that are implemented for the first time; past solutions may provide little guidance. Finally, *who makes the decisions?* Not surprisingly, non-programmed decisions typically are made by upper-level organizational personnel, whereas the more routine, well structured decisions are usually relegated to lower-level personnel.[7]

TABLE 13.1   *Programmed and Non-programmed Decisions: A Comparison*
As summarized here, *programmed* and *non-programmed* decisions differ with respect to the types of tasks on which they are made, the degree to which solutions can be found in organizational policies, and who makes the decisions.

	Type of decision	
Question	Programmed decisions	Non-programmed decisions
1. What type of tasks are involved?	Routine	Creative
2. How much reliance is there on organizational policies?	Considerable guidance from past decisions	No guidance from past decisions
3. Typically, who makes the decisions?	Lower-level workers	Upper-level supervisors

Certain versus uncertain decisions: How much risk is involved?   Just think how easy it would be to make decisions if we knew what the future had in store! Making the best investment in the stock market would simply be a matter of looking up the changes in tomorrow's newspaper. Of course, we never know exactly what the future holds, but we can sometimes be more certain than at other times.

Degrees of certainty and uncertainty are expressed as statements of *risk*. All organizational decisions involve some degree of risk—ranging from complete certainty (no risk), to complete uncertainty—"a stab in the dark" (high risk). What makes an outcome risky or not is the *probability* of obtaining the desired result. Decision-makers attempt to obtain information about the probabilities, or odds, of certain events occurring, given that other events have occurred. For example, a financial analyst may report that a certain stock has risen 95 percent of the time after the prime rate has dropped, or a TV weather forecaster may report that the probability of precipitation is 50 percent. These data may be considered reports of *objective* probabilities because they are based on objective, verifiable data. Many decisions are also based on *subjective* probabilities—personal beliefs or hunches about what will happen. For example, an investor who decides to purchase a stock because the name of the issue reminds him of his mother, or a person who suspects it's going to rain because he just washed his car is basing these judgments on subjective probabilities. (The riskiness of decisions made by individuals as compared to groups is an important topic that will be discussed later in this chapter.)

Obviously, uncertainty is an undesirable characteristic of decision-making situations. We may view much of what a decision-maker does in an organization as attempting to reduce uncertainty so that a better decision can be made. Studies have shown that decision uncertainty can be reduced by establishing linkages with other organizations. The more one organization knows what another organization will do, the greater certainty that organization will have in making decisions.[8]

In general, what reduces uncertainty in decision-making situations? The answer is *information*. Information about the past and the present can be used to help make projections about the future. A modern executive's access to the data needed to make important decisions may be as close as the nearest computer terminal. Not surprisingly, the faster an organization has to change to operate effectively, the greater uncertainty it faces in its decisions, and the more information upon which it must rely to make decisions.[9] A good example of this can be seen in today's rapidly changing microcomputer business. Winners and losers in this market will depend, in part, on how well they can predict what products will succeed.

THE IMPERFECT NATURE OF INDIVIDUAL DECISIONS

We all like to think that we are "rational" people who make the best possible decisions. What does it mean to make a *rational* decision? Organizational scientists view rational decisions as ones that maximize the attainment of goals, whether they are the goals of a person, a group, or an entire organization.[10] In this section we will present two different approaches to decision making that make different assumptions about the rationality of individual decision-makers.

The Rational-Economic Model: In Search of the Ideal Decision

What would be the most rational way for an individual to go about making a decision? Economists interested in predicting market conditions and prices have relied on a **rational-economic model** of decision making, which assumes that decisions are perfect and rational in every way. An economically rational decision-maker will attempt to maximize his or her profits by systematically searching for the best possible solution to a problem. For this to occur, the decision-maker must have complete and perfect information, and must be able to process all this information in an accurate and unbiased fashion.[11]

In many respects, rational-economic decisions follow the same steps outlined in our general model of decision making (refer to Figure 13.2 on page 396). However, what makes the rational-economic approach special is that it calls for the decision-maker to recognize *all* alternative courses of action, and accurately and completely to evaluate each one. As such, it views decision-makers as attempting to make **optimal** decisions.

Of course, the rational-economic approach to decision making does not fully appreciate the fallibility of the human decision-maker. It assumes that people can have access to perfect information and can use it to make perfect decisions. As such, the model can be considered a *normative* (also called *prescriptive*) approach—one that describes how decision-makers ideally ought to behave to make the best possible decisions. It does not describe how decision-makers actually behave under most circumstances.

The Administrative Model: Exploring the Limits of Human Rationality

Not only may people be incapable of acting in a completely rational-economic manner, but we should note that the cost of such so-called rationality may be very high. In fact, research findings have shown that it may be more rational to not try to be so rational, after all. For example, in one recent study, Fredrickson and Mitchell found that considering all possible solutions to problems might not be such an effective way of solving them.[12] They surveyed over one hundred executives in the forest products industry concerning how comprehensively and exhaustively their organizations were likely to act in making different types of decisions. It was found that using this seemingly rational strategy was not linked to organizational prosperity. In fact, the more comprehensive the executives reported their organizations' decision strategies were, the poorer their organizations performed financially. Particularly when organizations operate in very unstable environments (ones in which there is often a great deal of change), the effort involved in making completely rational decisions can actually interfere with economic progress. In other words, the cost of attempting to make a rationally economic decision sometimes may be so high that it cuts into economic gains.

As an example of this idea, consider how a personnel department might go about hiring a new receptionist. After several applicants are interviewed, the personnel director might then select the best candidate seen so far and stop the selection process. Had the interviewer been following a rational-economic model, he or she would have had to interview all possible candidates before deciding on the *best* one. However, by ending the search after finding a candidate that was just *good enough*, the manager was using a much simpler approach. The decision strategy used by the personnel manager in this example typifiies an approach to decision making known as the **administrative model**.[13] This conceptualization recognizes that decision-makers may have a limited view of the problems confronting them. The number of solutions that can be recognized or implemented is limited by the capabilities of the decision-maker and the available resources of the organization. Also, decision-makers do not have perfect information about the consequences of their decisions, so they cannot tell which one is best.

So, how are decisions made according to the administrative model? Instead of considering all possible solutions, as suggested by the rational economic model, the administrative model recognizes that decision-makers consider solutions as they become available to them. Then, they decide on the first alternative that meets the decision-maker's criteria for acceptability. As such, the decision-maker selects a solution that may be just good enough, although not optimal. Such decisions are referred to as **satisficing decisions**. Of course, it is much easier for a decision-maker to make a satisficing decision than an optimal decision. In most decision-making situations, March and Simon note, satisficing decisions are acceptable and are more likely to be made than optimal ones.[14] They use the following analogy to compare the two types of decisions: making an optimal decision is like searching a haystack for the sharpest needle, but making a satisficing decision is like searching a haystack for a needle just sharp enough to sew with.

Making satisficing decisions is often aided in organizational settings by the use of heuristics. A **heuristic** is a rule of thumb that is used to simplify complex decision-making situations.[15] In management science there are many well-known heuristics used to make a wide range of decisions, such as how to compose an investment portfolio, how to evaluate the progress of stocks, and how to determine the location of warehouses.[16] We use heuristics in our everday lives as well, such as when playing games. For example, in playing chess, we follow the rule of "controlling the center of the board," or in playing blackjack we may "hit on 16, stick on 17." These are all rules that help simplify potentially more complex problems by suggesting an appropriate decision to make. The decisions we make may not always be correct, but applying heuristics often helps make satisficing decisions possible.

As we have already noted, it is often impractical for people to make completely rational decisions. This is fortunate because people are incapable of making optimal decisions. The administrative model recognizes the **bounded rationality** under which most organizational decision-makers must operate. The idea is that people lack the cognitive skills required to formulate and solve highly complex business problems in an objectively rational way.[17]

It should not be too surprising that the administrative model does a better job than the rational-economic model of describing how decision-makers actually behave. As such, the approach is said to be *descriptive* (also called *proscriptive*) in nature. This interest in examining the actual, imperfect behavior of decision-makers rather than specifying the ideal, economically rational behaviors that decision-makers ought to engage in lies at the heart of the distinction between the administrative and rational-economic models (please refer to the summary of these two approaches in Table 13.2 on page 402). Our point is not that decision-makers do

TABLE 13.2   *Two Models of Decision Making: A Summary.*
As summarized here, the *rational-economic model* and the *administrative model* of decision making differ with respect to several important assumptions.

Assumption	Rational-economic model	Administrative model
Rationality of decision-makers	perfect rationality	bounded rationality
Availability of information	complete access	limited access
Process of selecting alternatives	optimal	satisficing
Type of model	normative	descriptive

not desire to behave rationally, but that restrictions imposed by people's innate capabilities and by the social environment in which decisions are often made sometimes discourage "perfect" decisions.[18] What, then, are some of the factors limiting optimal decisions? It is to this question that we now turn our attention.

Some impediments to optimal decisions.   This picture of a simple-minded decision-maker operating in a complex world is supported by many studies that point to the seemingly confused and irrational decisions made by people. The imperfections of decision-makers take many forms. For example, people often focus on irrelevant information in making decisions.[19] They also fail to use all the information made available to them.[20] Obviously, *limitations in peoples' abilities to process complex information* adversely influences their decisions.

But it would be a mistake to focus on human cognitive shortcomings and not to consider other social and organizational factors that also interfere with seemingly more rational decisions. The situations organizational decision-makers face may further impair their ability to make decisions. One obvious factor is *time constraints*. Many important organizational decisions are made under severe time pressure. Under such circumstances, it is often not possible for more thorough decision-making processes to occur.[21] This is particularly true when organizations face crisis situations requiring immediate decisions. In such situations, decision-makers have been found to limit their search for information that may help them make optimal decisions.[22]

The quality of many organizational decisions also may be limited by *political "face saving" pressure*. In other words, decision-makers may make decisions that help them save face in some way, although the resulting decisions might not be in the best interest of their organization. The concern for his or her survival within the organization may override an individual's concern for making an optimal decision.[23] Instead, organizational decision-makers may be most concerned with making the best decision for themselves. For example, one person might attempt to justify an apparent failure by continuing to pursue that course of action—a decision driven by the attempt to justify a previous solution rather than a concern for the problem itself.[24] (For a detailed description of such a strategy, please see the **Focus** insert on page 404.)

Imagine, for example, how an employee may distort the available information needed to make a decision if the decision would jeopardize this person's job. Unfortunately, such misuses of information to support desired decisions are common (recall our discussion of the problem of distorted communication in Chapter

10). One study reported that a group of businessmen working on a group decision-making problems opted for making an adequate—although less than optimal—decision rather than risk generating serious conflicts with their fellow group members.[25] In an actual case, a proponent of inoculation for the swine flu reported having decided to go ahead with the inoculation program on the basis of only a 2 percent chance of an epidemic.[26] What we are saying is that people may make the decisions they *want* to make even though these may not be the optimal ones for the organizations involved.

Besides time constraints and political pressures that limit the quality of organizational decisions, we should also note the limitations imposed by moral and ethical constraints—what is known as *bounded discretion*.[27] According to this idea, decision-makers limit their actions to those that fall within the bounds of current moral and ethical standards. So, although it may optimize an organization's profits to engage in illegal activities such as stealing, ethical considerations may—and we hope will—discourage such actions.

GROUP DECISIONS: DO TOO MANY COOKS SPOIL THE BROTH?

Decision-making groups are a well established fact of modern organizational life. Groups such as *committees, study teams, task forces,* or *review panels* are often charged with the responsibility for making important business decisions. They are so common, in fact, that it has been said that some administrators spend as much as 80 percent of their time in meetings.[31] Given this, it is important to consider the strengths and weaknesses of using groups to make organizational decisions (please refer to the summary in Figure 13.3).

FIGURE 13.3   *Group Decisions: Weighing the Advantages and Disadvantages.*
As summarized here, there are both advantages and disadvantages to using groups to make decisions.

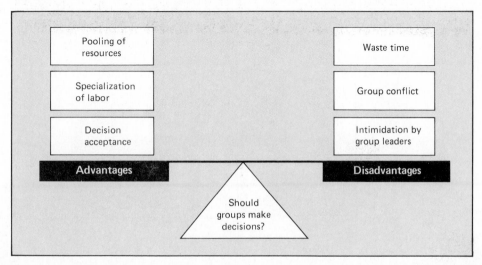

FOCUS ON BEHAVIOR

Commitment to Unsuccessful Decisions: Throwing Good Money after Bad?

Every day in organizations decisions are made, some of which are successful and some not. However, an unsuccessful outcome does not always lead the decision-makers involved to change their minds, back out, and pursue another course of action. To do so would be an admission of failure—an act that can be political suicide for a decision-maker. So, what do decision-makers do in the face of failure? Recent research has shown they often stand by their decisions in order to justify them.[28]

Recall how the United States government responded for many years to military losses in Vietnam. It escalated its involvement, because withdrawing troops would have been a costly admission of defeat.[29] The tendency for individuals and groups to escalate their commitment to a poor decision was studied in a

FIGURE 13.4 *Escalating Commitment to Unsuccessful Decisions: Some Evidence.*
Research has shown that individuals and groups responsible for making a previously unsuccessful decision (e.g., budgeting funds to a poorly performing organizational division) subsequently are more likely to escalate their commitment to that decision (such as by budgeting more funds to it) than are those who are not responsible for the decision. (Source: Based on data reported in Bazerman et al., 1984; see Note 30.)

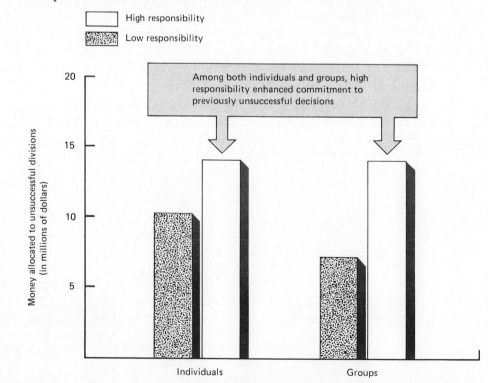

recent experiment by Bazerman, Giuliano, and Appleman.[30] The subjects in this investigation played the role of financial officers of an organization charged with the responsibility for deciding how to allocate funds to one of two organizational divisions. They either acted alone or as part of a small group working together as a decision-making committee. Participants were informed that three years ago one of these two divisions was given $10 million, and the other division was given no money. Subjects were asked to imagine either that they had made this past decision themselves (*high responsibility* condition), or that it had been made by other decision-makers (*low responsibility* condition). In the three years since the initial decision was made, the favored division was described as having suffered a steady loss in earnings. Now, subjects were given the opportunity to allocate $20 million—however they wanted—to the two divisions. How would they do it?

The results of the study, summarized in Figure 13.4, show the escalation of commitment we noted earlier, but only in the high-responsibility condition. This is, subjects (both individuals and groups), believing that the organizational division they previously favored had failed, now gave that group more money than they gave the other group (about $13 million out of $20 million). However, when subjects did not assume responsibility for the unsuccessful group's performance, they did *not* favor that group in their allocations. Not only did subjects in the high-responsibility condition show their commitment to their previously unsuccessful decision by making generous allocations to the poorly performing division, but they also reported feeling more committed to the previous decision and more confident that their funding decision would help "turn the situation around."

These results suggest that people may stick to decisions that appear to be irrational to others, but which are completely justifiable to themselves. Outsiders would claim that what the high-responsibility subjects in this study were doing was irrational: "throwing good money after bad." The decision-makers themselves, however, probably would claim that it would be irrational *not* to spend the extra money to support their past investments. If the investments made in this study were real rather than imaginary, time would tell how effective the decision really was. Regardless of the outcome, one thing is clear: what appears to be a "rational" decision is in the eye of the beholder.

There is little doubt that there is much to be gained from using decision-making groups. In fact, the authors of the bestselling book, *In Search of Excellence*, have claimed that the achievements of many of America's most successful business organizations are due, in part, to their effective use of decision-making groups—using their human resources to the fullest.[32] What potential advantages are to be gained from using groups? There are several. First, bringing people together possibly can increase the amount of knowledge and information needed to make good decisions. In other words, there may be a *pooling of resources*.[33] A related benefit is that in decision-making groups there can be a *specialization of labor*. With enough people around, it becomes possible for individuals to do only those tasks at which they are best, thereby also improving the potential quality of the group's efforts. Another benefit is that group decisions are likely to enjoy *greater acceptance* than individual decisions. People involved in making decisions may be expected to understand those decisions better and be more committed to carrying them out than decisions made for them by someone else.[34]

Of course, there are also some problems associated with using decision-making groups—ones that are probably only too familiar to you. One obvious drawback is that groups are likely to *waste time*. The time spent socializing before getting down to business may be a drain on the group and be very costly to organizations.[35] Another potential problem is that disagreement over important matters may breed ill-will and group conflict. Of course, constructive disagreement is not necessarily bad, and can actually lead to better group outcomes (see Chapter 12). However, with corporate power and personal pride at stake, it should not be at all surprising to find that lack of agreement can cause bad feelings to develop between group members. Finally, we may expect groups sometimes to be ineffective because of members' *intimidation by group leaders*. A group composed of several "yes-sayers" trying to please a dominant leader tends to discourage open and honest discussion of solutions.[36] Given these problems, it is no wonder that we often hear the old adage, "a camel is a horse put together by a committee."

As we have just observed, there are several pros and cons associated with using groups to make decisions (refer to the summary in Figure 13.3, page 403). A question arises, therefore, regarding when decisions should be made by groups and when they should be made by individuals. As we will see, there are circumstances under which one or the other is more appropriate.

Comparing Group and Individual Decisions: When Are Two (or More) Heads Better Than One?

An important determinant of whether decisions should be made by groups or individuals rests in one of the decision-making characteristics described earlier in this chapter—how well-structured or poorly structured is the problem about which a decision is to be made? As we shall see, the effectiveness of decisions made by groups and individuals differs greatly according to how well-structured the decision-making problem is.

Well-structured tasks. Imagine yourself working on a problem that requires several very specific steps and has a definite right or wrong answer—such as an arithmetic problem or an anagram puzzle. How would you expect to perform on such a *well-structured* task when working alone compared to when you are working with a group of people? Research findings indicate that groups performing well-structured tasks tend to make better, more accurate decisions, but take more time to reach them than individuals.

These effects are demonstrated in a study by Webber.[37] The subjects in this investigation worked either individually or in groups of five on several well-structured problems. Comparisons between groups and individuals were made with respect to accuracy (the number of problems solved correctly) and speed (the time it took to solve the problems). It was found that the average accuracy of groups of five persons working together was greater than the average accuracy of five individuals working alone. However, it was also found that groups were substantially slower than individuals in reaching solutions.

It is interesting to consider the reasons why these and other similar results arise. We already have noted the potential advantages that groups might enjoy in being able to pool their resources and combine their knowledge to generate a wide variety of approaches to problems.[38] For these benefits to be realized, however, it is essential that the group members have the necessary knowledge and skills to contribute to the group's task. In short, for there to be a beneficial effect of pooling of resources, there has to be something to pool. In other words, two heads may be better than one only when there is something in each of those heads.

This idea has been supported in a study in which lone individuals and pairs worked on solving several well-structured word problems.[39] On the basis of their performance on similar tasks performed one week before the experiment, subjects were classified according to their ability on the task. During the experiment, they performed the task either alone or in pairs of varying ability levels. It was found that two people of high ability working together performed better than any one person working alone. However, when two persons of low ability were paired, no such improvement occurred. These results suggest that pooling of resources may only help when there is something to pool. The "pooling of ignorance" does not help at all.

The practical managerial implications of this idea are clear: groups should be composed very carefully. It is not enough to consider how many persons are involved; the knowledge and skills they bring to the task must be evaluated too. Recall the group of experts Graham Vivaldi put together at Sunbelt Resorts in our opening story (page 393). There were accountants, lawyers, and several different specialists involved in this decision. Groups composed of complementary members having a variety of different perspectives have been found to perform better than groups composed of very similar members.[40] After all, two persons with similar perspectives may not add anything new to the group's task.

To summarize, groups tend to perform better than individuals on well-structured tasks. They can be expected to do so as long as the skills of the various group members complement each other, with each person adding something to the group. However, the slowness of group decisions on well-structured tasks may make them inappropriate in circumstances where quick decisions are critical.

Poorly structured tasks.　Most of the problems faced by organizations are *not* well-structured. They do not have any obvious steps or parts, and there is no obviously right or wrong answer. Such problems are reffered to as *poorly structured*. Creative thinking is required to make decisions on poorly structured tasks. A company deciding how to use a newly developed chemical in its consumer products is facing decisions on a poorly structured task. Similarly, the group at Sunbelt Resorts in our opening story (page 393) also faced a poorly structured problem. Although you would expect that the complexity of such creative problems would give groups a natural advantage, this is *not* the case. In fact, research has shown that on poorly structured, creative tasks, individuals perform better than groups.[41]

An approach to solving creative problems commonly used by groups is **brainstorming**.[42] This technique was developed by an advertising agency executive attempting to formulate creative, new ideas. The members of brainstorming groups are encouraged to present their ideas in an uncritical way and to freely and openly discuss all ideas on the floor. Specifically, members of brainstorming groups are required to: (a) avoid criticizing others' ideas, (b) share even far-out suggestions, (c) offer as many comments as possible, and (d) build upon others' ideas to create their own.

A laboratory study by Bouchard, Barsaloux, and Drauden compared the effectiveness of individuals and brainstorming groups working on creative problems.[43]

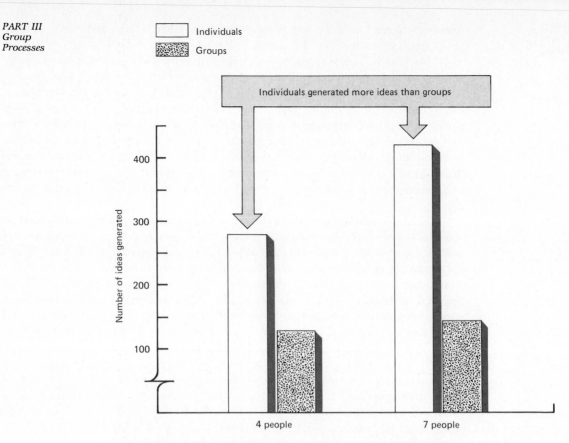

Individuals

Groups

FIGURE 13.5   *Brainstorming: Unsuccessful for Creative Problems.*
Research comparing brainstorming groups (composed of four members and seven members) to a like number of individuals has shown that individuals generate more solutions to creative problems. (Source: Based on data in Bouchard, Barsaloux, and Drauden, 1974; see Note 43.)

Specifically, subjects were given 35 minutes to consider the consequences of everybody suddenly going blind. Comparisons were made of the number of solutions generated by groups of four or seven people and a like number of individuals working on the same problem alone. As shown in Figure 13.5, individuals were far more productive than groups.

The relative ineffectiveness of brainstorming groups has also been demonstrated in a recent study by Yetton and Bottger.[44] The subjects, practicing managers and management graduate students, worked on the NASA moon survival problem described in earlier chapters. In it, participants imagine that they have crash-landed on the moon 200 miles from their base. They must then rank, in order of importance to their survival, fifteen pieces of equipment they have intact. It was found that the quality of the decisions made by interacting groups was no better than that of the best individual group member. In another study using this same problem, the investigators found that it is essential for the contributions of the most qualified group members to be counted most heavily in the group's decisions in order for the group to derive the benefits of that member's presence.[45] Thus, just as the pooling of

Preventing Groupthink: Some Guidelines

Considering how disastrous the effects of groupthink may be, it is important to examine some ways in which it can be avoided. Fortunately, several useful steps for minimizing the impact of groupthink upon group decisions exist, and can be readily summarized.[49]

1. Promote open inquiry. Remember, groupthink arises in response to group members' reluctance to "rock the boat." Group leaders should encourage group members to be skeptical of all solutions and to avoid reaching premature agreements. It sometimes helps to play the role of the "devil's advocate"—to intentionally find fault with a proposed solution. Although it doesn't pay to be argumentative, raising a nonthreatening question designed to force discussion of both sides of an issue can help.

2. Use subgroups. Because the decisions made by any one group may be the result of groupthink, basing decisions on the recommendations of two groups is a useful check. If the two groups disagree, a spirited discussion of their differences is likely to raise important issues. However, if the two groups agree, we can be relatively confident that they are both not the result of groupthink.[50]

3. Admit shortcomings. When groupthink occurs, group members feel very confident that they are doing the right thing. Such thoughts of perfection discourage people from considering opposing information. However, if group members acknowledge some of the flaws and limitations of their decisions, they may be more open to corrective influences. Try to keep in mind that no decision is perfect. Asking others to point out their misgivings about a group's decisions may help avoid the illusion of perfection that contributes to groupthink.

4. Hold second-chance meetings. Before implementing any decision it may be a good idea to hold a *second-chance meeting* in which group members are asked to express any doubts and to propose any new ideas they may have. Alfred P. Sloan, the former head of General Motors, is known to have postponed acting on important matters until some group disagreement developed.[51] As people get tired of working on problems they may hastily reach agreement on a solution. A second-chance meeting can be useful to see if the solution still seems as good after "sleeping on it."

We think that managers may find these suggestions simple enough to put into action. Given the alternative—facing the consequences of groupthink—they certainly warrant serious consideration.

---

resources influences the quality of decisions on well-structured tasks, it has a similar effect on poorly structured tasks as well.

Can the same adverse impact of decision-making groups be seen outside the laboratory? The answer is "yes." In fact, some of the most dramatic demonstrations of ineffective decision making by groups can be observed in the business world. Consider, for example, a recent comment by the successful chief executive officer of Chrysler Corporation, Lee Iacocca: "You always need committees, because that's where people share their knowledge and intentions. But when committees replace individuals—and Ford these days has more committees than General Motors—then productivity begins to decline."[46]

Groupthink. One reason why groups may fare so poorly on complex tasks lies in the dynamics of group interaction. As we have already noted in Chapter 11, when members of a group develop a very strong group spirit—or a high level of *cohesiveness*—they sometimes become so concerned about not disrupting the like-mindedness of the group that members may be reluctant to challenge the group's decisions. The tendency for group members to isolate themselves from information from outside the group that stems from group pressure is referred to as **group-think**.[47]

The concept of groupthink was proposed as an attempt to explain the ineffective decisions made by U.S. government officials that led to such fiascoes as the Bay of Pigs invasion in Cuba, the successful Japanese attack on Pearl Harbor, and the Vietnam war.[48] Analyses of these cases have revealed that, in each instance, the president's advisers actually *discouraged* the making of more effective decisions. Members of very cohesive groups may have more faith in their group's decisions than any discrepant idea they may have. As a result, they may suspend their own critical thinking in favor of conforming to the group. When group members become fiercely loyal to each other they may ignore information from other sources if it challenges the group's decisions. The result of this process is that the group's decisions may be completely uninformed, irrational, or even immoral. A more precise description of groupthink and its major symptoms are summarized in Table 13.3.

So as to not end this section on an entirely pessimistic note, we should point out that there are several strategies that can be effectively used to combat groupthink. Some of these are described in the **Perspective** insert on page 409.

TABLE 13.3   *The Warning Signals of Groupthink.*
Sometimes in highly cohesive groups the members become more concerned about maintaining positive group spirit than making the most realistic decisions—a phenomenon known as *groupthink*. The major symptoms of groupthink are identified and described here. (Source: Adapted from Janis, 1982; see Note 47.)

Symptom	Description
Illusion of *invulnerability*	Ignoring obvious danger signals, being overly optimistic, and taking extreme risks
Collective *rationalization*	Discrediting or ignoring warning signals that run contrary to group thinking
Unquestioned *morality*	Believing that the group's position is ethical and moral and that all others are inherently evil
Excessive negative *stereotyping*	Viewing the opposing side as being too negative to warrant serious consideration
Strong *conformity pressure*	Discouraging the expression of dissenting opinions under the threat of expulsion for disloyalty
Self-censorship of dissenting ideas	Withholding dissenting ideas and counterarguments, keeping them to oneself
Illusion of *unanimity*	Sharing the false belief that everyone in the group agrees with its judgments
Self-appointed *mindguards*	Protecting the group from negative, threatening information

Improving the Effectiveness of Group Decisions: Some Techniques

You may recall, from our discussion earlier in this chapter, that there are certain advantages to be gained from using individuals to make decisions and others to be gained from using groups. What would be an ideal decision-making technique would be one that combines the best features of groups and individuals while minimizing the disadvantages of both. Several techniques designed to realize the "best of both worlds" have been widely used in organizations.

The Delphi technique: Decisions by expert consensus.   According to Greek mythology, persons interested in seeing what fates the future held for them could seek the counsel of the Delphic oracle. Today's organizational decision-makers sometimes also consult experts to help them make the best decision. A technique developed by the Rand Corporation, known as the **Delphi technique**, represents a systematic way of collecting and organizing the opinions of several experts into a single decision.[52] The Delphi process starts by enlisting the cooperation of experts and presenting the problem to them, usually in a letter. Each expert then proposes what he or she believes is the most appropriate solution and sends these to the group leader. The leader them compiles all the individual responses and reproduces them so all opinions can be shared in a second mailing. At this point, each expert comments on the others' ideas and proposes another solution. These individual solutions are again returned to the leader, who compiles them and looks for a consensus of opinions. If a consensus is reached, that decision is made. If not, the process of sharing reactions with others is repeated until a consensus is eventually reached. (Please refer to the summary of the Delphi process in Figure 13.6, page 412.)

The obvious advantage of using Delphi groups to make decisions is that it makes it possible to collect expert judgments without the great costs and logistical difficulties of bringing many experts together for a face-to-face meeting. Unfortunately, the Delphi process can be *very* time consuming. The process of sending out the letters, waiting for everyone to respond, transcribing and disseminating the responses, and repeating the process until a consensus is reached can take quite a long time. Experts have estimated that the minimum time it would take to use the Delphi technique would be over forty-four days.[53] In one case the process took five months to complete.[54] Obviously, one wouldn't want to use the Delphi approach to make decisions in crisis situations, or whenever time is of the essence. However, the approach has been successfully employed to make decisions such as what items to put on a conference agenda, and what the impact would be of new land use policies.[55]

The nominal group technique: A structured group meeting.   In situations in which there are only a few hours available to make a decision, group discussion sessions can be held in which members interact with each other in an orderly, focused fashion aimed at solving problems. The **nominal group technique (NGT)** brings together a small number of individuals (usually seven to ten) who systematically offer their individual solutions to a problem and share their personal reactions to others' solutions.[56] The technique is referred to as *nominal* because the

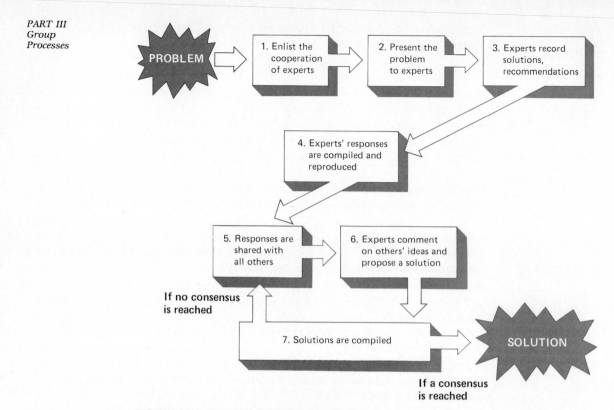

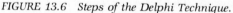

FIGURE 13.6 *Steps of the Delphi Technique.*
The *Delphi technique*, summarized here, allows decisions to be made by several experts without encountering many of the disadvantages of face-to-face, interacting groups.

individuals involved form a group *in name only*. The participants do not attempt to agree as a group upon any solution, but rather, vote on all the solutions proposed.

Specifically, the process begins by gathering the group members together around a table and identifying the problem at hand. Then, each member writes down his or her solutions to the problem. Next, one at a time, each member presents his or her solutions to the group and the leader writes these down on a chart. This process continues until all ideas are expressed. Following this, each solution is discussed, clarified and evaluated by the group members. Each member is given a chance to voice his or her reactions to each idea. After all the ideas have been evaluated, the group members then privately rank-order their preferred solutions. The idea that receives the highest rank is taken as the group's decision. (See the summary of this technique in Figure 13.7.)

Several advantages and disadvantages of NGT can be identified.[57] We have already noted that this approach can be used to arrive at group decisions in only a few hours. The benefit of the technique is that it discourages any pressure to conform to the wishes of a high-status group member because *all* ideas are evaluated and the preferences are expressed in *private* balloting. The technique must be considered limited, however, in that it requires the use of a trained group leader. In addition, the successful use of NGT requires that only one narrowly defined problem be considered at a time. So, for very complex problems, many NGT sessions

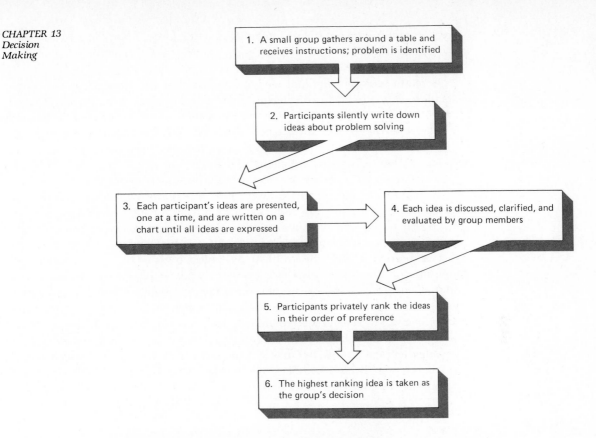

FIGURE 13.7   Steps in the Nominal Group Technique.
The *nominal group technique (NGT),* summarized here, structures face-to-face group meet-ings in a way that allows for the open expression and evaluation of ideas.

would have to be run—but that is only *if* the problem under consideration can be broken down into smaller parts.

Comparing the techniques.   It is important to consider the relative effectiveness of nominal groups and Delphi groups over face-to-face interacting groups. In gen-eral, research has shown the superiority of these special approaches to decision making in many ways on both structured and unstructured decision problems.[58,59] The effectiveness of both techniques has been demonstrated in a study by Van de Ven and Delbecq in which seven-member groups (nominal, Delphi, and interact-ing) worked on the task of defining the job of dormitory counselor.[60] Nominal groups tended to be the most satisfied with their work, and made the best quality judgments. In addition, both nominal groups and Delphi groups were much more productive than interacting groups.

However, as we have noted earlier, there is a benefit to be derived from face-to-face interaction that cannot be realized in nominal and Delphi groups—that is, acceptance of the decision. Groups are likely to accept their decisions and be committed to them if members have been actively involved in making them.[61]

Considering this, it is not surprising to find that the more detached and impersonal atmosphere of nominal and Delphi groups would make its members less likely to accept their groups' decisions.

Given the complex findings we have discussed in this section, you may find it difficult to draw any firm conclusions about which type of group is best. Clearly, there is no one best type of decision-making group. As we have noted throughout, the relative advantages of some types of groups may make them better suited for certain types of decision situations than others. (Some of the most important considerations we have discussed are summarized in Table 13.4.)

In what type of situation are interacting groups most appropriate? As you can see, their only strength seems to lie in their superiority with respect to decision acceptance. We have already discussed the tendency for interacting groups to perform poorly on creative tasks and to take a lot of time to make decisions. We also noted that groups may not do well unless there is someone in the group with the expertise needed to solve the problem. So, unless decision acceptance is the most important consideration, interacting groups may not be the best choice. By contrast, nominal and Delphi groups usually do better at creative tasks than interacting groups, although they may show less acceptance of the decision. Delphi groups may excel when expertise is crucial to task success, but not when decisions are needed quickly. On the other hand, nominal groups may provide the solutions more quickly than other types of groups, but may lack the expertise to make the best decisions. As you can see from Table 13.4, there is no one best type of group. Which type is most appropriate depends on the particular situation and the decision-maker's goals.

The Riskiness of Group Decisions: A Case of Group Polarization

At the beginning of this chapter we described two major characteristics of organizational decisions—how structured was the problem, and the degree of risk

TABLE 13.4 *Comparing the Effectiveness of Various Decision-Making Groups: A Summary.*
Different types of decision-making groups differ with respect to the level of decision creativity, member expertise, decision acceptance, and solution speed. The most appropriately used group depends on the tradeoffs between these considerations. (Source: Based on information in Stumpf, Zand, and Freedman, 1979; see Note 61.)

Consideration	Type of Group		
	Interacting	Nominal	Delphi
Decision creativity	Poor	Good	Good
Member expertise	Variable	Variable	Good
Decision acceptance	Good	Questionable	Poor
Solution speed	Slow	Fast	Slow

involved. Thus far, our discussion has focused on the quality of group decisions on tasks that are well-structured or poorly structured. Now, we will turn our attention to the matter of decision riskiness. We begin by posing a very basic, yet central, question: Do groups take greater risks or fewer risks than individuals do when making decisions?

Group shifts in decison riskiness.   Imagine that you are a corporate financial officer considering making a large investment for your organization as part of its diversification plan. Your present portfolio is adequate, and yields a modest profit each year. It is safe, very conservative, and unlikely to produce any great payoffs. Now, you have an opportunity to buy an interest in a new company that has a highly uncertain future. If the company succeeds, the payoff would be enormous. But you don't know how well it will do. Should you consider converting your safer investments into this much riskier, but potentially more lucrative, one?

What would the odds of the new company's success have to be before you would decide to "go for it" and make the investment? If you said that there would have to be a 90 percent chance of the company's succeeding before you would advocate making the investment, we could safely characterize your stance as very conservative, or cautious. However, if you were willing to make the investment when there was only a 10 percent chance of success, we would consider your position to be very risky. Now, suppose we asked a committee of corporate financial officers to consider this same investment decision. The question we are interested in is: Would the group make a riskier or a more conservative decision than an individual?

You might suspect that the give-and-take going on in a group's discussion sessions would make for more middle-of-the-road, neutral decisions to be made by groups—ones that shy away from risk. However, as we will see, a considerable amount of research conducted in the past quarter century seriously challenges this popular belief. In fact, systematic research has shown that *groups tend to make more extreme decisions than individuals.*[62]

This phenomenon was first discovered in 1961 when an M.I.T. graduate student in management, James Stoner, reported this effect in research conducted for his master's thesis.[63] Stoner developed a series of fictitious cases in which a person was confronted with the dilemma of having to choose between an attractive but risky alternative and a less attractive but more cautious alternative. Our example of the investment considered by the corporate financial officer is closely modeled after the types of cases about which Stoner's subjects had to make decisions. In one of the cases Stoner actually used, a character had to choose between taking a much higher-paying but less secure position with a new company and staying with his more secure but much lower-paying present job. Subjects read a series of cases like this and for each one selected the minimum odds of success there would have to be for them to recommend taking the riskier courses of action. After doing this alone, subjects were presented with the same cases a second time in small groups that had to discuss them and reach a unanimous decision. Time after time, it was found that the groups made riskier decisions than the same individuals. So, for example, if four individuals recommended that the riskier courses of action be taken if the odds of success were 40 percent, a group composed of these same individuals might recommend that the riskier courses of action be taken if the odds of success were lower,

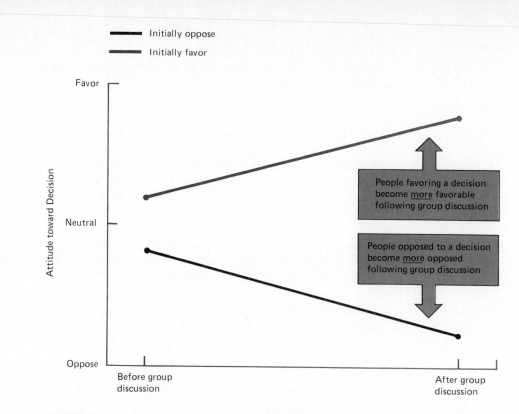

FIGURE 13.8   *Group Polarization: How It Works.*
According to the *group polarization effect*, people make more extreme decisions in the
direction of their initially held attitudes following group discussions.

say 20 percent. Because of this shift in direction of riskiness by groups compared to
individuals, the phenomenon became known as the **risky shift**.[64]

Scientists quickly became interested in the risky shift phenomenon. Their
curiosity was not only sparked by the surprising nature of the effect, but also, no
doubt, by the interesting implication that decision-making groups (such as juries,
business and governmental committees, just to name a few) might be biased toward
making risky—perhaps even dangerous—decisions. As a result, many scientists
became interested in comparing groups and individuals with respect to their tendency to make risky decisions. In the research that followed, there was a considerable amount of support found for the risky shift phenomenon. Many researchers
noted that the risky shift occurred under a wide variety of conditions.[65] However, it
was also found that in some cases groups shifted their decisions in the opposite
direction—towards caution. For example, groups tended to make more conservative decisions than individuals, as in one of Stoner's original cases—one involving
the decision to get married by a couple that had recently experienced some serious
disagreements. Eventually, other researchers reported shifts toward conservative
group decisions. It became clear that groups didn't *always* make more risky decisions than individuals, but that they did tend to make more *extreme* decisions.

Group polarization.   As researchers continued to study the decisions made by groups, it became apparent that they were not just more extreme when it came to riskiness, but on other dimensions as well. For example, studies have shown that liberal judges tend to hand down more liberal decisions when they convene in panels of three.[66] Other investigations have reported that jury members who believe a defendant is innocent or guilty before deliberations tend to be even more certain of these views after the deliberations. Apparently, the risky shift appears to be part of a more general tendency for group members to shift their individual views in a more extreme direction, a phenomenon known as **group polarization**.[67] Specifically, the group polarization effect refers to the tendency for group members to shift their views about a given issue to ones that are more extreme, in the same direction, as the views they held initially. This effect is summarized in Figure 13.8. As you can see, someone who is initially in favor of a certain decision will be more favorable toward it following group discussion, and someone who is initially opposed to a certain decision will be more opposed to it following group discussion.

Apparently, the group interaction makes people more extremely disposed to their initially held beliefs. Why does this happen? In other words, what causes group polarization? There appear to be two major explanations (see Figure 13.9).[68] One possibility, referred to as the *social comparison* explanation, suggests that group members may want to avoid leaving a bad impression on their fellow group

FIGURE 13.9   The Polarization of Group Decisions: Two Explanations for Its Occurrence. The two most popular explanations for the group polarization effect are based on *social comparison* (the desire to be favorably viewed by others encourages expression of extreme statements of positions favored by the group) and *persuasive information* (hearing convincing arguments strengthens support for the group's position).

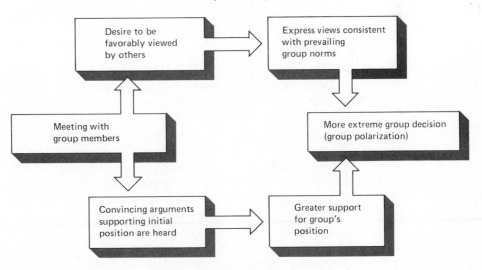

Social comparison explanation

Desire to be favorably viewed by others

Express views consistent with prevailing group norms

Meeting with group members

More extreme group decision (group polarization)

Convincing arguments supporting initial position are heard

Greater support for group's position

Persuasive information explanation

members, and try to avoid such negative outcomes by strongly endorsing predominant cultural values. For example, in considering one of the risky shift cases described earlier, group members may believe that other members will think better of them if they strongly endorse the cherished cultural value of riskiness. After all, some of America's greatest industrial heroes—such as Henry Ford, Andrew Carnegie, and John D. Rockefeller—are respected for the risks they took. Thus, they tend to adopt riskier positions than the ones with which they began. However, risk is not always valued. Recall the story about the troubled couple contemplating marriage. In cases such as these, risk is not valued, but instead, caution is considered prudent. Thus, people wanting to impress their fellow group members (or at least, to not embarrass themselves in front of them) in such cases embrace the predominant value of caution and express positions of a more cautious nature. In short, people who want to do the right thing in front of others will endorse more extreme positions with respect to whatever perspective seems "right."

However, this is not the only possible explanation for the group polarization effect. It is also possible that *persuasive information* is exchanged during the course of the group deliberations. As discussion progresses, some group members may be exposed to arguments they had not previously considered. Since most of these arguments will favor the views initially held by the majority of the group members, there may be a gradual shift toward extremity as more and more dissenters change their minds and join the "bandwagon." In addition, ideas coming out of the group deliberations can convince people that their initially held views were correct all along, leading them to more strongly endorse the favored course of action.

It is difficult to say which explanation of the group polarization effect is best, since both receive very good support.[69] It is conceivable that both processes play a role. Regardless of the precise basis for the group polarization effect, its existence has important implications for managers and organizations. Potentially, groups may make more and more extreme decisions, which can be dangerous. If this occurs, the results for both organizations and individuals can be disastrous. Clearly, the group polarization effect is a phenomenon well worth taking into account.

SUMMARY

Decision making is the multi-step process through which a problem is identified, solution objectives are defined, a *predecision* is made (a decision about how to make the decision), alternatives are generated and evaluated, an alternative is chosen, implemented, and then followed-up. The decisions made in organizations can be characterized as being either *programmed*—routine decisions made in accordance with pre-existing guidelines—or *non-programmed*—decisions requiring novel and creative solutions. Decisions also differ with respect to the amount of risk involved, ranging from those in which the decision outcomes are relatively *certain* to those in which the outcomes are highly *uncertain*.

Two major approaches to decision making have been identified. The **rational-economic model** characterizes decision-makers as completely searching through perfect information to make an *optimal* decision. In contrast, the **administrative model** recognizes the inherent imperfections of decision makers and the social and organizational systems within which they operate. Limitations imposed by people's ability to process the information needed to make complex decisions (*bounded rationality*), and by moral and ethical constraints (*bounded discretion*) restrict decision-makers to making *satisficing* decisions—solutions that are not optimal but are good enough.

In comparing the decisions made by groups and individuals on problem-solving tasks, research has shown that groups are more productive but much slower than individuals. However, groups perform less well than individuals on poorly structured, creative tasks, in part because of **groupthink**—the tendency for strong conformity pressures within groups to cause group members to accept solutions even if these are questionable. The quality of group decisions can be enhanced by using the **nominal group technique**—a method of structuring group meetings so as to systematically elicit and evaluate all opinions—and by use of **Delphi groups**—in which solutions proposed by experts are obtained through the mail.

Compared to individuals, groups tend to make more extreme decisions regarding the amount of risk they are willing to take (the famous *risky shift*), or the amount of caution they want to exercise. In general, following group discussions, group members tend to shift their opinions to more extreme positions in the direction they initially favored. This phenomenon, referred to as **group polarization**, has been explained in terms of members' desires to make favorable *social comparisons* with others and the impact of *persuasive information* presented during group meetings.

KEY TERMS

administrative model: The decision-making model that recognizes the bounded rationality that limits the making of optimally rational-economic decisions.

bounded discretion: The limitations imposed on decision-makers that result from moral and ethical constraints.

bounded rationality: The major assumption of the administrative model that organizational, social, and human limitations lead to the making of *satisficing*, instead of optimal, decisions.

brainstorming: A technique designed to foster group productivity by encouraging interacting group members to express all their ideas in a non-critical fashion.

decision making: The process through which a problem is identified, solution objectives are defined, a predecision is made, alternatives are generated and evaluated, an alternative is chosen, implemented, and then followed-up.

Delphi groups: A technique for improving group decisions in which the opinions of experts are solicited by mail and then compiled. The expert consensus of opinions is used to make a decision.

group polarization: The tendency for group members to shift to more extreme positions—in the direction they initially favored—following group interaction.

groupthink: The tendency for members of highly cohesive groups to conform to group pressures so strongly that they reject the potentially correcting influences of outsiders.

heuristics: Simple decision rules ("rules of thumb") used to make quick decisions about complex problems.

nominal group technique (NGT): A technique for improving group performance in which small groups of individuals systematically present and discuss their ideas before privately voting on their preferred solution. The most preferred solution is taken as the group's decision.

non-programmed decision: A decision made about a highly novel problem for which there is no pre-specified course of action.

predecison: A decision about how to make a decision.

programmed decision: A highly routine decision made according to pre-established organizational routines and procedures.

rational decisions: Decisions that maximize the chance of attaining an individual's, group's, or organization's goals.

rational-economic model: The model of decision making according to which decision-makers consider all possible alternatives to problems before selecting the optimal solution.

risky shift: The tendency for groups to make riskier decisions than individuals.

satisficing decision: A decision made by selecting the first minimally acceptable alternative as it becomes available.

NOTES

1. H. J. Mintzberg (1973). *The nature of managerial work.* New York: Harper & Row.

2. H. Simon (1977). *The new science of management decisions*, 2nd ed. Englewood Cliffs, N.J.: Prentice-Hall.

3. J. A. Seeger (1983). No innate phases in group problem solving. *Academy of Management Review, 8,* 683–689.

4. W. C. Wedley and R. H. G. Field (1984). A predecision support system. *Academy of Management Review, 9,* 696–703.

5. S. L. Alter (1980). *Decision support systems: Current practice and continuing challenges.* Reading, Mass.: Addison-Wesley.

6. K. R. MacCrimmon and R. N. Taylor (1976). Decision making and problem solving. In M. D. Dunnette (ed.), *Handbook of industrial and organizational psychology.* Chicago: Rand McNally.

7. K. J. Radford (1981). *Modern managerial decision making.* Reston, Va.: Reston.

8. K. G. Provan (1982). Interorganizational linkages and influence over decision making. *Academy of Management Journal, 25,* 443–451.

9. H. L. Tosi and S. J. Carroll (1982). *Management*, 2nd ed. New York: Wiley.

10. G. F. Pitz and N. J. Sachs (1984). Judgment and decision: Theory and application. In M. R. Rosenzweig and L. W. Porter (eds.), *Annual review of psychology*, vol. 35. Palo Alto: Annual Reviews.

11. H. A. Simon (1979). Rational decision making in organizations. *American Economic Review, 69,* 493–513.

12. J. W. Fredrickson and T. R. Mitchell (1984). Strategic decision processes: Comprehensiveness and performance in an industry with an unstable environment. *Academy of Management Journal, 27,* 339–423.

13. See Note 1.

14. J. G. March and H. A. Simon (1958). *Organizations.* New York: Wiley.

15. D. Kahaneman, S. Slovic, and A. Tversky (1982). *Judgments under uncertainty: Heuristics and biases.* Cambridge: Cambridge University Press.

16. R. N. Taylor (1984). *Behavioral decision making.* Glenview, Ill.: Scott, Foresman.

17. H. A. Simon (1957). *Models of man.* New York: Wiley.

18. K. R. Hammond, G. H. McClelland, and J. Mumpower (1980). *Human judgment and decision making.* New York: Praeger.

19. G. J. Gaeth and J. Shanteau (1984). Reducing the influence of irrelevant information on experienced decision makers. *Organizational Behavior and Human Performance, 33,* 263–282.

20. G. Ginrich and S. D. Soli (1984). Subjective evaluation and allocation of resources in routine decision making. *Organizational Behavior and Human Performance, 33,* 187–203.

21. A. Downs (1966). *Inside bureaucracy.* Boston: Little, Brown.

22. D. Tjosvold (1984). Effects of crisis orientation on managers' approach to controversy in decision making. *Academy of Management Journal, 27,* 130–138.

23. C. A. O'Reilly, III (1983). The use of information in organizational decision making: A model and some propositions. In L. L. Cummings and B. M. Staw (eds.), *Research in organizational behavior*, vol. 5. Greenwich, Conn.: JAI Press.

24. B. Staw (1980). Rationality and justification in organizational life. In B. Staw and L. Cummings (eds.), *Research in organizational behavior*, vol. 2. Greenwich, Conn.: JAI Press.

25. R. J. Johnson (1974). Conflict avoidance through acceptable decisions. *Human Relations, 27,* 71–82.

26. R. E. Neustadt and H. Fineberg (1978). *The swine flu affair: Decision making on a slippery disease.* Washington, D.C.: U.S. Department of Health, Education, and Welfare.

27. F. A. Shull, A. L. Delbeq, and L. L. Cummings (1970). *Organizational decision making.* New York: McGraw-Hill.

28. B. M. Staw (1981). The escalation of commitment to a course of action. *Academy of Management Review, 6,* 577–587.

29. A. I. Teger (1979). *Too much invested to quit: The psychology of the escalation of conflict.* New York: Pergamon.

30. M. H. Bazerman, T. Guiliano, and A. Appleman (1984). Escalation of commitment in individual and group decision making. *Organizational Behavior and Human Performance, 33,* 141–152.

31. A. L. Delbeq, A. H. Van de Ven, and D. H. Gustafson (1975). *Group techniques for program planning.* Glenview, Ill.: Scott, Foresman.

32. T. J. Peters and R. H. Waterman, Jr. (1982). *In search of excellence.* New York: Harper & Row.

33. G. Stasser and W. Titus (1985). Pooling of unshared information in group decision making: Biased information sampling during discussion. *Journal of Abnormal and Social Psychology, 48,* 1467–1478.

34. J. K. Murninghan (1981). Group decision making: What strategies should you use? *Management Review, 25,* 56–62.

35. R. A Guzzo and J. A. Water (1982). The expression of affect and the performance of decision-making groups. *Journal of Applied Psychology, 67,* 67–74.

36. L. N. Jewell and H. J. Reitz (1981). *Group effectiveness in organizations.* Glenview, Ill.: Scott, Foresman.

37. R. A. Webber (1974). The relationship of group performance to the age of members in homogeneous groups. *Academy of Management Journal, 17,* 570–574.

38. N. R. F. Maier (1967). Assets and liabilities in group problem solving: The need for an integrative function. *Psychological Review, 74,* 239–248.

39. P. R. Laughlin and H. H. Johnson (1966). Group and individual performance on a complementary task as a function of the initial ability level. *Journal of Experimental Social Psychology, 2,* 407–414.

40. R. Hall (1975). Interpersonal compatibility and work group performance. *Journal of Applied Behavioral Science, 11,* 210–219.

41. D. W. Taylor, P. C. Berry, and C. H. Block (1958). Does group participation when using brainstorming facilitate or inhibit creative thinking? *Administrative Science Quarterly, 3,* 23–47.

42. A. F. Osborn (1957). *Applied imagination.* New York: Scribner's.

43. T. J. Bouchard, Jr., J. Barsaloux, and G. Drauden (1974). Brainstorming procedure, group size, and sex as determinants of the problem-solving effectiveness of groups and individuals. *Journal of Applied Psychology, 59,* 135–138.

44. P. W. Yetton and P. C. Bottger (1982). Individual versus group problem solving: An empirical test of a best-member strategy. *Organizational Behavior and Human Performance, 29,* 307–321.

45. P. Yetton and P. Bottger (1983). The relationships among group size, member ability, social decision schemes, and performance. *Organizational Behavior and Human Performance, 32,* 145–159.

46. L. Iacocca (1984). *Iacocca: An autobiography.* New York: Bantam, p. 52.

47. I. L. Janis (1982). *Groupthink: Psychological studies of policy decisions and fiascoes,* 2nd ed. Boston: Houghton Mifflin.

48. P. E. Tetlock (1979). Identifying victims of groupthink from public statements of decision makers. *Journal of Personality and Social Psychology, 37,* 1314–1324.

49. See Note 47.

50. D. D. Wheeler and I. L. Janis (1980). *A practical guide for making decisions.* New York: Free Press.

51. A. P. Sloan, Jr. *My years with General Motors.* New York: Doubleday.

52. N. Dalkey (1969). *The Delphi method: An experimental study of group opinions.* Santa Monica, Calif.: Rand Corporation.

53. See Note 31.

54. A. H. Van de Ven and A. F. Delbeq (1971). Nominal versus interacting group processes for committee decision-making effectiveness. *Academy of Management Journal, 14,* 203–212.

55. See Note 31.

56. D. H. Gustafson, R. K. Shulka, A. Delbeq, and W. G. Walster (1973). A comparative study of differences in subjective likelihood estimates made by individuals, interacting groups, Delphi groups, and nominal groups. *Organizational Behavior and Human Performance*, 9, 280–291.

57. F. L. Ulshak, L. Nathanson, and P. B. Gillan (1981). *Small group problem solving: An aid to organizational effectiveness*. Reading, Mass.: Addison-Wesley.

58. T. T. Herbert and E. B. Yost (1979). A comparison of decision quality under nominal and interacting consensus group formats: The case of the structured problem. *Decision Sciences*, 10, 358–370.

59. R. E. Willis (1979). A simulation of multiple selection using nominal group procedures. *Management Science*, 25, 171–181.

60. A. H. Van de Ven, and A. L. Delbecq (1974). The effectiveness of nominal, Delphi, and interacting group decision making processes. *Academy of Management Journal*, 17, 605–621.

61. S. A. Stumpf, D. E. Zand, and R. D. Freedman (1979). Designing groups for judgmental decisions. *Academy of Management Review*, 4, 589–600.

62. H. Lamm and D. G. Myers (1978). Group-induced polarization of attitudes and behavior. In L. Berkowitz (ed.), *Advances in experimental social psychology*, vol. 11. New York: Academic Press.

63. J. A. F. Stoner (1961). *A comparison of individual and group decisions involving risk*. Unpublished master's thesis, M.I.T., Sloan School of Industrial Management.

64. E. Burnstein (1983). Persuasion as argument processing. In M. Brandstatter, J. H. Davis, and G. Stocker-Kreichgauer (eds.), *Group decision processes*. London: Academic Press.

65. See Note 64.

66. T. G. Walker and E. C. Main (1973). Choice-shifts in political decision making: Federal judges and civil liberties cases. *Journal of Applied Social Psychology*, 2, 39–48.

67. See Note 62.

68. D. G. Myers (1983). Polarizing effects of social interaction. In M. Brandstatter, J. H. Davis, and G. Stocker-Kreichgauer (eds.), *Group decision processes*. London: Academic Press.

69. See Note 62.

PART
IV

ORGANIZATIONAL
PROCESSES

CHAPTER 14

ORGANIZATIONS AS OPEN SYSTEMS

ORGANIZATIONAL STRUCTURE: The Basic Dimensions

Specialization: How Tasks Are Divided   Formalization: Rules and Documentation   The Chain of Command: Who Reports to Whom?   The Span of Control: Flat Structures and Tall Ones   Centralization versus Decentralization: Who Makes Decisions?   Line versus Staff: Production or Support?   Complexity: Internal Differentiation

ORGANIZATIONAL DESIGN: Two Early Perspectives

Scientific Management: Implications for Organizational Design   The Bureaucratic Model: The "Logical" Approach

BASIC ORGANIZATION DESIGNS: Function, Product, Matrix

Functional Designs: Organization by Tasks or Operations   Product Designs: Organization by Product, Service, or Market   Matrix Designs: A Hybrid Approach   Multinationals: A Note on Their Structure

SPECIAL INSERTS

FOCUS ON BEHAVIOR   Organizational Structure and Stress: Evidence for an Important Link

FROM THE MANAGER'S PERSPECTIVE   Organizational Design: Automatic Reaction or Conscious Choice?

Organization Design: The Structural Dimensions

The future looks bright for Restaurant Technologies, Inc. The company has been in business for only nine years, but in that short time has established a record of growth that is the envy of all its competitors. When it began, RT (as it is known to its employees) simply managed a number of units within an expanding fast-food chain. Since RT's top people seemed to possess an uncanny knack for choosing just the right locations, at just the right times, though, these businesses prospered greatly. In fact, their yearly volume was consistently double that of other outlets in the chain.

As if this success wasn't enough, the company soon moved into a new area. Sensing a shift in consumer habits, it gambled on a new operation of its own—restaurants specializing in "home-style" foods markedly different from the standard hamburger-fries-and-shake formula that had served it so well. Results here, too, were impressive. The first operation had been a huge success, so six additional units were opened in rapid succession during the next three years. Together, these had helped to multiply the company's earning severalfold. Then, to add icing to the corporate cake, two people in the accounting department, Tim Kowalski and Sheila Holcombe, came up with yet another brainstorm: why not develop and market software suitable for use in a wide range of high volume, limited menu restaurants? This idea proved remarkably easy to implement and, moreover, RT found virtually no competition in this new field. Thus, in a short time, the company was reaping handsome rewards from this business, too.

All in all, Restaurant Technology's short history reads like a textbook case of the entrepreneurial spirit in action, and most of its founders are already millionaires several times over. At present, though, the first visible clouds seem to be gathering on RT's horizon. Important problems have surfaced—ones that threaten to slow or even totally derail its growth. At first glance, these problems seem diverse. On closer examination, though, all seem to involve strains within its corporate structure.

As a small company RT had adopted a traditional, and simple, organizational chart. Separate departments for Marketing and Supply, Maintenance and Quality Control, Finance and Accounting, and Personnel had been established. All functioned well until the last year or two. Now, several seem on the very edge of chaos. The basic problem is simple: key people in each of these units feel that they are being asked to do too much, in too many different ways. A good example is provided by John Chandler, head of Marketing. In recent months, he has complained loudly and often about the frustrations of running a unit charged with the task of promoting both the company's fast-food outlets and its sophisticated line of software. In a similar vein, Chuck Scharf, the person in charge of Maintenance, has found it increasingly difficult to handle what amounts to two sets of personnel—people who can keep the kitchens in RT's restaurants going, and people who can deal with its increasingly complex computer facilities. Similar problems have arisen in relation to supply, where very different sources and procedures are required for the company's fast-food outlets and "home-style" restaurants. In sum, things are in a mess, and threaten to get even worse. But what should RT do? Should it undertake a major reorganization? And if so, what new internal set-up should it adopt? Unless something is done—and done soon—the situation threatens to get totally out of hand. But how should the company proceed? What goals should it seek? These are the key problems currently facing top management.

Once they exceed a minimum size (and this is small indeed!), all organizations require a formal *internal structure*. That is, they need a formal arrangement that allocates tasks and responsibilities among persons and departments, that determines who will report to whom, and that helps assure the communication, coordination, and integration essential for attainment of key organizational goals.[1] If such an arrangement does not exist, or, as is much more common, it proves to be ineffective, important problems usually follow. Decisions are delayed or turn out to be of low quality. The ability to adapt to changing external conditions is sharply lowered. Key employees experience high and unnecessary levels of stress; and excessive conflict between individuals or groups often erupts.[2] In short, the organization's effectiveness—or even its very survival—may be threatened.

Given the impact of an organization's structure on its outcomes and performance, an important question follows: What kind of internal arrangement is best? How should organizations be put together so as to maximize their efficiency, attainment of their major goals, and feelings of satisfaction among the people who work within them? These and related questions concerning **organization design** have long been central to our field. The reason for this interest should be clear: to the extent such questions can be answered, organizations should, quite literally, be able to plan their own success. They should be able to divide tasks, assign authority, establish communication, and attain coordination in the most effective manner possible.

Unfortunately, several decades of careful research on organization design suggest that framing such questions is one thing; obtaining comprehensive answers to them is quite another. Just as there is no single "best" style of leadership, and no single "best" technique for motivating employees, there appears to be no single "best" type of organizational structure. On the contrary, what works well for a given organization, facing a specific set of circumstances, often fails dismally for another organization, facing a different set of conditions. The appropriate question, then, appears *not* to be "what structure is best?" but rather "what structure is best for a specific organization facing a specific set of internal and external conditions?" We will focus on such complexities (and especially on the impact of both *technology* and the *environment*) in Chapter 15. Here, we will restrict our perspective somewhat and concentrate on a more basic topic: the precise nature of organizational structure itself. In order to accomplish this preliminary task, we will touch on several issues. First, we will take another—and closer—look at the nature of organizations, viewing them as **open systems** with an array of essential components. Second, we will consider the *basic dimensions* of organizational structure— important ways in which organizations can, and do, differ in their internal arrangements. Third, we will examine two early perspectives on organizational design— **scientific management** and the **bureaucratic model.** Finally, we will describe several basic organization designs in widespread use today, pointing out the advantages and disadvantages of each as we do.

ORGANIZATIONS AS OPEN SYSTEMS

In Chapter 1, we defined organizations as social structures in which two or more persons work together in a coordinated manner to attain common goals. This definition was useful, for it took account of several of the most important features of organizations: (1) they consist, ultimately, of people; (2) they are goal-directed in nature; and (3) they attain their goals through some form of coordinated activity. Our definition did not, however, take account of one additional feature of organizations also deserving of careful attention: the fact that they operate as **open systems.**[3]

To indicate what we mean by *open system,* we must first comment on the nature of systems generally. Briefly, a system is any set of parts or components linked together to form a whole, and that operates to attain certain objectives. Within a system, certain raw materials or *inputs* are somehow transformed or changed into desired products or *outputs.* While all systems share these basic features (i.e., all involve the transformation of inputs into outputs), they differ in their degree of contact with the external environment—the world around them. Some are *closed* in nature; they have little or no interaction with their environment. In a sense, each constitutes a sealed "world unto itself." One example of a closed system is provided by the space suits worn by astronauts. Within these suits, oxygen, water vapor, heat, and other substances circulate and recirculate freely, and are used and transformed by the occupants. However, the suits themselves are almost totally isolated from the external environment: deep space. In contrast, other systems are *open* in nature:

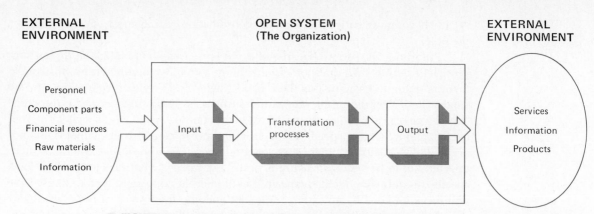

EXTERNAL ENVIRONMENT

OPEN SYSTEM (The Organization)

EXTERNAL ENVIRONMENT

Personnel
Component parts
Financial resources
Raw materials
Information

Input → Transformation processes → Output

Services
Information
Products

FIGURE 14.1   Organizations Operate as Open Systems.
Organizations operate as *open systems*. They receive input from the external environment, transform it in some manner, and then send their output back across their boundaries into the environment.

they have some degree of interaction with the external environment. In fact, they cannot survive in the absence of such contact, for it is from the world outside their boundaries that they obtain much of their input, and it is back across these boundaries that they send their final output (refer to Figure 14.1).

By now, it should be clear that organizations are indeed open systems. Their inputs (raw materials, information, financial resources, employees) often come from outside their boundaries. And their outputs, too (their products, services, etc.), flow back to the external environment. (Note, by the way, that not all outputs produced by an organization are positive in nature or intended. For example, the pollutants released by a large chemical company are certainly part of its outputs, but are clearly harmful and undesired.)

As we will see in more detail in Chapter 15, the fact that organizations operate as open systems is of crucial importance to understanding their internal structure. This is so because both the specific structures they adopt, and the success ultimately [enjoye]d by these arrangements (and so the success of the organizations themselves), [are sha]ped by the continuous flow of information, people, and resources back and [forth a]cross their boundaries.

[No]w that we have established the fact that organizations are open systems, it is [import]ant to note that they are composed of several essential *subsystems*.[4] Since the [functio]ns performed by these subsystems are essential to virtually all organizations, [they a]re worth mentioning here. (Please refer to Figure 14.2 as you read this [section.])

[Th]e first of these subsystems is the one concerned with **production.** This is [where] the primary transformation of input into output takes place. It is, in short, [where] the major work of the organization occurs. In a manufacturing concern, the [produc]tion subsystem would be represented by the Production Department. In a [school] it would involve the teachers; and in an insurance business, it might center [around] the company's agents. Whatever its precise form, the production subsystem lies at the heart of an organization, and all the remaining subsystems are usually oriented toward it.

A second key subsystem in most organizations is concerned with the task of **maintenance**—keeping the organization in a smoothly functioning state. This involves the repair and servicing of buildings, machinery, and other physical objects. In addition, it includes maintaining the health, comfort, and morale of employees. These functions are often divided among several units (e.g., Maintenance, Personnel, etc.).

Since organizations must both acquire necessary inputs (e.g., raw materials, supplies) and distribute outputs (e.g., finished products, services), a third key subsystem is concerned with these functions. This subsystem is usually described as **boundary spanning** in nature, since it handles transactions at the organization's boundaries (dealing with supplies, customers, regulatory agencies). These functions, too, are often divided among several units (e.g., Marketing, Supply).

Because the conditions under which organizations must operate frequently change, an additional subsystem is concerned with the task of **adaptation.** It is responsible for helping the organization meet and cope with new conditions. This function is often carried out by Research, Engineering, and Planning and Development units.

Finally, all of the subsystems discussed so far are overseen and directed by a fifth system—**management.** The essential task of the management subsystem is that of coordinating all the other subsystems. Thus, its major responsibilities include the formulation of organization-wide policies and long-range plans, the reso-

FIGURE 14.2   *Basic Organizational Subsystems.*
Most organizations contain the five subsystems shown here. Under ideal conditions, they are closely interconnected, and function as an integrated system.

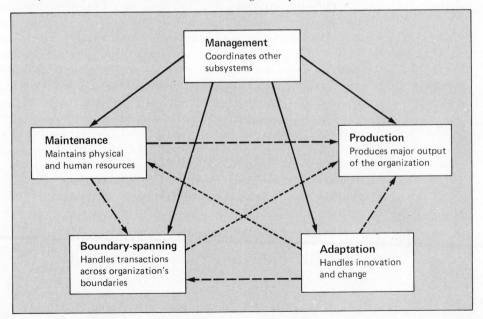

lution of conflicts between other subsystems, and development of an internal structure that allows for the smooth operation of the remaining subsystems.

As we will see in later sections of this chapter, the subsystems just described are present in all organizations. In a sense, they *must* be, for the functions they perform are essential to any operating, viable organization. However, the precise ways they are represented vary greatly—so greatly, that it is sometimes hard to discern their presence. Please try to keep this fact in mind as you read further; it may help you to perceive unifying themes in what can otherwise seem to be a complex and confusing topic: the nature of organization design. (For a summary of the various subsystems described above and the links between them, please refer to Figure 14.2, page 429.)

ORGANIZATIONAL STRUCTURE: THE BASIC DIMENSIONS

Orgnl' Structure :
1. Specialization
2. Formalization
3. Chain of command
4. Span of control
5. Centralization vs. Decentralization
6. Line vs Staff
7. Complexity

Consider the follo[w]

- Exxon
- Girl Scouts of A[merica]
- Sony
- Boston Pops Or[chestra]
- A.F.L.-C.I.O.
- Fraternal Order [...]
- United Federati[on ...]

All these entities e[xist] [...] in "Star Trek") qualify as organ[izations ...] [...] [requirements] [...] in the definition offered above. It is also clear, however, that while all are organizations, they differ tremendously in scope, nature, and purpose. Faced with such diversity, it might be tempting to conclude that organizations differ in so many ways, that it is impossible to describe them—let alone compare their internal structures—in a systematic manner. Fortunately, this is not the case. While organizations *do* differ along many dimensions, some of these appear to be key. That is, differences in some respects seem to be the ones that matter—the ones most likely to affect the behavior of individuals, the performance of specific units, or overall organizational effectiveness.[5] Before turning to specific (and often complex) organization designs, therefore, we will first acquaint you with several of these underlying dimensions. Knowledge of them is useful in several respects, but perhaps the following is most crucial: such information permits us to draw at least a rough road map or chart of the structure of virtually *any* organization.

Specialization: How Tasks Are Divided

One important way in which organizations differ concerns the extent to which tasks are subdivided. At the high end of this dimension of **specialization** are organizations (usually large ones) in which each person (or perhaps each subunit) performs a very narrow range of activities—one operation on the assembly line, one type of financial record-keeping, maintenance of one type of equipment. At the low end are organizations (usually smaller ones) in which employees perform a wide range of tasks or jobs—many steps in the manufacture of the company's products, a wide range of accounting operations, maintenance of many kinds of equipment plus painting, cleaning, and related activities. Because it can improve overall efficiency, a high degree of specialization (or *division of labor*) was strongly recommended by early management experts, especially Frederick Taylor and other adherents of **scientific management.**[6] (Refer to our discussion of this view in Chapter 1.) However, when carried to extremes, it can yield intense feelings of boredom, and so can adversely affect job satisfaction and other work-related attitudes. For this reason, specialization is far from the unmixed blessing some of its advocates once proposed.

Formalization: Rules and Documentation

Another basic dimension of organization structure involves **formalization**— the extent to which an organization possesses (and relies upon) written documentation. Such documents can take the form of policy manuals, lengthy job descriptions, sets of regulations, or handbooks. They specify how employees should act in certain situations, what their responsibilities are, to whom they should report, how decisions should be reached, and countless other things. Moreover, they often apply to departments, divisions, or units, as well as to individuals. Variations along this dimension of formalization are truly huge. At one extreme, some organizations (especially young or small companies) possess little in the way of formal documentation; people in them "play it by ear" most of the time. In contrast, others (especially mature and large organizations) can literally drown in their own documentation. The author had first-hand experience with this end of the formalization dimension when he worked in a large government agency. The manual of information and instructions he received on first joining the staff ran to several hundred pages, and attempted to touch on virtually *every* set of circumstances he could possibly encounter. Needless to add, when this degree of formalization prevails, a frustrating type of organizational paralysis may follow, with disastrous effects for both efficiency and morale.

The Chain of Command: Who Reports to Whom?

Almost every organization possesses a clearly defined hierarchy of authority: some people give orders to (or at least can influence) others. The length of this **chain of command,** however, can vary greatly. In some cases, only one or a few levels separate top persons from those on the lowest rung of the organizational ladder (usually, those who carry out the most basic aspects of production). In others, literally dozens of levels intervene. As you can readily imagine, organizations differing in these respects are sharply contrasting places in which to work. Thus, some knowledge of the chain of command within an organization is important to understanding just how it operates.

The Span of Control: Flat Structures and Tall Ones

Another aspect of organizational structure pertaining to authority is the **span of control.** This simply refers to the number of persons reporting to a single supervisor. In some cases, this number is fairly large (e.g., twenty to thirty), and the span of control is described as being *wide.* Such conditions often result in a *flat* structure—one in which a relatively small number of levels separate top management from persons on the shop or office floor (refer to Figure 14.3). In other instances, the span of control is *narrow* (i.e., only a few individuals report to each supervisor). This often results in a *tall* structure, in which many levels intervene between the top and bottom of the organization.

In the past it was often recommended that the span of control be kept quite narrow (e.g., no more that four to six subordinates under each supervisor). However, at present, it is widely recognized that the ideal span for a given organization or unit depends heavily on the tasks it performs and the goals it seeks. For example, the span may be greater when work is routine or repetitive than when it is not, and greater in large organizations than in small ones. Several other variables, too, may play a role. In view of these complexities, it is apparent that there can be no simple, hard-and-fast rule for setting this important aspect of organizational structure.

Centralization versus Decentralization: Who Makes Decisions?

In some organizations, important decisions are made only by top-level managers. In others, decision making (and the authority it implies) is shared quite widely, so that even persons at relatively low levels in the hierarchy of authority can offer input or participate in other ways. Organizations falling into the first category are described as showing a high degree of **centralization**; those falling into the latter are described as demonstrating **decentralization**.

At several points in this book, we have called attention to the benefits of permitting organization members to participate in decisions (e.g., increased motivation, higher job satisfaction, reduced stress). At first glance, therefore, you might assume that a decentralized structure is always preferable to a centralized one. In many cases this is true. However, decentralization, too, has certain drawbacks. For example, it can sometimes contribute to jurisdictional disputes, since different individuals or units feel equally responsible for key decisions. Similarly, it can actually tend to reduce coordination between various departments or groups, since each becomes accustomed to making its own decisions and operating independently. If such problems are overcome, a degree of decentralization *can* be a plus. However, once again, this aspect of organizational structure must be evaluated—and adjusted—on a case-by-case basis.

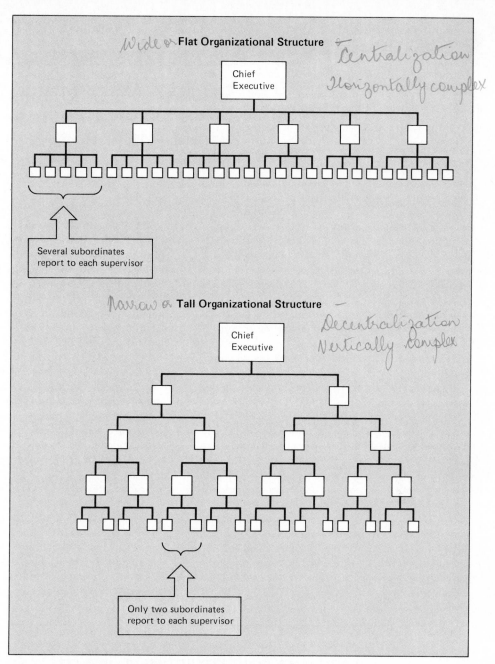

FIGURE 14.3 Flat and Tall Organizational Structures.
In a *flat* organizational structure (top illustration), a relatively small number of steps exist between top and bottom levels of the organization, and several subordinates report to each supervisor. In a *tall* organizational structure, many steps separate top and bottom levels of the organization, and only a few subordinates report to each supervisor.

Organizational Structure and Stress: Evidence for an Important Link

Stress, as we noted in Chapter 7, is an all too common aspect of life in modern organizations. Moreover, it exacts a costly toll in terms of personal health, reduced efficiency, and lowered morale.[7] Many different factors seem to contribute to work-related stress—everything from the demands of certain jobs through the personal characteristics of individual employees. Here, we can add yet another factor to this list of major stressors: organizational structure. Recent findings suggest that several types of stress are more likely to develop in organizations possessing certain structural features than in organizations possessing others.[8] A clear demonstration of this important relationship has been reported in a project conducted by Nicholson and Goh.[9]

Participants in this study were supervisors in two sharply contrasting organizations: the research and development department of a large public utility, and the production department of a manufacturing company. Subjects in both groups completed questionnaires designed to assess their perceptions of certain features of their organization's structure (e.g., its degree of formalization, span of subordination) and the amount of role conflict and role ambiguity they experienced. On the basis of previous findings, Nicholson and Goh predicted that in the relatively formal and structured work environment of the production department, *role conflict* would be related to various aspects of organizational structure. In the relatively informal and unstructured work environment of the research department, however, such links would not

be present. In contrast, they predicted that *role ambiguity* would be related to structural variables in both settings.

As you can see from Figure 14.4, results offered support for both of these predictions. Specifically, in the production department (but not in the research unit), the higher the degree of formalization present, the lower the level of role conflict reported by subjects. Further, in both organizations, role ambiguity was significantly related to structural variables (to formalization in the production department and to span of subordination in the research unit). The first of these findings indicates that under certain conditions (in a highly structured work setting), formalization can help to reduce feelings of role conflict among employees. Under other conditions (in an unstructured environment), however, it fails to yield such benefits. The second finding indicates that two structural variables (formalization and span of subordination) can reduce role ambiguity (uncertainty about job requirements) in both structured and unstructured organizational settings.

Since both role conflict and role ambiguity are important sources of stress, the evidence gathered by Nicholson and Goh, plus that reported by other investigators, points to the following conclusion: several features of organizational structure can play an important role in such reactions. Clearly, this is one more reason why managers should pay careful attention to structure when planning for overall effectiveness.

Line versus Staff: Production or Support?

As organizations grow in size and scope, they often find that they require the services of individuals possessing specialized knowledge or skills not directly linked to their principal work flow—that is, not directly related to the products or services they produce. For example, a company involved in the manufacture of equipment used in the television industry may discover that it needs the full time services of legal experts to advise it on matters relating to patents, and the services of a labor-

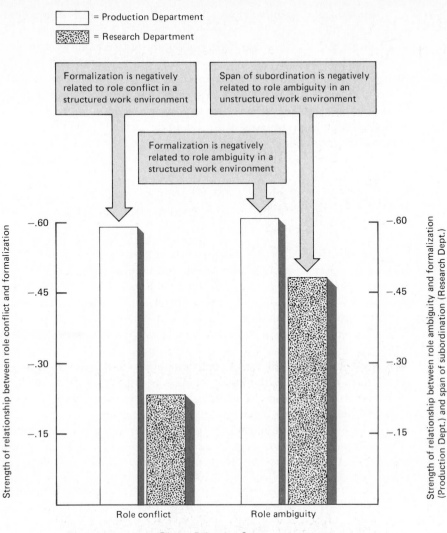

FIGURE 14.4 Organizational Structure and Two Sources of Stress.
In a highly structured work environment (a production department), the greater the degree of formalization, the less *role conflict* experienced by employees. This relationship was much weaker in a less structured research department. In both contexts, *role ambiguity* was significantly related to structural variables (to formalization for the production unit, and to span of subordination in the research department). These findings suggest that certain aspects of organizational structure can play an important role in stress. (Source: Based on data from Nicholson and Goh, 1983; See Note 9.)

management expert to handle dealings with the newly formed employee union. Such persons occupy **staff positions**—their primary task is that of offering support, advice, and service to individuals in **line positions**—jobs directly linked to the company's primary business.

Unfortunately, conflict between line and staff personnel is far from rare. Individuals directly concerned with the production of goods or services (i.e., line personnel) often feel that they know more about the organization's business and how it should be run than the "experts" occupying staff positions. Yet, top management often accepts the advice of such persons over their own. Conversely, staff personnel may conclude that individuals in line positions have a narrow perspective, and can't see beyond the confines of their own department or unit. In any case, the line-staff distinction is an important one, and should be carefully considered in any effort to understand an organization's structure.

Complexity: Internal Differentiation

Together, several of the dimensions we have examined so far constitute an additional aspect of organizational structure with important effects: **complexity.** This refers to the degree of internal differentiation present within an organization along two key dimensions: *vertical* and *horizontal.* Organizations may be described as *vertically* complex to the extent that they possess many levels in their chains of command. In contrast, they may be described as *horizontally complex* to the degree that they contain many departments or units. As organizations grow in size and scope, complexity, too, usually increases. This in itself is not necessarily a problem, provided that additional attention is directed to the task of maintaining coordination. When growing complexity is not matched by the development or refinement of integrating mechanisms, however, negative effects can result. Indeed, at extreme levels, communication, decision making, morale, and efficiency can all be adversely affected. (What are the effects of organizational structure on individual employees? For a discussion of recent findings on this issue, please refer to the **Focus** box on page 434.)

ORGANIZATIONAL DESIGN: TWO EARLY PERSPECTIVES

Now that we have considered some of the basic dimensions along which organizations differ, we can turn, briefly, to a closely related question: which of these possible internal arrangements is most effective? We say "briefly" with good reason. Our purpose here is *not* that of providing an exhaustive treatment of the complexities of organization design. Such a discussion requires detailed attention to the impact of technology and the complex interplay between organizations and the external environment—topics reserved for Chapter 15. Instead, we will merely provide you with some historical perspective—information about two early views of the "ideal" organization that have proven to be quite influential: **scientific management** and the **bureacratic model.**

Scientific Management: Implications for Organizational Design

As we have noted earlier (refer to Chapter 1), *scientific management* focused primarily on two issues: effective job design and enhanced work motivation.[10] With respect to job design, supporters of this approach (which was most popular in the early decades of the current century) suggested that high levels of efficiency could be obtained if (1) employees were carefully selected and trained for their jobs, and (2) procedures and tools were carefully standardized. Turning to motivation, advocates of scientific management held that most people are primarily concerned with financial gain. Thus, they felt that the key to higher motivation lay in offering such persons sufficient incentives for engaging in productive work. In addition, Taylor and his supporters emphasized the importance of cooperation between management and workers; they felt that without such conditions, and a fair division of both work and responsibility, high levels of productivity would be impossible to obtain.

While these assertions about the nature of effective management were not focused directly on organizational design, they appear to have direct implications for several of the aspects of structure we have already considered. For example, Taylor's emphasis on the scientific selection and training of employees seems to call for a high degree of specialization. Similarly, his concern with cooperative relations between management and employees implies at least some degree of decentralization and shared participation in decision making. Finally, Taylor's insistence on an equitable division of responsibility and work within an organization seems to imply a relatively short chain of command—one in which managers work side-by-side with their subordinates—and perhaps holding staff personnel to a minimum. (On the other hand, though, he also recommended the use of several specialized foremen, so there is some uncertainty on this score.) In these and other ways, some of the basic principles of scientific management bear at least indirectly on key dimensions of organizational design.

The Bureaucratic Model: The "Logical" Approach

At the present time, the term *bureaucracy* has a distinctly negative ring. For many persons, it conjures up images of huge organizations rigidly structured from top to bottom, filled with meaningless rules and regulations, and tied into helpless, seething knots by their own red tape (refer to Figure 14.5, page 438). Indeed, in some circles, labeling someone as a *bureaucrat* is the ultimate insult—something akin to writing this person off as a useful human being!

Given this prevalent view of bureaucracy, you will probably find it surprising to learn that at one time in the past, it was strongly recommended as the ideal form of organizational structure. The most famous advocate of this view was Max Weber.[11] Weber, a noted sociologist, first made a careful study of many organizations existing at the turn of the century. What he found appalled him. Most were based on favoritism, family connections, and friendship, rather than on principles of rationality and fair play. For example, people were hired because they were

FIGURE 14.5   Bureaucracy: The Prevailing View.
At present, most persons have negative associations with the terms *bureaucracy* and *bureaucrat*. (Source: By permission of Johnny Hart and News America Syndicate.)

related to those already in the organization, or because they belonged to the "right" social groups—not because of their qualifications. Similarly, employees were promoted because they were liked by their supervisors, or because of personal friendships—not on the basis of merit or past performance. And graft was rampant: many individuals with authority used their power to profit from the sale of organizational products or services. In short, everywhere he looked, Weber seemed to find inefficiency, waste, and corruption.

In response to such conditions, he proposed that organizations should adopt a new design—one based entirely on rational considerations. Only by doing so, Weber contended, could they hope to meet the complex challenges arising out of rapid industrialization. Specifically, he proposed a **bureaucratic model** consisting of seven basic principles.

First, this new structure would involve a high degree of *specialization* and division of labor. Specific duties should be divided among individuals in a clear manner, and each job holder should possess the authority necessary to perform these duties. Second, all positions within the bureaucracy would be arranged according to the principle of *hierarchy*. Each lower office would be under the control of a higher one, and there would be a clear chain of command. Third, all tasks would be carried out in accordance with *rules*. In this way, standard operating procedures would be established, and the impact of individual quirks or characteristics upon the central business or the organization would be minimized. Fourth, *impersonality* would apply throughout the organization. Individuals would be treated in an identical fashion, without regard to personal traits. This would go a long way toward eliminating the abuses of favoritism Weber observed in many situations. Fifth, employment would be based on *qualifications* and promotion on *merit*. Competence, not friendship or family ties, would be the guiding principle in such matters. Sixth, offices (i.e., specific positions) and persons would be viewed as separate. This would prevent specific individuals from "taking over" their positions, and using them for their personal benefit. Finally, all decisions, rules, and administrative acts would be *recorded* in writing, to provide the organization with a permanent record of past actions, and continuity over time. (Please refer to Table 14.1 for a summary of these basic principles.)

At present, few experts on organizational design would agree with Weber's assertion that bureaucracy is in fact the ideal—the goal toward which all organizations should strive. At the same time though, most would readily admit that several of the principles he recommended are widely accepted. While few "pure" bureaucracies exist, many modern organizations demonstrate at least some of Weber's principles within their structure. The key question, then, is not "Did bureaucracy ever catch on?" but rather "Is it as effective as Weber contended?" The answer, unfortunately, appears to be mixed.

On the one hand, it is hard to question the positive effects of such principles as hiring and promotion on the basis of merit, careful record-keeping, and the development of at least some clear rules. Further, there are certainly many organizations structured along bureaucratic lines that appear to be extremely efficient and productive. Indeed, in one study carried out by Child, it was found that as organizations grow larger, those that show high levels of bureaucracy tend to be more successful than those that do not.[12] Thus, it appears that at least under conditions of substantial size, bureaucracy may well contribute to organizational effectiveness.

On the other hand, however, bureaucracy also exacts important costs.[13] First, a bureaucratic structure may produce rigidity, and make it difficult for an organization to change. In the chaotic, modern world, this can be fatal. Second, the hierarchical nature of bureaucracy may tend to stifle upward communication, with all the problems this can generate. Third, as we have already noted, excessive reliance on rules, standard operating procedures, and the like can lead to a situation in which an organization chokes to death on its own red tape. At the very least, such factors can slow its response and produce rigidity. Fourth, by encouraging specialization, bureaucracy may reduce the motivating potential of many jobs, and so reduce employee performance (refer to Chapter 3). Finally, bureaucracies often stifle per-

Imp.

TABLE 14.1   *The Bureaucratic Model: Some Basic Principles.*
According to the *bureaucratic model* first proposed by Weber, organizations should operate in accordance with the rational principles outlined here.

Principle	Description
Specialization	Duties and responsibilities should be divided among organization members so as to maximize efficiency
Hierarchy	The organization should possess a clearly defined line of authority, with each lower position or office under the control of a higher one
Rules	Activities should be carried out in accordance with rules and standard operating procedures
Impersonality	Individuals should be treated in the same manner, regardless of their personal characteristics
Hiring by qualifications	Employees should be hired on the basis of past experience and qualifications, not their relationship with current organization members
Promotion by merit	Individuals should be promoted on the basis of past performance and merit
Written records	Decisions, rules, and administrative actions should be carefully and permanently recorded

sonal growth, innovation, and spontaneity. Since individual differences are viewed as a nuisance, conformity, groupthink, and a dull sameness are fostered. It is partly for this reason, of course, that bureaucracy suffers from such a negative image today.

We should hasten to add that none of these weaknesses are insurmountable. Through appropriate steps (e.g., the establishment of additional channels of communication, programs of job enlargement or enrichment) their impact can be reduced. However, to a degree, they are built into the system, and cannot be totally avoided. The result: despite good intentions, and a solid foundation in rational principles, bureaucracy often becomes a captive of the very characteristics claimed to be its strength. Contrary to enthusiastic statements by Weber, therefore, bureaucracy is *not* an ideal form of organizational structure. Several of its features are obviously useful, but under some conditions, at least, they seem more likely to block rather than enhance organizational effectiveness.

BASIC ORGANIZATION DESIGNS: FUNCTION, PRODUCT, MATRIX

Up to this point, we have described some of the basic dimensions along which organizations can differ in their internal structure, plus two historical perspectives on the issue of organization design. Now, we will turn to what is, perhaps, the most practical section of this chapter: a discussion of several basic contemporary designs. In short, we will now consider several designs (or, more accurately, *types* of designs) you are likely to encounter during the course of your own career. Many such designs exist. Indeed, from one point of view, there are almost as many unique internal structures as there are separate organizations. However, a sizable proportion, if not in fact a majority, seem to fall into three major categories. These are known, respectively, as **functional, product,** and **matrix** designs.

Functional Designs: Organization by Tasks or Operations

In one sense, **functional designs** can be viewed as being the most basic: many organizations begin with this type of design, and only shift to others as they grow in size and complexity. Within functional designs, departments, divisions, and units are based on specialized functions. That is, they are concerned with the performance of specific tasks or activities. A simple example of a functional design is presented in Figure 14.6. As you can see, separate departments exist for such basic tasks as sales, maintenance, production, and accounting. Almost any organization adopting a functional design would tend to possess such units: they reflect activities that must be performed in virtually any business. As a particular organization

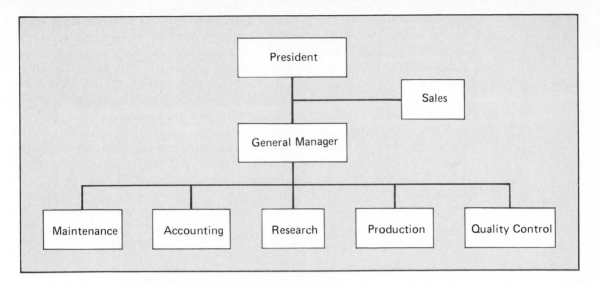

FIGURE 14.6   A Simple Functional Design.
In a *functional design,* separate departments or units perform specific tasks. Note that in this organization, Sales reports directly to the President, while the other departments report to the general manager.

grows and develops, however, it may well acquire additional units concerned with functions unique to itself, or to its basic industry. For example, a large chemical company might require separate departments concerned with transportation and storage, and would add these to its corporate structure. Similarly, a public utility might find that it needs a separate department charged with the task of managing pollution and assuring adherence to government standards. This potential for meeting needs as they arise through the creation of new departments is one of the major benefits conferred by a functional design.

In addition, such designs offer several other "pluses" as well. By combining activities within specific departments or units, they permit economies of scale and avoid unnecessary duplication. That is, all employees performing the same function work together, and share facilities. Similarly, they encourage units and individuals to specialize, and so to develop high level skills in their respective areas.

Partly offsetting these advantages, however, are several weaknesses. The most important of these stems from the fact that such designs encourage separate units to "go their own way" and develop their own perspectives. The result, of course, is that interunit coordination is often difficult to attain.[14] Second, top management, which has the task of integrating various activities, may soon find itself overloaded in a functional design. Specific departments, with their limited, focused views of the organization and its goals, can offer little help in this respect. Finally, functional designs encourage organization members to focus on routine tasks within their own units. As a result, the likelihood of innovations is reduced, and the organization as a whole may be relatively slow in responding to environmental change. In sum, while functional designs are certainly logical in nature, and have proved useful in a wide range of contexts, they are by no means a perfect solution to the problem of organization design.

Product Designs: Organization by Product, Service, or Market

Successful organizations do not stand still; on the contrary, they continue to grow in both size and scope. They develop new products, seek new customers, and enter new markets. As they do, the strains on a functional design may become intense. The production department may find it increasingly difficult to oversee the manufacture of a wide range of items; sales may find the task of promoting seemingly unrelated products unwieldy; and accounting may discover that keeping track of a growing number of local tax and business regulations, which come to apply as the company expands its operations, is pushing it to its limits. When such strains develop, organizations often shift to a **product design.** Here, self-contained units concerned with specific products or product groups are established. Each of these units contains all the resources and departments necessary for handling these products—everything from procuring needed supplies and personnel, through manufacture, sales, and delivery. Thus, in a sense, a single organization is divided into several independent units, each capable of operating as an entity by itself. Of course, the heads of each of these units still report to top management within the company. Moreover, some functions are generally performed at the organization's central headquarters, rather than in the individual product units (e.g., public relations, overall market research, legal arrangements). On a day-to-day basis, though, each unit operates in a largely independent fashion. (Please refer to Figure 14.7 for a concrete example of a product design.)

At this point, we should note that several variations on this basic theme exist. Self-contained operating units are sometimes established on the basis of specific markets, geographic regions, and even customers, rather than products or services. For example, a retail chain might establish separate units in different regions, states, or provinces. Similarly, a manufacturer of computer products might set up one division for dealing with business customers, and another for dealing with consumers. Regardless of the precise basis for the independent units, however, the basic rationale behind product designs remains the same: divide the organization's operations in such a way that efficiency (and flexibility) within each is enhanced.

Product designs offer several major benefits. Perhaps the most important of these is increased flexibility and ability to adapt to changing external conditions.[15] Since each unit specializes in a particular product line, service, or market, it can be highly sensitive to shifts in competition, customer needs, and related matters. Second, since each unit is largely self-contained, product designs heighten concern with overall results. Indeed, a degree of competition between an organization's operating units may develop, with each attempting to produce a better record of profits and sales than the others. This can contribute to overall effectiveness. Third, because divisions or units are held to manageable size, coordination within them may be enhanced.

On the other side of the coin, product designs suffer from certain drawbacks. The most obvious of these is the loss of economies of scale stemming from the

FIGURE 14.7   *A Simple Product Design.*
In a product design, separate units are established to handle different products or markets. Note that this necessarily leads to some degree of duplication in facilities and personnel.

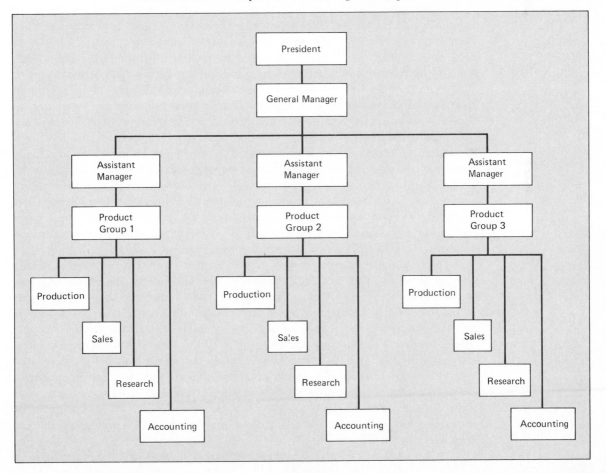

duplication of various departments within each operating unit. For example, if each unit carries out its own research and development functions, the need for costly equipment, facilities, and personnel may be multiplied severalfold. Another problem associated with product designs involves the ability of the organization to attract and retain talented employees. Since each department within operating units is necessarily smaller than a single combined one, opportunities for advancement and career development may be restricted; this may pose a serious drawback for at least some individuals. Finally, problems of coordination across product lines may arise. In fact, in exteme cases, actions taken by one operating division may have adverse effects upon the outcomes of one or more other units (e.g., one division may develop a product or service that siphons off business from others). Despite such disadvantages, though, when organizations find themselves facing an unstable and rapidly changing environment, an internal structure incorporating the basic principles of product design may be desirable.

Matrix Designs: A Hybrid Approach

As we have already seen, both functional and product designs offer important, but different, advantages. Is there any way of combining these approaches so as to obtain the best of each, while holding associated disadvantages to a minimum? In fact there is. Such a strategy is provided by **matrix designs.**[16] Basically, such designs are the result of superimposing a product structure on a functional one. In the design so produced, a dual system of authority is established. On the one hand, there are managers for various functional areas—people with authority over all aspects of production, engineering, marketing, and so on. On the other, there are also *product managers*—individuals whose authority extends to all processes connected with a specific product or project. The result is that some persons actually have two bosses—one in their functional department, and one who oversees the particular project or product to which they are currently assigned. (Please see Figure 14.8 for an illustration of a matrix design.) It is important to note, however, that this is the case only for a relatively small number of persons located near or at the top of the organization. Below this level, employees usually have only one supervisor, based either on functional or product considerations.

Perhaps our comments so far can be clarified by noting that within matrix designs, three major roles exist. First, there is the *top leader*—the person who has authority over both lines (the one based on function and the one based on product or project). It is this individual's task to maintain a balance of power between the functional and product managers. Second, there are the *matrix bosses*—people who head functional departments and product units. Since neither of these persons have complete authority over subordinates, they must work together to assure that their efforts coordinate rather than conflict. In addition, they must reach agreement on such issues as promotion and raises for specific individuals working under their joint authority. Finally, there are *two-boss managers*. These are the people who must report to both product and functional managers, and attempt to balance the demands of each.

Organizations are most likely to adopt matrix designs when they face certain

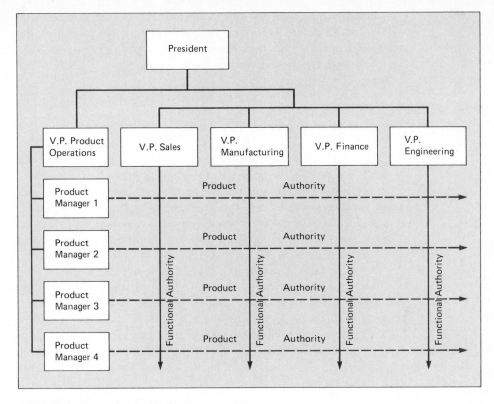

FIGURE 14.8 A Matrix Design.
In a matrix design, a product structure is superimposed on a basic functional structure. This results in a dual system of authority.

conditions. These include a complex and uncertain environment (one with frequent changes), and the need for economies of scale in the use of internal resources. Specifically, a matrix approach is often adopted by medium-sized organizations with several product lines, which do not possess sufficient resources to establish fully self-contained operating units. Under such conditions, a matrix design provides a useful compromise.

Key advantages offered by matrix designs have already been suggested by our discussion to this point. First, and of central importance, they permit flexible use of an organization's human resources. Individuals within functional departments can be assigned to specific products or projects as the need arises, but still be available for their regular, basic duties. Second, they offer medium-sized organizations an efficient means of responding quickly and adequately to a changing, unstable environment. Third, matrix designs often enhance communication among managers; indeed, they literally force matrix bosses to discuss and agree on many matters. Disadvantages of such designs include the frustration and stress faced by two-boss managers in reporting to two different supervisors, the danger that one of the two authority systems (functional or product) will gain supremacy over the other (performance is usually enhanced when these are perceived by employees as

445

being in balance[17]), and the fact that in order to succeed, it requires consistently high levels of cooperation from the people involved. Since organizations must often attempt to stretch their financial and human resources to the limit, however, matrix designs can be useful in many contexts.

Multinationals: A Note on Their Structure

In recent decades, the volume of world trade has increased to unprecedented levels. In fact, the flow of raw materials, finished products, technology, and labor is currently so great that many experts contend that there is now only a single, unified world economy.[18] The labels affixed to a wide range of products tell the story, even to a casual observer. It is common, today, to discover that the raw materials used in a specific product originated in one country, that its component parts were manufactured in several others, and that final assembly took place in yet another (refer to Figure 14.9). One effect of this shift toward a single worldwide economy has been tremendous growth in the number of **multinationals**—organizations that conduct their operations across international boundaries.[19] Since many, if not most, of these organizations previously existed within one country, an intriguing question pertaining to their structure arises: how have they handled the shift to international activities? In short, how have they built multinational operations into their structure?[20] Revealing information on this issue has recently been reported by Daniels, Pitts, and Tretter.[21]

These investigators were primarily interested in the question of how various operating characteristics of such companies (e.g., their product diversity, the ratio of foreign to total corporate sales) would affect their choice among potential multinational structures. To examine this issue, they first identified a number of large U.S.-based companies with significant foreign operations (at least 10 percent of their total business). Next, they assessed several operating characteristics of these organizations. Included were product diversity, investment in research and development, the ratio of foreign to total sales, and the way in which the companies entered foreign markets (e.g., acquisition of an existing foreign business, starting an entirely new one). A third step involved examination of the structures adopted by the chosen companies. Five distinct types were observed. These were: (1) *worldwide functional*—top-level executives had worldwide responsibility for dis-

FIGURE 14.9   *Today's Products: Multinational in Origin.*
Many products now move back and forth across international boundaries at several points during their manufacture.

Organizational Design: Automatic Reaction or Conscious Choice?

By now, it should be obvious that organizations differ greatly with respect to their internal structure. Some adopt a functional design, others are arranged according to products or markets, and still others combine these basic strategies in a matrix design. Further, an almost infinite number of variations on such patterns exist, and can be observed in operation. The existence of such diversity, in turn, raises an intriguing question: how, precisely, do organizations come to adopt their specific structures? One answer—by far the most popular one at present—is as follows: organizational structure is determined, to a large degree, by the *context* in which an organization operates. Contextual factors such as size, technology, and environmental uncertainty combine to mold organizational structure into specific forms.[22]

This reply makes a great deal of sense. As open systems, organizations *must* be sensitive to the contexts in which they exist. Thus, it is only reasonable to assume that their internal structure is largely a reflection of such circumstances. Moreover, as we will see in Chapter 15, an impressive body of evidence supports this *structure-contingency* approach, indicating that organizational effectiveness is often powerfully determined by the closeness of "fit" between internal structure on the one hand and various contextual factors on the other.[23] As you may already realize, however, there is one potential flaw in this perspective—a flaw noted by several recent critics.[24] This weakness can be summarized as follows: the structure-contingency approach seems to assume that organizational structure develops in an automatic manner, in reaction to external variables. It devotes little or no attention to the role of active decision-makers in this process. That managers do indeed matter in this respect is suggested by several considerations.

First, as pointed out recently by Keeley, human values are involved in, and shape, even the most scientifically oriented views of how organizations should be structured and managed.[25] For example, values relating to fairness in contractual arrangements, and goal-seeking by individuals or groups cannot help but shape certain aspects of *organization theory*. Second, as noted by Randolph and Dess, organization design is often the result of purposeful, strategic decisions by top managers.[26] These choices are, indeed, often constrained by contextual and situational factors, but they do enter into the process and play an important role. Finally, growing evidence suggests that managers often hold clear beliefs about the causal relationships between contextual factors (e.g., technology, size), key aspects of structure (e.g., formalization), and performance.[27] In short, they believe that certain conditions tend to produce specific internal structures, and that these, in turn, affect performance. Since beliefs often have a powerful self-confirming impact, it is clear that such views can influence decisions relating to organizational design in important ways.

In sum, there seem to be several compelling grounds for assuming that organizational design is influenced by the beliefs, values, and motives of decision-makers, as well as by the unavoidable constraints of contextual factors. This conclusion, in turn, holds an important message for practicing managers. Since organizational design stems, at least in part, from the cognitive processes of specific, high-level executives, it should *never* be viewed as an inevitable "given." On the contrary, since decisions by even the best informed and most rational individuals are subject to several sources of error (refer to Chapter 13), an organization's structure should be continually examined, with an eye toward improvement and refinement. In short, since organizational design is the product of *people*, as well as the result of powerful external constraints, it should be viewed as an ongoing process rather than as a past event now indelibly engraved upon the corporate chart. To the extent this perspective is adopted, organizations, as well as the persons within them, may reap substantial benefits.

tinct functions (e.g., sales, engineering); (2) *worldwide product*—top-level executives were responsible for one or more worldwide businesses; (3) *international division*—a separate division for foreign operations existed; (4) *area organization*—different executives head the company's operations in various regions; and (5) *matrix organization*—middle level executives report to two or more bosses.

When adoption of each of these structures was related to various operating characteristics of the companies studied, several interesting relationships were observed. First, as expected, no organizations rated high in product diversity adopted a worldwide functional design. Rather, most companies in this category chose a worldwide product design (64 percent) or an international division structure (32 percent). Second, it appeared that as dependence on foreign sales increased, organizations were more likely to adopt an international division approach (40 percent). Finally, it was observed that use of an area design was relatively rare among these U.S.-based multinationals, except in cases where dependence on foreign sales was especially high (e.g., among food, chemical, and auto supply companies).

In sum, there did appear to be numerous links between operating characteristics of these large and generally successful multinationals and the way in which they incorporated foreign business into their overall corporate structure. In this respect, the findings reported by Daniels and his colleagues serve to underscore what, we hope, has been a central theme of this entire chapter: the specific internal structure adopted by an organization both *reflects* the conditions under which it operates and *affects* its performance in many different ways. (Why do organizations adopt specific designs? And how can individual managers have an impact on this process? For some comments on these issues, please see the **Perspective** insert on page 447.)

SUMMARY

Organizations can be viewed as **open systems.** They receive input from the external environment, transform this into output, and then release their products and services back into the environment beyond their boundaries. Major subsystems within most organizations include production, maintenance, adaptation, boundary-spanning, and management.

The internal structure of organizations differs along a large number of dimensions. Among the most important of these are: *specialization*—the degree to which organizational tasks are subdivided; *formalization*—the presence of formal rules and regulations; length of the *chain of command*; *centralization*—the degree to which authority and decisions are reserved to persons high in the organization's hierarchy; and *complexity*—a composite of the number of levels in the organization's hierarchy and the number of different job titles, departments, and units it possesses.

Two early perspectives on organization design were provided by *scientific management* and the *bureaucratic model*. Basic components of scientific management imply the need for a short chain of command and at least a degree of decentralization. The bureaucratic model suggests that, ideally, organizations should be structured (and operate) in accordance with principles of *rationality* rather than favoritism or family ties. It recommends such specific steps as hiring on the basis of qualifications, promotion on the basis of merit, operating in accordance with clearly stated rules, a hierarchy of authority, and a high degree of specialization.

Most organizations adopt one of three basic types of design: **functional, product,** or **matrix.** In functional designs, separate departments are established to carry out specific activities (e.g., production, marketing, maintenance). Such designs provide important economies of scale, but are often slow to adapt to shifting environmental conditions. In product designs, separate self-contained units are established to handle specific products, markets, or geographic areas. Product designs permit rapid adjustment to changing environments, but face problems of interunit coordination and the loss of economies of scale. Matrix designs result when a product (or project) design is superimposed on a functional structure. Within such designs, a dual system of authority is established—one based on function and one based on product or project. As a result, some individuals must report to two different supervisors. Matrix designs afford medium-sized organizations some of the benefits of both functional and product designs. However, to succeed, they require a great deal of coordination among the units and persons involved.

Multinationals—organizations that conduct operations across international boundaries—can adopt any of several internal structures (e.g., worldwide functional, worldwide product, international division, area). Their choice among these seems to depend upon several operational factors (e.g., their degree of product diversity, the ratio of foreign to total sales).

KEY TERMS

adaptive subsystem: The subsystem within an organization responsible for dealing with change. Typically, this function is handled by such departments as research and development or engineering.

boundary-spanning subsystem: The subsystem within an organization that handles transactions across its boundaries. This function is often assigned to such departments as marketing and purchasing.

bureaucratic model: A model of organizational structure and function emphasizing rationality. According to the bureaucratic model, an "ideal" organization includes such features as adherence to formal rules, specialization, hiring on the basis of qualifications, and promotion on the basis of merit.

centralization: The extent to which authority and decision making are reserved for individuals high in the organizational hierarchy.

chain of command: Refers to the number of levels between the highest and lowest positions (in terms of authority) within an organization.

complexity: A composite index of the number of separate job titles and departments within an organization, plus the number of levels separating its highest- and lowest-ranking members.

formalization: The extent to which an organization possesses, and operates in accordance with, written documentation.

functional design: A basic type of organization design based on activities or functions. Within a function design, separate departments or units specialize in the performance of specific tasks (e.g., maintenance, production, sales).

line positions: Positions in an organization concerned with its major workflow (i.e., the goods or services it produces).

maintenance subsystem: The subsystem within an organization responsible for the smooth operation and upkeep of its physical and human resources.

management subsystem: The subsystem within an organization responsible for coordinating and directing the other systems.

matrix design: A form of organization design in which a product or project structure is superimposed upon a functional structure. This creates a dual system of authority, at least at high levels within the organization.

open system: A system that has some degree of interaction with its external environment. Organizations operate as open systems, receiving input from the environment, transforming it into output, and then send their products or services back across their boundaries.

organization design: The formal structure adopted by an organization to divide responsibility, enhance communication, and facilitate attainment of its major goals.

production subsystem: The subsystem within an organization concerned with its major workflow—the creation of goods or services.

scientific management: An early perspective on management that emsphasized the importance of effective job design and work motivation. Several aspects of this approach have implications for organization design.

span of control: The number of subordinates that report to a given supervisor.

specialization: The extent to which tasks performed by an organization are subdivided.

staff positions: Positions within an organization not directly concerned with its major workflow. Persons occupying such jobs offer their expertise and advice to other organization members (primarily, ones directly concerned with workflow).

NOTES

1. P. C. Nystrom and W. H. Starbuck, eds. (1984). *Handbook of organizational design.* New York: Oxford University Press.

2. R. L. Daft (1983). *Organizational theory and design.* St. Paul, Minn.: West.

3. J. D. Thompson (1967). *Organizations in action.* New York: McGraw-Hill.

4. D. Katz and R. L. Kahn (1966). *The social psychology of organizations.* New York: Wiley.

5. See Note 1.

6. F. W. Taylor (1911). *The principles of scientific management.* New York: Harper & Brothers.

7. J. E. McGrath (1976). Stress and behavior in organizations. In M. D. Dunnette (ed.), *Handbook of industrial and organizational psychology.* Chicago: Rand McNally.

8. J. H. Morris, R. M. Steers, and K. L. Koch (1979). Influence of organizational structure on role conflict and ambiguity for three occupational groupings. *Academy of Management Journal, 22,* 58–71.

9. P. J. Nicholson, Jr. and S. C. Goh (1983). The relationship of organizational structure and interpersonal attitudes to role conflict and ambiguity in different work environments. *Academy of Management Journal, 26,* 148–155.

10. See Note 6.

11. M. Weber (1947). *The theory of social and economic organizations.* Translated by A. M. Henderson and T. Parsons. New York: Free Press.

12. J. Child (1977). *Organization.* New York: Harper & Row.

13. See Note 2.

14. See Note 2.

15. R. Duncan (1979). What is the right organization structure? *Organizational Dynamics,* winter, 59–80.

16. S. R. Davis and P. R. Lawrence (1977). *Matrix.* Reading, Mass.: Addison-Wesley.

17. R. Katz and T. J. Allen (1985). Project performance and the locus of influence in the R&D matrix. *Academy of Management Journal, 28,* 67–87.

18. R. Moyer (1984). *International business: Issues and concepts.* New York: Wiley.

19. K. Paul and R. Barbato (1985). The multinational corporation in the less developed country: The economic development model versus the north-south model. *Academy of Management Review*, *10*, 8–14.

20. J. D. Daniels, E. W. Ogram, Jr., and L. H. Radebaugh (1982). *International business environments and operations*, 3rd ed. Reading, Mass.: Addison-Wesley.

21. J. D. Daniels, R. A. Pitts, and M. J. Tretter (1984). Strategy and structure of U.S. multinationals: An exploratory study. *Academy of Management Journal*, *27*, 292–307.

22. J. D. Ford and J. W. Slocum, Jr. (1977). Size, technology, environment, and the structure of organizations. *Academy of Management Review*, *2*, 561–575.

23. See Note 2.

24. H. R. Bobbitt, Jr. and J. D. Ford (1980). Decision-maker choice as a determinant of organizational structure. *Academy of Management Review*, *5*, 13–23.

25. M. Keeley (1983). Values in organizational theory and management education. *Academy of Management Review*, *8*, 376–386.

26. W. A. Randolph and G. G. Dess (1984). The congruence perspective of organization design: a conceptual model and multivariate research approach. *Academy of Management Review*, *9*, 114–127.

27. J. D. Ford and W. H. Hegarty (1984). Decision makers' beliefs about the causes and effects of structure: An exploratory study. *Academy of Management Journal*, *27*, 271–291.

CHAPTER 15

Organization Design: The Contextual Dimensions

These are grim days for Sober National Bank. For more than five decades SNB experienced steady, if modest, growth. Total assets increased, new branches were opened, and earnings rose in a consistent manner. The bank was viewed as a model of financial stability, and was justly proud of its record of having paid dividends in 168 consecutive quarters. During the past three years, however, the situation has altered sharply. Several factors have combined to threaten SNB's corporate health. First, new government policies favoring deregulation led to increased competition from larger banks, as well as from organizations outside the banking industry (e.g., money-market funds, national brokerage houses). Second, interest rates suddenly soared to record levels, leaving Sober in the bind of coping with thousands of low-yielding loans, while having to pay higher and higher rates to attract new deposits. A third problem faced by the bank has been its own inability to adapt to technological advances. Sober has been slower than several of its competitors to adopt such innovations as automated tellers, computerized payment of bills, and the like. On top of all these difficulties, the local economy has deteriorated badly, as growing numbers of businesses in SNB's home territory have departed for the friendlier environment of the "Sunbelt." In sum, SNB is an organization in crisis. The handwriting is clearly on the wall: if it doesn't change, and change soon, it is certain to disappear—probably into the hands of one of its larger competitors. But what steps should it take to adjust to these new conditions? It is to discuss this question that SNB's top executives are meeting today.

Graham Keefer, SNB's C.E.O., begins on a somber note. "I don't have to go into the situation in detail; you all know what's been happening. Our earnings are down and our customer-base is eroding. If you've got any bright ideas on how we can turn the situation around, now is the time to propose them. Two or three more quarters like the last one, and we'll be in serious trouble."

For a moment, there's only silence. Then, the suggestions begin to roll in. The first to speak is Sally Okun, one of SNB's senior vice presidents.

"Well, one thing we can do is get out there and fight for customers. A lot of our competitors are advertising, conducting mail campaigns, and drumming up new business in a lot of different ways. We've never done that sort of thing before, but now I think we have to."

"I agree," says Ray Cummings, another V.P., nodding his head vigorously. "We've got to let people know about our new services, and remind them of just how long we've been part of this region. Maybe we need a new department —one specializing in public relations and marketing. It would be a new move for us, but given the way things have changed, it makes a lot of sense."

"I'm with you there," Les Mitchell, head of Financial Services, comments. "Sprucing up our image *can* be a big plus. But I also think we've got to start targeting our branch offices for the type of customers they serve. That could save us a lot of unnecessary expense."

"Exactly what do you mean?" Graham asks.

"Just this. We've had some pretty big shifts in ethnic make-up in some of our towns and cities. A lot of Spanish-speaking people have moved in, and the proportion of retirees has literally exploded in recent years. Yet, we keep on offering the same mix of services at every branch. I think we should determine just what these different groups need or want, and tailor our local branches to provide it."

"Hmm . . ." Sally murmurs. "That sounds pretty good to me. There's no reason to have trust departments in locations where no one uses them, or a mortgage unit where most of our customers are renters. Yes, that's a good idea, all right."

Encouraged, Les continues. "If we do go that route, I also think we should make some adjustments in our style of operations. Primarily, we ought to give some thought to letting people in the branches make their own decisions. After all, they do know more about their local markets than anyone else. . . ."

Discussion of this and several other proposals for change at SNB continues for another half-hour. By the end of the meeting, two points have become clear: (1) Sober's current problems stem from its past inability (or unwillingness) to adapt to changing conditions, but (2) such change *is* possible, and if enacted promptly, can save SNB from extinction. In sum, the consensus might be summarized as follows: "SNB is down, but unless it continues to stand pat, it is definitely not *out!*"

As the preceding incident suggests, organizations do *not* exist in an environmental vacuum. On the contrary, as real entities embedded in a specific society at a given point in time, they are affected by a host of external forces. Government regulations,

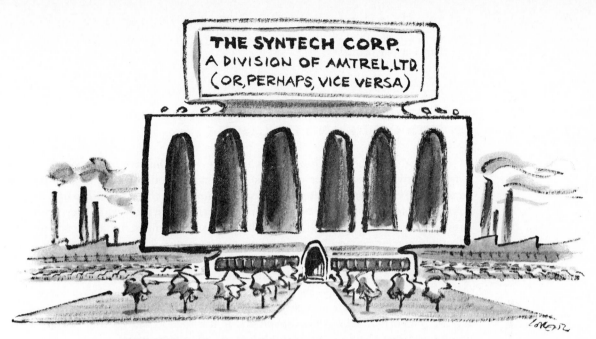

FIGURE 15.1   *The External Environment: As Complex as It Seems.*
As shown here, modern organizations must face a complex (and sometimes baffling!) external environment. (Source: Drawing by Lorenz; © 1982 The New Yorker Magazine, Inc.)

shifting patterns of competition, general economic conditions, technology, the skills and attitudes of employees—these are only a few of the environmental factors impinging on organizations at any time (refer to Figure 15.1). To reiterate our statement in Chapter 14, organizations are definitely *open* systems; and what they are open to, primarily, is influence from the external world around them.

Because the **external environment** exerts powerful and far-ranging effects upon most organizations, it is impossible to understand their nature, important processes within them, or key aspects of organizational behavior, in the absence of careful attention to this topic. The present chapter, therefore, will focus primarily upon this crucial *contextual dimension.* To provide you with a basic grasp of the complex interplay between various environmental factors on the one hand, and key organizational processes on the other, we will proceed as follows. First, we will describe those aspects of the environment most likely to influence organizations, and examine the key dimensions along which they, and external environments generally, seem to vary (e.g., complexity, stability). Next, we will examine some of the specific effects exerted by such factors. As will soon become apparent, the external environment surrounding a given organization can influence its *internal structure,* its overall *performance,* and even its general *management system* or approach.[1] After completing our discussion of the nature and impact of the external environment, we will turn to the role of another contextual factor—**technology**.[2] This refers to the knowledge, tools, and techniques used by organizations to perform their major work. It seems only reasonable that the kind of activities occurring within an organization will affect both its structure and function, and a substantial body of evidence suggests that this is actually the case. Under certain conditions, technology, too, appears to influence several aspects of organization design and organization performance.

THE ENVIRONMENT: EXTERNAL INFLUENCES ON STRUCTURE AND FUNCTION

To begin at the beginning, let's indicate just what we mean by the term **external environment.** For purposes of this discussion, it refers to *all elements outside the boundary of a given organization that have the potential to affect it (or certain of its component parts) in some manner.*[3] In a sense, virtually every aspect of the physical or social world surrounding a given organization has the potential to affect it in some manner. To mention just two examples, extremes in weather (e.g., a very hot summer or intensely cold winter) can cause an organization to use more energy, and changing fashions can alter the style of dress, and perhaps the behavior, of its employees. While such effects probably exist, there is general agreement that certain aspects of the outside world are crucial: they impinge more directly and forcefully on organizations than do others. In this section we will first identify these crucial *environmental domains,* and then examine their major effects.

The External Environment: Domains and Dimensions

While many aspects of the external environment might potentially influence organizations, nine seem most important. These have been labeled: *industry, raw materials, financial resources, human resources, market, government, economic conditions, culture,* and *technology.*

Nine key domains. The first of these factors, *industry,* refers primarily to the level of competition experienced by a given company. This varies greatly from industry to industry, and is an essential fact of life for most organizations. It determines how much must be spent on advertising, the size of profit margins, and several other important outcomes. *Raw materials,* of course, are the essential inputs required by an organization. They can range from various commodities for a manufacturing concern, through students in the case of universities, or patients for hospitals.

A third important aspect of the external environment is *financial resources.* This factor includes the availability of funds for performing normal functions (e.g., procurement, production, maintenance, sales), as well as resources for expansion and growth. It encompasses interest rates, insurance premiums, and even current conditions in bond and stock markets. The fourth factor on our list—*human resources*—might, at first, appear to be located within the organization. To an extent it is. But given that every organization experiences some degree of turnover, the supply of appropriate personnel in the job or labor market is an external factor of major importance. The term *market* refers primarily to customer demand for the goods and services produced by an organization. Since this can fluctuate greatly in response to many factors other than the quality or price of the organization's output, it is clearly an aspect of the external environment.

A sixth factor or domain involves the actions and policies of *government*.[4] Regulations, tax codes, and even the political system itself (e.g., capitalism, socialism) exert important effects upon organizations and must be dealt with on a daily basis. *General economic conditions,* too, are important. If these are favorable, an organization may prosper; if they are unfavorable, it may find it difficult to make a profit or even to remain in existence. Another aspect of the external environment that is often of major importance involves the *culture* or society in which an organization operates. Values can shift (e.g., from no concern with protecting the environment to major concern with this issue), and these, in turn, can strongly affect an organization's outcomes. Similarly, changes in the ethnic make-up of the population, shifts in average age, changes in birth rates, and related factors can all have profound long-term effects on organizations in many different fields. Finally, there is *technology*. Since this refers to techniques and methods used within an organization, it might, at first, appear to be an internal rather than an external factor. Because many advances in technology originate outside a given organization, however, technology, too, can be viewed as a part of the external environment. A summary of these nine major environmental domains is provided in Figure 15.2;

FIGURE 15.2   *Key Domains of the External Environment.*
As shown here, organizations are affected by many aspects of the external environment.

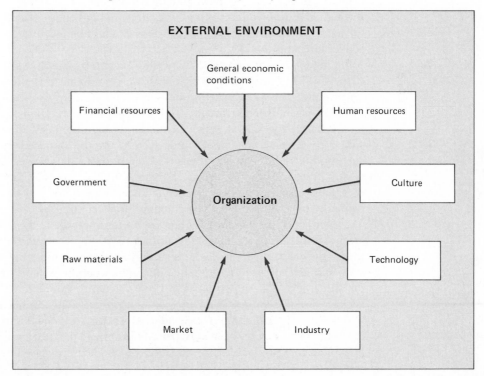

please consider it carefully before proceeding. As you do, you will probably come to realize that organizations, as entities, exist in, and are surrounded by, a complex external environment.

Complexity, stability, and uncertainty: The key environmental dimensions. A major goal in much recent organizational research has been that of establishing clear links between aspects of the external environment and the structure or performance of various organizations.[5] Given the diversity of the nine domains considered above, you may wonder whether this is really a feasible task. Since the environment faced by each organization is, in some respects, different from that faced by any other organization, how can general relationships be established? The answer lies in the following fact: while specific environments are indeed unique, all can be classified according to their position along certain underlying dimensions. The most important of these involve variations in terms of **complexity** and **stability.** Further, when combined, they yield a third basic dimension—one of **environmental uncertainty.**

As you can probably guess, the complexity dimension ranges from simple to complex, and involves the number of external elements that are relevant to, or play a role in, an organization's operations.[6] In a simple environment, few outside elements influence the organization; in a complex one, many exert such effects. In contrast, the stable-unstable dimension refers to the degree to which environmental elements change over time. In a stable environment, little change takes place; in an unstable one, major shifts occur. When these two factors are combined, they generate the third dimension mentioned earlier: environmental uncertainty. This ranges from low uncertainty—environmental conditions that are both simple and stable— through high uncertainty—conditions that are both complex and unstable. Perhaps the nature of all three of these dimensions can best be illustrated by means of several concrete examples.

First, consider a company that manufactures a single, simple product: paper clips. The environment faced by such an organization is probably quite low in uncertainty. This is so because the number of external elements impinging on the company is small. There are probably no government regulations, and few competitors. Further, the sale of paper clips is probably little affected by shifts in cultural values or changes in demographic factors. By the same token, the environment surrounding this company is also probably quite stable over time. Little change occurs in technology, the overall demand for paper clips, or the availability of raw materials. The result: environmental uncertainty is low. Decision makers in the company have little difficulty predicting future conditions.

Next, consider an organization facing a somewhat higher (but still moderate) level of uncertainty: a large life insurance company. Here, the environment is complex—the company must deal with a myriad of government regulations at both the state and federal level, with many financial matters (e.g., interest rates, changes in the value of its investment portfolio), with general economic conditions, and with various cultural values (e.g., the recent demand that premiums be identical for males and females). On the other hand, the changes in these and other factors tend to occur fairly slowly, over long periods of time. Thus, they are relatively predictable. The company, therefore, faces only a moderate degree of environmental uncertainty.

An even higher level of such uncertainty exists for an organization in the business of producing and marketing toys. Here, the environment is fairly simple—there are few major competitors, few government regulations, raw materials are rarely a problem, and appropriate employees are readily available. However, the environment is highly unstable: the company's intended market is notoriously fickle, often changing radically overnight, and it is virtually impossible to predict what toys will be "hot sellers" in any given season. As a result, it is difficult to adjust production to consumer demand. Environmental uncertainty is quite high, and decision-makers within the organization face a difficult and challenging task.

Finally, consider the level of environmental uncertainty faced by an international oil company. Here, the external environment is both highly complex (many elements impinge on the company in important ways) *and* highly unstable (oil supplies are unpredictable, government regulations shift from year to year, environmental groups institute legal actions on an irregular basis). This combination of conditions produces a high degree of environmental uncertainty. Decision-makers find it extremely difficult to estimate the potential costs and benefits associated with various courses of action, or even the probabilities that specific decisions will be successful. Thus, they must draw on all of their past experience and management skills in their efforts to forecast future trends and help their organization adapt accordingly.

A summary of these various combinations of complexity and stability, as well as the levels of environmental uncertainty they yield, is presented in Figure 15.3 on page 460. Since virtually any environment can be located along these dimensions, and since the degree of uncertainty confronting an organization has important implications for its future outcomes, attention to these factors can be useful in many different contexts.

The External Environment: An Overview of Its Major Effects

Earlier, we noted that organizations are strongly affected by the external environments in which they operate. Given the constant interaction between organizations and various environmental domains (e.g., economic conditions, human resources, market, competition), this is hardly surprising. Perhaps somewhat more unexpected, however, is the systematic nature of these effects. Growing evidence suggests that the internal structure of organizations is shaped in highly predictable and orderly ways by environmental factors.[6] Some of the research illustrating this important point will now be reviewed.

The environment and structural complexity. The modern world, it is widely agreed, becomes more and more complex with the passage of time. To the extent this is true, the external environment surrounding many organizations, too, tends to increase in complexity. How do organizations respond to such conditions? The answer seems to be: with growing internal complexity. That is, as a growing number of environmental elements impinge on an organization and affect its production and outcomes, it tends to add departments, new job titles, and levels within

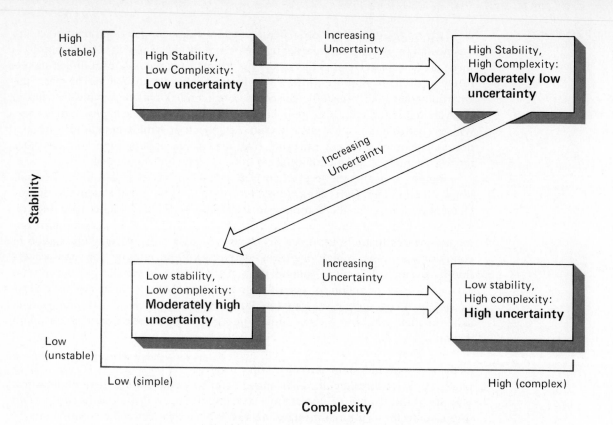

FIGURE 15.3 *Stability, Complexity, and Environmental Uncertainty.*
External environments vary in terms of *complexity* and *stability.* Various combinations of these conditions yield different levels of *environmental uncertainty.*

its authority hierarchy.[7] The basic reason for this is simple: these new units or positions are needed to deal with an ever-increasing array of external factors. For example, to return to the story at the start of this chapter, Sober National Bank found it necessary to establish a new department dealing with advertising and public relations because of increasing complexity in its external environment (e.g., growing competition from organizations outside the banking industry). Similarly, it seems likely that SNB would also soon create a separate unit charged with the task of forecasting economic trends, since these have become less and less predictable in recent years. The same process seems to be at work in real organizations as well as this hypothetical one: as the external environment becomes increasingly complex, this fact is mirrored in an organization's structure. In sum, growing external complexity generates corresponding internal adjustments.

Environmental uncertainty and boundary-spanning activities. All organizations must make contact, in some way, with important elements beyond their boundaries. Relationships with suppliers, customers, banks, government agencies, and many other entities are essential if they are to function and carry out their major work. In every organization, therefore, there are special individuals or units charged with the task of establishing and maintaining such relationships—with the task of performing what are usually known as **boundary-spanning** activities (refer to our earlier discussion in Chapter 14). Such activities involve two major roles: (1) obtaining and processing information about environmental conditions, and (2) representing the organization in its dealings with persons or entities beyond its boundaries.

While all organizations show some degree of boundary-spanning, however, it appears that the resources invested in such activities increase with environmental uncertainty.[8] As the external environment becomes less stable and more complex, organizations assign more and more employees to these tasks. For example, as government regulations become more and more complex, a company may increase the size of its legal department, or hire lobbyists to represent its views to the legislature. Similarly, as market conditions become more competitive, an organization may add staff to its marketing department, or perhaps establish new units to deal directly with the task of forecasting future trends.

That increased attention to boundary-spanning activities is often worth the effort is suggested by the findings of a recent study conducted by Dollinger.[9] He examined the relationship between boundary-spanning activities by the owners of eighty-two small businesses, and the success of their organizations. Boundary-spanning was assessed by asking participants to record the number of hours per week during which they had contact with people outside their company (e.g., customers, suppliers, potential new employees, bankers, union officials). Financial success was measured through data on current sales, and growth in net earnings. Results were quite clear: boundary-spanning activity was positively related to financial performance. The greater the proportion of their time spent by these entrepreneurs in contact with people outside their organizations, the more successful they tended to be.

The external environment and management style or approach. Another way in which the external environment influences organizations is illustrated by a classic investigation carried out some years ago by Burns and Stalker.[10] These researchers examined the organizational structure of twenty industrial firms in England. Included in their sample, and of special interest, were a rayon manufacturer, an engineering company, and a newly formed electronics-development firm. The external environment confronted by each of these organizations differed sharply. While environmental stability was high for the rayon manufacturer, it was lower for the engineering firm, and lowest of all for the electronics company. Burns and Stalker predicted that these differences in environmental stability would be reflected in the structure of the organizations, and results offered support for this prediction. The rayon company showed a relatively formal structure involving a high degreee of specialization and centralization, a strict hierarchy of authority, and vertical (mostly downward) patterns of communication. In contrast, the structure of the engineering company was more flexible. Tasks were not as clearly defined, and less emphasis was placed on the chain of command. Finally, the electronics firm showed the least formal structure of all. Decision making was more participative in nature, there was less specialization, and communication, too, was more open. Further study of additional companies confirmed these observations and led Burns and Stalker to a more general conclusion: many organizations tend to adopt either an **organic** or a **mechanistic** style of management (refer to Table 15.1). Moreover, which of these contrasting approaches is more effective depends upon the nature of the external environment they face. When conditions are relatively stable, a mechanistic approach may prove desirable. However, when they show rapid change, an organic approach may be more effective. In short, neither is necessarily "better" than the other; their relative success is *contingent* upon key aspects of the external environment.

The external environment and differentiation.   Earlier, we noted that as the external environment becomes increasingly complex, organizations adopt a more complicated internal structure. They create more departments, more jobs, and more levels of authority. The process does not stop there, however, and at this point, we wish to trace the impact of environmental factors one step further: to their role in **differentiation.**[11]

As organization structure becomes more complex, various departments become increasingly specialized. This is only reasonable, for they are designed with specific issues relating to certain environmental domains (e.g., market, financial resources, raw materials). One result of this process is that managers (and to a degree other employees) in various departments come to adopt different orientations and perspectives. In short, they come to view the world—and their organization—in contrasting ways. This process of *differentiation* helps the organization deal more effectively with environmental uncertainty. At the same time, though, it may create rising problems of **integration:** it becomes increasingly difficult for

TABLE 15.1   *Organic and Mechanistic Management Systems.*
Organizations often adopt either a relatively *organic* or a relatively *mechanistic* style of management. Major characteristics of each approach are summarized here.

Organic Style of Management	Mechanistic Style of Management
Task specialization is low	Task specialization is high
Communication is horizontal	Communication is mostly vertical
Hierarchy of authority is relatively open and flexible	A strict hierarchy of authority exists
Formalization is low	Formalization is high
Knowledge and control are spread throughout the organization	Knowledge and control are concentrated in a select group at the top of the organization
Conflicts are resolved through discussion	Conflicts are resolved through decisions by persons with authority

people or units with contrasting perspectives and orientations to collaborate with one another. Perhaps a specific example will help illustrate this point.

Imagine that in a large chemical company, there are separate functional departments dealing with production and with environmental control. (The latter unit is a fairly new addition to the corporate structure, created in response to increasingly complex government regulations, and legal actions by pro-environment groups.) Because their major task is that of manufacturing various chemicals as cheaply and efficiently as possible, managers in production devote little thought to preventing pollution, or protecting employees from contact with potentially harmful substances. In contrast, managers in environmental control focus precisely on these issues. The costs associated with reaching these goals are of less importance to them. The result: people in production become angry with those in environmental control for "meddling" with their operations and increasing their costs, while people in environmental control are constantly annoyed over the lack of cooperation they receive from those in production. In this and many other situations, therefore, increasing environmental complexity fosters growing differentiation and this, in turn, generates mounting problems of integration.

Evidence for the occurrence of such trends has been provided in well known studies conducted by Lawrence and Lorsch.[12] For example, in one of these projects, the investigators carefully examined three departments—production, sales, and research—in each of ten different corporations. Because these departments dealt with different aspects of the external environment, it was expected that they would become clearly differentiated over time. In fact, this was the case. For example, because it had to deal with the scientific community, the research department developed an informal structure, a long time horizon (it was willing to wait a long time for results), and an emphasis on quality. In contrast, the production department developed a formal structure, adopted a short time horizon, and focused on efficiency. Finally, the sales department, too, showed a formal internal structure and a short time horizon, but emphasized positive relations among employees.

In a subsequent study, Lorsch and Lawrence found support for the view that organizations devote increasing attention to the task of integration as environmental uncertainty rises.[13] Here, organizations in industries facing low (container), moderate (foods), or high (plastics) levels of uncertainty were studied. As expected, the degree of differentiation rose with increasing uncertainty. In addition, the proportion of managers assigned to integration activities (e.g., serving on task forces, committees, playing liaison roles) also increased with rising levels of environmental uncertainty. These findings, and those obtained in related research, underscore the impact of the external environment on these aspects of organizational structure.

In sum, existing evidence suggests that the external environment—and especially the degree of uncertainty it poses—affects the internal structure of organizations in several different ways. Complexity, boundary-spanning activities, general management system, and differentiation are all influenced in this manner. Clearly, then, if we wish to understand the structure of a particular organization, and comprehend how it developed, it is essential to consider factors beyond its boundaries, as well as within them. (Is the structure employed by organizations or work units fixed? Or does it vary with environmental conditions? For information on this issue, please see the **Focus** insert on page 464.)

Work Unit Structure: Fixed or Flexible?

Throughout this and the preceding chapter, we have assumed that any organization, department, or unit possesses a single unitary structure. That is, we have implied that there is one structure at a given time, and that it can be described and identified. In fact, this may not be the case. In almost any work setting, a variety of tasks are performed, and a wide range of situations is encountered. Some of these are routine and predictable. Others are nonroutine and unpredictable. It seems reasonable that an internal structure

effective in dealing with one of these types of situations might be less successful in handling the other. Thus, it may often be useful for departments or units to be flexible in this respect. In short, it may pay for them to be able to switch back and forth between contrasting structures or approaches. That this is actually the case is suggested by the findings of several studies. For example, Johnston found that depending on the goals being sought, a small consulting company switched back and forth between a mechanistic and an organic

FIGURE 15.4   *Work Unit Structure: Different in Certain and Uncertain Environments.* Members of work units reported that their groups showed less centralization and division of labor, but greater formalization when dealing with routine tasks/certain environments than when dealing with nonroutine tasks/uncertain environments. These findings suggest that work units adapt their internal structure to current environmental conditions. (Source: Based on data from McDonough and Leifer, 1983; see Note 16.)

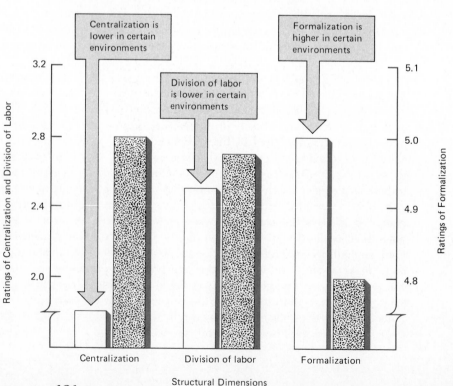

design.[14] Similarly, Duncan reported that decision units often employ a mechanistic structure for making routine decisions, but an organic one for making nonroutine ones.[15] That this type of flexibility in organization structure exists in other contexts, too, has recently been demonstrated by McDonough and Leifer.[16]

These investigators focused their attention on separate work units in a manufacturing firm and an insurance company. These units, which consisted of a supervisor and his or her subordinates, performed a number of different functions, ranging from purchasing and engineering through computer systems and quality control. Each supervisor was first asked to list four routine and four nonroutine tasks performed by their unit, and to indicate what environmental factors exerted an important impact upon the performance of these tasks. In addition, they indicated how unpredictable each of these factors was, thus providing information on environmental uncertainty. This information was then used to create sets of scenarios describing incidents involving routine tasks performed in a certain environment, and nonroutine tasks carried out in an uncertain environment. These scenarios were then presented to each supervisor's subordinates, who were asked to answer a series of questions relating to the structure adopted by their unit in each situation. These questions related to centralization, division of labor, and degree of formalization. Finally, ratings of the effectiveness of each work unit were obtained from executives familiar with them.

Findings were complex and not entirely consistent with initial predictions. However, they did provide support for the view that work units adopt somewhat different structures when dealing with routine tasks performed in the context of certain environments and nonroutine tasks performed in uncertain environments. Specifically, among work units rated as being effective, participants reported lower centralization and division of labor but higher formalization when dealing with routine tasks than when dealing with nonroutine ones (refer to Figure 15.4). Results for work units rated as less effective were identical, except that there were no differences between routine and nonroutine tasks with respect to division of labor.

Why should work units adopt lower centralization but greater formalization when dealing with routine as opposed to nonroutine tasks? Perhaps the answer lies in the fact that under such conditions, managers know what to expect (the tasks, after all, are routine, and environmental uncertainty is low). Thus, they are willing to rely on established rules and procedures as guides for subordinates, while at the same time allowing such persons to share in authority and decision making. In short, such conditions provide managers with an opportunity to "develop" their subordinates. Regardless of the reasons behind the specific pattern of findings obtained, however, it is clear that work units, as well as organizations and departments, are often flexible with respect to their internal structure. Like individuals, they tend to use whatever "works" in a given situation and in the context of specific environmental conditions.

Turning the Tables: Techniques for Controlling the Environment

In our discussion so far, we have examined the relationship between the external environment and organization structure from what might be termed a "passive" perspective. Briefly, we have focused on the ways organizations are shaped or molded by key features of the environment, especially uncertainty. As you already know, however, organizations are *not* passive entities. On the contrary, they are active, striving, goal-seeking systems, concerned with producing goods, services, and a wide range of outcomes. Given this fact, it seems only reasonable to turn the issue around and ask whether organizations also act upon their environments. The answer should be obvious: they do. In particular, they often attempt to change the environment, and so render it more favorable to them. This can be accomplished in several different ways.

Political action.   One of the most important strategies used by organizations to alter the external environment is political action. Typically, this involves contributions by specific companies to the campaigns of "friendly" candidates, or concerted lobbying efforts by trade associations representing entire industries. In both cases, the major goals are much the same: producing shifts in government policies so that they become more favorable to the interests of the organizations involved. Such changes can include the erection of trade barriers against foreign competitors, complex changes in certain portions of the tax code, or the removal of burdensome regulations and restrictions. That efforts along these lines often pay—and pay handsomely—is readily apparent. Consider the successful efforts of the U.S. automobile industry to restrict the importing of Japanese cars, and the "tax reform" act of 1982, which greatly increased the investment tax credit and other benefits for many companies. In these and numerous other cases, concerted political action by organizations has yielded an external environment that is much more predictable and advantageous than would otherwise be the case.

Contracts and mergers. Another general strategy employed by organizations to secure a more favorable environment is that of somehow attaining control over important (and especially unpredictable) domains. This can be accomplished either through appropriate contracts, which secure needed raw materials, markets, or financial resources on a long-term basis, or through acquisitions and mergers. For example, one large university has assured its supply of paper by signing a favorable long-term contract with a manufacturer of such products; indeed, the university is now the sole customer of this supplier. Going even further, an organization may actually purchase several of its suppliers, or acquire stores or other outlets for its products. To the extent an organization can engage in such actions, it may generate its own, favorable environment.

Cooptation. A third strategy for changing the external environment involves efforts to bring representatives of important environmental domains into the organization. For example, major customers and suppliers, or leaders of the local community can be appointed to the board of directors. Since they now have a stake in the future of the company, they can be expected to afford it "favored" treatment, or at least to take its interests into account in planning their own operations.

Advertising and public relations. Finally, organizations often attempt to secure stable or growing markets through advertising, and to improve their "image" through effective public relations. The latter strategy, of course, is related to political action. By creating a favorable impression among the public, organizations set the stage for follow-up actions by lobbyists, or by their friends in government. Safe-driving campaigns sponsored by the liquor industry, energy-conservation tips offered by oil companies, and warnings about smoking in bed by large tobacco companies provide good examples of such tactics.

Through these and related techniques, organizations take an active stance relative to their environment. Rather than merely adapting to external conditions, they seek to change them—to render them more favorable to their interests and goals. In short, they pursue an active, adaptive *strategy,* one designed to improve the alignment between their resources and capabilities on the one hand, and current environmental risks and opportunities on the other.[17] To the extent they succeed in such efforts, organizations may enhance, if not assure, their own success.

466

TECHNOLOGY: HOW TOOLS SHAPE STRUCTURE

Organizations differ tremendously in their **technology**—in the means they employ to transform inputs into outputs.[18] These can vary from simple hand tools at one extreme, through huge machines and complex computer-controlled equipment at the other. Clearly, the technology employed by a given organization is closely related to the work it performs, and the major goals it seeks. Thus, in an important sense, technology is shaped or chosen by the organization. But what about the reverse of this relationship? Are organizations themselves also shaped and affected by technology? In short, does the use of some specific set of knowledge, tools, or techniques make it more likely that an organization will adopt one type of internal structure rather than another? Research findings indicate that in some cases, at least, this may be so. Just as the design of a specific building reflects (or should reflect) the activities occurring within it, organization structure tends to mirror the technology employed. In the discussion that follows we will describe several major studies that have contributed to this conclusion. Because these investigations adopt contrasting frameworks for classifying technologies, and because they tend to focus on different levels (e.g., the entire organization, or units within it), they are often difficult to compare in a direct manner. However, in general, all point to the same general conclusions: technology plays an important role in shaping both the design and performance of many organizations.

Technology and Structure in Manufacturing Companies: The Woodward Study

Perhaps the best-known study on the impact of technology upon organization structure and performance is one conducted in England during the 1950s by Woodward.[19] At that time, it was widely assumed that the performance of virtually any organization could be maximized by following certain so-called *universal principles of management* (e.g., by adopting a specific span of control, a particular degree of centralization, and so on). To determine if these principles are indeed valid, Woodward and her associates collected information about one hundred different manufacturing firms. Data on many *structural characteristics* in these companies (e.g., span of control, management style, chain of command), as well as information on their success (e.g., profitability, market share) was gathered. Initially, Woodward expected that organizations classified as highly successful would share similar structural characteristics, while those classified as being low in effectiveness would share other characteristics. Surprisingly, though, results did not confirm this expectation. Instead, various aspects of organization structure appeared to be randomly distributed among successful and unsuccessful companies. Thus, there was little if any support for the accuracy of universal principles of management.

At this point, Woodward and her colleagues turned to the possibility that technology might act as a *mediating factor*, somehow determining the impact of various aspects of structure upon performance. To see if this was actually the case, they developed a system for classifying the firms in their study in accordance with the complexity of the technology they employed. Three major categories were established. In the first, labeled **small-batch and unit production,** custom work was the norm. Means of production were not highly mechanized, and the companies involved typically produced small batches of products to meet specific orders from customers. Firms included in this category produced such items as specialized construction equipment, or custom-ordered electronic items. In the second, known as **large-batch and mass production,** basic assembly-line procedures were prevalent. The companies in this group typically engaged in long production runs of standardized parts or products. Their output then went into inventory from which orders were filled on a continuous basis. The third category, **continuous-process production,** was the most technologically complex. Here, there was no start and no stop to production. Rather, output was generated in a continuous manner. Among the companies employing such advanced technology were oil refining and chemical corporations.

When companies employing these different types of technology were compared, important findings were uncovered. First, it was clear that they *did* differ with respect to internal structure. For example, the span of control (of first-level supervisors), formalization, and centralization were higher in companies employing mass production than in ones using small-batch or continuous process technologies. Similarly, chains of command were longest in organizations using continuous-process production, and shortest in those using small-batch methods. Complexity, too, varied with technology: companies using continuous-process production were highest on this dimension, while those using small-batch procedures were lowest. In short, it appeared that the type of technology employed in production was in fact an important variable with respect to organization structure (refer to Figure 15.5). As Woodward herself put it: "Different technologies imposed different kinds of demands on individuals and organizations, and those demands had to be met through an appropriate structure."[20]

Perhaps even more important than these findings was the fact that the characteristics distinguishing highly successful from unsuccessful companies also varied with technology. At the low and high ends of the technology dimension described above (small-batch production; continuous-process production), an *organic* management approach seemed best: companies showing this strategy were more successful than those demonstrating a *mechanistic* approach. In contrast, in the middle of the technology dimension (mass production), the opposite was true. Here, companies adopting a mechanistic approach tended to be more effective. Another finding was that successful firms tended to be those that had structures suited to their level of technology. Specifically, those with above-average performance showed structural characteristics similar to most other firms using the same type of production methods; in contrast, those with below-average records tended to depart from the median structure shown by companies in the same technology category. In sum, the results of Woodward's study indicated that there are important links between technology and organization performance.

Additional support for these conclusions was soon obtained in several other studies. For example, in a project involving fifty-five U.S. firms, Zwerman found that organizations employing small-batch or continuous-process technology tended to possess organic management systems. Those employing mass production methods generally showed mechanistic systems.[21] We should note, however, that other findings seem to point to the conclusion that *size* may sometimes be a more

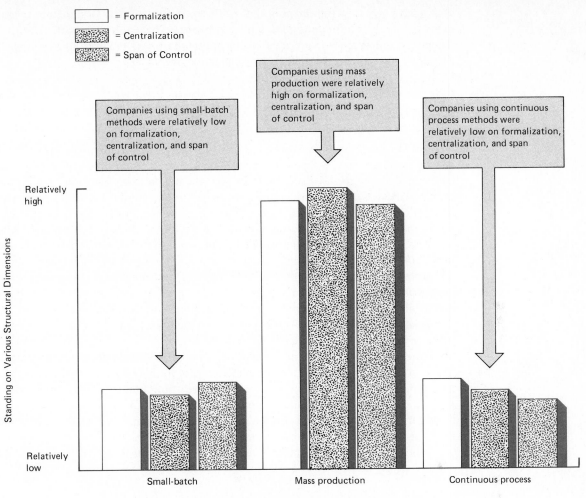

Key:
☐ = Formalization
▨ = Centralization
▨ = Span of Control

Companies using small-batch methods were relatively low on formalization, centralization, and span of control

Companies using mass production were relatively high on formalization, centralization, and span of control

Companies using continuous process methods were relatively low on formalization, centralization, and span of control

Standing on Various Structural Dimensions

Relatively high

Relatively low

Small-batch   Mass production   Continuous process

Type of Technology Employed

FIGURE 15.5   *Technology and Structure: Some Classic Findings.*
In a famous investigation, Woodward found that organizations employing contrasting types of technology differed in their internal structure. As shown here, companies using *mass production* technology demonstrated greater formalization and centralization, and larger spans of control than companies using either *small-batch* or *continuous-process* methods. Other differences in structure, too, were noted. (Source: Based on data from Woodward, 1965; see Note 19.)

important determinant of both internal structure and performance than technology.[22] We will have more to say about this issue below. At the moment, though, we wish to emphasize another point. Woodward's findings were extremely important in the following respect: they called attention to the fact that there is no single best organization structure. On the contrary, the characteristics that will prove most effective vary with (or are *contingent* on) technology and several other factors (e.g., key features of the external environment). Thus, in a sense, Woodward's research

was instrumental in establishing the *contingency approach* to organization structure—an approach that has guided most subsequent research in this area, and that,
despite recent criticism, remains highly influential even today.[23] In this respect,
certainly, the value of her efforts can hardly be overstated.

Workflow Integration: The Aston Studies

As the heading of the preceding section suggests, Woodward's project, and
several subsequent investigations of a similar nature, focused primarily on the links
between technology and structure in manufacturing companies. Thus, as thorough
as this work was, it left a basic issue unresolved: would similar findings be observed
in other types of organizations as well? Evidence on this question has been provided
by another team of British researchers affiliated with the University of Aston.[24] After
studying a wide range of both manufacturing and service organizations (e.g., savings banks, insurance companies, department stores), these investigators concluded
that technology can be described in terms of three basic characteristics: *automation
of equipment*—the extent to which work activities are performed by machines,
workflow rigidity—the extent to which the sequence of work activities is inflexible,
and *specificity of evaluation*—the degree to which work activities can be assessed
by specific, quantitative means. Since these three factors appeared to be highly
associated, they were combined into a single scale labeled **workflow integration.**
The higher an organization's score on this scale, the more likely it was to employ
automation, rigid task sequences, and precise, quantitative measurement of its
operations. The workflow integration scores obtained by various companies are
shown in Table 15.2. As you can see from this table, manufacturing firms generally
score higher than those whose primary output is service.

When workflow integration was related to structural characteristics in the

TABLE 15.2   *Workflow Integration: Some Representative Scores.*
Workflow integration scores for various companies included in the Aston studies. Note that
manufacturing firms generally receive higher scores than service organizations. (Source:
Based on data from Hickson, Pugh, and Pheysey, 1969; see Note 24.)

Organization	Classification (Manufacturing or Service)	Workflow Integration Score
Vehicle manufacturer	Manufacturing	17
Metal-goods manufacturer	Manufacturing	14
Tire manufacturer	Manufacturing	12
Printer	Service	11
Local water department	Service	10
Insurance company	Service	7
Savings bank	Service	4
Department stores	Service	2
Chain of retail stores	Service	1

organizations studied, no strong or general links were uncovered. Thus, at first glance, findings seemed contradictory to those reported by Woodward. Closer analysis of the data obtained, however, revealed that technological complexity *was* related to structural features in at least some ways. For example, as workflow integration increased, so did specialization, standardization, and decentralization of authority. The magnitude of these findings was small, and they seemed to involve mainly those aspects of structure closely connected to actual workflow. Moreover, *size* exerted stronger effects on several aspects of structure than technology.

These findings, plus those obtained in later studies, point to two conclusions. First, while technology does indeed seem to affect the internal structure of organizations, it is only one of several sources of influence in this regard. As a result, the so-called *technological imperative*—the view that technology always has a compelling influence on organization structure—clearly overstates the case. (This perspective gained a degree of popularity during the 1960s.) Second, technology probably exerts stronger effects upon structure in small organizations, where such characteristics impinge directly on workflow, than in large ones, where structure is complex, and often far removed from actual production. In any case, taken as a whole, the findings of the Aston studies can be interpreted as indicating that the impact of technology on organization structure is not restricted to manufacturing concerns; under certain conditions, it occurs in other types of companies as well.

Technology and the Structure of Work Units: Perrow's Model

Up to this point, we have focused on the impact of an organization's technology on its overall internal structure. As we noted in Chapter 14, however, different departments or units often specialize in performing different functions. To the extent that they do, it seems likely that they will also employ contrasting methods and tools. For this reason, it makes sense to inquire whether differences in technology can affect the internal structure and function of work units, as well as that of entire organizations. That this is in fact the case is suggested by a framework offered by Perrow.[25]

According to this model, two dimensions of technology are most directly relevant to an organization's structure: **exceptions** and **analyzability.** Exceptions refer primarily to level of variety associated with work activities. The greater the frequency of unexpected or novel events, the higher is a given technology on this dimension. Analyzability refers to the extent to which the process employed in converting inputs to outputs can be reduced to mechanical steps, or objective procedures. Combining these two dimensions yields four distinct categories of organizational or work unit technology: routine, craft, engineering, and nonroutine (refer to Figure 15.6, page 472). However, Perrow suggests that they can also be combined into a single dimension ranging from routine at one end through nonroutine at the other. *Routine* technologies involve little variety, and can readily be analyzed into simple, mechanical steps virtually anyone can follow. A good example is provided by standard production-line work. In contrast, *nonroutine* technologies involve

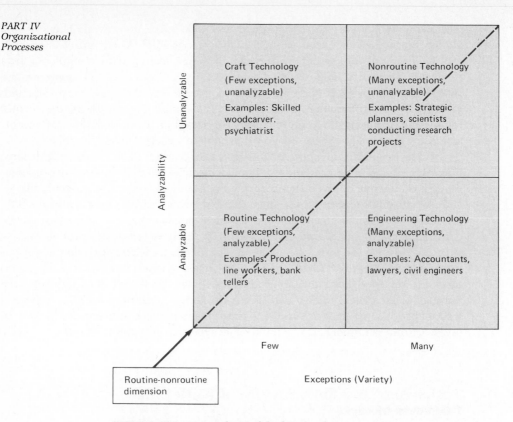

FIGURE 15.6   Perrow's Model of Technology.
According to a model proposed by Perrow, technology varies along two key dimensions: *analyzability* and *exceptions* (variety). When these are combined, four basic categories—routine, craft, engineering, and nonroutine—are generated. (Source: Based on suggestions by Perrow, 1967; see Note 25.)

considerable variety, and cannot be broken down into discrete, mechanical steps. Tasks using such technology include writing music, conducting basic research, or carrying out strategic planning.

Do departments or work units employing routine and nonroutine technologies differ in structure or function? The answer appears to be "yes."[26] First, units employing routine technologies appear to be mechanistic in orientation, while those employing nonroutine technologies tend to be organic. This is hardly surprising; since nonroutine technologies tend to call for creativity and can't be reduced to simple, mechanical formulas, it seems only reasonable that they would encourage a less formal, open, and free-flowing atmosphere than routine tasks. Such differences are often readily apparent on visits to different departments within a given organization (e.g., production on the one hand and research on the other). Second, as you might well anticipate, the span of control is often greater in work units employing routine technologies than in units employing nonroutine ones. A third difference involves communication. Often, this process is vertical in routine work units, but horizontal in nonroutine ones.[27] Finally, centralization is often higher in units employing routine technologies than in ones that make use of nonroutine proce-dures. Again, this makes good sense. When the tasks being performed are strictly mechanical, there is little reason to give employees much say in what happens, or much discretion in planning their own work activities. When tasks are more varied and complex, however, such latitude seems appropriate.

At this point we should note that the routine-nonroutine dimension (and the two factors underlying it—analyzability and exceptions) appears to be applicable to a very wide range of work units. For example in one recent study, individuals in many different units within a large organization (e.g., library, audit, computer programming, creative design, typing, personnel) were asked to answer questions about the technology used by their own unit.[28] Analysis of their responses indicated that the persons within a given unit tended to rate it in a fairly homogeneous way (i.e., they agreed about whether it was high or low in exceptions and high or low in analyzability). However, there were also significant differences *between* units: some were perceived by their members as employing routine technology, while others were viewed as using nonroutine procedures.

In sum, the technology used by various departments or units can range from being purely routine (unvaried, mechanical) at one extreme to being nonroutine (varied, unanalyzable) on the other. Further, such differences seem to be reflected in several features of internal structure. Where work units are concerned, therefore, technology is a factor well worth taking into careful account.

Technology and Interdependence

A final aspect of technology with important implications for organization structure is **interdependence.** This refers to the extent to which individuals, de-partments, or units within a given organization depend upon each other in accom-plishing their tasks. Under conditions of low interdependence, each person, unit, or group can carry out its functions in the absence of assistance or input from others. Under high interdependence, in contrast, such coordination is essential. A framework proposed by Thompson helps clarify the various types of interdepen-dence possible in organizations, and also the implications of this factor for effective structural design.[29]

The lowest level within this framework is known as **pooled interdepen-dence.** When such conditions prevail, departments or units are part of an organiza-tion, but work does not flow between them. Rather, each carries out its tasks in an independent fashion. One example of pooled interdependence is provided by the restaurants in a fast-food chain. Each contributes to the total earnings of the parent company, but there is little if any contact or coordination between them.

The next higher level suggested by Thompson is **sequential interdepen-dence.** Here, the output of one department or subunit becomes the input for an-other. For example, the advertising department of a large publisher cannot proceed with promotional campaigns until it receives information on forthcoming books from the editorial unit. Similarly, in a company that manufactures telephones, final assemblers cannot perform their jobs unless they receive a steady supply of compo-nent parts from other work units. Note that in sequential interdependence, informa-

Technology, the Environment, Structure and Performance: A Congruence Approach

If we were asked to extract the most crucial points made in the preceding thirty-odd pages, and to state them in a few simple sentences, this would be our reply: (1) the internal structure of an organization is strongly determined by the external environment in which it operates; (2) the internal structure of an organization is also determined by the technology it employs; and (3) the closer the congruence between these factors (i.e., between internal structure on the one hand, and environment and technology on the other), the better is the organization's performance.

These generalizations reflect the key findings of what, by and large, have been distinct lines of research. That is, many projects have been conducted to determine the impact of the environment on structure and performance, while many others have been performed to clarify the influence of technology on these factors.[31] This division in existing literature is readily understandable. As our discussion so far suggests, the complexities associated with each of these topics are quite staggering. Thus, it makes excellent sense to attempt to simplify matters by considering them separately. From the point of view of practicing managers, though, this division can be troublesome. Real organizations exist in a world where they must deal with a host of environmental factors, many aspects of technology, and their own performance simultaneously. For this reason, it is crucial that at some point, these separate bodies of knowledge about the environment and technology be combined into a unified framework. Unless they are, practical guidelines for maximizing efficiency and enhancing progress toward key organizational goals cannot be established. Can such integration be attained? The situation seems hopeful. During the past few years, attempts to develop such a multivariate framework have begun in earnest. One

FIGURE 15.7 *The Congruence Model of Organization Design: An Overview.*
According to the *congruence perspective,* an initial choice of product or service determines the specific environment faced by an organization. This, in turn, shapes the technology it uses, and the internal structure it adopts. Together, technology, the environment, and structure then determine organization performance. Feedback loops also exist between technology and product or market choice, and between performance and these choices. (Source: Based on suggestions by Randolph and Dess, 1984; see Note 5.)

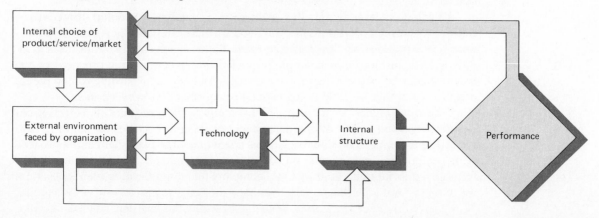

of the most interesting of these is the **congruence perspective** proposed recently by Randolph and Dess.[32]

According to these scholars, the process begins when a new organization or unit chooses its product or service, and so targets its potential market (the individuals, organizations, or other entities who will purchase its output). This initial choice then determines the environment in which it will operate. After all, depending on the particular product or service it produces, the organization will require certain inputs (e.g., raw materials, financial resources, human resources), and it will face specific types of competition, will have to deal with certain regulatory and legal systems, and will come face to face with certain cultural values relevant to its work.

The level of environmental uncertainty the organization or unit encounters will then play a role, along with product choice, in determining the specific technology it uses. The greater the uncertainty, the more nonroutine should be the technology selected. The choice of a specific technology, in turn, has implications for organization structure. To the extent technology is nonroutine and involves a high degree of interdependence between departments or units, an organic structure (i.e., one low in specialization, centralization, and formalization) should be adopted. If, instead, technology is routine and involves a low degree of interdependence, a mechanistic structure is more appropriate. Together, organization structure, technology, and the amount of environmental uncertainty remaining act to determine overall organization performance. This, in turn, forms a feedback loop with choice of product or market. If performance is high (the organization is successful), initial choices may be maintained. If it is low, they may be reassessed and altered. For example, if competition in one area is too intense to allow for profitable operations, the company may decide to shift to another, in which environmental conditions are more favorable. Similarly, technological advances, too, may affect managers' decisions to continue with the same products and services, or switch to others. (Please refer to Figure 15.7 for a summary of this model.)

It is important to note that at every step in this complex, ongoing process, the principle of *congruence* is of major importance. The closer the fit between environmental factors and choice of technology, the closer the match between technology and structure, and the closer the link between environmental factors and structure, the better the organization's performance.

At present, the congruence model is quite new, and still undergoing development. However, it already suggests a number of concrete hypotheses concerning the relationships between technology, the environment, internal structure, and performance. As these predictions are assessed in future research, it seems possible that the congruence model will form the basis for integrating current knowledge about all of these factors. To the extent it does, it will represent a major contribution to our knowledge of the complex ways in which organizations adapt to the world around them.

---

tion, products, and components flow in one direction. Thus, units further along the chain of production are dependent upon ones that precede it, but the reverse is not true.

The highest level in Thompson's model is known as **reciprocal interdependence.** Here, the output of each department or unit serves as the input for other departments or units in a reciprocal fashion. Thus, the output of Department A provides input for Department B, while the output of Department B serves as the input for Department A. An example of such reciprocal interdependence can be observed between the operations and maintenance departments of a large railroad. Here, the output of operations (from the point of view of maintenance) is rolling stock (engines, freight cars) in need of service: it is the input on which maintenance then works. Conversely, the output of maintenance (from the point of view of operations) is engines and railroad cars in good working order; this is the input the

Pooled interdependence

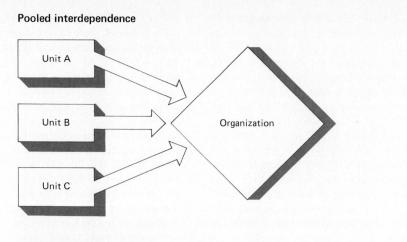

Sequential interdependence

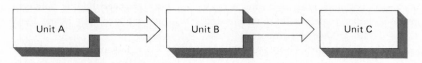

Reciprocal interdependence

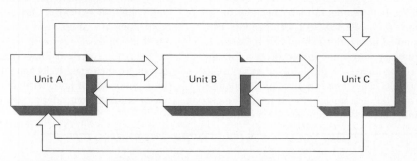

FIGURE 15.8 *Interdependence: Three Basic Types.*
Depending on the technology they employ, departments or units within an organization can show varying degrees of interdependence. Three important forms of such *interdependence—* pooled, sequential, and reciprocal—are illustrated here. Arrows indicate the flow of output between units. (Source: Based upon suggestions by Thompson, 1967; see Note 6.)

operations department then uses in its own work. The basic nature of all three types of interdependence described by Thompson are summarized in Figure 15.8.

As should be readily apparent, these three forms of interdependence require varying levels of coordination between the units involved. The need for coordination is quite low under conditions of pooled interdependence, since each of the departments or units involved is relatively independent. Rules and standard operating procedures can usually handle this task with little difficulty. In contrast, sequential interdependence requires substantially greater coordination. Here, formal meetings and vertical communication are often needed. Finally, reciprocal interdependence calls for strenuous efforts at coordination, including many unscheduled face-to-face meetings, and a high level of horizontal communication (recall our earlier discussion of coordination in Chapter 12).[30]

The level of interdependence existing between various units within an organization also has important implications for internal structure. Special attention should be directed, in planning organization design, to departments or units that are reciprocally interdependent. These should be grouped together so that they can engage in continuous, mutual adjustment (e.g., they should be close physically and should fall under the authority of the same person). Further, specific mechanisms for assuring a high degree of coordination between them (e.g., daily meetings, the creation of special liaison positions) should be developed. While top priority in devising internal structure should be devoted to reciprocal interdependence, efforts to establish effective communication between units that are sequentially interdependent is important, too. These should have ready access to one another, so that workflow between them can proceed in a smooth orderly manner.

In sum, the kind of work activities performed within an organization, and the specific technologies it employs, often determine the level of interdependence between its various units. Such interdependence, in turn, should be taken into careful account when planning internal structure. (Can the impact of the environment and the impact of technology be understood within a single conceptual framework? And if so, what is the relationship between these crucial factors? For some comments on these issues, please refer to the **Perspective** insert on page 474.)

SUMMARY

Organizations do not exist in a social or physical vacuum. On the contrary, they are surrounded by a complex and ever-changing **external environment.** Certain domains of the environment (e.g., competition, general economic conditions, government policies, raw materials) impinge on organizations, and affect them in important ways. Environments can be described in terms of their degree of *complexity* and their degree of *stability*. Together, these characteristics contribute to the important dimension of *environmental uncertainty.*

Research findings indicate that the external environment exerts important effects upon several aspects of organization structure. In addition, the environment affects the occurrence of *boundary-spanning* activities within organizations, their general *management systems* (whether these are *organic* or *mechanistic*), and their extent of *differentiation*. Organizations often attempt to influence the external environment, in order to make it more favorable to their operations. They seek to accomplish this goal through *political action, mergers and contracts, cooptation,* and *advertising or public relations.*

Technology refers to the tools, methods, or knowledge employed by an organization to transform inputs into outputs. Considerable evidence indicates that organization structure is affected by this factor in several ways. However, this relationship seems to be stronger and more consistent in small organizations than in large ones. Organizations employing *small-batch* or *continuous-process* technologies often show organic structure, while ones making use of *large-batch* methods demonstrate a more mechanistic approach. Technologies vary in terms of the extent to which they are *routine* or *nonroutine*. Organizations employing routine technologies show higher levels of formalization and standardization, and more vertical communication than organizations employing nonroutine technologies. Technologies also differ with respect to the degree of *interdependence* they require between departments or units. The higher the level of interdependence required, the greater the need for close coordination between the units involved.

KEY TERMS

analyzability: The extent to which the process employed to convert inputs into outputs can be reduced to mechanical steps or objective procedures.

boundary-spanning activities: Activities that link the organization to key elements of the external environment (e.g., suppliers, customers, sources of financial resources).

complexity: The number of external (environmental) elements relevant to an organization's operations.

congruence perspective: A perspective on organization design that seeks to link the environment, technology, internal structure, and performance within a single conceptual framework.

continuous-process production: Technology in which there is no start or stop to the production process.

differentiation: The extent to which managers and employees in different departments adopt contrasting orientations and perspectives.

environmental uncertainty: The extent to which key factors or elements in the external environment cannot be forecast or predicted accurately.

exceptions: The level of variety associated with work activities.

external environment: All elements outside the boundary of a given organization that have the potential to affect it in some manner.

integration: Efforts to overcome the loss of coordination that often results from differentiation.

interdependence: The extent to which units or departments within an organization depend upon each other to accomplish their tasks.

large-batch (mass) production: Technology based upon long runs of standardized parts or products.

mechanistic management approach: A management system characterized by a high degree of formalization and centralization.

organic management approach: A management system characterized by a relatively low degree of formalization and centralization.

pooled interdependence: A relatively low level of interdependence in which units within a given organization operate in a largely interdependent manner.

reciprocal interdependence: A high level of interdependence in which the output of each unit within an organization serves as the input for other units and vice versa.

sequential interdependence: An intermediate level of interdependence in which the output of one unit serves as input for another.

small-batch (unit) production: A technology in which products are custom-produced in response to specific customer orders.

stability (environmental):   Refers to the extent of change occurring in the external environment over time.

technology: The knowledge, tools, and techniques used by organizations to perform their work.

workflow integration: A measure of technology that takes account of the degree of automation, workflow rigidity, and specificity of evaluation within an organization.

NOTES

1. R. Jurkovich (1974). A core typology of organizational environments. *Administrative Science Quarterly, 19,* 380–394.

2. L. Fry (1982). Technology-structure research: Three critical issues. *Academy of Management Journal, 25,* 532–552.

3. R. L. Daft (1983). *Organization theory and design.* St. Paul, Minn.: West.

4. G. R. Ungson, C. James, and B. H. Spicer (1985). The effects of regulatory agencies on organizations in wood products and high technology/electronics industries. *Academy of Management Journal, 28,* 426–445.

5. W. A. Randolph and G. G. Dess (1984). The congruence perspective on organization design: A conceptual model and multivariate research approach. *Academy of Management Journal, 9,* 114–127.

6. J. D. Thompson (1967). *Organizations in action.* New York: McGraw-Hill.

7. J. Child (1972). Organizational structure, environment, and performance: The role of strategic choice. *Sociology, 6,* 2–22.

8. H. Aldrich and D. Herker (1977). Boundary spanning roles and organization structure. *Academy of Management Review, 2,* 217–239.

9. M. J. Dollinger (1984). Environmental boundary spanning and information processing effects on organizational performance. *Academy of Management Journal, 27,* 351–368.

10. T. Burns and G. M. Stalker (1961). *The management of innovation.* London: Tavistock.

11. J. W. Lorsch (1970). Introduction to the structural design of organizations. In G. W. Dalton, P. R. Lawrence, and J. W. Lorsch (eds.), *Organization structure and design.* Homewood, Ill.: Irwin.

12. P. R. Lawrence and J. W. Lorsch (1969). *Organization and environment.* Homewood, Ill.: Irwin.

13. J. W. Lorsch and P. R. Lawrence (1972). Environmental factors and organizational integration. In J. W. Lorsch and P. R. Lawrence (eds.), *Organizational planning: Cases and concepts.* Homewood, Ill.: Irwin.

14. H. R. Johnston (1976). Interactions between individual predispositions, environmental factors, and organizational design. In R. H. Kilmann, L. R. Pondy, and D. P. Slevin (eds.), *The management of organization design,* vol. 2. New York: North-Holland.

15. R. B. Duncan (1973). Multiple decision-making structures in adapting to environmental uncertainty. *Human Relations, 26,* 273–291.

16. E. F. McDonough III and R. Leifer (1983). Using simultaneous structures to cope with uncertainty. *Academy of Management Journal, 26,* 727–735.

17. E. E. Chaffee (1985). Three models of strategy. *Academy of Management Review, 10,* 89–98.

18. L. W. Fry and J. W. Slocum, Jr. (1984). Technology, structure, and work-group effectiveness: A test of a contingency model. *Academy of Management Journal, 27,* 221–246.

19. J. Woodward (1965). *Industrial organization: Theory and practice.* London: Oxford University Press.

20. See Note 19, p. vi.

21. W. L. Zwerman (1970). *New perspectives on organizational theory.* Westport, Conn.: Greenwood.

22. See Note 3.

23. C Schoonhoven (1981). Problem with contingency theory: Testing assumptions hidden within the language of contingency. *Administrative Science Quarterly, 26,* 349–377.

24. D. Hickson, D. Pugh, and D. Pheysey (1969). Operations technology and organization structure: An empirical reappraisal. *Administrative Science Quarterly, 14,* 378–397.

25. C. Perrow (1967). A framework for comparative organizational analysis. *American Sociological Review, 16,* 444–459.

26. C. A. Glisson (1978). Dependence of technological routinization on structural variables in human service organizations. *Administrative Science Quarterly, 23,* 385–395.

27. A. H. Van de Ven and D. L. Ferry (1980). *Measuring and assessing organizations.* New York: Wiley.

28. M. Withey, R. L. Daft, and W. H. Cooper (1983). Measures of Perrow's work unit technology: An empirical assessment and a new scale. *Academy of Management Journal, 26,* 45–63.

29. See Note 6.

30. See Note 3.

31. J. Pfeffer and H. Leblebici (1973). The effect of competition on some dimensions of organization structure. *Social Forces, 52,* 268–279.

32. See Note 5.

CHAPTER 16

Organizational Change and Development

Jim Brewster has just taken a position with Dallen Corporation, a leading manufacturer of industrial safety equipment. For years, Jim held a comparable post at Prime Industrial Systems, Dallen's arch rival. When he first joined Prime, it possessed a commanding lead in sales and earnings over its smaller competitor. Now, just eight years later, the situation is totally reversed: Dallen is the dominant company in the industry, and Prime is fighting for its very corporate life. The reason behind this dramatic shift is easy to spot: over the years, Dallen has been much more effective in coping with *change*. Time after time Jim had watched as Dallen launched new products that left its competition badly in the dust. Similarly, he had observed with growing awe the speed with which Dallen managed to adapt new technology to its manufacturing facilities. As a result, these are currently among the most efficient in existence. Yes, Dallen is a company on the move all right, and Jim is glad to be part of it. But what, precisely, lies behind Dallen's great success at innovation? He is still uncertain on this score, even after two weeks of thorough orientation. Since today marks the end of his official entry program, he hopes to raise this issue with Karen Von Duling, the V.P. responsible for his orientation, and with whom he's spent most of his time. The two executives are just completing a walking tour of one of Dallen's plants, when Jim sees a good opportunity to bring his question into the open.

"Look Karen," he begins, "you know how impressed I've been with everything I've seen. You've got a first-class operation here in every way, and I'm glad to be part of it. But there's one thing I'm still wondering about . . ."

"What's that?" Karen asks with interest.

"Just this: how do your people manage to be so flexible? I mean, all those innovations you're so famous for have to come from somewhere."

"Well, we've got a great R&D unit, and that helps a lot."

"I *know* you do; didn't I compete against it for years? But Prime has some good people in their operation too. Yet somehow, they never come up with the same kind of breakthroughs. And when they do, no one seems to do much about it."

"Well, that's part of the answer right there. We've got a real commitment to change at Dallen. When someone gets a good idea, we listen. And by 'we,' I mean everyone—from first-line managers on up to the C.E.O. himself."

"That's probably part of it, all right. We didn't have that kind of atmosphere at Prime."

"Oh, it's more than an atmosphere: it's a regular policy," Karen adds. "Dallen wants to be first with new methods, products, and everything else. That's practically carved in stone. And our top people are behind it 100 percent."

"O.K., I read you loud and clear. But getting the ideas in the first place is only part of the story. What about implementation? We had a heck of a job convincing people in our operations to accept new equipment or methods. And some of the people on our staff—whew!—they were always putting the brakes on new policies. How do you cope with those kind of things here?"

"Hm. . . that's a tough one." Karen comments, rubbing her chin. "I guess the best answer is that we have a kind of dual system. We're flexible and decentralized where new ideas or innovations are concerned—they can come from anyone at any level. But once a decision is made, or a new policy formulated, things get pretty firm. Rules come out of the woodwork, and we shift into a kind of "top-down" system. People at lower levels know that's how we operate, and they usually go along real well."

For a moment, Jim walks on in silence, thinking about Karen's words. Then, suddenly, he exclaims: "You know, I think I'm beginning to get it—it's a lot of things. First you go out of your way to encourage new ideas and flexibility, and then you sort of get tough, and make sure they're put to use. What a combination; no wonder you people were always so hard to beat! I don't envy my old friends at Prime. I hope they've been putting something away for a rainy day, 'cause from what I've seen so far, they may need it sooner than they expected . . ."

According to one old saying, "The more things change, the more they remain the same." This is a comforting thought, for most persons desire at least *some* degree of stability in their lives. Further, in certain respects, it appears to be true. Governments rise and fall, but taxes (in one form or another) are always present. Fashions come and go, but people remain interested in "looking good" and enhancing their appeal to others. And while individual leaders appear and disappear (sometimes with alarming speed), leadership itself—the functions it performs and the ways in which it is exercised—remains basically unchanged across the centuries. In these and other respects, stability *does* seem to be a fact of human life.

Such constancy is definitely lacking, however, where modern organizations are concerned. As we have noted in earlier chapters, they are open systems, existing in a complex, external world. Because of this fact, organizations must frequently cope with shifts in key environmental domains—trends that are, all too often, beyond their direct control. For example, among the important changes organizations have had to face in recent decades are these: vastly increased use of computers; the introduction of robotics and other automated means of production; rising competition across national boundaries; and major shifts in social attitudes and values, especially ones involving a decline in the "work ethic," and greater emphasis on personal freedom and fulfillment.

As you can readily guess, organizations effective in coping with such changes—companies like Dallen Corporation in our opening story—stand a good chance of success. By adapting to new conditions, they can continue to grow and prosper. In contrast, organizations unable to meet the challenge of change—companies like Prime Industrial Systems—tend to encounter serious problems. Indeed, in extreme cases, they may totally vanish from the scene (refer to Figure 16.1). It is on this key process of **organizational change** that we will focus in the present chapter.[1] Specifically, we will begin by considering some of the major *causes* of change—internal and external factors that lead organizations to alter their structure or functioning in some manner. Next, we will examine the major ways in which organizations respond to such pressures. These include shifts in their technology, the products and services they produce, and alterations in their internal structure and administrative systems. A fourth type of change, that involving people (efforts to alter their attitudes, skills or behavior), will be considered separately

FIGURE 16.1 Failure to Change: The Potential Costs.
If organizations fail to adapt to changing environmental conditions, they may soon meet the fate of the companies shown here.

under the heading of **organizational development**. Finally, we will also comment on the reasons why change is often strongly resisted, and on specific techniques for enhancing its acceptance.

ORGANIZATIONAL CHANGE: SOME BASIC CAUSES

Given a choice, most organizations prefer stability to change. The reason for this is obvious: the more predictable and routine major activities are, the higher the level of efficiency that can be obtained. Thus, "business as usual" is the preferred state in many cases. As you probably already realize, though, this goal of total stability is generally well out of reach. Too many forces conspire to make change both desirable and inevitable. Moreover, such forces are to be found within organizations themselves, as well as in the external environment. Several of the most important factors in each of these categories (internal and external) will now be considered. Please note: our purpose here is *not* that of providing an exhaustive list of the many factors responsible for organizational change—such a list would be practically endless. Further, we have already considered several of the key factors on it (e.g., various aspects of the external environment, technology) in Chapter 15. What we wish to do here is simply to emphasize the following fact: change, within organizations, does *not* occur in a random or unpredictable manner. On the contrary, it can usually be traced to specific factors that pave the way for its occurrence.

External Causes of Change

As we noted in Chapter 15, organizations are affected by many aspects of the external environment.[2] Not surprisingly, several of these domains also play a role in the process of organizational change. When they are altered, corresponding modifications in the structure or functioning of organizations soon follow.

Technology as a source of change. The space shuttle; genetic engineering; incredibly powerful microchips; wristwatch-size televisions; artificial hearts. The flow (should we say flood?) of new technological marvels seems endless. And of course, the ones just listed all fall into the "gee whiz!" category—they are the type journalists love to include in feature articles or in reports on the evening news. Many thousands of other advances are less dramatic in nature, and so tend to remain largely unknown outside the industries in which they are applied. Yet, they may literally revolutionize the ways in which many products are manufactured, or the manner in which thousands of companies conduct their operations. Clearly, then, technology—and especially advances in this crucial realm—serves as a basic stimulus for change in many organizational settings.

Economic factors. During the early 1980s, interest rates in the United States soared to previously unheard of levels. One result of this unsettling trend was that many organizations found it all but impossible to finance expansion, new construction, or other activities through traditional methods. This, in turn, led many to adopt new policies and procedures—ones designed to generate sufficient funds for high-priority projects in a purely internal manner. Moreover, such changes tended to become permanent: even when interest rates later fell, many companies continued to avoid financial markets, and retained their new strategies for obtaining needed capital.

This small slice of history serves to illustrate the impact of another external source of change within organizations: general economic conditions. Shifts in the business cycle, changes in interest rates, wild swings in inflation—these and other economic factors produce strong pressures for change. For example, recessions often necessitate reductions in work force, while high rates of inflation tend to push organizations in the direction of long-term contracts for raw materials, labor, and other essential inputs. In these and many other ways, shifts in economic conditions are reflected in important forms of change.

Shifts in cultural values and related government policies. As we noted in earlier chapters, organizations do not exist in a social or political vacuum. On the contrary, they are often strongly affected by prevailing values and beliefs.[3] When these shift, organizations must often scramble to keep up. They may find it necessary to alter the nature or "mix" of their products to take account of changing customer tastes. They may find it essential to change their policies toward labor, in order to respond to growing demands for long-term job security or more interesting work. And they may have to adjust their operations to comply with anti-pollution or affirmative action legislation adopted as a result of altered public attitudes toward the physical environment or ethnic discrimination. In short, organizational change often reflects important shifts in the values or attitudes of the surrounding culture.

Internal Causes of Change

While much organizational change occurs in response to trends or events in the external environment, a considerable amount derives from another major source: internal factors within organizations themselves. Among the most important of these are growing size, recognition of a *performance gap*, and internally generated changes in policy.

Size and organizational change. That organizations change as they grow in size is hardly surprising. As we noted in Chapter 14, increased size is often accompanied by major shifts in internal structure (e.g., growing complexity, increased specialization and differentiation). This is not the only way size can serve as a stimulus to change, however. As organizations prosper and grow in size, they often generate surplus resources (financial and otherwise).[4] These resources then permit them to seize upon new opportunities, and to experiment with various innovations. Thus, paradoxically, large organizations sometimes prove more flexible and open to change than smaller ones, in which such resources are lacking.

Performance gaps and change. Now, let's turn things around a bit and look at the other side of the coin. Imagine an organization in which everything is going wrong: market share is declining, profits are decreasing, and overall performance is

"Attention all department heads: From now on, we're just
going to make small, reliable cars."

FIGURE 16.2 Internal Shifts in Policy: One Potential Cause of Organizational Change.
As illustrated by this cartoon, organizations sometimes experience major change as a result
of internally generated shifts in policy. (Source: Drawing by Barsotti; © 1979 The New Yorker
Magazine, Inc.)

below expectations. How will management react? The answer is apparent: unless
they have already given up and decided that the case is hopeless they will make
vigorous efforts at change. That this is indeed the case is suggested by the findings of
several research projects.[5] In these investigations, recognition of a gap between
current and hoped-for performance was a good predictor of the adoption of subsequent innovations. This is only reasonable; when things are going poorly, most
people would agree that it's time for a change—and the sooner it is instituted, the
better. In any case, it appears that disappointing performance, as well as success,
can be a stimulus for change.

Adoption of new policy and change.   For ten years, the present author did
business with a local bank. During that period, it had always been possible to draw
on funds deposited into an account immediately, as long as the balance in the
account was larger than the new deposit. One day, however, the situation suddenly
changed. While depositing a large check, the author was informed by the teller on
duty that the funds in question would have to be "frozen" for two weeks. When
asked why this was so, the teller shrugged and indicated that it was just "a new
policy." Intrigued (and annoyed) by the change, the author spoke, in succession, to
the branch manager, an assistant vice president, and a vice president of the bank. In
no case was a clear explanation for the new policy offered. The bank had not lost
any funds as a result of its former policy, and did not expect to earn any extra
interest as a result of the new one. As far as the author could determine, this change
was simply "something the board of directors decided to institute." Annoyed, the
author transferred his business to a competing bank.

Obviously, this incident is far from earth-shaking in nature. Yet, it draws attention to another source of change that is sometimes overlooked: internally generated shifts in policy (refer to Figure 16.2). In some instances, organizations adopt new policies or procedures in what seems to be the total absence of external pressures for doing so. Why is this the case? No simple answer exists. Sometimes top managers develop new policies that, they believe, will improve performance of efficiency. In other cases, however, the process is somewhat less rational. Executives may simply want to try out new ideas, or change the company's "image." Alternatively, organizational politics may play a role, with each side pushing for adoption of its own pet change as a kind of power play. And sometimes, especially in large bureaucracies (e.g., government agencies), change may be insitituted merely for the sake of change itself—as a response to tedious boredom. The main point to keep in mind in all such cases is this: sometimes organizations seem to adopt change or innovation for internal reasons that have little, if any, connection with factors outside their boundaries. (What is the process of organizational innovation really like? What factors contribute to its occurrence? For information on these important issues, please refer to the **Focus** insert on page 488.)

ORGANIZATIONAL CHANGE: ITS SCOPE AND FORMS

Potentially, organizations can change in a great many ways. Careful study of the manner in which they actually *do* change, however, suggests that most of these alterations fall under four major headings: changes in technology, products, administrative systems, and employees (i.e., changes in their attitudes, skills, expectations, or motives). The first three of these categories are considered below. Change involving people will be examined separately, in a subsequent section on *organizational development*.

Change in Technology

Change in technology involves alterations in some aspect of an organization's transformation process—the ways in which it converts input into output (goods, products, services). For example, changes in technology in a manufacturing company might involve the introduction of new equipment, changes in the sequence of operations on the assembly line, or the application of new knowledge and processes. In contrast, changes in technology at a large university might involve shifts in the specific techniques of instruction employed.

At first glance, it is tempting to assume that the adoption of technological change is enhanced by an organic management approach. After all, the flexibility, decentralization, absence of rigid rules and procedures, and horizontal communication associated with such structure should encourage innovation at all levels within the organization. To some extent, this appears to be true. However, there is a complicating factor that should not be overlooked. While organic characteristics do

The Process of Organizational Innovation: A Policy Model

In almost every industry, some organizations are highly innovative: they develop new products, adopt new forms of technology, and are generally receptive to change. Others, in contrast, are slow to respond to shifts in environmental conditions; they hold back until it is clear that change is essential, or simply can't be avoided. What accounts for such differences? Some intriguing answers are provided by the **policy model of innovation**, proposed recently by Ettlie.[6]

According to this model, organizational innovation can be understood in terms of a three-step process involving certain *contextual factors*, key features of *organization policy*, and innovations themselves. With respect to contextual factors, two are most important: degree of environmental uncertainty (discussed previously in Chapter 15), and organization size. Turning to organization policy, such factors as policy concerning technology (e.g., the extent to which the organization is committed to adopting new methods and equipment) and policy concerning marketing (e.g., the extent to which top managers play an active role in

this process) are of central interest. In addition, the model posits that performance gaps, too, are important, and should be taken into account. Combining these factors, the policy model suggests that the contextual factors mentioned above (e.g., a high degree of environmental uncertainty, large organization size) lead to the development of certain organization policies (e.g., an aggressive approach to technological advances), and that these, in turn, enhance overall receptivity to innovations (refer to Figure 16.3). Evidence for the validity of this model is provided by the findings of a recent investigation conducted by Ettlie.[7]

In this study, executives at fifty-eight different companies supplying equipment or packaging to the food processing industry completed questionnaires designed to provide information on the variables included in the policy model of innovation. Thus, various items on these questionnaires asked respondents to report on the degree of environmental uncertainty faced by their company, its policies concerning technology and marketing, and the extent to which their

FIGURE 16.3   *The Policy Model of Innovation.*
According to the *policy model of innovation*, certain contextual factors (e.g., degree of environmental uncertainty, company size) cause organizations to adopt policies concerning technology and marketing that either favor or do not favor the adoption of innovations. Such policies, plus the recognition of performance gaps, then cause organizations to adopt or avoid innovations. (Source: Based on suggestions by Ettlie, 1983; see Note 4.)

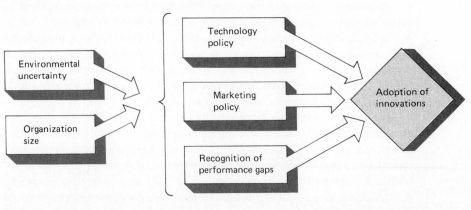

Contextual factors   **Organization policy**

company's performance was living up to expectations (the presence of a perceived performance gap). Additional information pertaining to company size was also collected. Finally, innovation within each company was measured in terms of the number of new products introduced during the past three years, and the introduction of one radically new product then gaining acceptance in the industry. When causal links between these various factors were examined, strong support for several portions of the policy model was obtained.

First, as expected, company size was positively related to both of the measures of innovation. Thus, the larger each company was, the greater its likelihood of adopting various innovations. Second, the greater the degree of environmental uncertainty faced by these companies, the more aggressive were their policies concerning the adopting of new technology. Third, and also consistent with the model, the more aggressive each company's technology policy, the greater its tendency to adopt innovations. Finally, environmental uncertainty was linked to the occurrence of performance gaps: the greater the uncertainty, the more likely were executives to report that their organizations were not living up to expectations.

In sum, the findings reported by Ettlie suggest that organizational innovation does indeed involve a process in which certain contextual factors (environmental uncertainty, organization size) influence key organization policies or the recognition of performance gaps, and where these, in turn, determine the rate of innovation. To the degree that contextual factors foster aggressive company policies, or the belief that the organization is not performing up to full potential, therefore, innovation will be encouraged. Thus, as noted earlier, the willingness of an organization to adopt innovations, or its ability to respond effectively to change, is *not* a random process. On the contrary, it can be both understood and predicted from thorough knowledge of appropriate environmental, policy, and attitudinal factors. Of course, other variables, too, probably play a role in this process (e.g., additional features of the external environment). Thus, further research designed both to extend and refine the policy model of innovation is clearly needed. As additional evidence along these lines is acquired, it may soon become possible for researchers to proceed with the next important step: identifying practical techniques for the encouragement of innovation in a wide range of organizational settings.

seem to facilitate the initiation of new ideas and a positive attitude toward innovations, they may also make it difficult to attain *implementation* of specific changes.[8] The reason for this should be apparent: since employees in an organically structured organization are accustomed to making their own decisions, and to a considerable degree of initiative and flexibility, they may simply decide to ignore innovations that do not meet with their approval. Implementation of specific changes, therefore, is often easier to obtain in organizations with a mechanistic structure—one in which employees are used to receiving directives from above, and to complying with specific rules. At the same time, though, such conditions tend to discourage new ideas or internally generated innovation.

Clearly, then, where technological change is concerned, we are left facing a dilemma. Conditions that create an atmosphere favorable to new ideas or approaches render their implementation somewhat uncertain. In contrast, conditions favoring ready implementation of proposals for change decrease the likelihood that they will be generated! How can this dilemma be resolved? One suggestion, offered by Duncan, is that organizations should learn to be somewhat *ambidextrous*.[9] That is, they should incorporate internal structures that favor, respectively, the initiation and implementation of change. In large companies, this can be accomplished through the establishment of different structures in different departments.[10] For example, such units as systems analysis, engineering, and research can be organically structured: this will aid in their task of generating new ideas and approaches.

In contrast, units responsible for implementing these innovations (e.g., operations, maintenance) should be mechanistic in orientation. In smaller organizations, similar results can be achieved by having the entire organization shift back and forth between organic and mechanistic modes as required. When new ideas and approaches are sought, participation from people at all levels should be encouraged, and an atmosphere free from the constraints of status or formalization adopted. Once desired innovations are selected, however, a return to mechanistic procedures, with their greater ease of implementation, should take place.

Before concluding, we should mention one additional factor that often plays an important role in the adoption of technological change: a *cosmopolitan orientation* on the part of key managers.[11] Briefly, a cosmopolitan orientation involves interest in and commitment to one's field that extends beyond the local community or a single organization. Individuals high on this dimension engage in such actions as publishing articles in appropriate journals, attending professional meetings, and holding offices in professional associations. In contrast, persons low on this dimension are oriented solely toward their local community or organization: they have little contact with colleagues outside these settings.

It seems only reasonable to predict that in situations where specific persons play an important role in the adoption of technological innovations, those with a cosmopolitan orientation will be more favorable to such change than those with a strictly local orientation. That this is indeed the case is indicated by the results of an intriguing study conducted by Robertson and Wind.[12] These investigators examined the purchase of innovative radiology equipment by more than two hundred hospitals. In each hospital, they measured the orientation (cosmopolitan or local) of two groups of people: radiologists and administrators. This was done since both groups play an important role in determining what equipment to purchase. It was predicted that the greatest degree of innovativeness would be observed in situations where both the radiologists and administrators were cosmopolitan in orientation, while the lowest level of innovativeness would occur when both groups were local in their perspective. Results offered only partial support for this prediction. While innovation was relatively high when both radiologists and administrators were cosmopolitan, it was even higher under intermediate conditions: when radiologists were cosmopolitan in outlook while administrators were local (refer to Figure 16.4). Robertson and Wind suggest that this pattern of results may stem from the fact that under these conditions, the radiologists were aware of and pushed for innovations, while administrators, because of their local orientation, had enough local power to secure such change. Whatever the specific explanation for these findings, they confirm the fact that in some settings, at least, the adoption of technological innovations is as much a function of the orientation of specific, key persons as it is of the internal structure or policies of the organizations in question.

Change in Products

A second major form of change often experienced by organizations involves shifts in their output: alterations in the products or services they produce. These can involve the introduction of totally new products, modifications in existing ones, or

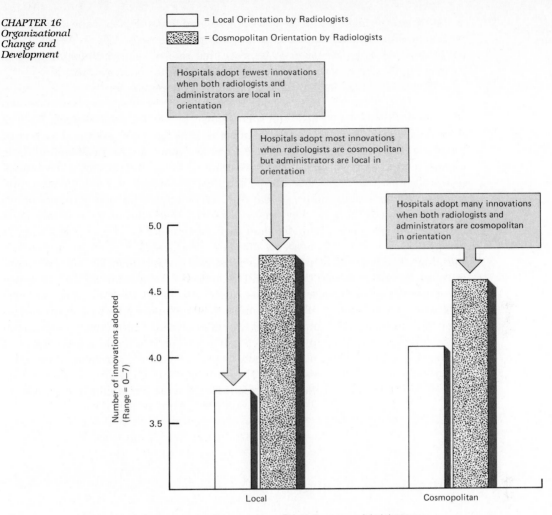

☐ = Local Orientation by Radiologists

▨ = Cosmopolitan Orientation by Radiologists

Hospitals adopt fewest innovations when both radiologists and administrators are local in orientation

Hospitals adopt most innovations when radiologists are cosmopolitan but administrators are local in orientation

Hospitals adopt many innovations when both radiologists and administrators are cosmopolitan in orientation

Number of innovations adopted (Range = 0–7)

5.0

4.5

4.0

3.5

Local   Cosmopolitan

Orientation among Administrators

FIGURE 16.4   Cosmopolitanism and the Adoption of Innovations.
Hospitals adopted most innovations when the professionals involved in such decisions (radiologists) were *cosmopolitan* in orientation, while administrators were *local* in their perspective. They adopted fewest innovations when both groups were local in orientation. (Source: Based on data from Robertson and Wind, 1983; see Note 12.)

the introduction of new product lines. In all of these cases, the major goals remain much the same: hold onto existing customers in the face of changing needs or tastes, increase market share at the expense of competitors, or acquire new and hitherto untapped markets.

As anyone who reads magazines or watches television well knows, the number of new products introduced each year is truly staggering. Thus, this is a major form of organizational change. Unfortunately, it is often also very costly, for only a small fraction of the new products developed are successful. It is estimated that fewer than one in three ever make it into the marketplace, and that only about one in eight ever yield economic benefits to the companies that produce them. Why is this the case? And what steps can be taken to improve this rate of return? Valuable insights concerning these issues are provided by the **horizontal linkage model**.[13]

This model suggests that three conditions are necessary for the effective development of new products. First, a high degree of specialization is needed in the two units most directly concerned with such change: marketing and research. Each of these departments must be competent at performing its major tasks, and each must possess internal structures appropriate to its key functions. Second, both of these departments must be closely linked to relevant sectors of the external environment. Research must maintain close ties with colleagues outside the organization, and with professional associations, so that research employees are aware of new developments and advances as they occur. Similarly, marketing must maintain close contact with customers, to understand their current needs, and a close watch on competitors, so as to be aware of any new products, tactics, or strategies they introduce. In short, both departments must engage in a high level of boundary-spanning activities. Finally, it is crucial that effective *horizontal linkages* be established between these key departments. A major factor in the failure of many new products is the reluctance of research units to invite input and advice from marketing people until quite late in the game. Effective horizontal communication between these departments can help avoid such problems, and can build a high degree of customer acceptance into new products or product lines. A summary of the horizontal linkage model is presented in Figure 16.5. Through careful attention to the steps it describes, organizations can greatly increase the probability that changes in their products or services will yield the positive outcomes they desire.

Administrative Change

A third major category of organizational change involves shifts in the overall management of a company. Such **administrative change** includes alterations in internal structure, specific policies, reward systems, accounting and budgeting systems, and major goals. Obviously, such change can be stimulated by any of the shifts in the external environment outlined above (e.g., changes in economic conditions, government policy, competition, technology), or by factors within an organization itself (e.g., a change in top management, increase in size, recognition of an important performance gap).

While it might again be tempting to conclude that such change is facilitated by an organic internal structure, this does not appear to be the case. In fact, rapid administrative change seems to occur more readily in the context of mechanistic than organic systems. The reason for this has been suggested by Daft in the *dual-core model* of organizations.[14]

According to Daft, many organizations, especially medium-sized ones, have two basic cores: *technical* and *administrative*. The technical core is concerned with the central work of the organization—the transformation of inputs into outputs. As a result, pressure for technical change should—and often does—flow *upward*,

FIGURE 16.5   *Product Innovations: The Horizontal Linkage Model.*
According to the *horizontal linkage model*, three conditions are essential to the successful development of new products: (1) both research and marketing departments must be highly competent, (2) both of these units must be closely linked to relevant sectors of the external environment, and (3) they must coordinate closely with one another.

from individuals in technical core departments possessing special skills or expertise. In contrast, the administrative core is concerned with the overall management of the organization—with tasks such as coordination, providing direction, setting goals and priorities, and so on. Because of this fact, change with respect to these matters should flow *downward*, in a top-to-bottom manner. Since such control is facilitated by a mechanistic structure, administrative change is often enhanced by this type of approach.

Evidence that the acceptance of administrative change is facilitated by existence of a mechanistic structure has recently been reported by Gaertner, Gaertner, and Akinnusi, in a detailed study of two large federal agencies in the United States: the Environmental Protection Agency (EPA), and the Mine Safety and Health Administration (MSHA).[15] These two organizations differ sharply in their overall orientation and in their internal structure. The EPA, which Gaertner and his colleagues describe as *entrepreneurial generalist* in nature, seeks to extend its base of operations into new areas and new opportunities; it is generally organic in internal structure. In contrast, the MSHA, described as *efficiency-based specialist* in orientation, focuses on performing a limited range of tasks, and does not seek to extend its activities; it is relatively mechanistic in structure. When the reactions of these two organizations to a specific administrative innovation (the Civil Service Reform Act of 1978) were compared, interesting differences emerged. First, high-level administrators at EPA were much more favorable to this innovation than their counterparts at MSHA. Given the different orientations of the two agencies, this is hardly surprising. Of greater interest, however, is the finding that operations-level managers at EPA actually voiced greater resistance to the new policies and procedures, and reacted less favorably to them, than corresponding persons at MSHA. Apparently, the overall "expansionist" orientation at EPA, coupled with its organic structure, encouraged a favorable attitude toward innovation among administrators, but in-

FROM THE MANAGER'S PERSPECTIVE

Organizational Change:
Enhancing Its Acceptance

Most people want to think of themselves as "modern" or "progressive." Thus, if you interviewed one hundred employees at almost any company and asked them how they felt about change, most would probably indicate positive views. "Change," they might comment, "sure—it's good. Without it we'd just kind of stagnate." On the basis of such statements, you might conclude that instituting change in organizations is a simple task. Just call the need for change to people's attention, and it will follow, effortlessly and swiftly. In fact, this is not usually the case. Regardless of what they say, many people often resist change, and resist it vigorously. Many factors contribute to such opposition or *resistance to change*, but here, we will mention only three.

First, as we have noted repeatedly throughout this volume, people strongly desire a sense of *personal control*. They want to believe that they can control (or at least influence) their own outcomes. Change, of course, introduces a large and unpredictable "X" into this equation. Such uncertainty, in turn, interferes with the sense of personal efficacy most people seek. Little wonder, then, that they often resist it with every trick and tactic at their disposal.

Second, opposition to change often stems from anxieties concerning its specific effects. In recent years, newspapers and magazines have been crammed full of stories about people who have lost their jobs to technological change, mergers, or foreign competition. When management starts talking about change in any of several major areas, therefore, employees often begin to worry about the future of their jobs. The result: they tend to dig in their heels and oppose change at every turn.

Third, resistance to change often stems from social factors. When people work together on a daily basis, they often develop strong mutual friendships. As a result, interacting with one another becomes an important source of on-the-job reward—perhaps as important as more formal rewards offered by the organization. Change, of course, often threatens to disrupt such positive social relations. Internal reorganizations

may result in the transfer of persons from one unit to another. Technological change, too, can break up long-standing social groups, as operations are shifted from one location to another, or different patterns of workflow are established. Faced with such negative outcomes, employees often adopt what, from their point of view, is a very rational posture: strong resistance to change, and efforts to return to previous patterns if it is actually instituted.

We should emphasize that these are only a few of the reasons why many persons fail to greet organizational change with open arms; many others exist as well. Regardless of its specific causes, though, resistance to change is a serious matter. The ability to adapt to shifting environmental conditions is essential in the late 1980s, and few organizations can afford to yield to the preference for total stability expressed by their employees. An important question for managers thus arises: What steps can be undertaken to reduce such resistance, and encourage more willing acceptance of necessary change? Fortunately, a number of techniques seem useful in this regard.

(1) *Participation: Involve affected persons in planning.* One of the most effective steps managers can take to increase the acceptance of change is that of involving the persons affected by it (or their representatives) in its planning. When this principle is followed, employees may feel that they have given their approval to change, and have helped shape its final form. When, in contrast, this principle is ignored, they may conclude that change has been "shoved down their throats." In such cases, they may do their best to block its implementation.

(2) *Need: Explain the necessity for change clearly.* One reason why many persons resist change is that they are not convinced of its necessity: they view it as one more meaningless step dreamed up by "those people up there" to make their lives more difficult. If, instead, they are made aware of the reasons requiring change, they may have more positive reactions to it, or at least refrain from working against it.

494

(3) *Benefits: Clarify what's to be gained.* Almost all change exacts some costs in terms of time, effort, and adjustment. Thus, the negatives associated with change are usually quite apparent to everyone concerned. What may not be nearly as obvious, however, are the potential benefits. These may be delayed for weeks or months, and may not be apparent unless one has a grasp of the total picture—the overall plan for future corporate development. It is crucial, therefore, that the future benefits of change be called to employees' attention. Once they are (and especially if they are substantial) resistance may fade with amazing speed.

(4) *Communication: Use the appropriate channels.* Some types of change are more complex and involve higher degrees of risk for employees than others. It seems only reasonable, then, that managers should take account of such factors in determining how to communicate information about change to the person affected. As Fidler and Johnson suggest, high-risk changes should be presented and discussed in a direct, face-to-face manner.[16] Such communication permits employees to ask questions, receive detailed information, and relieve anxieties. In contrast, less direct forms of communication (e.g., memos) may be more appropriate for handling less complex, low-risk innovations.

(5) *Idea champions: Secure the support of respected persons.* In every organization, there are individuals who are highly respected by many others. Members of their department or work group, and even persons outside these units, orient toward them, and use their actions as guides for their own behavior. Because of these positive reactions, gaining the support of such persons for proposed changes can greatly facilitate their acceptance. In some cases, idea champions will speak out on their own, as they become convinced of the need for specific innovations. In others, they can be assigned to play this role. In either case, their impact can be substantial.

Through these and related procedures, resistance to change can be markedly reduced. Once it is, organizations can proceed with a task that is essential for their continued survival: matching their technology, products, and administrative systems to the demands of a complex and ever-changing world.

terfered with its implementation at lower (technical) levels. In contrast, the more limited perspective at MSHA, plus its mechanistic structure, enhanced acceptance of administrative innovations once they were adopted. Once again, therefore, we see that as is true for other aspects of organization design, there are no simple answers where change or innovation are concerned. Rather, the specific needs of an organization, relevant environmental factors, the type of change in question, and the level at which innovations are to be implemented must all be taken into account. Only if they are can this crucial process unfold in an orderly and effective manner. (Resistance to change in organizations can sometimes be intense. Why is this so, and what steps can managers take to overcome its presence? For some comments on these issues, please see the **Perspective** insert on page 494.)

ORGANIZATIONAL DEVELOPMENT: CHANGE AND EFFECTIVENESS

One executive known to the author often makes the following remarks: "A company is only as good as its people. Show me an operation with good people, and I'll show you one bound to succeed." What he means by these comments, of course, is this: ultimately, an organization's effectiveness depends upon its employees—their commitment, motivation, skills, and abilities. The more positive these factors are, the more efficient and successful it will be. In recent decades, growing numbers of individuals, both practicing managers and experts in organizational behavior, have come to share this view. As they have, an active field of research known as **organizational development** (or **OD**) has emerged. The basic goal of this endeavor can be simply stated: enhancing organizational effectiveness through planned organization-wide change involving people. Specifically, it seeks to enhance organizational performance through improvements in the quality of work environments, positive shifts in the attitudes and motivation of employees, and furtherance of their health and wellbeing.[17] Another important feature of organizational development is that in devising such interventions, it draws heavily on knowledge provided by the behavioral sciences. As a result, many of the techniques it employs rest upon a firm foundation of scientific knowledge. In the remainder of this section, we will describe several techniques widely used for purposes of organizational development.

Survey Feedback: Change through Information

One popular technique of organizational development, **survey feedback**, rests primarily on the following principle: before useful change can take place in an organization, the people in it must understand both its current strengths and weaknesses. The basic task of survey feedback, then, is providing key individuals with such knowledge. In order to accomplish this goal, three basic steps are employed.[18] (It is important to note, by the way, that as is the case with most techniques of organizational development, survey feedback is best carried out by persons from outside the organization—expert consultants with special training and knowledge in this field.)

First, some (or even all) employees complete a carefully designed questionnaire. This survey is usually "custom-tailored" for a specific organization, so that it focuses on issues of greatest interest to it. However, it often seeks information on matters of general concern, such as the quality and style of leadership, current organizational climate, and employee satisfaction. The second step in the process

FIGURE 16.6 *Survey Feedback: An Overview.*
Survey feedback, a popular technique of organizational development, consists of three major steps.

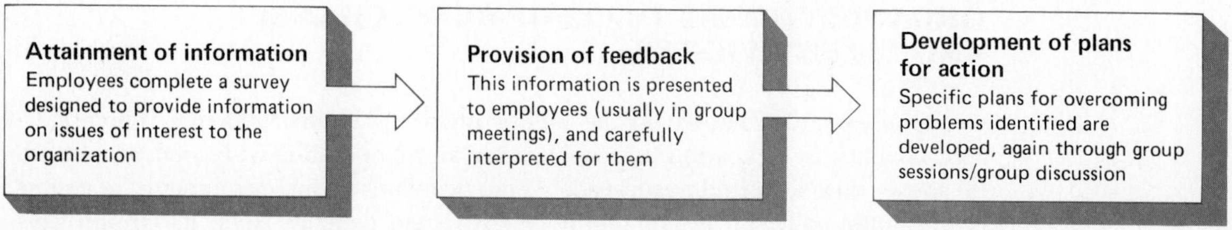

Attainment of information
Employees complete a survey designed to provide information on issues of interest to the organization

Provision of feedback
This information is presented to employees (usually in group meetings), and carefully interpreted for them

Development of plans for action
Specific plans for overcoming problems identified are developed, again through group sessions/group discussion

involves reporting the information obtained to employees, usually during group meetings. This requires considerable skill, for such information is often complex, and can also be quite threatening to specific persons or groups (e.g., it may indicate that some are viewed as failing to carry their weight by other members of the company). The persons who present this feedback, therefore, must be skilled at handling anxiety and other negative reactions, and at avoiding misinterpretation of the data presented. Finally, in a third step, specific plans for dealing with overcoming problems identified by the survey are developed. Again, this usually takes place in group sessions where open discussion is encouraged. (Please see Figure 16.6 for a summary of these steps.)

Survey feedback offers several key advantages. It is efficient, and can yield a large amount of useful data quickly. It is also quite flexible, and can be applied in a wide range of organizations facing many different problems. The results and recommendations obtained, however, are only useful to the extent that the following conditions prevail: (1) the questionnaires employed are both valid and reliable (i.e., they measure what they purport to measure, and do so in an accurate manner), (2) respondents are willing to describe their views and reactions honestly, and (3) top management is willing to act on the information gathered—to put plans based on the results into operation. When these conditions exist, survey feedback can be a valuable technique for enhancing organizational effectiveness.

Grid Training: Managerial Style and Enhanced Effectiveness

In our discussion of leadership (Chapter 9), we noted that leaders vary greatly in terms of their position along two key dimensions: concern with people and concern with production. Further, we noted that growing evidence suggests that leaders who are high on both dimensions are often the most effective.[19] This fact forms the basis for another popular technique of organizational development— **grid training**. This procedure, originally proposed by Blake and Mouton, is designed to shift existing leaders within an organization toward what is considered to be the ideal pattern: high concern with *both* people and production.[20] In order to accomplish this goal, it employs a number of distinct steps.

First, it is necessary to determine just where managers stand on these two dimensions. This is accomplished through a special questionnaire. On the basis of managers' answers to this survey, they are assigned two numbers—one representing concern with production and the other their concern with people. (Scores on both dimensions can range from 1 through 9.) Many different patterns are possible, and these are assumed to reflect contrasting management styles. For example, a manager who shows little concern with either people or production would receive a score of 1,1. This is described by Blake and Mouton as *impoverished management*. A manager who shows a great deal of concern for production but little interest in people would receive a score of 9,1. This is know as *task management*. In contrast, one who shows the opposite pattern—high concern with people but little interest in production—would receive a score of 1,9; this is described as

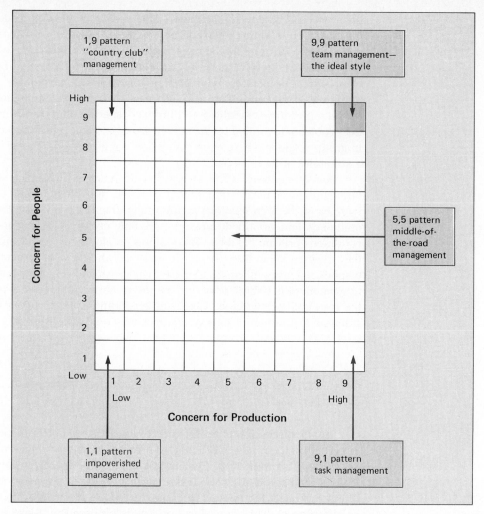

FIGURE 16.7   *The Managerial Grid.*
A given manager's standing along two key dimensions—concern with people and concern with production—can be illustrated by means of the *managerial grid*. According to Blake and Mouton, developers of *grid training* (a popular technique of organizational development), the ideal pattern involves high scores on both dimensions. (Source: Based on suggestions by Blake and Mouton, 1978; see Note 20.)

the *country club* style of management. These, and all other patterns, can be represented in the type of diagram show in Figure 16.7, know as the *managerial grid*.

Once a manager's current position within the grid is determined, training can begin. This involves a number of different steps. For example, managers themselves participate in designing plans for moving toward the preferred 9,9 pattern (which is termed *team management*). In addition, they discuss relations between various departments or units within the organization, and sources of conflict between them. Additional steps include efforts to devise an ideal model for their organization—one describing how it *should*, ideally, function—and the development of concrete plans for converting this model into reality. Later in the process, progress toward these goals is assessed, and areas requiring further work identified.

Grid training has been very popular in recent years. Indeed, to date, more than 250,00 people have participated in it. Further, some evidence, at least, suggests that it succeeds: it does assist managers in adopting a more effective leadership style.[21] In sum, it appears to be one useful technique for improving the quality of leadership within an organization, and so for enhancing overall effectiveness.

Sensitivity Training: Change through Insight

Interpersonal friction is an all too common part of life in many organizations. Individuals argue, cause each other to lose face, criticize one another's work, and generally manage to make life far more unpleasant and stressful than seems to be necessary (refer to our discussion of conflict in Chapter 12.) Needless to add, the negative feelings generated by such interactions can exert adverse effects upon organizational effectiveness. Indeed, when carried to extremes, persistent feuds, lasting ill will, and smoldering resentment can bring productive work to a virtual standstill.

Such friction derives from many different sources (e.g., conflicts of interest, marked differences in values or attitudes). Perhaps the single most important factor, though, is the absence of accurate social perceptions. Frequently, individuals lack insight into their own feelings and those of others. Even worse, they totally fail to understand the impact of their actions on the persons around them. The result: they anger, irritate, and annoy fellow employees unintentionally, and often unnecessarily. Can anything be done to reduce such problems? The answer appears to be "yes." In recent decades, several procedures for increasing individuals' understanding of and sensitivity to their own and others' behavior have been developed. Among these, the one that has been applied most often to the task of organizational development is **sensitivity training.**[22]

This procedure rests on three basic assumptions: (1) under ordinary conditions, individuals are far from open and honest with one another; (2) this lack of openness often blocks the development of important insights about oneself and others; and (3) such insights can be gained when persons are placed in a special setting where honest communication is the rule rather than the exception.

Putting these principles into operation, sensitivity training usually involves the participation of from ten to fifteen persons in extended group discussions. These take place away from the pressures and distractions of the home organization, and often last for several days. An expert trainer is present at all times, but he or she does not actively direct the group. Rather, the trainer's task is primarily that of assuring that the proper atmosphere of honesty and openness is maintained. During each session, participants are permitted to discuss anything they wish. However, it is emphasized that the major purpose is that of attaining greater understanding of oneself and others. To attain these goals, participants are encouraged to express their feelings directly and openly—not to hide or conceal them as they do when actually on the job. For example, if a manager feels that one of her subordinates has been goofing off, she should say so directly and forcefully—*not* keep this judgment to herself. Similarly, if the members of one department feel that the members of another are making their jobs harder, or failing to pull their weight, they should state these views openly. In addition, participants are encouraged to provide one another with *immediate feedback* during discussions. Whenever an individual states some feeling or reaction, other persons present should respond with their own interpretations. It is reasoned that under these conditions, individuals will learn much about themselves and others. In this way, they will become more skilled at handling interpersonal relations.

As you can probably guess, the outcomes of sensitivity training are difficult to assess. Insight into one's own personality and improvements in interpersonal skills are elusive and hard to measure. Partly for this reason, and partly because it seems applicable to only a limited range of organizational problems, sensitivity training is not currently as popular as it was in the past. However, some evidence suggests that it can contribute to improved relations among employees when applied by skilled and experienced trainers.[23] To the extent it does, it can also contribute to enhanced organizational effectiveness.

Management by Objectives: The Benefits of Having Clear-cut Goals

Since we have already referred to one old saying in this chapter ("The more things change . . ."), perhaps you'll forgive the use of just one more: "It's usually easier to get somewhere if you know where you're going." What this implies is that individuals (and organizations, too) have a better chance of reaching important goals if these are clearly defined or specified. On the face of it, this proposition makes good sense. After all, if persons or organizations are uncertain about their final objectives, they may experience confusion about how to reach them—and may not even know when such goals have been attained! You may be surprised to learn, therefore, that this basic principle is neglected in many large organizations. Goals are stated in very general terms (e.g., good performance, high efficiency, a positive public image), and little attention is directed to the task of specifying just what these mean. As a result, employees from the top on down may be uncertain as to just what they are trying to accomplish, and the entire organization can seem very much adrift. (Please refer to our discussion of the benefits of setting specific goals in Chapter 3.)

The potential costs of such uncertainty were forcefully stated several decades ago by Peter Drucker.[24] Drucker, who was then a vice president at General Electric, suggested that, contrary to what common sense indicates, an organization's goals are *not* always obvious. Rather, they must be carefully and clearly defined. Drucker, along with Harold Smiddy, noted that specifying concrete objectives is a key part of managing—perhaps the most important part of all. Thus, he urged careful attention to this issue. As Drucker himself put it: "The important factor is that every member of management should have *specific* goals which he agrees to attain by *specific* dates, and which will obligate him to examine and explain the reasons for variance or deviation. . . ."[25]

Drucker's suggestions were soon incorporated into an important approach to management we have already mentioned in Chapter 3: **management by objec-**

tives (or **MBO** for short).[26] Here, we will first describe the basic nature of MBO, and then indicate how it can be used as a technique of organizational development.

MBO: An overview.   At present, most experts in the use of MBO agree that it rests upon four central themes. First, it is crucial that managers and their subordinates agree on specific goals and objectives. Situations in which managers simply set such goals are not consistent with the spirit of MBO. Second, the goals selected must be *measurable, time-bounded*, and linked to a concrete plan for their attainment. Third, progress toward these objectives should be measured systematically, and on a regular basis. Finally, each employee's responsibilities should be clearly defined in terms of the results he or she is expected to achieve. In sum, MBO focuses on the development of specific, measurable goals, plans for attaining them, and regular assessement of progress toward them. In these respects, it is entirely consistent with the general notion that we should always try to know where we are going before we start out.

MBO and organizational development.   Now that we have described the major features of MBO, we can consider its use as a technique of organizational development. When used in this manner, MBO involves four distinct steps. First, the persons who will be involved in the MBO program are provided with a basic understanding of its major principles and procedures. In short, they undergo an adequate orientation to its use. Second, subordinates and supervisors meet in face-to-face sessions to discuss alternative goals, and select the ones they view as most important to the organization or their specific unit. At this time, specific steps for reaching these goals should also be determined. Third, after some predetermined interval, progress toward the chosen objectives is assessed, and feedback provided. (This step may be repeated on several different occasions.) Finally, an assessment of overall results is made, and in the context of this information, further goals are selected. Thus, the process is a continuous one, with new goals replacing former ones as these are met, or found to be unattainable. (Please refer to Figure 16.8 for a summary of these steps.)

FIGURE 16.8   *Management by Objectives: An Overview.*
When used for purposes of organizational development, *management by objectives (MBO)* involves four distinct steps. First, individuals are oriented to its basic principles. Next, subordinates and supervisors agree on specific goals and concrete steps for attaining them. Third, progress is assessed and feedback provided. (This step is usually repeated several times.) Finally, an overall assessment of progress is made, and additional goals are selected.

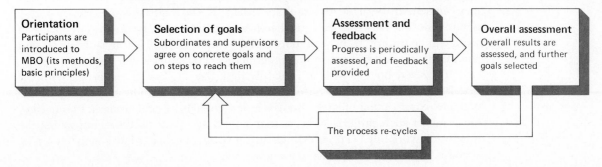

MBO, like grid training, has been a popular technique for a number of years. Indeed, in one form or another, it is now used by thousands of organizations. One reason for this popularity probably lies in the fact that it is largely "self-correcting" in nature. Since it states objectives in terms of quantifiable goals and assesses progress toward them on a periodic basis, it is continuously open to adjustment and feedback. Another attractive feature is its emphasis on close cooperation between supervisors and subordinates—something that is often lacking under other management approaches. That the popularity of MBO has been at least partially justified is suggested by the findings of a recent review of the results of more than 185 separate studies concerned with MBO's effectiveness.[27] While findings were not uniformly positive, a large majority of these investigations pointed to the conclusion that MBO is, indeed, often quite successful.

Of course, MBO, like all techniques of organizational development, suffers from certain drawbacks. Perhaps the most important of these lies in the fact that putting it into practice often requires a lengthy period of time—anywhere from two to five years.[28] Needless to state, many organizations are either unwilling or unable to meet this requirement. As a result, they may either avoid instituting MBO programs, or terminate them prematurely, before they have had a chance to reach their full potential. Despite this and other drawbacks, MBO does seem to be a useful technique in several respects. Thus, it will probably find continued use as one means for enhancing organizational effectiveness in the years ahead.

Quality of Work Life: The "Humanization" of Work and Work Settings

Work = Drudgery. This equation has been accepted without question throughout human history. Perhaps the major force behind its widespread adoption is the following assumption: positive organizational outcomes (e.g., high profits, high levels of efficiency) are basically incompatible with positive outcomes for individuals (e.g., a pleasant work setting, interesting and fulfilling jobs). Even today, many managers would agree with this assertion. They believe, perhaps implicitly, that work *has* to be unpleasant; this is part of its basic nature. Is this actually the case? In recent decades, an increasing number of experts on organizational behavior have begun to answer "no." Contrary to the traditional beliefs mentioned above, they feel that the goals of organizational effectiveness and employee satisfaction or fulfillment are not necessarily inconsistent; on the contrary, they can actually be achieved simultaneously.[29,30] The major task we face, therefore, is not choosing between them; rather it is determining how the quality of life at work can be improved in ways that enhance employee motivation, satisfaction and commitment—and so contribute to high levels of organizational performance. Research focused on this task is generally described as being concerned with the **quality of work life**; as we have just noted, however, it actually also focuses on the potential contribution of such changes to organizational effectiveness. In any case, the result of such projects indicate that several steps are useful in improving the quality of work life. (For an amusing illustration of techniques unlikely to be effective in this respect, please see Figure 16.9.)

*"Each employee can have one plant or one poster.
But they can't have both."*

FIGURE 16.9   *Enhancing the Quality of Work Life: An Inadequate Effort.*
The people in this cartoon seem to have the right goal (enhancing the quality of work life for
their employees), but little idea about how to reach it. (Source: Drawing by Vietor; © 1982
The New Yorker Magazine Inc.)

Perhaps the single approach to enhancing the quality of life at work (or QWL
as it is often termed) that has received most attention is that of *work restructuring*.[31]
Such procedures seek to change the nature or content of jobs in ways that make
them more interesting and varied. In addition, they attempt to provide employees
with greater autonomy—increased feelings of control over their outcomes. Since we
have already considered several aspects of this process in Chapter 3 in the context of
our discussion of *job enlargement* and *job enrichment*, we will not describe them
again here. But please note that these techniques often seem effective in enhancing
the quality of work life for employees.

A second tactic that seems useful in this regard involves changes in the nature
of the relationship between supervisors and their subordinates. Here, efforts are
made to reduce the gap in status existing in such relationships, and to train supervisors to treat their subordinates in a more democratic fashion. The overall goal is
that of creating a climate of mutual respect between managers and lower-level
employees, and to the extent this is accomplished, individuals *do* often feel better
about their jobs.

A third approach to enhancing QWL should also be quite familiar: a shift
toward more participative decision making. When employees are permitted to offer
input concerning decisions that affect their jobs, they generally report more positive
attitudes about their department, organization, and supervisor than is the case
when such participation is lacking.[32] Thus, this procedure, too, can be a plus.

Several other factors that may also contribute to enhanced QWL are noted by
Ouchi, in his widely read book, *Theory Z*.[33] According to Ouchi, the conditions
existing in many large Japanese companies (e.g., guarantees of long-term employment, concern for employees that extends beyond the work day, decision making by
consensus), contribute to very high levels of QWL. This, in turn, helps explain the

*Japanese Mgn't
Theory*

503

outstanding levels of commitment, motivation, and productivity demonstrated by Japanese workers. According to Ouchi, similar results might well be obtained by organizations in other countries if they adopted corresponding policies. At present, a degree of controversy exists concerning two points: (1) is it the policies mentioned above that have produced such high levels of commitment among Japanese workers, or do certain aspects of Japanese culture itself contribute to this outcome? and (2) to what extent will such procedures, which have worked so well in Japan, transfer readily to other cultures, and produce similar results?[34] Regardless of such questions, though, there is little doubt that some of the factors identified by Ouchi do play a role in overall QWL. Thus, they are worthy of careful attention for this reason.

In sum, the QWL existing in any given organization is determined by many different, interacting factors.[35] Thus, efforts to change these conditions, and so to enhance QWL itself, must be complex. The effort involved, however, is fully justified; to the extent QWL is improved, the benefits for individuals and organizations alike can well be substantial.

Organizational Development: A Note on Its Ethics

When organizations attempt to change their technology, products, or administrative systems, they generally do so on the basis of their own resources. That is, present members of the organization recognize the need for such alterations, and then attempt to both plan and implement them in an orderly manner. Techniques of organizational development, however, represent an exception to this general rule. In most cases, such interventions are conducted by persons from outside the organization—expert consultants who specialize in these procedures. Since many aspects of organizational development require detailed knowledge of the behavioral sciences plus extensive, specialized training, this is quite reasonable. Indeed, it would make little sense for most organizations to keep experts in organizational development permanently on their staffs. As noted recently by White and Wooten, however, the fact that practitioners of organizational development are *not* members of the organizations they assist raises several ethical issues that should not be overlooked.[36]

First, there is the possibility that the information collected by such consultants will be misused in some way within the organization. For example, certain people in the company may attempt to gain access to confidential statements by various employees, or to data concerning the personalities, career plans, and attitudes of these persons. Once they do, they may then use this information for their own benefit (e.g., for political maneuvering, to reward their "friends," and to punish their "enemies"). Clearly, ethical standards require that consultants resist such breeches of faith very vigorously. Since the company's management has hired them and pays the bill for their services, however, the pressures to release confidential information, at least to top-level people, may be great.

Second, since techniques of organizational development often focus on changing the attitudes and behavior of employees, the possibility of manipulation or coercion sometimes arises. Specific programs and interventions may put pressure on individuals to change in ways they find objectionable, or which are contrary to their personal values. For example, some persons may find participation in sensitivity training highly unpleasant: they dislike being blunt and hurting others' feelings, even for constructive purposes. Thus, they object to the pressure to act in these ways found in this setting. Similarly, some managers may discover that, try as they may, they simply do not have much interest in people. As a result, efforts to shift them in this direction (as, for example, during grid training) may be quite unpleasant. In these and many other cases, procedures of organizational development that can benefit an entire organization also have the potential for inducing conflict, anxiety, and other negative reactions among specific persons. As we're sure you can appreciate, permitting such outcomes to arise is questionable, at best.

Third, there is also the possibility that the values of organizational development consultants and those of the clients they serve will conflict in some manner. For example, consultants may feel that organizational effectiveness can be enhanced through a shift toward more organic procedures, and then design special programs to bring about such changes. The values implicit in this approach, however may be inconsistent with those held by some persons within the company (e.g., some managers may feel that *they*, not subordinates, should hold power and authority; others may strongly favor the presence of formal rules and procedures). Should the consultants proceed with their plan despite such value conflict, on the basis of the view that they "know best"? Or should they defer to the values of their clients, and seek some other plan for improving organizational performance? Clearly, situations such as this raise complex ethical questions.

In sum, because organizational development focuses primarily on efforts to change *people*—their attitudes, values, motives, and behavior—it raises many sensitive issues. Fortunately, because of their specialized training in the behavioral sciences, most experts in organizational development are quite aware of these dilemmas, and take active steps to deal with them in a fair and ethical manner. However, it is important to bring such issues sharply into focus whenever efforts at organizational development are contemplated. People, as we're sure you fully realize, are highly complex; and change, by its very nature, is unsettling. In combination, the two can be explosive—and woe to the manager or consultant who fails to take adequate account of this volatile potential!

SUMMARY

In order to survive and prosper, organizations must adapt to shifting conditions in the world around them. Thus, they must often alter their *technology, products*, or *administrative systems*. New ideas with respect to technological change are facilitated by an organic internal structure. However, actual implementation of innovations is often enhanced by a more mechanistic approach. Similar principles seem to apply to administrative change as well.

Resistance to organizational change stems from many sources (e.g., the strong desire of most employees for a sense of personal control; anxieties over the costs that may result). Such resistance can be overcome, or at least reduced, by allowing the persons affected to participate in the planning of change, by explaining the need for its implementation clearly and effectively, and by calling attention to the benefits that will be produced.

Ultimately, an organization's effectiveness depends upon its employees—their commitment, motivation, and attitudes. Systematic efforts to enhance such factors are known as **organizational development**. Among the most popular procedures employed for this purpose are *survey feedback, grid training, sensitivity tranining, management by objectives*, and efforts to enhance the *quality of work life*.

KEY TERMS

administrative change: Organizational change involving shifts in the overall management of a company. Administrative change includes alterations in internal structure, specific policies, and reward systems.

grid training: A technique of organizational development designed to shift managers toward a managerial style involving high concern with both people and production.

horizontal linkage model: A model specifying the conditions necessary for successful product innovation.

management by objectives (MBO): A technique of organizational development in which supervisors and their subordinates agree upon specific goals and steps for reaching them.

organizational change: Alteration of some aspect of the structure or functioning of an organization to take account of shifting external or internal conditions.

organizational development: Various techniques designed to enhance the overall effectiveness of an organization by inducing positive change in its employees (e.g., desirable shifts in their attitudes, level of commitment, motivation).

policy model of innovation: A model of the process through which innovations are adopted by organizations. According to this model, certain contextual factors (e.g., environmental uncertainty) cause an organization to adopt specific policies that either favor or do not favor the adoption of innovations.

quality of work life (QWL): Efforts to make work and work settings more pleasant and desirable for employees. It is assumed that changes in this respect will also enhance performance and efficiency.

sensitivity training: A technique of organizational development that seeks to enhance employees' understanding of their own behavior and its impact upon others. It is assumed that such enhanced sensitivity will reduce interpersonal friction within the organization.

survey feedback: A technique of organizational development in which questionnaires are used to obtain information about issues of concern to an organization, and such knowledge is then provided to employees.

NOTES

1. R. L. Daft (1983). *Organization theory and design.* St. Paul, Minn.: West.

2. W. A. Randolph and G. G. Dess (1984). The congruence perspective on organization design: A conceptual model and multivariate research approach. *Academy of Management Journal, 9,* 114–127.

3. See Note 1.

4. J. E. Ettlie (1983). Organizational policy and innovation among suppliers to the food processing sector. *Academy of Management Journal, 26,* 27–44.

5. T. D. Duchesneau, S. E. Cohn, and J. E. Dutton (1979). *A study of innovation in manufacturing: Determinants, processes, and methodological issues.* Orono, Maine: Social Science Research Institute, University of Maine.

6. See Note 4.

7. See Note 4.

8. J. Q. Wilson (1966). Innovation in organization: Notes toward a theory. In J. D. Thompson (ed.), *Approaches to organizational design.* Pittsburgh: University of Pittsburgh Press.

9. R. B. Duncan (1976). The ambidextrous organization: Designing dual structures for innovation. In R. H. Killman, L. R. Pondy, and D. Slevin (eds.), *The management of organization.* New York: North-Holland.

10. See Note 1.

11. J. L. Pierce and A. L. Delbecq (1977). Organization structure, individual attitudes and innovation. *Academy of Management Review, 2,* 27–37.

12. T. S. Robertson and Y. Wind (1983). Organizational cosmopolitanism and innovativeness. *Academy of Management Journal, 26,* 332–338.

13. See Note 1.

14. R. L. Daft (1982). Bureaucratic versus nonbureaucratic structure and the process of innovation and change. In S. B. Bacharach (ed.), *Research in the sociology of organizations.* Greenwich, Conn.: JAI Press.

15. G. H. Gaertner, K. N. Gaertner, and D. M. Akinnusi (1984). Environment, strategy, and the implementation of administrative change: The case of civil service reform. *Academy of Management Journal, 27,* 525–543.

16. L. A. Fidler and J. D. Johnson (1984). Communication and innovation implementation. *Academy of Management Review, 9,* 704–711.

17. E. F. Huse (1980). *Organizational development and change.* St. Paul: West.

18. See Note 1.

19. D. Tjosvold (1984). Effects of leader warmth and directiveness on subordinate performance on a subsequent task. *Journal of Applied Psychology, 69,* 422–427.

20. R. R. Blake and J. S. Mouton (1978). *The new managerial grid.* Houston: Gulf.

21. J. I. Porras and P. O. Berg (1978). The impact of organization development. *Academy of Management Review, 3,* 249–266.

22. See Note 1.

23. J. P. Campbell and M. D. Dunnette (1968). Effectiveness of T-group experiences in managerial training and development. *Psychological Bulletin, 70,* 73–104.

24. P. Drucker (1954). *The practice of management.* New York: Harper & Row.

25. See Note 24; p. 78 (italics added).

26. R. G. Greenwood (1981). Management by objectives: As developed by Peter Drucker, assisted by Harold Smiddy. *Academy of Management Review, 6,* 225–230.

27. J. N. Kondrasuk (1981). Studies in MBO effectiveness. *Academy of Management Review, 6,* 419–430.

28. See Note 1.

29. N. Q. Herrick and M. Maccoby (1975). Humanizing work: Priority goal in the 1970s. In L. E. Davis and A. B. Cherns (eds.), *The quality of working life,* vol. 1. New York: Free Press.

30. E. E. Lawler, III (1982). Strategies for improving the quality of work life. *American Psychologist, 37,* 486–493.

31. J. R. Hackman and G. R. Oldham (1980). *Work redesign.* Reading, Mass.: Addison-Wesley.

32. E. A. Locke (1976). The nature and causes of job satisfaction. In M. Dunnette (ed.), *Handbook of industrial and organizational psychology.* Chicago: Rand McNally.

33. W. G. Ouchi (1981). *Theory Z: How American business can meet the Japanese challenge.* Reading, Mass.: Addison-Wesley.

34. J. J. Sullivan (1983). A critique of Theory Z. *Academy of Management Review, 8,* 132–142.

35. R. W. Rice, D. B. McFarlin, R. G. Hunt, and J. P. Near (1985). Organizational work and the perceived quality of life: Toward a conceptual model. *Academy of Management Review, 10,* 396–410.

36. L. P. White and K. C. Wooten (1983). Ethical dilemmas in various stages of organizational development. *Academy of Management Review, 8,* 690–697.

NAME INDEX

SUBJECT INDEX

Some Major Contributors to the Field of Organizational Behavior

(Continued from inside front cover)

DECISION MAKING

Larry L. Cummings

A. L. Delbecq

Irving L. Janis

Terence R. Mitchell

Herbert A. Simon

Barry M. Staw

Andrew H. Van de Ven